SPAIN

SPAIN

Recipes and Traditions *from the* Verdant Hills *of the* Basque Country *to the* Coastal Waters *of* Andalucía

JEFF KOEHLER

Location photographs by Jeff Koehler
Food photographs by Kevin Miyazaki

CHRONICLE BOOKS
SAN FRANCISCO

FOR MY PARENTS, BILL AND JOANNE

Text copyright © 2013 by Jeff Koehler.

Location photographs and photographs on pages 19, 273 (top right), 274, 296, 319, 326, and 327 copyright © 2013 by Jeff Koehler.

Plated food photographs copyright © 2013 by Kevin Miyazaki.

All rights reserved. No part of this book may be reproduced in any form without written permission from the publisher.

Library of Congress Cataloging-in-Publication Data available.

ISBN 978-0-8118-7501-1

Manufactured in China

Designed by Alice Chau
Typesetting by Helen Lee
This book is typeset in Periódico, Block Berthold Condensed, Knockout, Duke, DuBois Block, and Rough Riders.

10 9 8 7 6 5 4 3 2 1

Chronicle Books LLC
680 Second Street
San Francisco, California 94107
www.chroniclebooks.com

ACKNOWLEDGMENTS

The list of those who helped this book in one way or another is long—especially as I began working on it officially four years ago, though in reality more than a decade before that, when I arrived in Spain and initiated my apprenticeship in its kitchen. To the vast number of butchers and bakers, farmers and fishermen, home cooks and chefs who have each offered a piece to this great culinary and cultural puzzle, I offer deep and sincere thanks.

There are a number of people in Spain for whose help I am particularly grateful: Tomàs Borràs and Rosa Ramírez; Carmina Borràs and Robert Cosials; Rosa María Borràs and Ramón Rovira; Marien Borràs and Xicu García; Tía Encarnita, Tía Angelita, Tía Fermi, Tía Rosa, and Tía Tere; Nicolas Morales and Pepe García; Albert and Jordi Asín; Antoni Cot; Natalia Reixach, Jaime Pascual, and Àvia Lola; Elisabet Ars; Mari-Luz Valero, Jesús Mansilla, Juana Ortega, Jesús Mansilla (padre), and Juan Aspas; Francisco Nuñez de Prado; Eduard Pons; Gerard Veà; David Montegut; José Manuel Arias; José Melero; Josep Ravell and Jesús Benevente; Manuel Pérez Pascuas and Juana González; Virginia Irurita and her staff at Made for Spain; Jorge González, Rúben Arnanz, and Inmaculada Casado; Apelio García Sánchez; Gregoria Carrasco Sánchez and family; Pedro Quijorna; Maria Pons and Pere Pons; Sandra Martínez; Eugenia Sarasqueta; Cesc Segura and Eli Jaso; Mark Gregory Peters and Olga Greño; Pilar Rodríguez, Cristina Chiva, and Dani Cárdenas; and Caspar.

Outside of Spain, to those in the food and publishing world who were particulary supportive, thank you: Naomi Duguid; Jodi Deleon; Leslie Jonath; Rebecca Staffel; Mary Risley; Sylvia Whitman and Heather Hartley; Mercedes Lamamie and Paz Tintoré; James Oseland and Dana Bowen; Justin Paul, Marika Cain, and Melanie Fowler; Jocelyn Zuckerman; Tina Ujlaki and Kate Heddings; Derk Richardson, April Kilcrease, and Tara Guerting; Dick Doughty and Sarah Miller; Jeanne McManus; Michelle Wildgen; Katie Workman and Mary Goodbody; and Sandy Gluck and Lisa Mantineo.

My agent, Doe Coover, and those in her office, including Francis Kennedy, deserve great thanks for their work on this from the very beginning.

And at Chronicle Books, a huge thanks for everything on this book, our fourth together. Warm appreciation to Bill LeBlond, Amy Treadwell, Sarah Billingsley, Vanessa Dina, Steve Kim, Ann Spradlin, Doug Ogan, Claire Fletcher, and Lorena Jones. Thanks to Peter Perez, David Hawk, and Alyson Pullman on the publicity side. And Ann Rolke for her copyediting. Thanks to Alice Chau for her design.

I would like to thank Kevin J. Miyazaki for his fantastic photographic work on the plated dishes. Appreciation also to Ana Torrontegui for her help in Barcelona and Dani Cárdenas in finding so much great tableware. And Rosa María Borràs and Ramón Rovira for use of their wonderful country place, which has always epitomized the best of the rural kitchen for me.

A huge thanks to my family—especially my parents, Bill and Joanne, and brother, Bill—for their support during the book.

My biggest thanks goes to my two girls—Alba and Maia—who have eaten everything in the book on numerous occasions (or as close to that as any father could ever wish). And to Eva, the reason I came to Spain all those years ago—and stayed.

CONTENTS

Introduction 10
Before Turning on the Stove 16

CHAPTER 1
SOUPS, BROTHS, STEWS, CREAMS, AND PULSES

The Ritz's Madrid-Style Cocido 20
Catalan Two-Course Soup.....................22
Castilian Garlic Soup 25
Basque Leek Soup 26
Creamy Artichoke and Leek Soup 27
Velvety Menorcan Fish Soup................28
Basque Fresh Tuna and
Potato Stew 31
Beef Stew...32
Cream of Seasonal Mushrooms...........35
Spinach with Garbanzo Beans.............36
White Beans with Clams 41
Pinotxo's Garbanzo Beans with
Blood Sausage, Raisins, and
Pine Nuts..42
Stewed Lentils with a
Nutty Chocolate Picada.........................43

CHAPTER 2
SALADS, COLD SOUPS, AND GAZPACHOS

Curly Endive with Xató Sauce 47
Belgian Endive with Cabrales Blue
Cheese Sauce and Anchovy Fillets......48
Winter Green Salad with Fresh
Cheese and Pomegranate Seeds..........49
Marinated Seafood Salad 50
Salt Cod, Orange, and Olive Salad 53
Catalan Shredded Salt Cod,
Tomato, and Olive Salad 54
White Bean Salad with
Bonito del Norte Tuna 55
Spanish Potato Salad..............................56
Melon or Fresh Figs with
Slices of Dry-Cured Jamón 57
Chilled Melon Soup with
Crispy Jamón 58
White Gazpacho with Grapes...............59
Classic Andalusian Gazpacho 60
Córdoba-Style Salmorejo.......................62

CHAPTER 3
TAPAS AND APPETIZERS

Country Bread Rubbed with
Tomato and Olive Oil.............................68
Catalan Flatbread with
Roasted Red Peppers 70
Roasted Red Peppers, Eggplant,
and Onions 72
Padrón Green Peppers............................73
Cádiz-Style Potatoes in Vinaigrette 74
Dates Wrapped in Bacon 75
Trout and Dry-Cured Iberian
Jamón Croquettes 76
Chicken Croquettes 79
Pork Ribs in Adobo Sauce...................... 81
Spicy Marinated Pork Skewers 83
Empanada with Marinated Pork
and Roasted Red Peppers 85
Salt Cod Brandade on Toast 87
Fresh Anchovies in Vinegar..................88
Galician Fair-Style Octopus with
Paprika on Potatoes 91
Deep-Fried Squid 92
Garlicky Shrimp in Olive Oil 93
Clams with Shrimp 94
Mussels in Vinaigrette 95

CHAPTER 4
VEGETABLES

Sautéed Wild Mushrooms 100
La Mancha–Style Sautéed Onions,
Zucchini, Tomatoes, and Peppers 102
Stuffed Tomatoes...................................103
Balearic-Style Baked Stuffed
Eggplant 104
Fried Eggplant Strips with
Salmorejo 106
Green Asparagus in
Vinegar Marinade 107
Fresh White Asparagus with Crispy
Shards of Dry-Cured Jamón 109
Spinach with Pine Nuts and
Raisins 110
Tender Spinach Leaves with
Spanish-Style Poached Eggs...............112
Roasted Artichokes 113
Roasted Beets in Vinegar..................... 114
Baker's Oven-Roasted Potatoes......... 116
Galician Boiled Potatoes with
Paprika 116
Puréed Potatoes with
Extra-Virgin Olive Oil.......................... 117
La Rioja–Style Stewed Potatoes
with Chorizo... 118
Smashed Potatoes and Cabbage
Topped with Streaky Salt Pork.......... 119

CHAPTER 5
EGGS

Potato and Onion Egg Tortilla 124
Artichoke Egg Tortilla..........................126
Salt Cod Egg Tortilla.............................127
Eggs Scrambled with
Tender Green Garlic Shoots,
Asparagus, and Shrimp 128
Eggs Scrambled with Mushrooms
and Dry-Cured Jamón 130
Fried Eggs with Fried Potatoes and
Slices of Dry-Cured Iberian Jamón.....132

CHAPTER 6
RICE, PASTA, AND MIGAS

Rabbit Paella with Artichokes
and Red Bell Peppers 138
Shellfish Paella....................................... 141
Black Rice with Allioli.........................144
Soupy Rice with Lobster 148
Soupy Rice with
Free-Range Chicken 150
Mountain-Style Rice with
Chicken and Fresh Sausage 151
Fideos in the Cazuela with
Pork Ribs 152
Seafood Fideuà with Allioli 153
Pyrenees Mountain–Style Penne
Pasta with Ground Meat and Pâté 155
Penne Pasta with Tomatoes
and Fresh Sausage au Gratin..............156
Cannelloni Stuffed with Meat 157
Cannelloni Stuffed with
Mushrooms and Pine Nuts 160
Shepherd's Migas with Grapes........... 161

CHAPTER 7
FISH

Andalucía-Style Deep-Fried Fish......164
Fisherman's Suquet 165
Monkfish Steaks with Saffron 166
Galician-Style Hake with
Garlic Ajada Sauce 169
Fish Braised in Romesco Sauce.........170
Baked Turbot with
Basque White Wine...............................173
Salt-Baked Gilt-Head Bream 174
Barbate-Style Tuna in
Caramelized Onions.............................175
Grilled Sardines with Slushy
Celery and Lemon Granita 176
Grilled Swordfish Steaks
with Piriñaca 178

Pan-Fried Trout with
Thyme and Walnuts 179
Navarra-Style Trout with
Dry-Cured Jamón 181
Marinated Salmon on the
Grill with Galician Potatoes 182
Biscay-Style Salt Cod with
Choricero Pepper Sauce 183
Grandma Lola's Lenten
Salt Cod with Raisins 185
Salt Cod Baked in the Tin 187
Piquillo Peppers Stuffed with
Salt Cod Brandade 188

CHAPTER 8
SHELLFISH

Grilled Razor Clams 195
Clams in Green Sauce 196
Clams with Oloroso Sherry 197
Steamed Cockles 198
Mussels in Sweet Sofrito
Tomato Sauce 199
Baked Scallops in the Shell 201
Grilled Shrimp 202
Lobster in a Nutty Chocolate
Sauce, Costa Brava Style 205
Small Squid in Their Own Ink 206

CHAPTER 9
POULTRY AND RABBIT

Duck with Pears 210
Chicken Braised in Saffron,
Almond, and Egg Yolk Sauce 212
Chicken with Shallots and
Orange and Cinnamon Sauce 214
Chicken with Samfaina 216
The Mayoress's Stewed
Christmas Chicken 217
Roast Chicken with Prunes 220
Grilled Rabbit with Eggplant,
Zucchini, and Allioli 221
Torre del Bosc Braised Rabbit
with Carrots 222

CHAPTER 10
GAME AND SNAILS

Grilled Marinated Venison Steaks 226
Toledo-Style Partridge 229
Grilled Quail with
Garlic and White Wine 230
Pilar's Cazuela with Snails
and Rabbit 231
New Year's Day Snails in
Spicy Tomato Sauce 232

CHAPTER 11
MEATS

Roast Shoulder of Kid Goat with
Potato and Shallot Confit 236
Shepherd's-Style Lamb Chops
with Potatoes and Zesty Vinegar-
Garlic Sauce 239
Grilled Lamb Rib Chops with
Quince Allioli 240
Grilled Lamb Chops with Honey 242
Chilled Pork Loin 243
Salt-Baked Pork Loin with
Two Sauces 245
Pork Tenderloin with
Purée of Chestnuts 246
Pork Tenderloin in Orange Sauce 248
Fresh Pork Sausages with
White Beans and Allioli 251
Seared Morcilla de Burgos
with Roasted Green Peppers
and Fried Eggs 252
Menorcan Meatballs in Tomato
and Pine Nut Sauce 257
Stewed Meatballs with Cuttlefish 258
Grilled Beef Tenderloin with
Blue Cheese Sauce 259
Braised Veal with
Dried Mushrooms 260

CHAPTER 12
INNARDS AND EXTREMITIES

Roasted Pig's Feet 265
Veal Kidneys in Sherry 267
Veal Tongue with Capers 268
Galician-Style Tripe with
Garbanzo Beans 269
Braised Oxtail Stew 271

CHAPTER 13
DESSERTS, SWEETS, AND FRUITS

Toasted Bread with Chocolate,
Extra-Virgin Olive Oil, and
Sea Salt Flakes 274
Creamy Vanilla Custard 275
Creamy Rice Pudding 276
Basque Walnut Pudding 277
Citrus-and-Cinnamon-Scented
Flan 278
Spongy Yogurt Cake 279
Spongy Cake with Pears and
Walnuts, Sinarcas Style 280
Country Muffins 282
Galician Crêpes with Fresh
Whipped Cream and Honey 285
Galician Almond Tart 286
Flatbread with Pine Nuts,
Sugar, and Anise 289
Marzipan Cookies Rolled in
Pine Nuts 291
Oranges with Extra-Virgin
Olive Oil and Honey 292
Early Spring Strawberries
with Red Wine Vinegar 293
Pears Poached in Red Wine 295
Baked Figs 296
Musicians' Dessert 297
Menorcan Gin Sorbet 299
Fresh Cheese with Honey 301

CHAPTER 14
DRINKS

Spanish Cinnamon-Scented
Drinking Chocolate in the Cup 306
Meringued Milk 308
Slushy Lemon Granita 309
Summer Red Wine Sangria 311
White Wine Sangria with
Fresh Berries 313
Menorcan Gin Cocktail with Fresh
Lemon Juice and Lemon Soda 315
Orense-Style Coffee Liqueur 316

CHAPTER 15
SWEET AND SAVORY
HOMEMADE CONSERVES

Christmas Cherries in
Aguardiente 320
Creamy Quince Paste 323
Creamy Lemon Curd 325
Dried Apricots Macerated in
Sweet Wine 326
Tomato Marmalade 327
Sweet Preserved Tomatoes
with Thyme 328
Sweet and Sour Preserved Onions ... 329
Quail in Escabeche Marinade 330
Fresh Sardines in Escabeche
Marinade 332

**A Glossary of Basic Recipes
and Techniques** 334
Selected Bibliography 344
Sources 345
Index 346

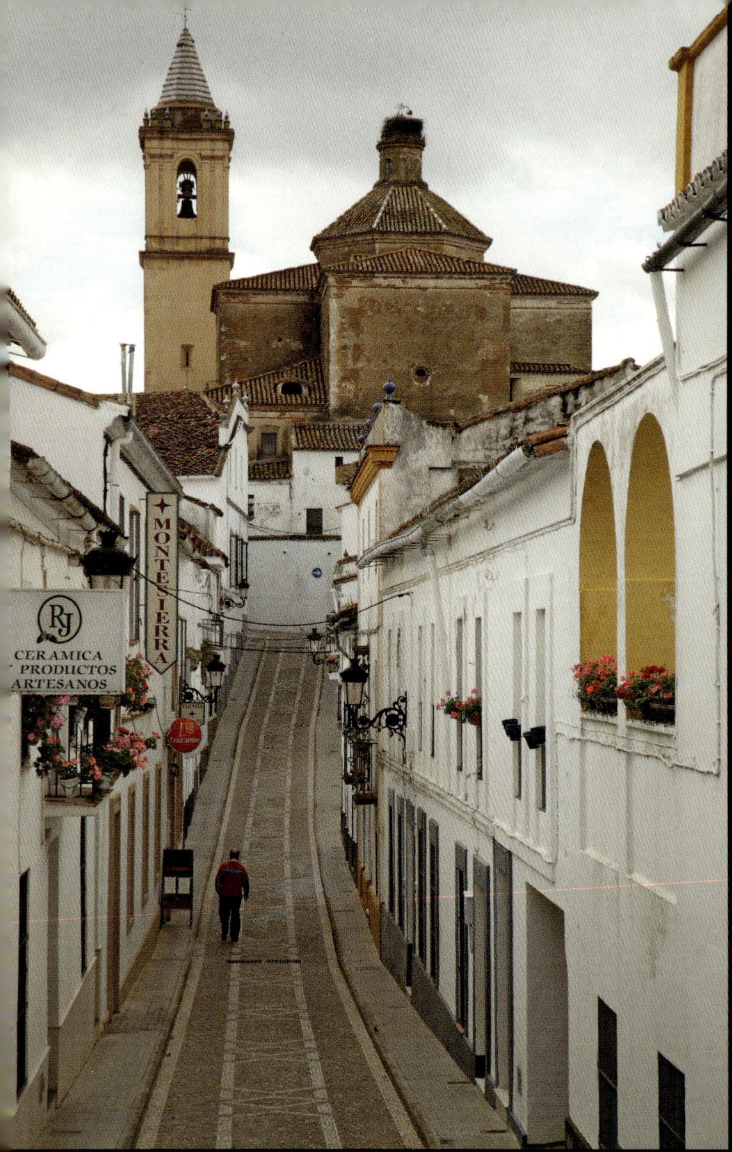
RJ
CERAMICA
PRODUCTOS
ARTESANOS

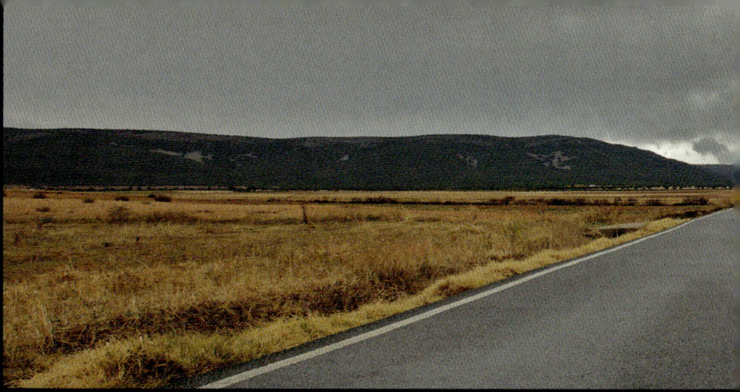

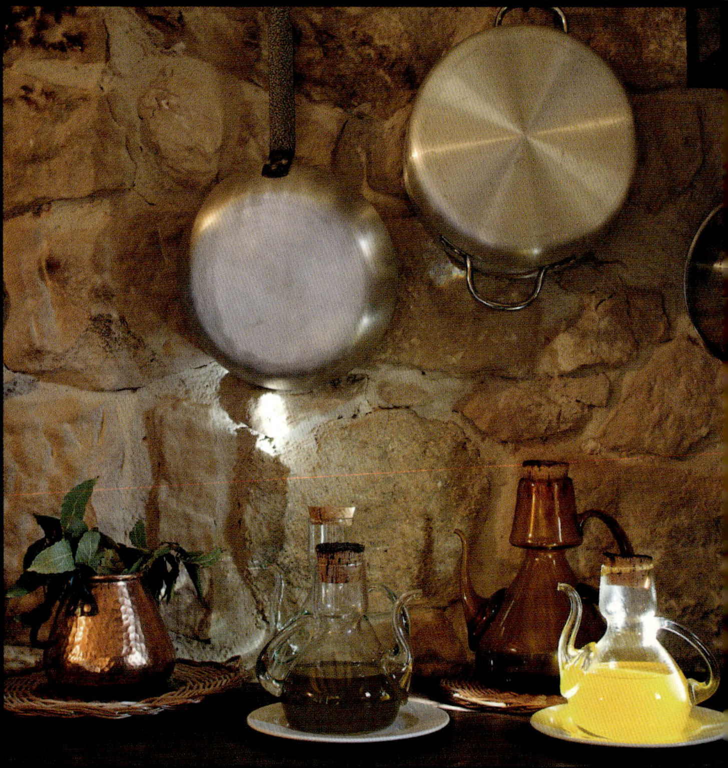

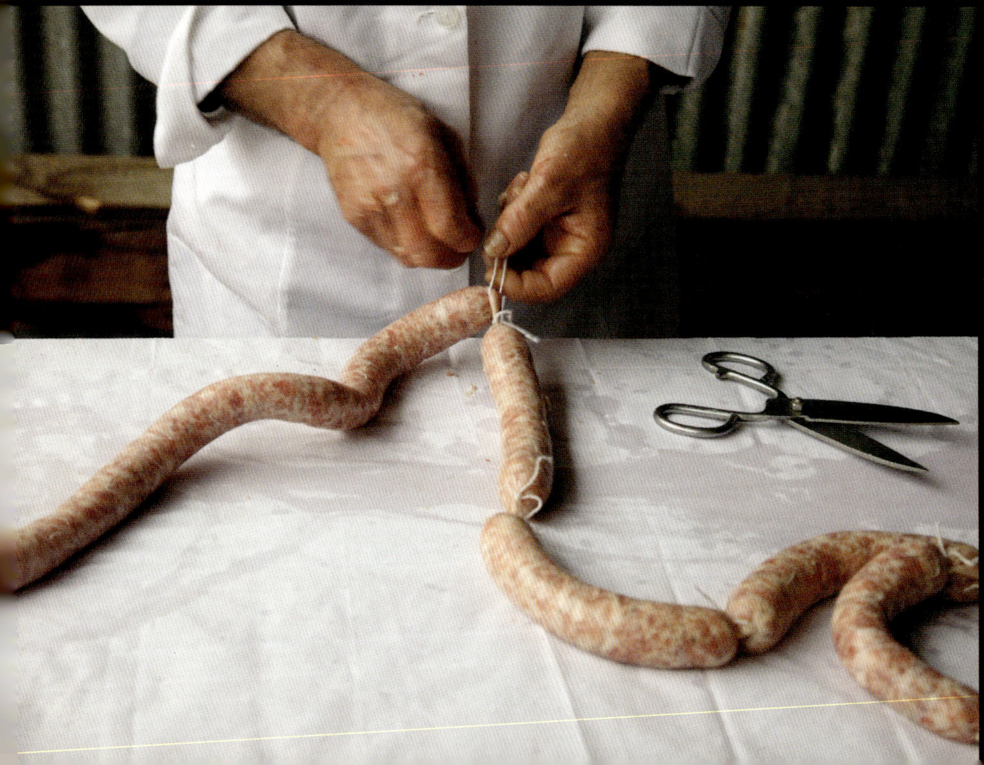

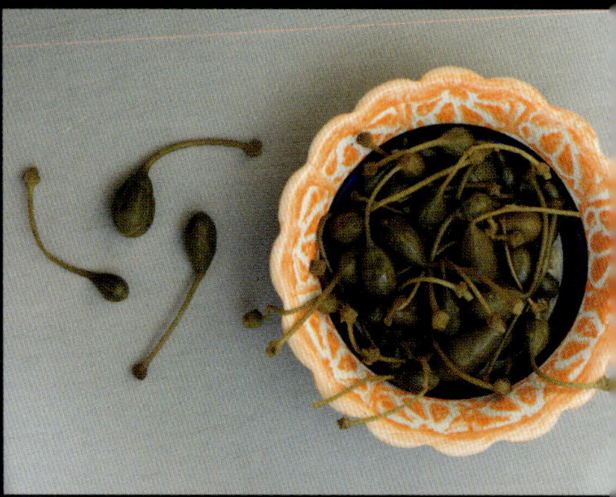

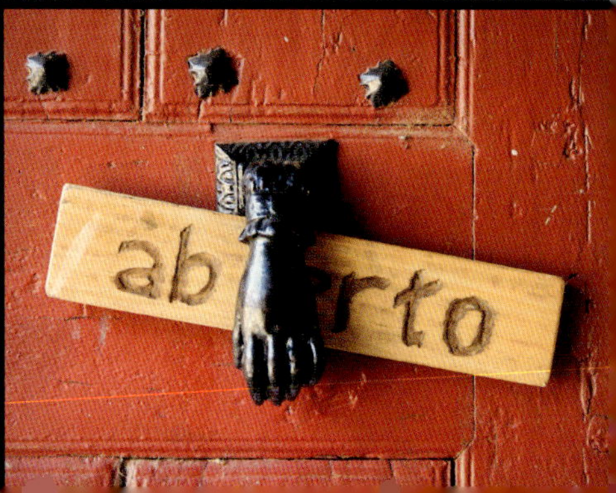

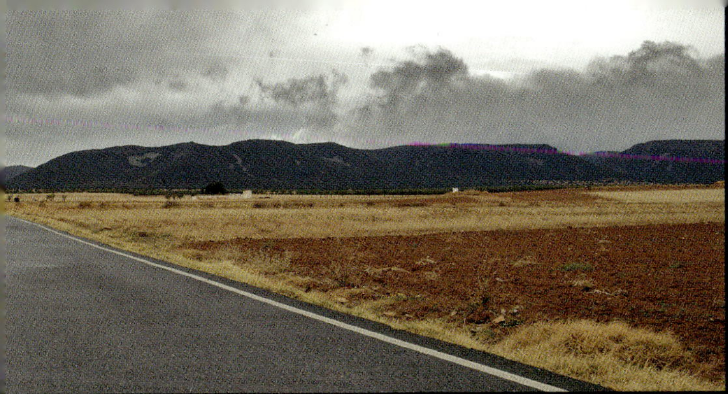
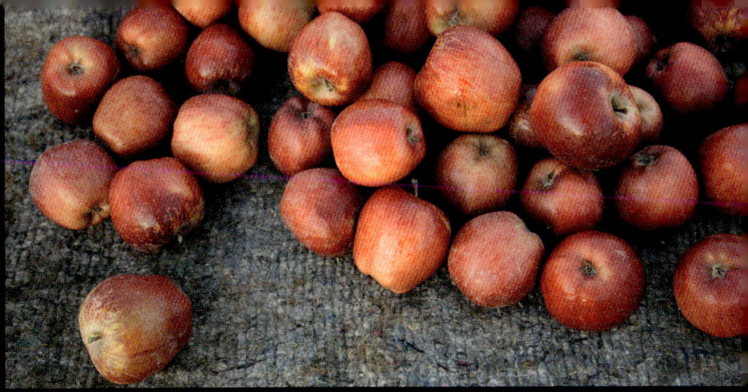
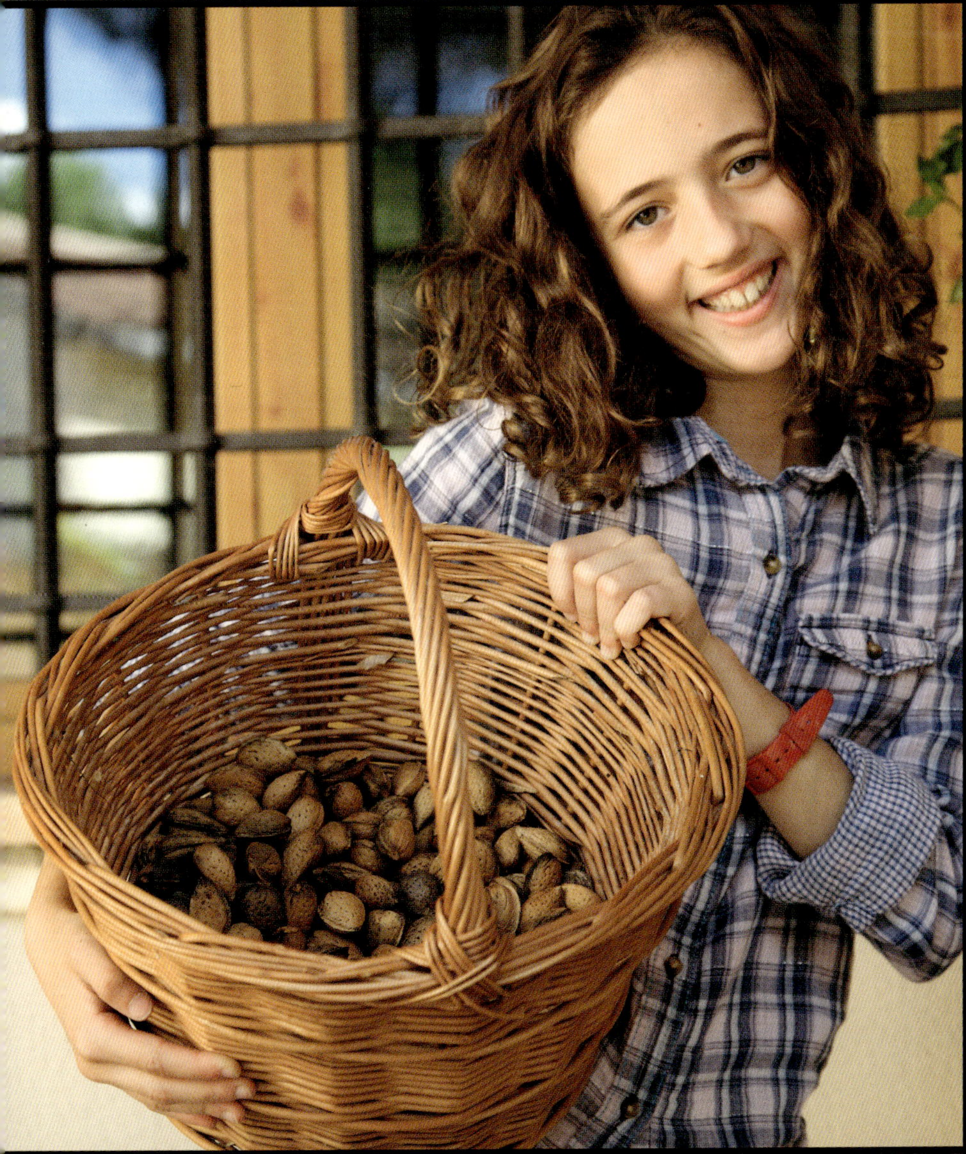
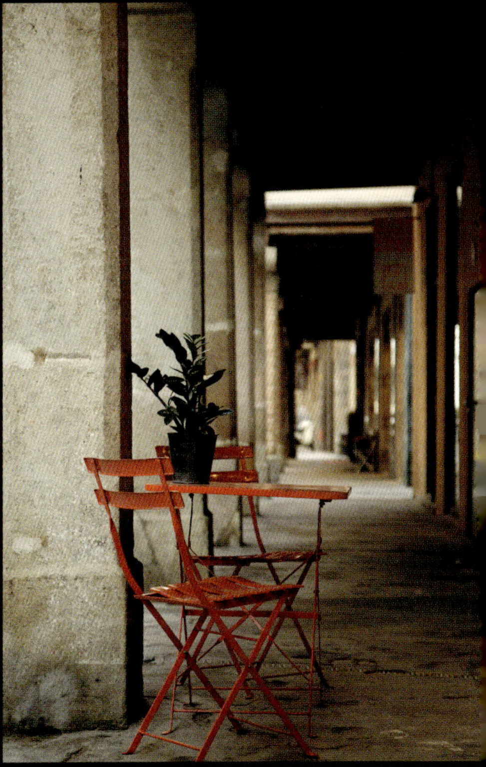
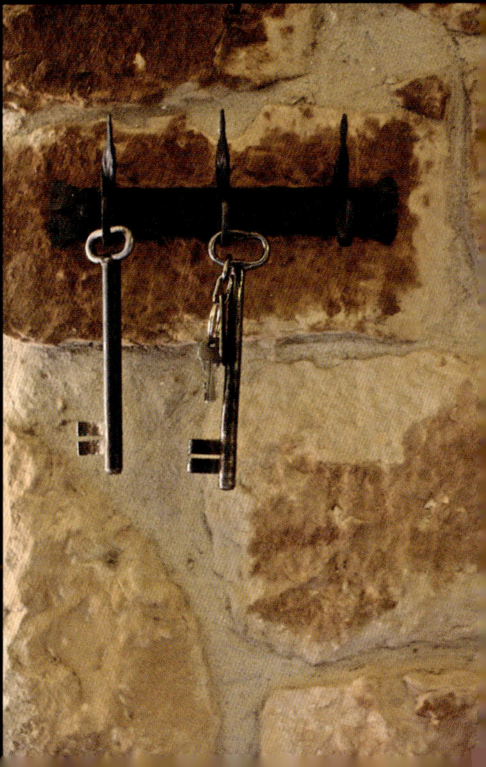
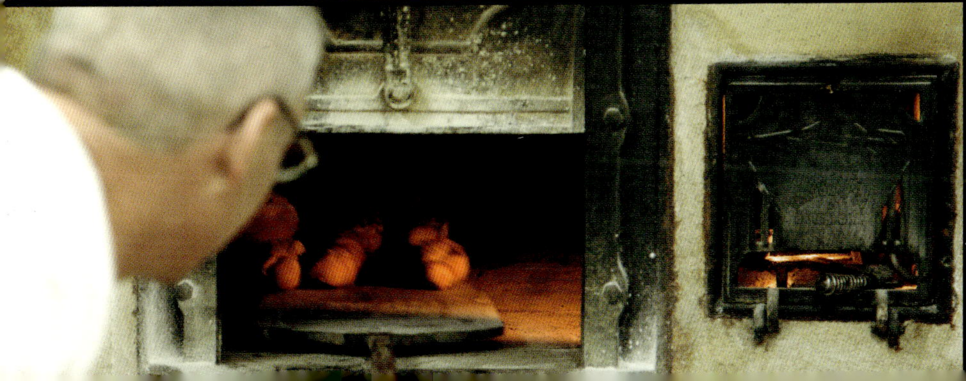

INTRODUCTION

Spanish cooking has never been more in fashion, nor has it ever elicited such interest as it does now. Magazines, newspapers, and TV programs have all tapped in to this cuisine that, apart from a handful of well-known dishes, remains relatively unknown to the average cook. And even tapas and paella, surely the two things that most people associate with the Spanish kitchen (along with molecular gastronomy foams), are largely misunderstood. Master chefs such as Ferran Adrià, Joan Roca, and Juan Mari Arzak have been instrumental in drawing attention to Spain and its gastronomy. At times, these culinary alchemists practice something more akin to chemistry in the kitchen, yet in many instances they are deconstructing or riffing on the most rustic of Spanish dishes, striving to elicit emotions frequently rooted in childhood.

I remember some years ago taking a visiting English friend to eat in one of Barcelona's temples of Catalan avant-garde cuisine headed by a prodigy of Adrià. The dazzling two-hour tasting menu ended with a finale of toasted bread topped with fruity, aromatic olive oil, swirled mounds of soft chocolate, and some flat flakes of sea salt. My friend was exuberant at such an original combination. I laughed. It was a barely disguised spin on the Friday afternoon snack that my youngest daughter was getting in daycare, the one my wife's school served when she was a girl (this or with quince paste—guess which disappeared first), the one her father ate in the countryside of Lleida as a boy.

Now, I am not suggesting that molecular gastronomy is a modern take on grandma's cooking, but rather that even at this level, with some of world's most celebrated chefs, many of the dishes, drawn on the flavors of memory, have their roots in the traditional Spanish kitchen. And the traditional kitchen in Spain is the country kitchen.

I moved to Spain over fifteen years ago and not long afterwards married the local girl I had followed here. (We met in London, in a residence hall for foreign graduate students, where we had, somewhat fittingly, shared a kitchen.) One of the things that I have learned during my time eating and cooking here, and traveling to all but one or two of Spain's fifty provinces, is that the country kitchen begins firmly with *las materias primas*, the fresh, high-quality ingredients cooks call "the raw materials." These are often simply prepared and presented, with usually just a few other components to draw out flavor. It's a largely straightforward cuisine, rarely overly laborious or complex (which isn't to say unsophisticated or lacking imagination), and more about ingredients than techniques or sauces. Meat, seafood, and poultry are not just vehicles for other, stronger flavors, nor simply bits of texture drowned in an overpowering sauce, but rather cooked for their own flavor. Sometimes that means quickly grilling, other times slowly cooking down to concentrate flavors. What's the point of buying a good sea bream if you aren't going to taste it?

To put that another way, if you are going to taste that sea bream—purely taste it and not the sauce—then it had better be a good fish, fresh, with the right texture, and cut or cleaned for the specific dish that you are preparing. When shopping, be ready for how you will cook it, because the fishmonger will want to know. A bream baked in the oven is cleaned differently than one baked in a salt crust. Butchers ask the same kinds of questions. Different dishes demand different cuts: a rabbit for a rice dish is trimmed into smaller pieces than rabbit for grilling, and so on.

This is one reason why the tradition of covered food markets and small specialty shops remains so important—and intact. Large supermarkets, of course, exist, but the butcher and fishmonger, the vegetable and fruit shop, the place on the corner selling cured *jamón* and cheese, the bakery beside it—these still dominate, even in cities. (Within two blocks of my residential Barcelona flat, I have five fruit stores—and three others that sell fruit—and six bakeries.) Small villages generally have a weekly *mercado* that gathers on the central square, usually on the open plaza fronting the church. These traveling markets act as a rural lifeline.

Markets also offer markers to the seasons and the seasonality of ingredients is always clear. What is most numerous is cheapest but also tastiest. It often feels like feast or famine regarding cherries and figs; tiny, crunchy mid-June pears (no bigger than the figs); asparagus and artichokes; wild mushrooms; certain fish, game birds, and fresh wild boar. Those who work in the markets and small shops are experts. They know their products. Their goods are usually marked with plenty of details, but if not, then ask where the fish was caught and how (in the Atlantic? the Mediterranean? line caught? netted or trawled? farm raised?). Look for freshness in the gloss of its eyes, the deep redness of its gills, the firmness of its flesh—but don't touch.

A guiding kitchen principle is this: The best is used—but nothing is thrown away. Spanish cooks have learned to eke everything they can out of their often undernourished land. What the garden, market, or refrigerator offers up must be utilized. Bones for stock, a pig's ear for flavor, kidneys to stew in sherry, the rabbit liver pounded with nuts and garlic and stirred into the dish at the end. Trotters, tongue, tail, tripe, even the blood (*sangre frita* with onions!): You name it, it's devoured somewhere by someone—with gusto.

Traditional Spanish cooking is flavorful but frugal, and many of its finest dishes originated not in palace kitchens, but as country fare. Take the iconic paella. Born in the fruit and vegetable fields around Valencia, it was a dish for farmers who could not make it back home for lunch. Vegetables from the fields, a few snails (or a sprig of rosemary), and perhaps some rabbit on a lucky day were sautéed and then simmered in a wide, flat pan until tender. Rice sprinkled into the pan absorbed the flavors and offered a filling, starchy base. The pan itself acted as a communal plate (who wanted to carry plates into the field, or wash them?) and the rice was eaten with spoons carved from boxwood crates. Even if paella can be gussied up like a princess with wallet-emptying red shrimp and saffron, or served in restaurants among velvet curtains, patinated silver, and a black-tied maestro on a baby grand piano in the corner, it is at heart a simple country dish where rice remains the star.

But what exactly is *la cocina española*—Spanish cooking? I can offer dozens of examples, but not one tidy definition. The country, and its kitchen, is simply too diverse, the range of flavors it produces too great. The gastronomy, like the landscape, like the country itself, is blessed with the riches of distinct regions.

Historically, Spain as a country has only been a reality since 1492, and in these five centuries it has resisted complete gastronomic unification. There are deep and distinct differences on many levels between Andalucía and the Basque Country, among Castilla, Galicia, and Catalunya, between the Balearic Islands and Cantabria. These are undeniable. There are the historical, social, and cultural differences that have produced four official languages—Castilian Spanish, Catalan, Basque, and Galician—and a handful of dialects, not to mention very distinctive ways of celebrating with food.

The diversity of the Spanish countryside is, in Europe, without rival. Ranging from the Atlantic Ocean to the Mediterranean Sea, the Pyrenees mountains that run along the northern border and the Sierra Nevada range in the south, the dry plateau that dominates the center of the peninsula, the rocky, fjord-like inlets of Galicia, the verdant greens of the Basque Country and Navarra, the olive-covered southern Andalucía, the spacious pasturelands studded with holm oak trees in Extremadura (where black-footed Iberian pigs roam semi-wild eating acorns) . . . the vast geographical cornucopia offers it all.

First and foremost, then, Spanish cuisine is regional, and the cooking of each region directly reflects the landscape, and changes as the landscape does. It is the landscape that, in many ways, has dictated the cuisine.

And there lies the pleasure in Spanish cuisine, the distinctive cooking that comes from different hamlets and corners, each with their own traditions, products, and dishes. Regionalism is a defining element of *la cocina española*.

The tastes of those rural landscapes, I have learned from living here, are not easily lost. They are still felt in the connection to the land and the cycles of the seasons: the seasonality of food; not wasting anything, whether yesterday's bread or the head of a fish (for stock!); long, multicourse meals; unfussy cooking styles and often unfussy flavors; the love of stews and hearty soups, of long-cooked pulses, game, salt cod, of roast suckling lamb and pig, of dishes with innards and extremities; in the tradition of curing and preserving that borders on obsession . . . these remain, making sure that the countryside is never far from any table in Spain, even in the cities.

Take my own in-laws. Tomàs and Rosa were part of a midcentury wave of urban migration that shifted the population, and workforce, from rural areas to the city. In the 1920s, 57 percent of the Spanish population was engaged in agricultural work. In 1960, a decade into an economic boom that was sending a massive influx of people into the cities, that number was steadily falling but still hovered at a whopping 42 percent. Although the percentage of those working in agriculture these days is down to a single digit, the shift came too abruptly for the traditions of the countryside to disappear, especially in the kitchen.

Tomàs grew up in the arid hills of inland Catalunya near Lleida and moved to Barcelona to study engineering; Rosa was born in Barcelona, but both her parents had come not long before from a small village surrounded by vineyards and cereal fields about an hour inland from Valencia on the Castilla–La Mancha border. Rosa's mother died when she was very young and, with her father owning a *colmado* (corner grocery store with staples) in Barcelona's dense Gothic Quarter, she spent large chunks of her childhood with the aunts back in the village. She and Tomàs married, had four girls, and spent their summers and holidays visiting family. They would return home laden with the plunders of the countryside. From one side of the family, they brought cases of wine—rough-edged table wine, but from the family grapes and thus drunk with stoic pride—and home-cured sausages from pigs butchered in the courtyard of an aunt's house and stored in lard-filled ceramic pots; from the other side of the family, jars of preserved tomatoes and stewed vegetables, quince paste made with the season's first fruit from the tree in the yard, home-brined Arbequina olives, even large jars of mallard duck legs preserved in olive oil, plus boxes of apples and peaches.

Like so many similar stories, Rosa's cooking—and Tomàs's palate—continues to reflect their roots: the long-simmered soups, the snails in spicy tomato sauce, even her weekend family paella. When she was a girl in the village, her aunts prepared paella of rabbit, chicken, snails, and green beans over vineyard cuttings in the courtyard of the house every weekend—and they still do. Sure, Rosa uses seafood in her paella now and cooks it over a wide gas burner on the stove, but the essence is the same, an anchor not just for the meal, but the family. Such tastes, and their accompanying recipes, have been passed down, and my wife—like her sisters, like most Spaniards—can scarcely imagine anything better.

Nor can I.

REGIONS

THE REGIONS OF SPAIN
las regiones de España

The Spanish countryside is ample and diverse, and its 200,000 square miles (518,000 sq km) range from the Atlantic Ocean to the Mediterranean Sea, the Pyrenees mountains to the Sierra Nevada, and dry plateaus to sprawling river deltas. First and foremost, Spanish cuisine is regional, and the cooking of each region directly reflects its landscape.

The northwest part of the country—Galicia, Asturias, and Cantabria—is generally green, hilly, and, in some places, mountainous, with an important dairy industry and one of the world's largest fishing fleets. The rugged, inlet-etched coastline of Galicia offers the country's finest fish and shellfish (clams, scallops, oysters, spider crabs, prawns) as well as much of its potato crop, while the valleys of Asturias produce celebrated cheeses, ciders, and white beans. Cantabria has its own culinary fame with its seafood canning industry (especially *bonito del norte* tuna and anchovies) and, in Potes, distillations of *orujo* (pressings of grape skins like grappa).

To the east of this lies the Basque Country, with its exquisite seafood; opulent, almost cultish cooking (exemplified in *txokos*, men-only gastronomic societies); obsession with salt cod; and *pintxos*, small and often highly creative tapas mounted on pieces of bread. Farther east are the nourished hills of Navarra, where asparagus and *piquillo* peppers grow, and mountain-river trout are cooked wrapped in slices of dry-cured *jamón*. Sitting snug on the south side of these provinces is the famed wine region of La Rioja, with its simple but flavorful cooking dominated by lamb and red peppers. Indeed, a plate of roasted peppers steeped in garlic-infused olive oil, a slowly roasted leg of suckling lamb, and a full-bodied bottle of Rioja red wine are some of Spain's unfailing gastronomic pleasures.

The Mediterranean coast, with its ancient seaports and wealthy Levantine fields of rice, vegetables, and citrus fruits, offers lively, diverse cooking. The marvelous Catalan and Valencian kitchens mix flavors with baroque abandon—seafood and meat are often found in the same dish; a piece of pork or cuttlefish can add flavor to about any savory dish—yet always strive to highlight the principal ingredients. A night's ferry ride away are the Balearic Islands, a stunning and rural archipelago that includes, in descending order of size, Mallorca, Menorca, Ibiza, and Formentera. Their Mediterranean cuisines are rich in olive oil and herbs, enlivened with a number of unique specialties, including silky fish stews, spiral *ensaïmada* pastries, cheeses, a spreadable paprika-red pork sausage called *sobrassada*, and even, on Menorca, gin—a legacy from the centuries when the English fleet harbored in the island's capital.

The south of the country is dominated by Andalucía; tough, dry, undulating hills—red-soiled, blanketed in olive groves, punctuated by tidy white villages and ancient Phoenician seaports. The base of the cooking here is olive oil, vinegar, and garlic, and incorporates plenty of lamb and pork, game, salt cod, and, along the coast, all manner of delicately fried fish. Tapas are a way of life, and often enjoyed with a local dry sherry. The lingering Moorish influence on the cuisine of Andalucía is clear in such typical dishes as garbanzo beans and spinach with cumin, lamb with honey, and monkfish with saffron, all calling on ingredients introduced during the 800-year-long Moorish reign of the region. (Its iconic gazpachos and *salmorejos*—thickened with bread in the purée—came later, incorporating tomatoes and peppers from the New World into already existing cool "soups.") As well, dishes here tend to have more spices—not that they are spicy, as in hot—than elsewhere in the country, and the tradition of sweets is particularly pronounced. For *dulces*, Andalusian chefs still use a base of sugar, eggs, lemon, and almonds to create countless delicacies.

To the northeast of Andalucía is Murcia, split between the glittering Mediterranean sea, with its delicious seafood dishes (gilt-head bream baked in a salt crust is a specialty) and the rural, often isolated mountain interior, where lamb dominates. To the northwest of Andalucía, landlocked on the inside of Portugal, is Extremadura, with its ancient monasteries, vast pastures of holm oak trees (*dehesas*) where black-footed pigs eat fallen acorns and wild grasses, and rustic, serious cooking. The valley of La Vera, where red peppers from America were first cultivated, dried, and ground into powder for cooking, produces the finest *pimentón* (smoked paprika), one of Spanish cooking's most important spices.

At the center is the vast central plateau known as *la meseta*, the dominating geographical feature of the Iberian peninsula, occupying nearly half of its land. Ringed with a turret of mountains, and commanding respect (or at least awe) in its vastness, it is a place of extremes—scorching summers, freezing winters, wind, and little rain. It is pale, austere, more pastoral than agricultural. Here, a windmill turns, sheep graze lazily in the sight of a shepherd, and, in the distance, a church steeple rises above a dun-colored village built around the ruins of an ancient crusader castle: the land of El Greco and Cervantes, saffron fields and honeybee hives, partridge hunts, *migas* (a dish made with breadcrumbs), *sopa de ajo* (garlic and bread soup), and aged Manchego cheeses. This is rural Spain at its purest.

In the dead middle of it all like a bull's-eye is the country's capital, Madrid. Urban and highly cosmopolitan, sure, but still dominated by the tastes of the countryside that is never far away.

Atlantic Ocean
France
A CORUÑA
ASTURIAS
BILBAO
BASQUE COUNTRY
GALICIA
CANTABRIA
PAMPLONA
PYRENEES
LEÓN
NAVARRA
LA RIOJA
CATALUNYA
BARCELONA
SALAMANCA
CASTILLA
MADRID
Portugal
VALENCIA
MENORCA
PALMA DE MALLORCA
VALENCIA
MALLORCA
LISBON
EXTREMADURA
IBIZA
MURCIA
SEVILLE
ANDALUCÍA
GRANADA
CÁDIZ
Mediterranean Sea
CANARY ISLANDS

BEFORE TURNING ON THE STOVE

A NOTE ON AMOUNTS, TIMES, AND TEMPERATURES

Apart from baking, cooking is for the most part lenient and generally forgiving in regards to precise amounts and times. Ingredients here are organic, which is to say not industrial (pasta aside), and exact times differ from cook to cook, kitchen to kitchen, product to product. Most Spanish cooks smile indulgently when prodded for specific times and measurements, and view such numbers, if given, as guidelines. Their advice: Watch, taste, and adjust as you cook. That's pretty good advice.

A NOTE ON INGREDIENTS

Unless otherwise specified, it is assumed that ingredients are cleaned, washed, peeled if needed, and so on. A few particular ingredients are worth highlighting:

Olive oil: While I acknowledge that extra-virgin olive oil is superior and should be used in just about every case, the reality is that many Spaniards often cook with a lighter (refined) olive oil called *suave* (soft) on bottles or 0.4° (also written as 0'4) referring to the degree of acidity, or else a "lighter" extra-virgin olive oil, by which I mean one that isn't too expensive or too heavy. But they will always reach for the good stuff in the pantry to dress salads, use in certain sauces (especially cold ones), drizzle over bread and fish, and so on.

Salt: Salt opens up flavors and accentuates them. The amount needed depends on many factors (including one's own personal level of "saltiness"), and specific quantities are given in only a few cases. When I call for "salt," I mean sea salt. I have specified "flaky sea salt" where the texture of the flakes can be fully appreciated, usually for "finishing" a dish. In a couple of cases, I have listed both "salt" and "flaky sea salt" in the ingredient list. There is no point in adding exquisite *flor de sal* to boiling water; use plain salt for that. Spanish brands of high-quality flaky sea salt may be harder to find than English Maldon salt, French *sel gris* or *fleur de sel*, kosher salt, and other fine options.

Dried red peppers: There are a number of mild, sweet dried red peppers whose pulp is soaked and scraped out before being used. *Romesco* and the slightly smaller *ñora* peppers are the most popular. Both are available outside Spain; see Sources, page 345. Darker, more earthy ancho chiles make a good substitution. They tend to be just slightly larger than romesco peppers. Romesco pulp is sold in jars (labels generally read *"carne de romesco"*). Choricero is a similar one popular in the Basque Country. Calculate about 2 teaspoons of pulp per dried pepper.

Dry-cured Spanish jamón: There is an entire world of Spain's legendary cured legs of ham. For the purpose of cooking with jamón in these recipes, use the least expensive options of Serrano ham (*jamón serrano* or *jamón del país*), or Italian prosciutto, which is often easier for many outside Spain to get. Eating a slice of jamón alone, though, is a different matter. In that case, go for *jamón ibérico* (from the black-footed Iberian pig; see page 133) and choose the best you can find—or afford.

Onions: Unless otherwise specified, "medium onions" can be either Spanish, yellow, or red. One of the finest onions in Spain—particularly nice in salads because of their mild, almost sweet taste—is the reddish purple, slightly flattened, and medium-size variety called Figueres.

Green peppers: Spanish *pimientos verdes* are long, tapered, and pointed, and about half the weight of a green bell pepper, with much thinner walls. In season, they can be found under the name "sweet Italian green pepper" or something similar. They are not hot! Do not confuse these with Anaheim chile peppers.

Stock: When using commercial stock in dishes that will simmer and reduce, dilute it with fresh water so that the stock doesn't overpower the other ingredients.

Vinegar: Dishes that include a significant amount of vinegar should be prepared in nonreactive cookware, such as stainless steel, glass, enamel, and so on; do not use copper or aluminum, as they will discolor.

A NOTE ON LANGUAGE AND TRANSLATIONS

While I have for the most part stuck to Castilian Spanish, certain dishes and products do carry their Catalan, Basque, or Galician names, from Spain's other three officially recognized languages. I have tried to offer the original names for dishes, traditions, and the like where possible. I would love to see these become more a part of the popular culinary lexicon in the manner of many Italian and French words now so commonly used.

Place names follow local versions and not Anglicized ones (so Sevilla and not Seville) or ones rendered into Castilian Spanish (so Lleida and not Lérida, A Coruña not La Coruña). Some names in the Basque Country are mentioned both in Basque and Castilian, such as Donostia (San Sebastián). These reflect not just standard usage, but what is found on both Michelin and Google maps.

All of the translations from Castilian and Catalan in the book are mine and I take complete responsibility for word choices and any errors. The handful of refrains, jingles, and songs included here—nearly all of them rhyming—I have translated more or less literally, getting their meaning but not necessarily their rhythm in English.

CHAPTER 1

SOUPS, BROTHS, STEWS, CREAMS, AND PULSES
cocidos, caldos, estofados, cremas y legumbres

Soup is surely the most fundamental of all of the country dishes. But as basic as it can be—and some soups *are* basic, so much so as to consist on a few bucolic occasions of little more than herbs, olive oil, a pinch of salt, and hot water—they tend to be nourishing, filling, and adaptable to what is in season or in the pantry.

For Spaniards, *sopa* usually means a broth made from boiling some bone-in meat or chicken, maybe beef or salted pork bones, chorizo, a handful of garbanzo beans, a couple of root vegetables—turnips, parsnips, carrots—and fresh herbs. These are cooked with patience, and given time for their goodness and flavors to seep into the *caldo*, or broth.

And then some fine *fideo* pasta noodles are tossed into the broth. But that "filler" can be even simpler—just a spoonful of chopped hard-boiled egg and cured jamón to give the soup some body. At the fullest, the soup becomes *cocido* (see page 24), eaten in two or three courses—first the broth with some pasta boiled in it, and the garbanzo beans and meats served afterwards.

There are stews, too: dark and rich ones with beef (see page 32) or oxtail (see page 271) in the interior provinces, and ones with seafood or fish from along the coasts. From Basque *marmitako* (see page 31) to Menorcan *caldereta* (see page 28), these were once largely humble concoctions, made on fishing boats or back on shore, with the small, bony fish that had little market value but packed a bold punch of flavor. "These are what our wives had to deal with at home," one elderly fisherman, lingering around the docks of a Mediterranean *lonja* (wholesale fish auction), told me once. "The better fish we sold to pay for the boat." And while soups are most often first courses, such stews can transform themselves into main ones.

Cremas (literally "creams") are usually a purée of vegetables—artichokes (see page 27) and wild mushrooms (see page 35) are two examples I chose to include here from the countless options. Perhaps these soups, more than their fellow *platos de cuchara* (dishes with spoons), echo the seasonal changes of the countryside, and reflect what is currently abundant in the garden, hills, or market.

For millennia, pulses have played a vital role in European civilization. They came largely from the east during antiquity—lentils from the Near East, garbanzo beans from the eastern Mediterranean—and their role in Spanish cuisine has been immense. And continues to be so. Filling, healthy, high in protein and fiber, and inexpensive, they form a cornerstone to the country diet, a foundation of countless meals, and are a staple in every sense.

The quantity and variety of pulses found in the Spanish pantry is wide. There is a range of white beans, from the large, meaty ones from Asturias to the tiny ones from the volcanic region of La Garrotxa near the Catalan town of Olot. There are various types of garbanzo beans, and two popular varieties of lentils: small brown Spanish Pardina lentils and larger, greenish brown ones called *castellana* or *rubia castellana* ("Castilian blond").

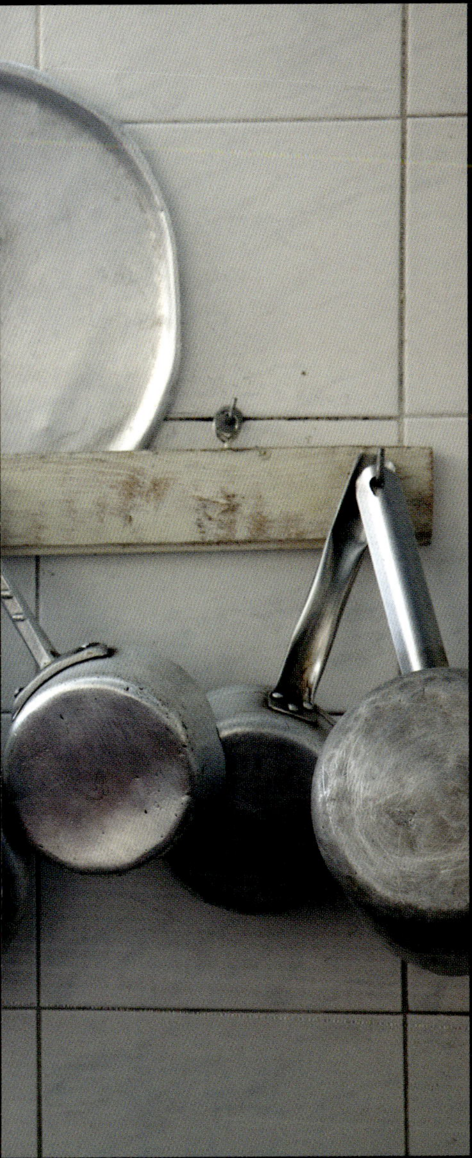
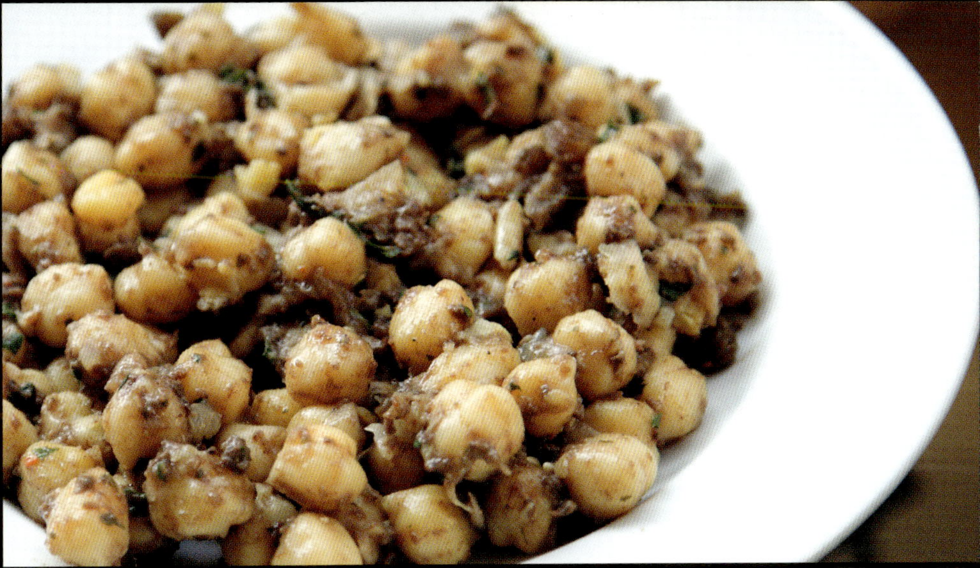
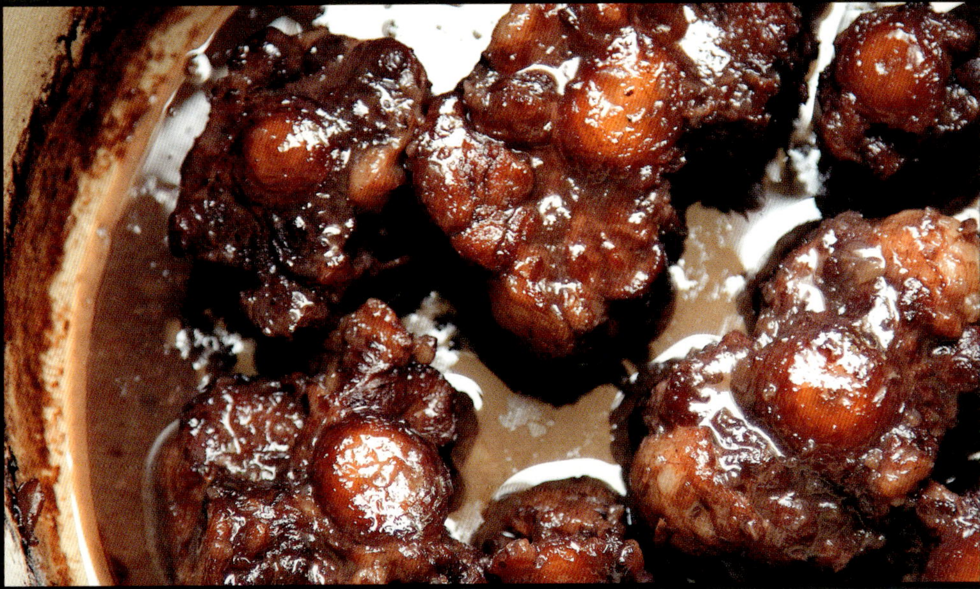
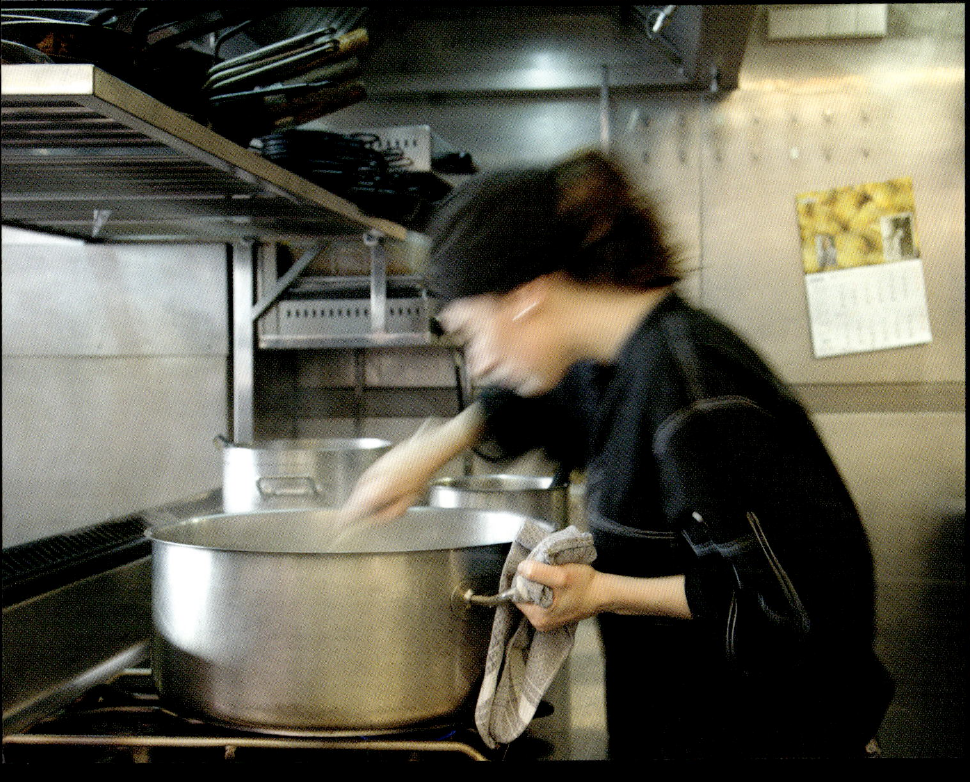

Across much of the central heartland of Spain, cocido is prepared in what today they call "Madrid-style." That the most country-esque dish in Spain is the one most associated with its capital city says a lot about the rustic nature of Spanish cuisine. Another winter dish synonymous with the capital is *callos a la madrileña*, a succulent stew of tripe with the pig's snout and feet, garbanzo beans, and plenty of spices. Both are typical examples of a dish's urban migration (in this case, from Extremadura and Andalucía) and continued popularity among the masses—of all classes.

As in some other of Madrid's finest, most classical restaurants (Lhardy comes to mind), cocido is a star attraction at the Ritz Hotel—one of the original three Ritz hotels (with Paris and London). Along with a sophisticated repertoire of game and wild mushroom dishes, cocido doesn't feel out of place in their Belle Époque–style Goya Restaurant. At the Ritz, they follow the age-old way of serving the cocido in *tres vuelcos*, literally "three overturnings," meaning courses: the soup, the vegetables, and then the meats. In the labyrinthine subterranean kitchen, I learned to prepare this signature plate, which I have adapted here for the home kitchen. One of the many nuances that separates their cocido from others is boiling the chorizos separately (with the blood sausage) so that the oily red color from the paprika doesn't bleed into the broth, and the final broth stays a rich golden color.

Some clients at the Ritz—and there are many who come faithfully for the cocido—request a small bowl of tomato sauce to spoon over the garbanzo beans. Here, I suggest adding a pinch of ground cumin to the sauce in the manner of some *madrileños*.

THE RITZ'S MADRID-STYLE COCIDO

COCIDO MADRILEÑO DE RITZ

SERVES 6

2 CUPS/375 G DRIED GARBANZO BEANS

1 POUND/455 G VEAL SHANK OR KNUCKLE, IN A SINGLE PIECE, OR OSSO BUCO

1 POUND/455 G BEEF BONES

8 OUNCES/225 G HAM BONES (SEE SOURCES, PAGE 345)

12 OUNCES/340 G OXTAIL (OPTIONAL)

8 OUNCES/225 G STREAKY SALT PORK, PANCETTA, OR UNSMOKED BACON, IN A SINGLE SLAB

2 LEEKS, TENDER WHITE AND GREEN PARTS ONLY, ROUGHLY CHOPPED

1 TO 1½ POUNDS/455 TO 680 G BONE-IN FREE-RANGE CHICKEN OR STEWING HEN, SKIN REMOVED AND FAT TRIMMED

1 EGG

2 TABLESPOONS MILK

6 OUNCES/170 G GROUND BEEF

6 OUNCES/170 G GROUND PORK

4 GARLIC CLOVES, MINCED

1 TABLESPOON MINCED FRESH FLAT-LEAF PARSLEY

SALT AND FRESHLY GROUND BLACK PEPPER

½ CUP/70 G PLAIN DRY BREADCRUMBS

3 TABLESPOONS EXTRA-VIRGIN OLIVE OIL

3 SMALL WHOLE SPANISH CHORIZO, ABOUT 6 OUNCES/ 170 G TOTAL

2 SMALL MORCILLA (BLOOD SAUSAGES), ABOUT 6 OUNCES/ 170 G TOTAL

½ HEAD GREEN CABBAGE, ABOUT 1½ POUNDS/680 G, CHOPPED

½ TEASPOON SPANISH PIMENTÓN DULCE (SWEET PAPRIKA)

3 CARROTS, PEELED AND CUT LENGTHWISE INTO THIRDS

8 OUNCES/225 G MEDIUM WHITE POTATOES, PEELED AND QUARTERED

3½ OUNCES/100 G FINE FIDEOS OR CRUSHED ANGEL HAIR PASTA

1 CUP/240 ML TOMATO SAUCE

1 PINCH GROUND CUMIN

1. The night before, rinse the garbanzo beans with water. Place them in a large bowl, cover with plenty of water, and soak for at least 12 hours. (If the water is "hard," add ½ teaspoon baking soda.) Drain, rinse away any yeasty or fermenting odors, and drain again. Tie the beans in a piece of cheesecloth, which will make removing them easier.

2. In a large soup pot, add the veal shank, beef and ham bones, oxtail (if using), and salt pork. Cover with 4 quarts/4 L cold water and bring to a boil. Skim off the foam. Add the beans and leeks. Reduce the heat to low and simmer uncovered for 1 hour. Add the chicken and simmer for 1½ hours.

3. In a bowl, whisk together the egg and milk and blend in the ground meats, 1 garlic clove, and the parsley. Season with salt and pepper and begin working in the breadcrumbs. Roll the mixture into two long cylinders, each about 1½ to 2 inches/4 to 5 cm in diameter and about 6 inches/15 cm long. In a sauté pan, heat 2 tablespoons of the olive oil over medium heat, add the meat cylinders, and brown, about 5 minutes, turning as needed. Remove and reserve.

4. In a saucepan, add about 1 cup/240 ml of the simmering broth, 1 cup/240 ml water, and the chorizo and morcilla. Bring them to a boil, reduce the heat to low, cover the pan, and gently boil until the sausages are tender, about 30 minutes. Remove from the heat and leave covered in the saucepan until ready to serve.

5. Bring a large pot of water to a boil. Add the cabbage and a generous pinch of salt; cover the pot and gently boil until the cabbage is tender, about 20 minutes. Transfer it to a colander to drain and cool. In a large, deep sauté pan, heat the remaining 1 tablespoon olive oil over medium heat, add the remaining garlic, the pimentón, and boiled cabbage; season with salt; and sauté for about 3 minutes to blend the flavors. Remove from the heat and cover the pan to keep warm.

6. Once the chicken has simmered for 1½ hours, add the carrots, potatoes, and meat cylinders to the pot. Simmer until the vegetables are tender and the beans can be easily pinched between thumb and forefinger, about 30 minutes.

7. Strain the broth into a clean saucepan. There should be between 7 and 8 cups/1.7 and 2 L. (Cover the meats, vegetables, and beans to keep warm.) Bring the broth to a boil, add the pasta, and boil until it is al dente, 2 to 3 minutes, following the time indicated on the package. Ladle the soup and pasta into bowls and serve as a first course.

8. Meanwhile, heat the tomato sauce, and stir in the cumin. Cover and set aside.

9. For the second course, remove the beans from the cheesecloth, arrange them with the vegetables on a large platter, and serve with the tomato sauce.

10. For the third course, cut the meats and meatballs into serving-size pieces and serve on another platter.

Catalan cocido is called *escudella*—or, more properly, *escudella i carn d'olla*, that second part literally meaning "and meat from the pot." One version—*olla de les quatre carns*—is supposed to have "four meats": veal, pork, chicken, and lamb. (But, unlike the cocidos from central Spain, there is no chorizo or blood sausage.)

It is a quotidian dish that still carries a deep cultural attachment. As Catalan food writer Néstor Luján (1922–1995) put it: "But in the subconscious of a Catalan persists a gratitude to the soup [pot], a nostalgia and maybe inextinguishable desire to return to the old life; good proof of this is that it's still eaten on Christmas Day for the large family meal." And so, in a slightly more elaborate form than this workday version here—with a pig's foot or a piece of ear, and, these days, *galets de Nadal* (large snail-shaped "Christmas" pasta)—it is prepared for the most important meal of the year in many households.

CATALAN TWO-COURSE SOUP

ESCUDELLA I CARN D'OLLA

SERVES 6

1½ CUPS/280 G DRIED GARBANZO BEANS

1 POUND/455 G VEAL SHANK OR KNUCKLE, IN A SINGLE PIECE, OR OSSO BUCO

8 OUNCES/225 G BEEF BONES

1 SMALL SALTED PORK BONE OR CURED JAMÓN BONE (SEE SOURCES, PAGE 345)

1 TO 1½ POUNDS/455 TO 680 G BONE-IN FREE-RANGE CHICKEN OR STEWING HEN, SKIN REMOVED AND FAT TRIMMED

3 CARROTS, QUARTERED LENGTHWISE

2 CELERY STALKS, FOLDED IN HALF

1 MEDIUM ONION, HALVED

1 TURNIP, HALVED LENGTHWISE

1 PARSNIP, HALVED

SALT

¼ HEAD GREEN CABBAGE, ABOUT 8 OUNCES/225 G

3 EGGS

8 OUNCES/225 G LEAN GROUND BEEF

8 OUNCES/225 G GROUND PORK

FRESHLY GROUND BLACK PEPPER

¾ CUP/110 G PLAIN DRY BREADCRUMBS

8 OUNCES/225 G SMALL (OR MINI) PASTA SHELLS FOR SOUP, SUCH AS CONCHIGLIETTE OR A VERY SMALL LUMACHE (SEE NOTE)

1. The night before, rinse the garbanzo beans with water. Place them in a large bowl, cover with plenty of water, and soak for at least 12 hours. (If the water is "hard," add ½ teaspoon baking soda.) Drain, rinse away any yeasty or fermenting odors, and drain again.

2. In a large stockpot over high heat, add the beans, veal shank, beef and pork bones and cover with 5 quarts/4.75 L water. Bring to a rolling boil and skim off any foam that comes up to the surface. Reduce the heat to low, cover the pot, and gently boil for 1 hour. Add the chicken, carrots, celery, onion, turnip, and parsnip; season with salt; cover the pot, and gently boil for 2 more hours.

3. Meanwhile, bring a large pot of water to a boil. Add the cabbage and a large pinch of salt and gently boil until it is tender, about 20 minutes. Remove from the heat and keep it in the pot until ready to serve.

4. Meanwhile, in a bowl, whisk the eggs. Add the beef and pork, season with salt and pepper, and begin working in most of the breadcrumbs, reserving a small amount. Form two large, elongated meatballs about 6 inches/15 cm long. Roll them in the remaining breadcrumbs.

5. After the broth has simmered for 3 hours, add the meatballs. (If needed, to keep the soup from overflowing the pot, remove some root vegetables.) Simmer for 45 minutes.

6. Strain the broth into a large saucepan, discarding the bones and herbs. Bring it to a boil over high heat. Add the pasta, cover the pot, and boil until it is al dente, 10 to 15 minutes, following the time indicated on the package.

7. Meanwhile, arrange the meats, meatballs, and beans on a large serving platter. Drain the cabbage and place it on the platter. Cover to keep warm.

8. Serve the soup with pasta in bowls as a first course. Follow this with the platter of meats and beans as a second course.

NOTE: If the pasta shells are quite large—meaning they take more than 10 minutes to boil—first partially boil them in plain water so that they don't suck up all of the broth. For pasta that takes 12 to 15 minutes, boil the shells in water for 2 to 5 minutes, drain, and immediately transfer them to the boiling broth. For even larger pasta shells, boil them first for about 7 minutes before draining and adding to the broth to finish cooking.

TRADITIONS

TWO-COURSE SOUP
cocido

So vast and varied is the Spanish landscape that there exists only one common dish across the country: cocido, a two-course soup made with meat, bones, fresh pork sausage, the foot or ear of a pig, a piece of stewing hen, garbanzo beans, some root vegetables, and herbs. After simmering for hours, these flavor-inducing ingredients are removed, and small pasta shapes are boiled in the broth. The first course is a bowl of broth with pasta; the second is a plate of the garbanzo beans, meats, and sausages. Of all of Spain's dishes, cocido most defines country cooking: economical but flavorful, simple, adaptable to what's in season. It's also filling, warm, and nourishing, three other important attributes of the rural kitchen.

But just as it's impossible to talk of a single *cocina española* (Spanish cuisine), it's impossible to talk about a single, nationwide cocido. Cocido can be defined only in regional terms, each with its distinct accent—*cocido andaluz* in Andalucía, with pieces of winter squash added to the vegetables and seasoned with saffron and even some sprigs of *hierbabuena* (mint); *escudella i carn d'olla* (see page 22) in Catalunya, with its different types of meats (chicken, pork, veal, lamb) and a large, oblong meatball or two; *cocido gallego* in Galicia, where the pig is the protagonist, and sometimes *grelos* (turnip greens) are added; and *cocido vasco* in the Basque Country, with other dried beans in addition to the garbanzos.

One of the most original versions in Spain is *cocido maragato* from around the area of Astorga in Castilla y León. *Maragatos* were muleteers (mule drivers) of still-disputed ethnic origin. (Some ethnologists think they are descendants of the original Berbers who came to Spain from North Africa in the eighth century.) While the ingredients might be similar to other cocidos in the interior of the country, the courses are eaten in reverse order: first the meat, then the vegetables and garbanzo beans (the local, tiny variety from nearby Fuentesaúco), then, finally, the broth.

Why the difference in order? I asked one of the Saez brothers who run, for the fifth generation, Restaurante La Peseta in Astorga, where cocido is a celebrated specialty. He repeated the saying about Maragato cocido that roughly translates to this: "If there is anything left over, then let it be the broth."

CASTILIAN GARLIC SOUP

SOPA DE AJO CASTELLANA

SERVES 4

Any rhapsodies made about soup's economy, warmth, and filling properties seem specifically aimed at *sopa de ajo castellana*. This soup takes its name from the central heartland of Spain, where it is a hugely popular dish. While some call it simply *sopa castellana*, others refer to it as *sopa de ajo*, literally "soup of garlic." This is a basic, classic version, though I have found many variations while traveling the back roads of Castilla. I always delight in the subtle differences from one house or rural restaurant to the next, such as a few added toasted cumin seeds.

5 CUPS/1.2 L MILD CHICKEN STOCK (PAGE 336)

6 TABLESPOONS EXTRA-VIRGIN OLIVE OIL

6 GARLIC CLOVES, THINLY SLICED

½ CUP/60 G FINELY CHOPPED DRY-CURED SPANISH JAMÓN (SEE INGREDIENT NOTE, PAGE 16)

½ CUP/60 G FINELY CHOPPED SPANISH CHORIZO

4 OUNCES/115 G SLICED COUNTRY-STYLE BREAD, DAY OLD OR TOASTED, CUBED

1 TEASPOON SPANISH PIMENTÓN DULCE (SWEET PAPRIKA) OR A BLEND OF SWEET AND PICANTE (SPICY) PAPRIKA

4 EGGS

1. Preheat the oven to 350°F/180°C/gas mark 4.

2. In a saucepan, bring the chicken stock to a boil. Reduce the heat, cover the pan, and keep it at a low boil.

3. In a large ovenproof terra-cotta cazuela or skillet, heat the olive oil over medium heat. Add the garlic, jamón, and chorizo, and cook until the garlic is golden and fragrant but not burned, about 2 minutes. Add the bread, sprinkle on the pimentón, stir to blend, and then quickly pour the boiling stock into the pan before the pimentón can burn and become bitter. Reduce the heat to low and gently boil for 5 minutes.

4. One by one, crack the eggs into the pan and gently transfer the pan to the oven, watching that the eggs don't huddle together. Bake until the egg whites are set but the yolks still runny, 6 or 7 minutes. Serve from the cazuela.

BASQUE LEEK SOUP

PORRUSALDA

SERVES 4

The Basque name translates to "broth of leek" and this soup is about as humble and homey as it sounds. Sometimes you find the soup with a bit of salt cod added for flavor. Of course, befitting the soup's humble nature, it doesn't get an expensive cut of salt cod, but usually a piece from near the tail or head.

2 TABLESPOONS EXTRA-VIRGIN OLIVE OIL, PLUS MORE FOR DRIZZLING

1 MEDIUM ONION, FINELY CHOPPED

SALT

6 CUPS/1.5 L MILD CHICKEN STOCK (PAGE 336) OR WATER

4 LEEKS, WHITE AND TENDER GREEN PARTS ONLY, CUT INTO 1-INCH-/2.5-CM-THICK ROUNDS

1 CARROT, CUT INTO THIN ROUNDS

2 MEDIUM WHITE POTATOES

1. In a large pot, heat the olive oil over medium heat and add the onion with a generous pinch of salt. Cook until the onions are soft and lightly golden, 8 to 10 minutes. Pour in the stock, add the leeks and carrot, and bring to a boil. Reduce the heat to low and gently boil for 15 minutes.

2. Peel the potatoes. Working over the pan and adding them directly to the stew, break the potatoes into generous bite-size pieces by making a small cut with a paring knife, twisting the blade, and snapping off a piece. (You will hear the noise.) Continue to gently boil for 20 minutes, or until all of the vegetables are tender.

3. Generously drizzle more olive oil into the pot, stir, and ladle the soup into bowls to serve.

CREAMY ARTICHOKE AND LEEK SOUP

CREMA DE ALCACHOFAS Y PUERROS

SERVES 4

Rich, silky *cremas*—literally "creams"—are a staple on the Spanish table, served as a first course or sometimes for a light dinner. Look for artichokes heavy for their size, with tightly packed leaves (opened leaves are a sign of being overripe), but not excessively hard. To check freshness, hold one to your ear and squeeze it—if you hear a slight crunch, then the artichoke is fresh. The soup is best with a textured creaminess—though without fibers. Purée it extremely well until it has a fine smoothness.

1 LEMON
2 POUNDS/910 G FRESH MEDIUM ARTICHOKES
¼ CUP/60 G BUTTER
2 CUPS/200 G FINELY CHOPPED LEEKS, WHITE AND TENDER GREEN PARTS ONLY
2½ CUPS/600 ML VEGETABLE STOCK (PAGE 335) OR CHICKEN STOCK (PAGE 336)
1½ CUPS/360 ML WHOLE MILK
PINCH FRESHLY GRATED NUTMEG
SALT AND FRESHLY GROUND BLACK PEPPER

1. Fill a large bowl with cool water. Cut the lemon into wedges, squeeze into the water, and then drop them into the bowl. Trim the artichokes following the directions on page 339, making sure the tough outer leaves have been stripped away. Leave the trimmed artichokes in the lemon water to keep from darkening until ready to use.

2. In a heavy soup pot, melt the butter over medium heat. Add the leeks and cook until they are soft and translucent but not browned, about 10 minutes.

3. Drain the artichokes, pat dry with paper towels, and add them to the pot. Cover the pot and cook, stirring frequently, until they are tender, 10 to 15 minutes. Pour in the stock and bring to a boil. Reduce the heat to low and simmer, covered, for 15 to 20 minutes or until the artichokes are extremely tender.

4. Remove the pot from the heat and let cool for 5 minutes, stirring from time to time. Check that the leaves are not still tough or fibrous; if so, either trim and discard the fibrous bits or cover the pot and cook for another 5 minutes or so.

5. Working in batches as needed, purée the pot contents in a food processor or blender until creamy smooth. Or, purée in the pot itself, using an immersion hand blender.

6. Return the puréed soup to the pot, stir in the milk and nutmeg, and season with salt. Over low heat and stirring frequently, slowly heat thoroughly without letting it reach a boil, about 10 minutes.

7. Ladle the soup into bowls, generously grind black pepper over the top, and serve hot.

Caldereta de langosta—a stew made with locally caught spiny lobster, a smaller and sweeter-tasting crustacean than the American lobster—is a legendary dish of Fornells, an isolated fishing village on the north coast of Menorca. The local season for spiny lobster runs from April 1 until August 31, and during this short season, the lobsters carry roe, which is incorporated into the dish. It's a silken stew, and served from the deep cazuela called a *caldera*, which gives the dish its name.

There are a couple of similar soups prepared in Fornell's calderas that are eaten year-round. One incorporates a range of shellfish, the other—this one—of fish. Specifically, it calls for *pescado de roca*, literally "rockfish," small, bony fish whose flavor drives Mediterranean dishes like this (as well as that classic from nearby Provence, bouillabaisse). This velvety Menorcan soup is topped with some flakes of a larger fish, such as bream or sea bass, and often served with very thin slices of toasted bread cut from the local low-salt country loaf.

VELVETY MENORCAN FISH SOUP

CALDERETA DE PESCADO

SERVES 4

2 POUNDS/910 G SMALL SOUP FISH OR ASSORTED HEADS AND BONES OF A FIRM, WHITE-FLESHED NON-OILY FISH

1 MEDIUM BREAM, SEA BASS, OR RED SNAPPER, CLEANED

2 MEDIUM LEEKS, WHITE AND TENDER GREEN PARTS ONLY, FINELY CHOPPED

2 MEDIUM ONIONS, FINELY CHOPPED

1 CELERY STALK, FINELY CHOPPED

3 TABLESPOONS EXTRA-VIRGIN OLIVE OIL

1 CARROT, FINELY CHOPPED

2 RIPE MEDIUM TOMATOES, PEELED, SEEDED, AND CHOPPED

¼ CUP/60 ML DRY WHITE WINE

½ TEASPOON SPANISH PIMENTÓN DULCE (SWEET PAPRIKA)

1 SMALL PINCH SAFFRON THREADS, DRY-TOASTED AND GROUND (SEE PAGE 340)

SALT AND FRESHLY GROUND BLACK PEPPER

DENSE COUNTRY BREAD, PREFERABLY ONE OR TWO DAYS OLD, FOR GARNISHING

1. Rinse all the fish and put them in a large stock or soup pot. Add half of the leeks, half of the onions, and the celery; cover with 8 cups/2 L water, and bring to a gentle boil over medium-high heat. Cover the pot, reduce the heat to medium-low, and gently boil for 20 minutes, until the essence of the sea has been poached from the fish. Strain, reserving the liquid. Remove the bream and any larger fish; skin, debone, and flake the meat. Set aside. Discard the vegetables and remaining fish.

continued

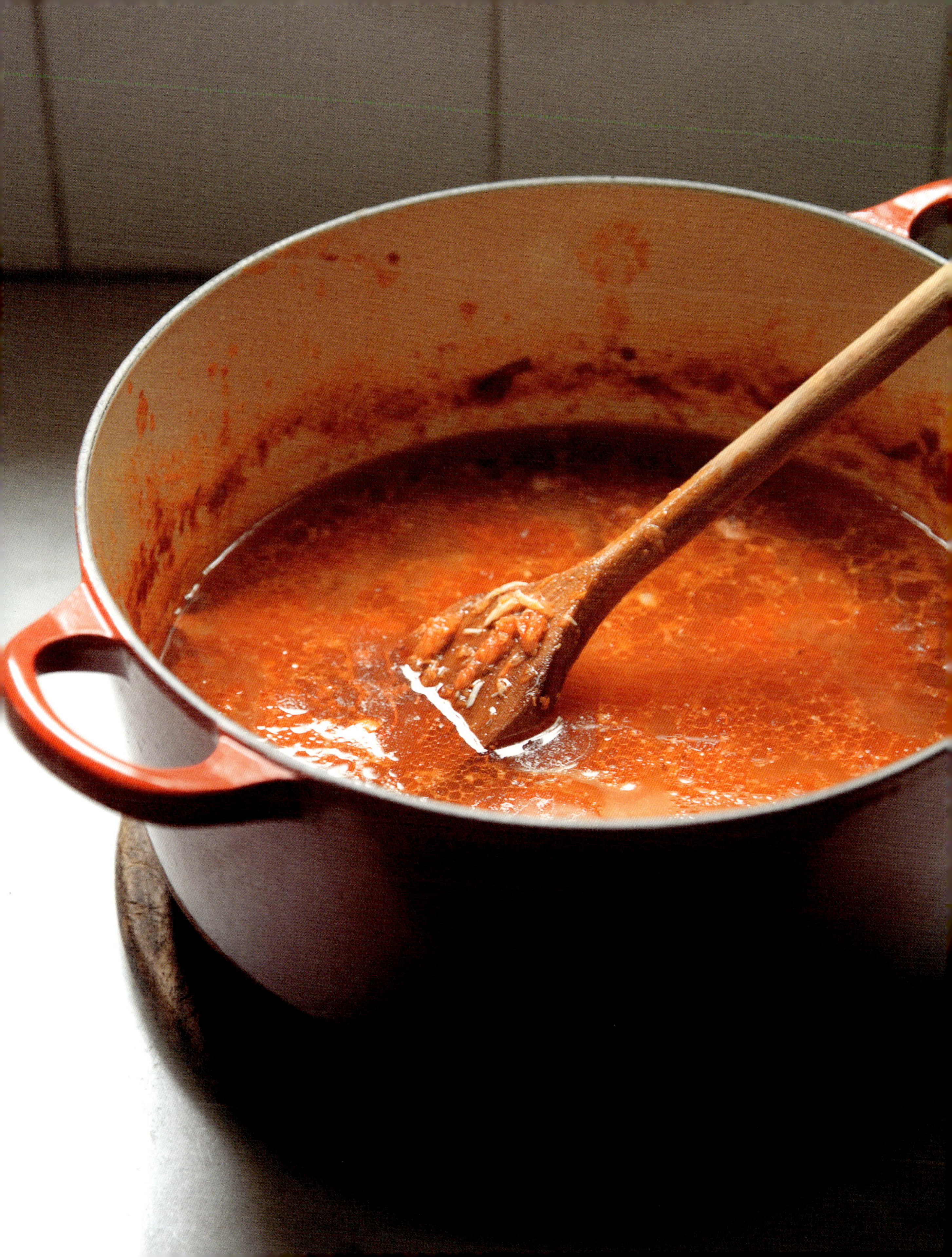

2. In a deep cazuela, Dutch oven, or large, heavy pot, heat the olive oil over medium heat and prepare a sofrito: Add the remaining leeks and onions and cook until they are pale and tender, about 8 minutes. Add the carrot and cook until it has softened somewhat and turned a yellowish orange color, about 8 minutes. Add the tomatoes and cook until pulpy and darker red, about 10 minutes, adding in a few tablespoons of simmering stock from time to time to keep it moist. Add the wine and cook for 2 minutes to burn off the alcohol. Stir in 1 cup/240 ml of the reserved stock, lower the heat, and simmer until the carrot is very tender and the sauce has concentrated down, about 15 minutes. Pass the sauce through a food mill and return it to the pan.

3. Stir in the remaining 7 cups/1.76 L reserved stock. Add the pimentón and saffron and season with salt and pepper. Bring to a simmer over medium heat and simmer uncovered for 30 minutes.

4. Meanwhile, preheat the broiler. Slice the bread as thinly as possible. Arrange it on a baking sheet, and place under the broiler until golden and toasted. Transfer to a bread basket.

5. Remove the pot from the heat and sprinkle the reserved flaked fish into the pot. Cover the pot for 1 to 2 minutes before ladling the soup into bowls and serving with the toast.

BASQUE FRESH TUNA AND POTATO STEW

MARMITAKO

SERVES 6

Like many Spanish fish stews—from *suquet* (see page 165) in Catalunya to *caldereta* (see page 28) in the Balearic Islands—the roots of this Basque dish lie with the humble fisherman. The name comes from the large cooking pots called *marmitas* used on boats from Basque *puertos pesqueros* (fishing ports) like Bermeo, Mundaka, and Lekeitio along the coast of Vizcaya. Potatoes kept well at sea, and fresh bonito was easy to catch in summer. This recipe calls for Spanish *pimentón dulce* (sweet paprika), but you often find the stew prepared using dried red *choricero* peppers. Use these instead of pimentón if you can get them. Soak the peppers in hot water for 30 minutes and scrape out the pulp following the directions on page 183.

If you can't find good fresh tuna, you can prepare this recipe using salmon steaks.

¼ CUP/60 ML OLIVE OIL

1 POUND/455 G FRESH BONITO TUNA OR ANOTHER FRESH TUNA, CUT INTO 1-INCH/2.5-CM CUBES

1 MEDIUM ONION, FINELY CHOPPED

3 GARLIC CLOVES, MINCED

½ GREEN BELL PEPPER OR 1 SWEET ITALIAN GREEN PEPPER, CUT INTO 1-INCH/2.5-CM PIECES

2 RIPE MEDIUM TOMATOES, PEELED, SEEDED, AND FINELY CHOPPED

½ TEASPOON SPANISH PIMENTÓN DULCE (SWEET PAPRIKA)

SALT

2 POUNDS/910 G MEDIUM WHITE POTATOES, CUT INTO 1-INCH/2.5-CM CUBES

1 BAY LEAF

5 CUPS/1.2 L FISH STOCK (PAGE 335) OR WATER

1. In a deep cazuela, Dutch oven, or large, heavy pot, heat the olive oil over medium-high heat. Working in small batches, add the tuna and sear the cubes on all sides, just 1 minute or less per batch. Transfer to a platter.

2. Add the onion and cook until it begins to soften and turn pale, about 5 minutes. Add the garlic and bell pepper and cook until fragrant and softened, about 5 minutes. Add the tomatoes and cook until pulpy and darker red, about 10 minutes. Stir in the pimentón, season with salt, and add the potatoes. Turn to coat and cook for 1 minute. Add the bay leaf and pour in the stock. Bring to a boil.

3. Once the liquid begins to boil, reduce the heat to medium-low, and simmer until the potatoes are tender and the tip of a knife can easily penetrate them, 20 to 25 minutes, stirring from time to time. Add the tuna, cover the pot, and cook until the tuna is just opaque throughout, 3 to 5 minutes. Immediately remove the pot from the heat.

4. Let the stew rest for a few minutes, ladle it into bowls, and serve.

Found from Asturias to Andalucía, and often using local breeds of cows that graze the fields, beef stew is a staple across Spain.

The key to keeping the meat tender is to *marcar*—literally "to mark," which means sear or quickly brown—the pieces first over high heat without crowding the pan and without the pieces losing their moisture. Then you cook it over low heat, very slowly, just letting the bubbles pop up on the surface. Cooking it like this is called *chup-chup*, pronounced "choop-choop." The word is onomatopoeiac, and the simmering should sound like it.

As with other stews that have potatoes, "snap" the pieces of potatoes directly into the soup (as opposed to cutting), so that they release more starch and help thicken the dish.

BEEF STEW

ESTOFADO DE BUEY

SERVES 4

2 POUNDS/910 G STEWING BEEF OR VEAL, CUT INTO 1-INCH/2.5-CM CUBES
SALT AND FRESHLY GROUND BLACK PEPPER
3 TABLESPOONS EXTRA-VIRGIN OLIVE OIL
4 RIPE MEDIUM TOMATOES, HALVED CROSSWISE, SEEDED, AND GRATED (SEE PAGE 339)
1 MEDIUM ONION, CHOPPED
1 CARROT, CUT INTO THIN ROUNDS
4 GARLIC CLOVES, GENTLY CRUSHED IN THEIR PEELS
½ CUP/120 ML DRY WHITE OR RED WINE
1½ CUPS/360 ML LIGHT BEEF STOCK (PAGE 336) OR WATER
1 BAY LEAF
3 MEDIUM WHITE POTATOES

1. Season the meat with salt and pepper. In a cazuela, heavy casserole, large sauté pan, or heavy skillet, heat the olive oil over high heat. Working in single-layer batches that don't crowd the pan, add the meat and sear it, turning as needed, 7 to 10 minutes total. Transfer to a platter and cover to keep warm.

2. Reduce the heat to medium, add the tomatoes, onion, carrot, and garlic and cook for 5 minutes. Stir in the wine, cook for 1 minute, allowing the alcohol to burn off, and return the meat to the pan. Turn the pieces to coat. Pour in the stock and add the bay leaf. Bring to a simmer, reduce the heat to low, partly cover the pot, and cook, just letting bubbles slowly break the surface for 1 hour (*chup-chup*). Stir from time to time to keep it from sticking.

3. Peel the potatoes. Working over the pan and adding them directly to the stew, break the potatoes into generous bite-size pieces by making a small cut with a paring knife, twisting the blade, and snapping off a piece. (You will hear the noise.)

4. Cook for a final 45 minutes over low heat, never letting it boil, until the meat is very tender and the potatoes are tender and slightly crumbling at the edges. Add a touch of water during cooking if needed to keep it loose. Serve in wide bowls.

TRADITIONS

HUNTING FOR WILD MUSHROOMS
buscando setas

"Mushrooms are the muse of the forest," the late, celebrated Catalan chef Santi Santamaria once wrote in his Sunday *La Vanguardia* newspaper magazine column, "that free us from the temptation to forget that nature is the creator and, at the same time, the most colossal, seductive, and mysterious creation. Only nature surpasses nature."

I love that kind of over-the-top sentiment that wild mushrooms have the ability to trigger—even in the likes of Santamaria, who had access to the finest of nature's products for his three-Michelin-starred restaurant Can Fabes in Sant Celoni, about halfway between Barcelona and Girona in the Montseny.

The intense, earthy flavors of mushrooms are well-loved across Spain, from chefs like Santamaria to school children, and legions of Spaniards from the Basque Country to Andalucía head to the hills to collect them themselves. For many, looking for *setas* or *hongos*, as some types are called in Spain, has tradition and ritual—getting up early, heading to a favorite, often secret spot in the hills (whose exact location will never be divulged), and walking and searching. Dark-gold *rebozuelos* (chanterelles) or meaty, brownish orange *níscalos* (delicious milk caps) are cut with a knife and gently set into a wicker basket to take back to the kitchen. Autumn and early winter is the main season, but there are varieties that appear in spring—most famously morels—and even during summer. Some are toxic, of course, and one should never eat a found mushroom unless it can be positively identified as a safe species. (Recently, there has been a spate of deaths and serious illnesses from urban foragers in Barcelona consuming the wrong kinds, reminders of the potential potency of the toxins.)

Mushrooms have an intense flavor that corrals the forest's humid essence. Every Spanish cook has a preferred way to prepare them—with pig's trotters, stewed with rabbit, scrambled with eggs (my own favorite; see page 130), or stuffed into cannelloni pasta (see page 160). For many, the best is also the simplest—sautéed in olive oil and seasoned with coarse sea salt, garlic, and some chopped fresh parsley, and perhaps a bit of jamón to give it a savory kick. After devouring a plate of these following a successful day's mushroom hunt, it is hard not to wax at least a little poetically *a la* Santamaria on these forest pleasures.

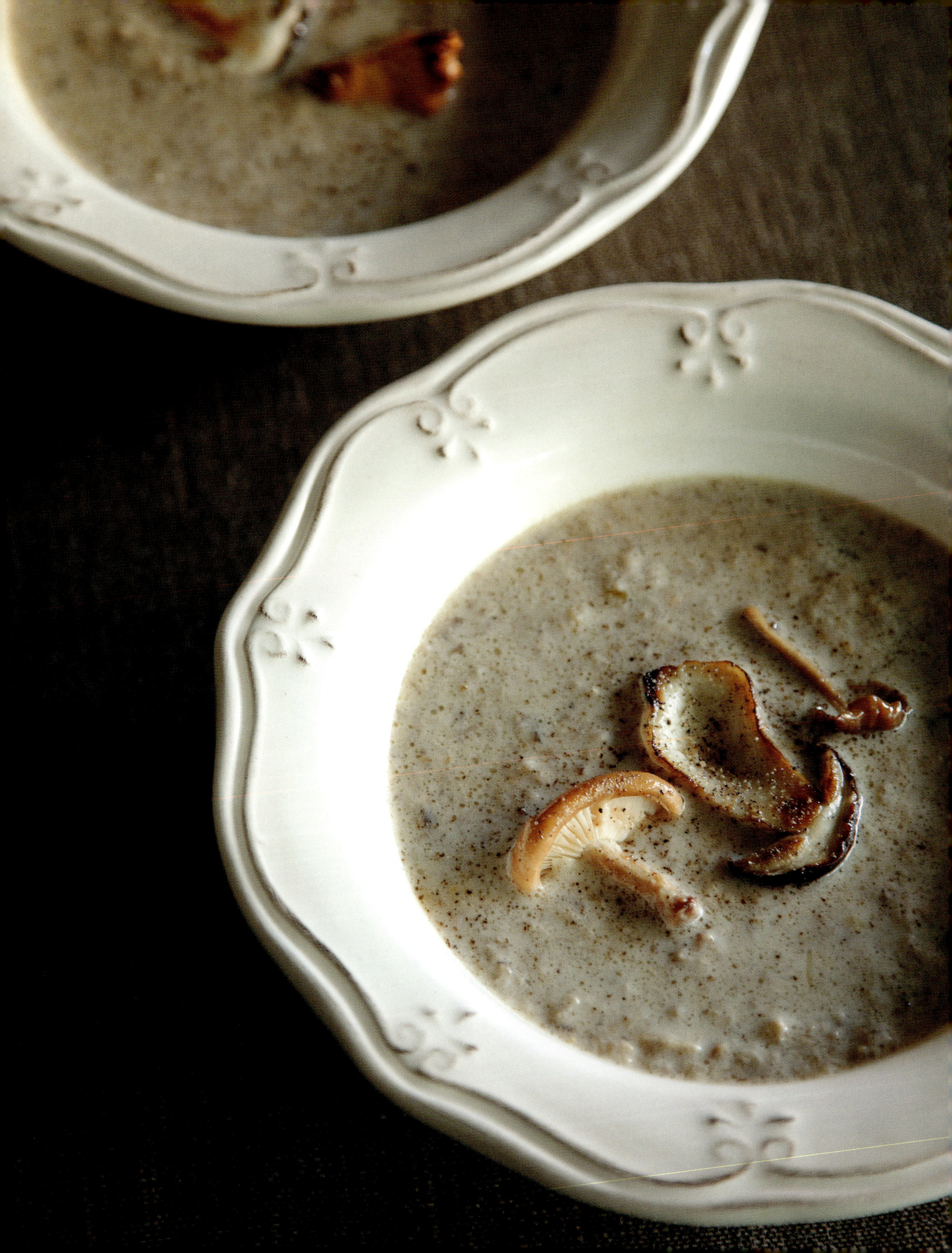

CREAM OF SEASONAL MUSHROOMS

CREMA DE SETAS DE TEMPORADA

SERVES 4

This warm and soothing soup brings the earthiness of wild mushrooms to the bowl. This really tastes like wild mushrooms—not the bland "cream of mushroom soup" found in cans on supermarket shelves. Use some button mushrooms for body, but be sure to blend in at least a handful of chanterelles or another bold-flavored wild variety. This is a perfect dish to use those imperfect and broken mushrooms from the bottom of the basket (they will be puréed anyway).

1 POUND/455 G ASSORTED WILD OR CULTIVATED MUSHROOMS

3 TABLESPOONS EXTRA-VIRGIN OLIVE OIL

2 CUPS/200 G FINELY CHOPPED LEEKS, WHITE AND TENDER GREEN PARTS ONLY

4 GARLIC CLOVES, CHOPPED

3 CUPS/720 ML MILD CHICKEN STOCK (PAGE 336), VEGETABLE STOCK (PAGE 335), OR WATER

¾ CUP/180 ML HEAVY CREAM

SALT AND FRESHLY GROUND BLACK PEPPER

1. Clean the mushrooms following the directions on page 339. Set aside a handful of the nicest ones for the garnish. Roughly chop the remaining ones.

2. In a heavy soup pot, heat 2 tablespoons of the olive oil over medium heat. Add the leeks and cook, stirring frequently, until they are golden and nearly translucent, about 5 minutes. Add the garlic and cook until fragrant, 1 to 2 minutes. Add the chopped mushrooms and cook for 5 minutes, stirring frequently. Pour in the stock and bring to a boil. Reduce the heat, cover the pot, and simmer for 30 minutes, or until the vegetables are very tender. Remove the pot from the heat, uncover, and let cool for 5 to 10 minutes, stirring from time to time.

3. Working in batches as needed, purée the soup in a food processor or blender, until creamy smooth. Or, purée in the pot itself, using an immersion hand blender.

4. Return the puréed soup to the pot, stir in the cream, and season with salt. Slowly heat over medium-low heat and stir frequently, without letting it reach a boil, 5 to 8 minutes.

5. Meanwhile, quarter or thinly slice the reserved mushrooms depending on their shape. In a skillet, heat the remaining 1 tablespoon olive oil over high heat and sear the mushrooms until golden, 2 to 3 minutes.

6. Ladle the soup into bowls, garnish with the seared mushrooms, and generously grind black pepper over the top. Serve hot.

SPINACH WITH GARBANZO BEANS

ESPINACAS CON GARBANZOS

SERVES 4

Garbanzo beans combine well with numerous other ingredients, while offering substance, texture, and their own earthy flavors. A small dish of stewed garbanzo beans with spinach is a popular bar tapa in Andalucía, and at home, it makes a comforting first course. The final texture should be moist but not watery. Serve in shallow bowls or, in the style of Andalusian bars, small terra-cotta *cazuelitas* (casseroles dishes).

3 CUPS/500 G CANNED GARBANZO BEANS
12 OUNCES/340 G FRESH TRIMMED SPINACH LEAVES
3 TABLESPOONS EXTRA-VIRGIN OLIVE OIL
2 THIN SLICES BAGUETTE, DAY OLD OR TOASTED
3 GARLIC CLOVES, PEELED
1 MEDIUM ONION, FINELY CHOPPED
1 TEASPOON GROUND CUMIN
1 TEASPOON SPANISH PIMENTÓN DULCE (SWEET PAPRIKA)
SALT
2 TEASPOONS SHERRY OR WINE VINEGAR

1. Drain, rinse, and place the garbanzo beans in a saucepan with about 2 cups/480 ml water. Bring to a boil, remove from the heat, cover the pan, and leave in the liquid until ready to use.

2. Wash the spinach in a couple of changes of water and drain. Put it in a large pot, cover with a lid, and wilt over medium heat, about 5 minutes.

3. In a large skillet or sauté pan, heat the olive oil over medium heat, add the bread and garlic, and cook until golden, 1 to 2 minutes. Remove when done and reserve. In the same oil, add the onion and cook until soft and translucent, 8 to 10 minutes.

4. Meanwhile, prepare a picada with the reserved bread, garlic, and 2 tablespoons of liquid from the beans, following the directions on page 39.

5. Drain the beans, reserving the liquid. Add them to the skillet and stir in the picada, cumin, and pimentón. Season with salt and moisten with the vinegar and 1½ cups/360 ml of the reserved liquid. Bring to a boil, reduce the heat to low, and cook mostly covered until tender and the flavors have melded, about 20 minutes. The dish should be moist. Stir in a bit more of the reserved liquid from the beans, if needed.

6. Drain off any excess liquid from the spinach and add the leaves to the skillet. Stir well and cook uncovered for 3 or 4 minutes. Spoon into bowls and serve hot.

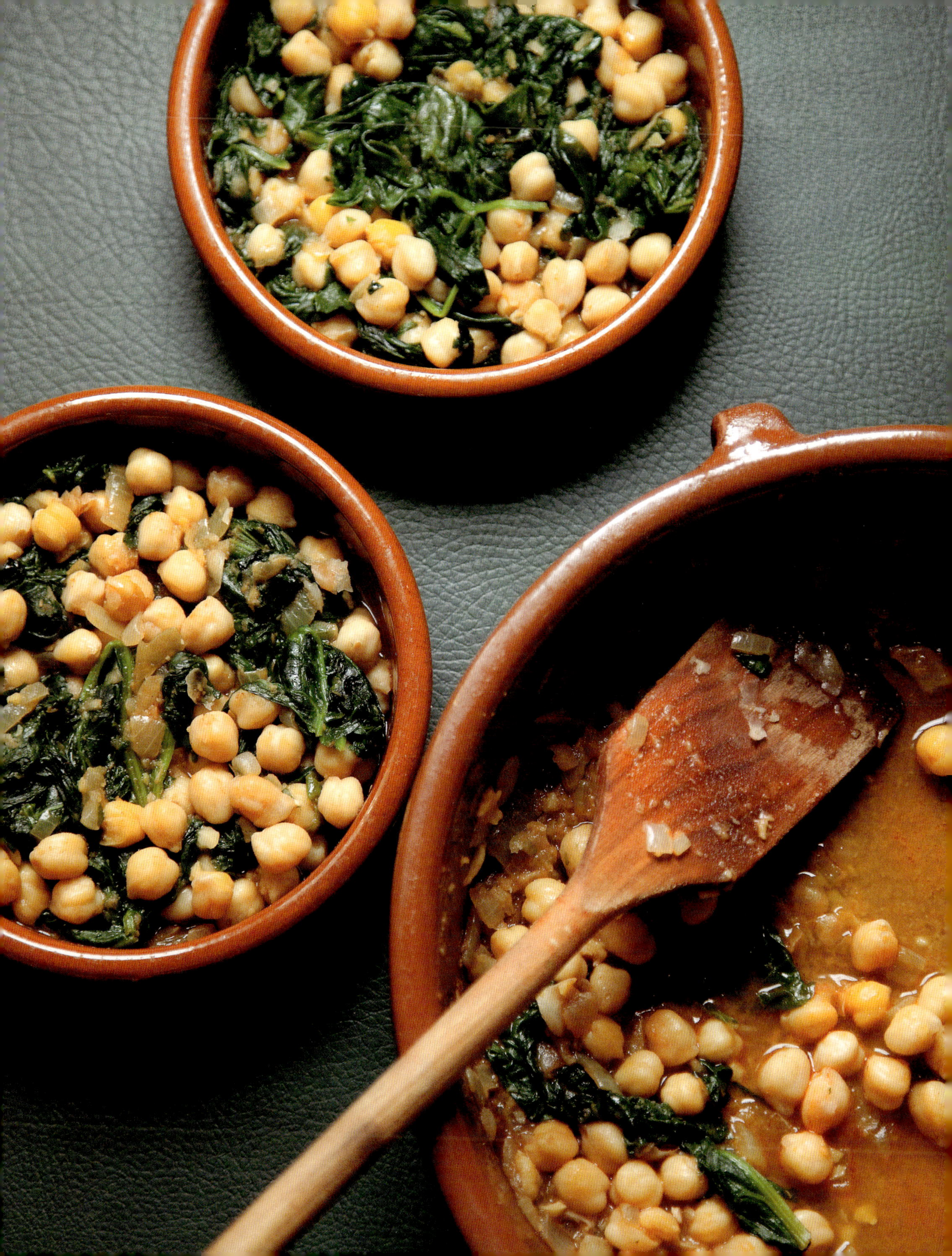

INGREDIENTS

EL SOFRITO AND LA PICADA

Many Spanish recipes, and particularly those from along the Mediterranean, begin with a *sofrito*, a slow-cooked aromatic base of (usually) onions and tomatoes. Called *sofregit* in Catalunya, Valencia, and the Balearic Islands, and *refrito* by some cooks in the center of the country, it often also includes garlic, sometimes sweet green pepper, and pieces of cuttlefish or squid. A good sofrito cannot be hurried: The onions should be slowly softened as their sweetness is drawn out without being scorched; tomatoes should cook equally without rush as their acidity dissipates, flavors deepen, color darkens, and texture becomes soft and pulpy.

Sofrito gives Spanish cooking a point of identity, and dozens of recipes in this book are built upon this base. Allow time for that foundation to be solid, for the sofrito's flavors to concentrate down and the consistency to thicken. That means 8 to 10 minutes for the onions, and between 10 and 20 (or even 30) minutes for the tomatoes. The final consistency should be moist but not runny, akin to a mushy marmalade, with a darkish red color. Longer cooking will yield a deeper, more flavorful sofrito. Dribble in a bit of water or stock a few times as it cooks to keep it moist. A pinch or two of sugar can be added to a sofrito if you're using out-of-season tomatoes that are a bit acidic.

It begins with onions. As they will stop browning once the tomatoes (which have moisture) are added, do not add the latter until the former have reached their desired tone. While I usually suggest using grated tomatoes, if using chopped ones, use a wooden spoon with a flattened end to tap down on the sofrito as it cooks to help break up pieces.

There are two ways to incorporate garlic into sofrito. The first is to add the finely chopped garlic to the onions just before they begin to turn brown; this method follows. There is a second way, ideal when the recipe also calls for a *picada* (a pounded paste of garlic, nuts, and parsley stirred in at the end of a dish; see following). Add the garlic to the oil *before* the onions, removing it once the garlic turns golden and aromatic. This nicely flavors the oil and softens the bite of the garlic, which will be pounded with the other ingredients in the picada and incorporated later into the dish.

A *picada* is a dense, pounded paste of (usually) toasted almonds or hazelnuts, fresh flat-leaf parsley, a small amount of bread, and garlic. Stirred into slow-cooked stews and braised dishes, certain rice dishes, stewed lentils and garbanzo beans, and soups toward the end of cooking, it acts as a thickener and offers a backbone of deep, rich flavors. In the south of Spain and elsewhere, it is known as a *majado* or even, by some, as a *picadillo*. It is a highly original element to the Spanish kitchen, especially in Catalunya and along the Mediterranean.

The garlic in the following recipe—a whole peeled clove—is quickly sautéed to soften its flavor, but, depending on the dish, it can be added raw. Only a handful of almonds or hazelnuts are used, and these should be well pounded or ground so that the picada can fully integrate into the sauce. In many rabbit dishes, the liver of the rabbit is commonly cooked and then pounded into the picada, too. This adds a rustic depth to flavors as well as creaminess to the dish. A picada can be quickly whirred in a food processor, but pounding a picada in a mortar with a pestle by hand gives more control over the final texture.

EL SOFRITO

MAKES ABOUT 1¼ CUPS/250 G

4 RIPE MEDIUM TOMATOES
3 TO 4 TABLESPOONS EXTRA-VIRGIN OLIVE OIL
1 MEDIUM ONION
SALT
1 GARLIC CLOVE, FINELY CHOPPED (OPTIONAL)

Halve the tomatoes crosswise, seed, and grate them following the directions on page 339. Alternatively, blanch and peel them following the directions on page 339, seed, and finely chop. Reserve all of the juices.

In a cazuela, heavy casserole, or large sauté pan or skillet, heat the olive oil over medium heat. Add the onion and a pinch of salt and cook, stirring frequently, as the onion turns pale and then translucent, 8 to 10 minutes. Add the garlic (if using) and cook, stirring almost continually, until aromatic, about 1 minute. Add the tomatoes and their juices and stir well. Cook uncovered over low heat, stirring often and tapping down on the ingredients with a wooden spoon to help break them down, until the tomato is dark, pulpy, and has lost its acidity, 10 to 20 minutes. Dribble in 2 or 3 tablespoons water two or three times during cooking to keep the sofrito from drying out. It can be made ahead and refrigerated for a day or two.

QUICKER SOFRITO: Once, many years ago—I hadn't lived in Spain for long—I remarked that I was going to make a "quick sofrito" to my mother-in-law. She looked at me almost in shock. "There is no such thing," she said. She was right. Indeed, a "quick sofrito" is somewhat of an oxymoron, but a *quicker* one can be prepared, using a wider skillet—to allow more onions to touch the skillet and the tomato to be spread out in order to accelerate the evaporation—and a bit more oil.

LA PICADA

MAKES ABOUT 3 TBSP/40 G

1 TABLESPOON EXTRA-VIRGIN OLIVE OIL
1 GARLIC CLOVE, PEELED
1 SLICE BAGUETTE OR SMALL PIECE CRUSTLESS COUNTRY BREAD, DAY OLD OR TOASTED
SALT
12 UNSALTED TOASTED ALMONDS OR HAZELNUTS (OR A MIX) WITHOUT SKINS
1 TABLESPOON MINCED FRESH FLAT-LEAF PARSLEY
1 TO 2 TABLESPOONS STOCK OR WATER

In a small skillet, heat the olive oil over medium heat and add the garlic, cooking until it is golden and fragrant, about 1 minute; remove and reserve. Add the bread and fry until golden, turning as needed, about 2 minutes.

To pound in a mortar: Add the garlic and bread along with a pinch of salt and pound with the pestle until pasty. Add the almonds, parsley, and, gradually, the liquid, pounding into a smooth paste.

To make in a food processor: Add all of the ingredients and grind using quick pulses, checking after each pulse for the desired consistency. Add in a bit more liquid if necessary and scrape down the sides of the bowl as needed.

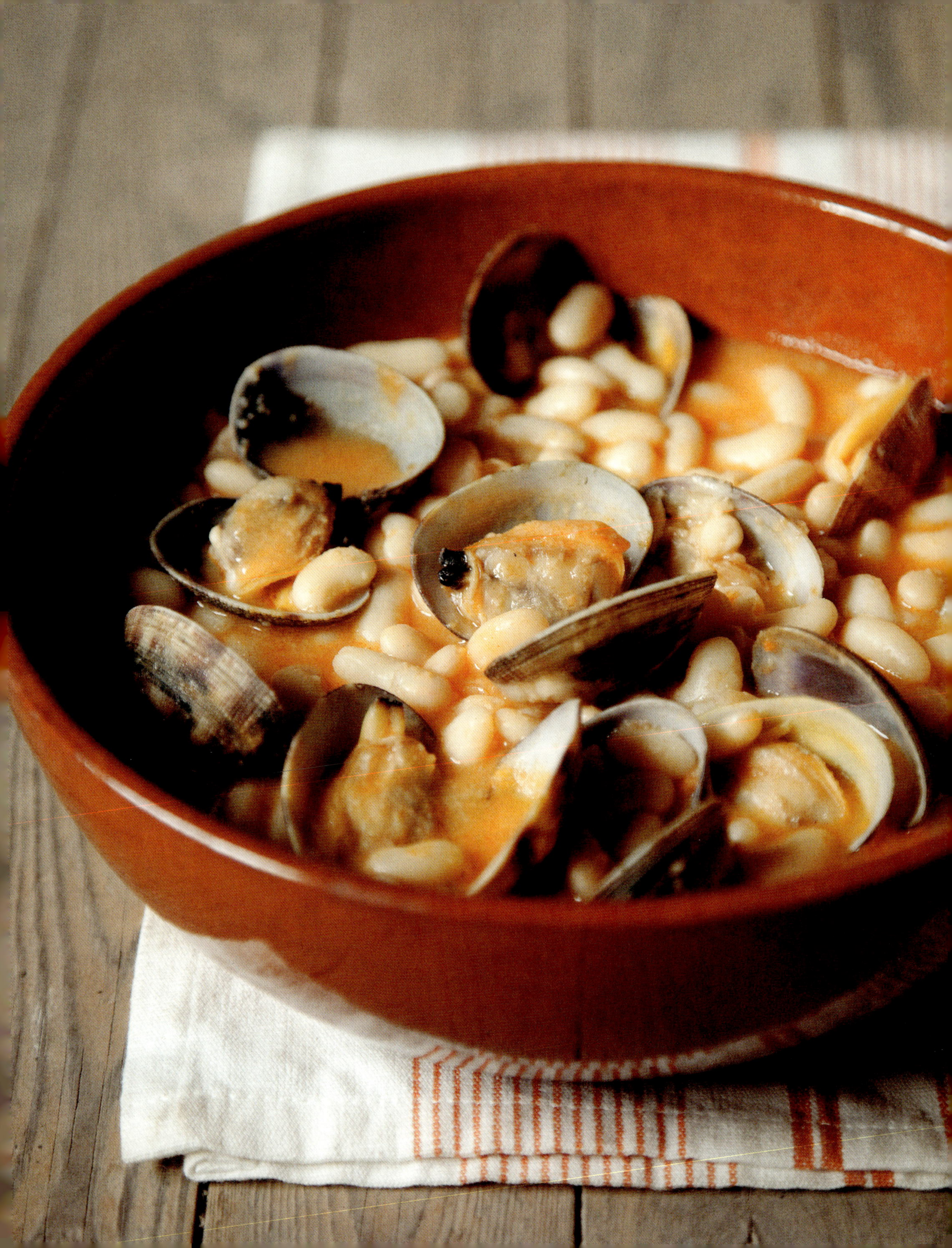

WHITE BEANS WITH CLAMS

ALUBIAS BLANCAS CON ALMEJAS

SERVES 4

Asturias is a verdant region along the northern coast between Galicia and Cantabria that still officially retains its title of Principality. The region is known for its *sidra* (hard apple cider) and sawdust-floored *sidrerías*, fishing, dairy farming, and mining—and its large, oblong white beans.

This is one of Asturias's most celebrated, and delicious, dishes. Prepare the clams separately and then add them to the beans, as a single clam still holding sand can wreck the dish. Serve with a dry white wine, or, more appropriately, with a glass of authentic Asturian *sidra*.

3 CUPS/525 G CANNED WHITE BEANS, SUCH AS CANNELLINI

1 POUND/455 G MEDIUM CLAMS, SCRUBBED

1 BAY LEAF

1 TABLESPOON EXTRA-VIRGIN OLIVE OIL

1 GARLIC CLOVE, PEELED

1 TEASPOON SPANISH PIMENTÓN DULCE (SWEET PAPRIKA)

3 TABLESPOONS PLAIN DRY BREADCRUMBS

SALT

1. Drain, rinse, and place the white beans in a saucepan with about 2 cups/480 ml water. Bring to a boil, cover the pan, and remove from the heat. Leave them in the liquid until ready to use.

2. Purge the clams of any sand by soaking them in salty water following the directions on page 341.

3. In a large sauté pan or skillet, add the clams, bay leaf, and ⅔ cup/165 ml water. Cover the pan and cook over medium heat, shaking the pan gently, until the clams have opened, about 5 minutes. Remove the pan from the heat and leave covered. Discard any clams that do not open.

4. In a small sauté pan or skillet, heat the olive oil over medium-low heat. Add the garlic and cook until golden and fragrant, about 1 minute. Transfer the garlic and the oil to a mortar. Add the pimentón and breadcrumbs, moisten with 2 or 3 tablespoons liquid from the beans, and mash with a pestle into a soft paste. Or mash with the back of a spoon in a bowl.

5. Drain off the liquid from the clams and add enough liquid from the beans to total 1½ cups/360 ml.

6. In a large saucepan or deep sauté pan, dissolve the garlic paste in the mixture of broths. Transfer the beans with a slotted spoon to the pan, season with salt, and add the clams. Cover the pan and simmer gently over low heat for 10 minutes. There should be just enough liquidy sauce so that the dish needs a spoon. Tip in some more broth from the clams or beans if needed.

7. Ladle into bowls and serve hot.

PINOTXO'S GARBANZO BEANS WITH BLOOD SAUSAGE, RAISINS, AND PINE NUTS

GARBANZOS DE PINOTXO

SERVES 4

For many, breakfast in Spain is all too often a coffee and a pastry while standing in a neighborhood bar or a roadside café. But when you go for something more substantial, it's called *desayuno de tenedor* (breakfast with a fork). This garbanzo bean dish is a classic *tenedor* breakfast at Bar Pinotxo inside Barcelona's iconic La Boqueria market. I have spent many mornings at their stainless-steel counter lingering over an order of these before picking up the day's provisions in the market. My friend, the late Albert Asín, was a fixture at the stoves for the past fifteen years that I have been eating at Pinotxo, and I learned much about the architecture of traditional cooking—building upward from a base—from him.

4 CUPS/275 G DRIED OR 4 CUPS/680 G CANNED GARBANZO BEANS

¼ CUP/35 G SEEDLESS RAISINS

8 TABLESPOONS EXTRA-VIRGIN OLIVE OIL

1 MEDIUM ONION, THINLY SLICED

6 OUNCES/170 G SPANISH BLOOD SAUSAGE (MORCILLA) OR CATALAN BOTIFARRA NEGRE, SLICED IN HALF LENGTHWISE

¼ CUP/35 G PINE NUTS

1 GARLIC CLOVE, FINELY CHOPPED

HEAPED 1 TABLESPOON MINCED FRESH FLAT-LEAF PARSLEY

BALSAMIC VINEGAR OR AGED SHERRY VINEGAR

FLAKY SEA SALT

1. If using dried garbanzo beans, soak them overnight and boil following the directions on page 343. If using canned garbanzos, drain, rinse, and place the garbanzo beans in a saucepan with about 2½ cups/600 ml water. Bring to a boil, remove from the heat, cover the pan, and leave in the liquid until ready to use.

2. Soak the raisins in a glass of warm water for 10 minutes; drain.

3. In a large skillet, heat 2 tablespoons of the olive oil over medium heat, add the onion, and cook until it begins to soften and turn pale, about 5 minutes. Add the blood sausage, pine nuts, and reserved raisins, and cook, stirring continually and breaking up the blood sausage, until it is completely crumbled, about 4 minutes. (Remove the casing from the pan and discard.) Reduce the heat to medium-low, add the garlic, and cook until the garlic is fragrant, about 1 minute. Drain the beans and add them to the skillet along with the parsley. Cook, stirring frequently, for 2 minutes, or until the ingredients are well mixed.

4. Divide among plates. Give each serving a generous drizzle of 1½ tablespoons of the remaining oil, a dash of vinegar, and some flakes of salt. Serve immediately.

STEWED LENTILS WITH A NUTTY CHOCOLATE PICADA

LENTEJAS ESTOFADAS

SERVES 6

Ships returning to Spanish ports from the New World in the sixteenth century unloaded many new products—from peppers to pumpkins to chocolate. Chocolate was almost immediately popular (unlike tomatoes, which took time to catch on), and Spaniards consumed it in a variety of ways. (See page 306 for hot Spanish-style drinking chocolate.) Today, some cooks still occasionally treat chocolate like a spice and crush a piece with nuts. In this dish, dark chocolate forms part of the picada that is stirred into the lentils toward the end of cooking to add body as well as a subtle hint of sweet, nutty fruitiness.

2 TABLESPOONS EXTRA-VIRGIN OLIVE OIL
2 GARLIC CLOVES, PEELED
1 SLICE BAGUETTE, DAY OLD OR TOASTED
1 MEDIUM ONION, FINELY CHOPPED
2 RIPE MEDIUM TOMATOES, HALVED, SEEDED, AND GRATED (SEE PAGE 339)
2 CUPS/400 G DRIED LENTILS, PREFERABLY SMALL BROWN SPANISH PARDINA VARIETY
1 PINCH SAFFRON, DRY-TOASTED AND GROUND (SEE PAGE 340)
½ TEASPOON SPANISH PIMENTÓN DULCE (SWEET PAPRIKA)
SALT AND FRESHLY GROUND BLACK PEPPER
12 UNSALTED TOASTED ALMONDS AND/OR HAZELNUTS, WITHOUT SKINS
½ OUNCE/15 G DARK CHOCOLATE, BROKEN INTO PIECES
1 TABLESPOON MINCED FRESH FLAT-LEAF PARSLEY
½ TEASPOON SHERRY OR WINE VINEGAR

1. In a large, heavy pot, heat the olive oil over medium heat. Add the garlic and bread and cook until golden, 1 to 2 minutes. Remove when done and reserve. In the same oil, prepare a sofrito with the onion and tomatoes, following the directions on page 39.

2. Meanwhile, put the lentils in a large bowl and pick them over for any debris. Rinse and drain.

3. When the sofrito is ready, add the lentils to the pot along with the saffron and pimentón, season with salt and pepper, and stir to blend. Cover with 6 cups/1.5 L water and bring to a boil. Reduce the heat to low, cover the pot, and gently boil until the lentils are tender but not mushy, 40 to 50 minutes. Add more water if necessary to keep the lentils loose.

4. Meanwhile, prepare a picada with the reserved garlic and bread, the almonds, chocolate, and parsley, following the directions on page 39.

5. Stir the picada and the vinegar into the lentils and cook for a final 5 minutes. Taste for seasoning and adjust as needed. Ladle into bowls and serve hot.

CHAPTER 2

SALADS, COLD SOUPS, AND GAZPACHOS
ensaladas, sopas frías y gazpachos

A simple green salad in the middle of the table is an omnipresent part of a Spanish meal, just as a filled fruit bowl appears at the end. Generally enlivened with a few thin slices of red onion, some wedges of tomato, and a handful of olives, the salad is dressed with only extra-virgin olive oil plus some drops of vinegar (ideally nutty sherry vinegar). This year-round accompaniment—so familiar, so stable—is to be stabbed at with a fork from the platter rather than served on individual "salad plates." (If the table is long, each end gets a platter.)

But in summertime, with salad greens vibrant and tomatoes bursting with sweetness, comes the desire to use the salad as a base for a first course or even a light meal. Bucked up with preserved white asparagus, fresh cheese, and maybe some cold cuts, whatever can be rummaged in the pantry or crisper drawer of the refrigerator, salads really begin to find their voice.

Or voices. Spanish salads go far, far beyond the lettuce ones in the center of the table. Across the country, traditional salads are prepared by combining such disparate ingredients as high-quality tinned bonito del norte tuna and small cooked white beans (see page 55); bitter curly endive in a robust sauce of garlic, dried red peppers, and almonds (see page 47); shredded salt cod with tomatoes and onions (see page 54); and even, a favorite of mine, flakes of just-grilled salt cod with orange segments and black olives (see page 53). All of these are inevitably given a generous dousing of extra-virgin olive oil. Perhaps one of the very few that doesn't get olive oil is the heavenly combination of cold wedges of melon (or fresh figs split in half) with slices of dry-cured jamón (see page 57).

I've put the classic Spanish gazpacho in this chapter with salads because it is really just that, a puréed salad (as opposed to a "soup"). Fresh and refreshing, it's ideal for those scorching summer days that blanket much of the country. *Salmorejo* (page 62) is gazpacho's thicker, richer, and more filling cousin that is eaten all year round.

The more elaborate salads tend to be first courses, but with slices of jamón or cured cheeses, some good bread— ideally rubbed with tomato and soaked in olive oil (see page 68)—and a cold bottle of Mahou or Alhambra beer on a still-warm evening, the last of the light draining from the sky, they make a wonderful dinner unto themselves.

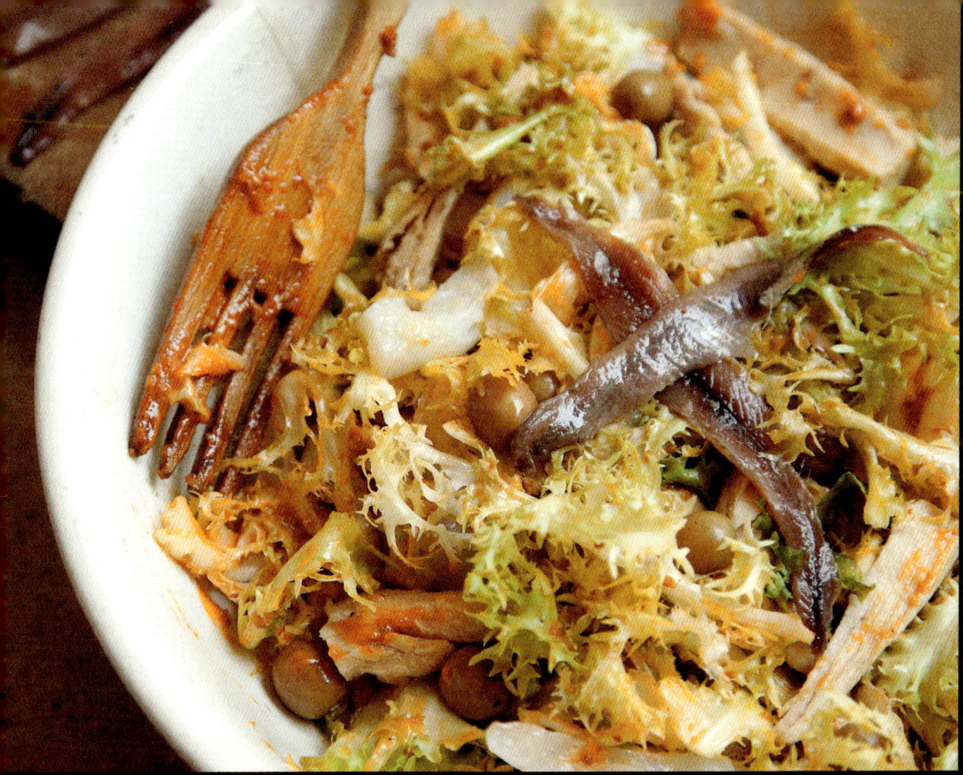
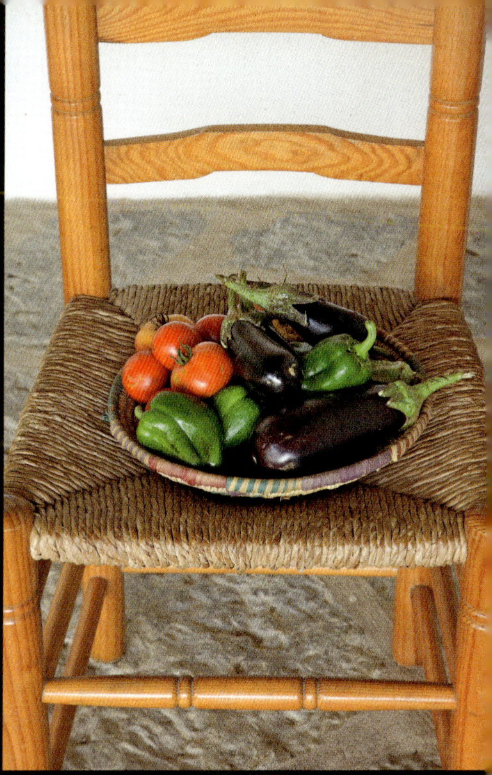
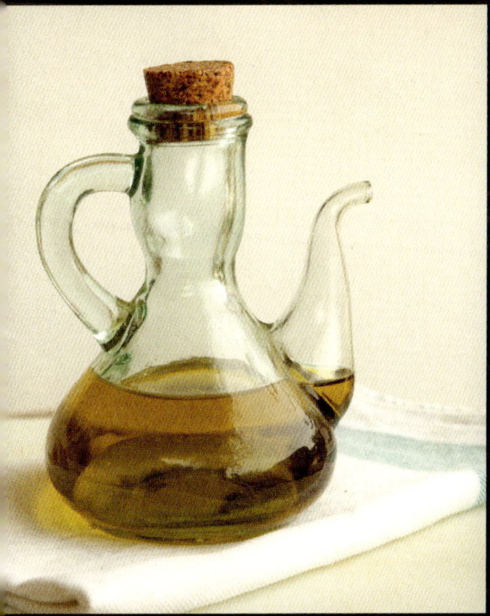
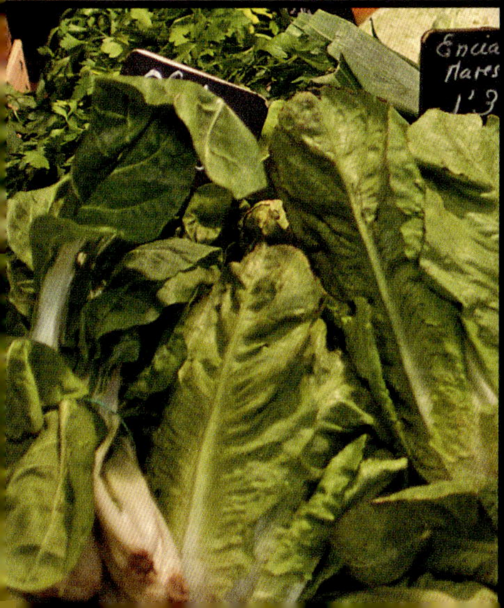
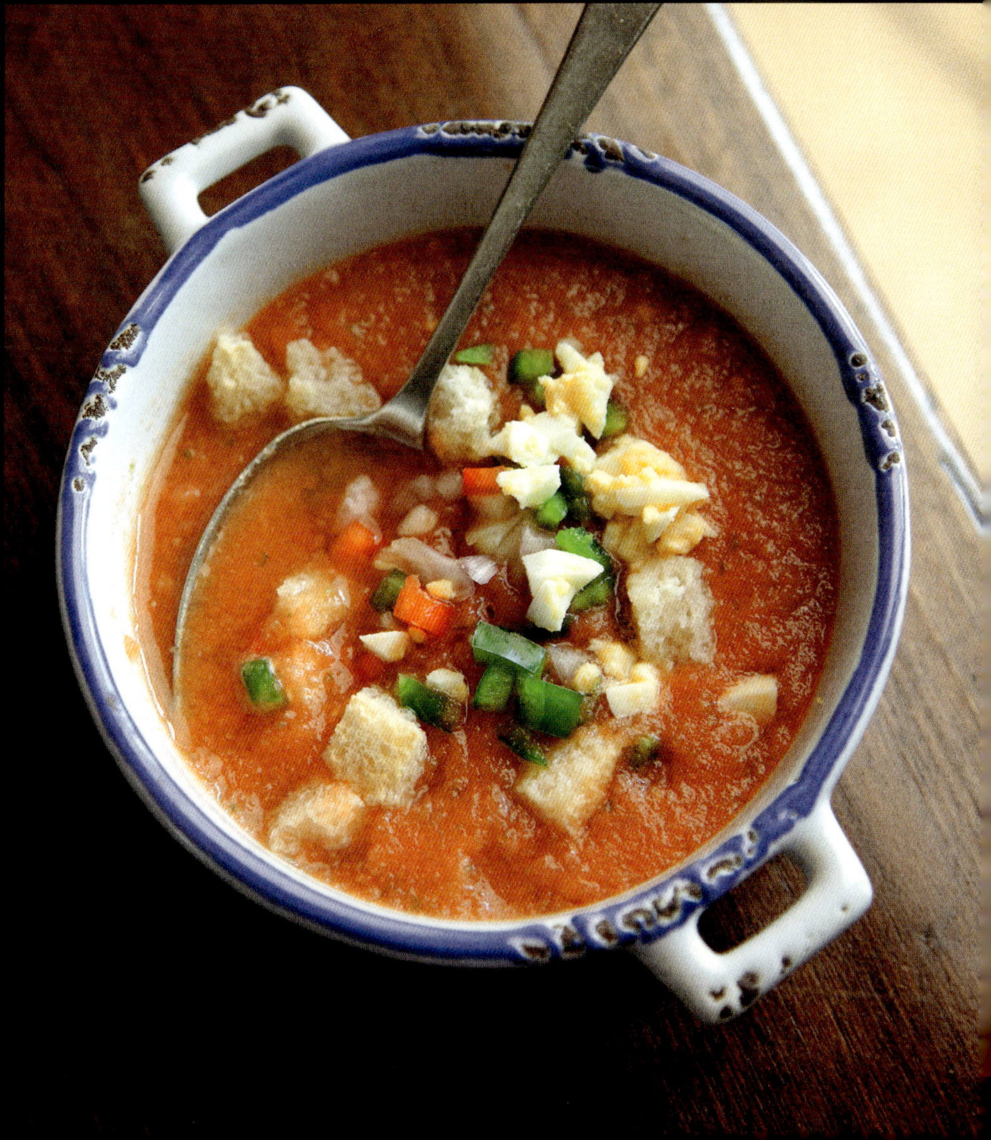

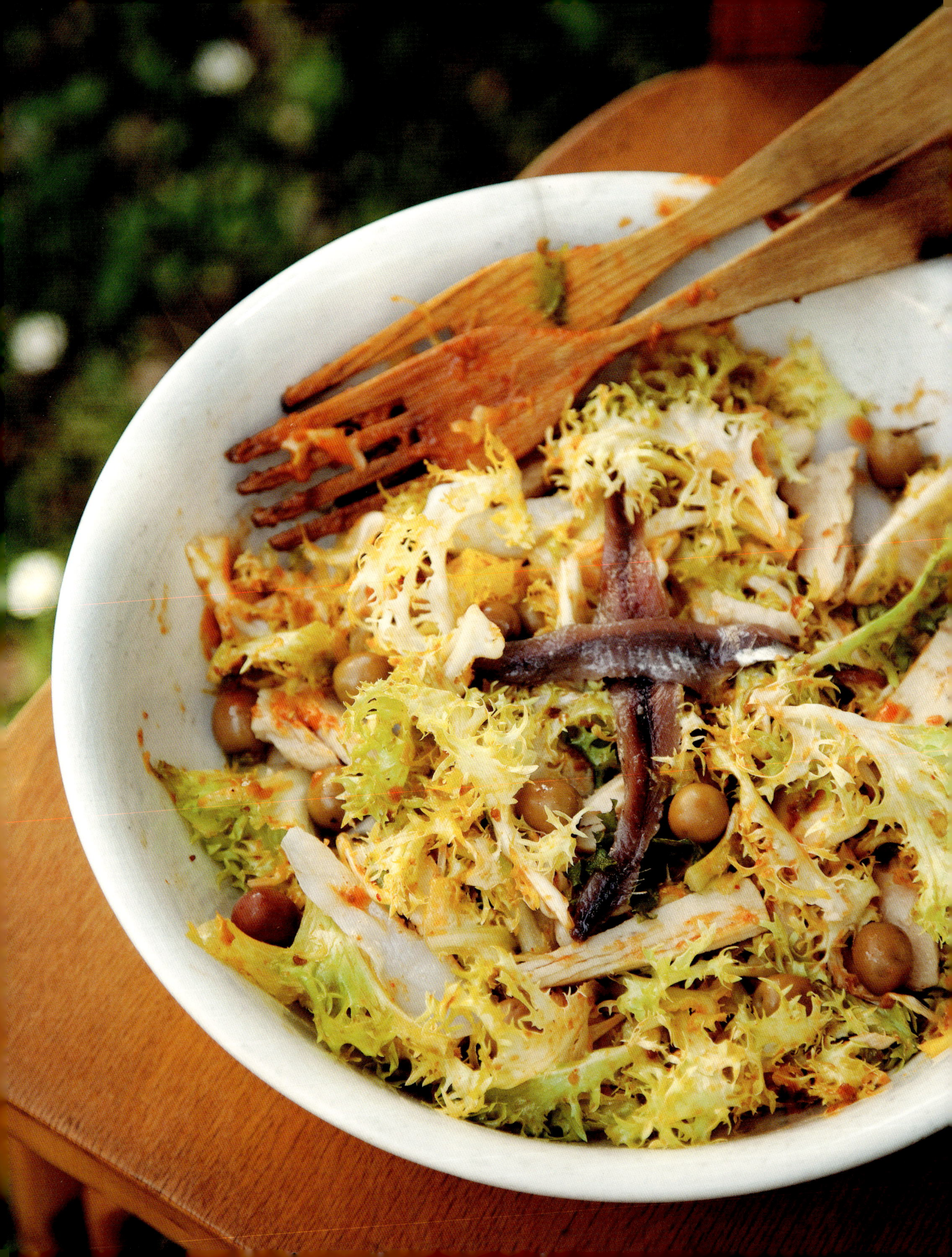

CURLY ENDIVE WITH XATÓ SAUCE

XATÓ

SERVES 4

Along the Garraf coast, south of Barcelona, are a handful of fishing villages that each claim the origin to this popular salad. The differences in the versions tend to be subtle, and each roughly adheres to the same list of ingredients. Bitter, curly endive leaves are tossed with a nutty sauce called *xató* prepared with garlic, roasted nuts, usually tomatoes, extra-virgin olive oil, and vinegar. Garnishes include olives and salted fish.

3½ OUNCES/100 G SALT COD (SEE NOTE, PAGE 54)

3 DRIED ROMESCO OR 4 ÑORA PEPPERS, OR ANOTHER MILD, SWEET DRIED RED PEPPER (SEE INGREDIENT NOTE, PAGE 16)

¼ CUP/30 G TOASTED ALMONDS WITHOUT SKINS

15 TOASTED HAZELNUTS WITHOUT SKINS

13 ANCHOVY FILLETS, RINSED AND PATTED DRY

2 SLICES BAGUETTE (ABOUT 2 OUNCES/55 G TOTAL), DAY OLD OR TOASTED

1 GARLIC CLOVE, PEELED

2 TEASPOONS RED WINE VINEGAR

PINCH DRIED RED PEPPER FLAKES

SALT AND FRESHLY GROUND BLACK PEPPER

1 CUP/240 ML EXTRA-VIRGIN OLIVE OIL

1 HEAD CURLY ENDIVE (SOMETIMES CALLED FRISÉE), ABOUT 1 POUND/455 G

3 OUNCES/85 G TINNED SPANISH BONITO DEL NORTE TUNA PACKED IN OLIVE OIL, DRAINED

24 TO 36 OLIVES WITH PITS, PREFERABLY ARBEQUINA

1. Begin desalting the salt cod 2 to 3 days before (depending on the cut), following the directions on page 341. Drain, rinse, and pat dry with paper towels. Shred the cod by hand into bite-size pieces following the flakes and fibers. Set aside.

2. Cut the peppers open and remove the seeds. Put the peppers in a bowl, cover with hot water, and soak for 30 minutes; drain. Scrape out the soft pulp with a spoon and transfer to a bowl. Discard the skins.

3. In the bowl of a food processor, add the almonds and hazelnuts, pepper pulp, one of the anchovy fillets, the bread, and garlic along with the vinegar. Add the pepper flakes and season with salt and pepper. Begin puréeing while slowly pouring in the olive oil. Grind into a moist, loose, and gritty paste.

4. Cover and refrigerate the sauce until chilled.

5. Clean and tear the endive into pieces. Rinse, drain, and spin or pat dry. Place in a large bowl and spoon over some of the sauce. Toss, add more sauce, toss, and so on until all of the sauce has been added and the endive is moist and covered. Transfer to a large platter or bowl.

6. Remove the tuna from the tin or jar in large flakes and place on the salad. Add the pieces of salt cod, crisscross the remaining anchovy fillets over the top, and scatter around the olives before serving.

BELGIAN ENDIVE WITH CABRALES BLUE CHEESE SAUCE AND ANCHOVY FILLETS

ENDIVIAS CON QUESO DE CABRALES Y ANCHOAS

SERVES 4

Of the various blue cheeses produced in Spain, the heavily veined and intensely pungent Cabrales from Asturias is, for me, the finest. Made from cow's milk or, during part of the year, cow's milk blended with that of goat or sheep, the heavy wheels are aged for at least two months inside natural caves around the Picos de Europa mountains. A piece of *queso de Cabrales*, with its milky, slightly acidic flavors and sharp, piquant notes, perfectly accompanies a handful of toasted nuts, some crisp apple slices, or a glass of Asturian *sidra* (cider).

But the cheese also makes an excellent base for sauces. You find these either warm and served over a grilled steak (see page 259) or, like this version, cold, and spooned over mildly bitter Belgian endive.

2 OUNCES/55 G CABRALES, ROQUEFORT, OR OTHER BLUE CHEESE, AT ROOM TEMPERATURE

½ CUP/120 ML HEAVY CREAM

4 HEADS BELGIAN ENDIVE

16 ANCHOVY FILLETS, RINSED AND PATTED DRY

FRESHLY GROUND BLACK PEPPER

1. In a small bowl, blend the cheese and cream into a runny, textured sauce with a fork by a combination of whisking and mashing.

2. Cut the endive in half lengthwise. Place a pair of endive halves on each salad plate with the cut center facing upward. Spoon the sauce over the endive. Top each endive half with two anchovy fillets in an "X" and generously grind over pepper before serving.

WINTER GREEN SALAD WITH FRESH CHEESE AND POMEGRANATE SEEDS

ENSALADA DE INVIERNO CON QUESO FRESCO Y GRANADA

SERVES 4

While summer salads burst with the spoils of the garden (tomatoes!), winter ones can contain a lovely blend of greens—some of them slightly bitter—like various chicories, radicchio, watercress, arugula, mizuna, and romaine. The vinaigrette here offers a tang and the anchovy fillets a snappy, salty pungency. And any bitterness in the greens is softened with the milky sweetness of the fresh cheese and the natural sugars in the pomegranate seeds.

Pomegranates are a pleasure of the winter fruit bowl. Brilliantly sweet, with a thick, leathery, and soft skin that protects their jewel-like seeds, the pomegranate—*granada*—was brought to Spain around 800 CE, and today the country is Europe's leading producer of the fruit. While grown extensively in Tarragona, Alicante, and Murcia, they famously gave the name to the most splendid city, Granada, during the later years of Muslim rule.

When the pomegranate season finishes at the end of January or early February, we start using pieces of pear in this salad instead.

8 OUNCES/225 G TRIMMED MIXED WINTER GREENS, SUCH AS CURLY ENDIVE, ESCAROLE, FRISÉE, RADICCHIO, AND MÂCHE

6 TABLESPOONS/90 ML EXTRA-VIRGIN OLIVE OIL

2 TABLESPOONS AGED SHERRY OR BALSAMIC VINEGAR

SALT AND FRESHLY GROUND BLACK PEPPER

36 GREEN OLIVES

6 OUNCES/170 G FIRM FRESH CHEESE, CUT INTO ½-INCH/1.25-CM CUBES

½ CUP/75 G POMEGRANATE SEEDS (SEE NOTE)

8 ANCHOVY FILLETS, RINSED AND PATTED DRY

1. Wash, drain, and spin or pat dry the greens.

2. In a small bowl, make a vinaigrette by whisking the olive oil and vinegar together until cloudy and blended. Season with salt and pepper and whisk again.

3. In a large salad bowl, toss the greens and the vinaigrette, turning over the leaves until moist and covered. Add the olives, cheese, and pomegranate seeds. Crisscross the anchovy fillets across the top. Serve from the bowl.

NOTE: To remove the pomegranate's seeds, slice off the top crown. Run the tip of a knife along the natural compartments, cutting just through the skin. Pull the sections outward to open up the fruit. Gently remove the seeds, without breaking and losing any of their juices.

Chilled seafood salads blending tomatoes, peppers, and a variety of shellfish and fish with a light vinaigrette are a coastal favorite from Galicia to Andalucía. Final flavors, though, depend somewhat on the season—steamed and shucked mussels or large clams make a typical winter addition—as well as how far south you travel in the country. Cooks in Andalucía tend to use a heavier hand with the vinegar, namely with the local tawny-colored sherry vinegar. This *salpicón* is one of those southern versions, the type found at tapas bars around Sanlúcar de Barrameda and Cádiz. At home, I like the large, meaty, and moist flakes of *dorada* (gilt-head bream), though any firm, white-fleshed fish will work.

MARINATED SEAFOOD SALAD

SALPICÓN

SERVES 4 TO 6

SALT

1 POUND/455 G FIRM, WHITE-FLESHED FISH FILLETS, SUCH AS BREAM, MONKFISH, COD, GROUPER, OR RED SNAPPER

1½ POUNDS/680 G WHOLE FRESH JUMBO SHRIMP OR PRAWNS WITH HEADS AND SHELLS, OR 1 POUND/455 G PEELED COOKED JUMBO SHRIMP OR PRAWNS

2 RIPE MEDIUM TOMATOES, CORED, SEEDED, AND CHOPPED

½ RED BELL PEPPER, CHOPPED

½ GREEN BELL PEPPER, CHOPPED

½ MEDIUM-SMALL ONION, FINELY CHOPPED

6 TABLESPOONS/90 ML EXTRA-VIRGIN OLIVE OIL

2 TABLESPOONS SHERRY WINE VINEGAR

FRESHLY GROUND BLACK PEPPER

2 LEMONS, CUT INTO WEDGES, FOR GARNISHING

1. In a large saucepan, bring 4 cups/1 L water to a boil and season with salt. Reduce the heat to medium-low. Gently lay in the fish fillets and poach until opaque throughout, 3 to 5 minutes depending on the thickness. Transfer them with a slotted spoon to a plate to drain. Once cool enough to handle, remove any skin and bones and discard, and break the fillets into generous pieces.

2. If using fresh (uncooked) shrimp, poach them in the same water over medium heat for 1 to 2 minutes, until just opaque throughout. Immediately transfer them with a slotted spoon to a bowl of ice water to stop any further cooking. Once cool, remove the heads and shells, leaving the tails attached. Devein if desired.

3. Place the tomatoes, bell peppers, and onion in a large salad bowl. In a small bowl, whisk together the olive oil and vinegar until cloudy and blended, and pour over the vegetables. Season with salt and a generous amount of pepper and toss. Add the fish and shrimp and gently turn over to coat without breaking the pieces of fish. Cover and refrigerate until chilled.

4. Before serving, gently toss again (adding more oil if desired). Serve with the lemon wedges on the side.

FINO SHERRY
fino

Fortified sherry wines are produced in the so-called Sherry Triangle in southern Spain between the towns of Jerez de la Frontera, Sanlúcar de Barrameda, and El Puerto de Santa María (across the bay from Cádiz). Sherries vary in type, color, and levels of dryness. They range from the palest, driest *finos* (literally "refined") and manzanilla, through the warmer, rounded amber-hued amontillado with its hazelnut aromas, slightly darker nut-brown and aromatic oloroso, the mahogany-colored palo cortado and pale cream to the sweet, ebony-toned Pedro Ximénez.

But it is fino that is the choice in the south to sip with a dish of olives or a couple of tapas. It's a crisp, light sherry, straw-colored, with a slightly edgy taste. As it ferments, a layer of yeast called *flor* forms, which protects the wine from the air and also imparts its own unique, tangy flavor. Fino is aged in American oak barrels using the *sistema de criaderas y solera*, basically a way of blending older sherries with younger ones and rotating casks among a pyramid of barrels. They generally age about eight years, though in reality are a final blend of different harvests, with at least a touch of the oldest in each barrel. Vintages, then, play no part in the conversation about finos.

Fino produced around the port of Sanlúcar de Barrameda is called manzanilla. The name is the same in Spanish as for chamomile tea, of which it is (vaguely) reminiscent in flavor. Manzanilla uses Palomino grapes grown in the chalky *albariza* soil, which are harvested during the first half of September. While the method of producing it is the same as with fino, the salty humidity of Sanlúcar de Barrameda, located at the mouth of the Guadalquivir River, means that a thicker, more protective layer of flor forms. Manzanilla is more delicate-tasting than other finos, and, aficionados like to say, carries salty hints from the sea estuaries where it is produced. It is best served quite chilled, ideally between 44 to 48°F/7 to 9°C. The public has latched on to this tremendous drink, and recently manzanilla has surpassed other finos in popularity.

Among the many excellent manzanilla producers, La Gitana and La Guita stand out. Both make bright manzanillas, the color of very pale straw, and carry clean, breezy aromas that recall green apples, yeast, and the humid seaside. On the tongue, the wines are light and dry, with a tangy but fresh finish.

Sitting in one of Sanlúcar's legendary tapas bars with a glass of manzanilla and a couple of tapas is one of Spain's culinary highlights.

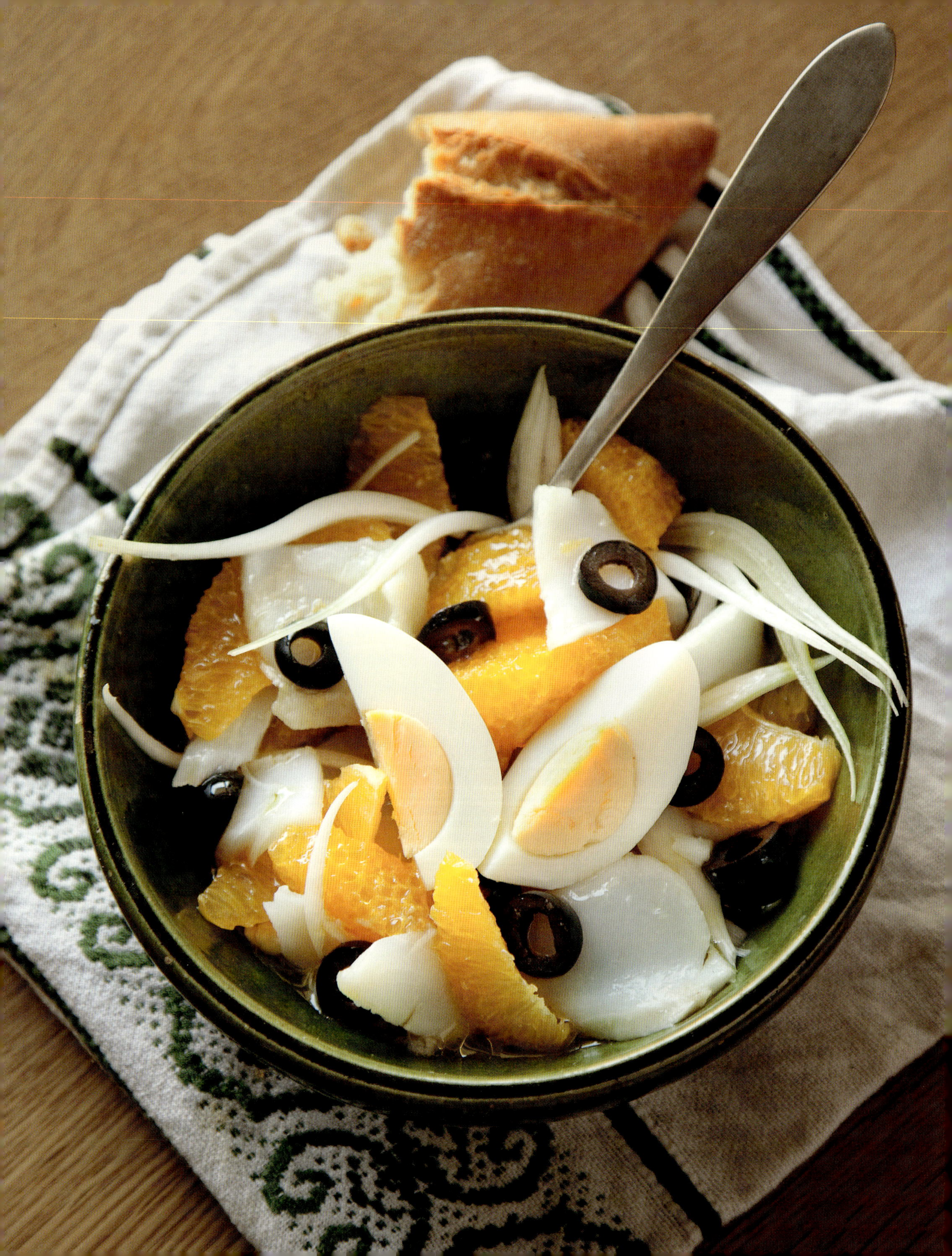

SALT COD, ORANGE, AND OLIVE SALAD

REMOJÓN DE NARANJA

SERVES 4

A favorite in Andalucía and Murcia, this winter salad offers a succulent combination of disparate and surprising flavors. Grilling the soaked salt cod for a couple of minutes allows the fish to be easily flaked apart, and offers a subtler texture and warmth to counter the orange segments. Use the strongest extra-virgin olive oil that you have, ideally a Spanish blend with plenty of the sharp Picual variety or even 100 percent Picual. It's a stunning, bold salad that is guaranteed to wow.

6 OUNCES/170 G SALT COD, PREFERABLY A SINGLE THICK CENTER-CUT LOIN PIECE

¼ CUP/60 ML EXTRA-VIRGIN OLIVE OIL, PLUS MORE FOR THE PAN

2 RIPE LARGE VALENCIA ORANGES

1 SCALLION, THINLY SLICED

12 TO 20 BLACK OLIVES, PITTED AND SLICED

2 HARD-BOILED EGGS (SEE PAGE 342), PEELED AND QUARTERED LENGTHWISE (OPTIONAL)

1. Begin desalting the salt cod 2 to 3 days before (depending on the cut), following the directions on page 341. Drain, rinse, gently squeeze out excess moisture, and pat dry with paper towels.

2. Preheat a skillet over high heat and lightly oil it. Lay on the cod and cook only until it can be flaked apart, 4 to 6 minutes depending on the thickness. Transfer to a plate. Remove the skin and gently flake apart, carefully checking for any bones.

3. Section the orange segments. To do this, peel the oranges and then trim any white pith with a sharp knife. Carefully cut along the membranes and remove the individual segments. Set the segments in a bowl along with any juices.

4. Add the cod to the bowl along with the scallion and olives. Drizzle over the olive oil and gently toss. Divide the salad among plates and garnish each with hard-boiled egg, if desired.

CATALAN SHREDDED SALT COD, TOMATO, AND OLIVE SALAD

ESQUEIXADA DE BACALLÀ

SERVES 6

While the Basques may have been the first to bring salted cod to Spain, *bacalao* soon spread, with the country's regions developing their own distinctive ways of preparing it. In Catalunya, one traditional favorite of using *bacallà* (as it is called in Catalan) is in *esqueixada*. Found in Catalan cuisine at least as far back as the sixteenth century, the name of the dish comes from the Catalan verb *esqueixar* (to shred). The salad should not need salt, but taste for seasoning before serving. This is a place to use the best extra-virgin olive oil kept in the cupboard for special occasions. It will be noted and appreciated.

1 POUND/455 G SALT COD (SEE NOTE)
8 PLUM TOMATOES, CORED, SEEDED, AND FINELY CHOPPED
1 MEDIUM RED ONION, FINELY CHOPPED
¼ GREEN BELL PEPPER, FINELY CHOPPED (OPTIONAL)
FRESHLY GROUND BLACK PEPPER
½ CUP/120 ML EXTRA-VIRGIN OLIVE OIL
36 TO 48 BLACK OLIVES

1. Beginning 2 to 3 days ahead, desalt the cod following the directions on page 341. Drain, rinse, gently squeeze out excess moisture, and pat dry with paper towels. Skin and carefully debone. Shred the cod by hand into bite-size pieces following the flakes and fibers.

2. In a large serving bowl, add the cod along with the tomatoes, onion, and bell pepper (if using) and season with pepper. Drizzle over the olive oil and toss to blend. (There should be enough oil that some pools in the bottom of the bowl; add more if needed.) Garnish with the olives. Cover and chill.

3. Before serving, re-toss. Serve slightly chilled or at least fresh.

NOTE: Use one of the more inexpensive cuts of salt cod, such as strips of esqueixada pieces. It soaks quicker and will be shredded, anyhow; save the fat loin cuts for dishes like Salt Cod, Orange, and Olive Salad (page 53) or Biscay-Style Salt Cod with Choricero Pepper Sauce (page 183), where the delicate texture of the large flakes can be fully appreciated.

WHITE BEAN SALAD WITH BONITO DEL NORTE TUNA

EMPEDRAT DE BONITO DEL NORTE

SERVES 6

In Spain's countryside, there grow different varieties of creamy, nutty-tasting local white beans, including the large *faba* in Asturias, medium-size *blanca riñón* (white kidney) in the provinces of León and Ávila, and small *fesol de Santa Pau* in the volcanic La Garrotxa region in Catalunya. For this earthy salad, choose smaller white kidney beans. Cannellini, great northern, or navy beans are excellent non-Spanish options.

Look for first-rate, line-caught tinned bonito tuna preserved in extra-virgin olive oil, such as those from Ortiz, Angelachu, Consorcio, or any of the other top Spanish producers along the northern Atlantic coast.

2½ CUPS/180 G DRIED OR 2½ CUPS/450 G CANNED SMALL WHITE BEANS, SUCH AS CANNELLINI, GREAT NORTHERN, OR WHITE LIMA

SALT

½ MEDIUM RED ONION, FINELY CHOPPED

2 RIPE MEDIUM TOMATOES, CORED, SEEDED, AND DICED

¼ GREEN BELL PEPPER OR ½ SWEET ITALIAN GREEN PEPPER, VERY FINELY CHOPPED

36 BLACK OLIVES

6 OUNCES/170 G TINNED SPANISH BONITO DEL NORTE TUNA PACKED IN OLIVE OIL

¼ CUP/60 ML EXTRA-VIRGIN OLIVE OIL

SHERRY OR RED WINE VINEGAR

FRESHLY GROUND BLACK PEPPER

1. If using dried beans, soak them overnight and boil following the directions on page 343. If using canned beans, drain, rinse, and place the white beans in a saucepan with about 2 cups/480 ml water. Bring to a boil, cover the pan, and remove from the heat. Drain and let cool completely.

2. Meanwhile, in a bowl, dissolve 1 teaspoon salt in about 2 cups/480 ml tepid water and add the onion. Stir to separate the onion layers. Let sit for 1 hour for the onion to lose its sharp bite. Drain, rinse well, and drain again.

3. In a large serving bowl, combine the beans, onion, tomatoes, bell pepper, and olives. Carefully remove the tuna from the tin or jar in chunks and add to the salad, reserving the oil. Add 1 tablespoon of the reserved oil to the bowl along with the olive oil and a few drops of vinegar. Season with salt. Mix carefully to avoid breaking the beans. Cover, refrigerate, and chill while allowing the flavors to blend.

4. Before serving, gently re-toss and generously grind some black pepper over top. Serve chilled.

SPANISH POTATO SALAD

ENSALADILLA RUSA

SERVES 6

The Spanish name means "little Russian salad." Some food writers even claim the salad's roots are in Russia, carried back to Spain by soldiers who fought during World War II and adapted using local ingredients—tinned tuna, olives for pickles, no cabbage, and so on. (While Spain did not join the war, Franco sent almost 20,000 volunteer soldiers to fight with Germany on the Eastern Front. They were known as the *División Azul*, the Blue Division.) Although that story makes sense, this is one of the most iconic Spanish dishes.

At its most basic, the creamy potato salad has a mix of boiled vegetables, hard-boiled eggs, olives, and, usually, tinned bonito del norte tuna. But there are countless variations. You can find it with boiled shelled shrimp, or roasted red bell peppers, or given a fresher tone with pieces of apple and walnuts. Normally, a handful of short breadsticks called *picos* or *bastones* are poked into a mound of the salad just before being served.

2 POUNDS/910 G MEDIUM WHITE POTATOES, PEELED AND CUT INTO ½-INCH/1.25-CM CUBES

1 MEDIUM CARROT, QUARTERED LENGTHWISE (CORED IF DESIRED) AND CUT INTO ¼-INCH-/½-CM-LONG PIECES

2 OUNCES/55 G FRESH GREEN BEANS, CUT INTO ½-INCH-/1.25-CM-LONG PIECES

SALT

½ CUP/70 G SHUCKED FRESH OR FROZEN PEAS

3 OUNCES/85 G TINNED SPANISH BONITO DEL NORTE TUNA PACKED IN OLIVE OIL, DRAINED

18 TO 24 SPANISH GREEN OLIVES

2 HARD-BOILED EGGS (SEE PAGE 342), PEELED AND CHOPPED

1 CUP/240 ML MAYONNAISE

6 TO 8 ANCHOVY FILLETS, RINSED AND PATTED DRY

PICOS, BASTONES, OR BREADSTICKS BROKEN INTO 2-INCH/5-CM LENGTHS FOR GARNISHING

1. In a large pot, combine the potatoes, carrot, and green beans; cover with abundant cold water; and bring to a boil over high heat. Add a pinch of salt, reduce the heat to low, and gently boil until the potatoes are almost tender, about 15 minutes. Add the peas and cook until the potatoes are tender but not crumbling and the peas done, another 10 minutes or so. Drain, gently rinse under cold water to cool, and thoroughly drain in a colander.

2. In a large bowl, break up the tuna with a fork. Add the boiled vegetables along with the olives and chopped eggs, and gently fold in the mayonnaise. Taste for seasoning and adjust as needed. Cover with plastic wrap and refrigerate for several hours, until thoroughly chilled.

3. Mound on a serving platter and crisscross the anchovy fillets over top. Serve with the picos to poke into the salad once dished up.

MELON OR FRESH FIGS WITH SLICES OF DRY-CURED JAMÓN

MELÓN E HIGOS FRESCOS CON LONCHAS DE JAMÓN

SERVES 4

Surely one of the great flavor combinations is chilled Spanish *melón*—an oblong summer melon with a webbed, dark-green rind and pale-green flesh—and dry-cured jamón. The honeyed sweetness of the former accentuates the earthy, salty flavors of the latter. Store the melon in the refrigerator and slice just before serving so that it is nicely chilled. Fresh figs make an excellent combo, too—sweeter even, more jammy, than fresh melon—and another perfect counter for the salty jamón.

The best season for melons is the hot one, as one is reminded by this old expression: *"En tiempo de melones, cortos los sermones."* (Basically, in the season of melons, the priest is advised to keep sermons short.) This dish is a perfect tonic for such summer days, and one that frequently begins lunch on the terrace of my in-laws' beach place. Or—if it doesn't begin the meal, then this combination often ends it. It is a typical dessert, too.

8 THICK SLICES OR WEDGES CHILLED SPANISH MELÓN OR ANOTHER SWEET SUMMER MELON, SUCH AS GALIA, HONEYDEW, CANTALOUPE, CRENSHAW, SANTA CLAUS (OR CHRISTMAS) MELON, OR CASABA, OR 12 CHILLED FRESH FIGS

8 THIN SLICES DRY-CURED SPANISH JAMÓN, PREFERABLY JAMÓN IBÉRICO (SEE INGREDIENT NOTE, PAGE 16), ABOUT 2 OUNCES/55 G TOTAL

SPRIGS FRESH MINT FOR GARNISHING

1. **To prepare with melon:** Place 2 slices of melon side by side on each plate.

To prepare with figs: Holding gently, cut the figs in half lengthwise. Place 4 halves on each plate, face up, with the stems facing inward to form an "X".

2. Drape 2 slices of jamón across each plate. Garnish with sprigs of mint. Serve immediately while the fruit is still chilled.

SALADS, COLD SOUPS, AND GAZPACHOS

CHILLED MELON SOUP WITH CRISPY JAMÓN

SOPA FRÍA DE MELÓN CON CRUJIENTE DE JAMÓN

SERVES 4

Over the last years, this soup has become something of a summer standard. Even my youngest daughter's second-grade summer-activity book included a recipe for it to prepare as an August family project. Just as gazpacho is essentially a puréed summer salad, this is a similar cool and thirst-quenching version of melon with slices of cured jamón (see page 57). It's simple, elegant, and refreshing (the pulp of the classic Spanish *melón* contains about 90 percent water), and offers a wonderful, surprising combination of flavors.

4 TO 4½ POUNDS/1.8 TO 2 KG RIPE SPANISH MELÓN OR ANOTHER SWEET SUMMER MELON, SUCH AS GALIA, HONEYDEW, CRENSHAW, SANTA CLAUS (OR CHRISTMAS), OR CASABA, WITH RIND AND SEEDS

SALT

WHITE PEPPER

¾ CUP/180 ML HEAVY CREAM OR PLAIN UNSWEETENED YOGURT

4 SLICES DRY-CURED SPANISH JAMÓN (SEE INGREDIENT NOTE, PAGE 16)

1. Slice the melon into thick wedges. Remove the rind and seeds, and cut the flesh into pieces. (The trimmed weight should be about half of the uncut weight.) Place it in a food processor or blender and purée the melon. There should be about 4 cups/1 L. Season with salt and white pepper, add the cream, and purée again until blended.

2. Pour the purée into a serving bowl, large pitcher, or jug and refrigerate for several hours, until the mixture is thoroughly chilled.

3. Preheat the oven to 350°F/180°C/gas mark 4. Line a baking sheet with parchment paper.

4. Lay the jamón on the sheet and bake until golden and nearly crispy, about 10 minutes. (It will get crispier once it cools). Do not let the jamón darken too much, as it can become bitter. Transfer it to paper towels to wick off some of the grease. Once cool, finely chop it into shards.

5. Before serving, whisk the soup. Ladle or pour it into soup bowls and garnish with about half of the jamón shards. Serve with the remaining jamón in a bowl on the side to add as desired.

WHITE GAZPACHO WITH GRAPES

AJO BLANCO CON UVAS

SERVES 4

Dating back to at least the centuries of Arab (and possibly even Roman) rule in the south of Spain, this ancient dish is the precursor to the classic chilled tomato-based gazpacho (see page 60). *Ajo blanco* ("white garlic") is, as one Andalusian chef told me on my first visit to Sevilla fifteen years ago, "the mother of all gazpachos," and long predates the arrival of tomatoes and peppers that define the better-known kin. This version of ajo blanco with grapes is now linked to the Mediterranean coastal city of Málaga.

Some cooks do not strain the ajo blanco before serving, but I find that doing so makes for a particularly refined dish.

1 CUP/140 G RAW ALMONDS
2 GARLIC CLOVES, PEELED
1 QUART/1 L ICE WATER
½ CUP/120 ML WHOLE MILK
½ CUCUMBER, PEELED AND ROUGHLY CHOPPED
½ CUP/85 G SEEDLESS WHITE GRAPES, PLUS 12 TO 16 WHOLE GRAPES FOR GARNISHING
¼ CUP/60 ML EXTRA-VIRGIN OLIVE OIL
2 TEASPOONS SHERRY VINEGAR
6 OUNCES/170 G COUNTRY-STYLE BREAD (ABOUT 4 THICK SLICES TOTAL), CRUSTS REMOVED AND TORN INTO CHUNKS (SEE NOTE)

1. Blanch and remove the skins of the almonds: Bring a saucepan of water to a boil, drop in the almonds, and blanch for 2 to 3 minutes. Remove with a slotted spoon and immediately dunk in cold water; drain. Place on an old but clean kitchen cloth, fold over, and vigorously rub until the skins slip off. Remove by hand the skins that did not come away.

2. In a food processor, grind the almonds and garlic with the ice water and milk. Add the cucumber, the ½ cup/85 g grapes, the olive oil, and vinegar and grind again. Gradually add in the bread while blending into a smooth, thin paste. Transfer to a bowl, cover, and refrigerate for at least 1 or 2 hours, stirring from time to time.

3. Strain the soup through a conical strainer or chinois into a clean bowl and press out all of the liquid with the back of a spoon; discard the solids. Cover and refrigerate the ajo blanco for several hours, until thoroughly chilled.

4. Stir before ladling into bowls. Quarter the remaining grapes and add a few to each bowl before serving.

NOTE: If using older, dried-out bread, cover the slices with water, soak for a few minutes, and then gently squeeze out the water before adding the bread to the food processor.

CLASSIC ANDALUSIAN GAZPACHO

GAZPACHO ANDALUZ

SERVES 4

Gazpacho is among Spain's most famous and iconic dishes, and combines some of Andalucía's key ingredients. It's so important to use good ingredients in the Spanish kitchen—and especially in dishes as unadorned as this one—that gazpacho is the base of an old saying: *"Con mal vinagre y peor aceite, buen gazpacho no puede hacerse"*—with bad vinegar and worse olive oil, good gazpacho cannot be made. Use the best that you have; you will be rewarded. That goes for the tomatoes, too. They need to be the ripest, freshest available.

The final consistency is one of personal taste, ranging from loose to very liquidy. In summertime, when temperatures soar, make it thinner and keep it in a jug in the refrigerator to drink by the glass. It's simple, nutritious, and delightfully refreshing.

2¼ POUNDS/1 KG RIPE TOMATOES, PEELED, SEEDED, AND QUARTERED, ALL JUICES RESERVED
1 CUP/90 G ROUGHLY CHOPPED GREEN BELL PEPPER
1 MEDIUM CUCUMBER, PEELED AND ROUGHLY CHOPPED
¼ MEDIUM SWEET ONION
½ GARLIC CLOVE, MINCED
3 TABLESPOONS EXTRA-VIRGIN OLIVE OIL
4 TEASPOONS SHERRY VINEGAR
SALT AND FRESHLY GROUND BLACK PEPPER

GARNISHES
2 HARD-BOILED EGGS (SEE PAGE 342), FINELY CHOPPED
½ CUP/65 G FINELY CHOPPED RED BELL PEPPER
½ CUP/65 G FINELY CHOPPED GREEN BELL PEPPER
½ CUP/65 G FINELY CHOPPED SWEET ONION
½ CUP/65 G FINELY CHOPPED CUCUMBER
½ CUP/40 G PLAIN SMALL CROUTONS

1. Working in batches as needed, in a food processor or blender, purée the tomatoes, green bell pepper, cucumber, onion, and garlic until silky smooth. Add the olive oil and purée again until smooth. Add the vinegar, season with salt, and then begin stirring in cold water until you find the desired consistency. About 1 cup/240 ml water should be enough.

2. Pour the gazpacho into a serving bowl, large pitcher, or jug, and refrigerate for several hours, until thoroughly chilled.

3. Before serving, whisk the gazpacho. Taste for seasoning and adjust as needed. Ladle or pour it into bowls and season with pepper. Place the garnishes in separate small bowls and serve on the side to add as desired.

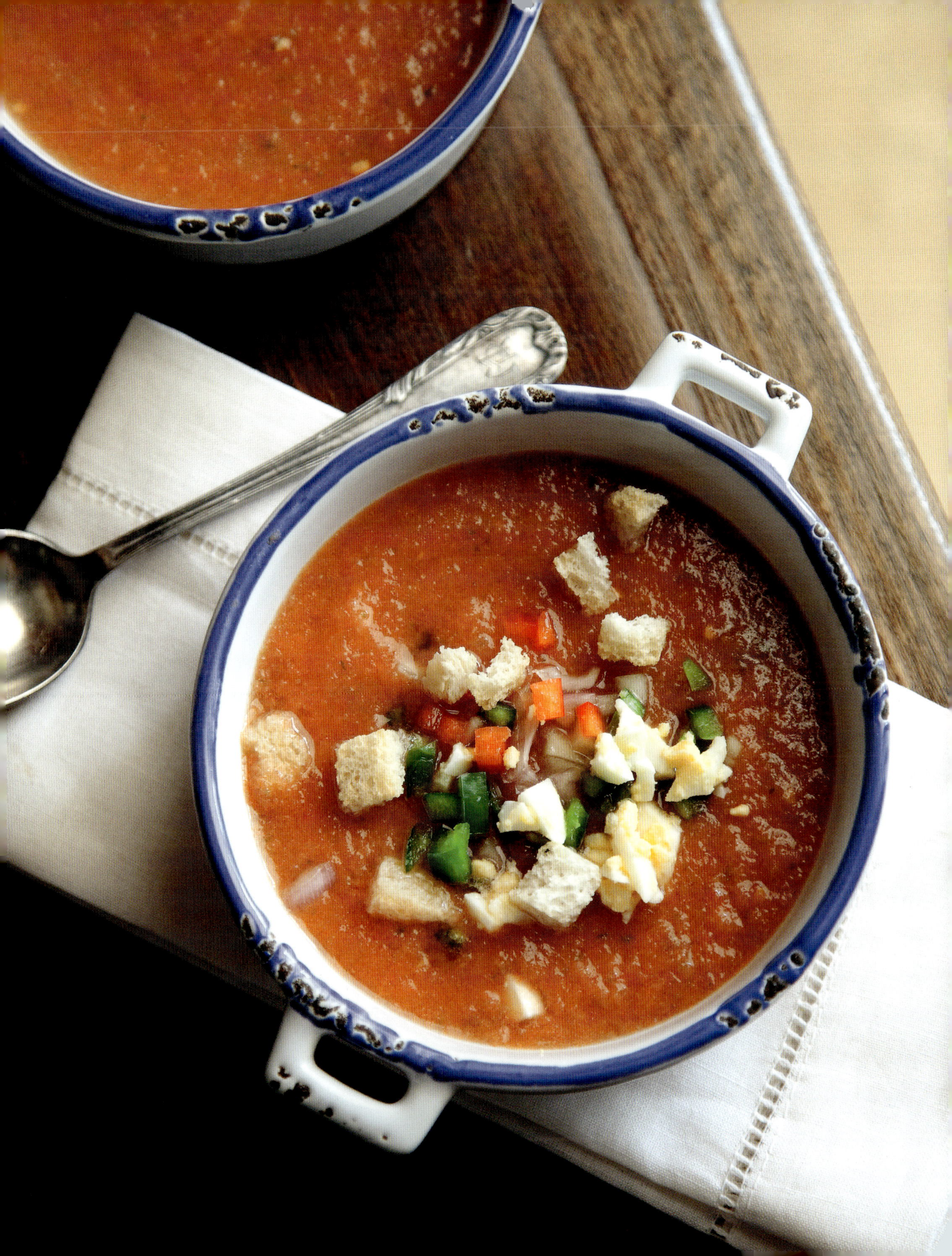

CÓRDOBA-STYLE SALMOREJO

SALMOREJO CORDOBÉS

SERVES 4

A specialty in the province of Córdoba, salmorejo is essentially a thicker version of gazpacho (see page 60). As in gazpacho, tomatoes, extra-virgin olive oil, and vinegar are three obligatory ingredients. But instead of being thinned with water, salmorejo has a significant amount more olive oil added as well as some bread puréed into the mixture to thicken it. Whereas gazpacho is a light, warm-weather favorite, *salmorejo* is eaten just about year-round.

This is adapted from a generations-old recipe of the Núñez de Prado family, which has been producing olive oil on their single-family estate since 1795. The old mill and compound still dominate one side of the main square in Baena, a lovely, ancient town 38 miles/61 km southeast of Córdoba. After a morning in their olive groves during a recent harvest with one of the brothers who runs the company, we returned for a lunch prepared by the family cook that included this dish.

2 POUNDS/910 G RIPE TOMATOES, CORED, QUARTERED, AND SEEDED, ALL JUICES RESERVED

4 OUNCES/115 G BAGUETTE (ABOUT A 10-INCH-/25-CM-LONG PIECE), SPANISH BREAD ROLLS (*PANECILLOS*), OR DINNER ROLLS (SEE NOTE, PAGE 59)

½ MEDIUM CUCUMBER, PEELED AND ROUGHLY CHOPPED

¼ CUP/30 G CHOPPED GREEN BELL PEPPER OR SWEET ITALIAN GREEN PEPPER

¼ CUP/30 G CHOPPED SWEET ONION

2 GARLIC CLOVES, PEELED

1 CUP/240 ML EXTRA-VIRGIN OLIVE OIL

1 TEASPOON SHERRY VINEGAR OR RED WINE VINEGAR

SALT AND FRESHLY GROUND BLACK PEPPER

2 HARD-BOILED EGGS (SEE PAGE 342), PEELED AND FINELY CHOPPED, FOR GARNISHING

½ CUP/60 G CHOPPED DRY-CURED SPANISH JAMÓN (SEE INGREDIENT NOTE, PAGE 16) FOR GARNISHING

1. Working in batches as needed, in a food processor or blender, combine the tomatoes and their juices, bread, cucumber, bell pepper, onion, garlic, and ½ cup/120 ml of the olive oil. Purée at high speed for at least 2 minutes, or until silky smooth, while gradually adding the remaining ½ cup/120 ml oil. Stir in the vinegar and season with salt.

2. Transfer the soup to a large serving bowl, cover, and refrigerate for several hours, until thoroughly chilled.

3. Before serving, whisk the salmorejo. Taste for seasoning and adjust as needed. Ladle it into wide bowls and grind some pepper over top. Serve the hard-boiled eggs and jamón in bowls on the side to garnish as desired.

OLIVE OIL
aceite de oliva

Spain is the world's largest producer of olive oil. Some 300 million olive trees—200 million of those in Andalucía—produce nearly 1.5 million tons of olive oil annually. The number has risen significantly over the last few years and, according to the International Olive Council, now totals three times more than Italy and well over four times more than Greece.

Cultivation in Spain goes back 3,000 years. The olive tree was brought to the Iberian Peninsula by the Phoenicians and the Greeks, the Romans expanded cultivation, and the Moors, who ruled the south for many centuries, perfected techniques of farming irrigation and pressing oil. Spain grows more than 250 varieties of olives, though only two dozen or so are used regularly in oil production.

The top producers still follow traditional, age-old methods of hand harvesting. To begin with, they never use fallen olives. During the November-to-January harvest, green tarps are laid out under the trees, and workers "rake" the branches using a small plastic brush (or sometimes vibrating "fingers") or else knock the fruit loose with a pole. The tarp is gradually rolled up, with the olives gathering in one end. They are transferred by the handful to buckets, and from there into a tractor trailer to be taken to the mill (*almazara*), where they are pressed within twenty-four hours of harvesting. As one producer told me, the quality of the olive oil is a reflection of the state of the olive when harvested and pressed.

In Andalucía, many oils are blended from different varieties. This tradition of diversification is "a way of making sure there are always ripe olives during the harvest," Francisco Núñez de Prado told me as we strolled through his family's ample groves containing some 100,000 trees. But it is also because the majority of the olives grown in Andalucía are the robust, deeply intense, and spicy Picual variety. These are generally blended with some smoother, more aromatic oil pressed from other varieties in the family's eighteenth-century mill.

Núñez de Prado, for instance, presses and blends three varieties of olives: Picual, mellow Picuda, and, for fruitiness and aroma, Hojiblanca (white-leaf). The result is a full-bodied oil with spicy aftertones. In dry years, the olives are spicy and bitter with little aroma; with rain, they become fruitier. "There are no fixed percentages in our blend."

Oils made from a single variety of olive are called monovarietals. Arbequina oil, in particular, stands out.

The center of Arbequina production is near Lleida in Les Garrigues, which lies about halfway between Barcelona and Zaragoza. It is the driest place in Catalunya, and has one of the most extreme climates. The steep ridges and tiered slopes of the craggy landscape are packed with olive and almond trees. The autochthonous olive here is Arbequina, a blueberry-size variety that ripens to greens and yellows blushed with purple, and produces the sweetest, most aromatic of any of the oils. The cold, first pressing of early harvested Arbequina olives yields little—perhaps just 7 percent of the olive's weight in oil. (Depending on the olive variety, maturity, and extraction process, that number can reach 30 percent.) But the result is hyper-aromatic oil, grassy and fresh, hinting of bananas and almonds and even tomatoes. In the mouth, the taste is smooth and fruity, almost sweet.

Each variety (or even blend) of olive oil has its optimal use in the kitchen. Bolder oils go well on toasted bread; cold "soups" like gazpacho (see page 60), salmorejo (see page 62), and ajo blanco (see page 59); and desserts like oranges with honey and olive oil (see page 292). I prefer fruitier Arbequina oils on green salads or oven-roasted fish. Like pairing wines with food, the key is not to overwhelm—or underwhelm—but to find the balance where the nuances can be fully appreciated.

CHAPTER 3

TAPAS AND APPETIZERS
tapas y aperitivos

Tapa means "lid," that is clear. But much else about the origins of Spain's famous little dishes is hard to pin down exactly. The tradition of having a small bite to eat with a drink in this manner probably began sometime in the eighteenth (or was it nineteenth?) century when a lid—in the form of a small saucer—was placed on top of a glass of sherry in the south of the country to keep out the flies. Crafty bar owners began to add a delicate slice of cured jamón, a couple of salty fried almonds, or maybe even a thin slice of salted and cured tuna loin known as *mojama* on the saucer as an enticement to come to the bar. (And the saltiness of the typical tapas surely was an enticement to drink more.) Tapas grew into an entire culture and way of eating, especially in the south, where many of the recipes in this chapter originated.

Apart from a small dish of olives, tapas are rarely free with your drink anymore, and it seems that bars rarely offer only one or two as they once did—though that doesn't mean that they don't have one or two *specialties* that people go there to eat. While just about every village has a bar serving at least a couple of tapas, some places in Spain are particularly well-known for them (Sanlúcar de Barrameda and San Sebastián, to name two of the most famous), while other towns have a street densely lined with tapas bars (such as Calle Laurel in Logroño, La Rioja). Galicia is known for its seafood tapas and the Basque Country for its mini-masterpieces called *pintxos*, a style of tapas that come mounted on a slice of baguette and held together by a toothpick. In those bars, with a small glass of local, spritely young white wine called Txakoli (or equally small glass of beer called a *zurito*), you generally pay by the number of toothpicks on your plate at the end. In the 1980s and 1990s, these were miniature showcases for the culinary creativity of *la nueva cocina vasca* (new Basque cooking), that led the wave of avant-garde Spanish culinary expression.

The key point about tapas is that they are social—something eaten among friends. You meet, have a drink, and enjoy something as simple as some mussels with a vinaigrette (see page 94) or more elaborate offerings like marinated and stewed pork ribs (see page 81). While some might go home for dinner after a tapa or two, others move on to another bar for their specialty, and then onto another. There is even a verb for this eating and traveling from bar to bar: *tapear*. In noun form, it's called a *tapeo*.

I have included a few typical tapas in other chapters, as you frequently find them also served as something more substantial. Spanish egg tortillas are an example, or potato salad (see page 56). Conversely, almost any savory dish in this book can be prepared and served in smaller portions as part of a spread of tapas. Meatballs, for instance, rolled a touch smaller, make an excellent tapas dish (serve with cocktail forks or even toothpicks). So do *callos* (Galician-Style Tripe with Garbanzo Beans, page 269), but serve these with spoons.

In preparing tapas, serving sizes vary greatly, and I have given them here assuming that the dishes will be served either as an appetizer with, say, a glass of iced dry *vermut* (vermouth) before a meal, or as part of a number of tapas for a rather festive gathering.

Alcorta RIOJA
Albóndigas de
Choco y gambas
Calamares
Ortiguillas
Tortillitas Camarón

Alcorta RIOJA
Pulpo Gallega
Brochetas
gambones
Surtido
gaditano

MESON CRIOLLO

SURTIDOS DE PESCADO

ATÚN

HUEVAS

GAMBONES

TORTILLITAS DE CAMARONES

MERLUZA

CALAMARES

GALLOS

PLATOS DEL DIA

BODEGA
DONOSTIARRA

PINTXOS

INGREDIENTS

SPANISH TABLE OLIVES
aceitunas de mesa

A dish of olives sitting on the long bar or a marble café table is a recurrent offering in Spain. Bold green Sevillanas or small, drab-green Arbequinas, purplish black almond-shaped ones, green ones stuffed with anchovies . . . table olives are one of the foodstuffs most associated with Spain, and rightly so. They form not just a favorite nibble, but an important part of the country's culinary heritage. Olives are grown both for olive oil (see page 63) and for use on the table. Spain is the world's largest producer of both.

Olives are hard, bitter, and inedible when picked from the tree. The process for preparing Spanish *aceitunas de mesa* usually takes two to three months and has three phases: *recolección* (harvesting and collecting), *conservación* (conserving), and *aderezo* (curing). Recolección takes place in late autumn and into the new year. Ranging from bright green to greenish yellow to violet to reddish black, the color of an olive shows its stage of ripeness. After being washed and soaked in an alkaline solution to rid them of some of the bitterness, the olives are washed again and then put to soak in a salt water brine to soften. The olives are then drained and rinsed. Still bland, they need to be cured with seasonings—aromatic herbs such as thyme, rosemary, bay leaves, sage, and oregano; spices like fennel, cumin, and cloves; as well as aromatic additions like lemon and orange peel and crushed garlic cloves. Flavoring changes from region to region. Campo Real olives, for instance, picked early in October and possessing a brilliant emerald green color, traditionally have thyme, fennel, oregano, and garlic in the aderezo.

Home curing was once done quite frequently. Like many in the countryside, my wife's grandmother cured her own olives, just as she put up batches of peaches and quince paste. It is still possible to buy freshly picked olives in certain markets during winter for home use, and of course many farmhouses, if the climate is right, have at least a handful of their own trees.

There is no disputing how tasty olives are. But with things that are so good, you need to use prudence when eating them, as the old Spanish refrain reminds us: *"Aceituna, una es oro, dos plata, y la tercera, mata"* (Olives: One is gold; two, silver; and the third kills).

But like many people, I don't follow that one. Rather, I heed another refrain that goes like this: *"Aceituna, una; y si es buena, una docena"* (One olive; and if it is good, then a dozen).

TRADITIONS

BREAD
pan

Flip open a book of Spanish *refranes* (refrains) and by far the most common food word used is *pan*—bread. (One recent search turned up 169 refrains with *pan*.) There is just simply nothing more fundamental than bread. These sayings range from the commonly uttered *"al pan, pan y al vino, vino"* (to call "bread *bread* and wine *wine*," essentially to call something by what it is, as in to "call a spade a spade"), to referring to someone as *"un trozo de pan"* (a piece of bread), which means a very good person.

There are about as many types of bread in Spain as there are refrains, from classic large, round country loaves to long, thin *barras de pan* (the word *barra* means "bar" or "rod"). Larger loaves are asked for by weight in the bakery, as in *un cuarto*, referring to a quarter of a kilo, or *una barra de medio*, referring to a half kilo loaf. Galician breads often include a bit of corn flour to keep them moist, while along the Mediterranean there is the wonderful *coca de pan*, a dense, and slightly chewy flat loaf rubbed with olive oil and sprinkled with salt flakes before being baked.

Bread is seldom made at home, but rather bought in the bakery. And while day-old bread is rarely thrown away—there are numerous recipes that utilize it in this book—buying fresh bread every day remains important.

"Bueno es pan, y mejor, con algo que agregar."—Bread is good, but better with something to go with it. Sometimes that means on the side, but other times it means cooked on top. *Cocas* are a flatbread popular in Catalunya topped with roasted peppers (see page 70), herring, spinach, or whatever can be rustled up and added. (Cocas can also be sweet; see page 289 for one with sugar, pine nuts, and anisette.)

Of course, old bread is not thrown away. Made from day-old bread, *migas* (see page 161)—which can be translated as "crumbs" and refers to the soft interior part of a loaf—is a famous shepherd's dish prepared with chorizo, bacon, and garlic, and often eaten with a fried egg. Substantial and filling, migas and a glass of red wine are about all that is needed for a day's work.

Or, as an old refrain goes, *"Con pan y vino se anda el camino"* (With bread and wine the trail can be walked). Shepherds know that one well.

COUNTRY BREAD RUBBED WITH TOMATO AND OLIVE OIL

PA AMB TOMÀQUET

SERVES 6

Perhaps invented as a way to rescue old, dry bread, and to take advantage of the tomatoes that grow so abundantly in the summer garden, there is probably nothing more typically (or uniquely) Catalan or Mallorcan than bread rubbed with tomato, drizzled with olive oil, and sprinkled with sea salt. *Pa amb tomàquet*—in Spanish, it is called *pan con tomate*—is commonly eaten with slices of cured cold cuts, cheeses, roasted *escalivada* vegetables (see page 72), or anchovy fillets. It can be part of a tapas spread, the basis of a meal, or an accompaniment to grilled meats, and is not infrequently prepared for breakfast. With some slices of aged cheese or chorizo (or, the best of the best, a wedge of leftover Potato and Onion Egg Tortilla, page 124) and a café con leche, it makes an ideal country breakfast.

The bread is generally wide slices of *pa de pagès* (crusty Catalan round-loaf country bread), but a baguette sliced horizontally will work, too. Toasting the bread makes it easier to rub with the garlic and tomato; if using baguette, skip the toasting. You can taste the olive oil here, so be sure to use the best in the pantry.

Some choose to rub the tomato and oil on both sides of the bread, in which case the slices need to be eaten with a fork and knife.

8 TO 12 SLICES HEARTY COUNTRY-STYLE BREAD
1 GARLIC CLOVE, PEELED (OPTIONAL)
3 TO 4 VERY RIPE MEDIUM TOMATOES, HALVED CROSSWISE
EXTRA-VIRGIN OLIVE OIL
FLAKY SEA SALT

1. Toast the slices of bread. If using the garlic, hold it like an eraser and rub the bread. Rub the tomatoes firmly over the bread while slightly squeezing to help release some of the juices, until the slices are reddish and moist.

2. If the slices are particularly large, cut them in half. On a large platter, place a bottom layer of bread. Generously moisten with olive oil and sprinkle with salt. Stack on another layer of slices and repeat with oil and salt. Repeat as necessary until all of the ingredients are used. Serve immediately.

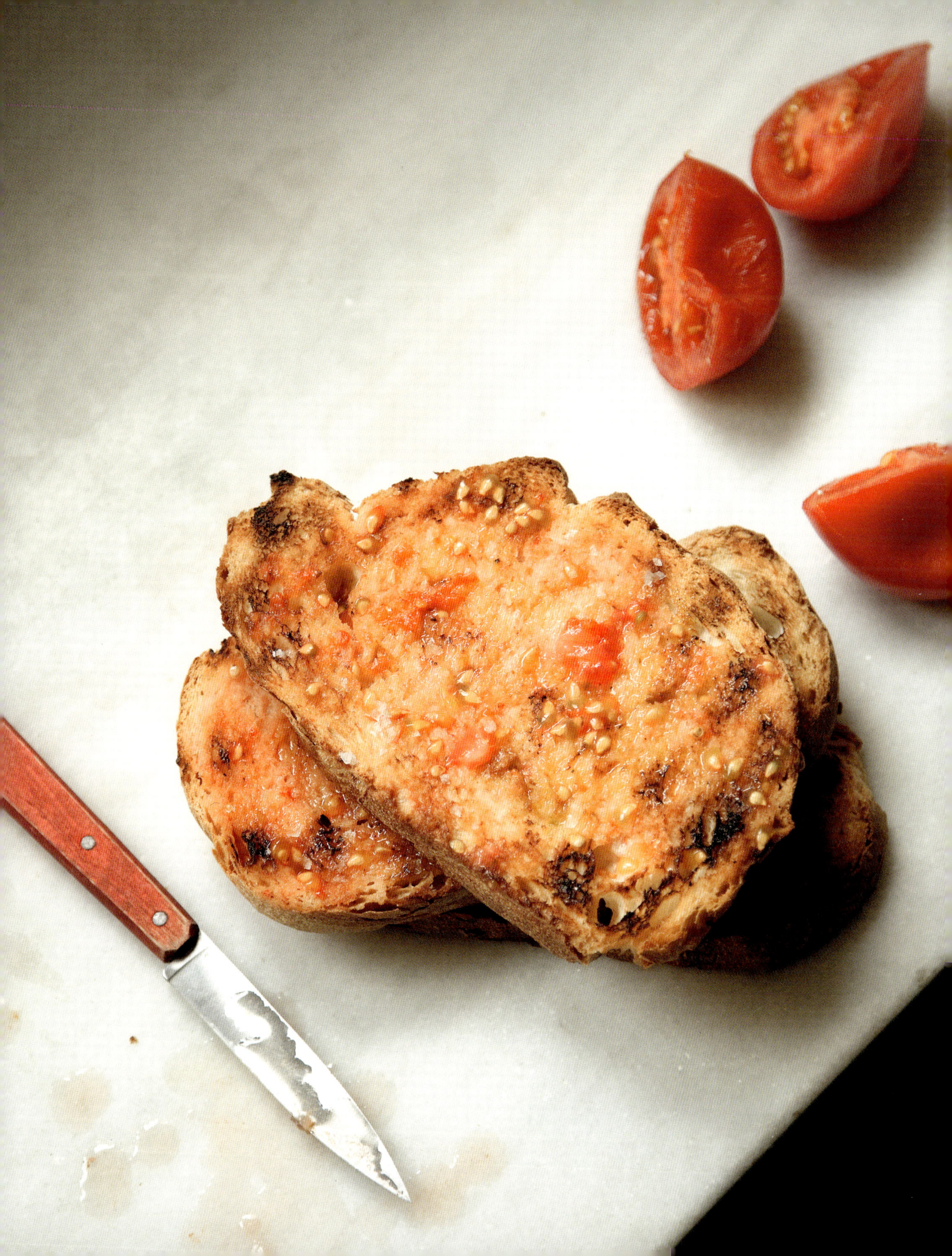

"The trick is to bake cocas hot and fast, or else they get drier than the feet of a saint." So began the advice of a baker named Carles Paricio—when I first met him, he was studying philosophy during the day and making bread at night—from Manlleu, a village in the foothills of the Pyrenees. This version is adapted from Carles's recipe and method of baking a single base and slicing it in half to make two open-faced cocas.

Coca can be either sweet or savory. *Coca de recapte* is the most popular savory version. In Catalan, *recapte* can loosely be translated as "provisions," and the topping can include a wide range of ingredients. Most typically it has roasted vegetables, herring or anchovies, and even some fresh pork sausage. (Recalling that Naples, Sicily, and Sardinia were medieval Catalan colonies, some have argued that coca is an ancient, older form of pizza, and that it was taken to Italy by merchants.)

CATALAN FLATBREAD WITH ROASTED RED PEPPERS

COCA DE RECAPTE

MAKES 2 COCAS, ABOUT 5 BY 13 INCHES/13 BY 33 CM

2 CUPS/250 G ALL-PURPOSE FLOUR
½ TEASPOON SALT
1 PACKAGE ACTIVE DRY YEAST (2¼ TEASPOONS)
OLIVE OIL FOR BRUSHING
2 RED BELL PEPPERS, WASHED AND DRIED
FLAKY SEA SALT
8 TO 12 ANCHOVY FILLETS, RINSED AND PATTED DRY
12 TO 16 BLACK OLIVES, PREFERABLY PITTED AND HALVED

1. In a large bowl, form a well with the flour and add the salt. Dissolve the yeast in ½ cup/120 ml warm water. In the middle of the well, add in the yeast. Mix, working in the flour from the center outward, until it forms a moist, sticky ball. Let sit for 5 minutes. Transfer to a lightly floured work surface and knead by hand for about 10 minutes, until the dough is supple and elastic and still slightly sticky. (Or use a bread hook and stand mixer.)

2. Place the dough in a large, lightly oiled bowl, cover with plastic wrap, and let rest at room temperature until it has doubled in size, 1 to 1½ hours.

3. Line a baking sheet with parchment paper or a silicone baking mat.

4. Transfer the dough to a work surface and form it into an oblong roll with your hands. Transfer to the sheet.

5. Working the dough as little as possible, gently stretch and press it out with your fingertips into an oval about ¾ inch/2 cm thick, 12 to 14 inches/30.5 to 35.5 cm long, and 5 to 6 inches/12 to 15 cm wide. Gently dimple it with your fingertips. Lightly brush with olive oil, cover with plastic wrap, and let sit for 30 minutes to rise again.

6. Preheat the broiler. Brush the bell peppers with olive oil and arrange on a baking sheet. Broil until charred in places, turning as needed with tongs, about 40 minutes. Immediately place them in a paper or plastic bag to cool and steam the skin to loosen before peeling. Once cool enough to handle, peel and strip. Working over a bowl to catch the juices, peel away the skin of the peppers, seed, and tear them into long, lengthwise strips ½ to 1 inch/1.25 to 2.5 cm wide.

7. Preheat the oven to 450°F/230°C/gas mark 8.

8. Remove the plastic from the dough and brush again with oil. Bake for 10 to 15 minutes, or until golden. Watch carefully during the final minutes. Remove from the oven and cool on wire racks.

9. Once cool, slice the bread flat through the middle to get two open-faced cocas.

10. Brush the soft, cut base with oil, lightly sprinkle with salt, and then lay on the roasted peppers. Criss-cross the anchovy fillets over the top, and place olives decoratively around.

11. Place the cocas into a hot oven for a couple of minutes until warm. Serve warm or at room temperature.

NOTE: The roasted and peeled red bell peppers will keep, covered, in the refrigerator for two days; the coca can easily be made half a day in advance. Do not slice it in half until ready to cover with the ingredients and serve.

ROASTED RED PEPPERS, EGGPLANT, AND ONIONS

ESCALIVADA

SERVES 4 TO 6

Escalivada derives its name from the Catalan words that mean "to cook on hot embers"—the traditional method of preparing this dish. These days, the vegetables are frequently roasted in the oven, the method given here. But for smokier, more rustic flavors, place the vegetables directly on hot charcoal or over a gas flame, turning frequently with tongs, until blackened. Place them in a paper sack or wrap in newspaper to cool and soften. Once cool enough to handle, peel and then follow the steps below.

Serve with wide slices of bread rubbed with tomato (see page 68), either alone or accompanied by anchovy fillets, cold cuts, or tinned bonito del norte tuna.

Escalivada keeps well for a few days in the refrigerator. The flavors will deepen as the garlic has time to embed its flavor into the vegetables.

⅓ CUP/75 ML EXTRA-VIRGIN OLIVE OIL, PLUS MORE FOR BRUSHING VEGETABLES
4 RED BELL PEPPERS, WASHED AND DRIED
1 MEDIUM GLOBE EGGPLANT, WASHED AND DRIED
2 UNPEELED MEDIUM ONIONS
6 GARLIC CLOVES, PEELED AND SLICED IN HALF LENGTHWISE INTO FLAT PIECES
SALT

1. Preheat the oven to 450°F/230°C/gas mark 8.

2. Lightly brush with oil the bell peppers, eggplant, and onions and then wrap them individually in aluminum foil. Place the vegetables on a baking sheet and bake until very tender and the skin of the peppers is falling away and the eggplant is charred in places and shriveled, about 1¼ hours. Remove from the oven and let cool in the foil for about 15 minutes.

3. Carefully open the foil (watch out for the steam escaping; it can burn) and let the vegetables cool further. Once cool enough to handle, begin working over a bowl to catch and save the juices. Peel away the skin of the peppers, seed, and tear them into long, lengthwise strips ½ to 1 inch/1.25 to 2.5 cm wide. Peel the eggplant, seed, and tear it into long strips the same size as the peppers. Remove the burnt outer skins of the onions, and cut them into slices.

4. In a large shallow serving dish, arrange the vegetables by type, with the brilliant red bell peppers in the middle. Dribble in 3 tablespoons of the reserved juice, tuck the garlic within the layers of vegetables, and season with a pinch of salt. Pour over the remaining oil and jiggle the dish to settle and distribute the oil. Let sit for at least 30 minutes to absorb the flavor of the garlic.

5. To store for up to 4 days, make sure the vegetables are covered with oil. Cover with a dish and refrigerate. Remove from the refrigerator with enough time before serving for it to return to room temperature.

PADRÓN GREEN PEPPERS

PIMIENTOS DEL PADRÓN

SERVES 4

Padrón is a village in the province of A Coruña (Galicia) famous for its short, slightly conical fresh green peppers not much bigger than a thumb. They are generally mild—which isn't to say sweet—and, when quickly fried until blistered in spots and then scattered with salt, make for a superb tapa. The oil needs to be hot (but not smoking) before adding so that they don't become soft and soggy, and they shouldn't be fried too long or they'll lose their natural flavor and aroma.

To eat, pick them up by the tail. You can eat the soft white core and seeds, if you want. Until recently, they were unavailable outside of Spain, but now are not infrequently found in the United States, carried by places like Whole Foods and in specialist Spanish shops such as La Tienda (see Sources, page 345). When buying, look for brilliant green peppers with firm, unwrinkled skin. If you can't find padrón peppers, look for Japanese shishito peppers.

One warning: While the level of heat is generally not something to be concerned about, every batch usually has one or two hot ones. Of course, whoever in the group can least handle the heat is bound to get it. I refer to this phenomenon as Padrón's Law.

32 FRESH PADRÓN GREEN PEPPERS
3 TABLESPOONS EXTRA-VIRGIN OLIVE OIL
FLAKY SEA SALT

1. Wipe the peppers with a cloth. Do not remove the stems or tails.

2. In a large skillet or sauté pan, heat the olive oil over medium-high heat. Add the peppers and quickly cook, turning as needed, until they are blistered in places but not blackened, 3 to 4 minutes. Use a splatter guard.

3. Quickly transfer the peppers with a slotted spoon to absorbent paper towels to wick away some of the excess oil, and then put them on a plate. Generously season with salt flakes. Serve hot.

CÁDIZ-STYLE POTATOES IN VINAIGRETTE

PAPAS ALIÑÁS

SERVES 6 TO 8

Brought to Spain from Peru in the sixteenth century, the potato carried its indigenous name *papa* for a couple of centuries before being largely replaced with the word *patata*. In parts of Andalucía (as well as in the Canary Islands), though, potatoes are still called papas just like they are today in South America. One of the favorite ways to eat papas around the region of Cádiz is boiled, sliced, and tossed with shallots in a heady vinaigrette. A simple, delightful bar tapa, you often find it topped with some flakes of tinned tuna or mackerel-like *melva* or a bit of chopped hard-boiled egg.

It is important to dress the potatoes while still warm and soft so that they can absorb more oil and vinegar and be more flavorful in the end. After blending, the potatoes should be moist but not soupy with the vinaigrette. While they are most commonly eaten at room temperature, if desired, you can cover and refrigerate until slightly chilled before serving.

2 POUNDS/910 G MEDIUM WHITE POTATOES
SALT
⅔ CUP/115 G FINELY CHOPPED SHALLOTS OR SPRING ONIONS
2 TABLESPOONS MINCED FRESH FLAT-LEAF PARSLEY
½ CUP/120 ML EXTRA-VIRGIN OLIVE OIL
2 TO 3 TABLESPOONS SHERRY VINEGAR
FRESHLY GROUND BLACK PEPPER

1. Wash but do not peel the potatoes. Place them in a large pot, cover with water, and bring to a boil. Add a generous pinch of salt, reduce the heat, partly cover the pot, and gently boil until they are tender and the tip of a knife can easily penetrate, 20 to 25 minutes. Transfer to a colander to drain and cool.

2. When the potatoes are cool enough to handle—but still warm—peel off the skin with your fingers. Cut the potatoes crosswise into ½- to 1-inch-/1.25- to 2.5-cm-thick slices and place them in a large glass or ceramic salad bowl. Add the shallots and parsley.

3. In a small bowl, whisk together the olive oil and vinegar (use a bit more for a bolder punch) until cloudy and blended. Pour over the potatoes, season with salt and pepper, and turn over to coat well. Let cool to room temperature before serving.

DATES WRAPPED IN BACON

DÁTILES CON BACÓN

SERVES 6

Few appetizers are as simple or more pleasantly surprising in taste than dates wrapped in bacon. For an added layer of texture and flavor, slip a toasted almond inside each date before wrapping with bacon. The dates can be wrapped in advance, covered with plastic wrap, and refrigerated until ready to fry and serve. Prepare them either on the stovetop or in the oven. Both versions follow.

Large—but not jumbo—size dates are best, as they can be popped in the mouth and eaten in a single bite. While North Africa produces most dates found in Spanish markets, Spain itself does grow them in Elche, south of Alicante. This ancient walled city was under Moorish rule for a few centuries, falling to the Christians in 1265 during the *reconquista*. During these centuries, palm trees were introduced. Today the *palmeral* (palm grove) has a total of 200,000 trees. These are so unique and important to the region, UNESCO named the grove a World Heritage Site.

8 TO 12 STRIPS LEAN BACON
24 LARGE DATES, PITTED
1 TABLESPOON OLIVE OIL

1. Cut each of the bacon strips into lengths about 3 inches/7.5 cm long. They need to be only long enough to wrap around a date a single time and just overlap. Wrap each date with a piece of bacon and secure with a toothpick.

2. *To prepare on the stovetop:* In a small skillet, heat the olive oil over medium heat and fry the wrapped dates until the bacon is golden and just crunchy and the dates warmed through and tender, about 4 minutes. Transfer to paper towels to drain.

To prepare in the oven: Preheat the oven to 350°F/180°C/gas mark 4. Line a baking sheet with parchment paper. Arrange the wrapped dates on the sheet and bake, turning if needed, until the bacon is golden and just crunchy, and the dates are warmed through and tender, about 6 minutes. Transfer to a plate.

3. Serve immediately while still hot.

TROUT AND DRY-CURED IBERIAN JAMÓN CROQUETTES

CROQUETAS DE TRUCHA Y JAMÓN IBÉRICO

MAKES ABOUT 30 CROQUETTES

At the end of an isolated mountain valley in Bierzo, in the far northwest corner of Castilla y León, is the tiny village of San Facundo. From the steep hills rising behind it comes a stream that passes through the center of town. The local park and swimming hole doubles as a trout fishing run. A small creek that feeds into it passes directly under a restaurant called Las Hoyas and is siphoned off into a private *vivero* (nursery) for trout and eel, two specialties of the house and its young chef, José Manuel Arias. When I ordered the eel, José brought me a plate of these *croquetas* and then went out to the vivero to net the rest of my lunch.

When frying various batches in a skillet, breadcrumbs gather in the bottom and burn. These tend to stick to the new batch and leave a bitter taste. After two batches, I very carefully filter the oil into a new skillet, bring it back to the correct temperature, and then continue frying.

7 TABLESPOONS EXTRA-VIRGIN OLIVE OIL

3 CLEANED FRESH MEDIUM RAINBOW TROUT, ABOUT 8 OUNCES/225 G EACH

SALT AND FRESHLY GROUND BLACK PEPPER

1 MEDIUM ONION, VERY FINELY CHOPPED

3½ OUNCES/100 G DRY-CURED SPANISH JAMÓN (SEE INGREDIENT NOTE, PAGE 16), VERY FINELY CHOPPED

1 GARLIC CLOVE, MINCED

3 CUPS/720 ML WHOLE MILK

PINCH FRESHLY GRATED NUTMEG

1 CUP/125 G ALL-PURPOSE FLOUR, PLUS MORE FOR DUSTING

1 HARD-BOILED EGG (SEE PAGE 342), VERY FINELY CHOPPED

2 EGGS

1 CUP/140 G FINE DRY BREADCRUMBS

SUNFLOWER OIL OR MILD OLIVE OIL FOR FRYING

1. In a large skillet or sauté pan, heat 1 tablespoon of the extra-virgin olive oil over medium-high heat until very hot. Season the trout with salt and pepper and lay them in the pan. Fry, turning once, until just opaque throughout (test for doneness along the backbone with the tip of a knife), about 4 minutes on each side. Transfer them to absorbent paper towels to drain off excess oil.

2. Once the trout are cool enough to handle, carefully and patiently remove all of the meat, discarding the skin and bones.

3. In a clean skillet or sauté pan, heat the remaining 6 tablespoons olive oil over medium heat and add the onion. Cook until soft and transparent but not yet browned, about 12 minutes. Add the jamón and garlic and cook, stirring frequently, for 2 minutes.

4. Meanwhile, in a medium saucepan, bring the milk to a simmer; season with salt, pepper, and nutmeg. Reduce the heat, cover the pan, and keep hot.

5. Sift the flour into the skillet over the onion and jamón, reduce the heat to medium-low, and cook, stirring constantly for about 2 minutes. It should be a compact and just-moist ball. Spread out the ball in the pan and begin slowly stirring in the hot milk until the mixture is creamy and not too sticky when touched, about 5 minutes. Reduce the heat to low and fold in the trout and the hard-boiled egg. Cook, gently stirring, for 2 minutes. The mixture should be spongy and can be touched without sticking to your finger.

6. Transfer the mixture to a large bowl to cool. Once cool, cover with plastic wrap and refrigerate for several hours until chilled. (This will make forming the croquettes easier.)

7. On a flat work surface dusted with flour, form croquettes into 2- or 2½-inch-/5- to 6.25-cm-long cylinders about 1 inch/2.5 cm in diameter. Lightly roll in flour.

8. Break the eggs in a bowl and thoroughly whisk. Place the breadcrumbs in a second bowl.

9. Dip the croquettes in the egg, and roll in breadcrumbs to completely cover.

10. In a skillet or sauté pan, heat at least ¾ inch/2 cm of sunflower oil over medium-high heat. Reduce the heat to medium-low.

11. Working in small batches that don't crowd the pan, fry the croquettes, turning frequently, until they are golden on the outside and hot and creamy at the center, 1 to 2 minutes. Gently transfer them to absorbent paper towels to drain off excess oil. Serve hot.

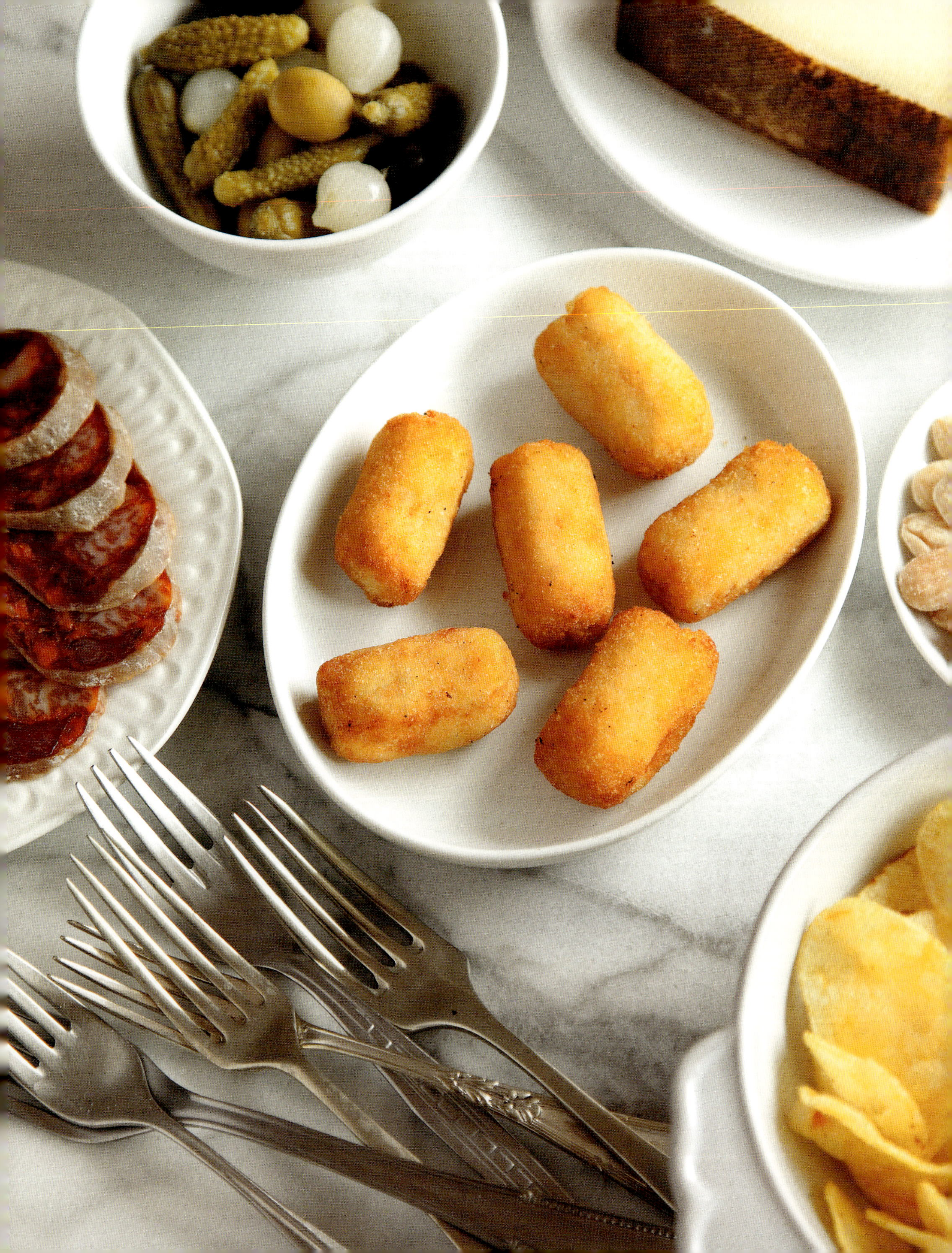

CHICKEN CROQUETTES

CROQUETAS DE POLLO

MAKES ABOUT 40 CROQUETTES

Spanish croquettes are not like French ones made with potatoes, or those large, round Sicilian *arancini* with rice. Rather, they use a thick, béchamel-like sauce as a base. To this, a host of flavors are added, ranging from cured jamón to salt cod. But chicken is perhaps the most common, and remains a beloved Spanish classic.

To freeze, roll the uncooked croquettes in egg and breadcrumbs and freeze in batches. Take them from the freezer and fry directly, without thawing. See the headnote on page 76 about changing the oil during frying.

1 TABLESPOON EXTRA-VIRGIN OLIVE OIL
12 OUNCES/340 G BONELESS SKINLESS CHICKEN BREAST
SALT
½ CUP/110 G BUTTER, CUT INTO PIECES
1 MEDIUM ONION, VERY FINELY CHOPPED
3 CUPS/720 ML WHOLE MILK
FRESHLY GROUND BLACK PEPPER
PINCH FRESHLY GRATED NUTMEG
1 CUP/125 G ALL-PURPOSE FLOUR, PLUS MORE FOR DUSTING
2 EGGS
1 CUP/140 G FINE BREADCRUMBS
SUNFLOWER OIL OR MILD OLIVE OIL FOR FRYING

1. In a skillet or sauté pan, heat the olive oil over medium heat. Season the chicken with salt and sauté until cooked through, about 10 minutes. Transfer to a platter to cool. Cut the chicken into pieces and grind with a food processor.

2. In a clean skillet or sauté pan, melt the butter over medium heat and add the onion. Cook over medium-low heat, until soft and transparent but not yet browned, about 12 minutes.

3. Meanwhile, in a medium saucepan, bring the milk to a simmer; season with salt, pepper, and the nutmeg. Reduce the heat, cover the pan, and keep hot.

4. Sift the flour into the skillet over the onion and cook, stirring constantly, for about 2 minutes. It should be a compact and just-moist ball. Spread out the ball in the pan and begin slowly stirring in the hot milk until the mixture is creamy and not too sticky when touched, about 5 minutes. Reduce the heat to low and fold in the ground chicken. Cook, gently stirring, for 2 minutes. The mixture should be spongy and can be touched without sticking to your finger.

continued

5. Transfer the mixture to a large bowl to cool. Once cool, cover with plastic wrap and refrigerate for several hours until chilled. (This will make forming the croquettes easier.)

6. On a flat work surface dusted with flour, form croquettes into 2- to 2½-inch-/5- to 6.25-cm-long cylinders about 1 inch/2.5 cm in diameter. Lightly roll in flour.

7. Break the eggs in a bowl and thoroughly whisk. Place the breadcrumbs in a second bowl.

8. Dip the croquettes in the egg and roll in breadcrumbs to completely cover.

9. In a skillet or sauté pan, heat at least ¾ inch/2 cm of sunflower oil over medium-high heat. Reduce the heat to medium-low.

10. Working in small batches that don't crowd the pan, fry the croquettes, turning frequently, until they are golden on the outside and hot and creamy at the center, about 2 minutes. Gently transfer them to absorbent paper towels to drain off excess oil. Serve hot.

PORK RIBS IN ADOBO SAUCE

COSTILLAS DE CERDO EN ADOBO

SERVES 6

This popular dish is a specialty of the sherry-producing triangle of Jerez de la Frontera, Sanlúcar de Barrameda, and El Puerto de Santa María, and in the ventas *(humble roadside eateries found between towns or at crossroads) around the hills above them. The tanginess of the dish comes from the region's sherry vinegar. If there is any sauce left over, spoon it into a bowl, refrigerate to solidify, and spread it on toast for a savory breakfast. That is exactly what they do in this part of Andalucía.*

6 GARLIC CLOVES, PEELED
4 TABLESPOONS SPANISH PIMENTÓN DULCE (SWEET PAPRIKA)
2 TABLESPOONS GROUND CUMIN
1 TABLESPOON DRIED OREGANO
¼ CUP/60 ML SHERRY VINEGAR
½ CUP/120 ML EXTRA-VIRGIN OLIVE OIL
3 POUNDS/1.4 KG BABY BACK PORK RIBS, CUT INTO SMALL PORTIONS OF 2 OR 3 RIBS
SALT AND FRESHLY GROUND BLACK PEPPER

1. In a mortar, mash the garlic with the pimentón, cumin, and oregano, and then stir in the vinegar to form a runny paste. Or in a food processor, purée the ingredients together with a touch of water to loosen them.

2. In a large, heavy casserole, sauté pan, or deep skillet, heat ¼ cup/60 ml of the olive oil over medium-high heat. Generously season the pork with salt and pepper and, working in single-layer batches that don't crowd the pan, cook, turning from time to time, until the pork is browned, 10 to 15 minutes.

3. Return all of the ribs to the pan, add the vinegary garlic paste, stir in the remaining ¼ cup/60 ml oil, and add about 2½ cups/600 ml water or just enough to cover. When it reaches a simmer, reduce the heat to medium-low and simmer uncovered, until the meat is very tender and begins to come away from the bone and the sauce has been largely reduced, about 1½ hours. Add in a touch more water as needed to keep it loose and moist.

4. Place a couple of ribs on each plate and cover with sauce. Serve warm.

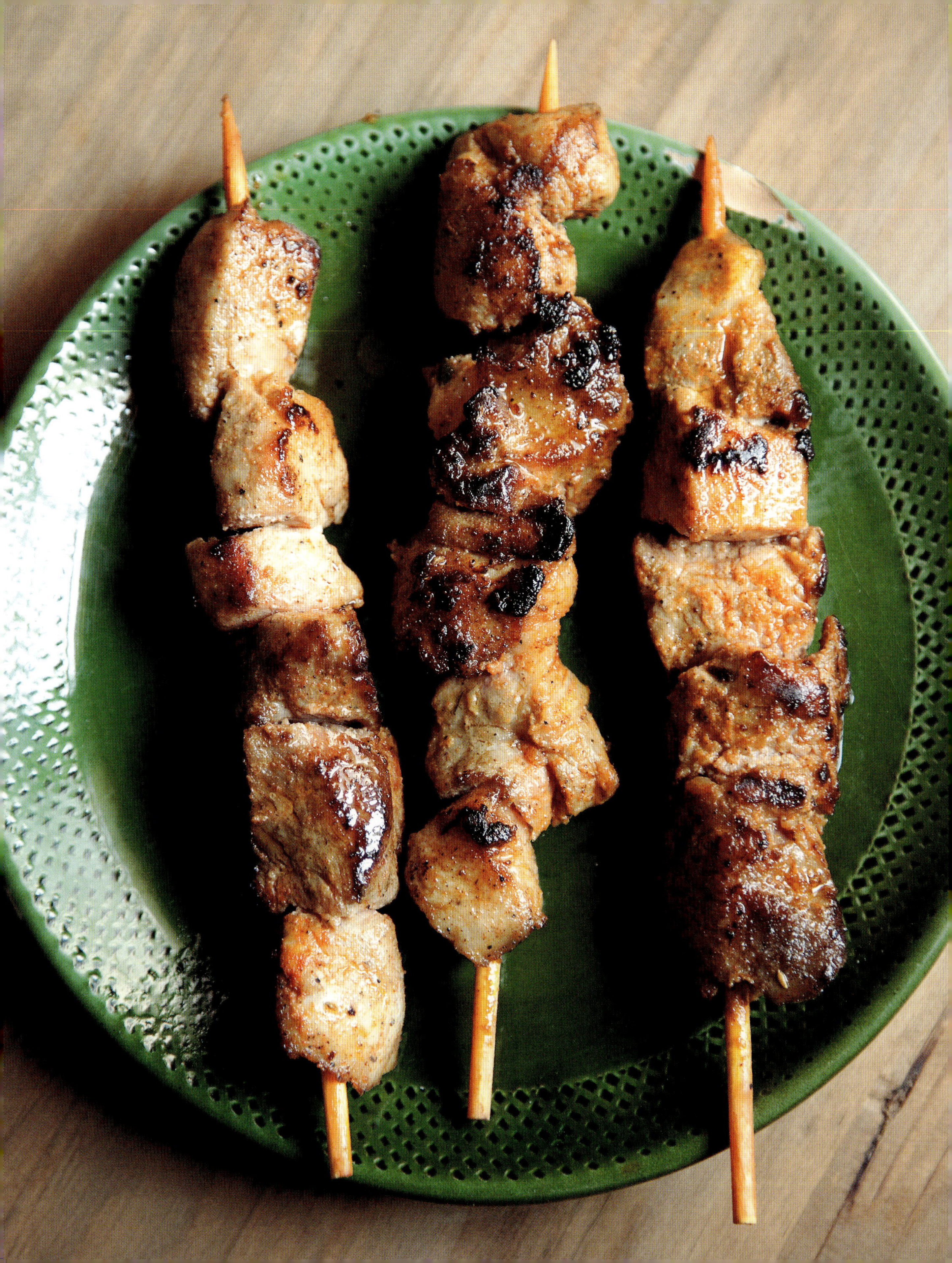

SPICY MARINATED PORK SKEWERS

PINCHOS MORUNOS

MAKES 8 TO 10 SKEWERS; SERVES 4

Heavily seasoned and marinated skewers of meat are a staple bar tapa. Originally lamb or beef was used, but these days pork is by far the most popular meat. And while this tapa is found across the breadth of the country, the unusually heavy use of spices reveals its southern origins.

Use the butt end of a pork loin or else the shoulder—both are tender, juicy cuts—and trim into same-size pieces to ensure even cooking. Serve with cold glasses of beer, preferably from one of the finer Spanish brewers like Alhambra, Moritz, or Estrella Galicia.

1 TEASPOON SPANISH PIMENTÓN PICANTE (SPICY PAPRIKA)
1 TEASPOON SPANISH PIMENTÓN DULCE (SWEET PAPRIKA)
1 TEASPOON GROUND CUMIN
1 TEASPOON DRIED OREGANO
1 TEASPOON FINELY CHOPPED THYME
1 TEASPOON GROUND CORIANDER
2 GARLIC CLOVES, MASHED OR FINELY CHOPPED
SALT AND FRESHLY GROUND BLACK PEPPER
5 TABLESPOONS EXTRA-VIRGIN OLIVE OIL, PLUS MORE FOR OILING PAN
SHERRY VINEGAR OR WINE VINEGAR
2 POUNDS/910 G BONELESS PORK, PREFERABLY BUTT OR SHOULDER, CUT INTO 1-INCH/2.5-CM CUBES
8 TO 10 SMALL PIECES CRUSTY BREAD (OPTIONAL)

1. In a large bowl, combine the spices, herbs, and garlic; season with salt and pepper; and blend in the olive oil and a few drops of vinegar. Mix into a moist paste. Add the pork and turn to coat well. Cover with plastic wrap, refrigerate, and marinate for at least 1 hour, though ideally a few hours longer. Toss the pork from time to time while it marinates.

2. Thread 4 to 6 pieces of pork on each skewer so that the pieces just touch.

3. Preheat a grill pan, griddle pan, or large, heavy skillet over medium-high heat and very lightly oil it. Lay on the skewers and grill, turning from time to time with the help of a spatula in order to cook them evenly on each side, until the meat is cooked through and firm to the touch, 8 to 10 minutes.

4. If desired, impale a piece of bread on the tip and serve hot on the skewer.

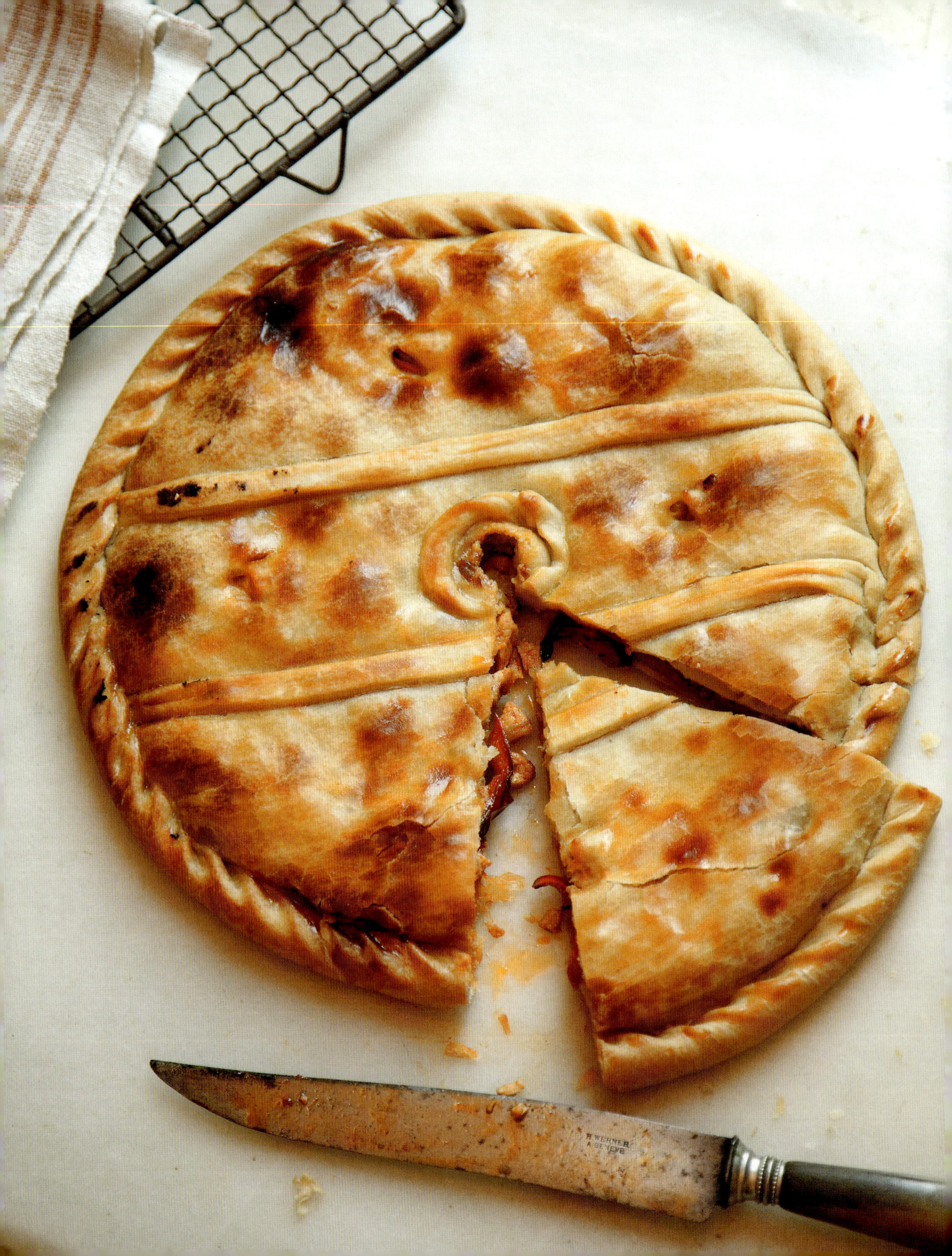

Galician cookbooks tend to be heavily weighted with recipes for seafood—no surprise there, as the region is one of the largest sources of it in Europe—and for empanadas. Empanadas are savory filled "pies" or pastries. These cookbooks often include a dozen or more traditional savory empanadas filled with everything from *bacalao con pasas* (salt cod with raisins), to *vieiras* (scallops), fresh *berberechos* (cockles, often made with a bit of corn flour in the dough), or *lomo* (pork). While they can make entire meals, they are excellent served as a generous, filling tapa.

This marinated pork empanada with onions and red bell pepper—called *empanada de raxo* in Galician—remains a classic from the region's interior. Many cooks add flakes of dried oregano to the marinade and a smashed hard-boiled egg to the stuffing to make it a bit more filling. A touch of sweet paprika in the dough gives it a distinctive golden tone.

EMPANADA WITH MARINATED PORK AND ROASTED RED PEPPERS

EMPANADA DE LOMO

MAKES ONE 10-INCH/25-CM EMPANADA; SERVES 6 TO 8

4 GARLIC CLOVES, PEELED

8 TABLESPOONS EXTRA-VIRGIN OLIVE OIL, PLUS MORE FOR OILING THE BOWL

2 TABLESPOONS DRY WHITE WINE

1½ TEASPOONS SPANISH PIMENTÓN DULCE (SWEET PAPRIKA)

1 TEASPOON DRIED OREGANO

SALT

1 BAY LEAF

12 OUNCES/340 G PORK FILLETS, THINLY CUT INTO ⅓-INCH-/1-CM-THICK STRIPS

3 CUPS/375 G ALL-PURPOSE FLOUR, PLUS MORE FOR WORK SURFACE AND PAN

1½ TABLESPOONS/20 G FIRMLY PACKED FRESH BAKER'S YEAST (SEE NOTE) OR 2 TEASPOONS ACTIVE DRY YEAST

½ CUP/120 ML WHOLE MILK, WARMED

2 EGGS, WHISKED

2 MEDIUM ONIONS, THINLY SLICED

1 RED BELL PEPPER, HALVED CROSSWISE AND SLICED INTO THIN LENGTHWISE STRIPS

BUTTER FOR GREASING PAN

continued

1. In a large bowl, blend the garlic, 3 tablespoons of the olive oil, the wine, 1 teaspoon of the pimentón, and the oregano. Season with salt and add the bay leaf and pork. Turn over to coat. Cover and marinate for at least a couple of hours.

2. Meanwhile, put the flour in a wide bowl and sprinkle in the remaining pimentón and 1 teaspoon salt, blend with your fingers, and make a crater in the middle. Dissolve the yeast in the milk and add along with one egg. Begin working into a ball while adding 2 tablespoons olive oil. (Add a touch more milk if needed.) Transfer the dough to a lightly floured work space and knead by hand for about 10 minutes, until supple and elastic and slightly tacky. Place it in a lightly oiled bowl, cover with plastic wrap, and let rise in a warm corner of the kitchen for about 1 hour, or until about doubled in size.

3. In a large skillet or sauté pan, heat the remaining 3 tablespoons olive oil over medium heat, add the onions, and cook until they begin to soften and turn pale, about 5 minutes. Add the bell pepper and cook until it and the onions are tender and sweet, about 25 minutes. Reduce the heat to low and cover the skillet toward the end. Transfer to a bowl.

4. Preheat a heavy skillet over high heat. Discard the garlic and bay leaf from the marinade. Working in single-layer batches that don't crowd the pan, quickly brown the pork in its marinade, 1 to 2 minutes per batch. Transfer to the bowl and blend with the onions and bell peppers.

5. Preheat the oven to 400°F/200°C/gas mark 6.

6. Butter and flour a 10½-inch/27-cm pie pan or line it with a piece of parchment paper cut to fit.

7. Divide the dough in half, with one piece slightly larger than the other. (The larger piece will be used for the bottom, the smaller for the top covering.) On a clean, lightly floured work surface, roll out the larger piece so that it will comfortably drape over the pie pan. Lay it over the pan, and gently tuck the inside against the sides of the pan.

8. Lay in the pork, bell pepper, and onions. Spread out in a thick, even layer.

9. Roll out the remaining piece of dough. Lay it on the top of the filling like a lid. Cut away and reserve the edges. Form a crimped edge by pinching the edges together with your fingers. Make a 1-inch/2.5-cm or so hole in the very center of the top to allow some steam to escape.

10. With the excess dough, decorate the top as desired. Roll out some pieces to run across the top or even make a cross, for instance, or make a simple braid to run along the edge.

11. Paint the top of the empanada with the whisked egg using a pastry brush.

12. Bake the empanada until the top is a lovely golden color, 20 to 25 minutes.

13. Let the empanada cool before slicing into portions and serving.

NOTE: Fresh baker's yeast is sold in compressed cakes that are ivory-colored, moist, and crumbly. In North America, it is often sold in 0.6-ounce/17-g foil packets.

SALT COD BRANDADE ON TOAST

BRANDADA DE BACALLÀ

MAKES 2 CUPS/480 ML; SERVES 4 TO 6

While this is perhaps best known outside Spain as a French dish from Languedoc-Roussillon and Provence, the deep, ancient links between these southern French regions and Spain's northeast mean that this fluffy salt cod and potato dish was incorporated centuries ago into traditional Catalan and Valencian cuisine. Here, it's commonly spread on slices of toasted bread. Not so in the Basque Country, where you find *brandada* frequently stuffed into red piquillo peppers (see page 188). As the salt cod will be puréed, buy a less expensive cut.

8 OUNCES/225 G SALT COD
1 MEDIUM WHITE POTATO WITH THE PEEL, SCRUBBED
6 TABLESPOONS/90 ML EXTRA-VIRGIN OLIVE OIL
3 GARLIC CLOVES, PEELED
6 TABLESPOONS/90 ML WHOLE MILK, WARMED
SALT
SLICED COUNTRY-STYLE BREAD

1. Begin desalting the salt cod 2 to 3 days before (depending on the cut), following the directions on page 341. Drain, rinse, gently squeeze out excess moisture, and pat dry with paper towels.

2. In a saucepan, add the potato, cover with about 1 inch/2.5 cm cold water, and bring to a boil. Partly cover the pan and gently boil, until the potato is tender and the tip of a knife can easily penetrate, 20 to 25 minutes. Transfer the potato to a colander to drain and cool. When cool enough to handle, peel away the skin, and cut the potato into four or five pieces.

3. Meanwhile, in another saucepan, add the salt cod and cover with 2 cups/480 ml cold water. Bring to a quick boil over high heat. As soon as the water breaks a boil, remove the pan from the heat and let the cod sit for 15 minutes in the water. Drain and rinse. Remove the skin and any bones.

4. In a small skillet, heat the olive oil over medium-low heat. Add the garlic and cook until just golden and fragrant, about 1 minute; do not let it burn. Transfer the garlic immediately to a plate. Reserve the oil.

5. In a food processor, purée the salt cod and garlic on low speed. Slowly add the reserved oil, potato chunks, and then the milk. Purée until creamy and fluffy, but not pasty. Taste for seasoning and add salt if needed.

6. To serve, toast the bread and cut it into triangles. Spoon the brandade into a bowl to spread on the toast as desired.

FRESH ANCHOVIES IN VINEGAR

BOQUERONES EN VINAGRE

SERVES 4

Tart, supple, straightforward—and so delicious. Be sure to use only very fresh anchovies. Look for ones that are 4 to 5 inches/10 to 13 cm long. Soaked for 3 hours in white wine vinegar, the fillets turn white. Drained, they are then submerged in olive oil with some herbs. Soaking the fillets first in a saltwater solution will help keep them firm and make them a more brilliant white.

12 TO 16 WHOLE FRESH ANCHOVIES (*BOQUERONES*) OR 6 FRESH SMALL SARDINES (SEE NOTE)

SALT

1 CUP/240 ML WHITE WINE VINEGAR OR ENOUGH TO COVER

1 CUP/240 ML EXTRA-VIRGIN OLIVE OIL OR ENOUGH TO COVER

2 BAY LEAVES

2 GARLIC CLOVES, LIGHTLY CRUSHED IN THE PEEL

12 BLACK PEPPERCORNS

FRESHLY GROUND BLACK PEPPER

1. Fill a bowl with water. Butterfly open the anchovies. Remove the heads and pull out the entrails. Using a thumbnail or paring knife, open the anchovies along the stomach. Using a thumbnail, loosen and then remove the central spine. Pick out any remaining bones. Gently rinse under running water and place the anchovies in the bowl of water. The fillets should be joined along the back, but it is fine if they separate into two fillets.

2. In a clean bowl, dissolve 1 teaspoon salt in 1 quart/1 L cold water. Drain the fillets and carefully place them in the bowl of salt water for 1 to 2 hours. Drain, gently rinse the fillets, and spread them out on paper towels to dry. Pat dry.

3. Lay the fillets in a shallow bowl and pour in enough vinegar to cover. Sprinkle with a few pinches of salt. Cover with plastic wrap, refrigerate, and marinate for 3 hours. While they soak, swirl the dish from time to time to keep the fillets from sticking together and allow them to marinate evenly. The fillets will turn white.

4. Remove the fillets from the vinegar, drain (but do not rinse with water), and gently pat dry with paper towels. Lay them in a clean dish or shallow bowl and cover with the olive oil. Add the bay leaves, garlic, and peppercorns and jiggle the dish to settle. Make sure the fillets are submerged. Let sit for at least 1 hour before serving.

5. To serve, remove the fillets and lay them on a plate. Spoon over a touch of the oil. Add a pinch of salt and grind some pepper over each fillet.

NOTE: If using fresh sardines, clean, scale, and fillet following the directions on page 332.

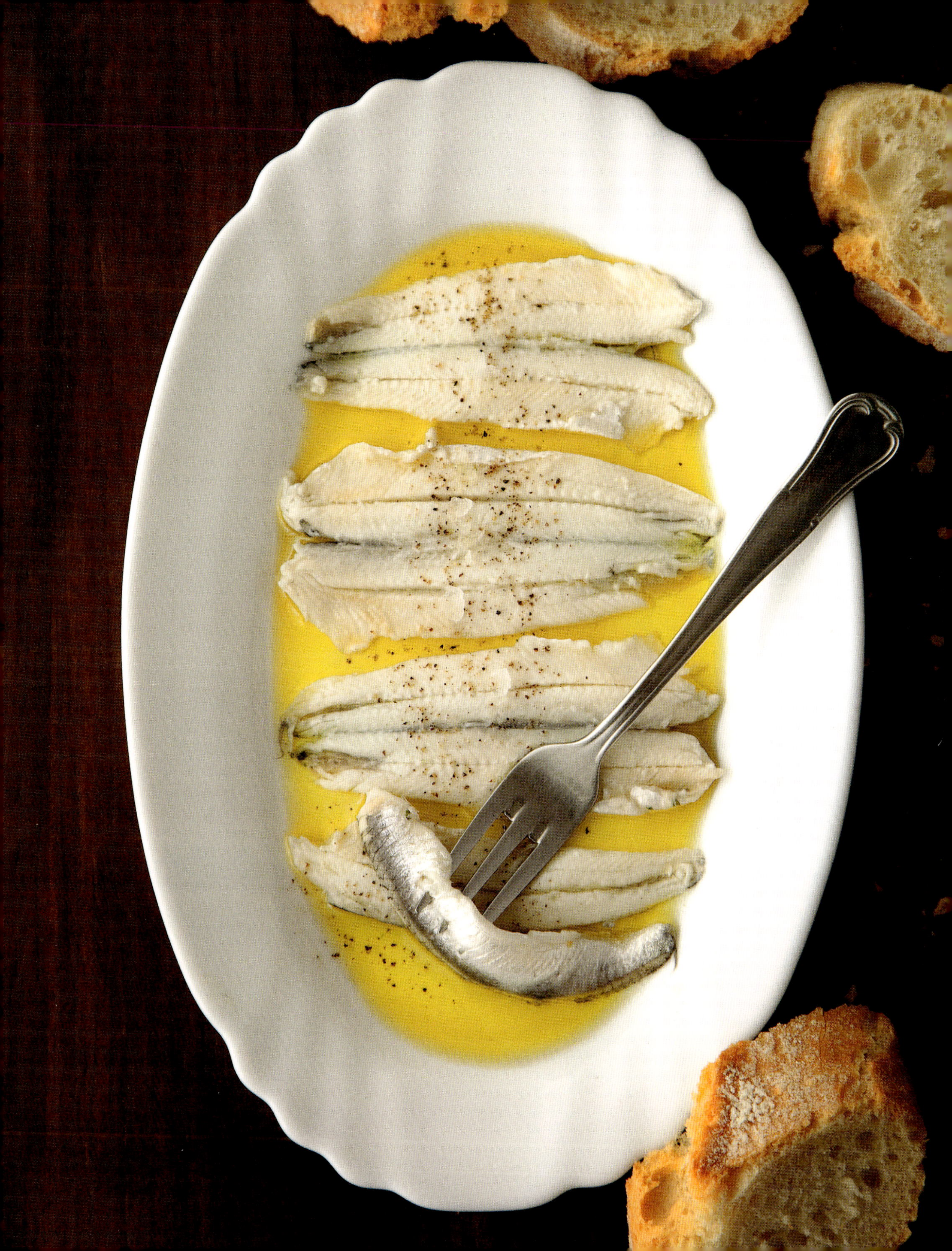

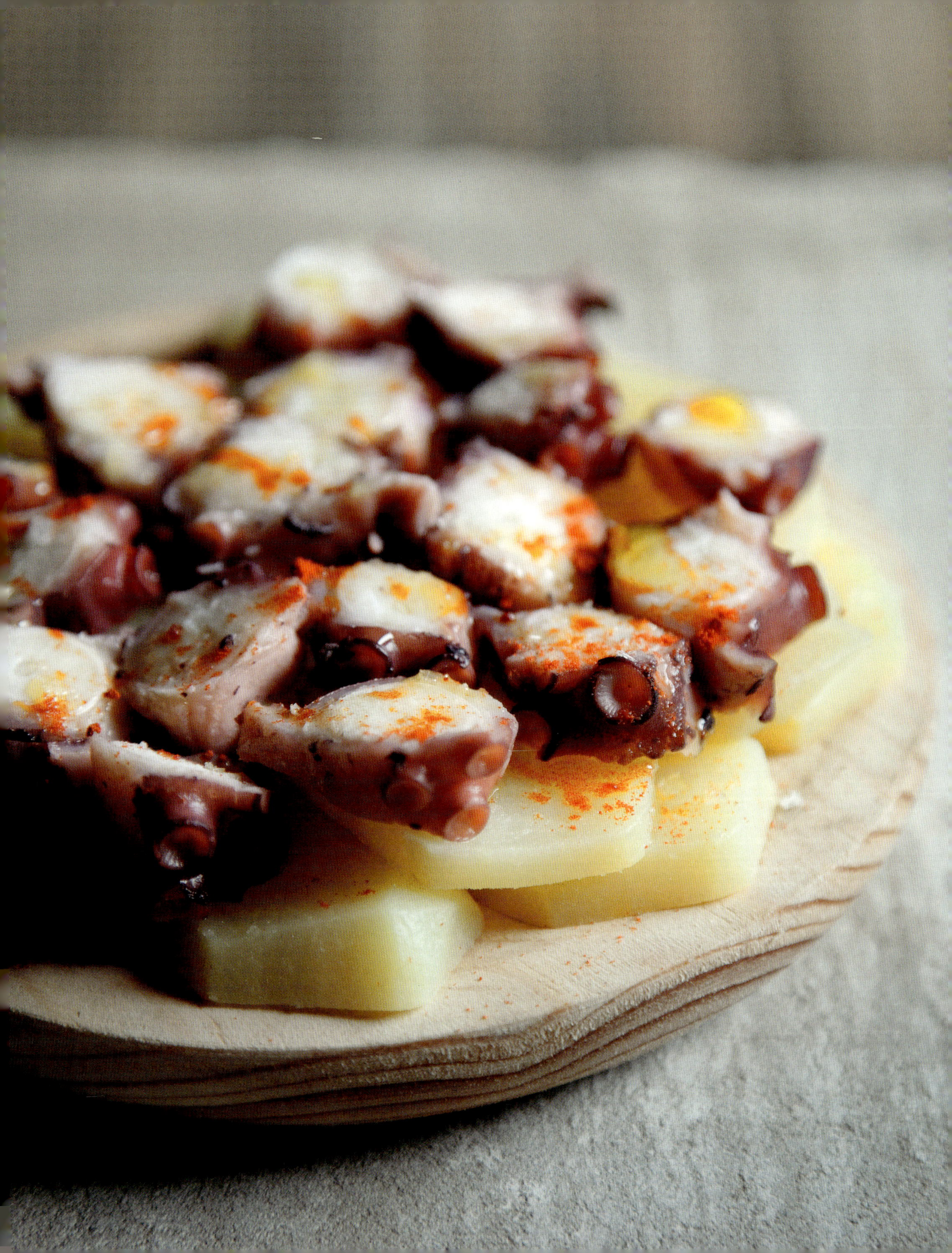

GALICIAN FAIR-STYLE OCTOPUS WITH PAPRIKA ON POTATOES

POLBO Á FEIRA CON PATATAS

SERVES 4

So associated with Galicia is this way of preparing octopus that while it is called *á feira* (fair style) in Galicia, in the rest of Spain it is generally called *a la gallega* (Galician style). Frequently nestled on a bed of potatoes to absorb the flavors, the tender octopus gets a drizzle of olive oil and a generous dousing of both sweet and spicy paprikas.

Freezing an octopus for at least 5 days will break down the hard fibers and make it more tender. Or, do what I have been shown by fishermen in Galicia: grasp the fresh creature by the head and swing it, giving it thirty-three powerful smacks against a hard surface. But this is advisable out on the docks, not on your kitchen counter.

Be careful not to overcook the octopus. It will be tender at 20 or 30 minutes, then toughen up and need to be boiled all day to become tender again.

1 CLEANED OCTOPUS, ABOUT 2¼ POUNDS/1 KG, FROZEN
SALT
1 ONION, PEELED AND HALVED
4 TO 6 MEDIUM WHITE POTATOES
1 BAY LEAF
FLAKY SEA SALT
EXTRA-VIRGIN OLIVE OIL FOR DRIZZLING
SPANISH PIMENTÓN DULCE (SWEET PAPRIKA) FOR SPRINKLING
SPANISH PIMENTÓN PICANTE (SPICY PAPRIKA) FOR SPRINKLING

1. Thaw the octopus gently in the refrigerator. Fill a large pot or stockpot with water and bring it to a rolling boil. Add a pinch of salt and the onion and, following tradition, dunk the octopus three times in the water "to frighten it." When the water returns to a boil, submerge the octopus in the water, cover the pot, and cook at a rolling boil over high heat for 20 minutes, or until tender. It's done when a toothpick or tip of a knife pricked quite deep into the upper part of a tentacle enters with little resistance. Remove the pot from the heat, leave covered, and let the octopus sit in the water for 15 minutes. Remove the octopus and place on a large platter to cool.

2. Wash but do not peel the potatoes. Place them in a large pot, cover with water, and bring to a boil. Add a generous pinch of salt and the bay leaf, reduce the heat to medium-low, partly cover the pot, and gently boil until the potatoes are tender and a knife tip penetrates with little resistance, 20 to 25 minutes. Transfer to a colander to drain and cool. Once cool, peel.

3. Cut the potatoes crosswise into ⅓-inch-/1-cm-thick slices and arrange them on a large round plate or wooden platter. Cut the tentacles of the octopus with kitchen shears into ¼- to ½-inch-/½- to 1.25-cm-thick rounds and arrange them, overlapping the rounds, on top of the potatoes. Season with salt flakes and drizzle liberally with olive oil. Mix the sweet and the spicy paprikas together as desired—half and half for sharper, more sweet for softer, and so on—and sprinkle over the top before serving.

DEEP-FRIED SQUID

CALAMARES FRITOS

SERVES 4 TO 6

Batter-coated and deep-fried squid rings called *calamares a la romana* are typical around Spain, especially in cheap bars, where they tend to be overbreaded and soggy. A much better way to fry good squid is with this coastal Andalusian method, which gives them just a light coating of flour. Here you taste not fried batter, but the squid. Given a pinch of salt and a squeeze of lemon, they make a quick and divine tapa.

2¼ POUNDS/1 KG SMALL OR MEDIUM SQUID (CALAMARI)
ALL-PURPOSE FLOUR FOR DREDGING
SALT
MILD OLIVE OIL OR SUNFLOWER OIL FOR DEEP-FRYING
1 LEMON, CUT INTO WEDGES

1. Clean the squid following the directions on page 342. Cut the smaller ones in half, and medium-size ones into ½-inch-/1.25-cm-wide rings. There should be about 18 ounces to 1¼ pounds/510 to 570 g of cleaned squid.

2. In a bowl, season the flour with salt and blend with your fingers.

3. Preheat the oven to 200°F/95°C.

4. In a deep skillet or sauté pan, heat at least 1 inch/2.5 cm of olive oil to 375°F/190°C. (The oil is the right temperature when a large cube of fresh bread dropped into it browns in about 60 seconds.)

5. Working in small batches that don't crowd the pan or bring the temperature of the oil below 350°F/180°C, flour about one third or one fourth of the squid, shake off any excess flour, and gently lower them into the oil with tongs. Fry until golden and tender, 1 to 3 minutes depending on the thickness of the squid.

6. Remove with a slotted spoon, and place on absorbent paper towels to drain. Transfer to a baking sheet and place in the oven to keep warm until all of the squid has been fried.

7. Flour and fry the remaining squid, being sure that the oil has returned to 350°F/180°C before adding the next batch.

8. Serve hot with lemon wedges on the side to squeeze over the top as desired.

GARLICKY SHRIMP IN OLIVE OIL

GAMBAS AL AJILLO

SERVES 4

Ajillo essentially means a sauce made with garlic and other ingredients—but garlic is the key and dominating flavor. That is the case here, though in this classic tapa, there is usually a red chile, too, a tiny ½-inch-/1.25-cm-long one called a *guindilla* or *bicho* (literally "bug"). Use fresh shrimp if possible, as frozen sweat too much water while cooking and finish with a blander texture. Serve with plenty of country-style bread or baguette to dip into the flavorful oil.

If you have heatproof *cazuelitas* (small round terra-cotta casserole dishes), prepare the servings individually in the dishes by dividing the ingredients among them.

⅔ CUP/165 ML EXTRA-VIRGIN OLIVE OIL
4 GARLIC CLOVES, MINCED
1 SMALL DRIED HOT RED CHILE OR PINCH DRIED RED PEPPER FLAKES
12 OUNCES/340 G SHELLED MEDIUM TO LARGE FRESH SHRIMP WITH TAILS
SALT
MINCED FRESH FLAT-LEAF PARSLEY FOR GARNISHING

1. In a large, deep sauté pan or skillet, heat the olive oil over medium-high heat. Add the garlic and chile and cook, stirring continually, until golden, 5 to 10 seconds. Add the shrimp and cook, stirring a few times, until pink throughout, 1 to 2 minutes. Remove the pan from the heat and season with salt.

2. Spoon the shrimp and some oil into individual bowls. Dust each bowl with parsley and cover with an overturned saucer or dessert plate until cool enough to eat. Serve with small forks or toothpicks.

CLAMS WITH SHRIMP

ALMEJAS CON GAMBAS

SERVES 4 TO 6

Most Spanish clam preparations are pretty straightforward, and cooked in a way that they won't lose their delicate sea flavors. There is usually some garlic, perhaps a bit of onion, and almost always a shot of white wine. This tapas recipe is no exception, except that it adds shrimp into that equation. In springtime, use the more mild tender garlic shoots (called *ajetes* or *ajos tiernos* in Spanish) or, in autumn, sauté a handful of wild mushrooms in the pan before adding the clams. Serve with some bread to soak up the liquid and a glass of crisp white wine.

1 POUND/455 G LARGE CLAMS, SCRUBBED

2 TABLESPOONS EXTRA-VIRGIN OLIVE OIL

½ CUP/65 G FINELY CHOPPED LEEKS OR SCALLIONS, WHITE AND TENDER GREEN PARTS ONLY

3 GARLIC CLOVES, MINCED

12 OUNCES/340 G SHELLED AND DEVEINED LARGE SHRIMP OR PRAWNS

1 TABLESPOON MINCED FRESH FLAT-LEAF PARSLEY

1 SMALL DRIED RED CHILE PEPPER OR PINCH DRIED RED PEPPER FLAKES (OPTIONAL)

½ CUP/120 ML DRY WHITE WINE, WARMED

1. Purge the clams of any sand by soaking them in salty water following the directions on page 341. Discard any with broken shells.

2. In a large sauté pan or skillet, heat the olive oil over medium heat, add the leeks and garlic, and cook until fragrant, about 1 minute. Add the shrimp, clams, parsley, and (if using) chile pepper and cook for 2 minutes, shaking the pot from time to time. Pour over the wine, partly cover the pan, and cook over high heat, shaking the pan from time to time and stirring, until the clams have opened and the shrimp are opaque throughout, about 4 minutes.

3. Transfer it all to a serving bowl (including the liquid), discarding any clams that did not open, and serve immediately.

MUSSELS IN VINAIGRETTE

MEJILLONES A LA VINAGRETA

SERVES 4

This delightful dish is a favorite in Galicia, where cooks use fat, juicy local mussels harvested in the *rías*, the deep inlets that furrow into the coastline. These mussels pack a bold punch and, as they have strong vinegar tones, pair best not with wine but with a glass of cold beer. A favorite *cerveza* brewed in this part of Spain is called Estrella Galicia, a pale lager-style beer with a distinctive red-and-black label.

16 MEDIUM TO LARGE MUSSELS, CLEANED, SCRUBBED, AND DEBEARDED (SEE PAGE 341)
3 TABLESPOONS EXTRA-VIRGIN OLIVE OIL
1 TABLESPOON SHERRY VINEGAR OR RED WINE VINEGAR
SALT
⅓ CUP/40 G VERY FINELY CHOPPED ONION
⅓ CUP/40 G VERY FINELY CHOPPED GREEN BELL PEPPER
⅓ CUP/40 G VERY FINELY CHOPPED RED BELL PEPPER

1. In a medium pot, bring ¼ cup/60 ml water to a boil over high heat. Add the mussels, cover the pot, and steam until the mussels have opened, 2 to 4 minutes. Transfer to a colander to drain and cool. Discard any mussels that did not open. Twist off the empty half of each mussel and discard.

2. In a medium bowl, whisk the olive oil and vinegar until cloudy and blended. Season with salt, add the onion and bell peppers, and whisk again.

3. Arrange the mussels spoke-like on a platter with the tips pointing to the center. Spoon 1 tablespoon of the pepper mixture into each shell and drizzle any remaining liquid from the bowl over the top. Cover and refrigerate to chill for at least 20 minutes before serving.

FIESTAS

TIÓ DE NADAL

Tió de Nadal, a "pooping" Christmas log, is an obsession among the kids in Catalunya for a few weeks leading into the holidays. Part of the ancient tradition of burning a Yule log in the hearth at Christmastime, these days it is a short trunk of wood propped up by two front legs, with a smile, pug nose, and floppy red felt Catalan hat called a *barretina*. Wrapped in a blanket and placed beside the fireplace, it is "fed" clementine and potato peels until the evening of the 23rd or 24th of December.

On that night, the family gathers around and the kids whack it with a heavy stick while chanting at the top of their voices "*Ca-ga-ti-ó! Ca-ga-ti-ó!*" ("Poop log! Poop log!") and singing a short song about pooping *torró* (almond and honey nougat, called *turrón* in Spanish) and oranges instead of salted herring or charcoal. Then they reach under the blanket and find pieces of torró (and often a small present) that have been "pooped out."

Around Catalunya, homes resound with chanting verses of the song. (Schools have an enormous Tió that kids bring scraps from home to feed. The offerings look like a rich mound of compost.) My two girls so beat up our Tió (and broke a number of my wooden spoons) in all their practicing over the last years, that we recently bought a new trunk (poor Tió!) at the centuries-old Christmas market in front of the Barcelona Cathedral.

There are many versions of the song, but one standard goes like this, with my (unrhyming) translation of the Catalan original beside it:

Caga tió,	Poop log,
tió de Nadal,	trunk of Christmas,
no caguis arengades,	don't poop herring,
que són salades;	which are salty;
caga torrons	poop nougat,
que són més bons,	which are much tastier,
caga taronges	poop oranges
que són ben dolces.	that are very sweet.

My girls know a half-dozen versions of similar songs. After singing one, pounding on Tió, and extracting a present from under the blanket, they go to a back bedroom to "rehearse" the next version while my wife or I secretly tuck another small gift under Tió's blanket for them to find in the next round.

One popular version that is a favorite of my girls goes like this, with the lyrics more about rhyming than making sense, especially at the end, which turns into almost scat singing of sounds.

Caga tió, tió de Nadal,
posarem el porc en sal,
la gallina a la pastera
i el pollí a dalt del pi;

toca, toca, Valentí.
Passen bous i vaques,
gallines amb sabates,
i galls amb sabatons.

Correu, correu minyons,
que la tieta fa torrons,

Poop log, log of Christmas, we will put the pork in salt, the hen at the trough and the chick on top of the pine tree;

play, play, Valentine. Oxen and cows pass, hens with shoes, and roosters with big shoes.

Run, run children, because the aunty is making nougat,

el vicari els ha tastat,
diu que són un poc salats.

Ai el ruc, ai el porc,
ai el cara, cara, cara,
ai el ruc, ai el porc,
ai el cara de pebrot.

the vicar has tasted them, and he says they are a bit salty.

Oh the donkey, oh the pig, oh the face, face, face, oh the donkey, oh the pig, oh the face of a pepper.

Sometimes, for good measure, these lines follow:

Tió de Nadal,
caga neules i torrons

i pixa xampany!

Trunk of Christmas, poop *neules* [a rolled wafer biscuit] and nougat, and piss champagne!

CHAPTER 4

VEGETABLES
verduras

A top-flight American chef once asked me, only partly in jest, if we eat any vegetables in Spain. He had been traveling here for two weeks and was overwhelmed by the vast amounts of lamb and kid, poultry, beef dishes, plates of fish and shellfish, and surely no shortage of pork and jamón. But vegetables?

The answer, of course, is a resounding yes—especially in homes. (He had been eating only in restaurants.) In southern Navarra along the Ebro River—an important center of the country's vegetable industry—the town of Tudela takes its vegetables so seriously that it offers a weeks-long spring celebration called the *Exaltación de la Verdura* (Exaltation of the Vegetable). There are samples, discussions, cooking workshops, and, of course, cooking contests with vegetables.

In homes, vegetable dishes tend to be served as a first course, rather than as a *guarnición* (garnish) or *acompañamiento* (accompaniment) to a main dish. A plate of sautéed wild mushrooms (see page 100), say, or stewed Manchego-style medley of vegetables (see page 102) will usually be served on its own, just as the fish or meat dish will be for the next course. Potatoes are perhaps the biggest exception. While there are a couple of notable first dishes based on potatoes—La Rioja-style with chorizo (see page 118) comes immediately to mind—they generally come alongside main dishes.

Of the vegetable treasures brought back from the New World—kidney and green beans, peppers, tomatoes, various members of the squash family—the potato has been one of the most important to the diet. The Spanish first encountered it in 1532 in modern-day Peru, though it didn't arrive in Spain until 1570. Cultivation began small and it was grown largely for cattle and pigs. Many considered the tuber venomous and a cause of leprosy. Not until the end of the eighteenth century was it integrated into the Spanish kitchen.

The most common Spanish potato is thin-skinned, with a waxy, pale-gold peel and white interior, akin to a Yukon gold or white round potato. Galicia has the best known potato culture (and grows the famous Kennebec variety around Ourense). Here, as elsewhere in the north of the country, they form the base for various stews, and are a key ingredient in many other dishes—including one with veal (see page 32) and another with bonito tuna (see page 31)—to give substance, thicken, and, ultimately, absorb the flavors of the pot. Boiled and sliced Galician *cachelos* (see page 116) make a great bed for seafood or skewers of marinated pork for the flavors to drain down into. A small book published by the Xunta de Galicia (the regional government) on its cuisine reported that potatoes are used in more than half of the dishes in Galicia. After spending much of a summer in the region, I believe it.

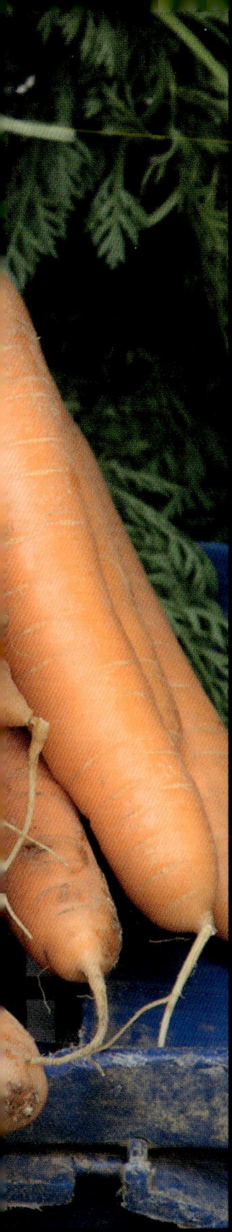
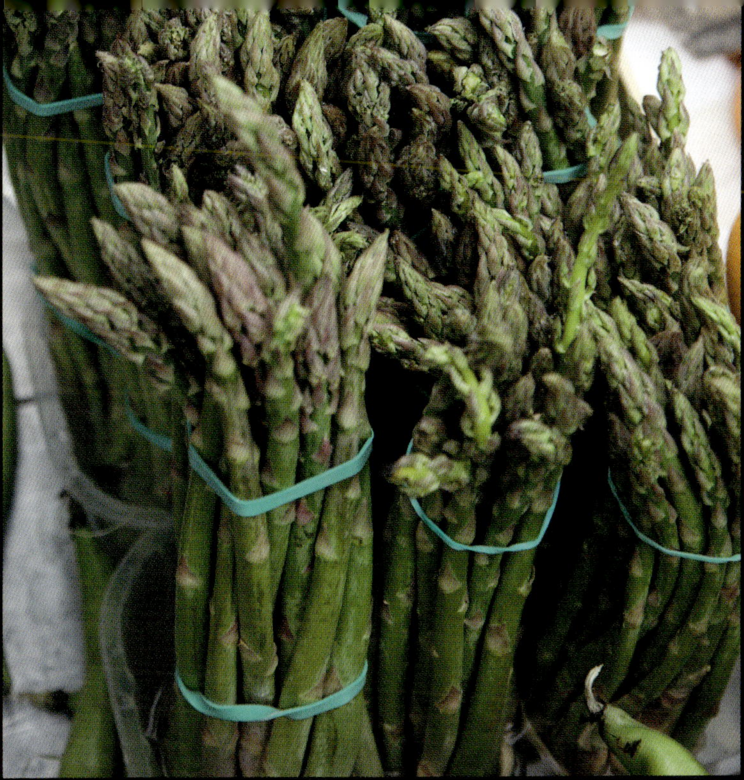
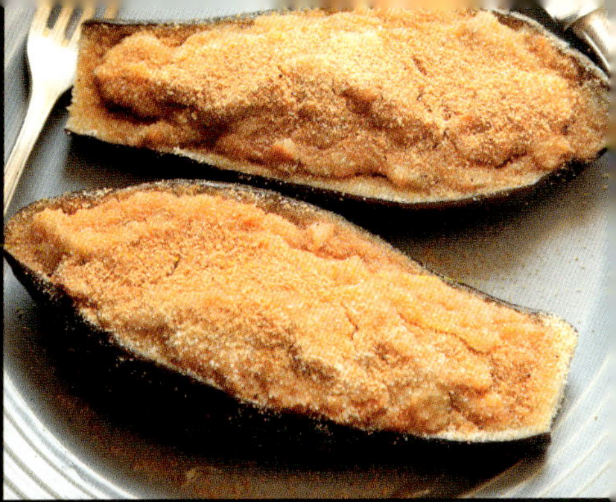
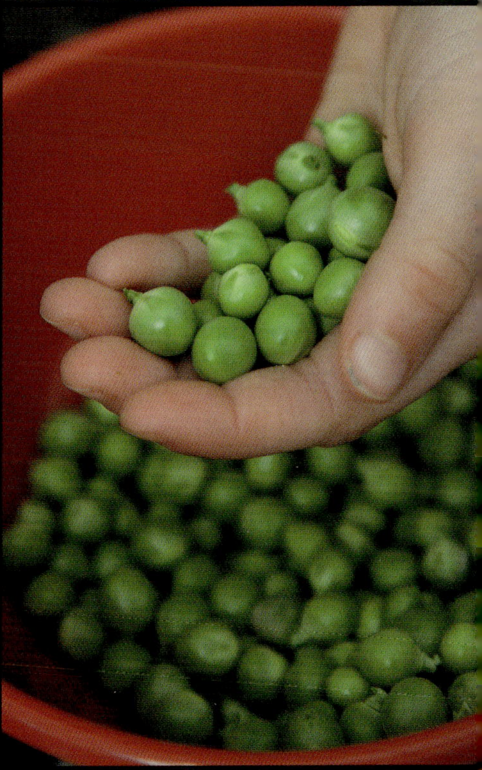
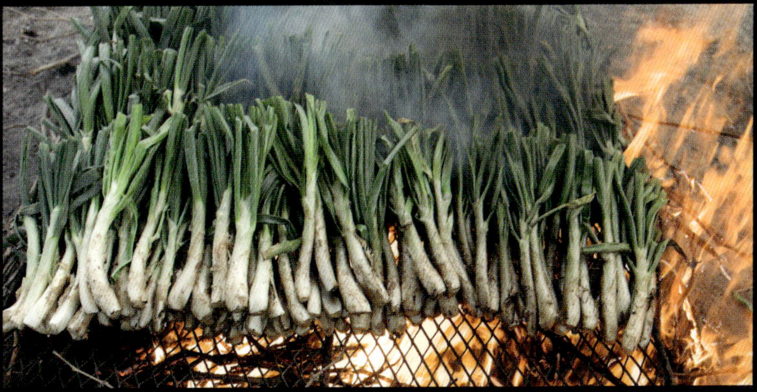
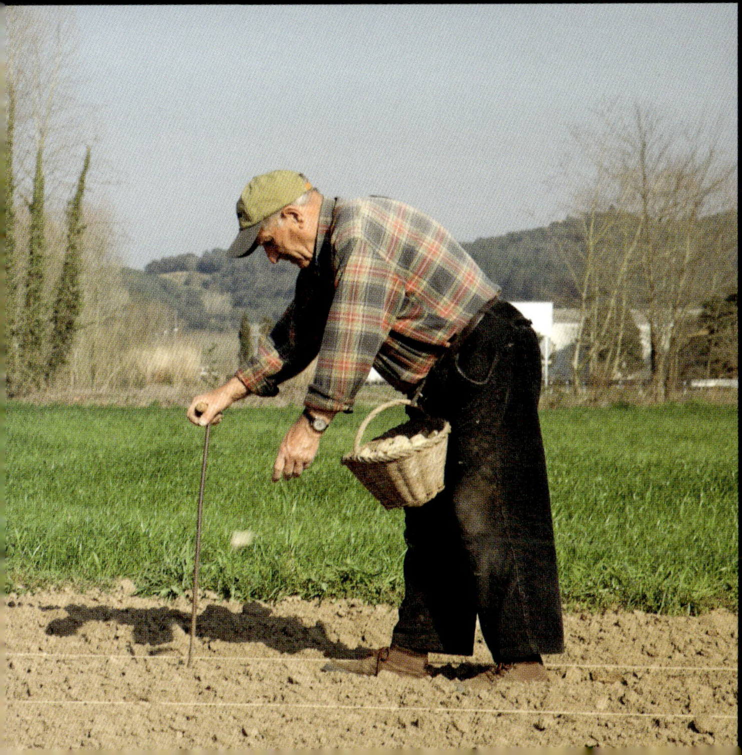
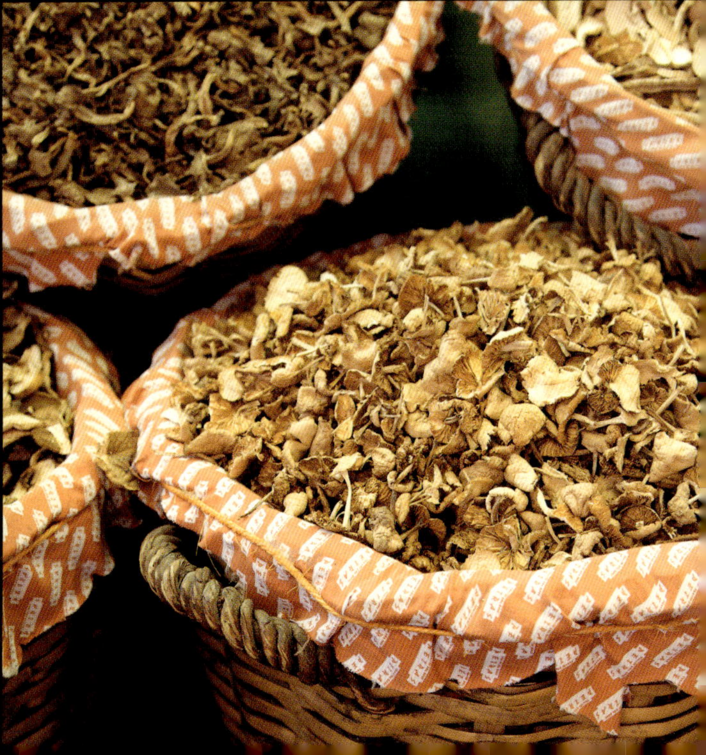

SAUTÉED WILD MUSHROOMS

SETAS SALTEADAS

SERVES 4

There are few better ways to appreciate the earthen, forest flavors of wild mushrooms than just quickly sautéing them in olive oil and seasoning with only salt and maybe some garlic and fresh parsley. But as with numerous traditional Spanish preparations, from artichokes to trout, adding some jamón, with its bold salty and savory flavors, pushes the dish up a notch. I've come across wonderful versions of this in La Rioja, in northern Navarra, and, most memorably, in the oak-covered hills of northern Andalucía around Aracena. The bar prepared it with some of the region's celebrated gurumelo mushrooms (firm and intensely aromatic, with muggy hints of the humid forest) and *jamón ibérico de bellota*—from acorn-fed Iberian black-footed pigs—from the nearby town of Jabugo. Celestial.

1½ POUNDS/680 G MIXED FRESH WILD OR CULTIVATED MUSHROOMS, IDEALLY 3 OR 4 DIFFERENT VARIETIES

4 TABLESPOONS EXTRA-VIRGIN OLIVE OIL, PLUS MORE FOR RE-OILING PAN

SALT AND FRESHLY GROUND BLACK PEPPER

4 GARLIC CLOVES, THINLY SLICED

½ CUP LOOSELY PACKED/60 G FINELY CHOPPED DRY-CURED SPANISH JAMÓN (SEE INGREDIENT NOTE, PAGE 16)

4 TEASPOONS MINCED FRESH FLAT-LEAF PARSLEY

1. Keeping the varieties separate, clean the mushrooms following the directions on page 339. Quarter or slice them depending on their shape.

2. In a large sauté pan or skillet, heat 3 tablespoons of the olive oil over high heat. Season the mushrooms with salt and pepper and cook each type of mushroom separately (to ensure even cooking), stirring frequently to help evaporate any moisture that they throw, until golden brown at the edges, 4 to 6 minutes, depending on the variety. Transfer the mushrooms to a serving bowl as they are cooked. Re-oil the pan between varieties as needed.

3. Meanwhile, in a small skillet, heat the remaining 1 tablespoon olive oil over medium heat, add the garlic, and cook until golden and fragrant, about 1 minute. Remove the pan from the heat and stir in the jamón.

4. Add the jamón mixture to the mushrooms and toss to blend well. Scatter the parsley over the mushrooms and serve immediately.

INGREDIENTS

PAPRIKA
pimentón

Christopher Columbus returned from one of his first journeys to the Americas with capsicum peppers, a significant and important New World export. Growing peppers for pimentón was first done in Extremadura, perhaps after they were presented by Columbus himself at the Monastery at Yuste to Hieronymite monks. The monks perfected the cultivation and drying of the peppers, and began using the ground pimentón in cooking.

Over the centuries, the ground spice spread around Spain, as seen in so many classic regional dishes: in empanada dough and vinegary *ajada* sauce fish (see page 169) in Galicia; potatoes in La Rioja (see page 118); with skate in Huelva; in numerous Andalusian marinades; chorizos from Navarra and La Rioja; soft, spreadable Mallorcan *sobrassada* sausage; cured pork loin in Extremadura; even rubbed into the rind of Mahón cheese in Menorca to give a characteristic reddish-gold color.

Long, red capsicum peppers—to be precise, of the Ocales group and the Bola variety—produce three flavors of pimentón: *dulce* (sweet), *agridulce* (bittersweet), and *picante* (spicy). Each has its own use in the kitchen, though sweet is by far the most common with the home cook.

The heart of the industry remains in Extremadura, above all in the valley of La Vera. Hand-harvested in October, the peppers are dehydrated and smoked slowly by oak-wood fires over ten or fifteen days, with workers turning the peppers by hand on the rack as needed. The peppers are then finely ground in traditional stone mills—slowly, avoiding excess heat from the friction, which might result in the spice becoming bitter—into a brilliant red brick–colored powder, silky in touch, and carrying strong smoky aromas and flavors. My favorite brand is La Dalia, but any with the *Denominación de Origen Pimentón de La Vera* seal is excellent.

The region of Murcia, too, has a long tradition of quality pimentón, and its industry has now overtaken Extremadura in size. While the first references to Murcian pepper production date from the sixteenth century (shared, no doubt, by friars at a brother-monastery), the industry grew dramatically during the middle of the 1800s. Pimentón here is dried in the sun or with hot air (but not smoked) before being ground.

While pimentón from Murcia does not have the smoky headiness of La Vera, the flavors give a rich, confident—but not dominating—boost to countless dishes. For many dishes, it is my preferred choice.

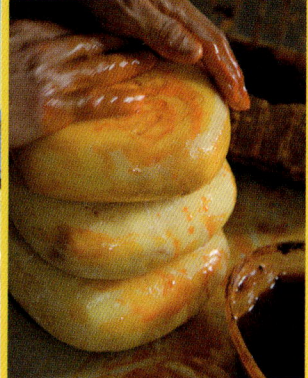

LA MANCHA–STYLE SAUTÉED ONIONS, ZUCCHINI, TOMATOES, AND PEPPERS

PISTO MANCHEGO

SERVES 4

From Spain's Castilian heartland of La Mancha—land of Don Quixote, ancient windmills along ridgelines, red-legged partridge in the fields, and its eponymous aged sheep's cheese—comes an unfussy stewed mélange of vegetables that grow abundantly in the region. It is typically served as a first course topped with a poached egg, though it also nicely accompanies grilled lamb or beef. You often find leftovers in homes served at room temperature or chilled with some wedges of Manchego cheese. Like many cooks, I prefer to use a can of good-quality peeled whole plum tomatoes for this, no matter the season. In Spain, I usually buy Cidacos brand (the label should read *tomate entero pelado*). Look for these or similar high-quality Italian San Marzano ones. The taste of the bell peppers should be prominent.

4 TABLESPOONS EXTRA-VIRGIN OLIVE OIL
TWO 14-OUNCE/400-G CANS WHOLE PEELED TOMATOES, ALL JUICES RESERVED
1 TEASPOON SUGAR
SALT
1 LARGE ONION, CHOPPED
1 RED BELL PEPPER, CHOPPED
1 GREEN BELL PEPPER, CHOPPED
2 MEDIUM ZUCCHINI, PEELED AND CHOPPED
½ TEASPOON SPANISH PIMENTÓN DULCE (SWEET PAPRIKA)

1. In a skillet or sauté pan, heat 1 tablespoon of the olive oil over medium heat. Add the tomatoes and all their juices and the sugar and season with salt. Cook, stirring frequently to break up the tomatoes, until the sauce has darkened and reduced, about 15 minutes.

2. Meanwhile, in a large skillet or sauté pan, heat the remaining 3 tablespoons olive oil over medium heat and add the onion. Cook until it begins to soften and turn pale, about 5 minutes. Add the bell peppers and cook until they, too, begin to soften, about 5 minutes. Finally, add the zucchini, stir to coat, and cook for 3 or 4 minutes to cut their rawness.

3. Add the tomatoes to the vegetables. Season with salt, add the pimentón, loosely cover the pot, and simmer over medium-low heat until the vegetables are very tender, about 20 minutes. The pisto should be very moist and loose, and needs a spoon to be eaten.

4. Divide the pisto among shallow bowls, and serve hot.

STUFFED TOMATOES

TOMATES RELLENOS

SERVES 4

Cooks around Spain love to stuff vegetables. Sometimes the filling is a vegetable mix (such as the stuffed eggplant on page 104), or puréed salt cod (such as the stuffed piquillo peppers on page 188). Usually, though, the filling has some meat. Ground beef is commonly blended with a bit of ground pork for flavor, but also to help keep it moist. The tomatoes should be tender, and just starting to crack. This recipe is from Natalia Reixach, an old friend from the foothills of the Pyrenees near Vic.

8 RIPE BUT FIRM LARGE TOMATOES
7 TABLESPOONS/105 ML EXTRA-VIRGIN OLIVE OIL
1 MEDIUM ONION, FINELY CHOPPED
12 OUNCES/340 G GROUND BEEF
4 OUNCES/115 G GROUND PORK
SALT AND FRESHLY GROUND BLACK PEPPER
1 TABLESPOON MINCED FRESH FLAT-LEAF PARSLEY
1 GARLIC CLOVE, MINCED
3 HEAPED TABLESPOONS PINE NUTS

1. Cut the caps out of the tomatoes as if carving a Halloween pumpkin; reserve. Using a medium spoon, hollow out the inside of the tomatoes, reserving everything in a bowl. Feel for the edge of the tomato shell from the inside with the spoon and scrape around it, leaving the shell intact. Shake any liquid or seeds into the bowl. Pick out the tender parts of the core and reserve. Strain the seeds, reserving the juice. In a food processor or blender, purée the reserved tender parts and the juice.

2. Preheat the oven to 400°F/200°C/gas mark 6.

3. In a large skillet or sauté pan, heat 3 tablespoons of the olive oil over medium heat and add the onion. Cook until soft and translucent, 8 to 10 minutes. Generously season the beef and pork with salt and pepper and add along with the parsley and garlic. Cook until the meat is just browned. Add in one-fourth of the tomato purée. Reduce the heat to medium-low and cook until the tomato begins to darken, about 5 minutes. Crush the pine nuts in a mortar or with the back of a spoon in a bowl and stir in. Remove from the heat.

4. Fill each tomato to the top with about ¼ cup/60 ml of the mixture. Replace the caps, fitting them on as well as possible. Arrange the tomatoes in a large baking dish or roasting pan. They can touch if they must, but only very lightly. Season the outsides with salt, and then pour the rest of the tomato purée over the stuffed tomatoes. Drizzle evenly with the remaining 4 tablespoons olive oil. Dribble about ¼ cup/60 ml water into the pan.

5. Bake uncovered for 40 to 45 minutes, or until the tomatoes are cooked through and just beginning to crack. Dribble more water into the pan if they threaten to scorch during cooking.

6. Place 2 tomatoes on each plate and spoon over some of the sauce. Serve hot.

BALEARIC-STYLE BAKED STUFFED EGGPLANT

BERENJENAS RELLENAS AL HORNO

SERVES 4

Stuffing vegetables in the Balearic Islands is a favorite way of utilizing the ample summer offerings of the *huerto* (garden)—zucchini, peppers, artichokes, and especially eggplant. Many in the islands call these by the descriptive name *barquetes d'aubergínia* (little boats of eggplant). Some stuff eggplant with ground meat, though as often as not, the stuffing is just a mixture of vegetables. These make a delightful first course.

4 SMALL TO MEDIUM GLOBE EGGPLANTS, ABOUT 10 OUNCES/280 G EACH
SALT
3 TABLESPOONS EXTRA-VIRGIN OLIVE OIL, PLUS MORE FOR DRIZZLING
1 MEDIUM ONION, FINELY CHOPPED
½ MEDIUM CARROT, FINELY GRATED
2 GARLIC CLOVES, MINCED
FRESHLY GROUND BLACK PEPPER
PINCH FRESHLY GRATED NUTMEG
⅓ CUP/50 G PLAIN DRY BREADCRUMBS

1. Trim the stems of the eggplants. Wash and cut the eggplants in half lengthwise. Place in a colander, generously sprinkle with salt, and let them sweat away some of their bitterness for 30 minutes. You will see dark beads appear on the surface. Gently rinse under cool running water. Place in a pot, cover with water, and bring to a boil. Reduce the heat to medium and simmer until tender but not mushy, 15 to 20 minutes. Remove with a slotted spoon and let drain and cool in a colander.

2. When the eggplants are cool enough to handle, carefully scoop out the insides, leaving the shells and shape intact; set the shells aside. Discard some of the seeds. Finely chop the eggplant pulp with a large knife.

3. In a large sauté pan or skillet, heat the olive oil over medium heat, add the onion, and cook until soft and translucent, 8 to 10 minutes. Add the carrot and cook until it softens, turning a yellowish orange color, and loses its rawness, about 5 minutes. Add the garlic and cook until fragrant, about 1 minute. Incorporate the eggplant pulp, mixing together and tapping down on it with the flat bottom of a wooden spoon, until pasty and very soft, about 10 minutes. Season with salt and pepper and the nutmeg. Remove from the heat and let cool slightly.

4. Spoon the filling into the eggplant shells. Arrange them on a baking sheet or in a baking dish. Spread a scant 1 tablespoon of breadcrumbs over each and drizzle with olive oil.

5. Preheat the broiler.

6. Broil until the tops of the eggplants are golden, about 10 minutes. Serve hot.

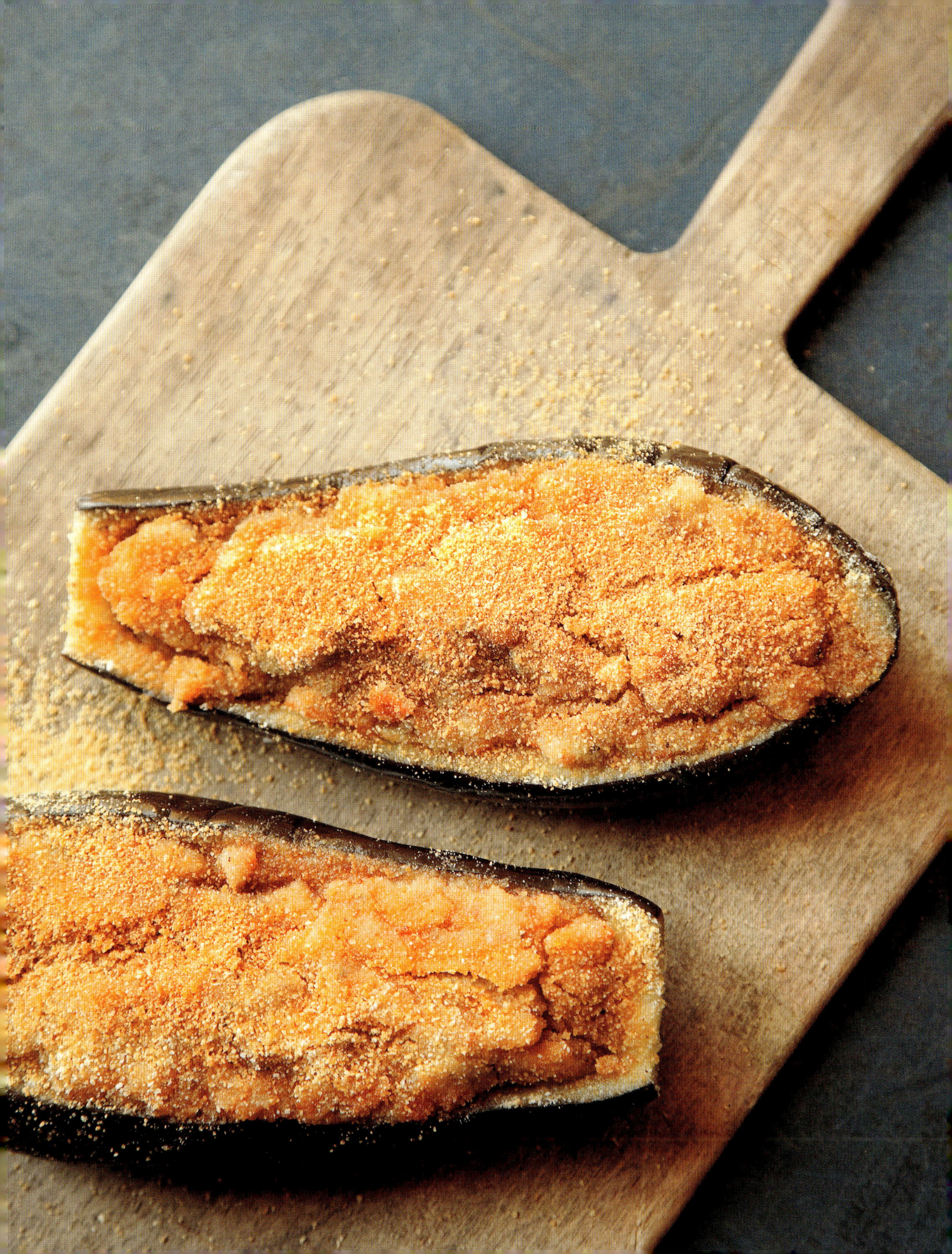

FRIED EGGPLANT STRIPS WITH SALMOREJO

BERENJENA FRITA CON SALMOREJO

SERVES 4

Winter evenings in the silvery, olive tree–blanketed hills of Andalucía can be cold, and this dish makes a rich and filling dinner—especially welcome after a day helping with the harvest. Combining lightly floured and deep-fried eggplant strips with silky, thick salmorejo remains for me an inspired combination.

5 CUPS/1.2 L CÓRDOBA-STYLE SALMOREJO (PAGE 62)

1 LEMON

3 MEDIUM GLOBE EGGPLANTS, ABOUT 10 OUNCES/280 G EACH

SALT

4 TO 6 CUPS/1 TO 1.4 L MILD OLIVE OIL OR SUNFLOWER OIL FOR FRYING

ALL-PURPOSE FLOUR FOR DREDGING

1. Cover and refrigerate the salmorejo to lightly chill until ready to serve.

2. Fill a large bowl with cold water. Halve the lemon, squeeze the juice into the water, and then drop in the halves.

3. Working one by one, stem and peel the eggplants. Cut into lengthy strips like French fries. Drop them into the water to keep them from discoloring. Soak for 10 to 15 minutes. Drain, and place on absorbent towels to dry. Place in a colander and liberally salt. Let the eggplants sweat away some of their bitterness for 1 hour. You will see dark beads appear on the surface. Rinse well under running water and pat dry with paper towels. Gently squeeze some moisture from the eggplants and pat dry again.

4. Preheat the oven to 200°F/95°C.

5. In a deep skillet, heat the olive oil to 375°F/190°C. (The oil is the right temperature when a large cube of fresh bread dropped into it browns in about 60 seconds.)

6. Lightly flour the eggplant strips. Shake off any excess flour in a sieve.

7. Working in batches that don't crowd the pan or bring the temperature of the oil below 350°F/180°C, gently lower the eggplant strips into the oil with tongs and fry until they are golden and slightly crunchy on the outside, 2 to 3 minutes.

8. Remove with a slotted spoon or tongs, and place on paper towels to briefly drain. Transfer to a baking sheet and place in the oven to keep warm until all of the eggplant has been fried.

9. Once the oil has returned to 375°F/190°C, fry the next batch of eggplant.

10. Once all of the eggplant has been fried, divide it among plates. Ladle the salmorejo into bowls. Serve immediately, spooning the salmorejo over top, if desired.

GREEN ASPARAGUS IN VINEGAR MARINADE

ESPÁRRAGOS VERDES EN VINAGRETA

SERVES 4

While small game birds—especially red-legged partridge and quail (see page 330)—and sardines (see page 332) are lovely preserved in an herby, garlic-filled marinade, so are asparagus. But these slender green vegetables quickly absorb the marinade's flavors and are meant to be eaten within hours as opposed to days. I first encountered this around Priego de Córdoba, and quickly adapted it into the pantheon of favorite vinegary dishes in my kitchen.

20 TO 24 MEDIUM-SIZE STALKS FRESH GREEN ASPARAGUS
SALT
1 CUP/240 ML EXTRA-VIRGIN OLIVE OIL, PLUS MORE AS NEEDED
½ CUP/120 ML WHITE WINE VINEGAR
2 GARLIC CLOVES, LIGHTLY CRUSHED IN THE PEEL
1 BAY LEAF
PEEL OF ½ ORGANIC LEMON, WHITE PITH SCRAPED AWAY
12 BLACK PEPPERCORNS
½ TEASPOON SPANISH PIMENTÓN DULCE (SWEET PAPRIKA)
FLAKY SEA SALT
FRESHLY GROUND BLACK PEPPER

1. Snap off the hard bottom part of each asparagus stalk at the natural break point and discard.

2. Fill a large bowl with ice water. In a large pot, bring an abundant amount of water to a rolling boil, add a generous 2 pinches of salt, and blanch the asparagus by boiling them for 2 minutes and then immediately transferring with a slotted spoon to the ice water to stop any further cooking. Once cooled, remove with the slotted spoon and drain. Spread out on paper towels to dry.

3. In a saucepan, add the olive oil, vinegar, garlic, bay leaf, lemon peel, and peppercorns and bring to a boil. Gently boil uncovered for 5 minutes. Remove the pan from the heat and let the mixture cool slightly before stirring in the pimentón (so that it doesn't scorch and become bitter).

4. In a rectangular earthenware, ceramic, or glass dish, arrange the asparagus stalks snugly side by side.

5. Swirl the marinade in the pan to blend and then pour the oil and herbs over the asparagus. The stalks should be covered. If not, add more oil as needed.

6. Let cool completely. Cover with plastic wrap and refrigerate until chilled. Serve chilled with a spoonful of the marinade over top, a pinch of salt flakes, and a fresh grinding of pepper.

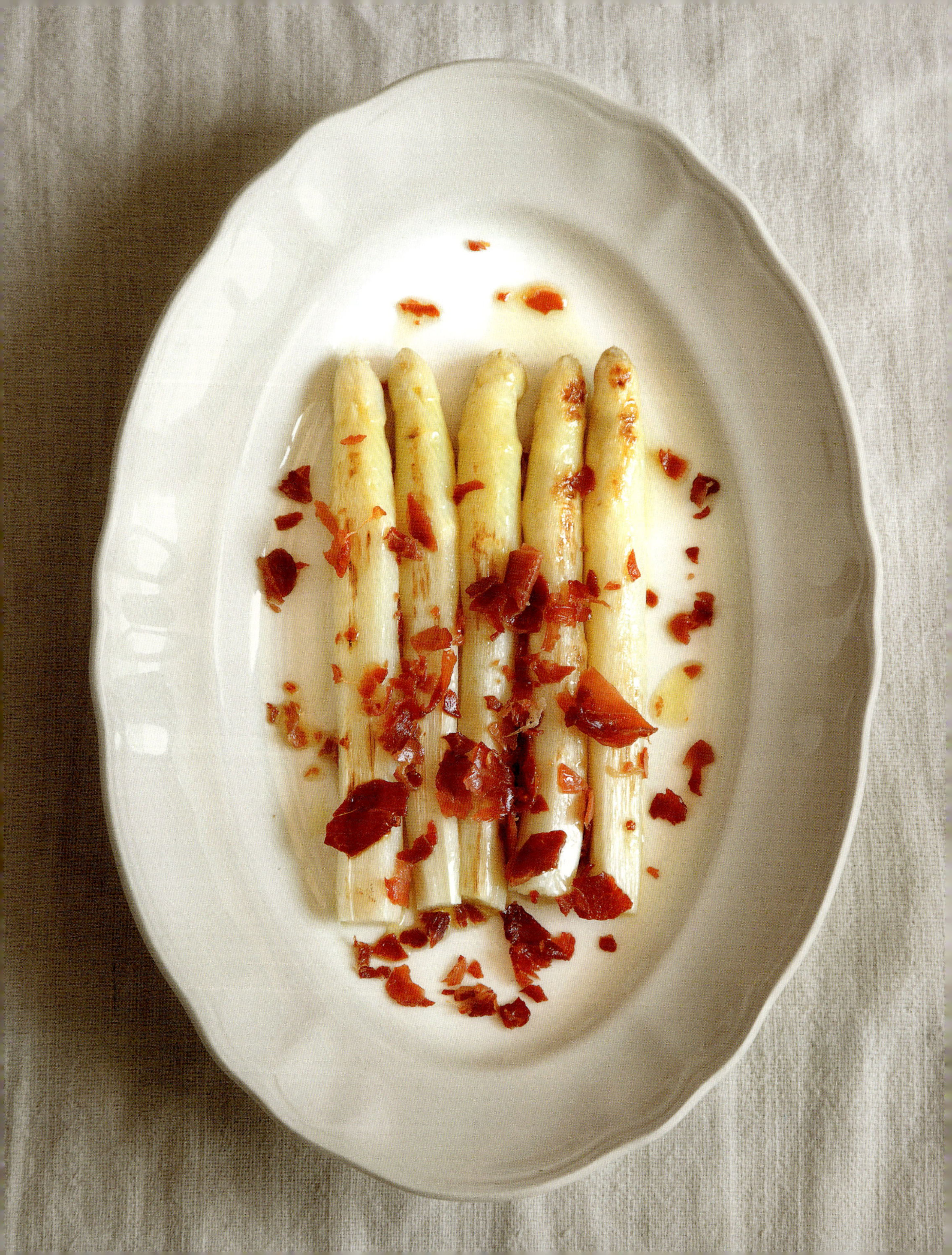

To stop ripening asparagus from turning green, they are kept from the sunlight. A mound of mulch is added gradually as they grow, and the tall, thick stalks are finally harvested in the dark. White asparagus are denser and have a higher sugar content than their green cousins, but also have a thicker, bitter outer skin that needs to be peeled away. May and early June is the time for these in Navarra and around La Rioja. As most of the harvest is preserved in tins to enjoy all year, this short season is the moment to take advantage of eating this distinctive vegetable fresh.

Traveling around La Rioja recently in late spring, I did just that and had them for lunch *and* dinner for more than a week. This recipe is inspired by my favorite version on that trip, Francis Paniego's, which is much more sophisticated than this. His more modern establishment is next door to his mother's classic, fourth-generation Echaurren restaurant in the mountain town of Ezcaray. While Francis's offerings tend to be more contemporary and free-flowing in their creativeness than his mother's, both celebrate the region's seasonal bounty.

FRESH WHITE ASPARAGUS WITH CRISPY SHARDS OF DRY-CURED JAMÓN

ESPÁRRAGOS BLANCOS FRESCOS CON VIRUTAS DE JAMÓN

SERVES 4

12 STALKS FRESH WHITE ASPARAGUS
SALT
2 TABLESPOONS EXTRA-VIRGIN OLIVE OIL, PLUS MORE FOR DRIZZLING
4 SLICES DRY-CURED SPANISH JAMÓN (SEE INGREDIENT NOTE, PAGE 16)
FLAKY SEA SALT

1. Snap off the hard bottom part of each asparagus stalk at the natural break point and discard. Using a vegetable peeler, peel the fibrous outer skin from each stalk from the tip down.

2. Fill a large bowl with ice water. In a large pot, bring an abundant amount of water to a rolling boil, add a generous 2 pinches of salt, and blanch the asparagus by boiling them for 4 to 5 minutes and then immediately transferring with a slotted spoon to the ice water to stop any further cooking. Once cooled, remove with the slotted spoon and drain. Spread out on paper towels to dry.

3. In a sauté pan or skillet, heat 1 tablespoon of the olive oil over medium-high heat and add the jamón. Cook, turning as needed, until golden, 3 to 5 minutes. Transfer the jamón to absorbent paper towels and dab off the excess oil. Chop it into shards.

4. Preheat a grill pan, griddle pan, or large, heavy skillet over high heat, and brush with the remaining 1 tablespoon olive oil. Lay on the asparagus and grill until golden and just tender, about 5 minutes, turning as needed.

5. Place the asparagus stalks parallel on a plate and drizzle liberally with oil. Dust with the reserved jamón shards and some salt flakes before serving.

SPINACH WITH PINE NUTS AND RAISINS

ESPINACAS CON PIÑONES Y PASAS

SERVES 4

Spinach was being grown in Sevilla by the eleventh century, brought, like many new products during those centuries, by Arab traders. It adapted well to the land and into the cuisine, and frequently partners now with a host of various other ingredients in the pan—both savory and sweet. One of the latter is raisins, which in Catalunya you find paired with pine nuts, while in Granada, cooks tend to toss in roughly chopped toasted almonds instead. This recipe is quick to prepare, especially using fresh baby spinach leaves. If using whole spinach leaves, closely trim the stems and thoroughly wash with plenty of fresh running water.

¼ CUP/35 G SEEDLESS RAISINS
12 OUNCES/340 G TRIMMED FRESH BABY SPINACH LEAVES
1 TABLESPOON EXTRA-VIRGIN OLIVE OIL
¼ CUP/35 G PINE NUTS
SALT AND FRESHLY GROUND BLACK PEPPER

1. In a small bowl, cover the raisins with warm water and soak for 10 minutes; drain. Spread out on paper towels to dry (to avoid splattering when cooking).

2. Meanwhile, wash the spinach in a couple of changes of water and drain. Put in a large pot, cover with a lid, and wilt over medium heat, about 5 minutes. Transfer to a colander to drain off excess liquid.

3. In a small sauté pan, heat the olive oil over medium heat. Add the raisins and pine nuts and cook, stirring frequently, until the pine nuts are golden and the raisins plump, about 2 minutes.

4. Put the spinach in a serving bowl and season with salt and pepper. Spoon in about half of the raisins and pine nut mixture with the oil from the pan and toss. Spoon the remaining mixture over top. Serve immediately.

INGREDIENTS

PINE NUTS
piñones

Growing up, my wife and her three older sisters spent a lot of time at their grandfather's summer house in the densely pine-forested hills outside Barcelona. By the time I moved to Spain in the mid-1990s, her grandfather was ailing, the house largely deserted, and the ample grounds unruly with unpruned and unharvested fruit trees—fig, persimmon, plum. Fallen fruit covered the grounds. And so did pine cones—and it was these that we collected.

We would sit for hours on the stone steps gently crushing the hard husks of pine nuts, extracting the oblong ivory seeds. Just as when she was a child, we followed her family's basic rule: Cracked seeds went into the mouth, perfect ones into a jar for later use in the kitchen. The creamy, toothy flesh has a piney, resinous flavor that hints of the wooded landscapes.

The house had a simple, two-burner stove with an aged orange gas canister, a couple of large and well-seasoned terra-cotta *cazuelas* (casseroles), and a grill outside that we used when the weather was pleasant. With vases of wild roses cut from the balcony balustrades and, from a dusty drinks cabinet, forgotten bottles of wine (always festive when one had turned), we ate late, pine nut–studded dinners by candlelight—spinach with pine nuts and raisins (see facing page); rice with rabbit and mushrooms, the sauce thickened by a picada of pine nuts and garlic; or grilled rabbit (see page 221) with dried fruits and pine nuts. After dinner, we'd drag chairs in front of the drafty fireplace to enjoy dessert: fresh cheese scattered with toasted pine nuts and honey (see page 301), and washed down with somewhat sticky dessert wine shot into the mouth in a streaming arc from a thin spouted *porrón*.

Along the Spanish Mediterranean, piñones have long played an integral culinary role, and are key to countless traditional dishes, from the type we prepared at the summer house to more complex ones made at home—roast duck stuffed with prunes and pine nuts; chicken or pork with orange sauce and pine nuts (see page 248); squid stuffed with pork and pine nuts; and marzipan cookies rolled in pine nuts (see page 291).

The house was sold not long after my wife's grandfather died, and we began to collect our piñones at the beach place of my in-laws south of Barcelona. Our daughters carry on this tradition and now sit patiently cracking the husks at a table in the breezy afternoon shade. The trick is to get them to follow that age-old rule of saving the whole ones for the kitchen. More often than not, it seems, these end up in their mouths, too.

TENDER SPINACH LEAVES WITH SPANISH-STYLE POACHED EGGS

SALTEADO DE ESPINACAS TIERNAS CON HUEVOS ESCALFADOS

SERVES 4

Spinach and eggs are an ideal combination, and I have encountered them served together from the Duero River in the north of Castilla y León to Jaén in Andalucía. I especially like the Andalusian touch of dashing the spinach with sherry vinegar after it has cooked—but just a dash. The flavors are quite mellow and the vinegar can easily dominate the dish.

1½ POUNDS/680 G TRIMMED FRESH BABY SPINACH LEAVES
SALT
3 TABLESPOONS EXTRA-VIRGIN OLIVE OIL
3 GARLIC CLOVES, PEELED
1 SMALL SLICE COUNTRY-STYLE BREAD, CRUSTS REMOVED
1 TEASPOON SPANISH PIMENTÓN DULCE (SWEET PAPRIKA)
SHERRY VINEGAR OR WINE VINEGAR (OPTIONAL)
4 EGGS

1. Wash the spinach in a couple of changes of water. Drain.

2. Bring a large pot of water to a boil, add a generous 2 pinches of salt, add the spinach, and boil until it begins to wilt but is still vivid green, about 3 minutes. Scoop out about ½ cup/120 ml of the liquid and reserve. Dump the spinach into a colander to drain.

3. In a large skillet or sauté pan, heat the olive oil over medium heat. Add the garlic and bread and cook until golden, 1 to 2 minutes. Remove and reserve. Remove the pan from the heat.

4. Prepare a picada with the garlic, bread, and the pimentón with 2 or 3 tablespoons of the reserved liquid from cooking the spinach, following the directions on page 39.

5. Transfer the spinach leaves to the pan, add about ¼ cup/60 ml of the reserved liquid, and stir in the picada. Add a dash of vinegar, if desired. Turn the leaves to coat and cook over medium-low heat for 2 minutes, until the flavors are combined. Divide the spinach among wide, shallow bowls, smoothing the spinach into a bed.

6. Bring a wide saucepan of water to a low boil and poach the eggs until the whites are set and the yolks firm on the edges but still very runny.

7. Using a slotted spoon, place 1 egg on each bowl of spinach. Serve immediately.

ROASTED ARTICHOKES

ALCACHOFAS AL HORNO

SERVES 4

Roasted artichokes are a classic garnish for meat on the grill. Usually just moistened with olive oil and seasoned with salt, the flavors of the artichokes are natural and delicious but do not distract from the main course they accompany. But hollowed slightly and filled with a bit of chopped dry-cured jamón, they become a delightful first course or tapa. To serve as a tapa, calculate one stuffed artichoke per person as part of a spread of various dishes.

1 LEMON, HALVED

8 MEDIUM ARTICHOKES

½ CUP LOOSELY PACKED/60 G FINELY CHOPPED DRY-CURED SPANISH JAMÓN (SEE INGREDIENT NOTE, PAGE 16)

SALT

2 TABLESPOONS EXTRA-VIRGIN OLIVE OIL

1. Preheat the oven to 350°F/180°C/gas mark 4.

2. Fill a large bowl with cool water. Cut the lemon into wedges, squeeze into the water, and then drop them into the bowl.

3. Working with one artichoke at a time, rinse under cold running water. Cut or pull away the toughest outer petals and then trim off the top section so that the center is revealed. Loosen the leaves by firmly rolling the artichoke under the palm of your hand until you hear a slight crunch. Immediately drop it into the lemon water to keep from discoloring. Repeat with the remaining artichokes. When ready to use, rinse, and turn the artichokes upside down on absorbent towels to drain.

4. Using a finger, make a space in the center of each artichoke. Fill the center of each with 1 tablespoon of jamón. Set the artichokes upright in a baking dish or roasting pan.

5. Sprinkle the artichokes with salt and drizzle the olive oil over the top. Pour about 1 cup/240 ml water around the bases of the artichokes. Cover with a tent of aluminum foil and bake for about 45 minutes, or until tender. Serve warm.

ROASTED BEETS IN VINEGAR

REMOLACHAS ASADAS EN VINAGRE

SERVES 4 TO 6

This lovely, vibrant dish, with its sweet tones and vinegary tang, comes from Alicante, a region south of Valencia with abundant fields of beets. Beet season is at its best during summer through fall, a time when beets are especially nice as a salad, tapa, or alongside a simple roasted chicken.

The beets can be boiled (about 45 minutes), but I prefer roasting them, which draws out a deeper, more nuanced sweetness. Note that roasting time varies from 30 minutes to 1 hour, depending on the beets. Begin checking for doneness after half an hour.

3 FRESH MEDIUM BEETS, BETWEEN 5 AND 7 OUNCES/140 TO 200 G EACH
¼ CUP/60 ML RED OR WHITE WINE VINEGAR
SALT AND FRESHLY GROUND BLACK PEPPER
3 TABLESPOONS EXTRA-VIRGIN OLIVE OIL
2 TABLESPOONS MINCED FRESH FLAT-LEAF PARSLEY

1. Preheat the oven to 400°F/200°C/gas mark 6.

2. Wash but do not peel the beets. Leave the root ends and at least 1 inch/2.5 cm of stems on them.

3. In a baking dish or deep, ovenproof pan, arrange the beets and pour 1½ cups/360 ml water around them. Cover with aluminum foil. Roast until tender, about 45 minutes. A knife tip poked into the center should enter with little resistance. Remove from the oven and let cool.

4. Trim the ends and slip off the skins. Halve the beets lengthwise and then cut them crosswise into slices slightly less than ¼ inch/½ cm thick. Place them in a wide bowl, cover with the vinegar, and season with salt and pepper. Let marinate for 1 hour.

5. Transfer the beets to a colander to drain for 10 minutes. (Do not rinse.) Arrange them on a platter or in a wide salad bowl. Drizzle with the olive oil, scatter over the parsley, and toss before serving.

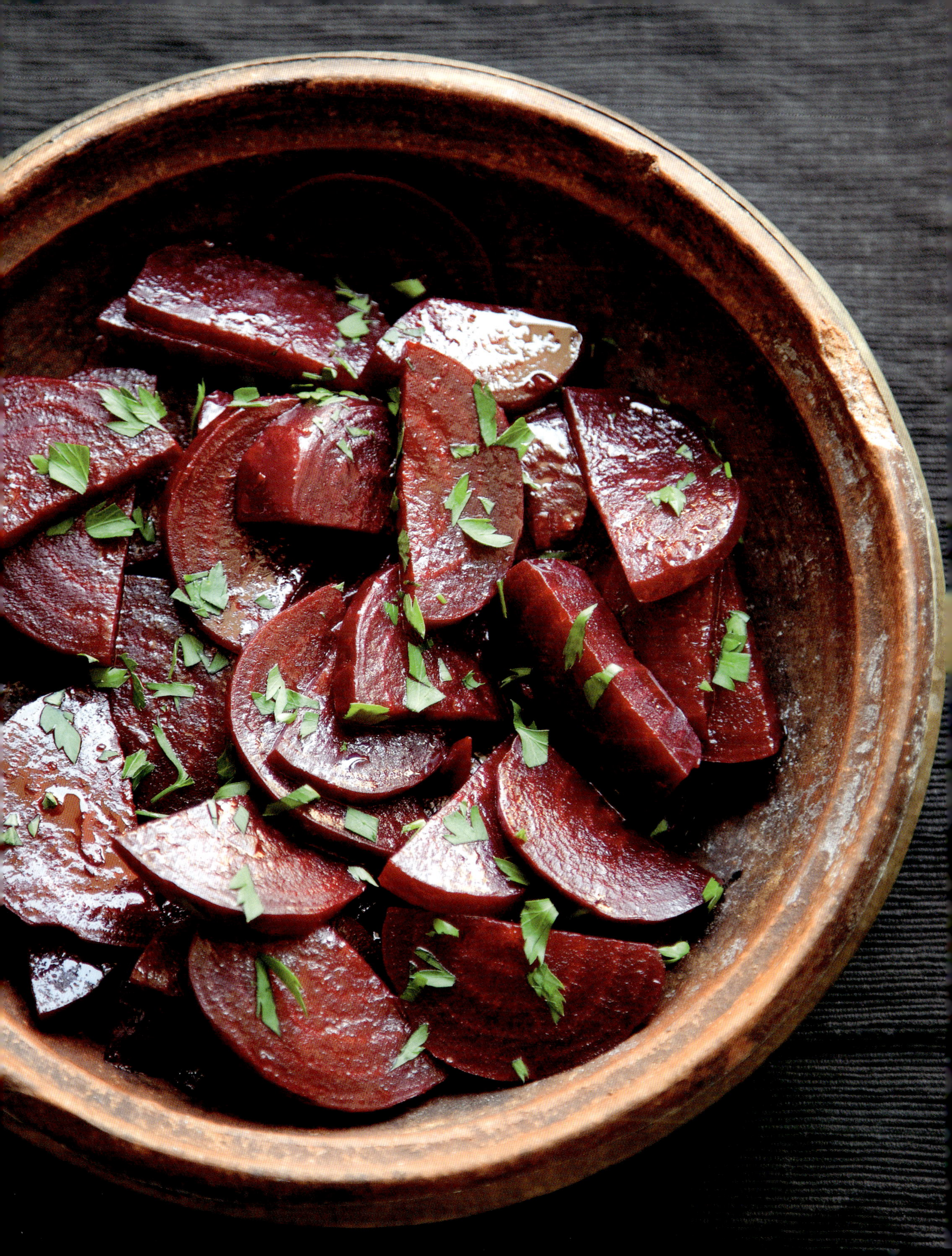

BAKER'S OVEN-ROASTED POTATOES

PATATAS PANADERAS AL HORNO

SERVES 6 TO 8 AS A SIDE DISH

This classic *guarnición* (side dish) is simple but devilishly tasty. Serve it with meat, poultry, or fish dishes, grilled quail, or game. The name comes from bakers who would put a big tray of these in their bread oven to cook.

3½ POUNDS/1.6 KG MEDIUM WHITE POTATOES, PEELED AND THINLY SLICED CROSSWISE
2 MEDIUM ONIONS, THINLY SLICED
SALT
½ CUP/120 ML EXTRA-VIRGIN OLIVE OIL

1. Preheat the oven to 400°F/200°C/gas mark 6.

2. In a large bowl, blend the potatoes and onions, season with salt, and add the olive oil. Toss to blend well. Transfer to a large ovenproof baking dish or roasting pan and cover with aluminum foil.

3. Bake until the potatoes are tender, about 45 minutes. Remove the foil and continue to bake until golden at the edges, about 10 minutes.

4. Remove from the oven. Until ready to serve, loosely cover with foil tented in the middle. This will keep them warm without steaming them.

GALICIAN BOILED POTATOES WITH PAPRIKA

CACHELOS

SERVES 4 TO 6

These Galician potatoes, boiled in the peel (*en la monda*, they call it in Galicia), are served with grilled fish and meats and, most famously, with boiled octopus (see page 91)—or, to be more precise, *under* the octopus in order to absorb the cephalopod's flavorful juices. These potatoes are especially nice in spring and summer, when the potato peel is fine and papery.

3 POUNDS/1.4 KG MEDIUM WHITE POTATOES
SALT
1 BAY LEAF
EXTRA-VIRGIN OLIVE OIL FOR DRIZZLING
SPANISH PIMENTÓN DULCE (SWEET PAPRIKA) FOR DUSTING
FLAKY SEA SALT

1. Scrub the potatoes but do not peel. Place them in a pot, cover with water, and bring to a boil over high heat. Add a generous pinch of salt and the bay leaf, reduce the heat to medium-low, partly cover the pot, and gently boil until tender and the tip of a knife penetrates with little resistance, 20 to 25 minutes. Drain.

2. Quarter the potatoes and slip off the peels with your fingers, if desired. Arrange them on a wide platter, generously drizzle with olive oil, and lightly dust with paprika and salt flakes before serving.

PURÉED POTATOES WITH EXTRA-VIRGIN OLIVE OIL

PURÉ DE PATATAS

SERVES 4 AS A SIDE DISH

Spanish mashed potatoes—or rather, translated more precisely, puréed potatoes—tend to be less fluffy than their American counterparts, but rather denser and creamier. They usually include a touch of milk and butter. But, this being Spain, mashed potatoes usually have some extra-virgin olive oil whipped in at the end. *Puré de patatas* is a classic guarnición to accompany grilled meats (especially good with marinated venison, see page 226), poultry and game birds, and fresh sausages.

A food mill (or else a potato ricer, so-called because of the form that the potatoes come out of the numerous tiny holes) is the typical way to make them. But they can be mashed by hand as well. Directions for both follow.

3 POUNDS/1.4 KG MEDIUM WHITE POTATOES
SALT
3 TABLESPOONS BUTTER, CUT INTO PIECES
⅓ CUP/75 ML WHOLE MILK, WARMED
FRESHLY GROUND WHITE PEPPER
3 TABLESPOONS EXTRA-VIRGIN OLIVE OIL

1. Peel the potatoes and cut into generous but equal-size pieces to ensure even cooking. Rinse with running water. Place in a pot, cover with plenty of cool water, add 1 teaspoon salt, and bring to a boil over high heat. Reduce the heat to low and gently boil until they are tender and a knife tip penetrates with little resistance, about 20 minutes. Transfer to a colander to thoroughly drain.

2. *Using a food mill:* Pass the potatoes through the food mill or potato ricer. Return to the (dry) pot and steam for 1 minute over medium-low heat while stirring continually. Begin folding in the butter and then milk with a wooden spoon. Season with salt and a pinch of white pepper.

Mashing by hand: Return the drained potatoes to the (dry) pot and steam for 1 minute over medium-low heat while stirring continually. Begin working in the butter and milk while mashing. Season with salt and a pinch of white pepper.

3. Whisk in the olive oil just before serving.

LA RIOJA-STYLE STEWED POTATOES WITH CHORIZO

PATATAS A LA RIOJANA

SERVES 4

Dishes a la riojana—*from La Rioja or La Rioja style—generally mean that they have chorizo and red bell peppers. The most famous riojana preparation is surely this one, with potatoes. A longtime friend (and dominoes partner) of my father-in-law from Logroño, La Rioja, Nicolas Morales, taught me his recipe. Nicolas was also the one who first taught me to "snap" the potatoes into irregular pieces—not cut them—before adding. This makes the potatoes sweat out more of their natural starches, which in turn thickens the sauce.* Chasquear *(or* chascar*)—it can mean "snap," "click," or "crack"—is the name for this technique widely used in many stewed dishes that include potatoes.*

¼ CUP/60 ML OLIVE OIL

1 MEDIUM ONION, FINELY CHOPPED

½ CUP/65 G FINELY CHOPPED GREEN BELL PEPPER

½ CUP/65 G FINELY CHOPPED RED BELL PEPPER

1 RIPE MEDIUM TOMATO, HALVED, SEEDED, AND GRATED (SEE PAGE 339)

6 OUNCES/170 G SPANISH CHORIZO, PREFERABLY FROM LA RIOJA OR NAVARRA, CUT INTO ⅓-INCH-/1-CM-THICK ROUNDS

1 TEASPOON SPANISH PIMENTÓN DULCE (SWEET PAPRIKA)

SALT

½ CUP/120 ML DRY WHITE WINE OR DRY SHERRY

3 POUNDS/1.4 KG MEDIUM WHITE POTATOES, PEELED

1 BAY LEAF

2 SMALL GARLIC CLOVES

1 TABLESPOON MINCED FRESH FLAT-LEAF PARSLEY

1. In a cazuela, Dutch oven, large sauté pan, or deep skillet, heat the olive oil over medium heat. Add the onion and cook until it begins to soften and turn pale, about 5 minutes. Add the bell peppers and cook for 5 minutes, stirring frequently. Add the tomato, chorizo, and paprika; season with salt; and pour in the wine. Stir and cook for 2 minutes to let the alcohol burn off.

2. Working over the pan and adding them directly to the stew, break the potatoes into generous bite-size pieces by making a small cut with a paring knife, twisting the blade, and snapping off a piece. (You will hear the noise.) Add the bay leaf, cover with 2 cups/480 ml water, and bring to a boil.

3. Prepare a picada with the garlic and parsley and a spoonful of the simmering liquid, following the directions on page 39; stir into the pan.

4. When the liquid reaches a boil, reduce the heat to low, and cook uncovered until the potatoes are very tender—the tines of a fork should easily pierce them—and the edges are beginning to crumble, about 45 minutes, although it depends on the type of potato. At the end, the sauce should be quite loose; add in bit of water during cooking if needed. Taste for seasoning and adjust as needed before serving.

SMASHED POTATOES AND CABBAGE TOPPED WITH STREAKY SALT PORK

TRINXAT DE LA CERDANYA AMB ROSTA

SERVES 4

This is the best known dish of La Cerdanya, the northern area of Catalunya that borders the mountainous French Cerdagne region. It has long been considered *un plato popular*. While in the early nineteenth century, when game and marmalades may have been found only on the tables of the upper classes, *trinxat* was enjoyed by every level of society. The name of the dish comes from the Catalan verb *trinxar*, which means to cut into small pieces. Here, it isn't exactly cut up, or even mashed, but rather smashed.

It is a winter dish that uses winter ingredients, with cabbage at its heart. Cabbage is tastiest when it has been, as they say in La Cerdanya, *tocades pel fred* (touched by the cold).

1 HEAD GREEN CABBAGE, ABOUT 1¾ POUNDS/800 G, HALVED AND RINSED
SALT
2 POUNDS/910 G MEDIUM WHITE POTATOES, PEELED AND CUT INTO 4 OR 5 PIECES
5 TABLESPOONS EXTRA-VIRGIN OLIVE OIL
4 GARLIC CLOVES, PEELED
8 OUNCES/225 G THICK-CUT STREAKY SALT PORK, BACON, OR PANCETTA

1. Bring a large pot of water to a boil. Add the cabbage and a generous pinch of salt and boil for 15 minutes. Add the potatoes and continue to boil until the potatoes are tender and the tip of a knife can easily penetrate, 15 to 20 minutes. Transfer to a colander and drain well.

2. Meanwhile, in a skillet or small sauté pan, heat 2 tablespoons of the olive oil. Add the garlic and cook until golden and fragrant, about 1 minute; remove and discard the garlic. Add the salt pork to the skillet and fry until golden and crunchy, 6 to 8 minutes; remove and drain on absorbent paper towels. Reserve the oil.

3. Chop two pieces of the fried salt pork; set the others aside until serving.

4. In a large sauté pan or skillet, heat the remaining 3 tablespoons olive oil. Add the vegetables and chopped salt pork and cook while tapping down on the ingredients with two flat-bottomed wooden spoons until mashy and pasty, about 5 minutes. Spoon off about 2 tablespoons of the reserved oil and stir it into the mash. Taste for seasoning and adjust as needed.

5. Serve with the remaining salt pork laid across the top.

VEGETABLES

TRADITIONS

CALÇOTADA

Calçots are a variety of long, thick green onions that look like slightly skinny leeks. They ripen in winter and have their peak season in January, February, and March. The center of production is in Tarragona, namely around the town of Valls. Like many in the northeast of the country, when calçots are at their peak, we head to Tarragona for a *calçotada*, a celebration of them grilled among friends.

For most, that means going to one of the rustic country restaurants in the area (my favorite is Masia Bou, which began grilling them for paying customers back in 1929; before that, they did it only for family and friends). For lucky others, though, it means heading to the farmhouse of friends. For many years, that is what we did on a Sunday in early February. We headed down to an old family hazelnut farm outside Falset with another forty or so others to devour the calçots planted on their land.

The routine was always the same. Calçots were arranged side by side on a wide metal screen, and once branches from hazelnut, almond, or olive trees were flaming, the screen was laid on top. The calçots were grilled until blackened on the outside, wrapped in newspapers, and kept warm in upturned terra-cotta roof tiles while the remaining ones were grilled. Once all of the calçots had been done, and the embers burned down, lamb chops, quartered rabbits, and fat, fresh pork sausages were laid across the screen to cook.

Meanwhile, in the courtyard of the house, makeshift tables were set up from sheets of plywood and benches from planks supported by upside-down plastic buckets. There were earthen bowls of olives, roasted vegetables in garlic-infused olive oil (escalivada, page 72), and bottles of hearty wine from a local cooperative in Priorat.

Calçots are eaten in a particular way. The blackened outside layer is peeled off with the fingers, exposing brilliant white flesh. Dragged through a flat bowl of salsa romesco (see page 170)—a sauce made from dried, sweetly mild red peppers, tomatoes, almonds and hazelnuts, garlic, and olive oil—the calçot is held above the head and lowered down into the mouth to eat the soft, sauce-slathered end. Eating calçots tends to be messy business, and long bibs are generally worn by all but the very confident. With groups like this, that meant no one had on a bib. If you weren't confident, then you wore old clothes. Bibs are considered the province of restaurants.

Twenty calçots per person is about the norm, but some of our friends devoured many times that. The brother of one friend was once the village champion. I read in the newspaper a few years ago that the winner of a contest in Falset had eaten 237 of them in a single sitting.

Once the spent remains of the calçots were cleared away, and char-blackened hands washed, we uncorked more wine and then set upon the platters of grilled meat that we dabbed with pungent *allioli* (see page 337). For dessert there were bowls of fruit—golden-speckled green apples, elongated *conferencia* pears, and, if we were lucky, some early strawberries—and usually a spongy *bizcocho* cake (see page 279) that someone had brought.

At that point, someone went into the kitchen to prepare coffee while a thin-spouted beaker of golden dessert wine went around the group. We lingered at the table, as jokes, stories, and compliments on the food flowed—and questions on the romesco recipe remained unanswered. (If the recipe is given on such an occasion, don't believe it: something will surely be "confused" or "forgotten.") People finally got up, sprawled under the long shadows of the old hazelnut trees, talked in low voices, or maybe read from the sports section of the Sunday newspaper about the previous evening's *fútbol* matches, and later, pulling on sweaters as it began to cool, strolled through the orchard, crunching twigs and spent hazelnut shells underfoot until it was time to drive back to Barcelona.

Not long ago, our friends uprooted the hazelnut trees and the patch set aside for calçots and planted grape vines, and the calçotada tradition came to an unfortunate halt. I am happy for them—their wine has been quickly successful, and, with bottles of it frequently gracing our table, their farm remains a year-round presence in our house.

But come February the urge for calçots returns, and we head south for a calçotada. But now, like most, we eat them in a country restaurant with long white bibs firmly tied around our necks.

CHAPTER 5

EGGS
huevos

The Spanish eat a lot of eggs, though just about never for breakfast. Apart from a mid-morning slice of *tortilla de patatas* (see page 124)—for me, nothing is better than a slice of yesterday's tortilla and a café con leche at about 11 a.m.—eggs are not considered morning food. But for a simple lunch or dinner, well, that's a different matter.

While Spanish egg dishes can be simple in preparation, their flavors are often rich and complex. A pair of eggs fried in extra-virgin olive oil and served with hand-cut slices of Iberian jamón and fried potatoes (see page 132) along with a glass of bold Ribera del Duero wine makes a most exquisite meal.

Excellent eggs are not hard to find. In the country's covered food markets, there is usually a stall or two dedicated to selling only eggs, offering a wide selection of options, from free-range, corn-fed chicken eggs to tiny speckled quail eggs.

While sold fresh across Spain, quail eggs seem to be most appreciated as part of a Basque pintxo, or tapa, fried and "mounted" on a slice of baguette with a slice of cured jamón. But they are tricky to crack into the pan to fry—you don't so much as *crack* them as cut off the end with the tip of a paring knife and gently tip the contents out of the shell and into the pan—and sometimes even more devilishly tricky to peel when boiled.

But never are eggs as delicious as when fresh—really fresh. In the summer we have a treat at the *finca* (estate) we've rented in Menorca. My girls head down the hill to the *gallinero* (henhouse) in the morning to pick up the eggs. The dozen hens at the finca are a local Menorcan breed—beautiful birds with brilliant black plumage and a great white spot on their heads—that, unfortunately, largely take the summer off from laying. But there are always one or two hens who indulge us, and offer a steady if slow supply. When asking about this summer recess, someone repeated the old saying, *"Por San Antón, huevos a montón."* (That is, on Saint Anthony's Day [January 17th], there are tons of eggs.) I looked up that expression later and found there was another, just as fitting: *"Por San Antón, todo ave pon."* (For Saint Anthony's Day, every bird lays.)

In the savory Spanish kitchen, eggs are probably most enjoyed in *tortillas* (Spanish egg omelets). While the potato tortilla—often with some onion to help keep it moist—remains *the* classic, it can be prepared with any vegetable, depending on the season. Eggplant. Zucchini. Mushrooms. Artichokes (see page 126). Asparagus. It is a happy coincidence that the hens' peak laying season is the same as many of the tortilla's more delicious fillings.

While the trick of a good egg tortilla largely rests in flipping it, a good *revuelto* is more about stirring. In revueltos, eggs are scrambled with sautéed ingredients. Well, scrambled is not exactly the correct word. The name comes from the verb *revolver*—to turn or to stir. That's a closer way of describing the light stirring used when cooking. Shrimp and asparagus (see page 128), say, or some wild mushrooms (see page 130), are quickly sautéed in a pan and then the whisked egg is poured over them. After a few seconds, the eggs are turned using just a couple of wide sweeps through the pan with a wooden spoon until the eggs are just set but still moist. Simple, perhaps, but also marvelous-tasting.

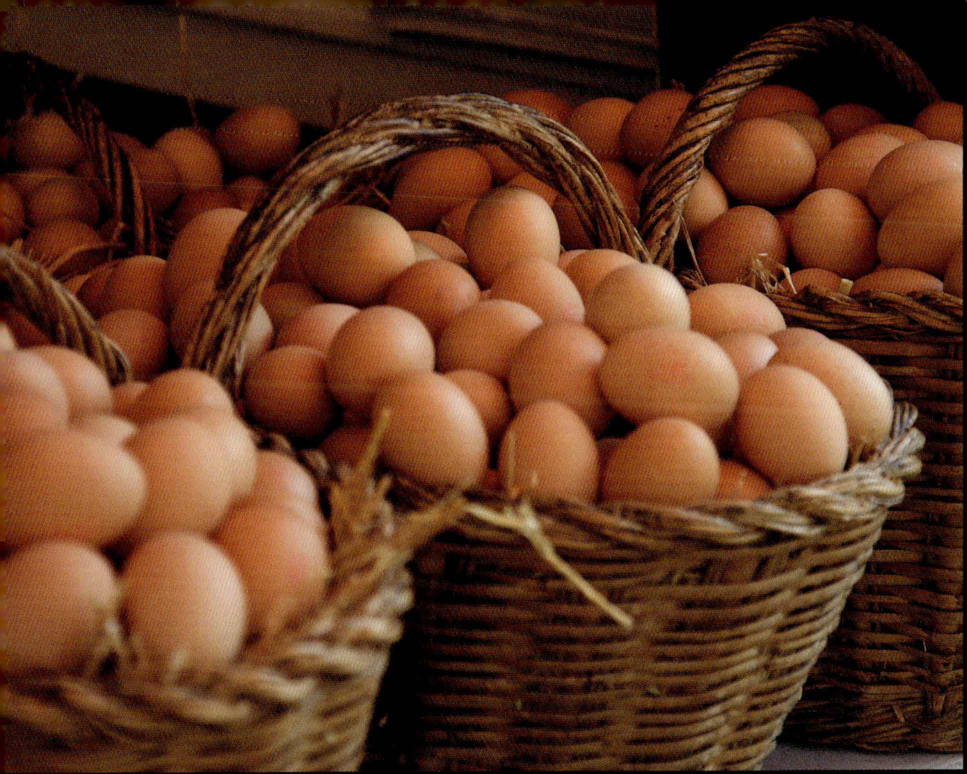

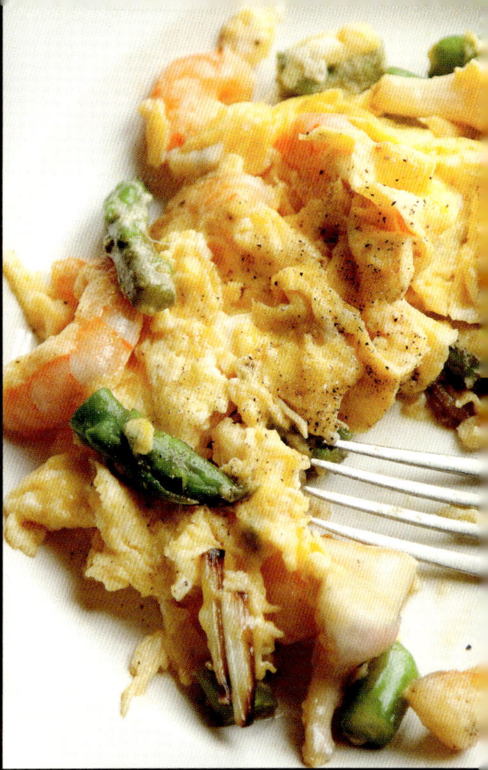

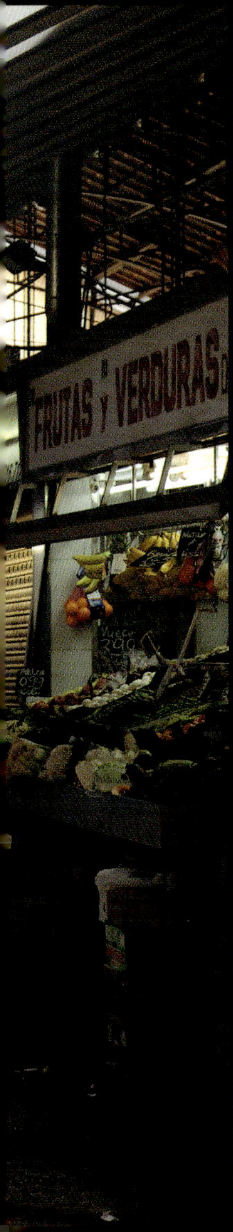
FRUTAS Y VERDURAS

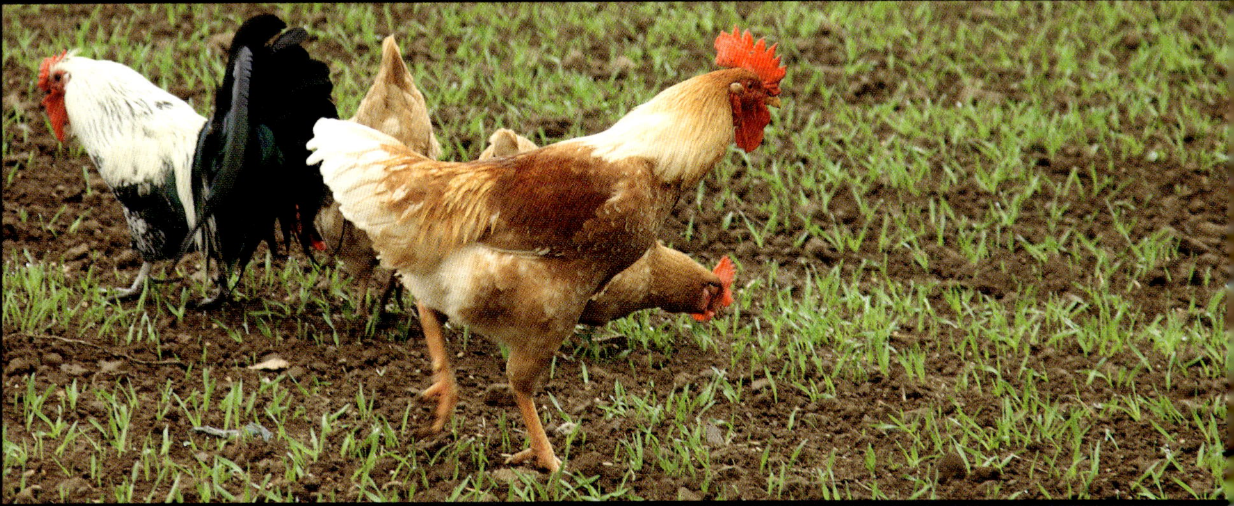

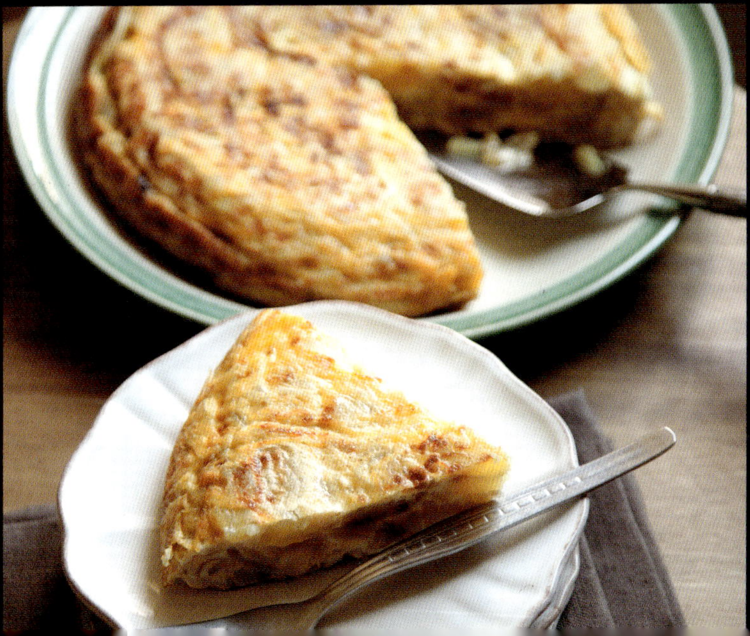

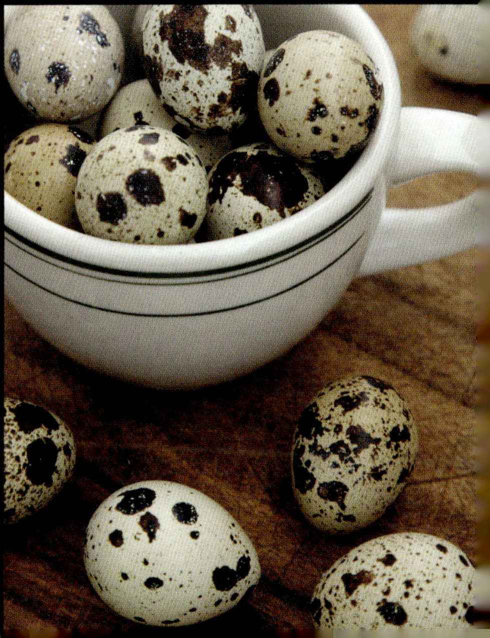

POTATO AND ONION EGG TORTILLA

TORTILLA DE PATATAS Y CEBOLLA

MAKES ONE 10-INCH/25-CM TORTILLA; SERVES 6 TO 8

One of the most classic and popular of all Spanish dishes, the egg and potato tortilla is, simply, iconic. It was, fittingly, the first dish I learned to make when I moved to Spain in 1996, in a lesson given to me by my future brother-in-law, Robert. Preparing a tortilla with potato alone is fine, but using an equal amount of onions produces a sweeter, moister, and, in my mind, superior result. While the key to a good tortilla is keeping it moist in the center, the real trick, he showed me, comes in flipping it. Or rather, flipping the tortilla without the bottom sticking.

1¼ POUNDS/570 G MEDIUM WHITE POTATOES
1¼ POUNDS/570 G MEDIUM ONIONS
1 QUART/1 L MILD OLIVE OIL OR SUNFLOWER OIL
10 EGGS
SALT

1. Peel the potatoes, halve lengthwise, and thinly slice crosswise. Peel the onions, halve lengthwise, and thinly slice crosswise.

2. In a large sauté pan or deep skillet, heat the olive oil over high heat until shimmering. Carefully add the potatoes and onions and cook over medium-high heat, stirring from time to time, until they soften and just begin to brown, about 15 minutes. Using a slotted spoon, transfer the potatoes and onions to a colander to thoroughly drain. Reserve 2 tablespoons of the oil.

3. In a large bowl, beat the eggs thoroughly with a hand whisk until frothy. Season with salt. Pour the drained potatoes and onions into the egg. Gently push down to cover with egg. Let sit and absorb for 10 minutes.

4. In a 10-inch/25-cm nonstick skillet, heat the reserved 2 tablespoons of oil over high heat. Pour in the egg mixture. Immediately turn the heat to low and swirl the pan in a circular motion for a few seconds to keep the egg from sticking. Cook until the bottom is golden and the tortilla set, about 6 minutes.

5. Wearing an oven mitt, place a flat, tight-fitting plate over the tortilla. Firmly pressing the plate against the pan, carefully and quickly turn the tortilla over onto the plate, and then slide the tortilla off the plate and back into the pan. Swirl the pan in a circular motion to settle the tortilla and keep it from sticking. Tuck any edges down with a spatula. Cook for another 3 to 4 minutes, until firm but still moist in the center.

6. Flip the tortilla onto a clean plate. Dab off any excess oil with a paper towel. Let cool before slicing it into fat wedges to serve.

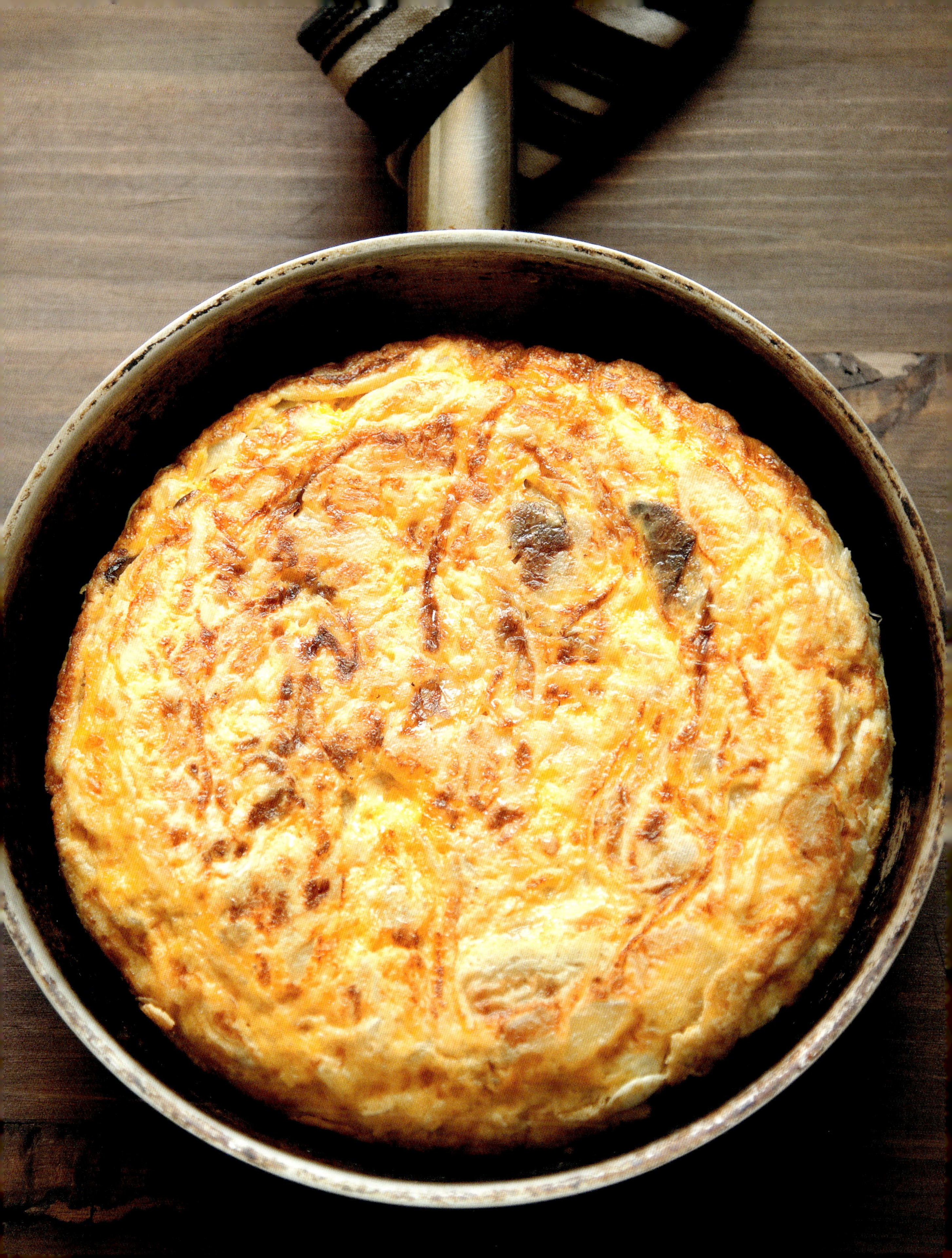

Like nearly all Spanish words that begin in *al*, the origin of *alcachofa* is Arabic, in this case from the Arabic *al-harsuf*. Artichokes were one of the key products introduced into Spain from North Africa during the Moorish rule of the country. Today, Spain is the world's second largest producer of artichokes (after Italy), and these thistle-like plants are widely farmed in Alicante, Murcia, Granada, south of Barcelona, and Navarra. The *alcachofa blanca de Tudela*—literally "white artichoke from Tudela," after a town in Navarra—is the one almost exclusively sold in local Spanish markets. (Other varieties are grown for export.) Medium-small, roundish, and compact, with green leaves, its season begins in October and winds down in spring, with the winter months marking its peak.

ARTICHOKE EGG TORTILLA

TORTILLA DE ALCACHOFAS

MAKES ONE 8-INCH/20-CM TORTILLA; SERVES 4 TO 6

1 LEMON
4 MEDIUM ARTICHOKES, ABOUT 2 POUNDS/910 G TOTAL
6 TABLESPOONS EXTRA-VIRGIN OLIVE OIL
7 EGGS
SALT

1. Fill a large bowl with cool water. Cut the lemon into wedges, squeeze them into the water, and then drop them into the bowl. Trim the artichokes following the directions on page 339, making sure the tough outer leaves have been stripped away. Cut the artichokes into eighths or even a bit smaller. Leave in the lemon water to keep from darkening until ready to cook.

2. In a large skillet or sauté pan, heat 4 tablespoons of the olive oil over high heat and add the artichokes. Cover and cook, stirring frequently, until golden and tender, 8 to 10 minutes. Reduce the heat to low, cover the skillet, and cook for 2 to 3 minutes to soften a touch more. Lift out with a slotted spoon and drain on paper towels.

3. In a large bowl, beat the eggs thoroughly with a hand whisk until frothy. Season with salt. Pour the artichokes into the egg. Gently push down to cover with egg. Let sit and absorb for 10 minutes.

4. In an 8-inch/20-cm nonstick skillet, heat the remaining 2 tablespoons olive oil over high heat. Pour in the egg mixture. Immediately turn the heat to low and swirl the pan in a circular motion for a few seconds to keep the egg from sticking. Cook until the bottom is golden and the tortilla set, about 6 minutes.

5. Wearing an oven mitt, place a flat, tight-fitting plate over the tortilla. Firmly pressing the plate against the pan, carefully and quickly turn the tortilla over onto the plate, and then slide the tortilla off the plate and back into the pan. Swirl the pan in a circular motion to settle the tortilla and keep it from sticking. Tuck any edges down with a spatula. Cook for another 4 to 5 minutes, until firm but still moist in the center.

6. Flip the tortilla onto a clean plate. Dab off any excess oil with a paper towel. Let cool before slicing it into fat wedges to serve.

SALT COD EGG TORTILLA

TORTILLA DE BACALAO

SERVES 4

In the apple orchard–filled hills outside San Sebastián, late winter and spring is the season to head to a country *sagardotegia* (cider house) for glasses of hard cider taken directly from massive chestnut barrels. Uncorked, the cider whizzes out in an arc and you simply hold your glass under the stream. Such visits are usually accompanied by a hearty, traditional set meal that includes a juicy salt cod tortilla. So associated with this splendid Basque city and its surrounding area is this dish, it is often called a *tortilla Donostiarra* after the Basque name for San Sebastián, Donostia.

This is a loose, open-topped version of a tortilla that isn't flipped but quickly "pulled" around the pan until set but still moist. As the salt cod will continue to sweat while cooking, the texture of the egg is better if the tortillas are small (or at least thinner) and very quickly cooked.

8 OUNCES/225 G SALT COD (SEE NOTE, PAGE 54)
6 EGGS
4 TABLESPOONS EXTRA-VIRGIN OLIVE OIL
1 MEDIUM ONION, FINELY CHOPPED
½ SWEET ITALIAN GREEN PEPPER OR ¼ GREEN BELL PEPPER, FINELY CHOPPED
3 GARLIC CLOVES, MINCED
1 TABLESPOON MINCED FRESH FLAT-LEAF PARSLEY, PLUS MORE FOR GARNISHING

1. Beginning 2 or 3 days ahead, desalt the cod following the directions on page 341. Drain, rinse, and pat dry with paper towels. Skin and carefully debone it. Shred the cod by hand into bite-size pieces following the flakes and fibers. Gently squeeze to remove any excess moisture.

2. In a medium bowl, beat 3 of the eggs with a hand whisk until frothy.

3. In a 9-inch/23-cm nonstick skillet, heat 3 tablespoons of the olive oil over medium heat. Add the onion and cook until it begins to soften and turn pale, about 5 minutes. Add the green pepper and cook until soft, 6 to 8 minutes. Finally, add the garlic and cook until fragrant, about 1 minute. Sprinkle in the parsley and add the salt cod. Cook, stirring continually, until the salt cod turns opaque and begins to flake apart, 2 to 3 minutes.

4. Remove half of the mixture from the skillet and set aside in a bowl.

5. Pour the eggs into the skillet. Immediately turn the heat to medium-high and move the pan quickly in a circular motion, pulling the pan back and forth to keep the eggs from sticking. Cook until the eggs are set but still very moist on top, 1½ to 2 minutes. Slide the tortilla onto a plate.

6. In the bowl, whisk the remaining 3 eggs until frothy.

7. Wipe the pan clean and heat the remaining 1 tablespoon of olive oil over medium-high heat. Return the remaining salt cod mixture to the pan, and prepare the second tortilla in the same manner as the first.

8. Sprinkle the tortillas with parsley and serve.

EGGS SCRAMBLED WITH TENDER GREEN GARLIC SHOOTS, ASPARAGUS, AND SHRIMP

REVUELTO DE AJETES CON ESPÁRRAGOS Y GAMBAS

SERVES 2

Ajetes or *ajos tiernos* are tender green garlic shoots, harvested before the clove forms. Showing up in markets in late winter and spring, they look like skinny green onions with ruddy pinkish-tipped ends, but have a smooth, powerful, and persistent garlicky taste and aroma. Cooked, though, they soften in flavor and offer a sweetness to their garlicky taste. You can also substitute two garlic cloves and two green onions.

As revueltos are best prepared in smaller batches, this recipe serves two. To serve four, double the ingredients, cook the vegetables and shrimp together, remove half, and prepare two tortillas with the eggs one after the other.

6 MEDIUM FRESH ASPARAGUS STALKS
8 TENDER GREEN GARLIC SHOOTS
4 EGGS
SALT
1 TABLESPOON EXTRA-VIRGIN OLIVE OIL
3 OUNCES/85 G PEELED MEDIUM FRESH SHRIMP
FRESHLY GROUND BLACK PEPPER

1. Snap off the hard bottom part of each asparagus stalk at the natural break point and discard. Blanch, chill, and drain the asparagus following the directions on page 107. Cut off the soft tips and then cut the remaining stalks into ½- to 1-inch/1.25- to 2.5-cm lengths, depending on their thickness. (The thicker the stalk, the shorter the piece.)

2. Trim the greenest part and root tip of each garlic shoot and discard. Peel off the outside layer. Cut into 1-inch-/2.5-cm-long pieces, with the final, thicker piece closest to the root end a touch shorter. There should be 24 to 32 pieces in total.

3. In a bowl, whisk the eggs with a pinch of salt until slightly frothy.

4. In a large nonstick skillet, heat the olive oil over medium heat. Add the garlic shoots and cook until tender, fragrant, and slightly golden, about 1 minute. Add the shrimp and cook until opaque throughout, about 2 minutes.

5. Pour the eggs into the pan. Let set for 10 seconds, and then stir two or three large, generous sweeps around the pan with a wooden spoon. Add the asparagus and stir again in generous sweeps around the pan, turning the eggs over, until the eggs are done but still quite moist, 30 seconds to 1 minute.

6. Divide among two plates and generously grind pepper over top. Serve immediately.

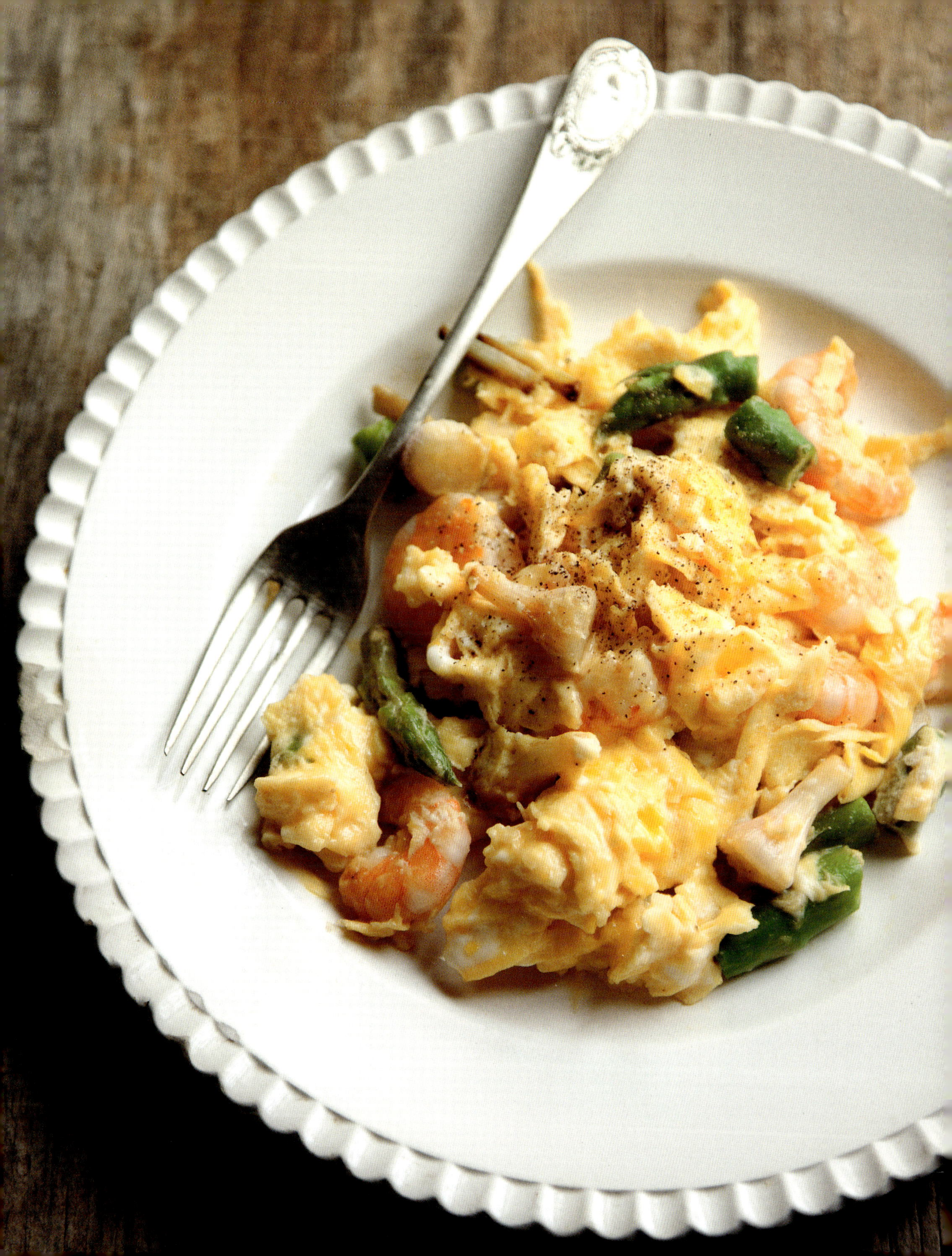

EGGS SCRAMBLED WITH MUSHROOMS AND DRY-CURED JAMÓN

REVUELTO DE SETAS Y JAMÓN

SERVES 2

Eggs are a wonderful way to appreciate the natural earthiness of mushrooms, especially wild ones. They soak up the flavors while acting as something of a binder, and offer their own fine texture and subtle taste. In making a good revuelto with them, it is important that all of the moisture from the mushrooms has been expelled before adding the eggs. If not, the eggs will be watery and the texture nubby as opposed to moist and silky. As revueltos are best prepared in smaller batches, this recipe serves two. To double, see the headnote on page 128.

6 OUNCES/170 G MIXED FRESH WILD AND CULTIVATED MUSHROOMS, PREFERABLY SEVERAL DIFFERENT VARIETIES

4 EGGS

SALT

1 TABLESPOON EXTRA-VIRGIN OLIVE OIL, PLUS MORE FOR DRIZZLING

1 GARLIC CLOVE, MINCED

1 OUNCE/30 G DRY-CURED SPANISH JAMÓN (SEE INGREDIENT NOTE, PAGE 16), FINELY CHOPPED

FRESHLY GROUND BLACK PEPPER

1 TABLESPOON MINCED FRESH FLAT-LEAF PARSLEY

1. Clean the mushrooms following the directions on page 339. Quarter or slice them depending on their shape.

2. In a bowl, whisk the eggs with a pinch of salt until slightly frothy.

3. In a large nonstick skillet, heat the olive oil over high heat. Add the mushrooms and cook until the moisture has been expelled and evaporated and the edges begin to brown, about 5 minutes. Reduce the heat to medium and add the garlic and jamón. Cook, stirring continually, until the garlic is fragrant, about 1 minute.

4. Pour the eggs into the pan. Let set for 10 seconds, and then stir six or eight large, generous sweeps around the pan with a wooden spoon, turning the eggs over, until the eggs are done but still quite moist, about 1 minute.

5. Divide among two plates, lightly drizzle with oil, generously grind pepper over the top, and garnish with a dusting of parsley. Serve immediately.

TRADITIONS

COVERED FOOD MARKETS
mercados

From Zamora's Mercado de Abastos and Zaragoza's Mercado Central to Bilbao's Mercado de la Ribera, covered food markets offer inspiration and ingredients to home cooks as well as chefs. The individually owned stalls offer the cured sausages and diverse cheeses, pulses, profusion of seasonal produce, mind-boggling seafood, fresh poultry and game, and innards and extremities that make Spain's cuisine so spectacular.

Many of the country's markets have open-air roots, and can trace their origins far back, to medieval times or even the Roman era. These ancient *plaza-mercados* eventually gained solid foundations and roofs with the advances in steel construction in the mid-nineteenth century. Market designs at that time often included the elegant, free-flowing curves of art nouveau, rich in ornamentation and lavished with decorative elements.

In Barcelona, La Boqueria is the city's most famous market and an icon for the food-conscious city. But it is just one of thirty-nine municipal food markets (and four specialist ones) scattered through Barcelona's neighborhoods. (It is the largest such network in Europe.) There are other markets closer to my home, though I go to La Boqueria for a handful of specific items brought in from the countryside—foraged wild mushrooms from Llorenç Petràs's stall, fresh thyme and rosemary from the vegetable stall behind it, the finest Arbequina olives from Olivas y Conservas Pinyol, and particular Galician seafood like large turbot, octopus, *percebes* (gooseneck barnacles), and *navajas* (razor clams).

Spain's markets are not only places to shop but also to eat. Tucked among the stalls, tiny and usually deceptively simple cafés serve splendid *cocina de mercado* (market cooking). Drawing on the fresh products that surround them in the market, they showcase bold flavors with straightforward cooking techniques.

Standing in a market like Valencia's Mercado Central, with its soaring, airy, mosaic-covered cupola above and splendid stalls of food all around, it truly feels like being in a cathedral of a faith that celebrates itself through its cuisine.

FRIED EGGS WITH FRIED POTATOES AND SLICES OF DRY-CURED IBERIAN JAMÓN

HUEVOS FRITOS CON PATATAS FRITAS Y LONCHAS DE JAMÓN IBÉRICO

SERVES 4

The town of Jabugo, located in the mountainous Sierra de Aracena along the Andalucía-Extremadura border, produces some of the most celebrated dry-cured *jamónes* in the country. Set at 2,150 feet/655 m in the mountains, with cold, dry winters and mild springs and summers, the climate is ideal for raising black-footed Iberian pigs that roam semi-wild in the vast *dehesas*—holm oak–filled pastures—that coat the region's hills. It is no surprise that many of Jabugo's dishes include slices of their marvelous jamón ibérico. Served over fried potatoes with a couple of eggs fried in local full-bodied extra-virgin olive oil, and a glass of red wine, it is divine simplicity.

2 POUNDS/910 G MEDIUM WHITE POTATOES
VEGETABLE OIL OR MILD OLIVE OIL, PLUS MORE FOR FRYING
4 TABLESPOONS EXTRA-VIRGIN OLIVE OIL, PLUS MORE AS NEEDED
8 EGGS
4 OUNCES/115 G SLICED HIGH-QUALITY DRY-CURED SPANISH JAMÓN IBÉRICO (SEE INGREDIENT NOTE, PAGE 16)
FLAKY SEA SALT

1. Scrub the potatoes, but do not peel. Cut them lengthwise into ⅓-inch-/1-cm-thick fries. Put them in a large bowl of water and soak for 15 minutes to leach out some of the starches. Rinse, drain, and spread out on paper towels to dry.

2. Preheat the oven to 200°F/95°C.

3. In a deep skillet, heat about 2 inches/5 cm of vegetable oil to 375°F/190°C. (The oil is right temperature when a large cube of fresh bread dropped into it browns in about 60 seconds.) Working in two batches that don't crowd the pan or bring the temperature of the oil below 350°F/180°C, add the potatoes and fry until golden, 12 to 18 minutes per batch. Remove with a slotted spoon or tongs, and place on paper towels to briefly drain. Transfer to a baking sheet lined with parchment paper and place in the oven to keep hot until all of the potatoes have been fried.

4. In a large nonstick skillet, heat the extra-virgin olive oil over medium heat and fry the eggs in batches as needed, re-oiling the pan if necessary.

5. Divide the fried potatoes among the plates and cover with slices of jamón. Place 2 eggs to the side on each plate, season with salt flakes, and serve immediately.

INGREDIENTS

ACORN-FED IBERIAN DRY-CURED HAM
jamón ibérico de bellota

A thin, nearly transparent slice of free-range, acorn-fed, and dry-cured Iberian jamón is surely Spain's most celebrated and delectable treat. Richly marbled with fat, deep ruddy red in color, and having a pleasant texture that is almost creamy in softness, its husky, marvelously nutty flavors just linger and linger.

Such perfection comes from a handful of specific factors that make it virtually unduplicated outside Spain. The first is the landscape, the *dehesas* where the pigs roam and forage. A dehesa is a pastureland planted with acorn-bearing holm oak and cork trees. It's not forest and not prairieland, but a mix, an airy space of wild grasses and tubers dotted with spacious, tightly foliaged trees. Dehesas cover some 9 million acres/3½ million hectares in the southwest of Spain. The cork produces about a quarter of the world's supply of wine corks.

The second factor is the animal itself. An ancestor of the wild boar, the black-footed Iberian pig is indigenous to Spain. Breeds of *cerdos blancos* (white pigs) have only been on the peninsula for the last few centuries and produce *jamón serrano* (Serrano ham). The darker Iberian pig has a longer snout, shorter, more slender legs, and more fat that tunnels through the muscle than its pinker relative, while their black hooves have given them the nickname *pata negra* (black foot).

The crucial stage in their rearing is the last one known as the *montanera*, the three or four final months of their lives when they rummage the ground for herbs, roots, aromatic grasses, and, most importantly, fallen acorns. Able to eat more than 20 pounds/9 kg of acorns a day and over 6 pounds/3 kg of grasses, they gain a staggering 2 pounds/1 kg a day, doubling in weight during this phase that runs some time between October into February or March. By the time the pigs head for the slaughterhouse, they weigh 375 to 420 pounds/170 to 190 kg. Indeed, the acorn is fattening, but it also contains a high percentage of oleic acids—the same as found in olive oil—which makes its way into the fat of the pigs.

To be clear, though, not all Iberian pigs are lucky enough to subsist solely on acorns for the last part of their lives. Pigs that have eaten only acorns during this montanera phase are known as *jamón ibérico de bellota*—the top, and most expensive. *Jamón ibérico de recebo* means that the pigs have had a mixed diet of acorns and grains during the last phase of life, and that they have gained only around 50 percent of their weight by eating acorns. And *jamón ibérico de cebo* are Iberian pigs that have been completely reared on a diet of grains and feed.

The third part of the equation is the curing, a process little changed since the days of the Romans. The hind legs, the most prized, are the *jamónes*, and the front shoulders are *paletas*, which are thinner, cured for a shorter time, and less expensive. A jamón weighs about 33 pounds/15 kg and, as one owner of a curing house told me, "Tradition says it needs to be salted for one day per kilo plus one more day." Cleaned, lard spread over the exposed cut, and a rope looped around the hoof, they're hung for two or even three years in cool cellars known as *secaderos* to slowly dry in the mountain air. (The best of the best can cure for as long as five years.) The final weight of a jamón is around 15 pounds/8 kg. The best ones can sell whole for well over $500, some even approaching double that amount.

The most famous jamón is produced by a quartet of regions under registered designation of origin seals and strict guidelines: Guijuelo (near Salamanca), Jamón de Huelva (the best known is from Jabugo), Jamón del Valle de Los Pedroches (from Córdoba), and Jamón de Trévelez (in the Sierra Nevada near Granada).

Hand-sliced paper thin using long, razor-sharp knives, the jamón is pure, natural, and simple excellence.

CHAPTER 6

RICE, PASTA, AND MIGAS
arroz, pasta y migas

Rice was introduced into Spain in the eighth century around the freshwater lagoon of the Albufera just south of Valencia. While Spain is Europe's second largest producer of rice—Italy produces some 48 percent of its total compared to Spain's 30 percent—the country's best and most sought-after rice still grows around the Albufera. Valencia and its environs remain the heart of Spanish rice culture. (See page 147 for more on Valencian rice.)

Most famous of all Spanish rice dishes is, of course, the iconic paella. Prepared in an eponymous wide pan, the rice remains in a thin layer. (The pan just gets wider, not deeper.) The authentic *paella valenciana* includes rabbit, chicken, snails, and three types of local green beans. But there are many traditional combinations, from rabbit with artichokes (see page 138) to the Mediterranean favorite with shellfish (see page 141). I tend to ignore the purists who dismiss such variations as "rice in a paella pan" rather than authentic paellas. But I do agree that to be a paella, it needs to be prepared in a paella pan.

Paella is considered an *arroz seco* (a dry rice) because of its final (dryish) consistency. There can be similar ingredients in other styles of rice dishes, with the difference found in the final texture. A *meloso*, or moist rice, is cooked in a *cazuela* (a round, flat casserole), while a *caldoso* (soupy or brothy) means you need a spoon to eat it. Though how soupy varies greatly, from *just* soupy to *really* soupy.

Importantly, in each of these variations, rice remains the protagonist: Everything is done to flavor the short, highly absorbent grains of rice that really just act as vehicles for the flavors. The most celebrated of the varieties is Bomba, which is a bit more resilient than other varieties in that it is less likely to "open." It is the main variety exported to North America, and also the one I recommend for anyone who doesn't frequently cook Spanish-style rice.

For these rice dishes, calculate about ½ cup/100 g of uncooked rice per person for paellas and moist rice dishes and ⅓ cup/66 g for soupy ones. These are generous servings. But if there is a spoonful left over, then you are lucky.

Spain has, too, its own pasta traditions, some going back to the Middle Ages and appearing in the earliest cookery books. Fideos are short, thin noodles that are cooked in the manner of a paella in a wide pan and called *fideuà* (see page 153), with the noodles absorbing (like rice) the flavors of the pan. There are also a couple of slightly moister country versions with thicker noodles cooked in a cazuela (see page 152).

Two other centuries-old pasta specialties stand out. *Macarrones*, or penne pasta with tomato sauce and fresh sausage (see page 156) is one. The other is *canelones*, stuffed cannelloni with ground meat (see page 157), mushrooms (see page 160), or spinach and pine nuts.

The rice and pasta dishes in this chapter are generally *platos únicos*, one-dish meals that break the Spanish tradition of first course–second course. There might be a few appetizers and probably a green salad in the middle of the table, but when the pan is carried to the table, the cook's work is done.

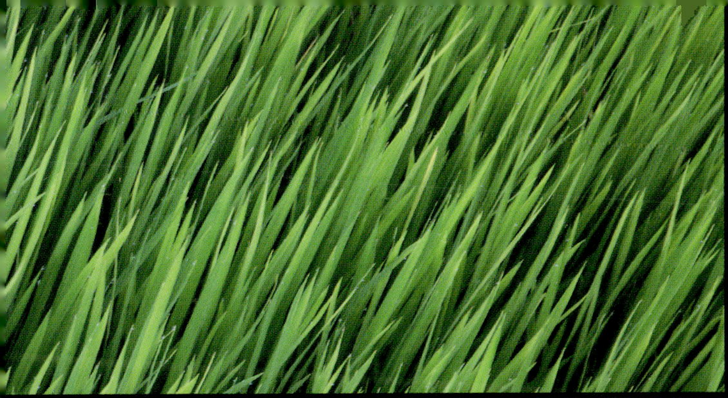
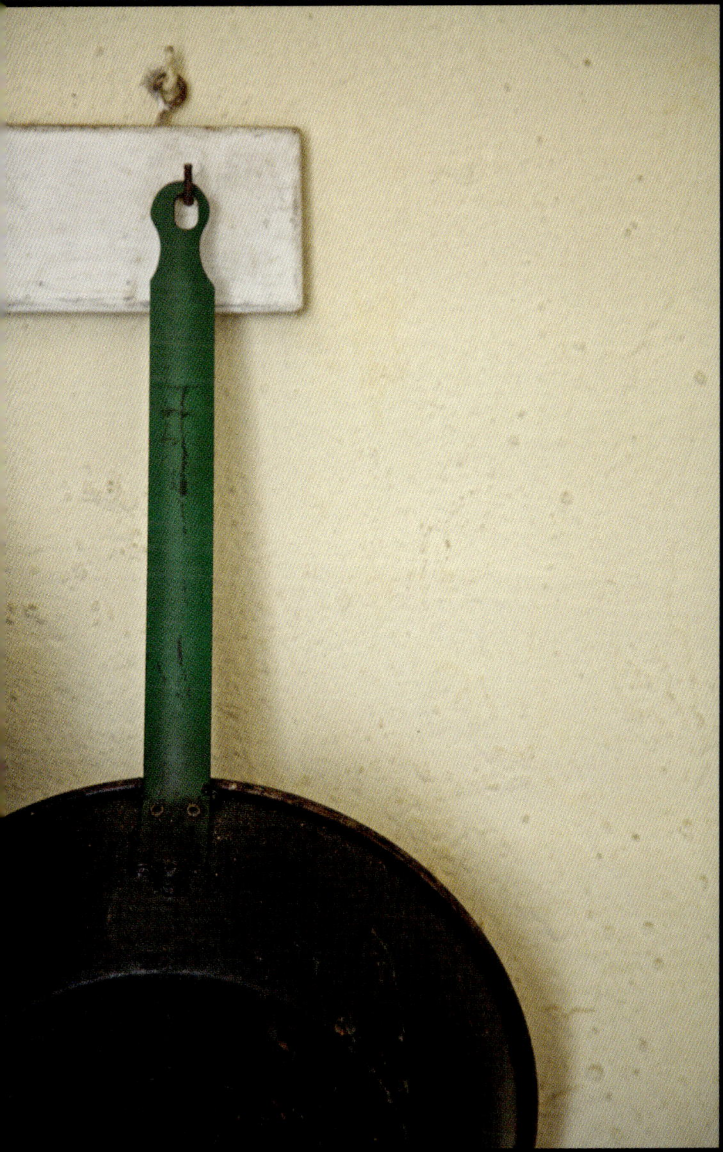
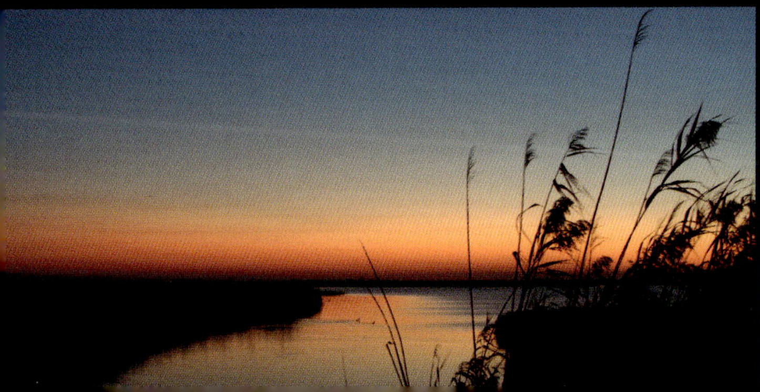
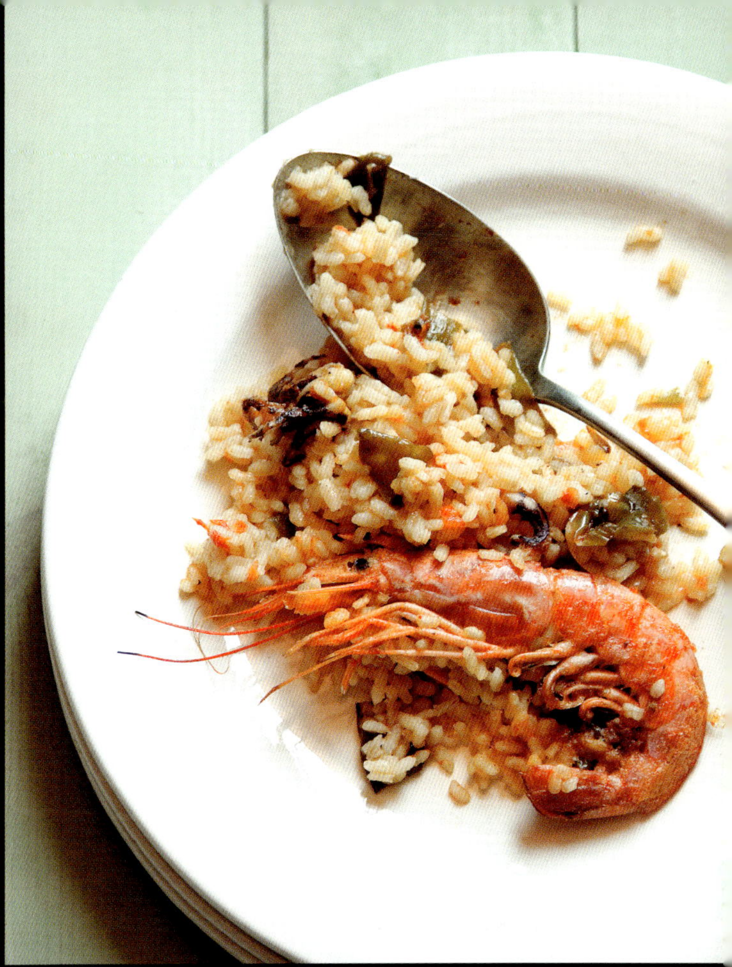
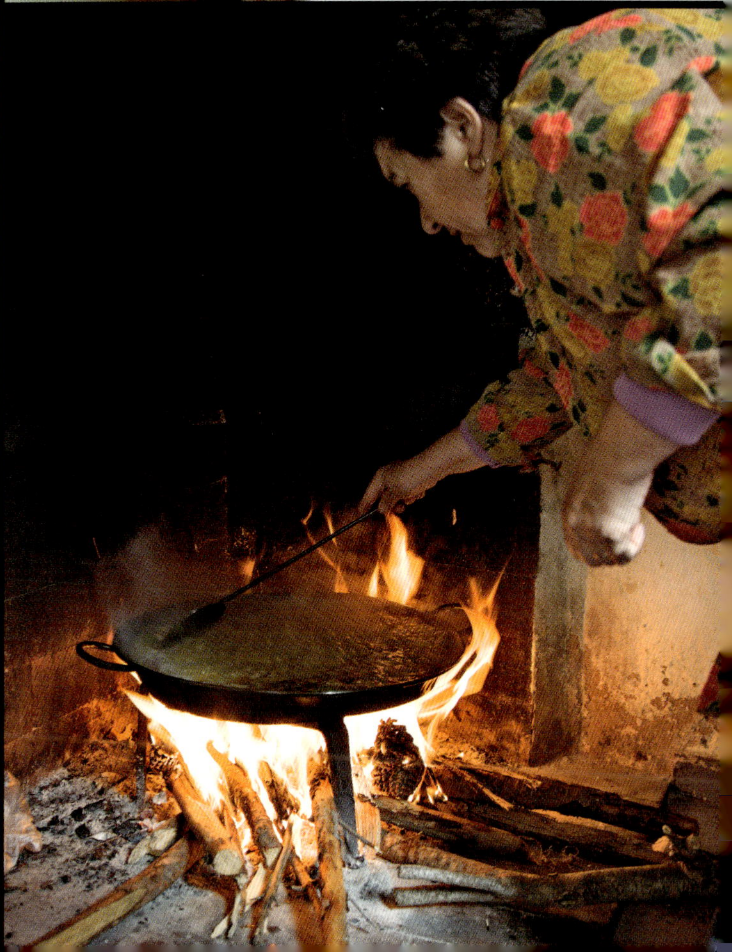

TRADITIONS

PAELLA: TECHNIQUES AND ADVICE
paella: técnicas y consejos

Getting a paella right can be a challenge. It isn't necessarily difficult, it just takes some practice. There are no easy "tricks" in making it work, but rather a series of techniques. Organized roughly by order of preparation, here is a list of some of the more important points—technical and otherwise—that I have learned over the years:

1. As Tía Encarnita (see page 138) says, "Paella is really just an excuse to gather people." A paella is always a festive occasion. But do not make a paella for the first time for a large group of people. Do a practice run first to be comfortable with the pan, heat source, rice, and amount of liquid. Take notes. And then repeat, using the same pan, same heat source, and same type of rice—and your notes.

2. Buy a paella pan, preferably an inexpensive one. Just be sure it is large. See page 143 for notes on types of paella pans, and Sources, page 345, for where to find them.

3. Paella is a lunch dish. It is considered too heavy for dinner. My mother-in-law has been preparing paellas almost weekly for five decades, and I am certain that in that time, not once has it been for dinner.

4. Prepare a couple of simple appetizers and a large green salad to put in the middle of the table. But no second course. Paella is a *plato único*, a one-course meal.

5. Buy the best and freshest ingredients you can. They will reward you with their flavors.

6. Use only natural saffron, not artificial paella coloring (powdered *colorante*). The rice should be a golden-brown, not neon yellow.

7. Use only pimentón dulce (sweet paprika), not picante (hot and spicy).

8. If using a really large pan on a kitchen stovetop, try straddling three burners, rotating the pan slightly every minute or two to ensure even cooking. Or prepare it outside on embers or the barbecue. See page 143 for how to do this.

9. Do not crowd the pan. The pan gets *wider*; the rice does not get *deeper*.

10. Paella is a rice dish. Rice is the protagonist and everything is done to flavor the grains of rice. Do not overwhelm the pan with other "stuff." A seafood paella is not a seafood dish with rice, but a rice dish flavored by seafood.

11. A paella can be made in advance—up to a point. That point is just before adding the rice. Remove the pan from the heat, and cover with sheets of aluminum foil to keep the liquid from evaporating (or add in a touch more water).

12. Use short- or medium-grain rice that can absorb the stock. Do not use long-grain rice or parboiled rice. Ever.

13. Do not rinse the rice before adding (to stop from washing away any nutrients and starches).

14. Use a light hand with the oil. It will coat the rice grains and too much oil will inhibit their absorption capabilities.

15. Do not add onions to paella. Paella is a "dry" rice. Onions are a "wet" vegetable. Add onions to other types of rice dishes, but never to a paella.

16. Do not add the rice until everybody is there. "There" means in the house. Not on the way. Not on the bus or in the metro. Not circling the block looking for parking. Not in the corner shop picking out a bottle of wine. *In the house!* And ready to eat. "I want to see your eyes!" my mother-in-law says. To repeat her mantra: "People can wait for rice, but rice can't wait for people."

17. As an expression goes, *"Arroz pasado, arroz tirado"* (literally "past rice, thrown rice"). That is, rice that is overcooked is tossed out. I tend to say this Catalan rhyme, though: *"Arròs passat, per el gat."* (Past rice, for the cat.)

18. After sprinkling in the rice, check with a wooden spoon that it is evenly distributed and that all of the grains are situated below the surface of the liquid. (If not, they won't cook fully.)

19. After checking that the rice is distributed, do not stir. Ever.

20. Do not cover the pan as the rice cooks. Ever.

21. Rice takes around 18 minutes to cook. The first half of that time the paella is cooked over high heat, the second half over low heat.

22. If the liquid has evaporated and the rice is not yet done, sprinkle drops of water over the rice.

23. If it smells like the bottom is beginning to burn, remove immediately from the heat and place the pan on damp kitchen towels for 5 minutes.

24. The finished paella needs to "rest" for 5 minutes after cooking to firm up the starches and to finish cooking any of the top grains. Cross a pair of wooden spoons over the pan and cover with paper towels.

25. Before carrying the pan to the table, make sure everyone is sitting down. If you are sitting at the table, applaud appreciatively when the paella is carried out.

26. If desired, place the pan in the middle of the table and eat directly from it with a spoon. In this case, it is considered bad manners to reach across the pan for that particularly plump shrimp. Stick to your own pie-shaped section of rice in front of you.

27. As paella is a *plato único* (see #4), that means no second course to fuss with. Your work as a cook is done. Sit down. And enjoy.

RABBIT PAELLA WITH ARTICHOKES AND RED BELL PEPPERS

PAELLA DE CONEJO CON ALCACHOFAS Y PIMIENTOS ROJOS

SERVES 6

In many ways, this popular paella is a variation on paella valenciana, the authentic and original paella from around Valencia. This one has just rabbit, leaving out the snails, and instead of green beans calls for artichokes. When the artichokes are in peak season in winter, Tía Encarnita—one of the "aunts" in the ancestral village of my mother-in-law, who frequently prepares dazzling paellas (always outside over embers, and always served in the center of the table to be eaten from the pan with a spoon)— likes to make this one. This paella is particularly nice over embers. To prepare it outside for smokier, earthier flavors, and an all-round most festive experience, see page 143. You can substitute bone-in chicken for the rabbit. Before preparing, see my list of hints, suggestions, and techniques on page 136.

1 WHOLE CLEANED RABBIT, ABOUT 2½ POUNDS/1.2 KG
SALT AND FRESHLY GROUND BLACK PEPPER
1 LEMON
4 MEDIUM ARTICHOKES
6 TABLESPOONS EXTRA-VIRGIN OLIVE OIL
½ RED BELL PEPPER, CUT INTO 1-INCH/2.5-CM PIECES
4 RIPE MEDIUM TOMATOES, HALVED CROSSWISE, SEEDED, AND GRATED (SEE PAGE 339)
2 GARLIC CLOVES, MINCED
1 TEASPOON SPANISH PIMENTÓN DULCE (SWEET PAPRIKA)
2 QUARTS/2 L CHICKEN STOCK (PAGE 336) OR VEGETABLE STOCK (PAGE 335)
1 PINCH SAFFRON THREADS, DRY-TOASTED AND GROUND (SEE PAGE 340)
3 CUPS/600 G BOMBA RICE OR ANOTHER SHORT- OR MEDIUM-GRAIN SPANISH RICE (SEE NOTE, PAGE 142)

1. Cut the rabbit into eight or nine pieces, following the directions on page 342 (or have your butcher do it). Season generously with salt and pepper.

2. Fill a large bowl with cool water. Cut the lemon into wedges, squeeze them into the water, and then drop them into the bowl. Trim the artichokes following the directions on page 339, making sure the tough outer leaves have been stripped away. Cut the artichokes into eighths and drop in the lemon water to keep from darkening until ready to cook.

3. In a 16- to 18-inch/40- to 45-cm paella pan, heat the olive oil over medium heat. Add the rabbit and cook, turning frequently, until well browned, about 10 minutes. Move the rabbit pieces to the outside of the pan (watching that they do not burn) and begin making a sofrito in the center of the pan: Drain the artichokes and add along with the bell pepper. Cook, stirring frequently, until tender, 8 to 10 minutes. Add the tomatoes, garlic, and 2 pinches of salt and cook, continuing to stir frequently, until the tomato begins to darken, about 8 minutes. If it begins to dry out, splash in a bit of water. Mix the rabbit into the sofrito and continue to cook for another 5 minutes or so, until the tomato is pulpy and has lost its acidity.

4. When the sofrito is ready, sprinkle in the pimentón, letting the flavors meld for a just few seconds while stirring constantly, and then immediately add 1 cup/300 ml of the stock. Simmer over medium heat until the liquid is just about evaporated and the rabbit is quite tender, about 30 minutes. Add in a touch more water if necessary to keep it moist.

5. Add the remaining 7 cups/1.7 L of stock with the saffron, increase the heat to high, and bring the liquid to a boil. When the liquid comes to a boil, sprinkle the rice around the pan. With a wooden spoon, check that the rice is evenly distributed and that the grains are below the surface of the liquid. Do not stir again.

6. Cook uncovered for 10 minutes over high heat. Reduce the heat to low and cook uncovered for 8 to 10 minutes more, until the liquid is absorbed and the rice grains are tender but still have an al dente bite to them. If all the liquid has evaporated and the rice is still not done, shake tepid water tablespoon by tablespoon over the rice where needed and cook for an additional few minutes.

7. Remove the paella from the heat, cross wooden spoons over top, cover with paper towels, and let rest for 5 minutes to allow the rice—particularly the grains on top—to finish cooking and the starches to firm up.

8. Carry the paella to the table and serve from the pan.

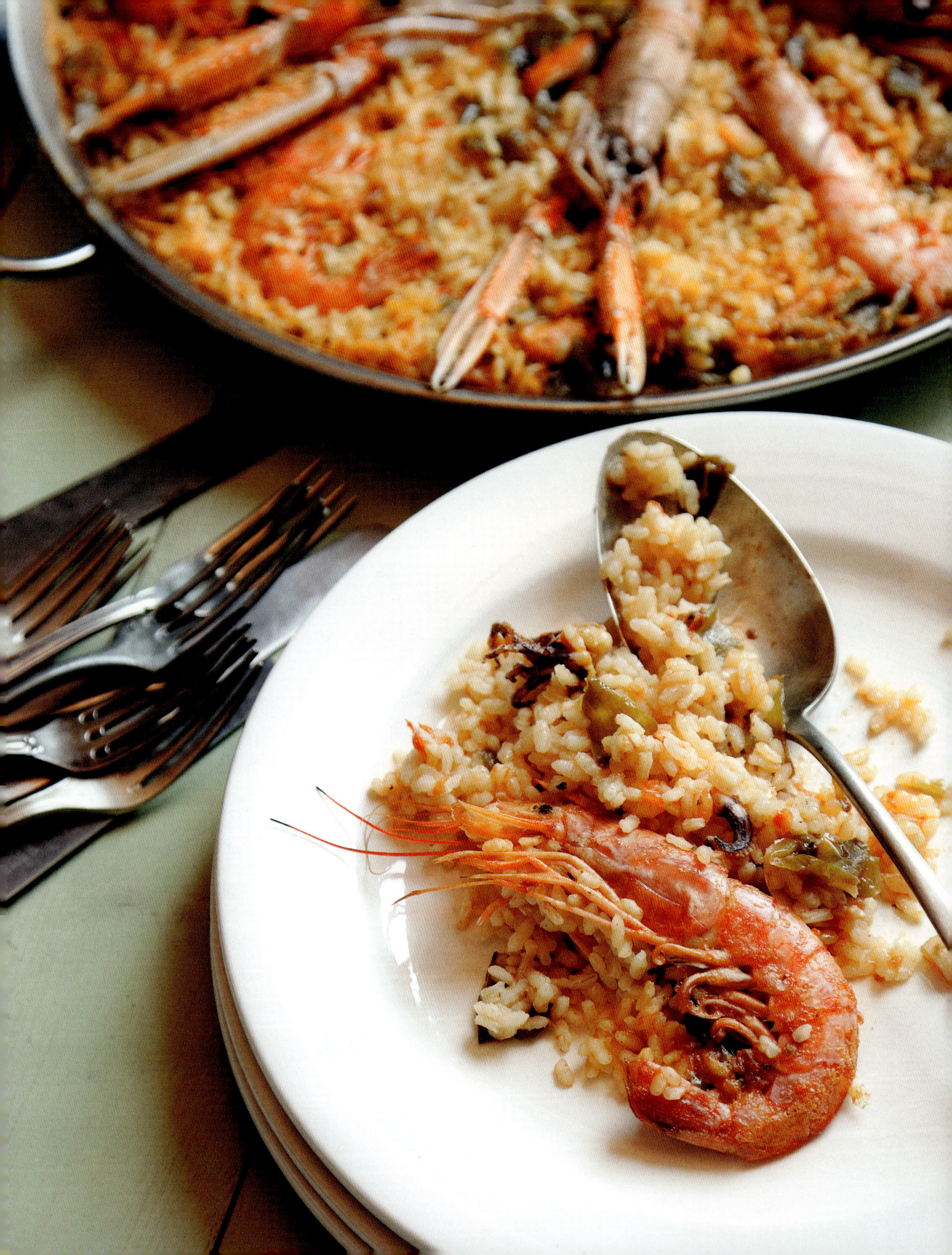

Baroque, regal, and always impressive carried out to the table, shellfish paella is one of Spanish cuisine's grandest dishes. For me, it also best represents this culture where food and family often swing hand and hand. My mother-in-law, Rosa, has been making one of these paellas nearly every weekend for fifty years. It was around her shellfish paella that I met the family of the woman I had followed to Barcelona in 1996, and where countless other memorable occasions have been announced and celebrated since. Over plates of her golden, flavorful rice, I learned how a simple staple could be converted into a family bond. I was so enamored with this concept that I wrote my first cookbook about Spanish rice dishes, with Rosa's paella at its center. And while this isn't exactly her recipe here—you can find it in that first book, *La Paella*—her influence is clearly discernible.

If there is anything that I have learned from Rosa about her paella, it is that it is a *rice* dish—not a seafood dish *with rice*. As I repeat elsewhere in the book, everything is done to flavor the rice. Using a good Spanish short- or medium-grain variety or one of the options listed in the Note following is crucial. As well, note that the clams are best prepared separately, because if they have any sand at all, they will wreck the rice. Before preparing, see my full list of hints, suggestions, and techniques on page 136.

SHELLFISH PAELLA

PAELLA DE MARISCO

SERVES 6

8 OUNCES/225 G SMALL CLAMS, SCRUBBED

8 OUNCES/225 G SMALL TO MEDIUM MUSSELS, CLEANED AND DEBEARDED

3 TABLESPOONS EXTRA-VIRGIN OLIVE OIL

6 LANGOUSTINES WITH HEADS AND SHELLS

2 SMALL SWEET ITALIAN GREEN PEPPERS OR 1 SMALL GREEN BELL PEPPER, CUT INTO ½-INCH/1.25-CM PIECES

1 POUND/455 G SMALL CUTTLEFISH OR SQUID, CLEANED AND CUT INTO ½-INCH/1.25-CM PIECES

18 FRESH WHOLE LARGE SHRIMP WITH HEADS AND SHELLS

3 RIPE MEDIUM TOMATOES, HALVED CROSSWISE, SEEDED, AND GRATED (SEE PAGE 339)

1 PINCH SAFFRON THREADS, DRY-TOASTED AND GROUND (SEE PAGE 340)

1 TEASPOON SPANISH PIMENTÓN DULCE (SWEET PAPRIKA)

7 CUPS/1.7 L FISH STOCK (PAGE 335) OR WATER

3 CUPS/600 G BOMBA RICE OR ANOTHER SHORT- OR MEDIUM-GRAIN SPANISH RICE (SEE NOTE)

1. Purge the clams of any sand by soaking them in salty water following the directions on page 341. Discard any with broken shells.

continued

2. In a saucepan, add the clams, cover with 1 cup/ 240 ml water, and bring to a boil. Cover the pot and cook, shaking from time to time, until the clams have opened, about 5 minutes. Transfer the clams to a bowl with a slotted spoon. Filter the liquid and reserve. Discard any clams that did not open. Twist off the empty half of each clam and discard.

3. Steam the mussels: Place them in a saucepan with ½ cup/60 ml water and bring to a boil over high heat. Lower the heat, cover the pot, and simmer, shaking the pot from time to time, until the mussels have opened, 3 to 5 minutes. Remove from the heat. Drain, reserving the liquid. (Strain and set aside.) Discard any mussels that did not open. Remove the meat from each shell; discard the shells.

4. In a 16- to 18-inch/40- to 45-cm paella pan, heat the olive oil over medium heat. Add the langoustines and cook, turning over until pink, about 5 minutes. Transfer to a platter. Add the green peppers and cuttlefish and cook until tender, 8 to 10 minutes. Add the shrimp and cook, turning over once, until opaque, 4 to 5 minutes. (Remove any stray legs or antennae from the pan and discard.) Add the tomatoes and cook until soft and pulpy, about 10 minutes. Tip in some of the reserved liquid from the clams to keep it moist. Stir in the saffron and pimentón.

5. Pour the stock into the pan and bring the liquid to a boil over high heat. When the liquid comes to a boil, sprinkle the rice around the pan. With a wooden spoon, check that the rice is evenly distributed and that the grains are below the surface of the liquid. Do not stir again.

6. Cook uncovered for 10 minutes over high heat. Arrange the reserved langoustines across the top of the rice. Reduce the heat to low and cook uncovered for 8 to 10 minutes more, until the liquid is absorbed and the rice grains are tender but still have an al dente bite to them. If all the liquid has evaporated and the rice is still not done, shake the reserved liquid from the clams (and, if needed, from the mussels) tablespoon by tablespoon over the rice where needed and cook for an additional few minutes.

7. Remove the paella from the heat, cross wooden spoons over top, cover with paper towels, and let rest for 5 minutes to allow the rice—particularly the grains on top—to finish cooking and the starches to firm up.

8. Carry the paella to the table and serve from the pan.

NOTE: Spanish Bomba rice is a highly absorbent short-grain Spanish variety. It is found at many supermarkets with a decent international section, as well as numerous specialty stores. See Sources, page 345, for where to look. The best substitute is the Italian rice Carnaroli. Alternatively use CalRiso, Calrose, or Japanese short-grain rice. For moister rice dishes (but not paellas), use the superfine-grade Italian varieties such as Arborio or Vialone Nano.

UTENSILS

THE PAELLA PAN

The iconic rice dish paella is named for the pan in which it is cooked. (In Catalan and Valencian, *paella* means "pan." The word derives from the Latin *patella*.) The wide, flat, and thin pan allows for the rice to cook evenly without stirring, the liquid to better evaporate, and for as much as possible of the rice to come in contact with the flavors in the bottom of the pan. The depth of the finished rice remains roughly the same (no more than ¾ inch/2 cm) no matter how many people the dish serves—the pan just gets wider. And wider.

Pan sizes range from the not-that-small to the gigantic, though the most common, and useful, sizes are 14 inches/36 cm for 3 to 4 people, 16 inches/40 cm for 4 to 6, 18 inches/45 cm for 6, and 20 inches/50 cm for 8. Note that the serving recommendations listed on most pans is woefully understated. A pan that says "Serves 6" on the packaging is more likely to serve closer to 3 or 4.

The most typical (and least expensive) paella pan is made of polished carbon steel, which quickly responds to the changes in heat. When the pan is removed from the heat, the rice stops cooking, which is exactly what you want to happen. (This pan also gives a slight and lovely minerally tang to the rice.) Stainless-steel pans work well for those who use them infrequently, as they store better. (Carbon-steel pans need to be either rubbed with oil or dusted with flour after use to keep from oxidizing.) Enameled-steel pans are an excellent choice between these—quicker to respond to heat changes than stainless steel, yet easier to maintain than carbon steel ones. Avoid cast iron, copper, and nonstick pans.

If you don't have a paella pan, I find the best substitution to be two very large skillets. Cook the sofrito base in a single skillet, transfer half to a second one, add liquid to each, bring to a boil, and then add the rice, cooking simultaneously. This is more preferable than crowding the pan and having a layer of rice that is too thick and will not cook evenly nor as intended.

The most evocative and traditional way of preparing a paella is over embers. The smoke will waft over the rice and perfume it in aromatic touches, giving it an incomparable final flavor. It is also inherently the most festive way to cook paella. Some thoughts:

- Grill-top recipes can be started on the stovetop and finished outside over a grill. Sauté the vegetables and meats or seafood in a very large skillet (or two, if needed) on the stove, transfer them to the paella pan on the hot grill outside, add the liquid, and carry on with the recipe. This not only gives better control when cooking the meats, but reduces grilling time significantly—thus staving off some worries of the coals having enough heat to finish the rice.

- You can either cook with kindling in a fire pit or similar space, or else on a barbecue using charcoal or gas.

- For kindling, use a stand or a couple of bricks to hold the paella pan above the flames.

- The rice takes about 18 or so minutes to cook; the first 10 minutes are over a hot fire, the remainder over a low one. If using logs, they should be burned down by then. If not, pull some out of the fire to reduce the heat to low.

- If using a grill, be sure that it is at least as large as the paella pan.

Rice colored black from the ink of squid or cuttlefish is a specialty of the Empordà region of the Costa Brava. But the ink here does more than offer its dark color. It also gives the rice a tight, almost tinny sea flavor as well. Mercury-colored ink sacks are found beneath the tentacles of cuttlefish and squid; remove them carefully when cleaning—see page 342 for instructions—or ask your fishmonger to do so. Certain Asian and Italian markets sell packets of preserved squid ink, as well as the Spanish specialty stores listed in the Sources, page 345. They generally come in 4-gram packets (slightly more than 1/8 ounce). Two packets are enough for this rice.

Perhaps an even more original twist to this traditional dish than the ink is the addition of pieces of pork ribs to add an almost baroque range of flavors. *Allioli*–a garlic emulsion–is an obligatory accompaniment.

BLACK RICE WITH ALLIOLI

ARROZ NEGRO CON ALLIOLI

SERVES 4

3 TABLESPOONS EXTRA-VIRGIN OLIVE OIL

8 FRESH WHOLE JUMBO SHRIMP OR PRAWNS WITH HEADS AND SHELLS

1 MEDIUM ONION, FINELY CHOPPED

½ RED BELL PEPPER, CUT INTO 1-INCH-/1.25-CM-SQUARE PIECES

1 POUND/455 G CUT-UP CUTTLEFISH OR SQUID STEAKS

4 RIPE MEDIUM TOMATOES, HALVED CROSSWISE, SEEDED, AND GRATED (SEE PAGE 339)

SALT

6 CUPS/1.4 L FISH STOCK (PAGE 335)

¼ OUNCE/235 ML SQUID (CALAMARI) INK

2 GARLIC CLOVES, MINCED

1 TABLESPOON MINCED FRESH FLAT-LEAF PARSLEY

1 TEASPOON SPANISH PIMENTÓN DULCE (SWEET PAPRIKA)

2 PINCHES SAFFRON THREADS (ABOUT 20 TOTAL), DRY-TOASTED AND GROUND (SEE PAGE 340)

2 CUPS/400 G BOMBA RICE OR ANOTHER SHORT- OR MEDIUM-GRAIN SPANISH RICE (SEE NOTE, PAGE 142)

ALLIOLI (PAGE 337)

1. In a large cazuela, heavy casserole, Dutch oven, large sauté pan, or deep skillet, heat the olive oil over medium-low heat. Add the shrimp and cook, turning over until pink, about 5 minutes. Transfer to a platter. (Remove any stray legs or antennae from the pan and discard.)

2. In the same pan, prepare a sofrito: Add the onion and cook until soft and translucent, 8 to 10 minutes. Add the bell pepper and cook, stirring frequently, for another 5 minutes. Add the cuttlefish and cook for 5 minutes, stirring frequently. Finally, add the tomatoes and 2 pinches of salt, and cook, stirring from time to time, until the tomato has darkened and is pasty, 10 to 15 minutes. Moisten with a spoonful of water if needed to keep it from drying out.

3. Meanwhile, in a large saucepan, heat the stock over medium heat. Stir in the ink. Cover the pan and keep hot until ready to add.

continued

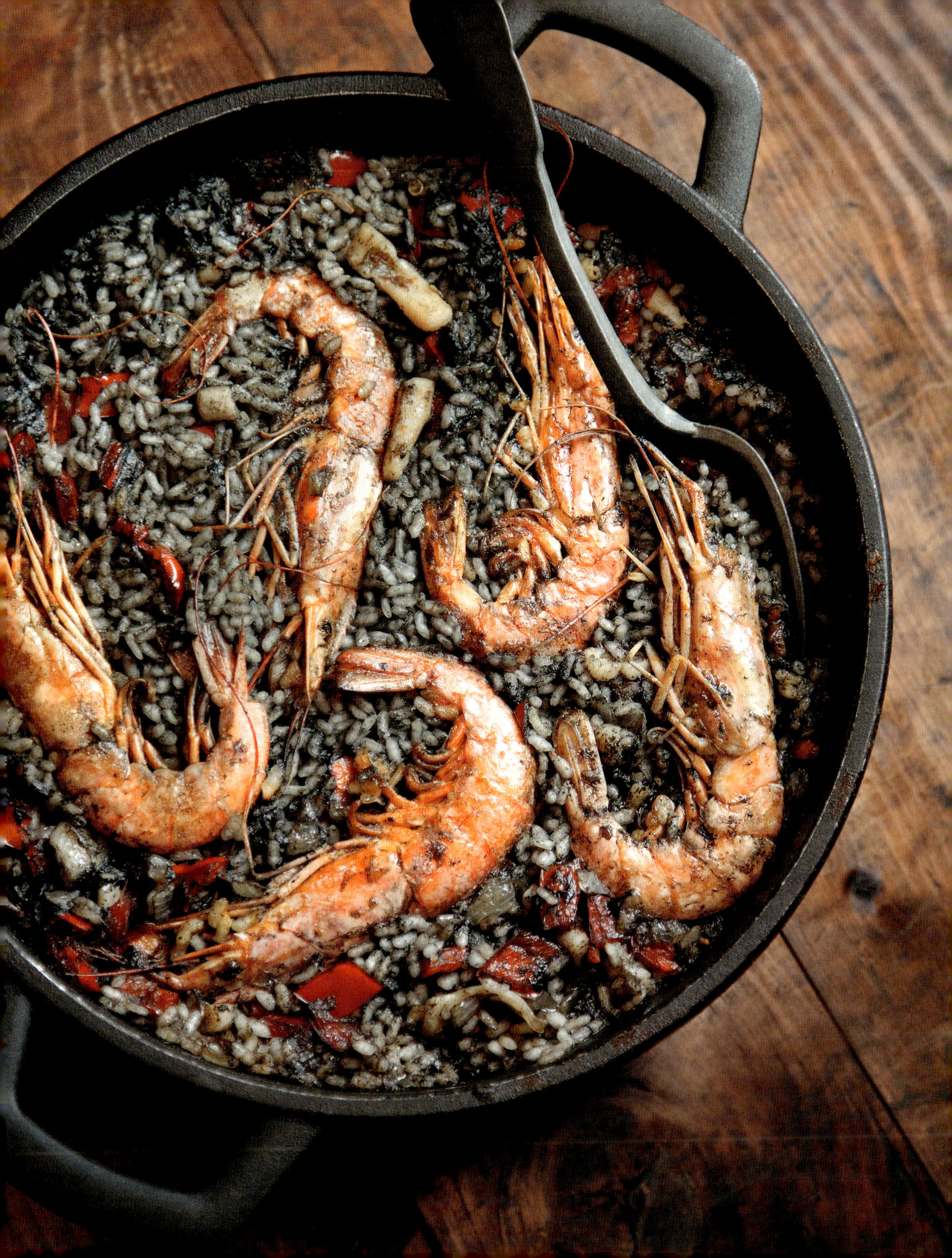

4. Prepare a picada with the garlic, parsley, and 1 to 2 tablespoons of the simmering stock, following the directions on page 39.

5. When the sofrito is ready, add the pimentón and saffron, stir, and then pour in the stock. Bring to a boil over high heat, add the rice and stir in the picada. Cook uncovered over high heat for 10 minutes, stirring from time to time. Lay the reserved shrimp across the top of the rice, reduce the heat to low, and cook for another 7 to 8 minutes, or until the rice grains are tender but still have an al dente bite to them.

6. Remove the rice from the heat and let rest for a few minutes. Serve with the allioli on the side to dollop on the rice as desired.

INGREDIENTS

VALENCIAN RICE
arroz de Valencia

Just south of Valencia lies the Albufera, a freshwater lagoon separated from the Mediterranean by a thin string of dunes. The name comes from the Arabic word *al-buhaira*, a diminutive of "the sea" (*al-bhar*). It was along the fringes of this lagoon that the Moors introduced rice into Spain, not long after they conquered the peninsula in the early eighth century. Valencia was under Moorish rule for five centuries, and when Jaume I triumphantly entered the city in 1238 during the lengthy Christian *reconquista* of Spain, his army found the Albufera fringed with rice and, growing in nearby fields, oranges, lemons, artichokes, and eggplants. With the rice paddies extending to the edge of the city, according to Lourdes March in her authoritative *El libro de la paella y de los arroces* (The Book of Paella and of Rice Dishes), the new ruler dictated laws that limited the cultivation of rice to the area around the Albufera to avoid *paludismo* (what we now call malaria), which was blamed on the flooded fields. The Spanish word *arroz* (rice) and the Catalan and Valencian *arròs* both come from the Arabic *ar-ruzz*.

Rice does grow elsewhere in Spain—most notably, quality-wise, in the Ebro Delta, where the fields grid the delta that juts into the Mediterranean like an arrow; and in Calasparra, in the low mountains of northwest Murcia, where the paddies have moving (as opposed to stagnant) water, forming a slightly harder grain.

Yet it is this area around the Albufera that, although only harvesting about one fifth of Spain's total crop, remains the most important rice-growing area in the country. Sueca, Sollana, Cullera, and Silla are four of the best-known rice towns. The Spanish government has bestowed protective *Denominación de Origen* (D.O.) status on Arroz de Valencia. Under this seal, farmers can produce just three varieties of rice grains: medium-grain Senia and Bahía and short-grain Bomba. (There are more than 5,000 varieties of rice—*Oryza sativa*—around the globe.)

Like the Senia and Bahía, Bomba is a japonica type of rice. The stubby, short grain has a dense concentration of starch that allows for a high level of absorption. For the Spanish way of cooking rice, this is key, as the grains merely act as vehicles for the flavors in the pan. The grains themselves of these varieties taste identical, but Bomba has the advantage of being slightly more resistant to "opening" and losing its consistency if slightly overcooked. For this reason, I recommend it for those who infrequently cook Spanish rice dishes.

SOUPY RICE WITH LOBSTER

ARROZ CALDOSO DE BOGAVANTE

SERVES 4

This is one of the country's most spectacular dishes and holds a prominent place in many seafood and rice restaurants and in homes, including ours. It incorporates the best of the Spanish Mediterranean kitchen, from a sofrito and a picada to a bold fish stock and ñora peppers.

There is a difference between the European lobster and the American one, and it's not just where fishermen catch them. The *bogavante europeo* has some bluish green to the body, sometimes speckled with browns and oranges, while the *bogavante americano* is redder and a bit larger.

- 4 TABLESPOONS EXTRA-VIRGIN OLIVE OIL
- 2 LEEKS, WHITE AND TENDER GREEN PARTS ONLY, ROUGHLY CHOPPED
- 2 CARROTS, CUT CROSSWISE INTO 10 OR SO PIECES
- 2 POUNDS/910 G SMALL SOUP FISH OR ASSORTED HEADS AND BONES OF FIRM, WHITE-FLESHED NON-OILY FISH
- 1 CELERY STALK, CUT CROSSWISE INTO THIRDS
- 12 SPRIGS FRESH FLAT-LEAF PARSLEY, PLUS 1 TABLESPOON MINCED FRESH FLAT-LEAF PARSLEY
- 8 BLACK PEPPERCORNS
- SALT
- ½ CUP/120 ML DRY WHITE WINE
- 2 SMALL DRIED ÑORA PEPPERS OR ANOTHER SWEET, MILD DRIED RED PEPPER (SEE INGREDIENT NOTE, PAGE 16)
- 1 FRESH LOBSTER, ABOUT 2 POUNDS/910 G
- FRESHLY GROUND BLACK PEPPER
- 2 GARLIC CLOVES, PEELED
- ½ MEDIUM ONION, FINELY CHOPPED
- 4 OUNCES/115 G SQUID (CALAMARI) OR CUTTLEFISH, CUT INTO ½-INCH-/1.25-CM-SQUARE PIECES
- ¼ GREEN BELL PEPPER, CUT INTO ½-INCH-/1.25-CM-SQUARE PIECES
- 2 RIPE MEDIUM TOMATOES, HALVED CROSSWISE, SEEDED, AND GRATED (SEE PAGE 339)
- 8 UNSALTED TOASTED ALMONDS WITHOUT SKINS
- 8 TOASTED HAZELNUTS WITHOUT SKINS
- ½ TEASPOON SPANISH PIMENTÓN DULCE (SWEET PAPRIKA)
- 2 PINCHES SAFFRON THREADS (ABOUT 20 TOTAL), DRY-TOASTED AND GROUND (SEE PAGE 340)
- 1⅓ CUPS/265 G BOMBA RICE OR ANOTHER SHORT- OR MEDIUM-GRAIN SPANISH RICE (SEE NOTE, PAGE 142)

1. In a stockpot or other large pot, heat 1 tablespoon of the olive oil over medium-high heat. Add the leeks and carrots and cook, stirring frequently, until they begin to brown and release their juices, about 5 minutes. Add the fish, celery, parsley sprigs, peppercorns, and 2 pinches of salt. Pour in the wine, stir, let the alcohol burn off for 1 minute, and then add 8 cups/2 L water. Bring to a boil, reduce the heat to medium-low, and cook, partly covered, for 30 minutes. Remove from the heat and cover the pot.

2. Meanwhile, cut the ñora peppers open and discard the seeds. Place the peppers in a bowl, cover with hot water, and soak for 20 minutes. Drain. Using a coffee spoon, scrape the soft pulp from inside the skin and reserve. Discard the skins.

3. Clean and cut the lobster in half lengthwise down the middle. If it is female, reserve the red roe for the picada. Season the lobster generously with salt and pepper.

4. In a Dutch oven or another heavy pot, heat 2 tablespoons olive oil over medium heat. Add the lobster and cook for 2 minutes, flesh-side down, then for another 2 minutes, shell-side down. Transfer to a platter. Trim away the antennae and appendages and add them to the stock. Set the rest of the lobster aside.

5. Add the remaining 1 tablespoon of olive oil to the pot and prepare a sofrito: Add the garlic and cook over medium heat until golden and fragrant, about 1 minute; remove and reserve. Add the onion and cook until soft and translucent, 8 to 10 minutes. Add the squid and bell pepper, and cook, stirring frequently, for another 5 minutes. Add the tomatoes and 2 pinches of salt, and cook, stirring from time to time, until the tomato has darkened and is pasty, 10 to 15 minutes.

6. Meanwhile, cut the lobster tail crosswise in half with a heavy knife or kitchen scissors, leaving the meat attached to the shell. Crack the large claws slightly or "mark" them with the knife so they remain intact but the meat will be easily accessible when served.

7. Prepare a picada with the reserved ñora pulp, garlic, and lobster roe (if there was any) the almonds, hazelnuts, and the minced parsley, and 1 tablespoon of stock, following the directions on page 39.

8. Strain the stock through a colander, pressing out any remaining liquid from the fish and vegetables.

9. When the sofrito is ready, sprinkle in the pimentón and saffron, stir, and let the flavors meld for a few seconds. Add 6 cups/1.4 L of the stock. Increase the heat and, when the liquid reaches a boil, add the rice and the pieces of lobster along with any juices from the platter.

10. Cook uncovered over medium-high heat for 10 minutes, gently stirring occasionally. Stir in the picada, reduce the heat to low, and cook for a final 4 to 6 minutes, or until the rice grains are nearly tender but still have a definite al dente bite to them. Tip in more stock if needed to keep it nice and soupy.

11. Remove the pot from the heat and let sit covered for 3 to 4 minutes. Ladle into bowls and serve immediately.

SOUPY RICE WITH FREE-RANGE CHICKEN

ARROZ CALDOSO DE POLLO DE CORRAL

SERVES 4

This is a delightful dish for a rainy evening. It uses corn-fed pollo de corral *(free-range chickens). These tend to be generously sized, weighing up to 8 pounds/3½ kg, and carry the flavors of the past—those flavors that have disappeared from certain ingredients in the rush to grow them too quickly. In autumn, add a handful of mushrooms, or in spring, some trimmed artichokes or fresh-shucked peas or fava beans.*

2 WHOLE FREE-RANGE CHICKEN LEGS

3 TABLESPOONS EXTRA-VIRGIN OLIVE OIL

1 MEDIUM ONION, FINELY CHOPPED

1 SWEET ITALIAN GREEN PEPPER OR ½ SMALL GREEN BELL PEPPER, FINELY CHOPPED

2 RIPE MEDIUM TOMATOES, HALVED CROSSWISE, SEEDED, AND GRATED (SEE PAGE 339)

SALT

3 GARLIC CLOVES, MINCED

1 CUP/240 ML DRY WHITE WINE

12 UNSALTED TOASTED ALMONDS WITHOUT SKINS

1 TABLESPOON MINCED FRESH FLAT-LEAF PARSLEY

1⅓ CUPS/265 G BOMBA RICE OR ANOTHER SHORT- OR MEDIUM-GRAIN SPANISH RICE (SEE NOTE, PAGE 142)

1 PINCH SAFFRON THREADS, DRY-TOASTED AND GROUND (SEE PAGE 340)

1. Remove the skin from the chicken. Split the legs into drumsticks and thighs, and then cut each in half crosswise through the bone to get eight bone-in pieces. Pick out any small bone shards.

2. In a Dutch oven or another heavy pot, heat the olive oil over medium heat. Add the chicken, onion, green pepper, and tomatoes. Season with salt and cook until the chicken is browned, about 12 minutes. Stir in the garlic and cook until fragrant, about 1 minute. Pour in the wine and simmer for 10 minutes. Cover with 8 cups/2 L water, bring to a low boil, lower the heat, and gently simmer uncovered for about 45 minutes, until the chicken is tender and the liquid has reduced by about one-third.

3. Meanwhile, prepare a picada with the almonds, parsley, and 1 tablespoon of the simmering liquid, following the directions on page 39.

4. Sprinkle in the rice and the saffron and stir in the picada. Cook uncovered until the rice grains are nearly tender but still have a definite al dente bite to them, 14 to 16 minutes, depending on the rice. Add more water if needed to keep it nice and soupy.

5. Remove the pot from the heat and let sit covered for 3 to 4 minutes. Ladle into bowls and serve immediately.

MOUNTAIN-STYLE RICE WITH CHICKEN AND FRESH SAUSAGE

ARROZ DE MONTAÑA

SERVES 4

This moist rice dish, common in the mountainous parts of Spain, is sometimes called *arroz a la cazuela*, after the round terra-cotta casserole (*cazuela*) used to prepare it. Sometimes it has chicken or fresh sausage, and not infrequently some pork ribs are added. I like stirring in a pounded picada of nuts to thicken the dish slightly and give it an earthy backbone.

- 4 BONE-IN CHICKEN THIGHS, ABOUT 18 OUNCES/510 G TOTAL
- SALT AND FRESHLY GROUND BLACK PEPPER
- 3 TABLESPOONS EXTRA-VIRGIN OLIVE OIL
- 2 GARLIC CLOVES, PEELED
- 8 OUNCES/225 G FRESH PORK SAUSAGE, SQUEEZED FROM THE CASING AND PINCHED INTO MARBLE-SIZE PIECES (SEE NOTE, PAGE 156)
- 1 MEDIUM ONION, FINELY CHOPPED
- 3 RIPE MEDIUM TOMATOES, HALVED CROSSWISE, SEEDED, AND GRATED (SEE PAGE 339)
- ½ TEASPOON SPANISH PIMENTÓN DULCE (SWEET PAPRIKA)
- 1 SMALL PINCH SAFFRON THREADS, DRY-TOASTED AND GROUND (SEE PAGE 340)
- 7 CUPS/1.7 L LIGHT CHICKEN STOCK (PAGE 336) OR WATER
- 12 UNSALTED TOASTED HAZELNUTS OR ALMONDS (OR A MIX) WITHOUT SKINS
- 1 TABLESPOON MINCED FRESH FLAT-LEAF PARSLEY
- 2 CUPS/400 G BOMBA RICE OR ANOTHER SHORT- OR MEDIUM-GRAIN SPANISH RICE (SEE NOTE, PAGE 142)

1. Remove the skin from the chicken and trim any excess fat. Cut the thighs into two pieces each, keeping the knife blade along the bone, leaving the bone attached to one of the pieces. Generously season with salt and pepper.

2. In a cazuela, heavy casserole, large sauté pan, or deep skillet, heat the olive oil over medium heat. Add the garlic and cook until golden and fragrant, about 1 minute. Remove and reserve.

3. Add the chicken and sausage and cook, stirring frequently, until browned, about 5 minutes. Transfer with a slotted spoon to a platter.

4. In the same pan, prepare a sofrito with the onion and tomatoes, following the directions on page 39. Stir in the pimentón and saffron, return the chicken and sausage to the pan, and turn over to coat. Add 1 cup/240 ml of the stock. Cook over medium-low heat for 20 minutes, stirring from time to time, until the liquid has mostly reduced and the chicken is quite tender.

5. Prepare a picada with the reserved garlic, the hazelnuts, parsley, and 1 tablespoon of liquid from the pan, following the directions on page 39.

6. Add the remaining 6 cups/1.4 ml stock to the pan and bring to a boil. Add the rice and cook uncovered over medium-high heat for 10 minutes. Stir in the picada, reduce the heat to low, and cook uncovered for a final 7 to 8 minutes, or until the rice grains are tender but still have an al dente bite to them.

7. Remove from the heat and let rest for 2 to 3 minutes before serving.

FIDEOS IN THE CAZUELA WITH PORK RIBS

FIDEOS A LA CAZUELA

SERVES 4

Fideos are short, thin strands of pasta that are usually cooked like Spanish rice—that is, cooked to absorb the flavors of the pan. Along the Mediterranean coast, you find a couple of different fideo dishes, including the famous seafood version that is prepared in a wide paella pan (facing page). This, though, is an inland version, made with thicker noodles and the pork-rich flavors of the countryside.

1¼ POUNDS/570 G PORK BABY BACK RIBS, INDIVIDUALLY SEPARATED AND CHOPPED INTO 1½-INCH/4-CM LENGTHS

SALT AND FRESHLY GROUND BLACK PEPPER

3 TABLESPOONS EXTRA-VIRGIN OLIVE OIL

1 MEDIUM ONION, FINELY CHOPPED

3 RIPE MEDIUM TOMATOES, HALVED CROSSWISE, SEEDED, AND GRATED (SEE PAGE 339)

1 TEASPOON SPANISH PIMENTÓN DULCE (SWEET PAPRIKA)

1 BAY LEAF

1 GARLIC CLOVE, PEELED

1 TABLESPOON MINCED FRESH FLAT-LEAF PARSLEY

8 UNSALTED TOASTED ALMONDS WITHOUT SKINS

1 SLICE BAGUETTE, DAY OLD OR TOASTED

1 POUND/455 G THICK FIDEOS (SEE NOTE)

½ CUP/70 G FRESH SHUCKED PEAS OR FROZEN PETIT POIS (OPTIONAL)

ALLIOLI (PAGE 337)

1. Generously season the ribs with salt and pepper. In a cazuela, heavy casserole, large sauté pan, or deep skillet, heat the olive oil over medium heat. Add the ribs and brown, turning from time to time, about 10 minutes. Reduce the heat to medium-low, add the onion, and cook until it begins to soften and turn pale, about 5 minutes. Add the tomatoes and 2 tablespoons water and cook, stirring frequently, until the tomatoes are dark and pasty, 10 to 15 minutes. Add 1½ cups/360 ml water, the pimentón, and the bay leaf and simmer uncovered over medium-low heat for 30 to 45 minutes, or until the pork is quite tender. Tip in a bit more water during cooking if needed to keep the sauce loose.

2. Prepare a picada with the garlic, parsley, almonds, bread, and 1 tablespoon of the simmering liquid from the pan, following the directions on page 39.

3. Add 6 cups/1.4 L water to the cazuela, increase the heat to medium-high, and bring to a boil. Add the fideos and peas (if using) and cook uncovered until the fideos are al dente, 12 to 15 minutes (follow the time indicated on the pasta package). About halfway through cooking, stir in the picada, making sure that it completely dissolves into the sauce. Add in a touch more water if it threatens to dry out.

4. Remove from the heat, cover with paper towels, and let sit for 3 minutes or so before serving with the allioli on the side.

NOTE: Use No. 2 fideos or break or cut long, thin pasta, such as spaghettini, vermicelli, or tagliarini, into 1-inch/2.5-cm lengths.

SEAFOOD FIDEUÀ WITH ALLIOLI

FIDEUÀ AMB ALLIOLI

SERVES 4 TO 6

Just as short-grain rice absorbs and cooks in the flavorful broth of the paella, the thin pasta noodles here do the same. As one story of the dish's conception goes, a century or so ago a cook on a fishing boat from Gandia, south of Valencia, forgot to stock the larder with rice and instead added small fideos to the paella pan for lunch.

4 TABLESPOONS EXTRA-VIRGIN OLIVE OIL

12 MEDIUM FRESH SHRIMP, PEELED OR WITH HEADS AND SHELLS

4 TO 8 FRESH PRAWNS OR JUMBO SHRIMP WITH HEADS AND SHELLS

4 OUNCES/155 G THICK FILLETS MONKFISH, PORGY, BREAM, OR ANOTHER FIRM, WHITE-FLESHED FISH

8 CUPS/2 L FISH STOCK (PAGE 335; PREPARED WITHOUT THYME)

8 OUNCES/225 G CLEANED CUTTLEFISH OR SQUID (CALAMARI), CUT INTO PIECES

2 GARLIC CLOVES, MINCED

3 RIPE TOMATOES, HALVED CROSSWISE, SEEDED, AND GRATED (SEE PAGE 339)

½ TEASPOON SPANISH PIMENTÓN DULCE (SWEET PAPRIKA)

1 PINCH SAFFRON THREADS, DRY-TOASTED AND GROUND (SEE PAGE 340)

1 POUND/455 G MEDIUM-THICK (NO. 2) FIDEOS (SEE NOTE, FACING PAGE)

SALT

ALLIOLI (PAGE 337)

1. In a 15- to 16-inch/28- to 30-cm paella pan or very large skillet, heat the olive oil over medium heat. Add the shrimp and prawns and cook, turning over until pink, 3 to 5 minutes. Transfer to a platter. (Remove any stray legs or antennae from the pan and discard.) Add the fish and cook until opaque, about 5 minutes.

2. Strain the stock into a clean saucepan and bring to a boil. Reduce the heat, cover the pan, and keep at a low boil.

3. Add the cuttlefish to the pan and cook, stirring frequently, until it has browned and released its liquid, about 5 minutes. Add the garlic, cook for about 20 seconds until fragrant, stirring continually. Add the tomatoes and about ½ cup/100 ml of the stock, and cook until dark and pulpy, about 10 minutes. Stir in the pimentón and saffron, sprinkle in the fideos, and add the reserved shrimp. (Don't return the prawns yet.) Skin and debone the fish, break into large pieces, and add.

4. Pour over the remaining 7½ cups/1.8 L stock and season with salt. Cook uncovered for 4 minutes. Arrange the prawns across the fideos, and then continue to cook uncovered until the fideos are tender and the liquid has been largely absorbed by the pasta, 6 to 8 minutes.

5. Remove from the heat, cover with paper towels, and let sit for 5 minutes or so. The tips of the pasta on the top layer should curl slightly upward. Serve with the allioli.

NOTE: Use No. 2 fideos or break or cut long, thin pasta, such as spaghettini, vermicelli, or tagliarini, into 1-inch/2.5-cm lengths.

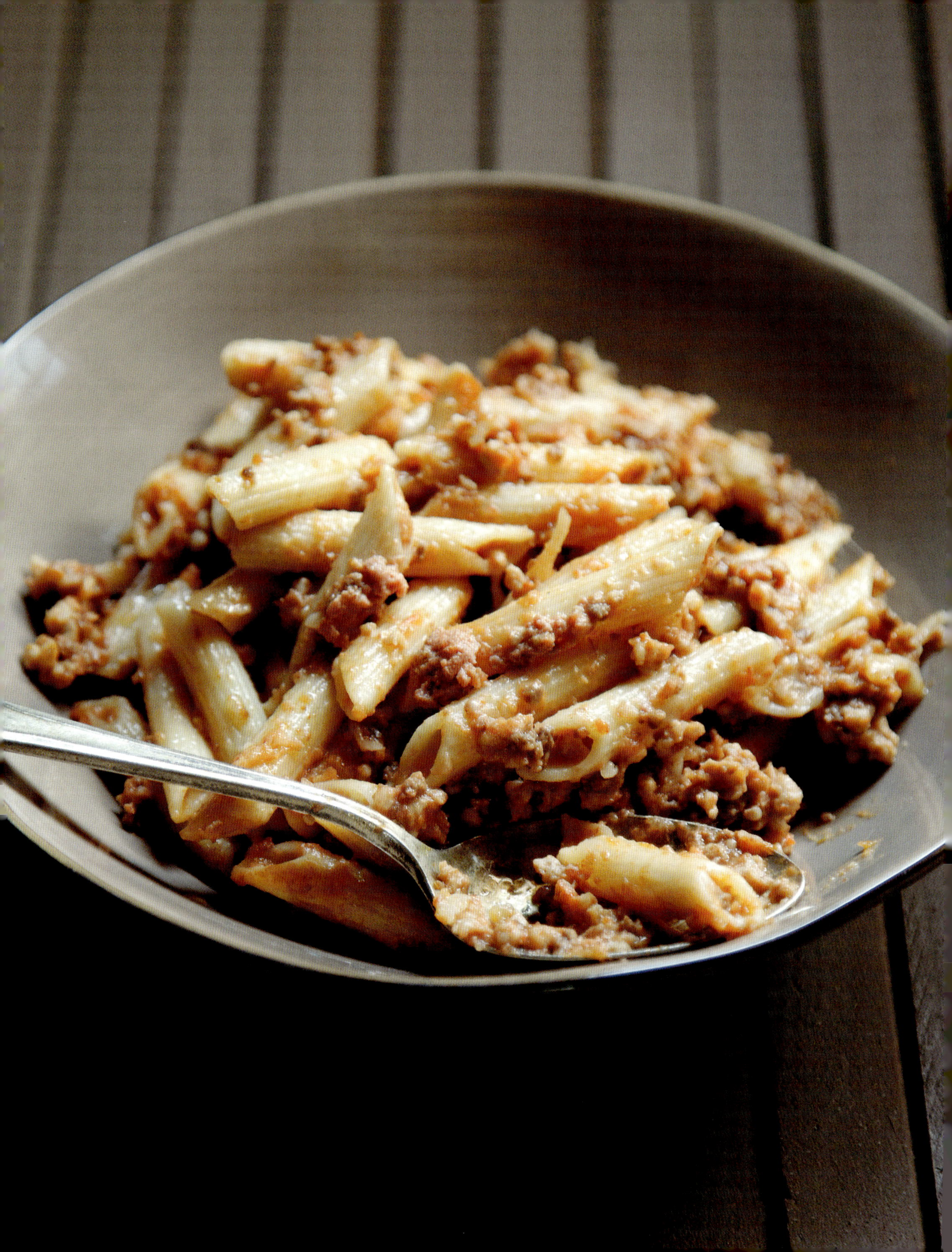

PYRENEES MOUNTAIN–STYLE PENNE PASTA
WITH GROUND MEAT AND PÂTÉ

MACARRONES DE LOS PIRINEOS

SERVES 4

The Pyrenees mountain range divides the Iberian Peninsula from continental Europe, Spain from France. Running more than 300 miles/nearly 500 km in length, with peaks rising to more than 11,000 feet/3,400 m, the range stretches across the north of Spain from the Bay of Biscay on the Atlantic Ocean to the Mediterranean Sea. This variation of macarrones comes from the eastern part of the range. The addition of pâté—use a smooth, spreadable type, not coarse country-style—gives the pasta dish a satiny, almost creamy finish. A handful of sliced and seared wild mushrooms blended in at the very end makes an excellent autumn addition. In winter, you find this on tables after a long walk in the hills or a day on the ski slopes.

2 TABLESPOONS EXTRA-VIRGIN OLIVE OIL
1 MEDIUM ONION, FINELY CHOPPED
8 OUNCES/225 G GROUND BEEF AND/OR PORK
1 CUP/240 ML TOMATO SAUCE
SALT
¼ CUP/50 G SMOOTH PÂTÉ
14 OUNCES/400 G PENNE OR ANOTHER TUBULAR PASTA
1 CUP/70 G LOOSELY PACKED, FRESHLY GRATED MILD PASTA CHEESE, SUCH AS MOZZARELLA

1. In a large skillet or sauté pan, heat the olive oil over medium heat, add the onion, and cook until soft and translucent, 8 to 10 minutes. Add the meat and cook, stirring frequently, until browned, about 5 minutes. Add the tomato sauce and season with salt. Bring to a simmer and cook, stirring occasionally, until the tomatoes have darkened and the sauce has thickened, 10 to 15 minutes. Add a small amount of water if the sauce needs more time to sweeten. Remove the pan from the heat and stir in the pâté until dissolved.

2. Meanwhile, in a large pot, bring 4 quarts/4 L water to a boil and season with salt. Add the pasta and cook, stirring from time to time to keep the pasta from clumping together, until al dente (follow the time indicated on the pasta package).

3. Drain the pasta in a colander but do not rinse. Shake off any water that clings to the pasta. Return the pasta to the pot and blend with the sauce and half of the cheese until thoroughly coated and the cheese has melted. Serve immediately with the remaining cheese on the side to add as desired.

PENNE PASTA WITH TOMATOES AND FRESH SAUSAGE AU GRATIN

MACARRONES GRATINADOS

SERVES 4

This is the mac and cheese of Spain, the dish that, as every Spanish grandmother (and restaurant cook) knows, kids love and will be sure to finish. And perhaps because it's a kids' favorite—kids grow up after all—it's beloved by adults, too. To offer more savory, robust flavors, cut the nutmeg and cinnamon and add some finely chopped pieces of Spanish chorizo to the sofrito.

3 TABLESPOONS EXTRA-VIRGIN OLIVE OIL

8 OUNCES/225 G FRESH PORK SAUSAGE, SQUEEZED FROM THE CASING AND PINCHED INTO MARBLE-SIZE PIECES (SEE NOTE)

1 MEDIUM ONION, FINELY CHOPPED

4 RIPE MEDIUM TOMATOES, HALVED CROSSWISE, SEEDED, AND GRATED (SEE PAGE 339)

1 OR 2 PINCHES FRESHLY GRATED NUTMEG

1 OR 2 PINCHES GROUND CINNAMON

SALT

14 OUNCES/400 G PENNE OR ANOTHER TUBULAR PASTA

1 TABLESPOON BUTTER, CUT INTO SMALL PIECES

1 CUP/70 G LOOSELY PACKED, FRESHLY GRATED MILD PASTA CHEESE, SUCH AS MOZZARELLA

1. In a cazuela, heavy casserole, large sauté pan, or deep skillet, heat the olive oil over medium heat. Add the sausage and brown, about 5 minutes. Transfer with a slotted spoon to a plate. In the same oil, prepare a sofrito with the onion and tomatoes, following the directions on page 39.

2. When the sofrito is ready, stir in the nutmeg and cinnamon, season with salt, return the sausage and any juices to the pan, and add ¼ cup/60 ml water to loosen the sauce. Cook for 5 minutes, or until the sausage is hot and cooked through.

3. Meanwhile, in a large pot, bring 4 quarts/4 L water to a boil and season with salt. Add the pasta and cook, stirring from time to time to keep the pasta from clumping together, until al dente (follow the time indicated on the pasta package).

4. Meanwhile, preheat the broiler.

5. Drain the pasta in a colander but do not rinse. Shake off any water that clings to the pasta. Return the pasta to the pot, spoon over the sofrito, and turn to blend well. Transfer to a large ovenproof baking dish. Place the butter around the top and evenly sprinkle over the cheese. Broil until the cheese is melted and golden, 2 to 3 minutes. Serve immediately.

NOTE: Be sure the pork sausages are not sweetened breakfast links.

Though these days it's considered a local dish, this is one of the plates that clearly shows the influence of Italians and Swiss working in Barcelona in the nineteenth century. That began, according to gastro-historian Néstor Luján, with the celebrated restaurant El Suizo, found along Barcelona's Las Ramblas. *Canelones* went from the public—the finest restaurants of the time—to the private—home cooking. And, almost uniquely, it made the reverse trek of many dishes, moving from the city to the countryside, where canelones are now considered a supreme country classic.

Canelones are traditionally prepared for San Esteban (December 26, St. Stephen's Day), and for many families are an unfailing part of the holidays. My mother-in-law makes a couple of trays of them—some eighty-five or ninety canelones—for the family every year. The labor is intense. But she would never give it up.

CANNELLONI STUFFED WITH MEAT

CANELONES DE CARNE

MAKES 20 CANNELLONI; SERVES 4 TO 5

FILLING

2 TABLESPOONS EXTRA-VIRGIN OLIVE OIL

8 OUNCES/225 G CHICKEN BREAST, CUT INTO 2 LARGE PIECES

8 OUNCES/225 G PORK LOIN, PREFERABLY BUTT END, CUT INTO PIECES ABOUT 1 X 1½ X 3 TO 4 INCHES/2.5 X 4 X 7.5 TO 10 CM

4 OUNCES/115 G STEWING VEAL, CUT INTO PIECES ABOUT 1 X 1½ X 3 TO 4 INCHES/2.5 X 4 X 7.5 TO 10 CM

2 CHICKEN LIVERS (OPTIONAL)

SALT

¼ CUP/60 ML BRANDY OR WHITE WINE

1 MEDIUM ONION, FINELY CHOPPED

2 RIPE TOMATOES, PEELED, SEEDED, AND FINELY CHOPPED

4 GARLIC CLOVES, PEELED

1 SMALL PIECE CINNAMON STICK

¼ CUP/60 ML MILK

2 TEASPOONS SALT

20 CANNELLONI SHEETS (SEE NOTE)

SAUCE

3 CUPS/720 ML MILK

3 TABLESPOONS BUTTER

2 TABLESPOONS ALL-PURPOSE FLOUR

2 PINCHES FRESHLY GRATED NUTMEG

1 CUP/70 G LOOSELY PACKED, FRESHLY GRATED MILD PASTA CHEESE, SUCH AS MOZZARELLA

continued

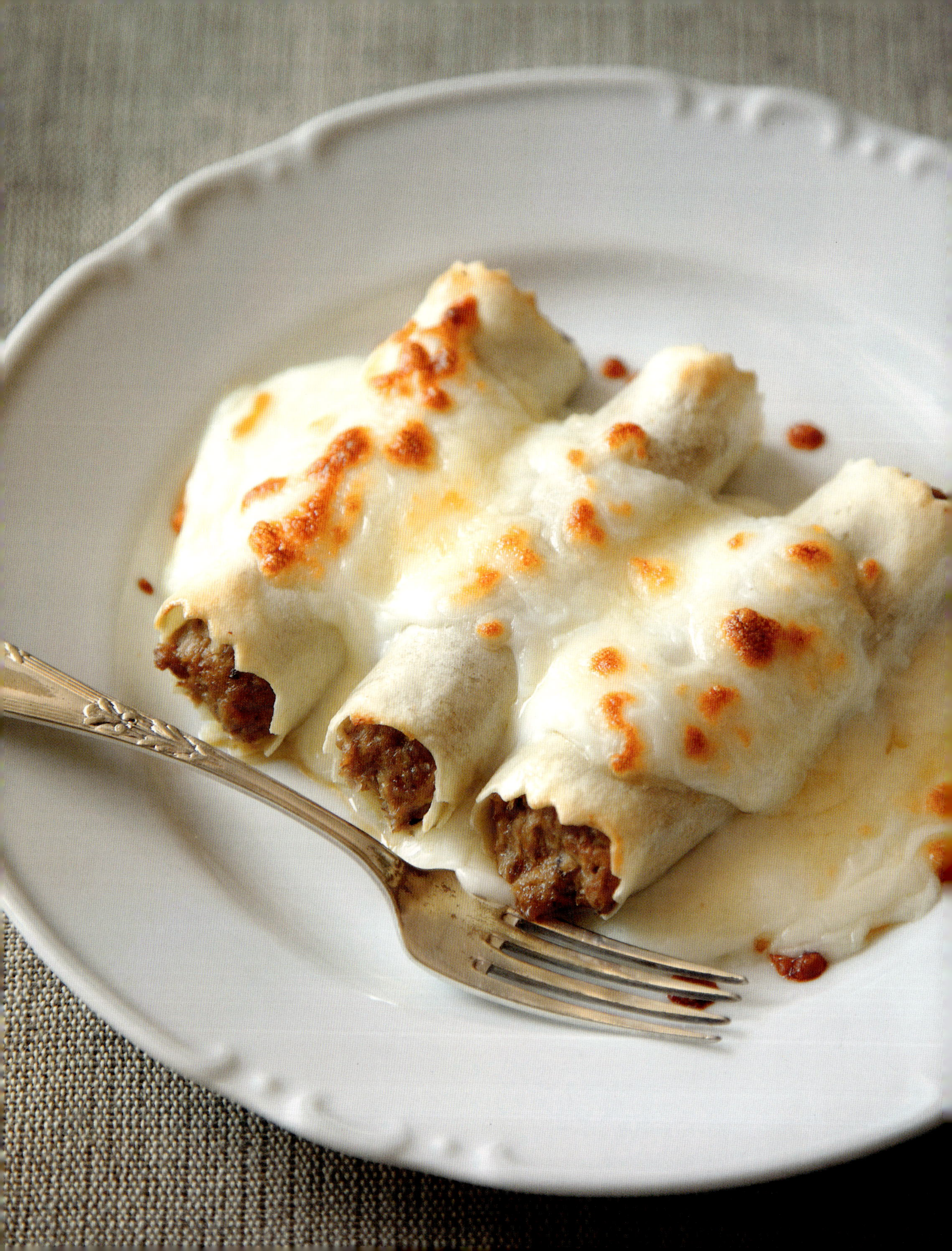

1. **To make the filling:** In a cazuela, Dutch oven, large sauté pan, or deep skillet, heat the olive oil over medium-high heat. Season the chicken, pork, veal, and the chicken livers (if using) with salt; add to the pan; and brown, turning as needed, about 5 minutes. Pour in the brandy, cook for 2 minutes, and then add the onion, tomatoes, garlic, and cinnamon. Dribble in ½ cup/120 ml water, reduce the heat to medium-low, and simmer until the meats are tender and the liquid has been reduced to a sauce, about 1¼ hours. Remove the pan from the heat and let cool. Discard the cinnamon. In a food processor or meat grinder, finely grind the meats and sauce. Transfer to a large bowl. Moisten with the milk.

2. Meanwhile, prepare the cannelloni sheets: In a large pot, bring 3 quarts/3 L water to a rolling boil and add the salt. Add the cannelloni squares one by one. Gently boil, swirling the water with a wooden spoon from time to time to keep them from sticking together, until al dente, 12 to 15 minutes (follow the time indicated on the package). Remove the pot from the heat and pour in some cold water to begin the cooling process. Fill a bowl with cold water, and transfer the squares with a slotted spoon to the cold water to finish cooling. Carefully drain. Cover a large work surface with clean kitchen cloths. Arrange the squares in a single layer on the towels to absorb excess water.

3. **To make the sauce:** Prepare a thin béchamel with the milk, butter, flour, and nutmeg, following the directions on page 338. Remove from the heat.

4. Onto each cannelloni square, place 2 tablespoons of the filling and roll the squares into tubes with the sides just overlapping. Place them tightly together in a large baking dish with the seams facing either downward or upward.

5. Preheat the broiler.

6. Spoon the béchamel sauce over the top of the cannelloni and then sprinkle with the cheese. Broil until the cheese is golden brown in places, 5 to 10 minutes.

7. Use a small flat spatula to remove the cannelloni from the baking dish without breaking them. Start with three per plate. Spoon some sauce from the dish over the top. Serve hot.

NOTE: Spanish cannelloni sheets (called *placas* or *láminas*) are flat and square with fluted edges. A standard package contains 20 sheets and weighs 125 g, or about 4½ ounces. See Sources, page 345, for where to find them. You can also substitute lasagna sheets broken into about 3-inch/7.5-cm squares.

CANNELLONI STUFFED WITH MUSHROOMS AND PINE NUTS

CANELONES RELLENOS DE SETAS

MAKES 20 CANNELLONI; SERVES 4 TO 5

> While canelones are typically stuffed with ground meats, spinach and raisins are another popular filling. My favorite version, the one I prepare more frequently at home and also order in country restaurants when in the mountains, has mushrooms. Blending cultivated mushrooms with some wild ones makes for the best filling.

20 CANNELLONI SHEETS (SEE NOTE, PAGE 159)

FILLING
5 TABLESPOONS EXTRA-VIRGIN OLIVE OIL
1 MEDIUM ONION, FINELY CHOPPED
3 TABLESPOONS PINE NUTS
1½ POUNDS/680 G CLEANED ASSORTED CULTIVATED AND WILD MUSHROOMS, CHOPPED (SEE PAGE 339)
SALT AND FRESHLY GROUND BLACK PEPPER

SAUCE
3 CUPS/720 ML MILK
3 TABLESPOONS BUTTER
2 TABLESPOONS ALL-PURPOSE FLOUR
1 PINCH FRESHLY GRATED NUTMEG

¾ CUP/50 G LOOSELY PACKED, FRESHLY GRATED MILD PASTA CHEESE, SUCH AS MOZZARELLA

1. Prepare the cannelloni sheets following the instructions on page 159.

2. To make the filling: In a small sauté pan or skillet, heat 2 tablespoons of the oil over medium heat. Add the onion and cook until it begins to soften, about 5 minutes. Add the pine nuts and cook until the onion is soft and the pine nuts golden, about 5 minutes. Transfer to a large bowl.

3. In a large sauté pan or skillet, heat the remaining 3 tablespoons olive oil over high heat. Add the mushrooms, season with salt and pepper, and cook until the moisture has been thrown and the edges begin to brown, about 8 minutes. Transfer to the bowl.

4. To make the sauce: Prepare a thin béchamel with the milk, butter, flour, and nutmeg, following the directions on page 338. Remove from the heat.

5. Stir 3 or 4 tablespoons of the béchamel into the mushroom mixture. Turn over until evenly blended.

6. Roll the cannelloni and set into a large baking dish following the directions on page 159. Preheat the broiler.

7. Spoon the remaining béchamel sauce over top of the cannelloni and then sprinkle with the cheese. Broil until the cheese is golden brown in places, 5 to 10 minutes.

8. Use a small flat spatula to remove the cannelloni from the baking dish without breaking them. Start with three per plate. Spoon some sauce from the dish over top. Serve hot.

This recipe comes from the village of Checa, high up in the mountains of eastern Guadalajara, where I stayed recently with friends from the village. One morning, with the season's first snow falling—heavy, pregnant flakes covered the cobblestone streets, public fountain, and terra-cotta roof tiles—we headed into the nearby Parque Natural del Alto Tajo, where we met a shepherd on a narrow gravel road moving his flock of 500 sheep down to a corral in the village. When we finally made it back to the house for lunch, the mother of my friend Jesús, Juana Ortega, had made the same thing that the shepherd had eaten that morning: *migas*. Migas are, essentially, cubes of bread cooked down to small pellets, and served with any number of garnishes. This recipe is adapted from the one prepared that day in Checa.

SHEPHERD'S MIGAS WITH GRAPES

MIGAS DE PASTOR CON UVAS

SERVES 3 TO 4

8 OUNCES/225 G DENSE, THIN-CRUSTED COUNTRY BREAD OR BAGUETTE, 1 OR 2 DAYS OLD

1 TEASPOON SALT

¼ CUP/60 ML EXTRA-VIRGIN OLIVE OIL

3 GARLIC CLOVES, PEELED AND THINLY SLICED CROSSWISE

5 SLICES STREAKY SALT PORK, PANCETTA, OR UNSMOKED BACON, OR ½ CUP/60 G THINLY SLICED SPANISH CHORIZO

1 MEDIUM ONION, CHOPPED

1 SWEET ITALIAN GREEN PEPPER OR ½ GREEN BELL PEPPER, CHOPPED

1 TEASPOON SPANISH PIMENTÓN DULCE (SWEET PAPRIKA)

FRESH GRAPES, WASHED AND CHILLED, FOR GARNISHING

1. The night before, slice the bread as thinly as possible and then cut the slices into small pieces. Place them in a large bowl. Dissolve the salt in ½ cup/120 ml tepid water and sprinkle it over the bread, turning and tossing to slightly dampen. Cover with a kitchen cloth and leave overnight.

2. In a very large skillet or deep sauté pan (or wok), heat the olive oil over medium heat. Add the garlic and cook until golden and aromatic, about 1 minute. Remove and reserve. Add the salt pork and cook until browned, 5 to 7 minutes. Transfer to a plate. In the same oil, add the onion and green pepper and cook until they begin to soften, about 5 minutes. Add the pimentón and immediately stir in ¼ cup/60 ml water to keep it from burning. Begin working in the bread, stirring until coated and then adding more.

3. Cook until the migas have formed golden brown pellets, continually stirring to keep them from scorching, 20 to 30 minutes. Toward the end, chop two slices of the cooked salt pork and add along with the reserved garlic.

4. Serve hot with the remaining salt pork. Place the grapes in the middle of the table to eat alongside.

CHAPTER 7

FISH
pescados

The Spanish consumption of fish per capita is among the largest in the world, with each Spaniard devouring, on average, about 100 pounds/45 kg a year. To give that number some perspective, the European Union average is exactly half that amount, and the United States, according to the Food and Agriculture Organization, is even lower, with just under 16 pounds/7 kg a year.

Visit any of the covered food markets along the coast and the importance of fish and seafood is clear. In many *mercados*, these stalls are in the center of the market, an apt symbol for the diet. The markets offer choices from the Atlantic Ocean and the Mediterranean Sea that bracket Spain.

But there are freshwater fish, too, eels from the Ebro Delta and the Albufera lagoon south of Valencia, trout from the streams of Navarra, Cantabria, and Granada, and salmon in the rivers of Asturias.

Such a variety of species means a variety of methods of preparation: lightly flouring and deep-frying in Andalucía, the fish stews of the Mediterranean and the Basque Country, braising with spices like saffron or mild dried red peppers, or cooking in a parsley-rich "green sauce."

But often the best way to prepare fish is the simplest. Simple, though, doesn't necessarily mean easy. Perhaps it is here that the theory of Spanish cooking and tasting the principal ingredient is at its most obvious. When buying a gorgeous turbot or porgy, why would you want to bury it under a heavy sauce and disguise its lovely sea flavors?

While Spain consumes a huge amount of fish, not all of it is fresh. The importance on the Spanish table of dry-salted cod is hard to underestimate, especially in the years before freezing and refrigeration. Back then, it was just about the only fish available to much of the country.

The Basques were the first great salt-cod fishermen, and they traveled long distances to Newfoundland and Iceland at first to whale and then to fish the rich banks of cod. The Spanish word *bacalao* and Catalan *bacallà* come from the Basque, *bakailao*. The medieval Catholic Church gave the salt cod a final, solidifying role (and the Basques a massive, lucrative market in Europe) when it prohibited meat all year on Fridays and during Lent. While such rigorous abstinence is rarely practiced today, and fresh fish is available even in the most rural of Castilian villages, salt cod dishes remain firmly present on the year-round contemporary table.

The prominence of salt cod in so many regional cuisines is impressive. Some of the most classic, even celebrated, dishes in Spain are made with bacalao. Because it is so versatile, I have included some salt cod recipes in other chapters on tapas, salads, and egg dishes.

Outside of Spain, salt cod can be found in certain gourmet grocers, but also in many Spanish, Portuguese, and Italian markets. Look for pieces that are white (not yellowish). While the best pieces are cut from the *lomo* (loin), not every dish needs such an expensive cut. Desalting takes at least a couple of days; plan ahead. See page 341 for more on this process. Note that the soaked weight of salt cod increases by about 20 percent (or, rarely, as high as 25 percent) from the dried weight.

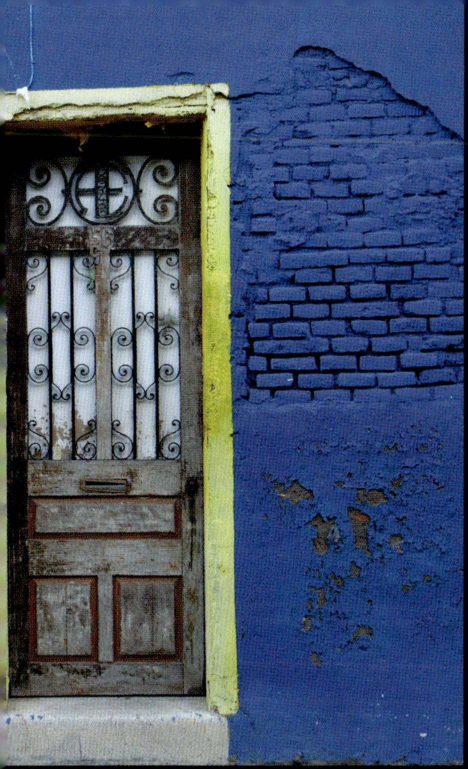

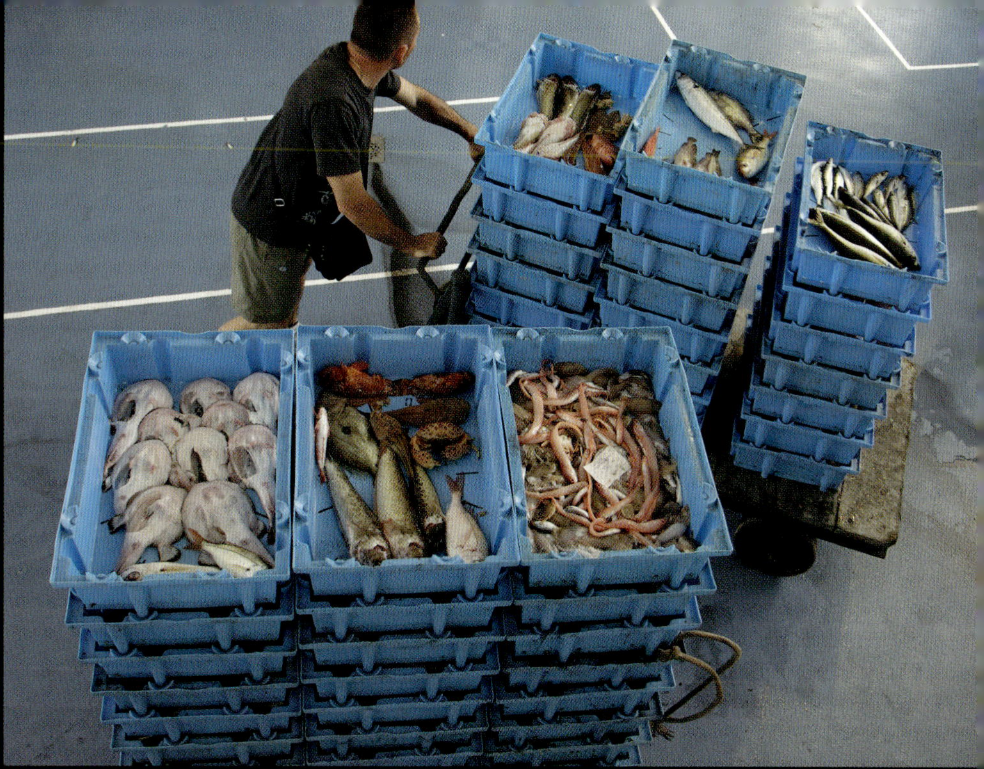

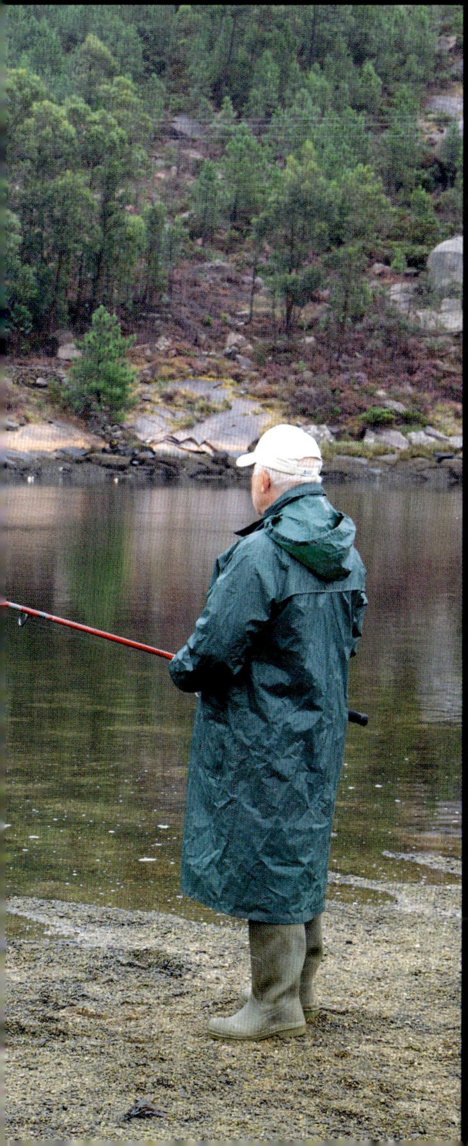

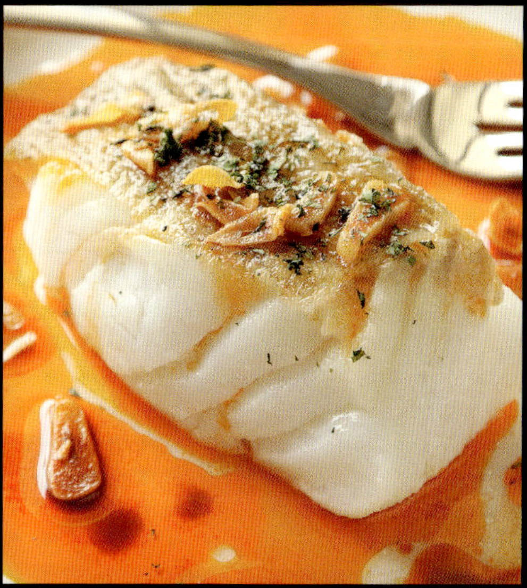

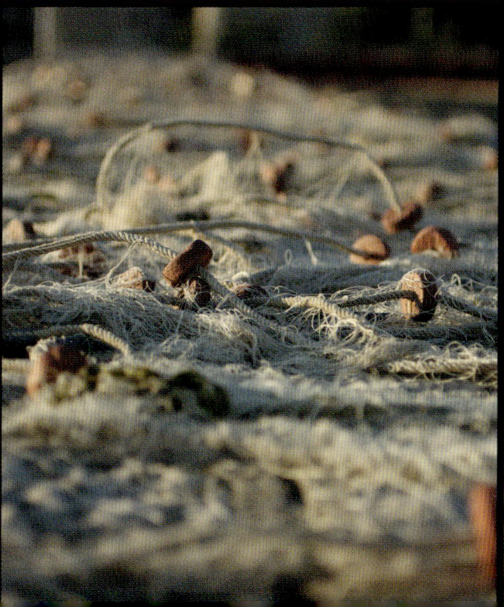

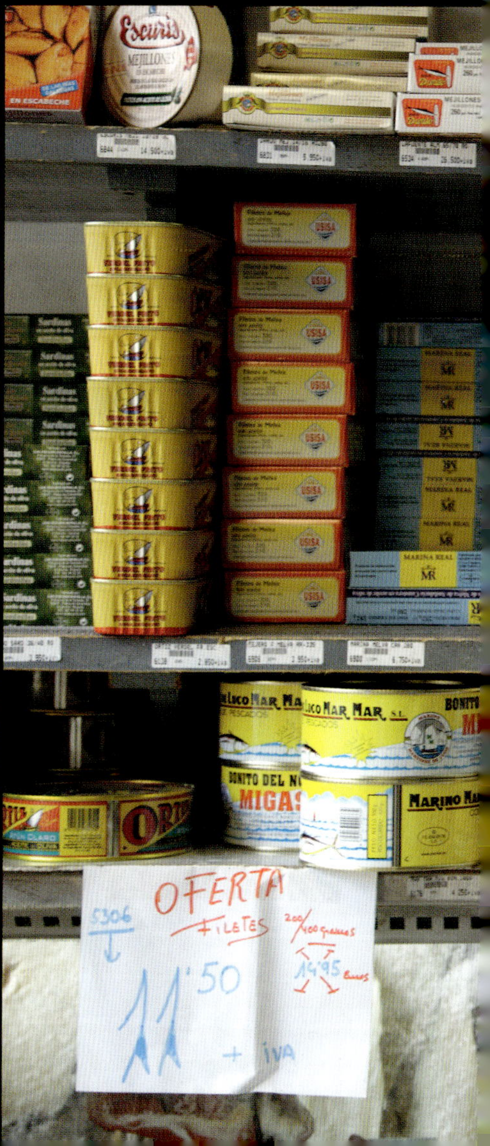
Escuris
MEJILLONES
ORTIZ
OFERTA
FILETES
11'50
+ iva

The southern coast of Andalucía is the land of excellent *fritura*, small fish (and sometimes vegetables) perfectly deep-fried in a light flouring (rather than a thick batter). Also called *pescadito frito* (literally "little fried fish"), the most famous version comes from Cádiz and can include a large selection of different seafood.

The key to getting the fish golden brown on the outside while juicy and tender on the inside, with a light, crispy texture, is using abundant and hot oil. Do not crowd the pan, because it cools the temperature of the oil. If the oil is not hot enough, the fish will get soggy and perhaps break apart. (If it is too hot, though, the fish will burn on the outside before the center can cook.) Fry the fish by types and in small batches. Fry one complete batch at a time, rather than adding more as space allows in the pan. Between batches be sure that the oil returns to an adequate temperature.

ANDALUCÍA-STYLE DEEP-FRIED FISH

FRITURA DE PESCADO

SERVES 4

3½ POUNDS/1.6 KG FRESH FISH, SUCH AS SMALL HAKE, SOLE, ANCHOVIES, AND RED MULLET, AND WHOLE FRESH SHRIMP
MILD OLIVE OIL OR SUNFLOWER OIL FOR FRYING
SALT
ALL-PURPOSE FLOUR FOR DREDGING
1 LEMON, CUT INTO WEDGES

1. Do not rinse the small fish and shrimp; instead wipe them with a damp towel. Clean the larger fish and, if needed, cut them in half or into thick steaks; leave the smaller fish whole. Scale the red mullet. Refrigerate until ready to fry.

2. Preheat the oven to 200°F/95°C.

3. In a deep skillet, heat about 2 inches/5 cm of olive oil to 375°F/190°C. (The oil is the right temperature when a large cube of fresh bread dropped into it browns in about 60 seconds.)

4. Season the fish with salt and then dredge in flour, covering each part. Shake off any excess flour in a sieve.

5. Working in small batches that don't crowd the pan or bring the temperature of the oil below 350°F/180°C, gently lower a batch of fish or shrimp into the oil with tongs and fry until golden and slightly crunchy on the outside, 1 to 2 minutes.

6. Remove with a slotted spoon or tongs, and place on paper towels to briefly drain. Transfer to a baking sheet lined with parchment paper and place in the oven to keep warm until all of the fish have been fried.

7. Fry the remaining fish, being sure that the oil has returned to 350°F/180°C before adding the next batch.

8. Serve immediately with lemon wedges on the side.

FISHERMAN'S SUQUET

SUQUET DE PESCADORS

SERVES 6

How to translate the name of this dish? It's not really soup or stew—there is little liquid in the end, just enough to dip bread into. But it's that bit of sauce—the *suquet*, Catalan for "little juices"—that gives the dish its name. Suquet hails from the fishing villages of the Costa Brava, where fishermen cooked the fish that were beaten up when they were caught, the odds and ends, or the fish that didn't fetch such high prices at the market. (Incredibly, that once included monkfish.)

¼ CUP/60 ML OLIVE OIL

2 GARLIC CLOVES, PEELED

2 THIN SLICES BAGUETTE, DAY OLD OR TOASTED

1 MEDIUM ONION, FINELY CHOPPED

2 RIPE MEDIUM TOMATOES, PEELED, SEEDED, AND CHOPPED, ALL JUICES RESERVED

4 CUPS/1 L FISH STOCK (PAGE 335)

2¼ POUNDS/1 KG MEDIUM WHITE POTATOES, PEELED AND CUT CROSSWISE ABOUT ⅓ INCH/1 CM THICK

16 TOASTED ALMONDS WITHOUT SKINS

1 TABLESPOON MINCED FRESH FLAT-LEAF PARSLEY

½ TEASPOON SPANISH PIMENTÓN DULCE (SWEET PAPRIKA)

1 SMALL PINCH SAFFRON THREADS, DRY-TOASTED AND GROUND (SEE PAGE 340)

2¼ POUNDS/1 KG MONKFISH STEAKS OR ANOTHER FIRM, WHITE-FLESHED FISH, SUCH AS GROUPER, ROCK COD, PACIFIC SNAPPER, OR RED SNAPPER

SALT AND FRESHLY GROUND BLACK PEPPER

1. In a cazuela, heavy casserole, large sauté pan, or deep skillet, heat the olive oil over medium heat. Add the garlic and bread and cook until each is golden, 1 to 2 minutes. Remove as done and reserve.

2. In the cazuela, prepare a sofrito with the onion and tomatoes, following the directions on page 39.

3. In a saucepan, heat the stock over medium heat, cover the pan, and keep hot.

4. When the sofrito is ready, add the potatoes and cook, turning over a few times to coat with sofrito, until they lose their rawness, about 10 minutes. Pour in 2 cups/500 ml of the stock and simmer until the potatoes are quite tender and nearly cooked, 10 to 20 minutes, depending on the potato.

5. Meanwhile, prepare a picada with the reserved garlic and bread, the almonds, parsley, and 1 to 2 tablespoons of the simmering liquid, following directions on page 39.

6. Stir in the picada, pimentón, and saffron. Season the fish with salt and pepper and lay them in the pan. Pour over the remaining 2 cups/500 ml stock and simmer until the fish is opaque throughout and the potatoes tender, jiggling the pan from time to time, about 10 minutes. Taste for seasoning and adjust as needed. Serve from the cazuela.

FISH

Monkfish are wedge-shaped, thick, and have a wide, toothy mouth in a massive head that comprises over half of its total weight. The head makes some of the richest stock, while the meat on the fleshy tail has a texture often likened to very tender lobster.

I first encountered this delicious, straightforward recipe in the deep south, an area steeped in Moorish influences. This recipe showcases one of their most important introductions to the Spanish countryside—saffron. Use whole saffron threads, preferably those from La Mancha, where the severe climate gives Spain's most distinguished spice its potent aromas and bold, brilliant color. See page 168 for more on La Mancha's *oro rojo* (red gold).

MONKFISH STEAKS WITH SAFFRON

RAPE CON AZAFRÁN

SERVES 4

1¾ POUNDS/800 G MONKFISH, HAKE, OR GROUPER STEAKS ABOUT ¾ TO 1 INCH/ 2 TO 2.5 CM THICK

SALT AND FRESHLY GROUND BLACK PEPPER

3 TABLESPOONS EXTRA-VIRGIN OLIVE OIL

ALL-PURPOSE FLOUR FOR DREDGING

2 MEDIUM ONIONS, FINELY CHOPPED

20 SAFFRON THREADS; 10 DRY-TOASTED AND GROUND (SEE PAGE 340), 10 WHOLE

1. Generously season the fish with salt and pepper. In a large cazuela, heavy casserole, skillet, or sauté pan, heat the olive oil over medium-high heat. When the oil begins to shimmer, dredge the fish piece by piece in flour and then cook in batches as needed, turning only once, until golden on the outsides and just opaque throughout, about 3 minutes per side. Transfer to a platter.

2. Add the onions to the cazuela, reduce the heat to medium-low, and cook until soft and translucent, 8 to 10 minutes. Add all of the saffron, stir, and immediately cover with ½ cup/120 ml water. Bring the liquid to a boil and then reduce the heat to low. Return the monkfish and any drippings to the pan and cook, shaking the pan from time to time, until the liquid has reduced down almost completely and the onions are still very moist, about 5 minutes.

3. Divide the fish among plates and cover with the onion sauce. Serve immediately.

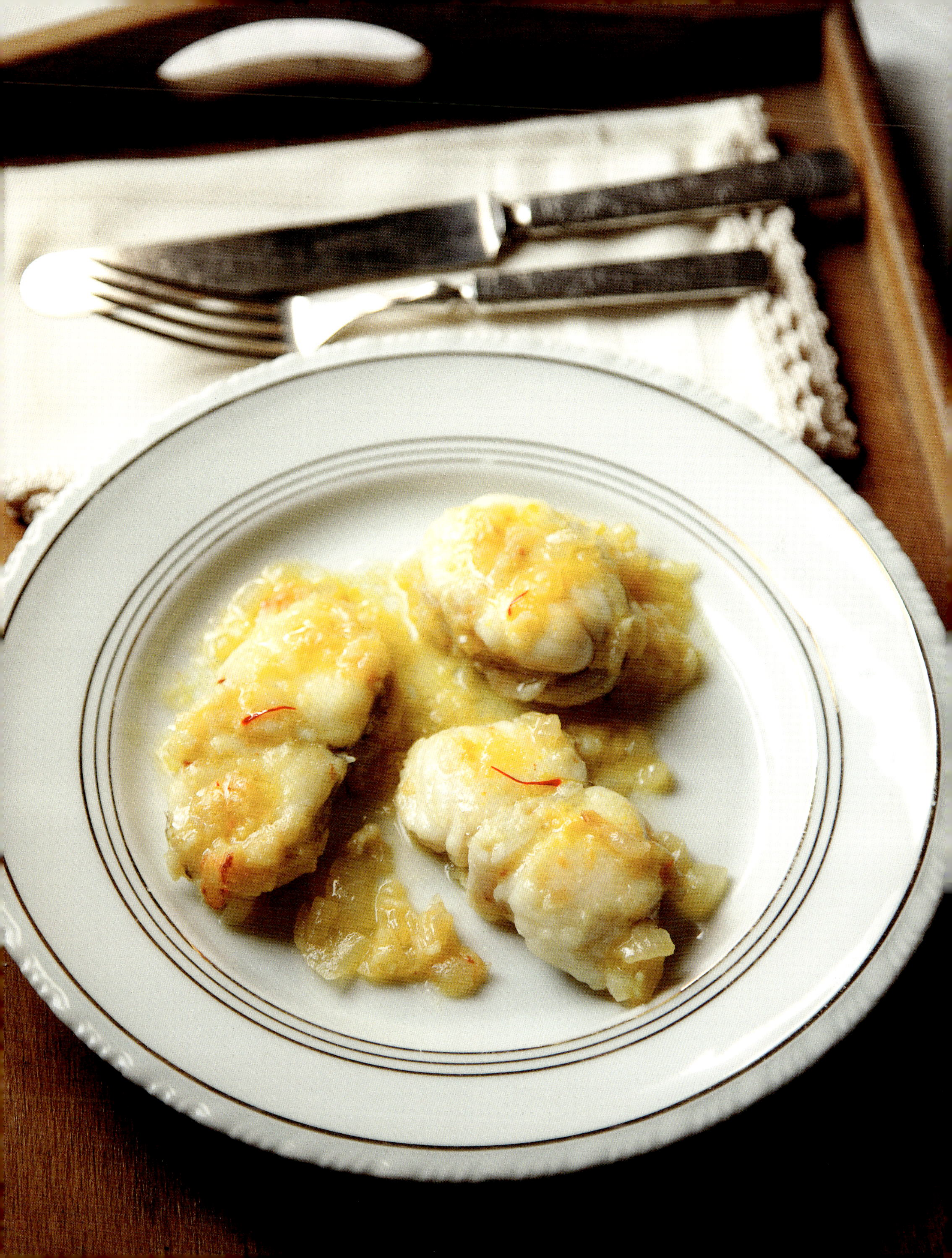

INGREDIENTS

SAFFRON
azafrán

As I entered a converted garage in the Castilla–La Mancha town of Madridejos on a cold winter afternoon, the smell was overpoweringly tropical in its heady floral aromas. Mounds of purplish saffron flowers picked that morning covered a long table topped with a bright yellow tablecloth. Sitting around it was Gregoria Carrasco Sánchez, her three daughters, and her husband, working quickly but patiently, extracting the three scarlet-red stigmas from each flower. They placed the 1- to 1½-inch-/2.5- to 4-cm-long threads in a small dish and dropped the rest of the flower to the floor, where they piled around their feet.

Arab traders introduced saffron into Spain sometime around 900 CE. The Spanish word *azafrán* comes from the Arabic *za'faran*. The center of the industry is in Castilla–La Mancha, where the brutally hot summers and bitter cold winters give the saffron its vivid color and intense aromas. The saffron bulbs are planted between June and September, and the short-lived but beautiful flowers are picked from mid-October to mid-November. During the harvest, entire families help out in *la monda*, as the process to remove the stigmas is known. As a girl, my mother-in-law sat with her aunts to separate threads from the flowers, and still remembers a few weeks every autumn, plucking out the fine filaments and listening to the stories and songs of these women.

Saffron is famously the world's most expensive spice. Gregoria told me that it takes the stigmas of 260,000 to 265,000 flowers to make a single kilogram of the spice—about 132,500 for one pound.

That family I visited in Madridejos is typical in that they grow a small plot of their own saffron, remove the threads, and toast them over a small heater (where they lose 80 percent of their weight), and then sell them to a wholesaler. "It's the only industry left in Spain that pays its workers in the product by weight," Gregoria told me. They receive one third of the threads that they separate as payment.

But saffron isn't just a commodity. It plays an important role in the Spanish kitchen, too. If it's good saffron, just a pinch of threads is enough. (Too many and the flavors can be almost medicinal.) That pinch gives many Spanish dishes their defining color or aroma—chicken in pepitoria sauce (see page 212), monkfish with saffron (see page 166), and, most famous of them all, paella (see page 136).

GALICIAN-STYLE HAKE WITH GARLIC AJADA SAUCE

MERLUZA A LA GALLEGA CON AJADA

SERVES 4

The highly popular *merluza* (hake) is a long and thin fish, nickel-gray, with flaky, soft flesh. (Hake is generally cut into steaks because the fillets are hard to handle.) The best ones are line-caught in Galicia. Called *merluza de pincho*, these are sold in markets with the hook and a short length of fishing filament still attached—there is no mistaking them. Use fresh cod or snapper for this recipe if you can't find hake. And though steaks are preferable, fillets will also work.

In Galicia, preparing hake with this vinegary, sweet paprika sauce called *ajada* is typical. This version is simple, and requires just a single pot for cooking the potatoes and the fish. It's pure Galician country cooking, with few ingredients and none of the flavors lost.

GALICIAN AJADA SAUCE

½ CUP/120 ML EXTRA-VIRGIN OLIVE OIL

2 GARLIC CLOVES, MINCED

SALT

1 BAY LEAF

1 TEASPOON SPANISH PIMENTÓN DULCE (SWEET PAPRIKA)

1 TABLESPOON SHERRY VINEGAR OR RED WINE VINEGAR

1 BAY LEAF

SALT

2 POUNDS/910 G MEDIUM WHITE POTATOES, PEELED AND CUT CROSSWISE INTO ¼-INCH-/½-CM-THICK SLICES

2 POUNDS/910 G HAKE CUT INTO ¾- TO 1-INCH-/2- TO 2.5-CM-THICK STEAKS

FRESHLY GROUND BLACK PEPPER

1. **To make the Galician Ajada Sauce:** In a small skillet, heat the olive oil over medium-low heat. Add the garlic and cook until aromatic, about 1 minute. Immediately remove the pan from the heat, stir in a pinch of salt, and add the bay leaf. Let cool for a few minutes and then stir in the paprika and vinegar.

2. In a large pot that will comfortably hold the potatoes as well as the fish, bring about 5 quarts/5 L water to a boil. Add the bay leaf, season with salt, and add the potatoes. Boil until tender but not crumbling, 10 to 15 minutes. Reduce the heat to low. Season the hake with salt and pepper and set it in the water with the potatoes. Poach until opaque throughout, 3 to 5 minutes.

3. With a wide slotted spoon, transfer the fish and potatoes to a platter to drain off any excess liquid. Arrange the potatoes on a serving platter with the fish on top.

4. Scoop out ¼ cup/60 ml of the liquid from the pot and whisk it into the ajada sauce. Spoon about half of the sauce over the fish. Serve with the remaining sauce in a bowl on the side to spoon over as desired.

FISH BRAISED IN ROMESCO SAUCE

ROMESCO DE PESCADO

SERVES 4

During the 600-year Roman rule of the Iberian Peninsula (from 218 BCE to 409 CE), one of the provincial capitals of Hispania was Tarraco, modern-day Tarragona. It is a lovely spot along the Mediterranean that has long been rich in almond and olive trees. Some historians date Tarragona's famous romesco sauce to this era. Well, sort of. One of the key ingredients—indeed the ingredient that gives it its name!—is a sweetly mild dried red pepper that didn't arrive in Spain from the New World until over a thousand years after the fall of the Roman Empire. But as David Solé i Torné wrote in his authoritative book on romesco, the sauce began as a sauce for stewing fish from Tarragona and incorporated the peppers later.

To use the romesco as a stand-alone sauce, eaten cold with grilled vegetables, fish, snails, or—my favorite—dolloped on a hard-boiled egg, stir 1 or 2 tablespoons of red wine vinegar into it. It can be stored, covered in a sealed container in the refrigerator, for up to 1 week.

ROMESCO SAUCE

3 DRIED ROMESCO OR ÑORA PEPPERS OR ANOTHER SWEET, MILD DRIED RED PEPPER (SEE INGREDIENT NOTE, PAGE 16)

1 RIPE MEDIUM TOMATO

SALT

5 TABLESPOONS EXTRA-VIRGIN OLIVE OIL

2 GARLIC CLOVES, PEELED

20 TOASTED HAZELNUTS WITHOUT SKINS

10 UNSALTED TOASTED ALMONDS WITHOUT SKINS

1 SLICE BAGUETTE, DAY OLD OR TOASTED

FRESHLY GROUND BLACK PEPPER

1¾ TO 2 POUNDS/800 TO 910 G MONKFISH, HAKE, AND/OR SEA BASS CUT INTO ¾- TO 1-INCH-/2- TO 2.5-CM-THICK STEAKS

SALT AND FRESHLY GROUND BLACK PEPPER

3 TABLESPOONS EXTRA-VIRGIN OLIVE OIL

ALL-PURPOSE FLOUR FOR DREDGING

¼ CUP/60 ML DRY WHITE WINE

1 CUP/240 ML FISH STOCK (PAGE 335)

1. Prepare the Romesco Sauce: Cut the peppers open and remove the seeds. Put the peppers in a bowl, cover with hot water, and soak for 30 minutes; drain. Using a coffee spoon, scrape the soft pulp from inside the skins and reserve. Discard the skins.

2. Stem the tomato, halve crosswise, and seed. Season the face with salt.

3. In a medium skillet, heat 1 tablespoon of the olive oil over medium-low heat. Add the garlic and cook until fragrant, about 1 minute. Transfer to a plate to cool. Place the tomato facedown on the skillet and cook until browned and fragrant, turning from time to time, about 5 minutes.

4. *Using an immersion hand blender:* Add the romesco pulp, tomato, and garlic to a tall, cylindrical, and narrow container along with the remaining 4 tablespoons olive oil, the nuts, and baguette and season with salt and pepper. Grind, moving the blender up and down, into a moist, gritty paste.

Using a food processor: Add the romesco pulp, tomato, and garlic to the bowl along with the remaining 4 tablespoons olive oil, the nuts, and baguette and season with salt and pepper. Grind into a moist, gritty paste. Wipe down the bowl between pulses to keep the sauce within reach of the blades.

5. Season the fish generously with salt and pepper. In a large cazuela, heavy casserole, heavy skillet, or sauté pan, heat the olive oil over medium-high heat. When the oil begins to shimmer, dredge the fish piece by piece in flour and then cook in single-layer batches, turning only once, until golden on the outsides, 1 to 2 minutes on each side. Transfer to a platter.

6. Pour the wine and then the stock into the cazuela, stir in the romesco sauce, and bring the liquid to a boil. Return the fish to the pan, reduce the heat to medium-low, and gently simmer for 10 minutes, until the fish is cooked through and the sauce slightly thickened. The sauce should be loose but not watery. (If needed, remove the fish and reduce the sauce over high heat. Return the fish to the pan when ready.) Serve from the cazuela.

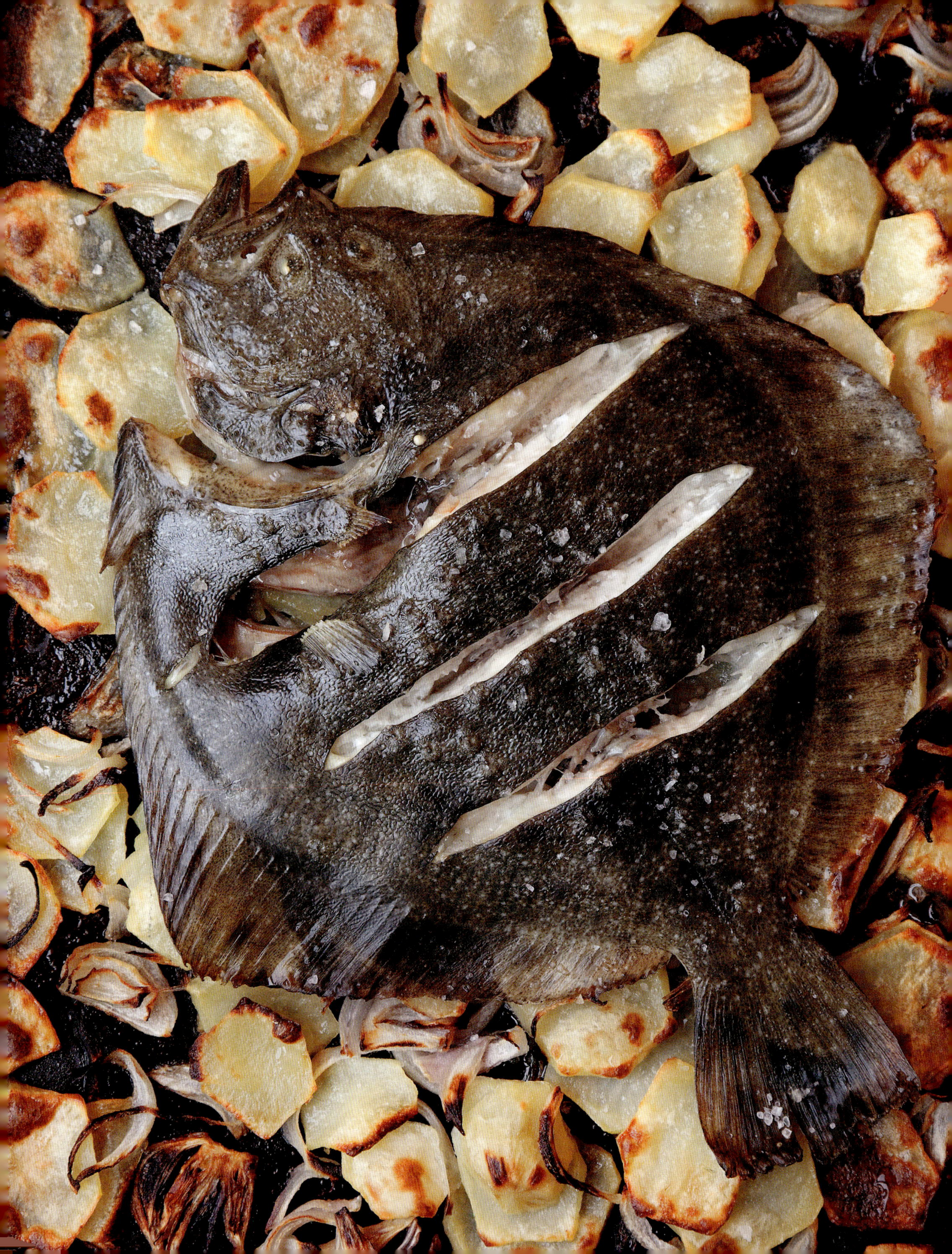

BAKED TURBOT WITH BASQUE WHITE WINE

RODABALLO AL HORNO CON TXAKOLI

SERVES 4 TO 6

The most sublime of all of the fishes in the sea! The greenish, almost round flatfish, with a tiny mouth and eyes pinched together on top of the head, has succulent meat bursting with concentrated flavors. The best turbot are caught in the Atlantic off Europe, especially in the Bay of Biscay. When buying, try to find one of these.

The best way I have discovered to prepare them is on a bed of potatoes and onions in the oven with a good drizzle of Txakoli. Txakoli is a Basque white wine with lovely acidic notes and some natural bubbles. It is consumed very young—its optimal drinking season runs November to March, following the harvest. Happily, this season coincides with that of turbot. (You can also substitute another young, fruity white wine.) The wine gives only a slight flavor to the fish—its main function here is to seep down into the potatoes and, as it cooks, moisten and gently flavor the fish with its vapors.

3 POUNDS/1.4 KG MEDIUM WHITE POTATOES
1½ POUNDS/680 G MEDIUM ONIONS, THINLY SLICED
3 TABLESPOONS EXTRA-VIRGIN OLIVE OIL, PLUS EXTRA FOR DRIZZLING
SALT
1 CLEANED TURBOT WITH HEAD AND TAIL, 3 TO 4½ POUNDS/1.4 TO 2 KG
FRESHLY GROUND BLACK PEPPER
1 CUP/240 ML TXAKOLI OR ANOTHER YOUNG DRY WHITE WINE

1. Preheat the oven to 425°F/220°C/gas mark 7.

2. Peel the potatoes and cut into ¼-inch-/½-cm-thick slices. Soak them in a large bowl of cold water for 1 hour to leach out some of the starches. Drain, rinse, and then let drain well.

3. In a rimmed baking sheet or large roasting pan that can comfortably fit the fish, toss the potatoes and onions with the olive oil, season with salt, and spread them evenly across the tray. Cover with aluminum foil. Bake until they begin to soften, about 30 minutes. Uncover and bake for 10 minutes more, or until the edges are beginning to brown.

4. Meanwhile, make (or ask your fishmonger to do this when buying) three or four deep crosswise cuts through the central section of the fish (including spine), leaving at least 1 inch/2.5 cm of the fish uncut (thus remaining "joined") around the edges. This will allow the fish to cook evenly, keep its shape for presentation, and be easier to serve. Generously season with salt and pepper.

5. Place the fish on top of the bed of potatoes, pour over the wine, and bake until the fish is just opaque throughout, 15 to 30 minutes, depending on its size. Test for doneness along the backbone with the tip of a knife; the meat should be just opaque and still very moist.

6. Separate the pieces of fish and divide among plates with the potatoes. Serve with extra-virgin olive oil to drizzle over as desired.

SALT-BAKED GILT-HEAD BREAM

DORADA A LA SAL

SERVES 4

There is no better way to harness the briny flavors of a whole fish, or to keep the meat moist and juicy, than to cook it packed in a salt crust. It is important to use a thick-skinned fish, so that the saltiness can't penetrate. The favorite choice for this is dorada, a tin-colored gilt-head bream with a distinguishing gold spot on the cheek and a crescent-shaped mark above the eye. (*Dorada* means "golden.") Once you crack the salt shell open, work quickly to keep the juices of the fish from dissolving the salt and making the dish too salty. *Dorada a la sal* is a specialty of Murcia and Alicante.

TWO 1-POUND/455-G OR THREE 10-OUNCE/280-G WHOLE SEA BREAM WITH HEAD AND TAIL, OR GROUPER, RED SNAPPER, ROCKFISH, OR ANOTHER NON-OILY WHITE FISH

4½ POUNDS/2 KG KOSHER SALT

3 EGG WHITES

ALLIOLI (PAGE 337) OR HOMEMADE MAYONNAISE (PAGE 337)

1. Preheat the oven to 400°F/200°C/gas mark 6.

2. Trim the fish's gills and pull out the intestines through the gills (or ask your fishmonger to do it). If the fish has already been cleaned, tuck a small piece of aluminum foil around the outside of the belly to keep salt from entering the cavity. Leave on the head and tail. Do not wash; just gently wipe with a damp cloth.

3. In a large bowl, mix the salt with the egg whites until the salt feels slightly damp.

4. On a rimmed baking sheet or large roasting pan that can comfortably fit the fish, lay down a piece of parchment paper or aluminum foil (for easier cleanup). Spread about one-fourth of the salt in a layer approximately ½ inch/1.25 cm thick across the bottom; pat down. Lay the fish on top, keeping them at least a generous finger's width apart. Cover completely with the remaining salt in an even ½-inch-/1.25-cm-thick layer, patting it down around the fish. Be sure the fish are thoroughly and evenly covered.

5. Gently—without shifting the packed salt—place the fish in the oven. Bake until the fish are just done and the salt forms a hard, lightly browned shell, 10 to 15 minutes. (Calculate about 15 minutes per 1 pound/455 g of whole fish.)

6. Have a large bowl ready for the salt crust. Using a wooden mallet or hammer, carefully break open the salt shell by tapping gently. Pull off the larger chunks of salt. Using a pastry brush, brush away any salt grains from the fish. Lift out the fish; brush away any salt from the skin. Working quickly on a clean surface, remove the skin and bones and transfer the fillets to a clean platter.

7. Serve immediately with the allioli on the side.

BARBATE-STYLE TUNA IN CARAMELIZED ONIONS

ATÚN ENCEBOLLADO AL ESTILO DE BARBATE

SERVES 4

This classic dish comes from the section of Spain's Atlantic coast that slopes toward the Strait of Gibraltar. There, the schools of tuna that migrate each spring into the Mediterranean to spawn are funneled past the fishing towns of Conil de la Frontera, Barbate, and the wonderfully named Zahara de los Atunes (Zahara of the Tunas) that still catch *atún rojo de almadraba*—trap-netted bluefin tuna—following ancient methods.

While there is no single recipe for this dish, the variations tend to be slight—some cooks add parsley and nutmeg and leave out the oregano, others use aged vinegar instead of white wine or sherry. Without a doubt, the finest version I've had was at El Campero, José Melero's restaurant in Barbate. Instead of the fino sherry, José uses some twenty-five-year-old sherry vinegar, and chooses fat-marbled *mormo*, a hard (if not impossible) cut to buy, from the top of the head at the neck of the tuna. Use a cut with a bit of fat—like *ventresca*, the belly—which will keep it moister. It makes an exquisite tapa.

⅓ CUP/75 ML EXTRA-VIRGIN OLIVE OIL
6 GARLIC CLOVES, LIGHTLY CRUSHED IN THE PEEL
1½ POUNDS/680 ML MEDIUM ONIONS, THINLY SLICED
SALT
3 PINCHES DRIED OREGANO
3 PINCHES SPANISH PIMENTÓN DULCE (SWEET PAPRIKA)
1 TEASPOON ALL-PURPOSE FLOUR
1 POUND/455 G FRESH TUNA, CUT INTO ¾- TO 1-INCH/2- TO 2.5-CM CUBES
1 BAY LEAF
½ CUP/120 ML DRY SHERRY

1. In a cazuela, heavy casserole, Dutch oven, large sauté pan, or deep skillet, heat the olive oil over medium heat. Add the garlic and cook, stirring frequently, until fragrant, about 1 minute. Add the onions, season with salt, and cook over medium heat for 5 minutes, until they begin to soften and turn pale. Reduce the heat to low, cover the pan, and cook, stirring from time to time, until the onions are tender and translucent, about 40 minutes.

2. Add the oregano, paprika, and ¼ cup/60 ml water. Sprinkle in the flour and stir until it is dissolved. Arrange the tuna in the pan, add the bay leaf, and drizzle over the sherry. Simmer uncovered over low heat, until the tuna is just warmed through and still a touch purple in the very center, about 5 minutes. The sauce should be thickish and the onions meltingly smooth. Taste for seasoning and adjust as needed. Remove from the heat and let cool for a few minutes before serving.

"*Las sardinas, virgen a virgen*" ("Sardines, from virgin to virgin"), goes fishermen's wisdom on when to best catch these small, flavorful fish. While available year-round in Spain, their peak runs from the feast day of the Virgen del Carmen (July 16) to the feast day of the Virgen de la Victoria (September 8). With the sardines loaded with fats and oils, it is also the best time of year to grill them *a la brasa* on the beach. Across coastal Spain, and especially in Andalucía, groups gather for informal *sardinadas* to celebrate these tiny fish cooked over embers as their fragrant, briny smell fills the air.

Every summer, one of my father-in-law's closest friends, Pepe García from Almería, throws a sardinada. And following the age-old tradition of *granizados*, drinking granitas flavored with citrus juices, he serves this *granizado de apio y limón*, made with celery and lemon, to refresh the palate between batches of sardines. The combination is as original as it is perfect. Prepare the granita ahead of time, as it takes some hours to freeze.

GRILLED SARDINES WITH SLUSHY CELERY AND LEMON GRANITA

SARDINAS A LA BRASA CON GRANIZADO DE APIO Y LIMÓN

SERVES 6

24 TO 36 FRESH WHOLE MEDIUM SARDINES
FLAKY SEA SALT
SLUSHY CELERY AND LEMON GRANITA (FACING PAGE)

1. Prepare a grill with coals, preferably from hardwood briquettes. Be patient and let the embers burn down low. Rake them out into an even layer.

2. Do not remove the head of the sardines, nor clean, nor rinse with water. Rather, wipe them with a damp cloth. Set the sardines in a grill basket and generously season with salt flakes.

3. Once the embers are ready, set the grill basket 3 to 5 inches/7.5 to 13 cm above the coals and grill for 2 to 4 minutes on each side, depending on the sardines' size, or until the skin is tinny and the eyes have gone white.

4. Remove the sardines from the rack, transfer them to a platter, and loosely cover with foil tented in the middle. This will keep them warm while not steaming them. Grill the remaining sardines. Serve with glasses of the granita.

SLUSHY CELERY AND LEMON GRANITA

GRANIZADO DE APIO Y LIMÓN

Pepe uses the more white-colored stalks of celery, which tend to be less bitter. Directions follow on making this in a bowl as well as in water bottles. Both methods work.

MAKES 1½ QUARTS/1½ L

6 OUNCES/170 G CELERY STALKS
1½ CUPS/315 G SUGAR
1¼ CUPS/300 ML FRESH LEMON JUICE

In a large pot, combine the celery and sugar and cover with 1½ quarts/1½ L water. Bring to a boil, stirring to dissolve the sugar, and boil uncovered for 5 minutes. Remove from the heat and let cool for 5 minutes.

Using an immersion hand blender, roughly purée the celery in the pot. Alternatively, using a food processor or blender, working in batches as needed, roughly grind it with a couple of quick pulses.

Strain the purée through a colander into a large bowl, pressing all of the liquid from the celery; discard the solids. Stir the lemon juice into the liquid. Allow the liquid to completely cool.

To freeze using a bowl: Pour the liquid into a large glass or plastic bowl. Cover tightly. Place in the freezer. When it begins to freeze, stir with a whisk. Repeat two or three times, never letting it completely freeze, until slushy, at least a couple of hours.

To freeze using plastic bottles: Place a funnel over a clean 2-quart/2-L plastic bottle (or two smaller ones) and pour in the liquid. Close tightly. Place in the freezer. When it begins to freeze, shake. Repeat two or three times, never letting it completely freeze, until slushy, at least a couple of hours.

Serve in tall glasses with straws.

In Spanish, the mighty swordfish is called by a variety of names. The most common is *pez espada* (*pez* means "fish" and *espada* "sword"), although *emperador* (emperor) is perhaps more fitting for this long, magnificent bluish-black fish with silver flanks that can measure up to 15 feet/4.5 m in length and top 550 pounds/250 kg. Like tuna, this winter favorite is often best when prepared simply—on the grill and slightly undercooked to keep the rather lean meat from drying out. (Do not cut the steaks too thin.)

A classic companion in the south to marinated and grilled swordfish is this salad of diced vegetables, whose name changes from place to place in Andalucía even more frequently than swordfish. In Cádiz they call it *piriñaca*, for instance, but elsewhere you find it (with subtle differences in the salads) referred to as *pipirrana*, *picadillo*, or *almorraque*.

GRILLED SWORDFISH STEAKS WITH PIRIÑACA

PEZ ESPADA A LA PLANCHA CON PIRIÑACA

SERVES 4 TO 6

PIRIÑACA
2 RIPE PLUM TOMATOES, CORED, SEEDED, AND FINELY DICED
½ GREEN BELL PEPPER, FINELY DICED
¼ RED BELL PEPPER, FINELY DICED
1 CUCUMBER, PEELED AND FINELY DICED
½ MEDIUM RED ONION, FINELY DICED
SALT
3 TABLESPOONS EXTRA-VIRGIN OLIVE OIL
1 TABLESPOON SHERRY VINEGAR

4 GARLIC CLOVES, MINCED
2 TABLESPOONS MINCED FRESH FLAT-LEAF PARSLEY
2 TABLESPOONS EXTRA-VIRGIN OLIVE OIL
SALT AND FRESHLY GROUND BLACK PEPPER
2¼ POUNDS/1 KG SWORDFISH STEAKS ¾ TO 1 INCH/2 TO 2.5 CM THICK

1. Make the piriñaca: In a salad bowl, combine the diced vegetables and season with salt. Drizzle over the olive oil and vinegar and toss. Refrigerate to chill for about 1 hour and allow the flavors to meld.

2. Meanwhile, in a large bowl, blend the garlic, parsley, and olive oil, and season with salt and pepper. Add the swordfish and turn to coat. Cover with plastic wrap, refrigerate, and marinate for about 1 hour, turning occasionally.

3. Preheat a grill pan, griddle pan, or large, heavy skillet over medium-high heat and lightly oil. Lay on the fish steaks and sear, turning once, 2 to 3 minutes on each side, leaving the centers still moist and just warm.

4. Divide the swordfish among plates. Toss the piriñaca and place a generous spoonful beside the fish before serving.

In Spain, rivers have both rainbow trout, called *trucha arcoíris*, and brown trout, which is the native variety and known as *trucha común* (common trout). These are golden-hued with black and red spots that the Spanish call *lunares* (freckles), though in a rather poetic sense. (The word derives from *luna*, "moon.") Navarra, Guadalajara, and the Sierra Nevada in Andalucía each have well-known streams to fish for trout. I have adapted this recipe from Antonio Díaz Lafuente's *Fogones granadinos* (Granada Stoves).

While I call for butterfly-filleting the trout, you can prepare the recipe using pan-fried whole fish (fry for about 4 minutes on each side). For larger trout, use fillets.

PAN-FRIED TROUT WITH THYME AND WALNUTS

TRUCHAS CON TOMILLO Y NUECES

SERVES 4

4 CLEANED WHOLE TROUT, WITH HEADS AND TAILS, ABOUT 8 OUNCES/225 G EACH
SALT
3 TABLESPOONS EXTRA-VIRGIN OLIVE OIL
1 CUP/100 G BROKEN WALNUT PIECES
4 GARLIC CLOVES, MINCED
2 TEASPOONS FINELY CHOPPED FRESH THYME
2 TABLESPOONS MINCED FRESH FLAT-LEAF PARSLEY
SHERRY VINEGAR

1. Butterfly fillet the trout. Wash the insides of the cavities. Remove the heads, cutting at an angle through the backbone. Working from the inside of each cavity, run the tip of a sharp knife along both sides of the backbone, cutting through the ribs (but not the skin); gently pull out the backbone, leaving the two fillets attached. Using the tip of the knife and your fingers, remove the rib bones. Wash and pat dry with paper towels. Lightly season with salt.

2. In a large skillet or griddle pan that can comfortably hold the fish (if you don't have anything large enough, divide the ingredients and prepare in two batches), heat the olive oil over medium-high heat and lay the trout opened flat, skin-side down. Sprinkle over the walnuts, garlic, thyme, and parsley. Cook for 4 minutes and then carefully turn them over with a wide spatula and a wooden spoon without breaking the fillets. Cook for 2 minutes more, or until opaque throughout.

3. Transfer to plates, skin-side down, lightly dash with vinegar, and serve immediately with the remaining warm walnuts from the pan scattered over top.

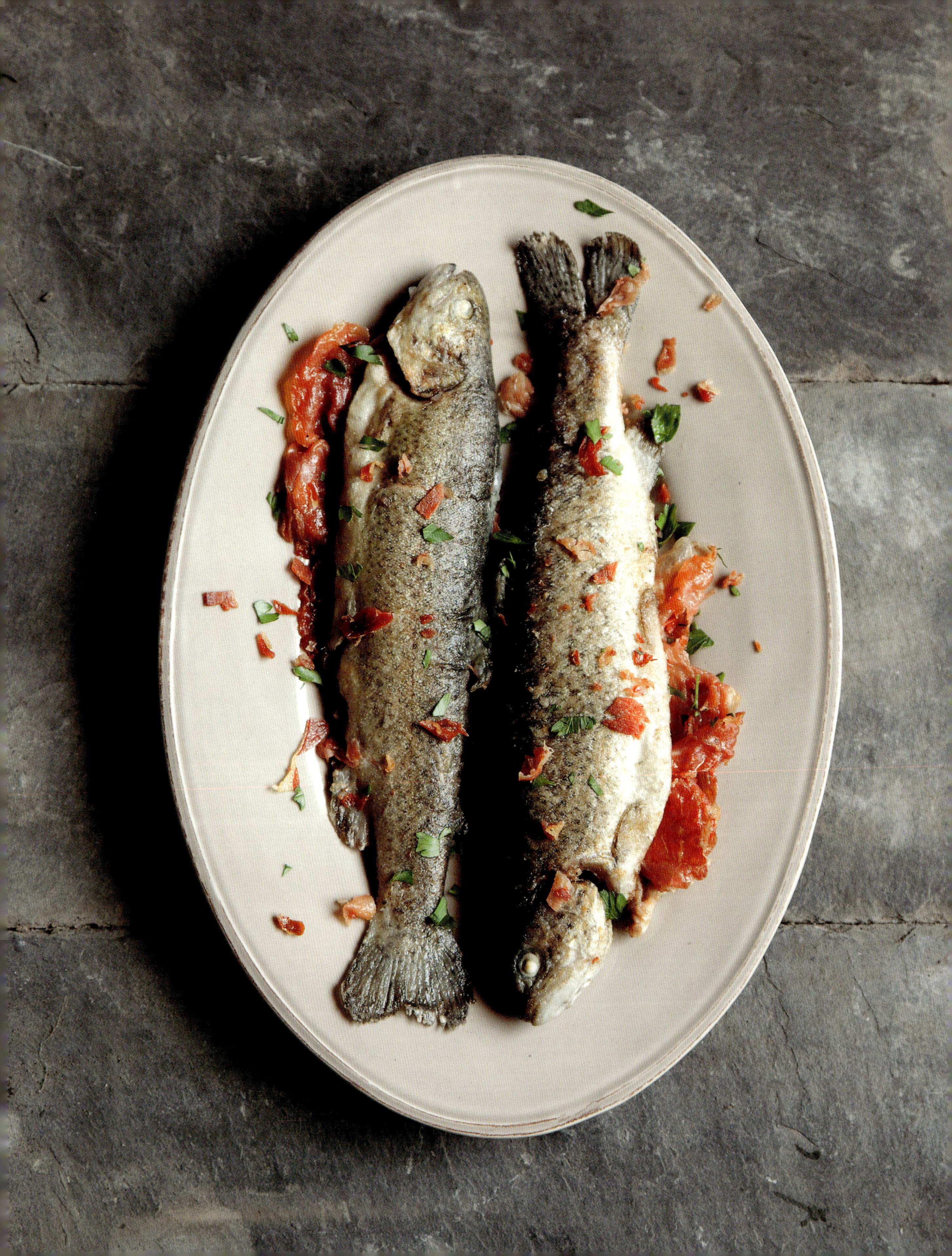

NAVARRA-STYLE TROUT WITH DRY-CURED JAMÓN

TRUCHAS A LA NAVARRA

SERVES 4

The most famous way to prepare trout in Spain comes from Navarra, a fertile region in northern Spain bordering the Basque Country, La Rioja, and Aragón. The saltiness of the jamón offers a perfect counter to the delicate flavors of the fish. Like many cooks, I use the least expensive cured jamón called jamón serrano (as opposed to the much more expensive jamón ibérico) for this dish. Look for wide, moist, and fatty slices.

4 CLEANED WHOLE TROUT, WITH HEADS AND TAILS, ABOUT 8 OUNCES/225 G EACH
SALT
¼ CUP/60 ML EXTRA-VIRGIN OLIVE OIL
8 GENEROUS SLICES DRY-CURED JAMÓN (SEE INGREDIENT NOTE, PAGE 16)
ALL-PURPOSE FLOUR FOR DREDGING
1 LEMON, HALVED
2 TABLESPOONS CHOPPED FRESH FLAT-LEAF PARSLEY

1. Rinse the trout and pat dry with paper towels. Lightly season with salt.

2. In a large skillet or sauté pan, heat the olive oil over high heat and add the jamón. Cook, turning as needed, until golden, 3 to 5 minutes. Transfer the jamón to paper towels and dab off the excess oil.

3. Lightly dredge the trout in flour and add to the skillet. Cook until the trout are golden and just cooked through, turning very carefully just once, about 4 minutes on each side. Test for doneness along the backbone with the tip of a knife; the meat should be just opaque and still very moist. Cook for 1 to 2 minutes more if needed. Transfer to a serving dish.

4. Tuck a slice of jamón into the cavity of each fish. Finely chop the remaining four slices of jamón into shards.

5. Squeeze the lemon over the fish and dust with the chopped jamón and the parsley. Serve immediately.

MARINATED SALMON ON THE GRILL WITH GALICIAN POTATOES

SALMÓN MARINADO A LA PARRILLA CON CACHELOS

SERVES 6

The tradition in Spain for salmon comes from the northwest, in Galicia, Cantabria, and, principally, Asturias, where they migrate from the sea up rivers like the Sella and Narcea. The first fish caught each season is called *el campanu*, as the church bell (*campana*) is rung to announce the news. The fish is sold by auction in the village square, usually to a restaurant for a newsworthy sum of money. A recent campanu, weighing 13½ pounds/6.2 kg, sold to an Asturian cider house in Madrid for an even €10,000 ($13,000). In the flush days of 2007, the campanu went to a restaurant in the Asturian port city of Gijón for €18,000.

1 MEDIUM ONION, FINELY CHOPPED
¼ CUP/60 ML EXTRA-VIRGIN OLIVE OIL
2 TABLESPOONS MINCED FRESH FLAT-LEAF PARSLEY
6 SALMON STEAKS ABOUT 1 INCH/2.5 CM THICK
SALT AND FRESHLY GROUND BLACK PEPPER
GALICIAN BOILED POTATOES (PAGE 116), BUT DO NOT ADD THE PAPRIKA
HOMEMADE MAYONNAISE (SEE PAGE 337)

1. In a wide, shallow bowl, blend the onion, olive oil, and parsley. Season the salmon with salt and pepper and lay them in the onion mixture, turning over to coat. Cover, refrigerate, and marinate for about 1 hour, turning from time to time.

2. Preheat a grill pan, griddle pan, or large, heavy skillet over medium-high heat.

3. Remove the salmon from the marinade and place on the grill pan. Grill, about 5 minutes on each side, turning carefully with a wide spatula just once. Test for doneness near the bone with the tip of a knife; the meat should be just opaque and still very moist. Cook for 1 to 2 minutes more if necessary.

4. Serve with Galician potatoes on the side along with a bowl of mayonnaise to dollop as desired.

Vizcaya is a Basque province, a maritime region with a dramatic coastline dotted with small fishing villages. (It is spelled Bizkaia in Euskera, the Basque language, and called Biscay in English. The region's capital, Bilbao, is by far its largest city.) Its well-known red sauce—*salsa vizcaína*—is served with vegetables, snails, and fish, especially salt cod. The sauce's main ingredient is the dried red pepper called choricero. There are also many excellent commercial brands that sell small jars of pasty choricero pulp (the labels usually read *carne de pimiento choricero*). Calculate about 2 teaspoons of paste per choricero pepper, or, for this recipe, about 3 tablespoons total.

BISCAY-STYLE SALT COD WITH CHORICERO PEPPER SAUCE

BACALAO A LA VIZCAÍNA

SERVES 4

1½ POUNDS/680 G BONELESS SALT COD LOIN, CUT CROSSWISE INTO 4 PIECES

6 DRIED RED CHORICERO PEPPERS OR ANOTHER SWEET, MILD DRIED RED PEPPER (SEE INGREDIENT NOTE, PAGE 16)

8 TABLESPOONS EXTRA-VIRGIN OLIVE OIL

2 MEDIUM ONIONS, THINLY SLICED

3 GARLIC CLOVES, MINCED

1. Beginning 2 to 3 days ahead, desalt the cod following the directions on page 341. Do not remove the skin. Drain in a colander skin-side up for at least 1 to 2 hours. Pat dry with paper towels. There should be about 1¾ pounds/800 g of desalted fillets.

2. Cut the peppers open and remove the seeds. Put the peppers in a bowl, cover with at least 2 cups/480 ml hot water, and soak for 30 minutes. Drain, reserving the liquid. Using a coffee spoon, scrape the soft pulp from inside the skins and reserve. Discard the skins. There should be 3 to 4 tablespoons of pulp.

3. In a large skillet or sauté pan, heat 5 tablespoons of the olive oil over medium-low heat and add the onions, cooking until pale and tender, about 20 minutes. Add the garlic and cook until fragrant, about 1 minute. Stir in the pepper pulp and cook over medium heat for 5 minutes to concentrate the flavors. Stir in 1 cup/240 ml of the reserved liquid from the peppers and simmer until the onions are very tender, 5 to 10 minutes. Remove from the heat and let cool slightly. Pass the sauce through a food mill and then strain it through a conical strainer or chinois. The sauce should be fine and a bit loose. Stir in a bit more of the reserved liquid from the peppers if needed. Return the sauce to the skillet.

4. Meanwhile, in a clean skillet or sauté pan, heat the remaining 3 tablespoons olive oil over medium heat. Set the cod skin-side up in the oil and gently cook, only nudging from time to time to keep it from sticking, for 15 minutes. Transfer with a wide spatula to a plate with the skin side up.

5. Gently set the fish in the sauce, still keeping the skin side facing upward. Cook over medium-low heat in the sauce until warmed through, about 5 minutes. Serve immediately.

FIESTAS

LENT
cuaresma

The forty-day period before Easter known as *Cuaresma* (Lent) is a period of abstinence and fasting meant to imitate the example of Christ. (The Spanish name comes from the Latin *quadragesima*, meaning "fortieth.") On the Spanish table, it is marked by the Catholic prohibition of eating red meat. Although such dietary restrictions have largely become quite relaxed, there are still many traditional Lenten dishes that reflect this ancient practice. These are usually based on fish, eggs, vegetables, and pulses, especially garbanzo beans. In Andalucía, a stewed garbanzo bean and spinach dish (see page 36), typical nearly year-round as a bar tapa as well as homey comfort food, is sometimes called *cazuelita de Cuaresma* (small Lenten casserole).

The food most associated with Lent, though, is *bacalao*, salt cod. Salting cod is a way of preserving fish that was perfected by the Basques more than a thousand years ago. Until quite recently, bacalao was Spain's most important fish. This wasn't only because it could be easily transported and stored, but also because salt cod was an acceptable substitution for red meat during Lent (and on Fridays). Traditional cookbooks often have just a couple of recipes for chicken—and usually rather elaborate, celebration-worthy preparations—but dozens for salt cod. Cooks prepare numerous favorite recipes during this time, including ones with honey, with raisins (see facing page), in "green sauces" heavy with parsley or red sauces with dried peppers (see page 183), made into croquettes, into fritters, as salads, and so on.

And, of course, there are some popular Lenten sweets, too. The most famous are fried sweet fritters called either *buñuelos de Cuaresma* (literally "fritters of Lent") or *buñuelos de viento* ("fritters of the wind"). The latter is a more poetic description of their fluffy texture. A couple placed in a small paper sack when buying bread make a lovely Sunday treat.

GRANDMA LOLA'S LENTEN SALT COD WITH RAISINS

BACALAO CON PASAS DE AVIA LOLA

SERVES 4

During Lent, the number of salt cod dishes you find on tables flourishes. This rather baroque one comes from the grandmother of a Catalan friend in Torreló, a village at the foothills of the Pyrenees mountains north of Vic. Àvia Lola—Grandma Lola (short for Dolores)—prepares this on her saint's day, *El Viernes de Dolores*, the Friday before Easter Sunday. Making the dish over the last few years, I have found that it is key, after soaking the salt cod, to drain it very well, ideally overnight, to keep any salty moisture from seeping into the sweet tomato sofrito at the very end of cooking.

1½ POUNDS/680 G BONELESS SALT COD LOIN, CUT CROSSWISE INTO 4 PIECES
¼ CUP/60 ML EXTRA-VIRGIN OLIVE OIL
ALL-PURPOSE FLOUR FOR DREDGING
1 MEDIUM ONION, FINELY CHOPPED
2 GARLIC CLOVES, MINCED
4 RIPE MEDIUM TOMATOES, HALVED CROSSWISE, SEEDED, AND GRATED (SEE PAGE 339)
½ CUP/120 ML DRY WHITE WINE
1 TABLESPOON MINCED FRESH FLAT-LEAF PARSLEY
¼ CUP/35 G SEEDLESS RAISINS
¼ CUP/35 G PINE NUTS, DRY-TOASTED (SEE PAGE 340)
2 HARD-BOILED EGGS (SEE PAGE 342), PEELED AND HALVED LENGTHWISE

1. Beginning 2 to 3 days ahead, desalt the cod following the directions on page 341. Do not remove the skin. Drain in a colander skin-side up for at least 6 or 8 hours. Pat dry with paper towels. There should be about 1¾ pounds/800 g of desalted fillets.

2. In a cazuela, heavy casserole, large sauté pan, or deep skillet, heat the olive oil over medium heat. Lightly dredge the cod in flour and fry until golden and not yet flaking apart, about 4 minutes total, turning once. Transfer to paper towels to drain.

3. In the same oil, prepare a sofrito with the onion, garlic, and tomatoes, following the directions on page 39. When the sofrito is ready, stir in the wine, parsley, and ¼ cup/60 ml water and bring to a simmer. Reduce the heat to medium-low and simmer uncovered for 15 minutes. Add a bit more water if needed to keep it moist and slightly loose.

4. Meanwhile, bring a pan of water to a boil and drop in the raisins. Boil for 5 minutes and then drain.

5. Gently place the salt cod skin-side down into the sofrito, reduce the heat to low, and let it slowly cook until opaque throughout, about 10 minutes. The final consistency of the sofrito should be quite moist; dribble in water as needed during cooking.

6. Sprinkle the raisins and the pine nuts over the fish. Serve the salt cod garnished with the hard-boiled eggs.

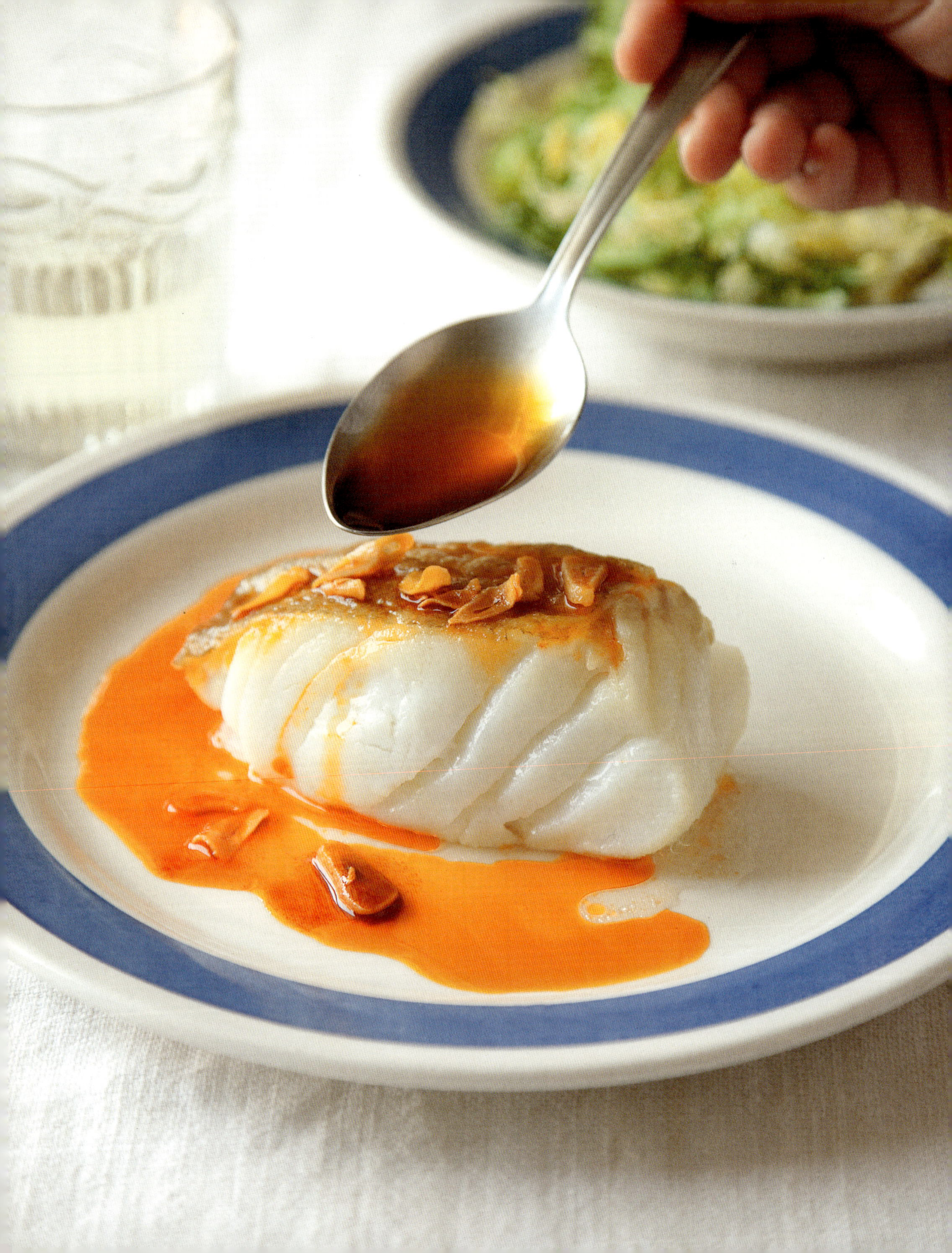

SALT COD BAKED IN THE TIN

BACALLÀ A LA LLAUNA

SERVES 4

This simple, flavorful dish got its start, according to respected Spanish culinary historian Néstor Luján, in nineteenth-century Barcelona, and still recalls the inns and small taverns of the time.

A *llauna* is a rectangular pan with low, straight sides. Use a rimmed baking sheet, rectangular cake pan, or a roasting pan. It is important that you don't overcook the cod in the skillet. The fish should just flake away in moist pieces on the plate—that's it. And there should be plenty of oil to spoon over the top and to soak up with bread.

1¾ POUNDS/800 G BONELESS SALT COD LOIN, CUT CROSSWISE INTO 4 OR 8 PIECES
½ CUP/120 ML EXTRA-VIRGIN OLIVE OIL
ALL-PURPOSE FLOUR FOR DREDGING
6 GARLIC CLOVES, CUT INTO THIN, FLAT LENGTHWISE SLICES
1 TABLESPOON SPANISH PIMENTÓN DULCE (SWEET PAPRIKA)
MINCED FRESH FLAT-LEAF PARSLEY FOR GARNISHING (OPTIONAL)

1. Beginning 2 to 3 days ahead, desalt the cod following the directions on page 341. Do not remove the skin. Drain in a colander skin-side up for at least 1 to 2 hours. Pat dry with paper towels. There should be about 2¼ pounds/1 kg of desalted fillets.

2. Preheat the oven to 350°F/180°C/gas mark 4.

3. In a large skillet, heat the olive oil over medium heat. Lightly dredge the cod in flour and fry until golden and not yet flaking apart, about 4 minutes total, turning once. Remove the skillet from the heat. Transfer the pieces of cod to paper towels to briefly drain. Arrange the salt cod skin-side up on a rimmed baking sheet.

4. Return the skillet to the stove. Add the garlic and cook over medium heat until fragrant and just golden, about 45 seconds. Do not let it burn. Remove the skillet from the heat, let the oil cool for a few moments, and then stir in the pimentón until dissolved.

5. Immediately spoon the oil and garlic over the fish. Dribble 1 tablespoon water around the base. Bake for 3 minutes, or until warmed throughout.

6. Carefully transfer the salt cod to plates, spoon over the sauce, and, if desired, lightly garnish with parsley before serving.

PIQUILLO PEPPERS STUFFED WITH SALT COD BRANDADE

PIMIENTOS DEL PIQUILLO RELLENO DE BRANDADA DE BACALAO

SERVES 4

Red piquillo peppers are nearly inedible when fresh. But fire-roasted and preserved, they transform into a sublime and perfectly stuffable vegetable. Most often sold packaged in flat tins or sometimes glass jars, they have a distinctive triangular shape. Look for ones that are whole (*entero*), roasted (*asados*), and hand-peeled (*pelados a mano*). The best come from Lodosa, a town in Navarra. A quicker and not uncommon version of this Basque Country and Navarra classic substitutes the brandade with high-quality tinned bonito del norte tuna mixed with mayonnaise. In nearby La Rioja, the peppers are also stuffed with ground meat or mushrooms blended with some béchamel sauce. The possibilities are deliciously wide. Remember, brandade can take several days to prepare, so be sure to plan ahead and start soaking the salt cod in advance.

10 CANNED ROASTED WHOLE PIQUILLO PEPPERS
1 CUP/240 ML SALT COD BRANDADE (PAGE 87)
1 CUP/240 ML HEAVY CREAM
SALT
MINCED FRESH FLAT-LEAF PARSLEY FOR GARNISHING

1. Open the tin(s) of piquillo peppers. Drain the liquid and reserve. Gently remove the peppers. Set aside any that are broken.

2. Fit a pastry bag with a round tip and fill the bag with the brandade. Select the best 8 peppers and carefully fill each with about 2 tablespoons of brandade. The filling should just spill out of the ends.

3. Purée the remaining 2 peppers with the cream. In a saucepan, add the puréed mixture, season with salt, and gently heat over medium heat; do not let it reach a boil.

4. Drizzle some warm sauce on a platter and place the stuffed peppers on top. Lightly garnish with parsley. Serve with the remaining sauce in a bowl on the side to add as desired.

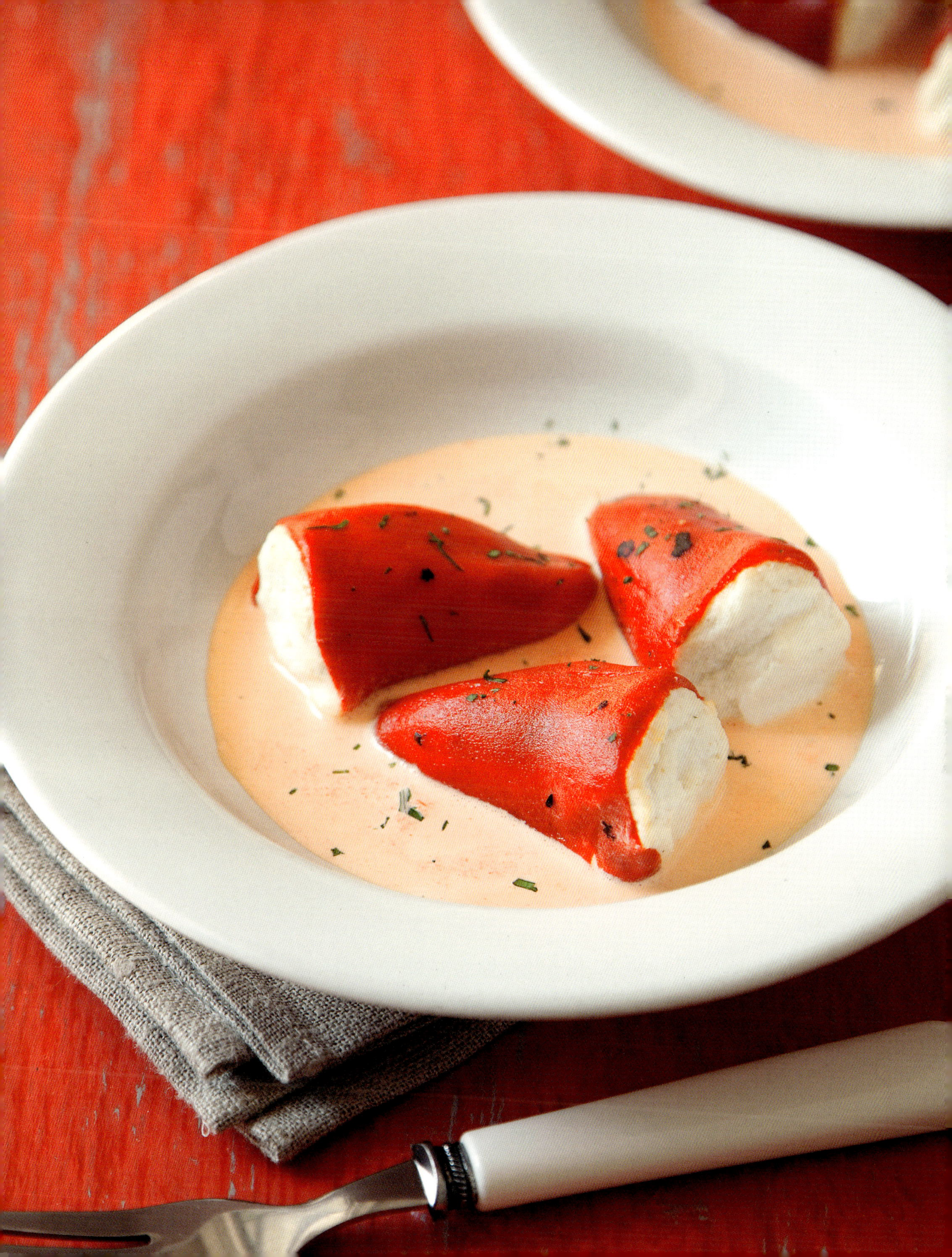

INGREDIENTS

TINNED DELICACIES
las latas

The traditional function of *conservas* (preserves) is to prolong the life of seasonal ingredients, from the abundance of summer fruits and tomatoes to pork from pigs slaughtered during the cold weather. In Spain, this has been done with salt, smoke, alcohol, vinegar, and olive oil. Seafood and vegetables, especially, benefitted greatly from mid–nineteenth century advances in canning. Over the years, the practicalities of these ancient traditions graduated into what can only be called art forms in *latas* (tins).

Numerous companies continue to follow traditional methods. It begins with buying the finest raw materials available in the markets. As Nely Concheiro, the proprietor of one such company—the exquisite Conservas Ramón Peña in Cambados, Galicia—bluntly put it to me: "The best goes in the tin." She was referring to the goods in the numerous *lonjas* (wholesale seafood auction markets) that dot the Galician coastline, but could have been referring to the entire philosophy of the vast industry of conservas processed by artisanal methods.

Conservas like those from her company are the blue chip products of the Spanish seas and fields. Work is detailed and meticulous, with shortcuts never taken, especially when it comes to flavors. Whereas inexpensive versions might use a chemical essence for flavor, at places like this, Nely emphasized, "everything is natural." The day I visited Conservas Ramón Peña (it is more workshop than factory), a woman was peeling and adding garlic cloves to an escabeche marinade for mussels. "*Como hago yo en casa*," Nely said. (Just as I do at home.) Another dozen women sat along a high bench patiently trimming the last strands of beard from shucked mussels with tiny scissors. Once the women hand-packed the mussels into tins, a bay leaf would be delicately laid into each one before being sealed.

There are many fine producers that pay such attention to details. Here is a list of the most common types of latas, with a few highly recommended brands. Prices can be astronomical. But the splurge is usually worth it. Just open the tin (or jar) and enjoy the best of Spain's countryside and coastline.

Anchovy fillets from the Cantabrian Sea *(anchoas de Mar Cantábrico)*: Lolín, Angelachu, La Brújula, Don Bocarte

Anchovy fillets from the Mediterranean *(anchoas de l'Escala)*: Anxoves de l'Escala

Artichoke hearts *(corazones de alcachofa)*: Rosara, Leyenda, La Catedral de Navarra

"Baby" fava or broad beans in extra-virgin olive oil *(habitas baby en aceite de oliva virgen extra)*: Viuda de Cayo, Ferret, La Catedral de Navarra

Bonito del norte tuna *(bonito del norte)*: Acromar, Angelachu, Ortiz, Consorcio

Chestnuts in syrup *(castañas en almíbar)*: Moncloa de San Lázaro, Prada a Tope

Clams in natural brine *(almejas al natural)*: Los Peperetes, Dardo, Paco LaFuente

Cockles in natural brine *(berberechos al natural)*: Paco Lafuente, Pay-Pay, Dardo, Ramón Peña

Garbanzo beans *(garbanzos)*: Rosara, Vitra, El Navarrico

Mussels in escabeche marinade *(mejillones en escabeche)*: Dardo, Ramón Peña, Consorcio

Partridge in escabeche marinade *(perdiz en escabeche)*: La Ponderosa de Cuenca, Lahoz

Razor clams in natural brine *(navajas al natural)*: La Brújula, Los Peperetes

Roasted piquillo peppers *(pimientos del piquillo)*: El Navarrico, La Catedral de Navarra

Small sardines in escabeche marinade *(sardinillas en escabeche)*: El Porrón

Small sardines in extra-virgin olive oil *(sardinillas en aceite de oliva virgen extra)*: Real Conservera Española, Ramón Franco

Small squid in their own ink *(chipirones en su tinta)*: La Brújula, Los Peperetes

White asparagus in natural brine *(espárragos blancos)*: El Navarrico, La Catedral de Navarra

CHAPTER 8

SHELLFISH
mariscos

Shellfish is so key to the diet in parts of Spain—especially in Galicia—that more than one regional cookbook on my shelf *opens* with the shellfish chapter. Fish follows, and then soups, breads, pulses, and other staples. "Shellfish," begins the introduction of Matilde Felpeto Lagoa's wonderful *Recetas de la cocina familiar gallega* (Recipes from the Galician Family Kitchen), "is our 'jewel in the crown,' one of the greatest treasures to enjoy." Indeed. The wholesale seafood market in Madrid is the largest in Europe and second in the world only to Tokyo's Tsukiji market. It sells around 290 million pounds/132 million kilograms annually, and an important part of that is shellfish. Spanish fleets bring back to port the largest percentage of Europe's collective haul—some 16 percent of the catch.

While Galicia is the dominant force and key source, it is by no means the only region with significant seafood industries. Along the Atlantic Ocean, Asturias, Cantabria, and the Basque Country all have extensive fishing fleets and well-known ports. In the south, Andalucía straddles the Atlantic and the Mediterranean. On the Atlantic side, the provinces of Cádiz and Huelva draw from the waters below Portugal, while Spain's 1,000-mile-/1660-km-long Mediterranean coast has its own important seafood industry.

Although many species come from either the Atlantic or the Mediterranean, there are species found in both—though usually with a difference between them. *Navajas* (razor clams), for instance, gathered in Galicia tend to be larger and meatier than those from the Mediterranean, which are more delicate in texture as well as flavor. Among many celebrated varieties of shrimp, the *gamba blanca* (literally "white shrimp," but correctly called rose shrimp, *Parapenaeus longirostris*) from Huelva and the *gamba roja* ("red shrimp," *Aristeus antennatus*) from Dénia in Alicante are two of the jewels previously mentioned.

With such fine *materias primas* (raw materials), preparations are often straightforward, and allow the shellfish to properly and loudly express their potent flavors. As I learned in Galicia, the classical way to prepare most shellfish is in boiling salted water with a bay leaf. It is only a matter of buying fresh products and calculating—and respecting—cooking times. Cooking shellfish, then, doesn't only begin in the market, but that is often the most important step in the process.

The best season tends to be winter. There is a saying in Spanish that you should eat shellfish during the months with an "r"—*septiembre, octubre, noviembre, diciembre, enero, febrero, marzo y abril*. That is because the waters are colder, there are less algae blooms, and the cooler weather often means that the shellfish make their way from sea to market to table in better condition.

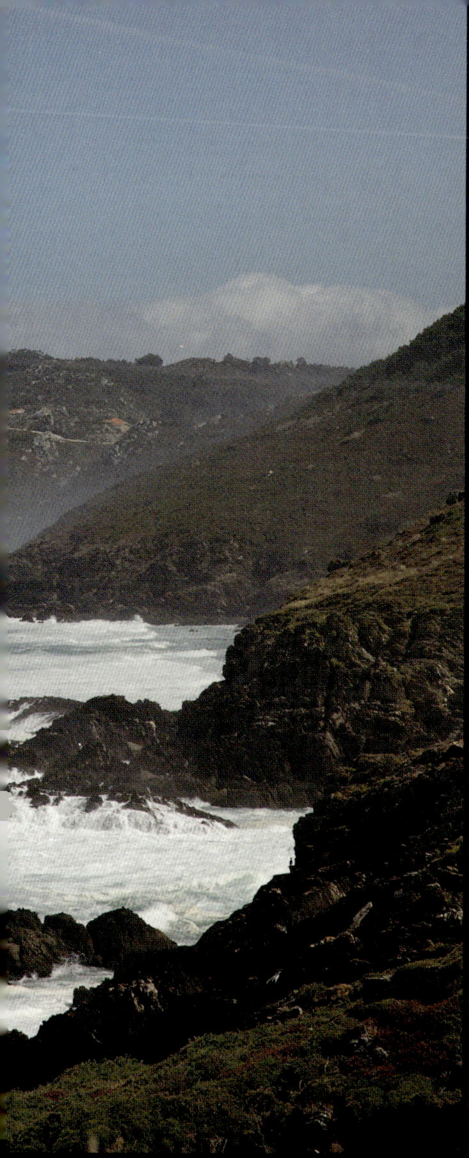
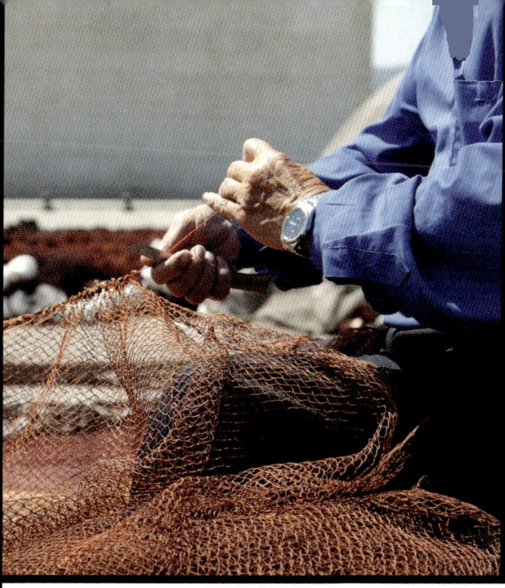
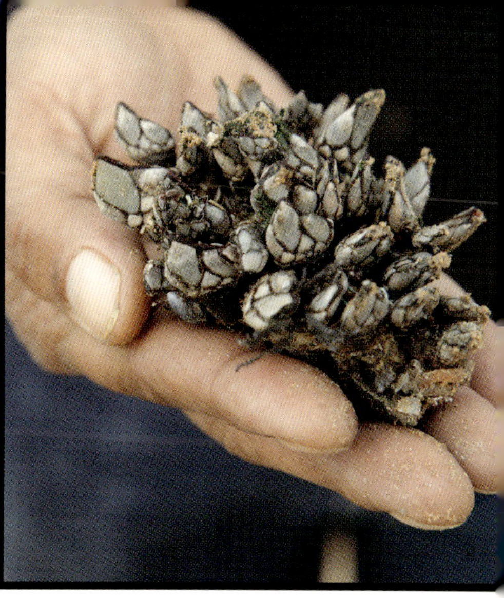
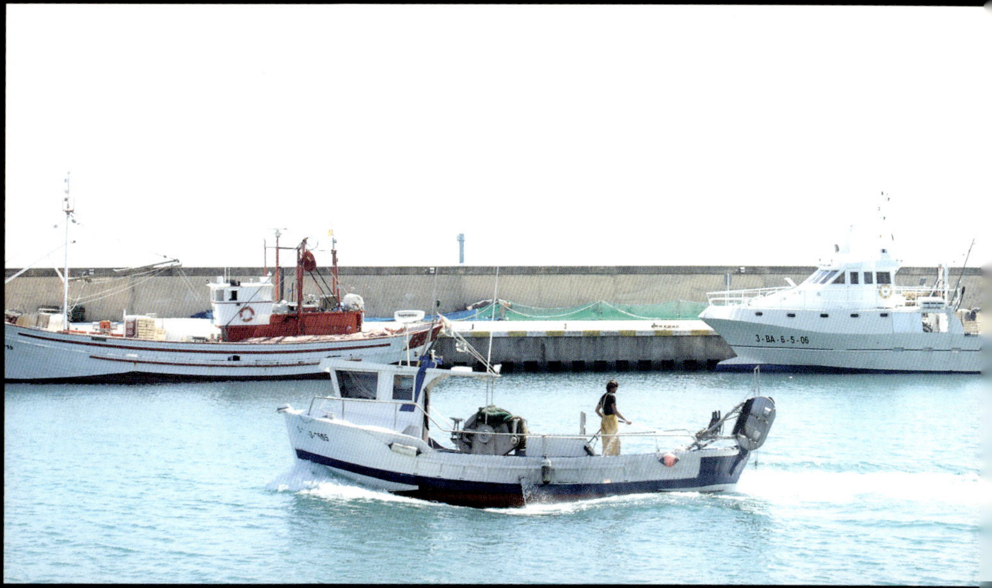
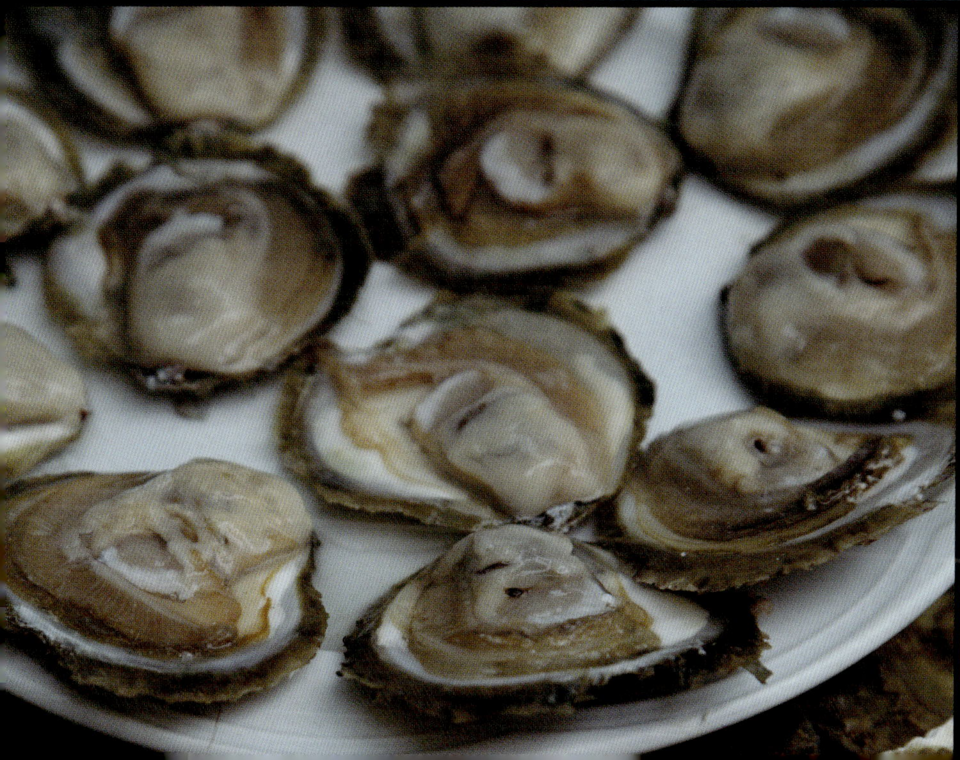
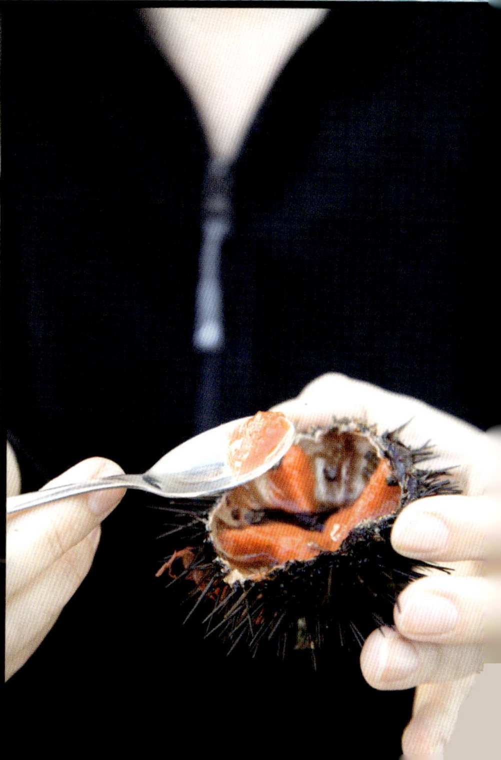

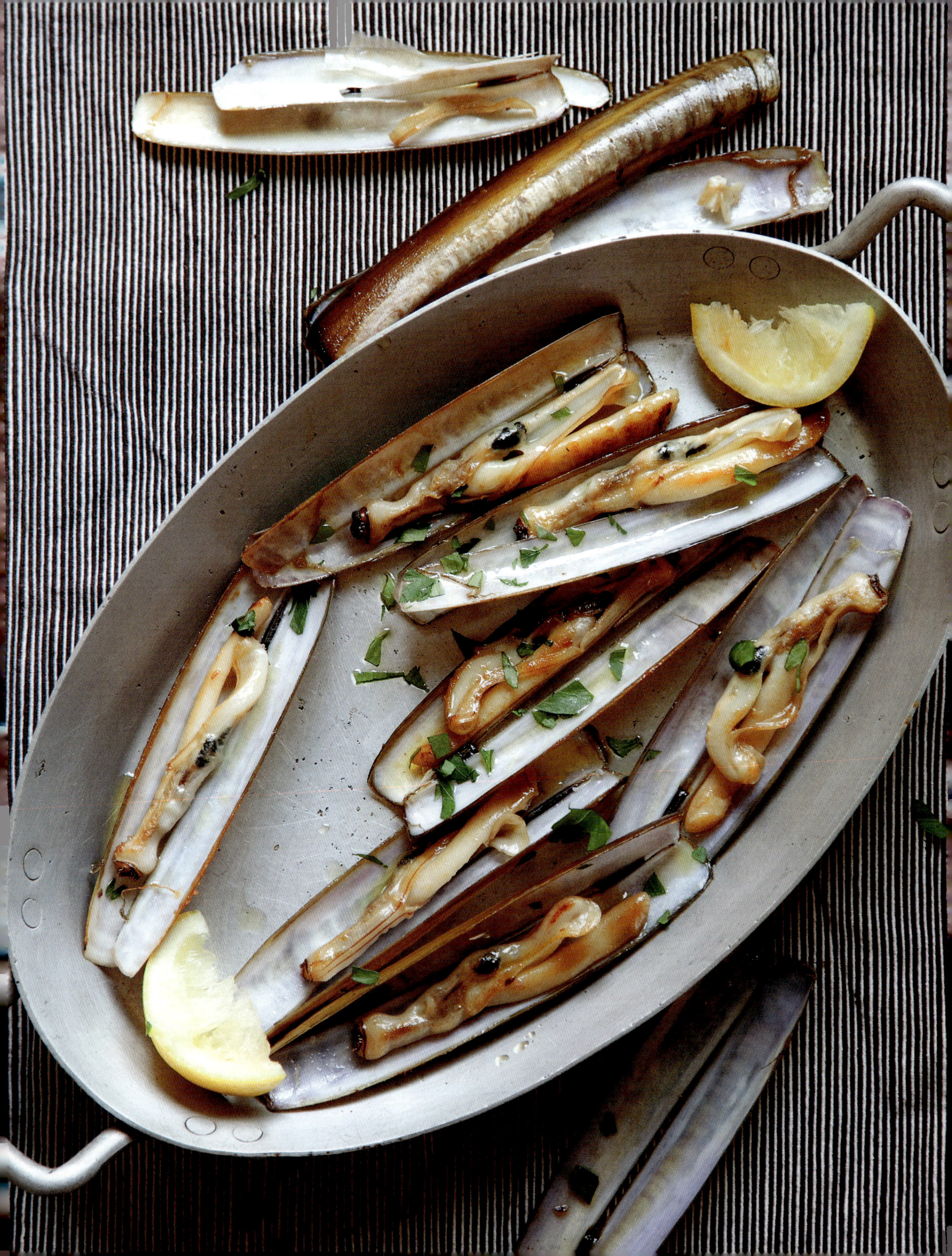

GRILLED RAZOR CLAMS

NAVAJAS A LA PLANCHA

SERVES 4

These long, meaty clams, shaped like old-fashioned straight razors (*navajas*) are, for me, Spain's preeminent shellfish. There are two closely related varieties found in the markets—the larger, meatier ones from the Atlantic coast (namely from Galicia) that measure about 6 inches/15 cm long, and the smaller, often sweeter-tasting ones from the Ebro Delta that are just 3 to 4 inches/7.5 to 10 cm long. Both are found buried in sand vertically, and both are superb tasting, with a fine texture. Keep them rubber-banded snugly together until ready to grill.

Grilling navajas is the most typical and by far the best way to prepare them. It's simple. Put them on the hot pan, and when the shell opens, turn them meat-side down and grill until golden and tender. Prepared like this, they make a finger-licking dish. Or rather, shell-licking. Lick the shell, too, as that is where the real flavors concentrate.

EXTRA-VIRGIN OLIVE OIL FOR OILING PAN AND DRIZZLING
FLAKY SEA SALT
12 TO 16 RAZOR CLAMS
1 TABLESPOON MINCED FRESH FLAT-LEAF PARSLEY
1 LEMON, CUT INTO WEDGES

1. Preheat a grill pan, griddle pan, or large, heavy skillet over medium-high heat, lightly oil, and scatter with salt flakes. Without crowding the pan, lay on the clams. Once the shells open, flip them over so that the meat is against the pan. Gently press down on the back of the shells. Cook until the meat is golden and still tender, 3 to 5 minutes, depending on the size of the razor clams.

2. Transfer to a platter, generously drizzle with oil, and scatter some parsley over the top. Garnish with lemon wedges and serve immediately.

SHELLFISH

CLAMS IN GREEN SAUCE

ALMEJAS EN SALSA VERDE

SERVES 4

From the Atlantic fishing communities of the north—Galicia, Cantabria, Asturias, and the Basque Country—comes this classic dish prepared with either clams or hake, or a combination of the two. The green in the sauce is from a generous amount of fresh parsley. Use flat-leaf Italian parsley, not the curly variety. (Parsley is so common in the Spanish kitchen that it is given free in fishmongers' and butchers' shops.)

2 POUNDS/910 G MEDIUM TO LARGE CLAMS, SCRUBBED
1 BAY LEAF
3 TABLESPOONS EXTRA-VIRGIN OLIVE OIL
1 MEDIUM ONION, FINELY CHOPPED
2 GARLIC CLOVES, MINCED
½ CUP/120 ML DRY WHITE WINE
3 TABLESPOONS MINCED FRESH FLAT-LEAF PARSLEY
SALT
2 TEASPOONS ALL-PURPOSE FLOUR

1. Purge the clams of any sand by soaking in salty water following the directions on page 341. Discard any clams with broken shells.

2. In a large pot, add the clams, bay leaf, and ½ cup/120 ml water, and bring to a boil over high heat. Lower the heat, cover the pot, and simmer, shaking the pot from time to time, until the clams have opened, 2 to 4 minutes. Remove from the heat. Drain, reserving the liquid. Discard any clams that did not open.

3. In a cazuela, heavy casserole, large sauté pan, or deep skillet, heat the olive oil over medium heat and cook the onion until soft and nearly translucent, 8 to 10 minutes. Add the garlic and cook until fragrant, about 1 minute, stirring frequently. Combine the reserved liquid from the clams with water to make ¾ cup/180 ml and add to the pan along with the wine and parsley. Season with salt and whisk in the flour. Bring to a boil and cook uncovered, stirring from time to time, over a low boil for 5 minutes to thicken the sauce.

4. Add the clams to the pan and cook uncovered, shaking the pan from time to time, for 5 minutes. Transfer to a shallow serving bowl, pour over the sauce from the pan, and serve immediately.

Most Spanish clam preparations are pretty straightforward, and cooked so that the shellfish don't lose their delicate flavors. Steaming them open in a pot with some white wine is common across Spain, with the differences mostly in the type of wine. In Galicia, cooks reach for their minerally, fruity Albariño (see page 204), while in the Basque Country they might tip in some young Txakoli. In Andalucía, they add a *chorro* (shot) of one of the various dry sherries produced around Jerez.

My favorite way to prepare clams is using an aged sherry like amontillado, with its rich hazelnut and, at times, tobacco notes, or else oloroso. Deep amber-toned and highly aromatic—the name means "scented"—oloroso carries hints of toasted nuts, dried fruits, even raisins. If you don't have either of these, use a trick that I learned from one wine store owner who was loath to sell me such an elegant, unique wine for cooking: Use a dry white wine and some drops of brandy to give it some depth of color and flavor. Try to find large, meaty clams that will absorb the sherry's perfume.

CLAMS WITH OLOROSO SHERRY

ALMEJAS AL OLOROSO DE JEREZ

SERVES 4 TO 6

2 POUNDS/910 G MEDIUM TO LARGE CLAMS, SCRUBBED
1 TABLESPOON EXTRA-VIRGIN OLIVE OIL
4 GARLIC CLOVES, CHOPPED
½ CUP/120 ML OLOROSO, AMONTILLADO, FINO, OR ANOTHER DRY SHERRY
1 TEASPOON ALL-PURPOSE FLOUR
1 TABLESPOON MINCED FRESH FLAT-LEAF PARSLEY

1. Purge the clams of any sand by soaking in salty water following the directions on page 341. Discard any clams with broken shells.

2. In a large pot, heat the olive oil over medium heat and add the garlic. Cook until fragrant and just golden, about 1 minute. Do not let it burn. Add the sherry, stir in the flour, and bring to a boil. Boil for 2 minutes to burn off the alcohol, and then add the clams. Cover and cook, stirring and shaking the pan, until the clams have opened, about 5 minutes. Discard any clams that did not open.

3. Transfer the clams and sauce to a deep serving platter, sprinkle with the parsley, and serve immediately.

STEAMED COCKLES

BERBERECHOS AL VAPOR

SERVES 4

Berberechos are fat, almost heart-shaped clams about 1 or 1½ inches/3 or 4 cm across with some two dozen distinct, deeply marked ridges in the shell. The best come from the *rías* (inlets) of Galicia, specifically around Muros and Noia. Their season begins in autumn and winds down in March or so, as the weather warms. They are gathered by women known as *mariscadoras* who scour the beaches with rakes. Although most commonly preserved in tins in natural brine, they are at their plumpest and sweetest when steamed and eaten with a few drops of lemon. That is all they need—and all they ever get.

2 POUNDS/910 G FRESH COCKLES
1 BAY LEAF
SALT
4 LEMON WEDGES

1. If needed, purge the cockles of any sand by soaking in salty water following the directions on page 341. Discard any cockles with broken shells.

2. In a large pot, add 3 tablespoons water, the cockles, bay leaf, and a pinch of salt and snugly cover the pot with a lid. Over high heat, bring the water to a boil and steam the cockles, shaking the pot from time to time, until they have opened, 2 to 3 minutes. Discard any cockles that did not open.

3. Transfer to a serving bowl with a slotted spoon. Serve immediately with the lemon wedges to squeeze over the tops.

MUSSELS IN SWEET SOFRITO TOMATO SAUCE

MEJILLONES CON SOFRITO

SERVES 4

Pocketed with fishing villages, riddled with inlets, and blessed with protective coves for its colorful fleets, Spain's northern Atlantic coast is a source of much of the country's shellfish, from lobsters to prehistoric-looking *centollas* (spider crabs), from the spectacular razor clam dug in the sand to the humble mussel cultivated on floating wooden rafts called *bateas*. This preparation elevates the inexpensive mussel beyond its modest status into one of those dishes that is nearly impossible to stop eating. The slow-cooked tomato sofrito gives the dish a sweetness, the sherry a lovely aroma, and the mussels more than a glint of the sea.

2 POUNDS/910 G SMALL TO MEDIUM MUSSELS, CLEANED, SCRUBBED, AND DEBEARDED (SEE PAGE 341)

4 TABLESPOONS EXTRA-VIRGIN OLIVE OIL

1 MEDIUM ONION, FINELY CHOPPED

4 RIPE MEDIUM TOMATOES, HALVED, SEEDED, AND GRATED (SEE PAGE 339)

SALT

SUGAR

1 GARLIC CLOVE, MINCED

1 TABLESPOON MINCED FRESH FLAT-LEAF PARSLEY

¾ CUP/180 ML DRY SHERRY

1 TABLESPOON PLAIN DRY BREADCRUMBS

1. In a large pot, add the mussels and ½ cup/120 ml water and bring to a boil over high heat. Lower the heat, cover the pot, and simmer, shaking the pot from time to time, until the mussels have opened, 3 to 5 minutes. Drain, reserving the liquid. Discard any mussels that did not open. Twist off the empty half of each mussel and discard.

2. In a cazuela, heavy casserole, large sauté pan, or deep skillet, heat the olive oil over medium heat and prepare a sofrito with the onion and tomatoes, following the directions on page 39. Allow plenty of time for it to become particularly dark, pulpy, and sweet. Season with salt and a generous pinch of sugar during cooking and moisten from time to time with a touch of reserved liquid from cooking the mussels to keep the sofrito from drying out.

3. When the sofrito is ready, stir in the garlic and parsley. Arrange the mussels facing upward in the pan, moving them gently around the sofrito with a wooden spoon. Drizzle over the sherry and sprinkle with the breadcrumbs. Cover the pan and cook over low heat for 15 minutes. Transfer the mussels to a serving platter and spoon the sofrito over top. Serve immediately.

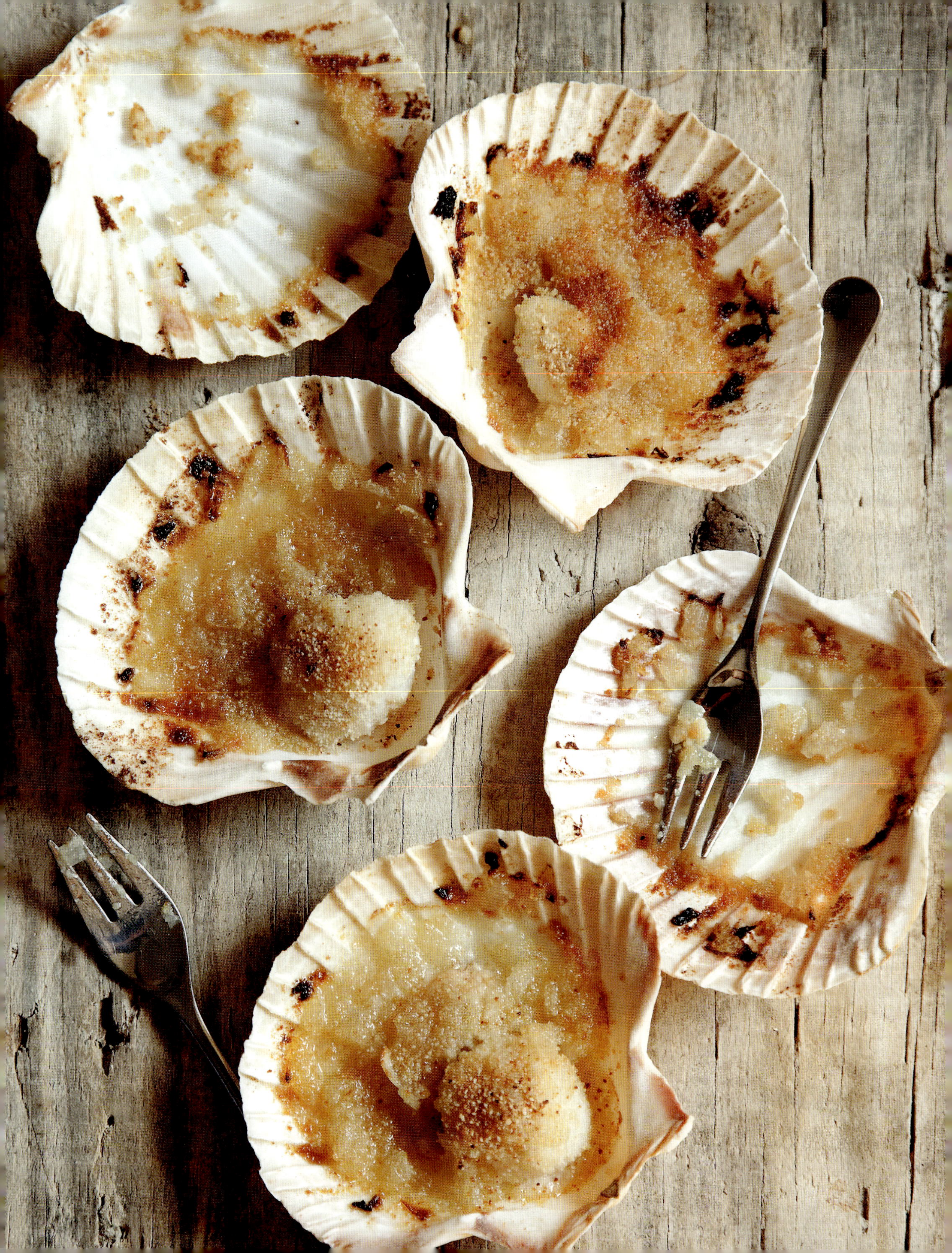

BAKED SCALLOPS IN THE SHELL

VIEIRAS AL HORNO

SERVES 4

In Spain, scallops are particularly associated with Galicia and the lengthy pilgrimage route, the Camino de Santiago. *Peregrinos* (pilgrims) symbolically carry a scallop shell on a necklace or fastened to their pack as they walk to Santiago de Compostela. Scallops on the half-shell, sweetened with some tender sautéed onions, moistened with a bit of white wine, sprinkled with breadcrumbs, and slid into the oven, is a superb Galician specialty. A similar treatment is given to smaller, bright orangish red scallops called *zamburiñas*. (*Vieiras* have one rounded and one flat shell, while the smaller *zamburiñas* have two equally rounded shells.) A pinch of finely chopped dry-cured jamón or some sweet pimentón (paprika) will add an interesting touch of flavor. But do not overwhelm the lovely natural taste of the scallops. This serves four as a first course, but you can serve double that number as a rather elegant part of a tapas spread.

4 TABLESPOONS EXTRA-VIRGIN OLIVE OIL
1 MEDIUM ONION, FINELY CHOPPED
SALT
½ CUP/120 ML FRUITY WHITE WINE
8 SCALLOPS IN THE SHELL
⅓ CUP/50 G PLAIN DRY BREADCRUMBS

1. In a medium skillet, heat the olive oil over medium heat and add the onion and a pinch of salt, cooking until soft and translucent, 8 to 10 minutes. Stir in the wine and cook for 3 minutes to let the alcohol burn off and reduce slightly. The onion should be very moist and juicy. Remove from the heat.

2. Preheat the broiler.

3. Rinse the scallops, leaving the meat in the half shell.

4. On a baking sheet, arrange the scallops. Spread about 1 tablespoon of the onion inside each shell around the scallop meat. Sprinkle a thin layer of breadcrumbs over top. (Depending on the size of the shell, there may be some of each left over at the end.) Broil until the breadcrumbs are golden, 5 to 10 minutes. Transfer to plates and serve hot.

GRILLED SHRIMP

GAMBAS A LA PLANCHA

SERVES 4

Gambas cooked *a la plancha*—on a flat grill pan—exemplify one of the delights of Spanish cooking: few ingredients and intense flavors. After all, what's the point of buying good, fresh shrimp and then cooking them in a manner where you can't fully appreciate their exquisite briny flavors or enjoy their firm, juicy texture?

I learned to cook shrimp when living in Spain, but that is also where I learned to eat them. There *is* a proper (or at least recommended) way to do so. First, break off the head, pinch it between your thumb and forefinger, and noisily slurp out the juice (that is where the flavors are most concentrated); then attack the body with your fingers, freely licking the salty, flavorful oil from them. Cloth napkins in Spain tend to be extra-large, and this is a reason why. Some like to dollop a spoonful of minced garlic and fresh parsley on top before serving, but I find that if the shrimp are of the highest caliber, it isn't necessary or even advisable.

These make great tapas, but also a spectacular first course—one that is now traditionally found at even the most special of occasions, Christmas lunch.

2 POUNDS/910 G FRESH LARGE SHRIMP OR PRAWNS WITH THE HEADS AND SHELLS
2 TABLESPOONS EXTRA-VIRGIN OLIVE OIL
FLAKY SEA SALT

1. Do not rinse the shrimp; instead wipe them with a damp towel.

2. Preheat a grill pan, griddle pan, or large, heavy skillet over high heat. Lightly coat with the olive oil and sprinkle with salt flakes.

3. Place the shrimp on the pan, sprinkle a pinch of salt over top, and grill, turning once, until opaque throughout, about 2 minutes on each side. Serve immediately.

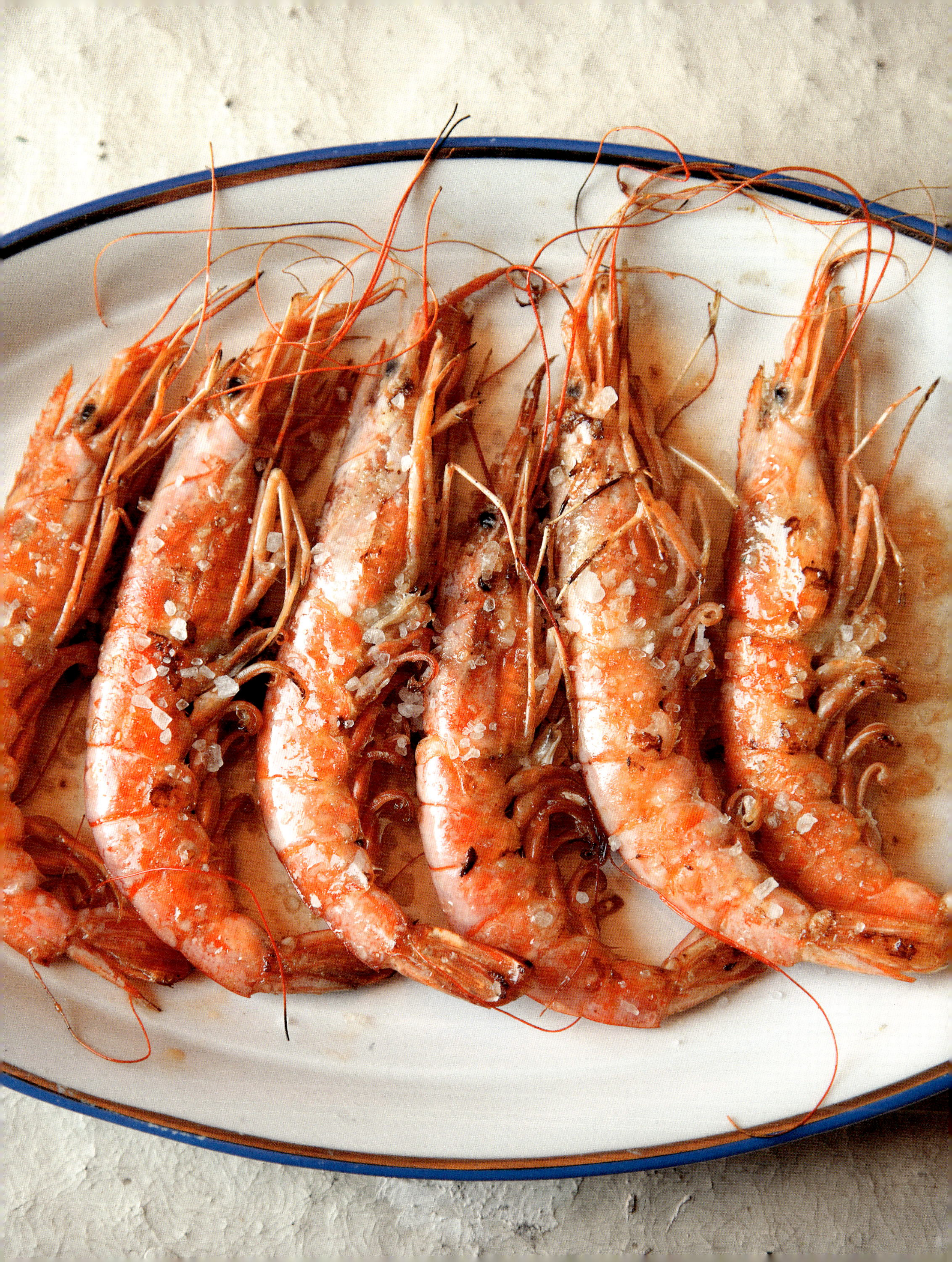

ALBARIÑO

Far from the arid plateaus of the Ribera del Duero, or the steep slate and shale slopes of Priorat, and across the palate from husky, structured red wines, comes the crisp and refreshing Albariño, produced along the wild coasts and *rías* (inlets) of southwestern Galicia. Made from an eponymous grape grown in the Rías Baixas, the lower section of Spain's Atlantic coast to the north of Portugal, this is one of the country's most pleasant, easiest drinking wines.

It is an ancient, regional vino, dating perhaps as far back as Roman times, two thousand years ago, though at least to the twelfth century, when records show Cistercian monks making Albariño wine near Cambados. In the 1980s and 1990s, the industry exploded in popularity, taking Albariño from a local wine to a national, and global, one.

Still today, you find dense pockets of vines behind houses and three-hundred-year-old *pazos* (stone manor houses), rather than undulating hills of vineyards. The small, thick-skinned grape is planted on tall granite pylons and trestles 6 or 8 feet/2 or 2.5 m high. This keeps the grapes off the moist ground while allowing them to catch more ocean breezes. By allowing the air to circulate like this, it better dries away the moisture, avoids rot, and exposes the tight clusters of ripening grapes to more sunshine.

The resulting wines are bright and refreshing, with touches of minerals and often hints of stone fruits—peaches, apricots, nectarines—citruses, and melons, and with aromas of wildflowers and honeysuckle. These are springy wines meant to be drunk young.

Perhaps not coincidentally, they are perfectly paired with the region's even more celebrated seafood. A chilled glass of Albariño with a plate of grilled razor clams (see page 195), steamed cockles (see page 198), baked scallops (see page 201), or a half-dozen shucked oysters from Soutomaior is one of the country's coastal highlights.

LOBSTER IN A NUTTY CHOCOLATE SAUCE, COSTA BRAVA STYLE

BOGAVANTE CON CHOCOLATE

SERVES 2 TO 4

Chocolate made a not-infrequent appearance as an ingredient in Catalan cooking during the nineteenth century, a time when many from coastal Catalunya were going to the Antilles for business. While something of a specialty dish these days, recipes for lobster in chocolate that I have found in traditional Catalan cookbooks are strikingly similar. This one is adapted from their comparable versions. The chocolate here is treated like a spice and goes into the pounded picada stirred into the sauce. The outcome is baroque, tasty, and highly original.

2 FRESH LOBSTERS, 1½ TO 2 POUNDS/680 TO 910 G EACH

SALT AND FRESHLY GROUND BLACK PEPPER

¼ CUP/60 ML OLIVE OIL

2 GARLIC CLOVES, PEELED

2 MEDIUM ONIONS, FINELY CHOPPED

½ TEASPOON SPANISH PIMENTÓN DULCE (SWEET PAPRIKA)

2 PINCHES SAFFRON THREADS (ABOUT 20 TOTAL), DRY-TOASTED AND GROUND (SEE PAGE 340)

¼ CUP/60 ML BRANDY

1½ CUPS/360 ML FISH STOCK (PAGE 335)

1 OUNCE/30 G DARK UNSWEETENED CHOCOLATE

16 UNSALTED TOASTED ALMONDS WITHOUT SKINS

1 TABLESPOON MINCED FRESH FLAT-LEAF PARSLEY

2 THIN GALLETA MARÍA COOKIES OR ANOTHER ROUND, FLAT TEA BISCUIT, OR 1 GRAHAM CRACKER

1. Clean and cut the lobsters in half lengthwise down the middle. (If female, reserve the roe for the picada.) Crack the large claws slightly or "mark" them with a knife so they remain intact but the meat will be easily accessible when served. Season the lobster generously with salt and pepper.

2. In a cazuela, heavy casserole, or large sauté pan, heat the olive oil over medium heat. Add the lobsters and cook for 2 minutes, meat-side down, then for another 2 minutes shell-side down. Transfer to a platter.

3. Add the garlic to the pan, reduce the heat to medium-low, and cook until golden and fragrant, about 1 minute; remove and reserve. Add the onions, and cook until soft and translucent, about 10 minutes.

4. Cut away and discard the antennae and small legs on the lobsters.

5. Return the lobsters and any juices to the pan, add the pimentón and saffron, and then pour in the brandy. Let the alcohol burn off for 1 minute, and then pour in the stock. Simmer for 10 minutes.

6. Meanwhile, prepare a picada with the reserved garlic and lobster roe (if there was any), the chocolate, almonds, parsley, cookies, and 2 tablespoons of simmering stock from the pan, following the directions on page 39.

7. Stir the picada into the sauce and simmer for a final 10 minutes. The sauce should be loose but not watery. Remove the lobsters and reduce the sauce over high heat if needed. Serve from the cazuela.

For me, this is one of the great traditional Basque dishes. The small stuffed squid are braised in a sauce that includes their own ink, which adds dense sea flavors, not to mention an impressive black color. (Packets of squid ink can be bought at many Italian and Asian markets as well as specialist Spanish ones; see Sources, page 345.) Many formal Spanish cooks have a tendency to purée sauces before serving—here I agree that it is necessary. Some Basques add a couple of spoonfuls of tomato sauce to soften the final result. Serve the squid with some *pan frito*, slices of bread quickly fried in a bit of olive oil, as I learned to do from friends in the Basque Country.

SMALL SQUID IN THEIR OWN INK

CHIPIRONES EN SU TINTA

SERVES 4

2 POUNDS/910 G SMALL WHOLE SQUID (CALAMARI) ABOUT 4 INCHES/10 CM LONG (MEASURING THE TUBES)

5 TABLESPOONS EXTRA-VIRGIN OLIVE OIL

3 MEDIUM ONIONS, FINELY CHOPPED

3 GARLIC CLOVES, PEELED

1 SWEET ITALIAN GREEN PEPPER OR ½ SMALL GREEN BELL PEPPER, FINELY CHOPPED

½ CUP/120 ML DRY WHITE WINE

½ TABLESPOON SQUID (CALAMARI) INK OR INK RESERVED FROM A FRESH SQUID OR CUTTLEFISH

SALT

1. Clean the squid. Pull out the head and entrails. Carefully remove the ink sac(s) found beneath the tentacles, and reserve. Trim off the tentacles and reserve. Remove the hard, clear quill from inside of the tubes and any innards that remain. Wash the tubes well and set aside. Finely chop the legs plus four to six of the tubes—use any that are broken first.

2. In a skillet or sauté pan, heat 2 tablespoons of the olive oil over medium heat. Add 2 of the onions and cook until soft and translucent, 8 to 10 minutes. Mince 1 of the garlic cloves, add it to the pan, and cook until aromatic, about 1 minute. Add the chopped squid and cook until the moisture has been expelled and then has evaporated and the pieces begin to brown slightly, about 5 minutes. Spoon the mixture into a bowl and let cool.

3. Loosely stuff about 1 tablespoon of the mixture inside each of the remaining tubes. They should not be tightly stuffed nor overstuffed, as the tubes will shrink somewhat when cooking. Secure the end of each with a toothpick.

4. In a cazuela, Dutch oven, large sauté pan, or deep skillet, heat the remaining 3 tablespoons olive oil over medium-high heat and brown the stuffed squid. Cook, turning as needed, until golden, about 3 minutes. Transfer to a platter.

5. In the same pan, add the remaining 2 garlic cloves and cook until golden and aromatic, 1 to 2 minutes; remove and reserve. Add the remaining onion and cook until soft and translucent, 8 to 10 minutes. Add the green pepper and cook until tender, 8 to 10 minutes. Pour in the wine and cook for 2 minutes to burn off the alcohol and then moisten with ½ cup/120 ml water. Simmer for 5 minutes, until the onion and green pepper are tender. Remove from the heat and let cool slightly. Pass the sauce through a food mill or chinois, or purée in a blender, and return to the cazuela.

6. Meanwhile, pound the reserved garlic in a mortar or mash with the back of a spoon in a bowl. Loosen the ink with a touch of water and carefully blend it with the garlic into a runny paste. Add to the cazuela. Swirl a bit of water in the mortar to get any remaining traces of the ink. Stir in ½ cup/120 ml water to loosen the sauce.

7. Carefully remove the toothpicks from the squid. (Having constricted slightly in size, they will keep their shape.) Add to the cazuela. Simmer over low heat until tender, 20 to 30 minutes. Add in a touch more water if needed. The sauce should still be quite loose. Taste for seasoning and add salt if needed.

8. Divide the squid among plates and spoon over the sauce before serving.

CHAPTER 9

POULTRY AND RABBIT
aves de corral y conejo

Aves de corral, they call them. *Aves* refers to *pollos* (chickens) and *gallinas* (hens), *patos* (ducks), and *pavos* (turkeys) domesticated and raised for consumption like they have been since ancient times. The *corral* is just that, a pen, and reminds us of the appreciation for birds that still peck around the side of the farmhouse and continue to carry their rich, slow-grown flavors.

Whereas now chicken often occupies a second tier of meats, it once reigned supreme, and was prepared for most auspicious occasions. This is because chickens were largely raised for eggs, and only butchered when they were old and had stopped laying, or else to cook for a particularly important meal. Flip through any traditional Spanish cookbook. There are very few—if any—plain or straightforward chicken recipes. Rather, they all seem to be highly elaborate preparations. Just look at one typical preparation from La Mancha called *pepitoria* (see page 212) that dates from at least the sixteenth century. It uses not just a valuable hen, but also includes almonds, saffron, and hard-boiled egg yolks. If this is one of the most splendid ways to prepare a chicken today—just imagine hundreds of years ago when butchering the hen was truly a festal act, and such ingredients only available to the wealthiest.

It's not surprising, then, that many traditional poultry dishes get regal consorts: chicken stewed with prunes (see page 220), ducks and geese with pears (see page 210), even olives. And capons! *Capones* are male birds neutered young and slowly fattened over eight months to be eaten at Christmas. As the saying goes, *"Capón de ocho meses, comida de reyes"* (literally "Capon of eight months, food of kings"). The most famous capones in Spain come from the old Roman town of Villalba de Lugo (population 15,000), in the Galician province of Lugo. Capons begin arriving in the market in mid-December and peak over the holidays. Plump ones weigh some 9 to 12 pounds/4 to 5.5 kg and are generally stuffed with dried fruits and nuts and roasted in the oven.

The texture of poultry is special, and should be treated carefully—cooked until done, but no more. It should be juicy and tender. Keep in mind that a good free-range chicken will take a bit longer to cook. The flavors will be richer, though, and the sturdier bones of these *aves* make noticeably stronger, deeper-tasting stock.

It wasn't until I moved to Spain that I discovered what a marvelous meat rabbit is—healthful and high in protein but low in fat, cholesterol, and sodium, tender, and, most important, delicious. It's versatile, succulent and relatively mild-tasting on its own, and about once a week we either grill, roast, stew, or use a rabbit in a rice dish. In the United States, many butcher shops sell rabbit or can get hold of it as a special order, and it is easily obtainable from specialist purveyors like D'Artagan and Nicky USA (see Sources, page 345). Hare and mountain rabbits are leaner and more flavorful than farm-raised rabbits, and need to be cooked much longer to be tender, but the meat is also more aromatic, reflecting their diet of wild herbs. These combine well with a range of flavors, especially bold, earthy ones like bacon, mushrooms, onions, chestnuts, and white beans.

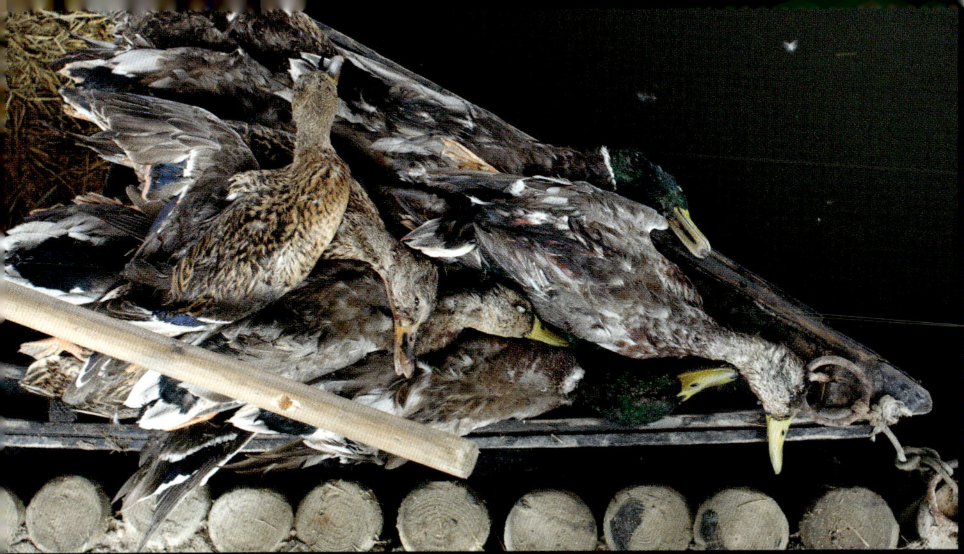
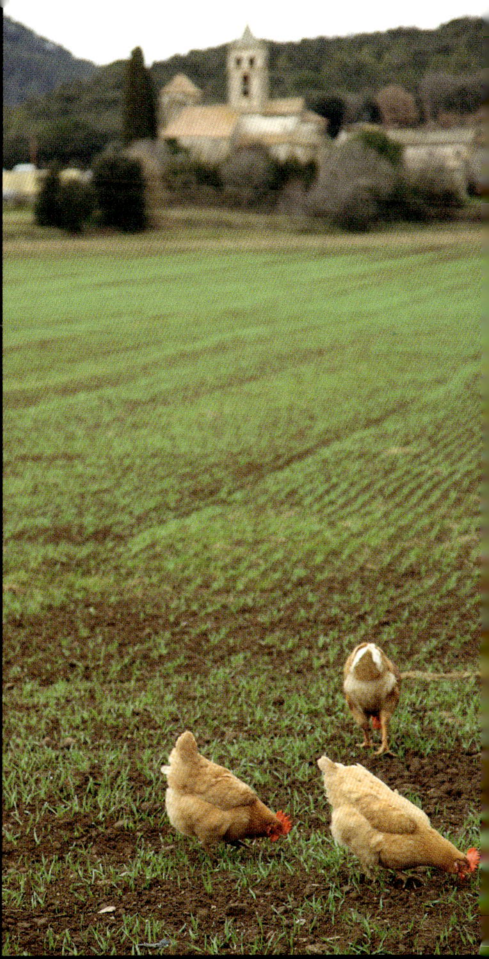
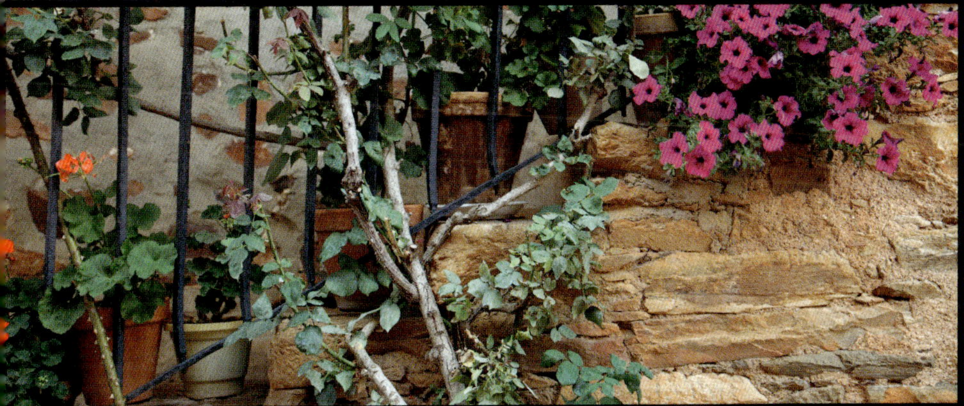
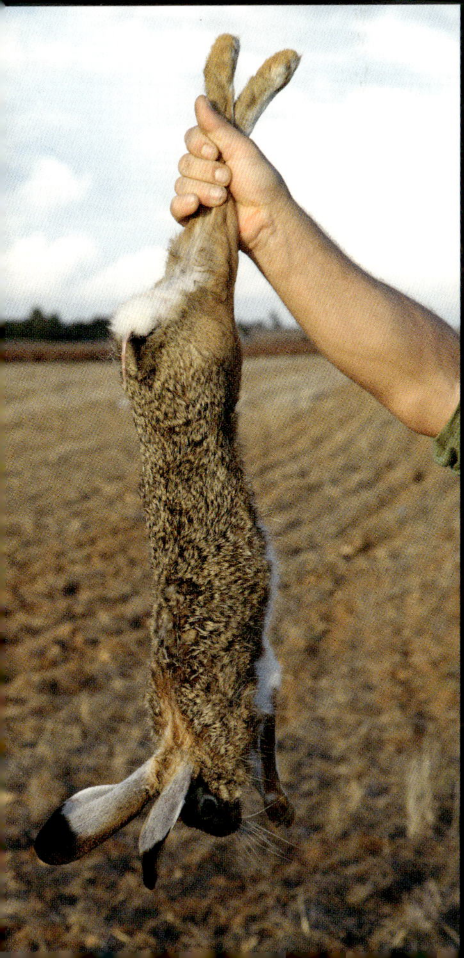
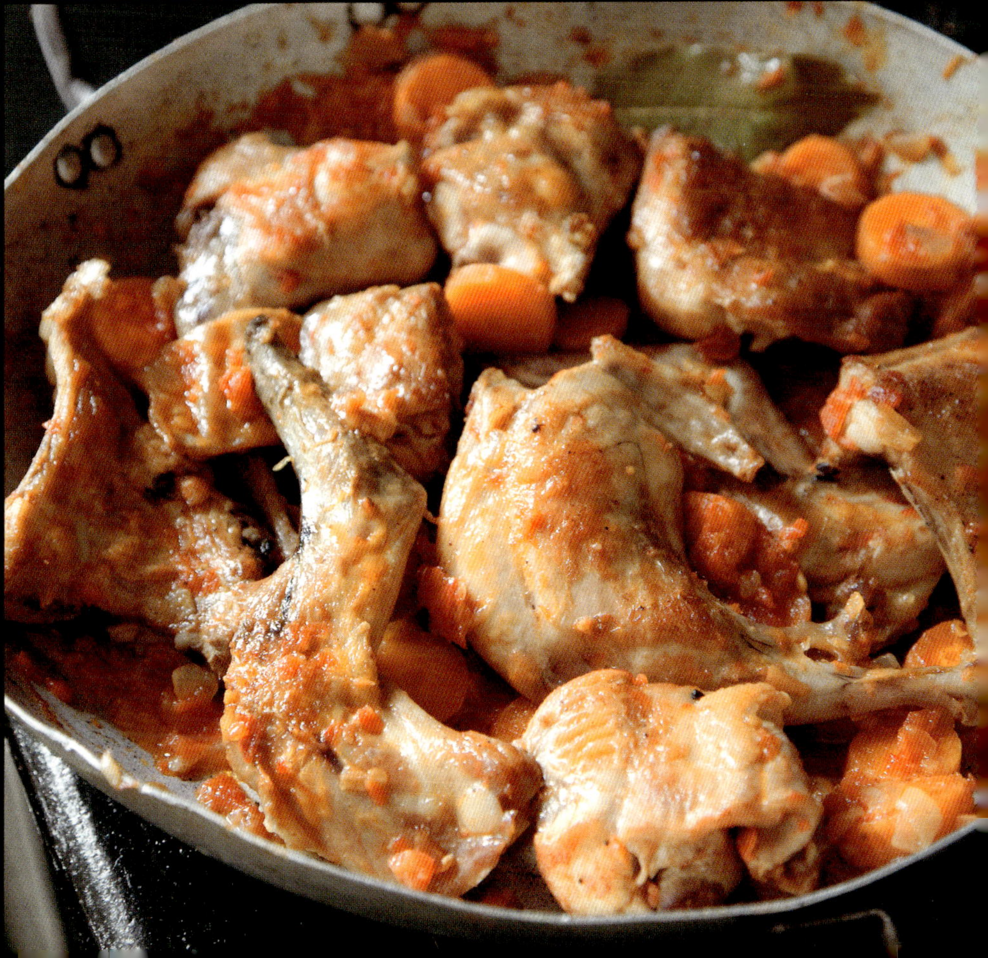

DUCK WITH PEARS

PATO CON PERAS

SERVES 4 TO 6

Over the years in Spain, I have come across a number of spectacular dishes with duck, including in various rice ones south of Valencia. But three in particular immediately spring to mind. In Sevilla, duck with olives is superb, as is, in La Cerdanya, at the other end of the country on the border with France, duck with local black turnips. Most stunning of all, though, must be duck with pears, one of the great dishes of the Catalan kitchen.

I have stuck close to the traditional preparation and have adapted this recipe from the rather grandiose but fittingly named *Corpus del patrimoni culinari català* (The Corpus of Catalan Culinary Heritage) put out by the Fundacío Institut Català de la Cuina (The Catalan Culinary Institute Foundation). As the *Corpus* duly notes, you can substitute firm peaches for the pears, cooking them for the final 15 minutes.

- 1 MEDIUM CLEANED BARBARY (OR MUSCOVY) DUCK, 4 TO 5 POUNDS/1.8 TO 2.3 KG
- SALT AND FRESHLY GROUND BLACK PEPPER
- 1 TABLESPOON EXTRA-VIRGIN OLIVE OIL
- 2 ONIONS, FINELY CHOPPED
- 2 LEEKS, WHITE AND TENDER GREEN PARTS ONLY, CUT INTO THIN ROUNDS
- 2 CARROTS, CUT INTO THIN ROUNDS
- 2 RIPE MEDIUM TOMATOES, PEELED, SEEDED, AND CHOPPED
- ½ CUP/120 ML BRANDY OR COGNAC
- 1 SMALL CINNAMON STICK
- 2 BAY LEAVES
- 1 SPRIG FRESH THYME
- 1 SPRIG FRESH ROSEMARY
- 4 FIRM WINTER PEARS, SUCH AS CONFERENCE, ANJOU, OR WILLIAMS, PEELED AND SLICED
- 2 GARLIC CLOVES, PEELED
- 12 TOASTED ALMONDS WITHOUT SKINS
- 2 THIN GALLETA MARÍA COOKIES OR ANOTHER ROUND, FLAT TEA BISCUIT, OR ½ GRAHAM CRACKER

1. Cut the duck into eight or ten pieces following the directions on page 336 for chicken (or have your butcher do it). Rinse and pat dry with paper towels. Prick the skin with a fork to help render the fat when the duck cooks. Generously season with salt and pepper.

2. In a cazuela, large sauté pan, or deep skillet, heat the olive oil over medium heat. Working in single-layer batches, add the pieces of duck, skin-side down, until browned and the fat has been rendered, 5 to 10 minutes total. Transfer to a large platter. Remove all but a thin coating of fat from the pan.

3. Add the onions, leeks, and carrots and cook over low heat until they begin to brown, about 5 minutes. Add the tomatoes. Cook for 5 minutes or so, until darker and slightly pasty. Stir in the brandy, let the alcohol burn off for 1 to 2 minutes, and return the duck to the pan, turning over to coat in the sauce. Add the cinnamon stick, bay leaves, thyme, and rosemary and cover with 2 cups/480 ml water. Simmer over medium-low heat for 45 minutes, turning the duck and basting from time to time.

4. Add the pears and a touch more water if needed to keep them moist, reduce the heat to low, partly cover the pan, and gently simmer until the pears are nearly tender and the meat of the duck begins to come away from the bone, about 30 minutes.

5. Meanwhile, prepare a picada with the garlic, almonds, cookies, and 1 or 2 tablespoons of simmering liquid from the cazuela, following the directions on page 39.

6. Stir the picada into the sauce, season with salt, and simmer until the pears are tender but not mushy, about 10 minutes.

7. Transfer the duck to a serving platter. Arrange the pears on top. Pass the sauce through a food mill (or a colander, pushing out the vegetables); discard the herbs. Spoon some of the sauce over the duck before serving and put the remaining sauce in a bowl to add as desired.

CHICKEN BRAISED IN SAFFRON, ALMOND, AND EGG YOLK SAUCE

POLLO EN PEPITORIA

SERVES 4

*If there is a richer or more delicious way of braising chicken than in a pepitoria sauce from La Mancha, thickened with pounded almonds, hard-boiled egg yolks, and the region's celebrated saffron, then I haven't come across it. An ancient dish dating back centuries, it remains festive, even celebratory. While once prepared using a young hen (*gallina*), it is perfect—and more commonly prepared these days—with a plump, free-range chicken. I like to use whole legs, but you can prepare it with only drumsticks or only thighs if desired.*

2 HARD-BOILED EGGS (SEE PAGE 342)
5 TABLESPOONS EXTRA-VIRGIN OLIVE OIL
2¼ POUNDS/1 KG FREE-RANGE CHICKEN DRUMSTICKS AND THIGHS
SALT AND FRESHLY GROUND BLACK PEPPER
ALL-PURPOSE FLOUR FOR DREDGING
1 MEDIUM ONION, FINELY CHOPPED
2 SMALL BAY LEAVES
15 UNSALTED TOASTED ALMONDS WITHOUT SKINS
4 GARLIC CLOVES, ROUGHLY CHOPPED
2 SMALL SLICES BAGUETTE, DAY OLD OR TOASTED
1 PINCH SAFFRON THREADS, DRY-TOASTED AND GROUND (SEE PAGE 340)
1 CUP/240 ML DRY WHITE WINE
2 CUPS/480 ML CHICKEN STOCK (PAGE 336)

1. Peel the eggs and remove and reserve the yolks. Roughly chop the whites and set aside.

2. In a cazuela, heavy casserole, large sauté pan, or deep skillet, heat 3 tablespoons of the olive oil over medium heat. Season the chicken with salt and pepper, lightly dredge in flour, and cook until golden, turning as needed, about 8 minutes. Transfer the chicken to a platter. Add the remaining 2 tablespoons olive oil, the onion, and the bay leaves. Reduce the heat to medium-low and cook until the onion is soft and nearly translucent but not browned, 8 to 10 minutes.

3. Meanwhile, prepare a picada with the almonds, garlic, bread, saffron, and 1 tablespoon water, following the directions on page 39. Add the reserved egg yolks and 1 tablespoon water and mash into a moist paste.

4. When the onion is ready, return the chicken to the pan along with the picada, turn to coat the chicken, and then pour in the wine. Let the alcohol burn off for 2 minutes, pour in the stock, and bring to a simmer. Cook uncovered over low heat for about 50 minutes, or until the chicken is very tender but not falling off the bone and the sauce thickened.

5. To serve, divide the chicken among plates, cover with the sauce, and garnish with the chopped egg white.

UTENSILS

CAZUELA

Perhaps the most classic and all-purpose piece of Spanish stovetop cookware, the round, flat cazuela is used to stew, simmer, braise, and prepare moist rice dishes. In Valencia, it is also used for preparing rice dishes in the oven. Traditional cazuelas are sturdy and made from glazed terra-cotta, though heavy coated aluminum and cast-iron versions have become popular in recent years.

Terra-cotta cazuelas need to be "seasoned" before using the first time. Soak overnight in water and then allow to dry completely. Never place a cold cazuela (holding, say, leftovers) directly on the stovetop heat or it risks cracking. The same goes for a hot cazuela on a cold (say, marble) surface.

In general, a cazuela that measures 12 to 13 inches/30 to 32 cm in diameter is ideal for serving four to six people. This is the correct size for the recipes in this book.

Spanish terra-cotta cazuelas are easy to buy outside of Spain these days—see Sources, page 345, for a few places to start looking.

For excellent alternatives, look for anything that cookware shops classify as "low casseroles" or "buffet casseroles." The best ones are heavy, and allow for slow cooking. I find that pots like Le Creuset's "round casserole"—it is more like a Dutch oven—work well, too. A large sauté pan or deep skillet is also fine.

Many cooks use small *cazuelitas*—usually around 5 or 6 inches/13 or 15 cm in diameter—to serve, or even prepare, certain tapas and individual desserts. They also make great dishes to serve olives, Spanish almonds, and other nibbles.

INGREDIENTS

TURKEYS

Those New World imports, turkeys, get similar treatment and starring roles on the festive table as capons and farm-raised hens (like the Mayoress's Stewed Christmas Chicken, page 217). The first turkeys arrived in Spain in the early sixteenth century from the island of Hispaniola—the Caribbean island divided by modern-day Haiti and the Dominican Republic, where Columbus had landed on his voyage to "the Indies"—and spread rapidly around Spain and then Europe. The breeding was no doubt helped by King Ferdinand sending out instructions that every ship returning from the New World should bring back ten turkeys, half males and the other half females, to breed.

The central market in Valencia is one of the most spectacular in the country, with soaring cupolas, ceilings that reach 100 feet/30 m, and ample windows that infuse it with Mediterranean light. And that is only the architecture! Nearly one thousand food stalls offer the spectacular makings of Valencia's rather baroque cuisine. The city was under Muslim rule for five centuries (until 1238), and that legacy can clearly be tasted. One prominent influence is the frequent combination of sweet and savory. This chicken dish is one such example, and is adapted from a small book that the stall holders put together a few years ago.

CHICKEN WITH SHALLOTS AND ORANGE AND CINNAMON SAUCE

POLLO CON CHALOTES Y SALSA DE NARANJA Y CANELA

SERVES 4

3 POUNDS/1.4 KG FREE-RANGE CHICKEN DRUMSTICKS AND THIGHS
SALT
GROUND WHITE PEPPER
18 WHOLE SHALLOTS
¼ CUP/60 ML EXTRA-VIRGIN OLIVE OIL
1 TEASPOON ALL-PURPOSE FLOUR, PLUS MORE FOR DREDGING
GENEROUS 1 CUP FRESH VALENCIA ORANGE JUICE
1 CINNAMON STICK, BROKEN IN HALF

1. Remove the skin and trim the excess fat from the chicken. Rinse and pat dry. Season with salt and white pepper.

2. Peel the shallots. Finely chop two of them and set aside.

3. Preheat the oven to 375°F/190°C/gas mark 5.

4. In a cazuela, heavy casserole, large sauté pan, or deep skillet, heat the olive oil over medium heat. Lightly dredge the chicken in flour and brown in single-layer batches that don't crowd the pan, about 5 minutes per batch. Transfer to a platter.

5. Add the whole shallots to the cazuela and cook until golden, 2 to 3 minutes, and then transfer with a slotted spoon to the platter with the chicken. Add the chopped shallots and cook until tender and golden, about 2 minutes. Stir in the 1 teaspoon flour and then add the orange juice and cinnamon stick. Bring to a boil and boil for 2 minutes, stirring continually. Remove the pan from the heat.

6. In a large baking dish or roasting pan, arrange the chicken without overlapping the pieces, scatter around the whole shallots, and pour over the sauce. Loosely cover with aluminum foil and bake for 30 minutes, or until the chicken is done and just starting to separate from the bone.

7. Spoon the sauce into a saucepan and reduce by about one-fourth over high heat into a thickish glaze, about 3 minutes. To serve, place a drumstick and a thigh with some whole shallots on each plate and ladle over some sauce.

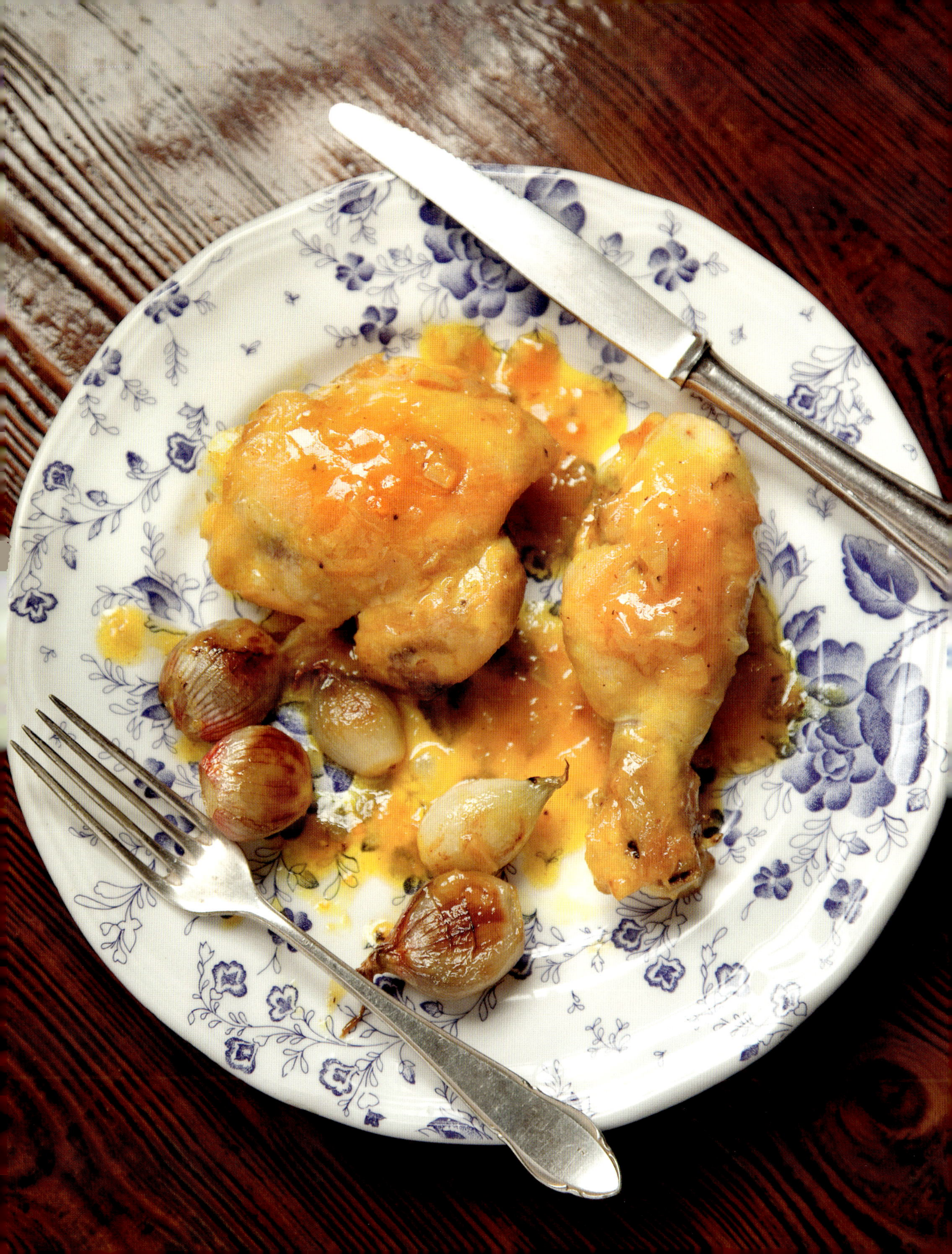

CHICKEN WITH SAMFAINA

POLLO CON SAMFAINA

SERVES 4

My wife's earliest memories of her grandmother's kitchen in Lleida, on the flat, fruit-rich plain of western Catalunya, are of the pantry behind it. Among the preserves, canned fruits, and olives that lined the tall shelves were jars of *samfaina*, a stewed mélange of onions, tomatoes, and eggplant. She garnished grilled meats with it, spooned it over pig's feet, and added it to the pot as a sauce for braising chicken, rabbit, and, during Lent, salt cod. This recipe makes a generous amount of samfaina; enough, if you are lucky, for leftovers to eat at room temperature as a thick relish. We spread it over pieces of toasted bread, just as my wife remembers her grandmother doing.

1 MEDIUM GLOBE EGGPLANT
SALT
5 TABLESPOONS EXTRA-VIRGIN OLIVE OIL
1 MEDIUM ONION, THINLY SLICED
1 RED BELL PEPPER, CUT INTO ½-INCH/1.25-CM PIECES
½ SMALL GREEN BELL PEPPER, CUT INTO ½-INCH/1.25-CM PIECES
4 RIPE MEDIUM TOMATOES, PEELED, CORED, SEEDED, AND CUT INTO LARGE PIECES
2½ POUNDS/1.2 KG BONE-IN CHICKEN LEGS OR BREASTS, SKIN REMOVED AND EXCESS FAT TRIMMED
FRESHLY GROUND BLACK PEPPER
ALL-PURPOSE FLOUR FOR DREDGING

1. Rinse and stem the eggplant, but do not peel. Cut it into ½-inch/1.25-cm cubes. Place them in a colander, salt liberally, and let them sweat away some of their bitterness for 1 hour. Rinse well under running water and pat dry with paper towels. Gently squeeze some moisture from the eggplant and pat dry again.

2. In a cazuela, heavy casserole, large sauté pan, or deep skillet, heat 3 tablespoons of the olive oil over medium heat. Add the onion and cook until soft and translucent, 8 to 10 minutes. Add the bell peppers and cook about 8 minutes, stirring frequently, and then add the eggplant. Cook for 5 minutes and add the tomatoes. Cook until the vegetables are pasty and soft, about 15 minutes. Add a touch of water if needed to keep it from drying out.

3. Meanwhile, in a large skillet or sauté pan, heat the remaining 2 tablespoons olive oil over medium heat. Season the chicken with salt and pepper and then lightly dredge in flour. Cook until golden, turning as needed, about 8 minutes.

4. When the samfaina is ready, transfer the chicken to the cazuela and turn to coat. Add 1 cup/240 ml water, partly cover, and cook over low heat for about 50 minutes, until the chicken is very tender but not falling off the bone.

5. To serve, divide the chicken among plates and generously cover with the samfaina.

THE MAYORESS'S STEWED CHRISTMAS CHICKEN

POLLO NAVIDEÑO DE LA ALCALDESA

SERVES 4 TO 5

This recipe is from Juana González, the *alcaldesa* (mayoress) of the small but very important wine-producing town of Pedrosa de Duero. It is a recipe that her mother prepared at Christmas, and now she does, in an old terra-cotta cazuela blackened from years of use. The recipe calls for an authentic *pollo de corral*, a large free-range, corn-fed chicken. These birds might take longer to stew, but their flavors are deeper. Watch that the sauce doesn't dry out during stewing.

- 1 PLUMP FREE-RANGE CHICKEN, 4 TO 4½ POUNDS/1.8 TO 2 KG
- SALT AND FRESHLY GROUND BLACK PEPPER
- 3 TABLESPOONS EXTRA-VIRGIN OLIVE OIL
- 2 SLICES BAGUETTE, DAY OLD OR TOASTED
- 4 GARLIC CLOVES, PEELED AND HALVED LENGTHWISE
- 1 MEDIUM ONION, FINELY CHOPPED
- ½ SMALL GREEN BELL PEPPER OR 1 SWEET ITALIAN GREEN PEPPER, FINELY CHOPPED
- ½ RED BELL PEPPER, FINELY CHOPPED
- 2 RIPE MEDIUM TOMATOES, PEELED, SEEDED, AND CHOPPED
- 6 TABLESPOONS/90 ML BRANDY OR COGNAC
- 16 UNSALTED TOASTED ALMONDS WITHOUT SKINS
- 2 TABLESPOONS MINCED FRESH FLAT-LEAF PARSLEY

1. Clean the chicken, remove the skin, and trim any excess fat. Cut it into 10 pieces following the directions on page 336. Season with salt and pepper.

2. In a cazuela, heavy casserole, large sauté pan, or deep skillet, heat the olive oil over medium heat. Add the bread and garlic and cook until each is golden, 1 to 2 minutes. Remove and reserve. Add the chicken and brown in single-layer batches that don't crowd the pan, 6 to 8 minutes per batch. Transfer to a platter and cover to keep warm.

3. In the same oil, prepare a sofrito: Add the onion and cook until soft and translucent, 8 to 10 minutes. Add the bell peppers and cook for 8 to 10 minutes, stirring frequently. Add the tomatoes and cook until darker and pasty, 10 to 15 minutes. Add water if needed to keep it from drying out.

4. Return the chicken to the pan. Add the brandy and cook uncovered, turning the chicken over a couple of times, for 2 minutes to let the alcohol burn off. Add 1½ cups/360 ml water, partly cover the cazuela, and simmer over low heat for 1 hour.

5. Meanwhile, prepare a picada with the reserved garlic and bread, the almonds, parsley, and 1 to 2 tablespoons of the simmering liquid from the cazuela, following the directions on page 39.

6. Loosen the picada with 3 to 4 tablespoons water and stir it into the chicken. Cover the cazuela and cook until the sauce has thickened and the chicken is tender, about 45 minutes. Stir in water if needed to keep the sauce loose, or remove the lid to let it evaporate if watery. Serve from the cazuela.

RIBERA DEL DUERO

The Río Duero runs across the northern part of the meseta (plateau). Although it is the third largest river in the peninsula, it does little to temper the austere, arid landscape that is best suited for flocks of grazing sheep.

But along the way to Portugal (where it changes its name to Douro, eventually entering the Atlantic at Oporto), the Duero waters hundreds of bodegas that produce some of the most spectacular and sought-after wines in Spain. The stellar roster of vineyards includes such well-known names as Vega Sicilia, Pingus, Pesquera, Protos, and Viña Pedrosa. These are powerful, elegant wines, plummy and full of berries and leathers, clay and spice, and hints of oaks for structure. Along with La Rioja and Priorat, the Ribera del Duero has been awarded the top-level *Denominación de Origen Calificada* (Qualified Denomination of Origin or D.O.C.) status. There are also three other wine areas along the river that have *Denominación de Origen* (Denomination of Origin or D.O.) status: Toro, Rueda, and Arribes del Duero.

Although recently uncovered Roman mosaics—including a particularly large (710 square feet/66 square metres) and well-preserved one of Bacchus, the god of wine, discovered in the village of Baños de Valdearados—show that wine was being produced in the Ribera del Duero some 2,000 years ago, it was Middle Age plantings by Cistercian and Benedictine monks that formed the origins of the modern tradition. By the thirteenth century, the monks were using underground cellars to protect their wines from the region's rather extreme climate.

On the northern end of the D.O.C. Ribera del Duero area, where vineyards give way to cereals, sits the tiny village of Pedrosa. "We don't have a bakery, but we have a number of world-class wineries," Manuel "Manolo" Pérez Pascuas told me. He is one of the three Pérez Pascuas brothers behind the legendary Viña Pedrosa wines. The vineyards had been their father's, and in the early 1980s the trio decided that the quality of the grapes was sufficient to produce better, and better-aging, wines. They were right. Their *crianzas* (aged for two years), *reservas* (aged for at least three years), and, in exceptional years, *gran reservas* (aged at least five years) all stand out.

Sitting in the shade behind the winery having a late breakfast, something of a tradition with the family—a plate of jamón ibérico and chorizo, wedges of aged, almost crystallized Manchego cheese, and bread from the truck that passed through town in the morning, with, of course, a bottle of Viña Pedrosa—certain descriptions kept coming up in reference to their wines: *personalidad, elegancia, mucho carácter,* and that it keeps and ages well.

Why was this? I asked. What gave them such a distinct character? "Quality begins in the vineyard," Manolo said. That means many things, but he honed in on two. The first was the rather extreme and dry climate. Ribera del Duero has some of the highest vineyards in the world (and the last to be harvested in Spain). Viña Pedrosa's land is at around 2,700 feet/850 metres above sea level. The sharp difference between daytime and nighttime temperatures helps the growth of the grapes during the day, but allows them, at night, to balance acidity and aromas. Or, as Manolo put it, "The grapes have time to recuperate from the heat." (I laughed when he likened it to "having a cold beer after a hot day.")

The second reason he named was the grapes themselves. The main varietal is called Tinto Fino or Tinto del País, the local name for Tempranillo, which is well adapted for the conditions. Later, as we strolled the fields together, Manolo showed me clusters of these with paternal tenderness. He kept picking and popping grapes into his mouth. "Taste one!" he said a dozen times. The grapes were ripe and plump. The harvest was just days from beginning.

I had been hearing excellent predictions for the year. Manolo was more prosaic when I asked him about this. "My father always said, 'Until the last day of the harvest, when you shut the bodega door, you don't know if you've got a good wine.'"

It reminded me of a Catalan expression that my wife likes to say: "*No diguis blat fins que sigui al sac i ben lligat.*" That translates to something like, "Don't say you have wheat until you have it in the sack and tightly knotted," the equivalent of "Don't count your chickens until they hatch."

But Manolo was not offering me country wisdom. He meant it literally. Anything could happen between now and the end of the harvest. Having spent his life among these fields, he had seen it all.

ROAST CHICKEN WITH PRUNES

POLLO ASADO AL HORNO CON CIRUELAS PASAS

SERVES 4 TO 6

In the Spanish kitchen, chicken and dried fruits are natural and frequent partners. And while prunes and apricots are often stuffed *inside* the birds (along with, not uncommonly, fresh sausage), they also go well *alongside* the bird in a roasting pan. This dish makes a simple, delicious Sunday lunch. I like to soak the prunes in wine before adding. Sometimes I take a few apricots from my jar of them macerating in muscatel (see page 326) and add along with the prunes. Delightful.

1 CUP/160 G PITTED PRUNES
½ CUP/120 ML DRY WHITE WINE
1 WHOLE CLEANED CHICKEN, ABOUT 4 POUNDS/1.8 KG
3 TABLESPOONS EXTRA-VIRGIN OLIVE OIL
SALT AND FRESHLY GROUND BLACK PEPPER

1. Place the prunes in a bowl and cover with the wine.

2. Preheat the oven to 400°F/200°C/gas mark 6.

3. Rinse the chicken on the inside as well the outside. Pat dry with paper towels.

4. In a roasting pan, place the chicken breast-side down. Lightly rub with the olive oil and season with salt and pepper. Roast it until golden, about 25 minutes, and then turn the chicken breast-side up. Drain the prunes, reserving the wine. Arrange the prunes around the chicken and drizzle the wine over the top. Dribble in ½ cup/120 ml water around the base. Reduce the heat to 350°F/180°C/gas mark 4 and continue to roast until the chicken is golden and an instant-read thermometer probed in the thigh reads at least 165°F/74°C, about 30 minutes. Remove from the oven and let rest for 10 minutes before carving.

5. Arrange the chicken on a serving platter and surround it with prunes. Ladle the sauce around the sides and serve.

When the Phoenicians arrived on the Iberian Peninsula in 1100 BCE, they found rabbits so plentiful that, according to *El gran diccionario de cocina* (The Grand Dictionary of Cooking), they named the peninsula *I-saphan-im*, literally "land [or island] of rabbits." This Punic word morphed into *Hispania* and eventually *España*. Rabbit remains abundant and popular. Healthful and mild-tasting, rabbit meat nicely absorbs the flavors of the stewing pot. But it is also exceptional when grilled, especially when marinated in plenty of Mediterranean herbs.

GRILLED RABBIT WITH EGGPLANT, ZUCCHINI, AND ALLIOLI

CONEJO A LA BRASA CON BERENJENAS, CALABACINES Y ALLIOLI

SERVES 8

2 WHOLE CLEANED RABBITS, ABOUT 2½ POUNDS/1.2 KG EACH, QUARTERED

6 SPRIGS FRESH THYME

6 SPRIGS FRESH ROSEMARY

6 GARLIC CLOVES, GENTLY CRUSHED IN THE PEEL

6 TABLESPOONS EXTRA-VIRGIN OLIVE OIL, PLUS MORE AS NEEDED

2 FAT GLOBE EGGPLANTS

SALT

4 FAT ZUCCHINI, STEMMED AND WASHED

FRESHLY GROUND BLACK PEPPER

ALLIOLI (PAGE 337)

1. Trim any excess fat from the rabbit quarters. Put the pieces in a large baking dish. Strip the flowers from one of the thyme sprigs and the needles from one of the rosemary sprigs and sprinkle over the rabbit. Add the remaining sprigs of thyme and rosemary along with the garlic to the dish. Drizzle the 6 tablespoons olive oil over the dish and mix. Cover, refrigerate, and marinate for at least 2 hours, turning the pieces from time to time.

2. Wash the eggplants and cut crosswise into ½-inch-/1.25-cm-thick rounds. Place in a colander, liberally salt, and let them sweat away some of their bitterness for 1 hour. (You will see dark beads of moisture appear.) Rinse well under running water and pat dry with paper towels. Gently squeeze some moisture from the eggplant and pat dry again.

3. Meanwhile, prepare the grill for medium-high heat. If using charcoal, allow the embers to burn down until surrounded by a layer of grayish white ash. Rake into an even layer. Brush the grill grate with olive oil.

4. Wash the zucchini. If they are fat, cut crosswise into ¾-inch-/2-cm-thick rounds (slightly thicker than the eggplant); if they are skinny, cut them lengthwise in half. Season with salt. Brush the eggplant and zucchini rounds with olive oil and arrange on the grill grate (or in a perforated grill pan), grilling for 3 to 4 minutes on each side, or until charred in places. Transfer as done to a platter. Loosely cover with foil tented in the middle until ready to serve. This will keep them warm while not steaming them.

5. Remove the rabbit from the marinade, generously season with salt and pepper, and arrange on the grill grate. Grill, turning from time to time, until cooked through and the internal temperature of a thigh is 160°F/71°C, 10 to 15 minutes, depending on the heat of the grill. Do not overcook.

6. Serve the rabbit with the grilled vegetables and the allioli on the side.

TORRE DEL BOSC BRAISED RABBIT WITH CARROTS

CONEJO DE TORRE DEL BOSC

SERVES 4

My sister-in-law, Rosa María, and her husband, Ramón, have the old summer house that his grandfather built in the Pre-Pyrenees mountains back in the early 1900s and christened Torre del Bosc. *Torre* is a way of referring to a country house in Catalan, but the word also means "tower," perhaps a more fitting description of its towering stories and sharply peaked slate roof that reaches up 72 feet/22 m.

There are a dozen rooms, including a cavernous kitchen lined with the original okra- and azure-hued ceramic wall tiles. The original woodstove is still there, too, with a makeshift pair of butane-driven burners sitting on top of it. With these, Rosa María regularly cooks for two dozen of us when the family gathers for Easter, someone's birthday, or a special anniversary. This dish is one of my favorites of her many stews that she prepares when my wife and kids and I go to spend a long weekend there.

- 1 WHOLE CLEANED RABBIT, ABOUT 2½ POUNDS/1.2 KG, LIVER RESERVED
- SALT AND FRESHLY GROUND BLACK PEPPER
- 4 TABLESPOONS EXTRA-VIRGIN OLIVE OIL
- 3 GARLIC CLOVES, PEELED
- 1 ONION, FINELY CHOPPED
- 2 RIPE TOMATOES, PEELED, SEEDED, AND FINELY CHOPPED
- 2 CARROTS, CUT INTO ¼-INCH-/½-CM-THICK ROUNDS
- 1 BAY LEAF
- ½ CUP/120 ML DRY WHITE WINE
- 1 CUP/240 ML CHICKEN STOCK (PAGE 336) OR WATER
- 8 TOASTED ALMONDS WITHOUT SKINS
- 1 TABLESPOON MINCED FRESH FLAT-LEAF PARSLEY

1. Cut the rabbit into eight or nine pieces, following the directions on page 342 (or have your butcher do it). Trim any excess fat. Season generously with salt and pepper.

2. In a cazuela or heavy casserole, heat the olive oil over medium-high heat and add the rabbit along with its liver. Cook until the liver is cooked through and the other pieces are browned, about 8 minutes. Transfer to a platter.

3. Reduce the heat to medium. Add the garlic to the cazuela and cook until fragrant, about 1 minute. Remove and reserve. Prepare a sofrito with the onion and tomatoes, following the directions on page 39. Return the rabbit (except the liver) to the pan. Turn the rabbit over to coat well with sofrito. Add the carrots and bay leaf, cover with the wine and stock, and bring to a simmer. Reduce the heat to low, and stir from time to time, gently cooking by just letting bubbles slowly break the surface, for 1 hour or until the rabbit is tender. Stir in water if needed to keep the sauce moist.

4. Meanwhile, prepare a picada with the reserved garlic, the liver, the almonds, parsley, and 2 tablespoons of simmering liquid from the cazuela, following the directions on page 39.

5. Stir the picada into the cazuela and cook for a final 10 minutes. Serve from the cazuela.

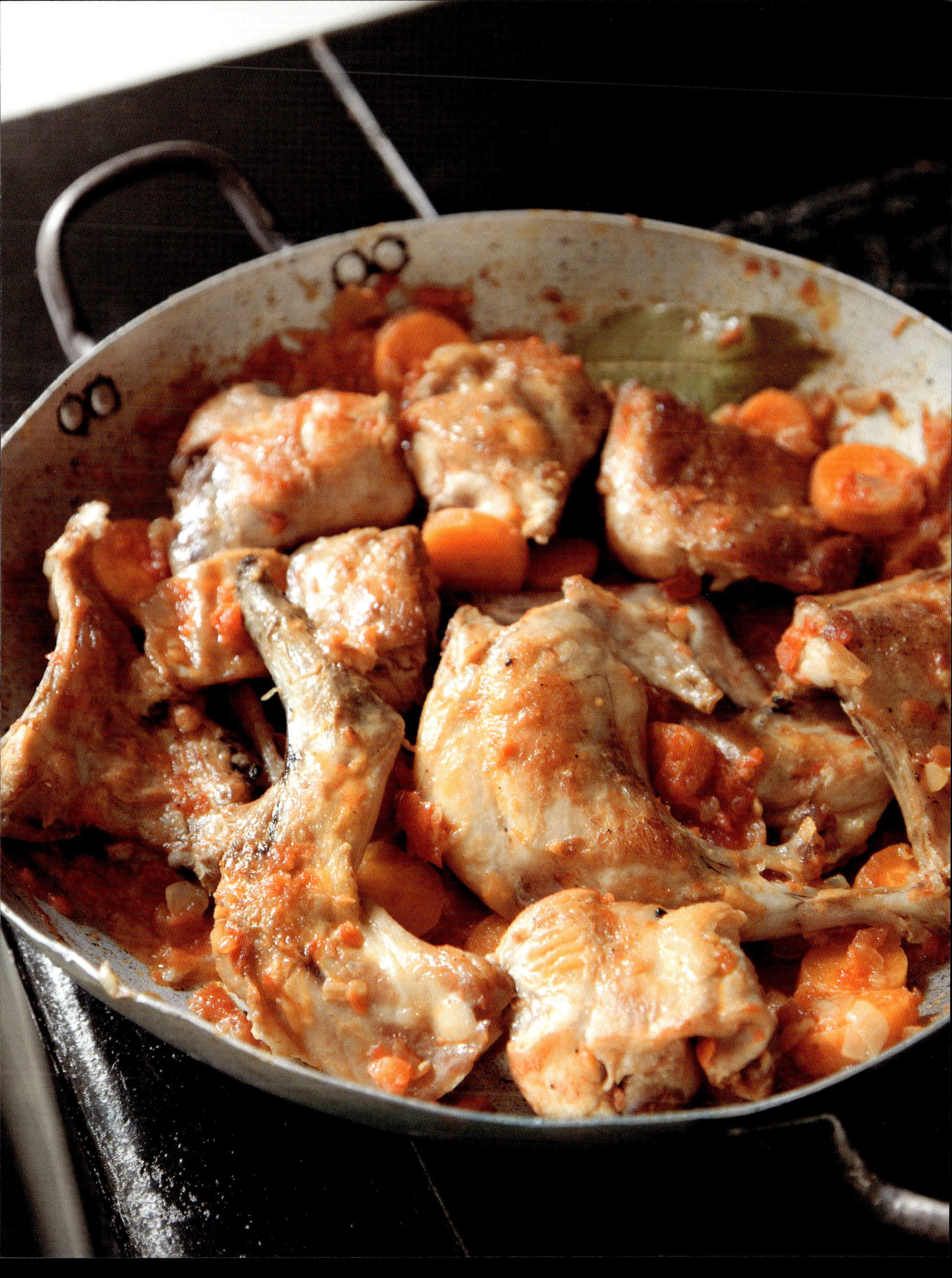

CHAPTER 10

GAME AND SNAILS
caza y caracoles

Hunting is as old as the human race. The famous Paleolithic-age paintings inside the cave of Altamira in Cantabria, dating back to sometime after the first *Homo sapiens* arrived in northern Spain around 35,000 years ago, depict in charcoal and ochre animals that they no doubt hunted—deer, boar, and, across the ceiling, a herd of stampeding bison (long since extinct). Hunting, of course, is still practiced today, though often more for sport than necessity—in the impoverished midcentury years following the Spanish Civil War, my wife's grandfather frequently hunted small game, but never for the thrill of the shot. That doesn't mean that nowadays the spoils of the hunt are not keenly sought nor deeply appreciated.

Although certain food markets sell hunted game in their feathered dress, most game cooked these days is farm-raised. (In general, birds sold in markets with feathers are wild, while those without are not.) The flavor of farm-raised animals is usually less "gamey" than their wild brethren, and the meat more tender and milder.

Of the larger game, *jabalí* (wild boar) has the most widespread tradition on the peninsula. This beast has been scavenging Spanish forests since the beginning, and continues to do so. They have a stocky, compact body, squat legs, and short tail that ends in a stiff tuft of hair. The head is large and elongated, with a long snout and two fierce, protruding horns. This ancestor of the domesticated pig is a powerful, smart animal with an acute sense of hearing and smell. Walking in wooded areas, you often see signs of their foraging—but you will very rarely see the secretive, elusive animals themselves. From a cook's point of view, the finest are younger ones, under a year old. Boar meat is usually marinated, often in red wine and herbs, and then stewed.

Spain has excellent venison, too. The word *venado* (venison) comes from the Latin word *venatus*, meaning "to hunt." The word originally meant any kind of edible game, but now it usually refers to the meat of deer—in Spain that means specifically roe deer or red deer. Like boar, venison is frequently marinated before being cooked. The loin is the choicest for grilling, while the shoulder and leg are preferably stewed.

Of the game birds, partridge, quail, and pheasant are the most typical, with partridge considered by many to be the finest.

And there are snails. Although not game, these can be gathered in the wild. Snails caught like this need to be purged of impurities for three days—usually on a diet of bran and then hung in net baskets—though most snails sold in markets these days have already gone through this process. See page 340 for how to clean and prepare them before adding to the dish.

Shopping recently in Valencia's Mercado Central, I counted no less than five varieties of snails. The main Spanish ones include the classic Burgundy or vineyard snail (*Helix pomatia*); a smaller, common snail usually called in English by their French name, *petit-gris* (*Helix aspersa*); and the smaller-yet forest snail (*Helix lucorum*). In general, smaller snails or petit-gris are best for rice dishes, and petit-gris or vineyard snails in stews.

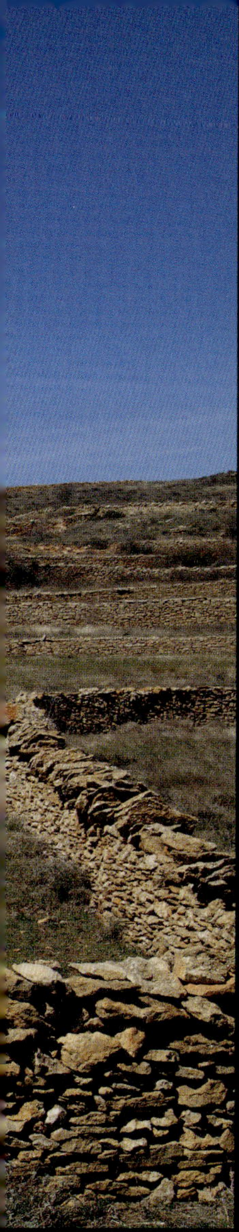
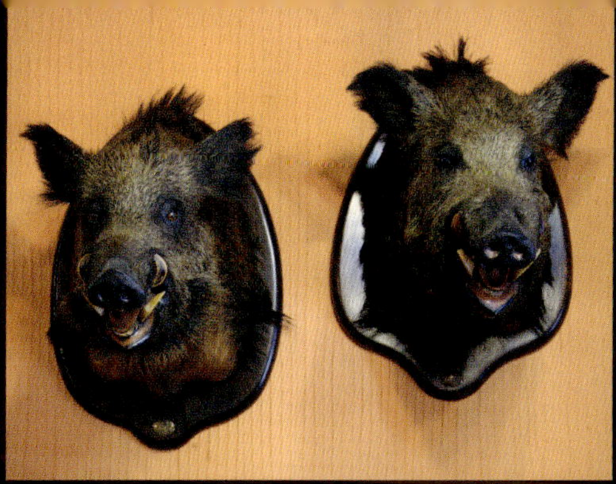
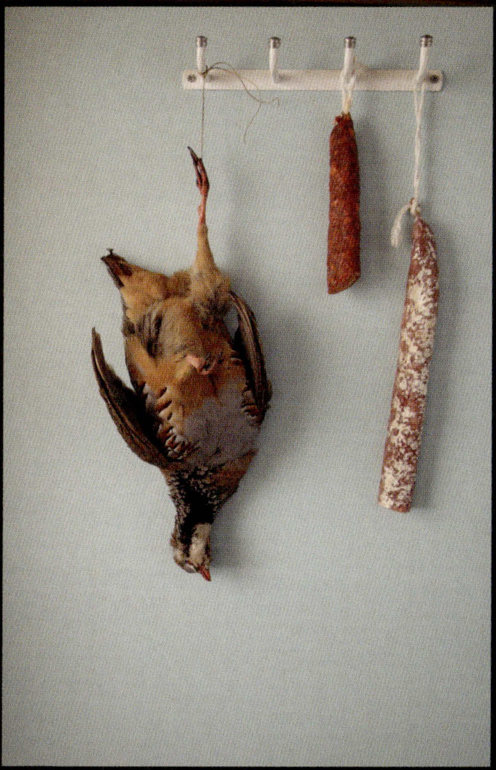
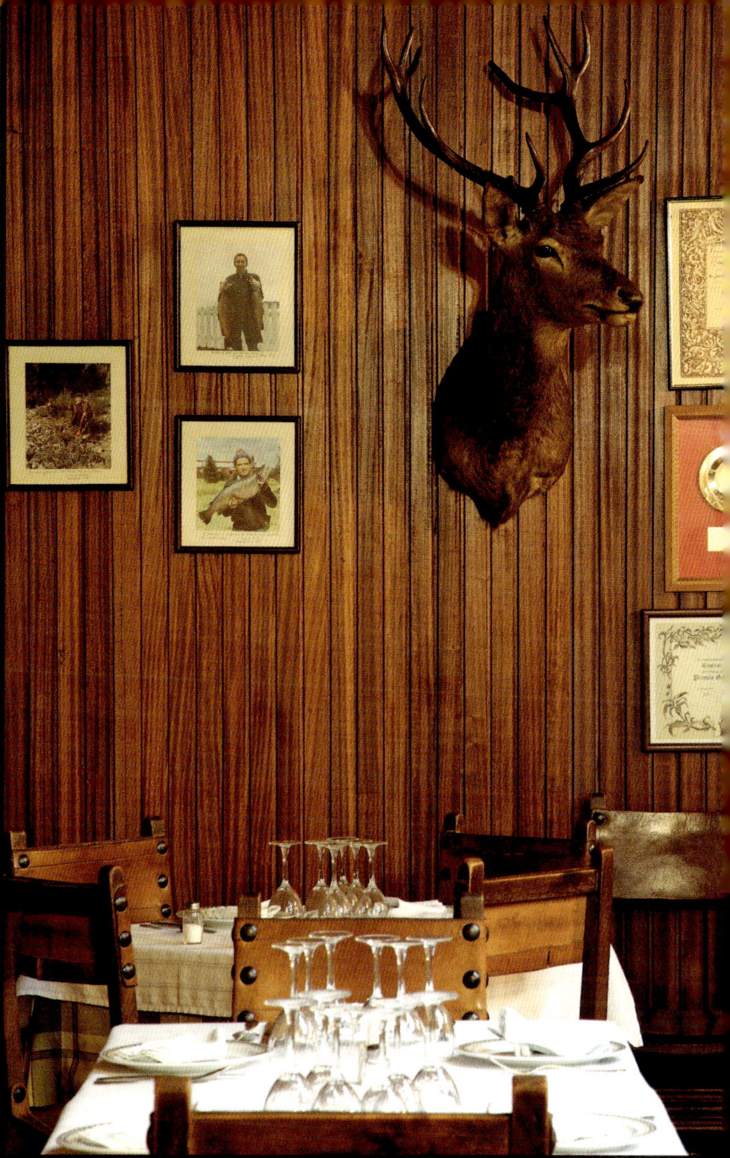
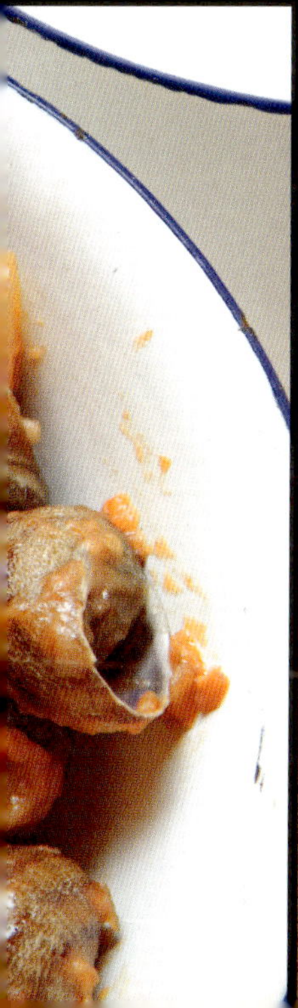
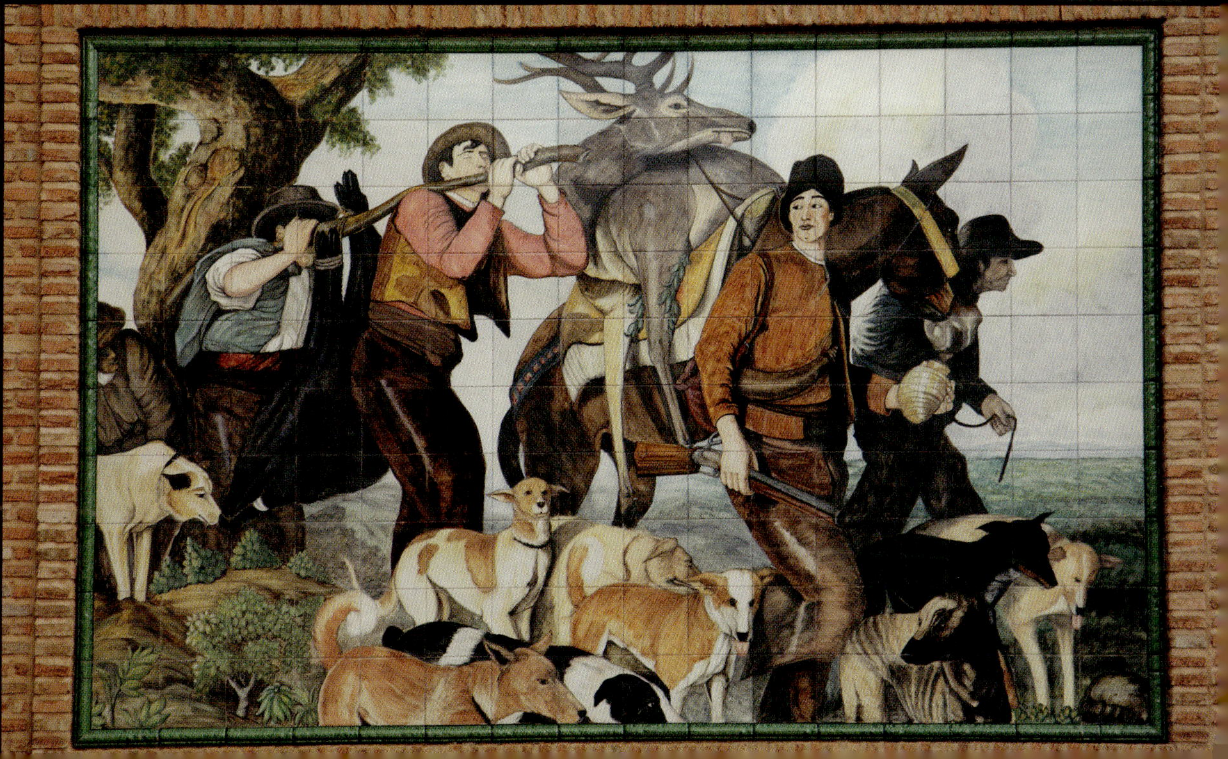

GRILLED MARINATED VENISON STEAKS

CIERVO ADOBADO A LA PLANCHA

SERVES 4

The village of Los Yébenes, in the Montes de Toledo mountain range, is the center of Spain's big-game hunting, namely deer. The town itself is set on the slope of a steep hill, with a commanding view down over the fertile valley to the south. At the top of town, next door to the *Ayuntamiento* (town hall), sits Casa Apelio, a small hotel and restaurant that was opened in 1937 by the current proprietor's grandfather. Now in its third generation of management, little has changed—at least in the kitchen. Venison is, not surprisingly, a specialty. This recipe is adapted from the restaurant.

Of the various cuts of venison, medallions sliced from the loin are the most tender. If using the leg or shoulder, cut thin steaks crosswise against the grain to make the pieces more tender. A few hours of marinating is usually enough, especially with game bought in markets, though longer surely won't hurt the steaks.

Serve with puréed potatoes (see page 117) or fried potatoes (page 132). If the weather is decent, grill the venison outside over embers.

1½ POUNDS/680 G BONELESS VENISON LOIN, LEG, OR SHOULDER
2 GENEROUS PINCHES CUMIN SEEDS
3 GARLIC CLOVES, PEELED
2 GENEROUS PINCHES DRIED OREGANO
2 GENEROUS PINCHES DRIED THYME
2 GENEROUS PINCHES SPANISH PIMENTÓN DULCE (SWEET PAPRIKA)
SALT AND FRESHLY GROUND BLACK PEPPER
¼ CUP/60 ML EXTRA-VIRGIN OLIVE OIL
2 TEASPOONS WHITE WINE VINEGAR

1. Trim any fat or nerves from the venison. If using loin, slice the venison into round ½-inch-/1.25-cm-thick medallions. If using leg or shoulder, slice them crosswise against the grain into thin filets.

2. Crush the cumin in a mortar. Add the garlic, oregano, thyme, and pimentón; season with salt and pepper; and pound into a paste. Moisten with the olive oil and vinegar and blend. In a large baking dish or bowl, put the venison, add the marinade, and turn to coat. Cover and refrigerate for at least a few hours or overnight. Remove from the refrigerator an hour or so before grilling.

3. Preheat a grill pan, griddle pan, or large, heavy skillet over high heat. Remove the venison from the marinade and, without wiping off any marinade, lay the meat on the pan. Grill hot and fast, turning just once, until medium-rare, 1 to 2 minutes. Serve immediately.

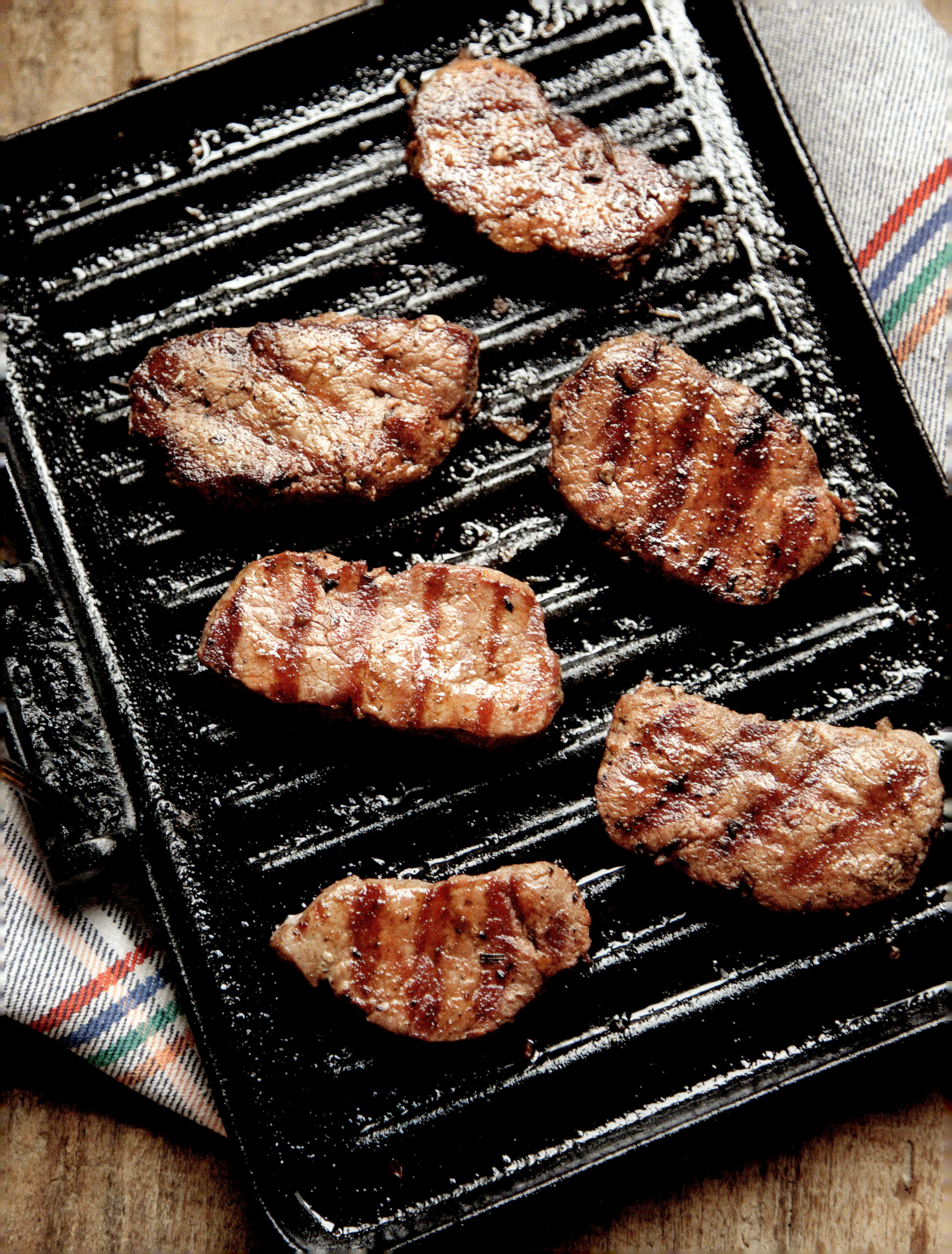

TRADITIONS

RED-LEGGED PARTRIDGE
perdiz roja

Though red-legged partridge inhabit much of Spain, the *llanuras* (high central plains) of the Castilian meseta south of Madrid, along with some areas of Extremadura and Andalucía, are the best place in all of Europe to find them. They are a sedentary (rather than migratory) bird, and live in fields of grains, groves of olive trees, and vineyards. Walking in this region, I have seen a dozen partridge, even two dozen, moving slowly across a field at a time. They will only fly when they must, and then alight with quick, short, and powerful flights.

Native to Spain, the perdiz roja is a beautifully feathered bird with a cinnamon-colored top, white throat, bluish gray chest, cinnamon belly, and wings with alternating stripes. The beak, legs, and around the eyes are all red. Weighing around 16 to 18 ounces/455 to 510 g, partridge have lean, smooth, and slightly aromatic meat thanks to their diet which includes plenty of wild herbs. Stewed (see facing page), grilled, or prepared in escabeche marinade, it is an exquisite bird for cooks.

But they are also the most prized game bird for hunters. The most famous (and expensive) way to hunt perdiz is in a formal, traditional driven hunt called an *ojeo*. Like many Spanish kings before him (and one notable twentieth-century dictator after), Alfonso XIII, the grandfather of the current king, was a keen bird hunter, and made it popular for aristocracy across Europe to hunt on the vast Spanish estates. Ojeos have changed little since, and remain, if not an exclusively aristocratic way of hunting, then a wealthy, genteel one.

Shooters sit behind a blind with a brace of shotguns and await birds winging by at 55 to 75 miles/90 to 120 km per hour, driven by a line of beaters progressing toward them. Traditionally, each shooter is accompanied by two assistants, a *cargador*, who helps with loading the shotguns and gathering fallen birds, and a *secretario*, who keeps track of counts and fallen birds. There are generally five beatings in a morning, with short breaks between.

As with nearly every tradition in Spain, food forms a key part of the hunt. The morning *taco*, or snack, is brought out to the field—chorizo and jamón, aged cheeses, *migas*, (essentially fried breadcrumbs, see page 161), and bottles of supple red wine. After the fifth beating, the hunters, helpers, and assistants adjourn to the manor house for a hearty lunch.

Even when the shooting is good (and perhaps even great), the taco and the post-shoot meal are surely among the day's most important and enjoyable parts.

TOLEDO-STYLE PARTRIDGE

PERDICES A LA TOLEDANA

SERVES 2 TO 4

Sitting protectively encircled on three sides by the Río Tajo (Tagus River), Toledo—one-time capital of the country, immortalized by El Greco, its tastes shaped by a strong Moorish, Jewish, and Christian heritage—is probably best known to the epicure for its fabulous marzipan. But Toledo is also surrounded by the finest partridge hunting (and eating) in Europe.

The emblematic way to prepare Spain's most sought-after game bird is Toledo style, that is, slowly stewed in white wine, olive oil, vinegar, herbs, and plenty of onions. The partridge should take about an hour, but I have cooked ones fresh from the finca (first laboriously plucking and then picking out buckshot with the tip of a knife) for twice that long.

2 WHOLE PARTRIDGE (NOT BONELESS), PLUCKED
SALT AND FRESHLY GROUND BLACK PEPPER
¼ CUP/60 ML EXTRA-VIRGIN OLIVE OIL
2 ONIONS, FINELY CHOPPED
1 CUP/240 ML DRY WHITE WINE
¼ CUP/60 ML SHERRY VINEGAR
6 SPRIGS FRESH PARSLEY
1 SPRIG FRESH THYME
1 SPRIG FRESH ROSEMARY
2 FRESH BAY LEAVES

1. Wash and dry the birds. Singe off any remaining hairs or feathers over an open flame. Wipe clean with a damp cloth. Clean the cavities while leaving the birds whole. Truss the legs with cotton kitchen string to help them keep their shape and cook evenly. Generously season with salt and pepper.

2. In a large, deep skillet, heat the olive oil over medium heat. Add the partridge and brown, turning as needed, about 5 minutes. Add the onions and cook until they begin to soften and turn pale, about 5 minutes. Pour in the wine, vinegar, and 2 cups/480 ml water. Tie the parsley, thyme, rosemary, and bay leaves together with cotton kitchen string and add. Partly cover the pan and simmer, swirling the pan from time to time, for 45 minutes to 1 hour. The partridge are done when the meat begins to come away from the bone and a leg jiggles in the socket. Discard the herb wrap.

3. Transfer the partridge to a cutting board. Using kitchen shears, cut the birds in half lengthwise through the breast and the backbone. Lay cut-side down on a plate and cover with the onions and sauce. Serve hot.

GRILLED QUAIL WITH GARLIC AND WHITE WINE

CODORNICES A LA PLANCHA CON AJO Y VINO BLANCO

SERVES 4

This simple grilled quail dish topped with a fragrant, garlic-laden olive oil and white wine sauce is perfect for an end-of-summer lunch, when this migratory bird is prevalent across much of Spain. (Farm-raised ones are found in markets year-round.) I first encountered this typical and straightforward country way of preparing quail in a *venta* (simple roadside restaurant) in the rolling, red-soiled hills of central Andalucía. Serve it with a green salad and a plate of potatoes, either fried (see page 132), puréed (see page 117), or made in the oven baker's style (see page 116). Don't overcook the birds. They should be moist, and the breast meat still a bit pink.

8 CLEANED WHOLE QUAIL (NOT BONELESS), ABOUT 7 OUNCES/200 G EACH
SALT AND FRESHLY GROUND BLACK PEPPER
½ CUP/60 ML EXTRA-VIRGIN OLIVE OIL, PLUS MORE FOR OILING PAN
4 GARLIC CLOVES, CHOPPED
¼ CUP/60 ML DRY WHITE WINE
2 TABLESPOONS MINCED FRESH FLAT-LEAF PARSLEY

1. Using poultry or kitchen shears, and beginning in the cavity, cut the quail through the breast and open like a book until flat. Trim the neck and the tips of the legs. Tap on the ribcage with the closed shears to slightly loosen the meat from the bones. Generously season both sides with salt and pepper.

2. Preheat a grill pan, griddle pan, or large, heavy skillet over medium-high heat and lightly oil. Working in batches as needed, grill the quail until done but still pink in the breast, about 10 minutes, being careful not to break the skin. (Smaller birds take 1 to 2 minutes less.) Transfer to a platter and loosely cover with aluminum foil tented in the middle to keep warm. Re-oil the pan if necessary between batches.

3. Meanwhile, in a small saucepan or skillet, heat the ½ cup olive oil and garlic over medium-low heat until the garlic is tender and fragrant but still pale, about 2 minutes. Carefully add the wine and bring to a boil. Remove the pan from the heat and whisk until cloudy.

4. Place two quail on each plate, spoon over some of the sauce with pieces of garlic, and sprinkle with the parsley. Serve immediately.

PILAR'S CAZUELA WITH SNAILS AND RABBIT

CAZUELA DE PILAR

SERVES 4 TO 5

This is from Pilar Rodriguez, the mother of a friend and a great cook who had a stall that sold cured jamónes and cheeses in one of Barcelona's finest covered food markets.

18 OUNCES/510 G SNAILS IN THEIR SHELLS, FRESH OR PRESERVED

4 GARLIC CLOVES; 1 UNPEELED, 3 PEELED

2 BAY LEAVES

1 SPRIG FRESH THYME

1 WHOLE CLEANED RABBIT WITH LIVER, ABOUT 2½ POUNDS/1.2 KG

SALT AND FRESHLY GROUND BLACK PEPPER

4 TABLESPOONS EXTRA-VIRGIN OLIVE OIL

2 SMALL SLICES BAGUETTE, DAY OLD OR TOASTED

1 ONION, FINELY CHOPPED

3 RIPE MEDIUM TOMATOES, PEELED, SEEDED, AND FINELY CHOPPED

½ CUP/60 G FINELY CHOPPED DRY-CURED SPANISH JAMÓN (SEE INGREDIENT NOTE, PAGE 16)

½ CUP/60 G FINELY CHOPPED SPANISH CHORIZO

½ CUP/120 ML DRY WHITE WINE

1 TABLESPOON MINCED FRESH FLAT-LEAF PARSLEY

DRIED RED PEPPER FLAKES

1. Clean and boil the snails with the unpeeled garlic, bay leaves, and thyme, following the directions on page 340 (for fresh) or page 341 (for preserved). Leave the snails in the water.

2. Cut the rabbit into eight or nine pieces, following the directions on page 342 (or have your butcher do it). Trim any excess fat. Reserve the liver. Season with salt and pepper.

3. In a cazuela, heavy casserole, large sauté pan, or deep skillet, heat the olive oil over medium-high heat. Add the bread and fry until golden, turning once, 1 to 2 minutes. Remove and reserve. Add the rabbit to the cazuela along with its liver. Cook until the liver is cooked through and the other pieces are well browned, about 8 minutes. Transfer to a platter.

4. Prepare a sofrito in the cazuela with the onion, tomatoes, and one of the garlic cloves, following the directions on page 39. When the sofrito is ready, add the jamón and chorizo, stir well to coat, and then add the wine. Return the rabbit (except the liver) to the pan along with any juices and turn over the pieces with a spoon to coat well with sofrito.

5. Using a slotted spoon, transfer the snails to the pan, reserving the liquid. Filter 1 cup/240 ml of the liquid from the snails into the cazuela. Bring to a simmer, reduce the heat to medium-low, and simmer for 30 minutes.

6. Prepare a picada with the reserved bread and liver, the remaining garlic cloves, the parsley, and 2 tablespoons of liquid from the snails, following the directions on page 39. Season with 1 or 2 pinches of red pepper flakes. Loosen with ½ cup/120 ml reserved liquid from the snails and stir into the cazuela.

7. Cook until the sauce has thickened and the rabbit is tender, 20 to 30 minutes. Taste for seasoning and add salt, if needed, before serving.

In Spanish, they say that snails (like shellfish) are best during months with an "r"—that is, September through April. January sits on that list, and it's something of a tradition with my mother-in-law to prepare a big pot of snails in a slightly *picante* tomato sauce for New Year's Day lunch. My father-in-law comes from around Lleida, a heartland of snail eating, and one of his culinary passions is these gastropods. Like most snail dishes around Spain, it has a slightly spicy touch to it. The trick, my mother-in-law taught me, is to sprinkle in a bit of flour at the end. This thickens the sauce slightly but, more importantly, gets the sauce to coat the snails as opposed to remaining in the bottom of the pan.

The best snails to use here are a medium-size variety such as *pequeño gris* (brown garden snail, or *petit-gris*). The next size larger will work, too. These are called *los viñedos* (vineyard or Burgundy snail). Fresh snails can be hard to find in North America, but preserved ones ready to cook are certainly available. The artisanal preserves company Rosara from Navarra exports them preserved in brine. Delicias de España carries them and will ship. See Sources, page 345, for where to find these and start looking for live ones.

NEW YEAR'S DAY SNAILS IN SPICY TOMATO SAUCE

CARACOLES DE AÑO NUEVO

SERVES 4

18 OUNCES/510 G SNAILS IN THEIR SHELLS, FRESH OR PRESERVED

2 GARLIC CLOVES; 1 UNPEELED, 1 MINCED

2 BAY LEAVES

1 SPRIG FRESH THYME

3 TABLESPOONS EXTRA-VIRGIN OLIVE OIL

1 MEDIUM ONION, FINELY CHOPPED

⅓ CUP/45 G LOOSELY PACKED FINELY CHOPPED SPANISH CHORIZO

⅓ CUP/45 G LOOSELY PACKED FINELY CHOPPED DRY-CURED SPANISH JAMÓN (SEE INGREDIENT NOTE, PAGE 16)

4 RIPE MEDIUM TOMATOES, HALVED CROSSWISE, SEEDED, AND GRATED (SEE PAGE 339)

DRIED HOT RED CHILES OR RED PEPPER FLAKES

HEAPED 1 TABLESPOON ALL-PURPOSE FLOUR

1. Clean and boil the snails with the unpeeled garlic, bay leaves, and thyme, following the directions on page 340 (for fresh) or page 341 (for preserved). Drain and discard the herbs.

2. In a cazuela, heavy casserole, large sauté pan, or deep skillet, heat the olive oil over medium heat and add the onion. Cook until soft and translucent, 8 to 10 minutes. Add the minced garlic and cook until fragrant, about 1 minute. Stir in the chorizo and jamón and then add the tomatoes. Cook, stirring from time to time, until the tomatoes have darkened and the sauce is pasty, about 10 minutes.

3. Add the snails, season with red chiles (1 or 2 tiny ones should be enough), and pour in ½ cup/120 ml water. Cook uncovered over medium-low heat for 20 minutes, until the sauce is thickened and the flavors blended. Sprinkle in the flour and stir until the sauce coats the snails, 2 or 3 minutes. Serve with toothpicks or small snail forks to extract the meat.

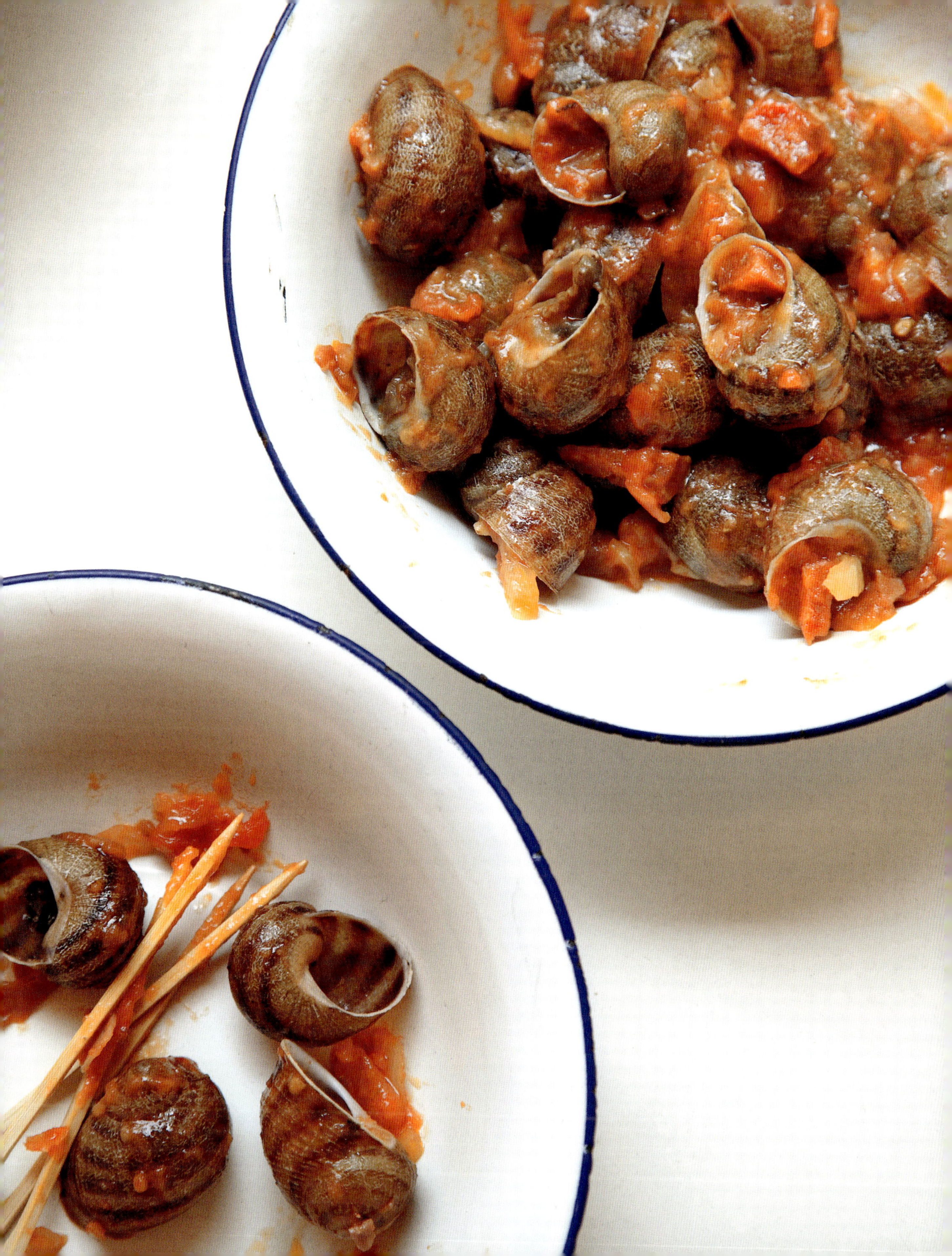

CHAPTER 11

MEATS
carnes

Consumption of beef in Spain is among the lowest per capita in Europe. My own theory is that this is for a handful of reasons. First is the excellent pork and lamb available—Spain is a top European producer of both of these; only Germany raises more pigs and Britain more sheep—as well as high-quality rabbit and poultry. Just as significant is the vast quantity of seafood. The Spanish are among the world's biggest consumers of fish and shellfish. And pulses are extremely important. All of this is a way of saying there is a balance in the diet and plenty of other ways to get protein. Besides, Spain was poor for much of the twentieth century, and beef was comparatively expensive.

And of course there is the fact that much of the country is arid, with vast regions lacking grasslands or suitable terrain. This has focused the beef industry to a handful of pockets, namely in the mountain areas of the central meseta and in the north. In the past years, ten different regions have been awarded protective regulatory status for their cattle, often local, autochthonous breeds like the long-horned Tudanca from Cantabria and muscular, grayish black Morucha from Salamanca.

I should say something about beef terminology in Spanish. *Ternera* means veal and usually refers to a younger animal less than one year old. (Sometimes they are older. For instance, under the Basque Country's guidelines for Protected Geographic Indication Euskal Okela, *ternera* can mean from eight to twenty months.) *Ternera lechal* is milk-fed veal, more similar to the pale pink veal in the English and American tradition. *Buey* means ox, a castrated bull whose meat is slightly darker, deeper red, and more flavorful. Uncastrated bulls are called *toros*, and its meat is something of a specialty. It tends to be tougher and require longer cooking.

For many, the animal most associated with the Spanish countryside is the sheep. The image of flocks of sheep moving across a barren hillside remains an iconic one. Roasted, stewed, or grilled, lamb is a fine, flavorful meat, fatty (therefore usually moist) and aromatic, and fundamental in the kitchen.

In some places—take the mountainous, often rugged province of Guadalajara in Castilla–La Mancha—*cabrito* (or *choto*, kid goat) takes pride of place on many people's tables. They are small, tender, and delicately flavored, and especially appreciated in winter and spring.

But it's the pig that is arguably the most important four-footed animal in the Spanish kitchen—and on the farm.

Fresh pork and pork sausages are found in numerous dishes. Among cuts, center-cut loins are prized. When buying loin, I nearly always ask for the blade or butt end, which stays moister as it cooks. In Spanish, it is referred to as the end of *dos colores* (two colors). The blade end has a near-S-shaped division of leaner whiter meat and darker, fattier meat, which is more tender. My favorite way to prepare this is to roast it in a salt crust (see page 245), where it literally cooks in its own juices, and comes out gamey, almost wild, as opposed to salty.

Cuarenta sabores tiene el cerdo y todos son buenos, goes one saying: "The pig has forty flavors and they are all tasty."

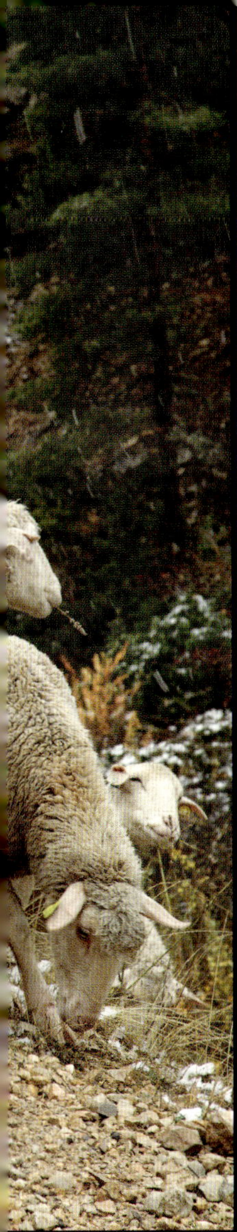
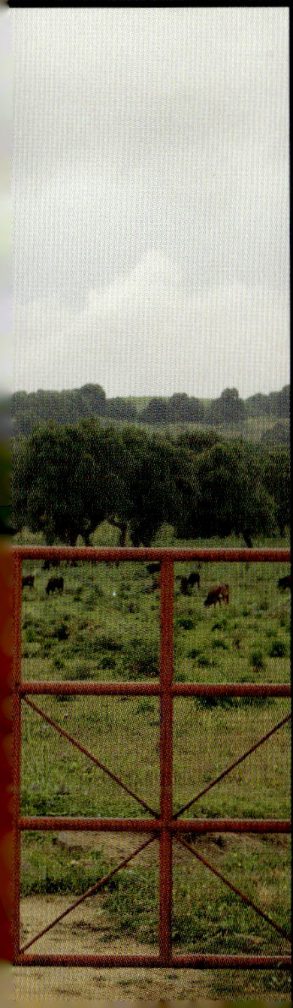
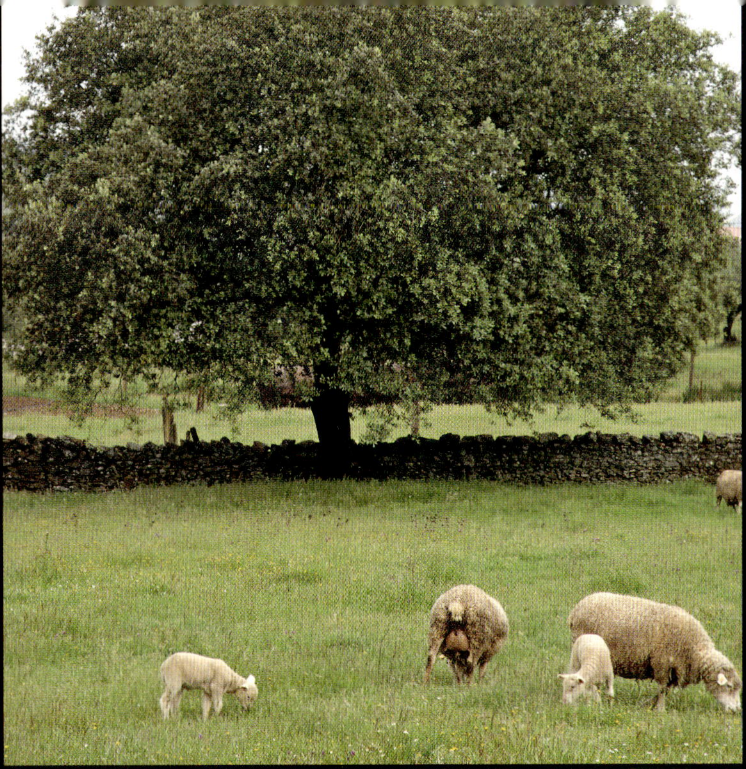
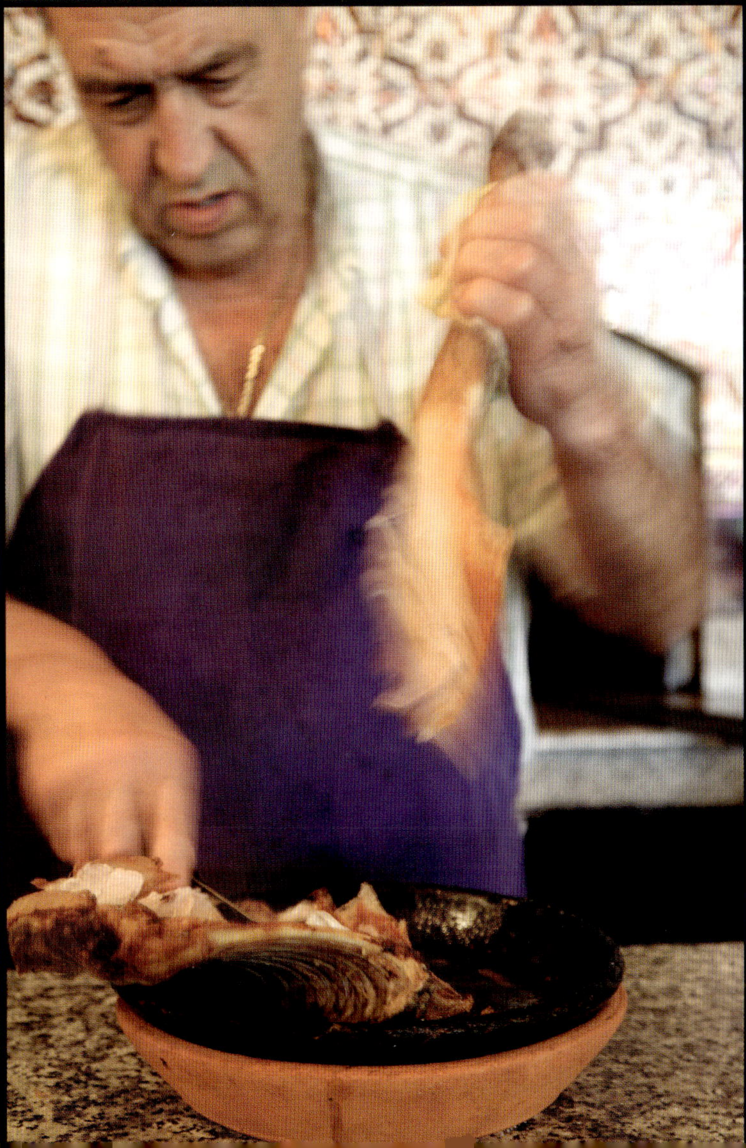
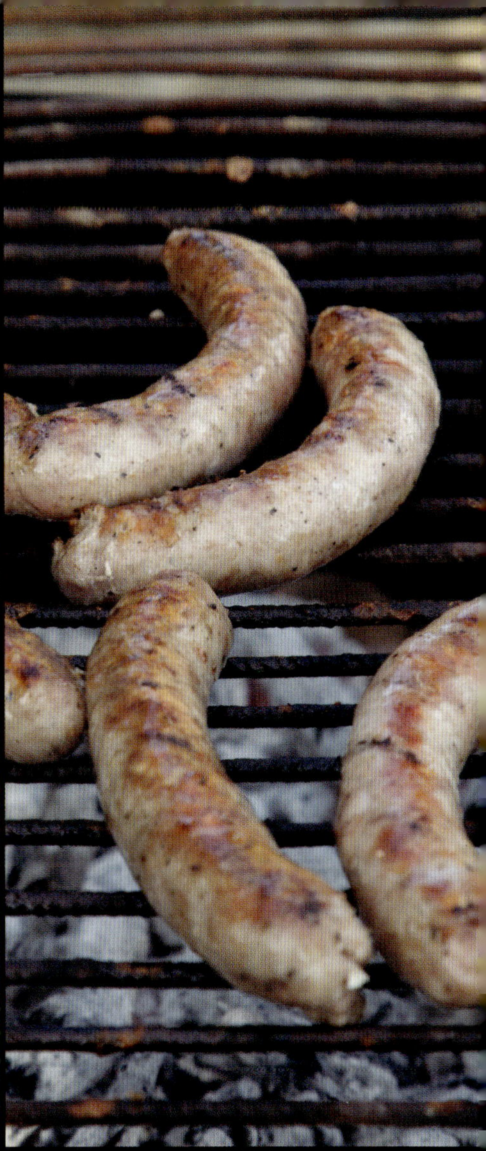
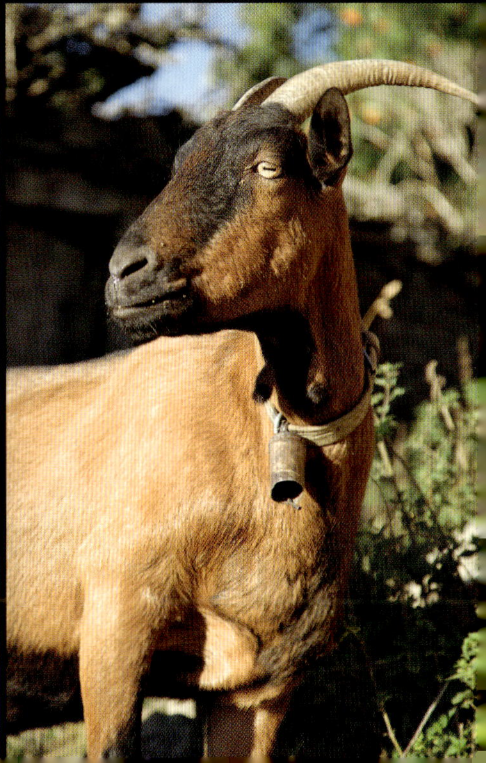

ROAST SHOULDER OF KID GOAT WITH POTATO AND SHALLOT CONFIT

ESPALDITA DE CABRITO AL HORNO CON PATATAS Y CEBOLLITAS CONFITADAS

SERVES 4

The tender, delicate meat of kid goat remains something of a treat. So highly regarded is cabrito in Guadalajara and parts of Castilla that it is the choice for many Christmas tables. The shoulder is a tender, juicy cut, a choice piece of the kid. (*Cabrito* means that the goat is usually not more than six months old.) The recipe is adapted from Jesús Benavente, the long-serving chef at the Can Ravell delicatessen in Barcelona. His versions of country classics are so popular that at Christmastime, Can Ravell gets some four hundred orders for this kid dish, nearly all as take-out for family meals. (That is nothing compared to the six thousand meat-stuffed cannelloni they sell in the same time period, again largely as take-out.)

1 POUND/455 G MEDIUM WHITE POTATOES
8 OUNCES/225 G SHALLOTS
1 MEDIUM ONION, FINELY CHOPPED
1 CARROT, FINELY CHOPPED
1 LEEK, WHITE AND TENDER GREEN PARTS ONLY, FINELY CHOPPED
1 CELERY STALK, FINELY CHOPPED
1 GARLIC CLOVE, LIGHTLY CRUSHED IN THE PEEL
3 TABLESPOONS EXTRA-VIRGIN OLIVE OIL, PLUS MORE FOR THE PAN
4 KID GOAT SHOULDERS, ABOUT 10 OUNCES/300 G EACH
SALT AND FRESHLY GROUND BLACK PEPPER
½ CUP/120 ML MEDIUM RED WINE
6 SPRIGS FRESH THYME
4 TO 6 CUPS/1 TO 1.4 L SUNFLOWER OIL OR MILD OLIVE OIL FOR FRYING
2 OR 3 TABLESPOONS SHERRY OR SWEET WINE
3 TABLESPOONS BUTTER

1. Preheat the oven to 325°F/165°C/gas mark 3.

2. Peel the potatoes and finely slice them crosswise, ideally with a mandoline so that they are similar in thickness and will cook evenly. Soak the potatoes in a large bowl filled with cold water for 30 minutes to leach out some of the starches.

3. Bring a small pot of water to a boil. Blanch the shallots in the boiling water for 2 minutes, then rinse and peel under cold water.

4. In a roasting pan, place the onion, carrot, leek, celery, and garlic and moisten with the olive oil.

5. Preheat a grill pan, griddle pan, or large, heavy skillet over high heat and lightly oil. Generously season the kid goat with salt and pepper and, working in batches as needed, quickly sear, turning with tongs as needed, until lightly browned, 2 to 3 minutes on each side. (It is fine if not every part of the kid gets browned.) Place on top of the vegetables. Drizzle with the red wine and arrange the thyme around the kid.

6. Roast for 40 minutes, turning the kid from time to time. Drizzle in about ½ cup/120 ml water. Cover with aluminum foil and roast until done, 20 to 30 minutes more, turning the kid from time to time to cook evenly. Transfer the kid to a platter and loosely cover with foil tented in the middle to keep warm. Strain the vegetables through a chinois, gently pressing out the moisture. Reserve the liquid, and discard the solids.

7. Meanwhile, drain the potatoes, gently rinse, drain again, and then gently pat dry with paper towels. In a sauté pan or deep skillet, heat the sunflower oil until shimmering. Add the potatoes and cook over medium-high heat, gently moving from time to time without breaking. After about 10 minutes, once they have begun to soften, add the shallots. Reduce the heat to medium and cook until the potatoes are golden at the edges and the shallots very tender, about 20 minutes. Using a wide, flat, slotted spoon, transfer the potatoes and shallots to a colander to drain well.

8. Transfer the potatoes and shallots to a clean skillet. Add 2 tablespoons of the reserved liquid from the roasting pan, drizzle the sherry over the skillet, and add the butter. Cook over medium-low heat until the vegetables are tender and the flavors have been absorbed, about 10 minutes.

9. Place one shoulder on each plate along with some potatoes and shallots. Drizzle over some sauce and serve.

TRADITIONS

Can Ravell

Opened in 1929, this slender "deli" is a gourmand's delight. Ignasi Ravell began working in a neighborhood *colmado* (a small general store) before he was a teenager, helping all day and sleeping under the counter at night. At eighteen, he took a job at another colmado, one beside the magnificent art nouveau La Concepió market in Barcelona's Eixample neighborhood. A year later he bought it from the owner. He changed the name to Can Ravell and called it a *mantequería*. It had little to do with butter (*mantequilla*), his son told me, but rather was a refined version of a colmado, with more selective food items. Ignasi eventually bought land in Castilla to grow some of his own products, and also traveled frequently, meeting producers and bringing his finds back to the shop's clients. In the 1960s, Can Ravell began preparing a handful of traditional dishes in the small kitchen and serving them at long marble tables among bottles of wines and spirits. Ignasi ran the shop until his death in 1994 at eighty-four years old.

Like many such establishments, Can Ravell is a family one, and the son, Josep—who began working in the shop in the late 1970s—took it over. He refurbished the store and increased the staff from three to fifteen. But the founding and fundamental principles remained exactly the same.

TRADITIONS

SHEEP
cordero

There are few images of rural Spain more classical (or idealistically painted) than flocks of sheep grazing across the dry, golden landscape of the country's interior. A *pastor* (shepherd) follows—walking stick in hand, a knapsack slung over a shoulder—watching, seemingly with casual attention, as a small dog bounds somewhere around the animals.

Sheep have long played an important part in Spanish history, especially in Castilla and the central meseta tablelands. The animals are smart, but also extraordinarily resistant and extremely adaptable to the harsh climate of the meseta, with its scorching, dry summers, and bitter, cold winters. Merino sheep were introduced into Spain from North Africa around the twelfth century, and the line was bred and refined for their fleecy wool. Between the fourteenth and sixteenth centuries, the European wool market was centralized in Burgos, capital of Old Castile for five hundred years and home to one of the most spectacular Gothic cathedrals in the country. In the heady days of the 1500s, there were some three million sheep in Spain, with spun wool flowing north through ports like Bilbao and Santander en route to the important cloth industries of Flanders, the great medieval principality that today is divided among Belgium, the Netherlands, and France. For centuries, Spain held a monopoly on merino wool, and until the eighteenth century, it was forbidden to export the sheep.

In the autumn, great flocks of migrating sheep moved (and still move!) from summer pastures in the north down to winter pastures in the south, and then back in springtime, following long pathways called *Cañadas Reales*. In 1273, King Alfonso X *el Sabio* ("the Wise") guaranteed and protected these paths by royal edict, and also set up an organization called the Concejo de Mesta to govern them. The cañadas had to be a width of 90 *varas castellanas* (that is, 237 feet/72.22 m), and generally run for distances over 300 miles/480 km. Numerous smaller routes fed into these. Of the nine key routes in Spain, the longest runs from Soria to Sevilla, some 500 miles/800 km south in Andalucía. The vast web of routes, sprawling across much of the center of the country, totals some 78,000 miles/125,000 km.

And while sheep are a symbol of the Castilian landscape, they are also an emblem of its kitchen. What could be more characteristic than a wedge of nutty, aged Manchego cheese, or a quarter of roast suckling lamb slid from the wood-burning oven of a centuries-old, tile-walled *mesón*? And, for that matter, what could be tastier?

The name *cabañil* refers to the mules that traveled with flocks of sheep moving between summer and winter pastures, or to market. It is a recipe found, in numerous variations, across the mountainous region of southern Murcia that borders Andalucía, where lamb and goat form the centerpiece of the local cuisine, and offer it something of a culinary identity. This humble mountain dish adds a zesty, tangy sweetness to the savory flavors of the lamb.

SHEPHERD'S-STYLE LAMB CHOPS WITH POTATOES AND ZESTY VINEGAR-GARLIC SAUCE

CHULETAS DE CORDERO AL AJO CABAÑIL

SERVES 4

1 SMALL GARLIC HEAD, CLOVES PEELED

SALT

3 TABLESPOONS WHITE WINE VINEGAR

6 TABLESPOONS EXTRA-VIRGIN OLIVE OIL

2¼ POUNDS/1 KG MEDIUM WHITE POTATOES, PEELED AND CUT CROSSWISE INTO ¼-INCH-/½-CM-THICK SLICES

1 MEDIUM ONION, SLICED

1 TEASPOON SUGAR

12 BONE-IN LAMB LOIN CHOPS, ABOUT ½ INCH/1.25 CM THICK

1. In a large mortar, mash the garlic with a few generous pinches of salt. Stir in the vinegar and ¾ cup/180 ml water. Or quickly pulse the ingredients in a food processor.

2. In a large skillet or sauté pan, heat 4 tablespoons of the olive oil over medium heat. Add the potatoes and onion, cover the skillet, and cook until the potatoes are nearly tender, about 20 minutes, turning from time to time. Pour over a generous half of the garlic sauce, add ½ teaspoon of the sugar, and cook uncovered until the potatoes are tender and the liquid reduced, 20 to 25 minutes. Remove from the heat and cover to keep warm until ready to serve.

3. In a large skillet or sauté pan, heat the remaining 2 tablespoons olive oil over high heat. Season the lamb with salt and cook in single-layer batches until browned, about 1½ minutes on each side. Return all of the lamb to the pan, sprinkle over the remaining ½ teaspoon sugar, and pour over the remaining garlic sauce. Reduce the heat to low and cook, turning from time to time, until done but still medium-rare, about 5 minutes.

4. Place the potatoes on a large serving platter and arrange the lamb chops on top. Drizzle any remaining sauce from the pan over the dish. Serve immediately.

GRILLED LAMB RIB CHOPS WITH QUINCE ALLIOLI

COSTILLAS DE CORDERO CON ALLIOLI DE MEMBRILLO

SERVES 6

As well as in making quince paste (see page 323), some of the hard fruit from the pear and apple family in the foothills of the Catalan Pyreness is used in this oil-and-garlic emulsion. It's fruity without being sweet, and has the background bite, flavor, and aroma of garlic. It pairs well with grilled meats and poultry, and in Tremp—the Pallars Jussà town of my father-in-law's family—it is frequently spread over toasted country bread.

QUINCE ALLIOLI

½ SMALL QUINCE, PEELED, CORED, AND CUT INTO SMALL PIECES

½ SMALL WINTER PEAR, PEELED, CORED, AND CUT INTO SMALL PIECES

2 SMALL GARLIC CLOVES, PEELED

1 EGG

SALT

WHITE WINE VINEGAR

1 CUP/240 ML MILD OLIVE OIL OR A BLEND OF OLIVE OIL AND SUNFLOWER OIL

EXTRA-VIRGIN OLIVE OIL FOR OILING PAN

FLAKY SEA SALT

4 POUNDS/1.8 KG BONE-IN LAMB RIB CHOPS OR SHOULDER BLADE CHOPS

1. To make the allioli: In a small saucepan, combine the quince, pear, and 1 cup/240 ml water and bring to a boil. Reduce the heat to low, cover the pan, and gently boil until very tender, almost mushy, 20 to 30 minutes, depending on the ripeness of the fruit. Transfer to a strainer to let the fruit drain and to cool. Mash into a paste with the back of a fork and remove any hard fibers.

2. *To prepare using an immersion hand blender:* In a tall, narrow, and cylindrical container, add the fruit paste, garlic, egg, a generous pinch of salt, some drops of vinegar, and the olive oil. While still turned off, place the blender shaft in the bottom of the container. Turn the blender on to three-fourths speed and begin blending. Once the emulsion begins to form, slowly bring the hand blender up through the oil and just out, and then slowly back down to the bottom. Bring it up once more and out. Total blending time is 30 seconds to 1 minute. The allioli should have thickened to the consistency of mayonnaise; if not, lower the shaft slowly back down to the bottom and out again.

To prepare using a food processor: Add the fruit paste, garlic, egg, a generous pinch of salt, and some drops of vinegar. Begin whirring the food processor and add the olive oil in a very slow but steady stream until all of the oil has been used and the emulsion has thickened to the consistency of mayonnaise, about 1 minute.

3. Transfer the allioli to a small serving bowl. Cover with plastic wrap and refrigerate until ready to use.

4. Preheat a grill pan or large, heavy skillet over high heat, lightly oil, and scatter with salt flakes. Lay on the rib chops, scatter salt flakes over the top, and grill for 2 to 3 minutes on each side, turning just once with tongs. Serve the chops immediately with the allioli on the side.

TRADITIONS

SUCKLING LAMB
lechazo

For five generations, the Cristóbal family has been preparing one dish to perfection at their Restaurante Asados Nazareno in the ancient market town of Roa: *lechazo*, or roast *cordero lechal* (unweaned suckling lamb). The dry Castilian landscape along the Ribera del Duero, where vineyards meet golden fields of cereals, is the heartland of lechazo. *Asadores*, or traditional restaurants that roast these as well as suckling pigs in wood ovens, abound, and are championed with cultish loyalty. Many aficionados—me among them—consider Asados Nazareno to be the regions's best.

Until recently, Asados Nazareno opened only on Tuesdays (market day in Roa) and weekends. Quarters must be ordered before noon, when master roaster, octogenarian Javier Cristóbal, places them on wide earthenware dishes and slides them into the restaurant's deep, wood-burning ovens. No herbs, no garlic, just some *manteca* (lard), salt, and a touch of water. That's it. And only for lunch.

With such straightforward cooking, what is the key to such perfection? "The most important thing is the quality of the animal," Javier told me, dismissing his own well-honed touch. The best lechazo are twenty-four days old, he said, and weigh 22 to 24 pounds/10 to 11 kg.

I was eating with Manuel "Manolo" Pérez Pascuas of Bodegas Pérez Pascuas—Viña Pedrosa (see page 218). It was Tuesday and packed with winemakers. (The Consejo Regulador for Ribera del Duero wine is located in Roa.) With the harvest beginning later that week, the mood was buoyant if a bit nervy.

When our quarters were ready, Javier slid the earthenware dishes from the oven and carved some of the meat off the bone for easier eating, adding a final pinch of salt. When the large dishes were set down in front of us along with a simple green salad, the first thing Manolo did was to soak a piece of bread in the pooled juices.

"The sheep are nearly wild," Manolo explained as we dug into the long, tender strips of succulent meat. "They need to walk for food, the mothers eating the dry herbs." He took a bite and then added, *"Son deportistas."* (They're sportswomen.)

As we worked through our quarters, Manolo repeated the wisdom that where there is good wine, good food follows. I raised my glass of lusty Viña Pedrosa reserva.

We finished the meal with a couple of slices of chilled green melon. Green salad, roast suckling lamb, and melon—the Jack-Queen-King of Castilian cooking.

GRILLED LAMB CHOPS WITH HONEY

CHULETAS DE CORDERO CON MIEL

SERVES 4

Lamb roasted with honey is surely one of the most sophisticated Moorish-influenced dishes in Andalucía. One winter, in the village of Montefrío, perched dramatically on a cliff above hills of olive groves near Granada, I discovered a quicker way to prepare this spectacular combination. Instead of roasting a large cut of lamb, chops were grilled and then immediately drizzled with a touch of honey before being served. It's a simple but striking preparation. Use a strong, natural honey, such as an aromatic monofloral one from bees that gather nectar from rosemary or thyme. For smokier tones, grill the lamb outside over embers.

EXTRA-VIRGIN OLIVE OIL FOR OILING PAN
FLAKY SEA SALT
12 BONE-IN LAMB LOIN CHOPS, ABOUT ½ INCH/1.25 CM THICK
2 TABLESPOONS HONEY

1. Preheat a grill pan, griddle pan, or large, heavy skillet over high heat, lightly oil, and scatter with salt flakes. Lay on the loin chops, scatter salt flakes over the top, and grill for about 2 minutes on each side, turning just once with tongs.

2. Transfer the chops to plates. Smear ½ teaspoon of the honey across each chop; turn over and smear another ½ teaspoon honey on each one. Serve immediately.

CHILLED PORK LOIN

CARNE MECHADA

SERVES 6 TO 8

One spring day, driving through the rolling, red-soiled, and olive-studded hills east of Jerez de la Frontera, the landscape broken by hilltop *pueblos blancos* (white towns) huddled around ancient Moorish castles, I stopped at a simple *venta* (roadside eatery) and had this pork for lunch. The loin had been cooked, chilled, and then very thinly sliced like a cold cut. Served as a first course, the owner brought it out with a small dish of flaky sea salt and an ample bottle of heady local extra-virgin olive oil to drizzle over the top. At home, look in the pantry for inspiration—I like a dollop of pear compote (see page 245) or some sweet-and-sour onions (see page 329). When served with a lovely green salad, Spanish Potato Salad (page 56), or fried potatoes (see page 132), it becomes a full meal.

2 TABLESPOONS EXTRA-VIRGIN OLIVE OIL, PLUS MORE FOR DRIZZLING

2¼ POUNDS/1 KG BONELESS CENTER-CUT PORK LOIN ROAST, PREFERABLY THE BLADE (OR BUTT) END, IN 1 PIECE

SALT AND FRESHLY GROUND BLACK PEPPER

½ CUP/120 ML DRY WHITE WINE OR ⅓ CUP/75 ML DRY SHERRY

1 TEASPOON DRIED OREGANO

1 TEASPOON SPANISH PIMENTÓN DULCE (SWEET PAPRIKA)

2 PINCHES FRESHLY GRATED NUTMEG

2 CLOVES

1 BAY LEAF

FLAKY SEA SALT

½ LEMON, CUT INTO 4 WEDGES

1. In a large, heavy skillet or sauté pan, heat the olive oil over medium-high heat. Generously season the loin with salt and pepper and add to the pan, cooking and turning from time to time, until well-browned, 6 to 8 minutes.

2. Carefully pour the wine over the loin and then add 1½ cups/360 ml water to the pan. Add the oregano, pimentón, nutmeg, cloves, and bay leaf and cook uncovered until the loin is still pink in the middle and an instant-read thermometer probed to the center of the loin reads at least 145°F/63°C, 50 minutes to 1 hour.

3. Remove from the heat and let cool to room temperature. Cover with plastic wrap and refrigerate for several hours, until thoroughly chilled.

4. Slice the loin as thinly as possible, like a cold cut. Serve with salt flakes and olive oil to drizzle as desired. Garnish with lemon wedges.

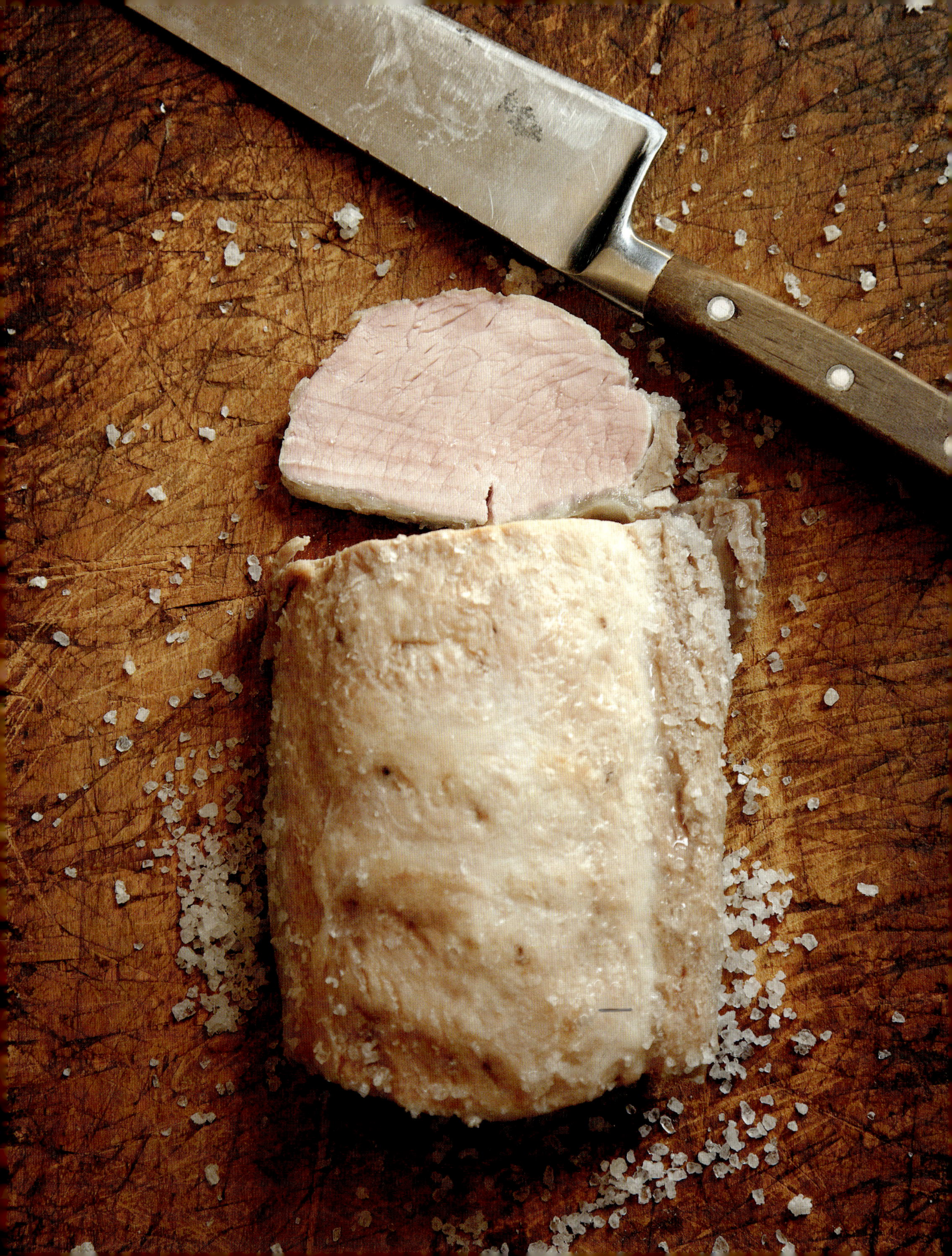

SALT-BAKED PORK LOIN WITH TWO SAUCES

LOMO DE CERDO A LA SAL CON DOS SALSAS

SERVES 4

Baking a loin in a salt crust gives the pork gamier, earthier flavors that combine perfectly with a host of juxtaposing sauces—from sweet compotes of apples or pears to a purée of chestnuts (see page 246) to blue cheese sauces.

4½ POUNDS/2 KG COARSE KOSHER SALT

3 EGG WHITES

2¼ POUNDS/1 KG BONELESS CENTER-CUT PORK LOIN ROAST, PREFERABLY THE BLADE (OR BUTT) END, IN 1 PIECE

BLUE CHEESE SAUCE (PAGE 259)

PEAR COMPOTE

2 POUNDS/910 G RIPE BUT FIRM PEARS, SUCH AS CONFERENCE, CONCORDE, ANJOU, OR WILLIAMS

1/2 LEMON

3 TABLESPOONS SUGAR

1 SMALL CINNAMON STICK

1/4 CUP/60 ML WHITE WINE

1. Preheat the oven to 400°F/200°C/gas mark 6.

2. In a large bowl, mix the salt with the egg whites until the salt feels slightly damp.

3. Line a roasting pan or an ovenproof baking dish large enough to accommodate the loin with a piece of parchment paper or aluminum foil (for easier clean up). Spread about one-fourth of the salt in a layer approximately ½ inch/1.25 cm thick across the bottom; pat down. Lay the loin on top, and cover completely with the remaining salt, in an even ½-inch-/1.25-cm-thick layer, patting it down around the loin. Be sure the entire piece of pork is thoroughly and evenly covered.

4. Gently—without shifting the packed salt—place the covered loin in the oven. Bake for about 50 minutes. The salt will form a hard, browned shell. Remove from the oven. An instant-read thermometer, worked through the salt and into the center of the loin, should read at least 145°F/63°C.

5. Have a large bowl ready for the salt crust. Using a wooden mallet or hammer, carefully break open the salt shell by tapping gently. Pull off the chunks of salt and then remove the loin. With a pastry brush, sweep away any salt grains. On a clean surface, cut the loin crosswise into pencil-thin slices and layer on a serving platter or plates.

6. To make the compote: Quarter, peel, and core the pears. Cut them into ½- to 1-inch/1.25- to 2.5-cm pieces of roughly equal size. Squirt with lemon juice to keep them from turning brown. In a large saucepan, dissolve the sugar in ½ cup/120 ml water and bring to a boil. Add the pears and cinnamon and pour in the wine. When the liquid returns to a boil, lower the heat and gently boil, stirring frequently, until the pears are very tender but still holding their shape and the syrup has thickened, about 20 minutes. Add some water if it threatens to dry out. Remove from the heat and let cool.

7. Serve with the pear compote and blue cheese sauce to spoon over the pork as desired.

PORK TENDERLOIN WITH PURÉE OF CHESTNUTS

SOLOMILLO DE CERDO CON PURÉ DE CASTAÑAS

SERVES 4

The humble and ancient chestnut was once fundamental to the Galician diet, though it was largely displaced by the sixteenth-century introduction of potatoes (and corn). A favorite way to cook them is as a purée to accompany roasted or grilled meats and sausages.

Searing the tenderloins will keep them juicy and tender. Be sure to turn them with tongs, not with a fork, which will release some juices.

1 POUND/455 G WHOLE CHESTNUTS
2½ CUPS/600 ML MILK
¼ CUP/60 G BUTTER, CUT INTO PIECES
2 TABLESPOONS SPANISH BRANDY OR COGNAC
FLAKY SEA SALT
EXTRA-VIRGIN OLIVE OIL FOR OILING PAN
2 PORK TENDERLOINS, ABOUT 14 OUNCES/400 G EACH
½ CUP/120 ML SWEET SHERRY OR PORT

1. Peel the chestnuts: Score the flat side of the chestnuts with a short, cross-shaped incision through the leathery surface using the tip of a sharp knife. Bring a saucepan filled with water to a rolling boil. Drop in the chestnuts and boil for 2 to 3 minutes. Fill a bowl with cold water. Transfer the chestnuts with a slotted spoon to the cold water. Cover the saucepan and keep the water at a low boil. Once the chestnuts are cool enough to handle, take them from the water one by one and peel away both the outer layer and the thin, membrane-like inner one that covers the nut. Use a paring knife if needed to help. If the inner covering does not easily come away, drop the chestnut back in the boiling water for 1 minute, transfer with a slotted spoon to the bowl of cold water to cool, and then peel. Place the peeled chestnuts on paper towels to dry. There should be about 10 ounces/280 g of peeled chestnuts.

2. In a saucepan, add the milk and chestnuts, cover the pan, bring to a simmer over medium heat, and simmer until the chestnuts are tender, about 30 minutes. Purée them in the pan with an immersion hand blender or transfer to a food processor, purée, and then return to the pan. Stir in the butter, brandy, and a pinch of salt and cook, stirring continually, over low heat for 2 to 3 minutes to burn off the alcohol. The texture should be creamy and thickish; it will thicken a bit more as it cools. (Add a touch more butter if necessary.) Remove from the heat.

3. Meanwhile, preheat the oven to 350°F/180°C/gas mark 4.

4. Preheat a grill pan, griddle pan, or large, heavy skillet over high heat, lightly oil, and scatter with salt flakes. Lay the tenderloins in the pan and quickly sear, turning with tongs as needed, until they are browned and have a slight crust, about 5 minutes.

5. Transfer the pork to a roasting pan, slide it into the oven, and roast until done and the insides are still rosy, 15 to 20 minutes, depending on the thickness of the tenderloins. An instant-read thermometer poked into the center of the tenderloin should read at least 145°F/63°C. Drizzle with the sherry about halfway through cooking.

6. Transfer the loins to a cutting board and let rest for 3 minutes before slicing into generously sized medallions, about two or three fingers thick. Arrange a couple of medallions on each plate, sprinkle with salt flakes, and garnish with a generous dollop of the purée of chestnuts. Serve with the remaining purée in a bowl on the side.

PORK TENDERLOIN IN ORANGE SAUCE

SOLOMILLO DE CERDO A LA NARANJA

SERVES 4 TO 6

I like this dish for the way the flavors accent each other. I like the way it smells when it's cooking on the stove, once the tenderloin's juices begin to run into the simmering orange juice. And I like how it looks on the plate, and for this reason always arrange the medallions on a white platter to show off the brilliant glistening deep-orange sauce that is ladled over the top. There are a number of ways to make this dish more complicated—adding some Cointreau to tighten the orange flavor, a piece of orange peel—but the simplicity here is another reason why I like it so much.

1 TABLESPOON EXTRA-VIRGIN OLIVE OIL
2 PORK TENDERLOINS, 14 OUNCES TO 1 POUND/400 TO 455 G EACH
2 CUPS/480 ML FRESHLY SQUEEZED ORANGE JUICE
1 CUP/200 G SUGAR
½ CUP/70 G PINE NUTS, DRY-TOASTED (SEE PAGE 340)

1. In a large skillet or sauté pan, heat the olive oil over high heat. Add the tenderloins and sear on each side, turning with tongs, 3 to 5 minutes. Transfer to a platter and cover with aluminum foil tented in the middle to keep warm.

2. Add the orange juice to the skillet and bring to a boil. Stir in the sugar, reduce the heat to medium, and simmer into a loose, runny glaze that can coat the back of a spoon, about 30 minutes.

3. Return the tenderloins to the pan and cook, turning from time to time, until done but still rosy on the inside, 10 to 15 minutes more, depending on the thickness of the tenderloin. An instant-read thermometer poked into the center of the tenderloin should read at least 145°F/63°C.

4. Transfer the loins to a cutting board and let them rest for 3 minutes before slicing into finger-thick medallions at a slight diagonal angle. Arrange on a long serving platter, spoon the sauce over the top, sprinkle with the pine nuts, and serve.

TRADITIONS

ROAST SUCKLING PIG
cochinillo asado

At the foot of the Sierra de Guadarrama, northwest of Madrid, lies the ancient city of Segovia. In a region specializing in wood-roasted meats, Segovia stands out for its numerous centuries-old *mesones* serving *cochinillo* (suckling pig). A certified *Cochinillo de Segovia* is no more than twenty-one days old and weighs between 10 and 12 pounds/4.5 and 5.5 kg. These are slow-roasted whole in oval earthenware dishes with the most minimal of condiments—a bit of lard, salt, and a touch of water—until the skin is crispy and the meat succulent and tender.

To show just how tender, the late Cándido, namesake and founder of the town's most famous mesón, used to come to the table, brandish a plate, and "slice" the pig with the plate's edge. A plate! Good theater, but it never took away from the meat that was so tender it didn't need a knife to be cut.

On my first visit to Segovia nearly fifteen years ago, friends took me there for lunch. By then Cándido had passed away, but his son, Alberto, ran the restaurant and carried on the tradition. The cochinillo was as good as its reputation. While I have had cochinillo many times since, the memory of that meal remains particularly vivid. (A close second is of roasting one in the large, wood-burning oven of a friend's *cortijo*, an Andalusian farmhouse, in the olive-covered hills outside Ronda.)

That day in Segovia, we had joined an exodus of *madrileños* fleeing the city for a sunny spring Sunday in the mountains, and after a lengthy post-meal stroll among the ancient backstreets and the Roman aqueduct, and a coffee in one of the terraces on the plaza, we joined the caravan of traffic for the return drive to the capital. A day's excursion built around a worthy meal. Something that is an all-too-common Spanish activity.

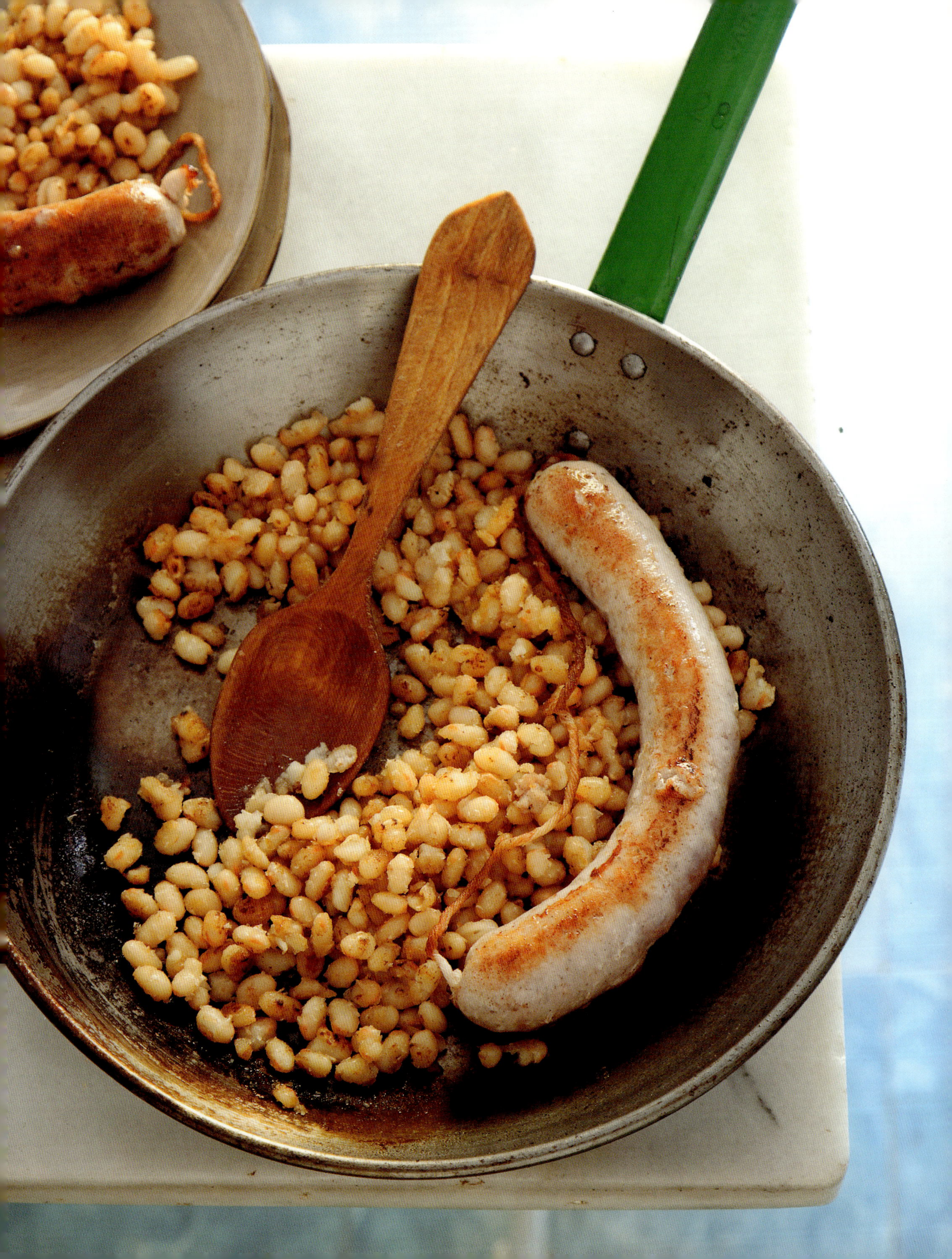

This is pure Catalan country food, and quite nearly the region's national dish. This almost-holy trio of grilled sausages, white beans, and *allioli* (garlic sauce) is served for a farmer's lunch and at village celebrations. With that lingering link to the countryside, it remains a part of many urban festivities, too. During the autumn revelries in my Barcelona neighborhood, there is a massive *botifarrada*—basically a celebration centered around grilled fresh sausages—with rows of tables set up in the small square. A couple of euros gets you a long, thick sausage, more white beans than you can—or rather, should—eat, and a generous amount of allioli. For another euro, you get a bottle of rather sturdy red table wine (that some of my neighbors are known to cut with *gaseosa*, a sweet carbonated soda water). An allioli-making competition takes place beforehand, and after all of the sausages have been polished off, an orchestra strikes up, the tables are cleared from the center of the square, and there is dancing until late at night. It ends with cups of hot, thick drinking chocolate (see page 306) served from a massive pot sometime after midnight.

The standard botifarra is around 1¼ inches/3 cm thick. Adjust the cooking time here if using thinner sausages. Outside of Spain, it is often easier to find fresh Italian sausages; use plain ones made without fennel or other dominating spices.

FRESH PORK SAUSAGES WITH WHITE BEANS AND ALLIOLI

BOTIFARRA AMB MONGETES I ALLIOLI

SERVES 4

3½ CUPS/700 G CANNED WHITE BEANS, SUCH AS CANNELLINI OR WHITE LIMA BEANS
2 TABLESPOONS EXTRA-VIRGIN OLIVE OIL
4 FAT FRESH PORK SAUSAGES, ABOUT 8 OUNCES/225 G EACH
SALT
ALLIOLI (PAGE 337)

1. Drain, rinse, and place the white beans in a saucepan with about 2 cups/480 ml water. Bring to a boil, cover the pan, and remove from the heat. Leave in the liquid until ready to use.

2. In a large skillet or sauté pan, heat the olive oil over medium heat. Pierce the sausages in a dozen places with the tines of a fork and lay them in the pan. Grill, turning occasionally, until cooked through, about 25 minutes. Transfer to a platter and loosely cover with aluminum foil tented in the middle to keep warm.

3. Drain the beans and add to the pan. Season with salt and cook over high heat, turning in the pan but being careful not to mash, until some of the beans are golden at the edges, 1 to 2 minutes.

4. Serve the sausages alongside the beans and a generous dollop of allioli.

SEARED MORCILLA DE BURGOS WITH ROASTED GREEN PEPPERS AND FRIED EGGS

MORCILLA DE BURGOS CON PIMIENTOS ASADOS Y HUEVOS FRITOS

SERVES 4

During the matanza, when pigs are butchered, the first chore is to capture the blood, and then keep it moving to stop it from coagulating so that it can be used to make blood sausage, morcilla. While morcilla can be plain, often a bit of rice or onion is added for texture and filler as well as flavor. The most famous morcilla comes from around Burgos, the ancient city in the arid northern meseta, where there is rice (and often onion) inside. (La Tienda and Despaña both stock morcilla from Burgos; see Sources, page 345.) The best way to eat this type of morcilla is to cut it into thick rounds and sear it on the exposed ends, giving the edges a nice chewy texture. Do this by using a nonstick pan and very little oil. Note that other types of blood sausages—that is, plain or with only onions—tend to come apart if cut into neat rounds. Grill these types whole.

4 SWEET ITALIAN GREEN PEPPERS OR 2 GREEN BELL PEPPERS

½ TABLESPOON EXTRA-VIRGIN OLIVE OIL

2 POUNDS/910 G SPANISH MORCILLA WITH RICE FROM BURGOS OR ANOTHER BLOOD SAUSAGE (SEE HEADNOTE), CUT INTO ½- TO ¾-INCH-/1.5- TO 2-CM-THICK ROUNDS

8 EGGS

1. Preheat the broiler.

2. Wash the green peppers and pat dry with paper towels. Place them on a baking sheet and broil, turning from time to time, until soft and blistered in places, 10 to 15 minutes. Transfer to a plate and loosely cover with aluminum foil tented in the middle to keep warm.

3. In a nonstick skillet, heat the olive oil over medium heat. Add the pieces of morcilla and sear the ends until the edges are crispy and the centers warm, about 2 minutes on each end. Transfer to a plate and loosely cover with foil tented in the middle. This will keep them warm without steaming them.

4. In the same skillet, immediately fry the eggs sunny-side up or as desired. (Re-oil the pan if needed.)

5. Serve the morcilla with a pair of eggs and the peppers alongside.

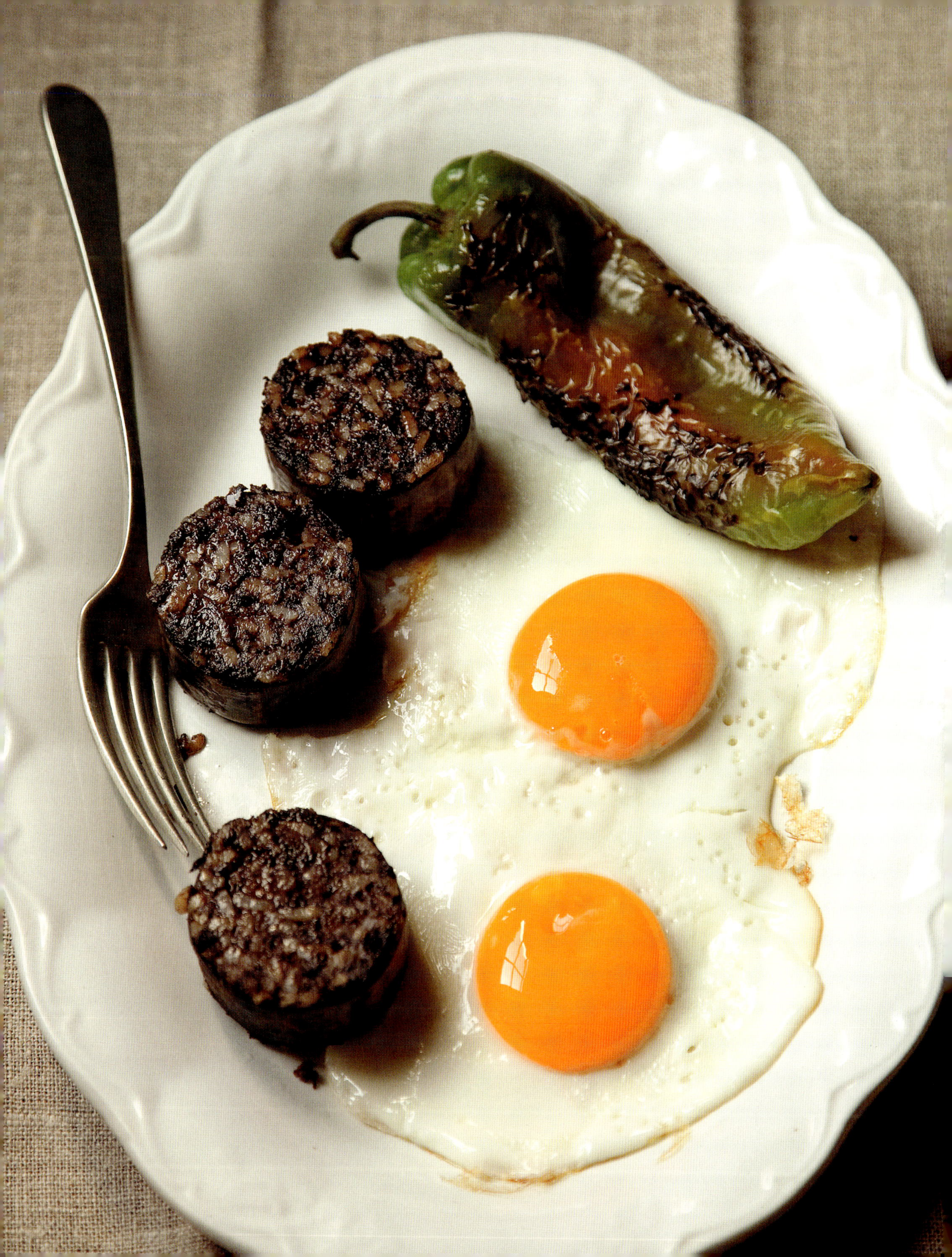

INGREDIENTS

CURED PORK PRODUCTS
embutidos

The deep reverence and long tradition in curing pork products is hard to overstate. These can be a single cut—like a leg, shoulder, or tenderloin—though they are often a ground blend of parts seasoned and stuffed into natural intestinal casing. Such practices date back to, or even before, the time when the Romans ruled Spain (218 BCE to 409 CE). Cured legs of ham from Extremadura might be shipped to Tokyo and (at last!) New York today, but 2,000 years ago they were sent across the Roman Empire.

These traditions have remained hugely important in part because of the abundance of pork over the centuries. How to utilize the whole animal, and keep it—in the time before refrigeration and freezing—before it could go bad? From this came a range of *embutidos*—the general name for products cured this way—that often have strong regional differences.

While most embutidos can be considered *curados* (dry-cured), such as the well-known legs of jamón, there are also a number that are *cocidos* (literally "cooked").

The principal dry-cured embutidos include:

chistorra A thin, soft paprika-red sausage that is only lightly cured. A specialty in Navarra and the Basque country, chistorra is usually fried in olive oil and served in a small terra-cotta casserole dish or else skewered to a piece of bread with a toothpick and eaten as a tapa.

chorizo An emblematic sausage with spices including pimentón (paprika), which gives it its distinctive red color and smoky flavor. One of the most popular embutidos in the country. A specialty of La Rioja and Pamplona. Note that Mexican chorizo is unsmoked and usually fresh rather than cured, the pork is ground and not chopped, and the texture moister and softer than its firm Spanish cousin.

fuet Typically Catalan, this dense sausage flavored with black pepper usually measures about 12 inches/30 cm in length and about 1 inch/2.5 cm in diameter. A white mold forms on the outside.

jamón (curado) A cured leg of ham, specifically the thicker, choice back leg, is the jamón, while the front leg (the shoulder) is the smaller *paleta*. Curing is done with both the standard "white" (serrano) pig and the black-footed Iberian pig. Jamón serrano and jamón del país denote less-expensive versions from common pigs, while jamón ibérico is produced from the Iberian breed. Slices of the latter have a wonderful marbling, lusher taste, and are significantly more expensive. (See page 133 for more on jamón ibérico.)

lomo embuchado or ***caña de lomo*** The long, thick tenderloin is first marinated in an adobo sauce seasoned with garlic, salt, paprika, marjoram, nutmeg, and other spices. After draining and drying, it is matured for at least two months. It is lean, exquisite, and very expensive (especially when it comes from an Iberian pig).

salchichón A firm sausage, slightly thicker than fuet, that often includes whole black peppercorns in the ground mixture. Aragón, Zamora, and Vic (in the Montseny region of the Pre-Pyrenees mountains) have well-known versions.

sobrassada A soft, spreadable minced pork sausage with characteristic deep red color, aromas, and flavors from smoky pimentón (paprika). Found across the Balearic islands, most famously in Mallorca.

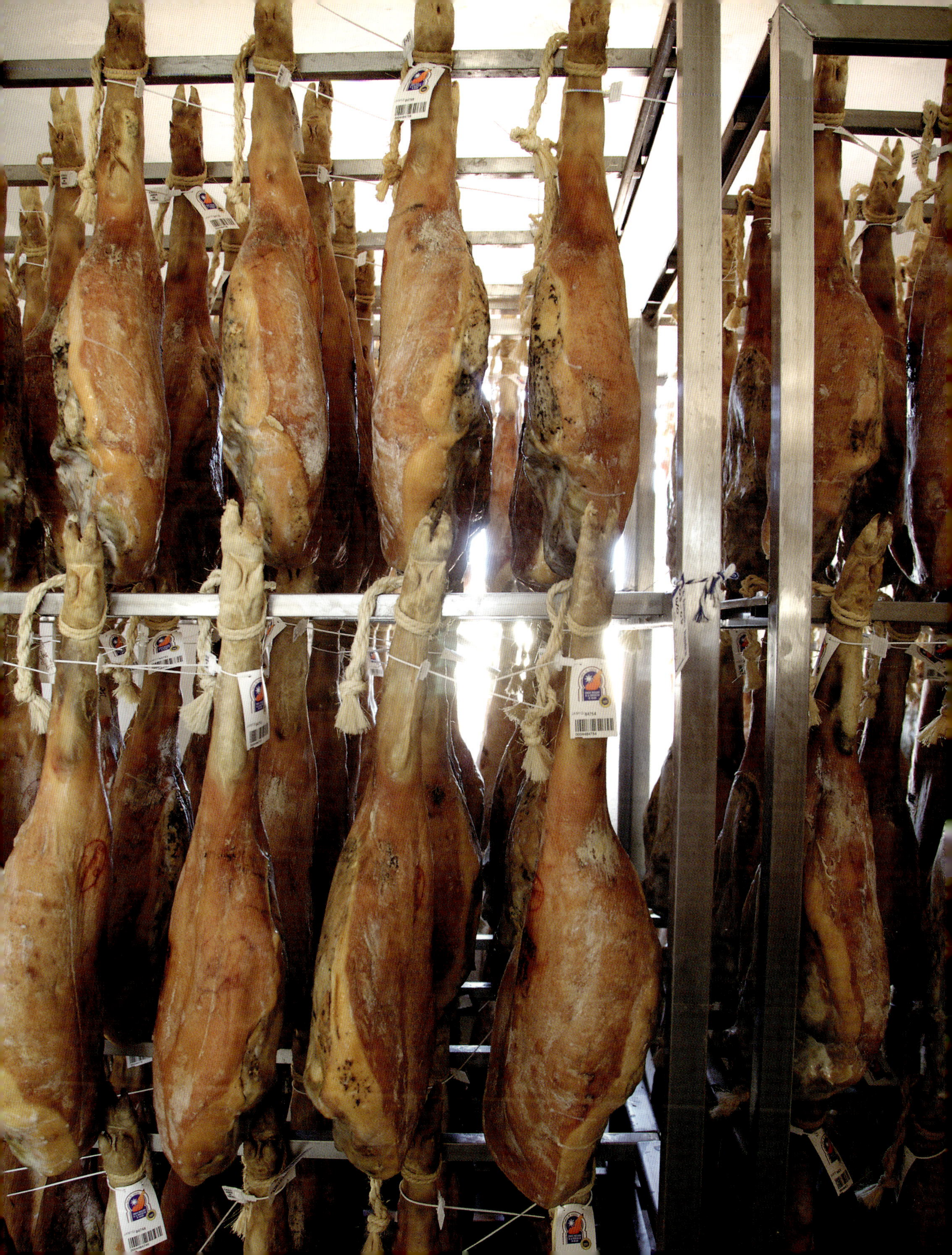

The main embutidos that have been cooked (*cocidos*) as opposed to dry-cured include:

butifarra blanca or butifarra cocida A white pork sausage seasoned with spices such as black pepper, nutmeg, and cinnamon, depending on the producer. In Catalunya, there is a similar version called *bull blanc*.

butifarra negra Blood sausage made with offal and cooked with various spices, such as black pepper, nutmeg, and cinnamon. It tends to be denser and chewier than *morcilla* (see following). It is called *botifarra negre* in Catalunya, Valencia, and the Balearic Islands, where it is popular.

jamón cocido The classic bright-pink cooked and deboned ham. It is also called *jamón dulce* (sweet ham), to distinguish it from the salty variety, or *jamón de York*, which refers to the English town where this style of preparing was popularized.

morcilla Blood sausage made with minced pork. The stuffing can include rice, onions, pine nuts, and/or aniseed. Often cooked and served hot.

And one important embutido that isn't made from pork:

cecina The hind leg of beef that has been salted, smoked, and then air-dried. Dark, lean, and carrying clear smoky, ancestral flavors, it is served very thinly sliced. The best is moist and tender. Superb with a drizzle of bold extra-virgin olive oil. A specialty of León.

Typically prepared in homes across Menorca, these have also become a favorite bar tapa in the island's market towns, Alaior, Es Mercadal, Ferreries, and Es Migjorn Gran. Some Menorcan cooks add a soft, spreadable pork sausage called sobrassada to the ground meat mixture. The paprika-flavored sobrassada adds a perfect contrast to the sweet tomato sauce. (See Sources, page 345, for where to find sobrassada.) I learned in Menorca to moisten my hands with white wine before rolling the meatballs. It makes the process easier and slightly perfumes the meatballs.

MENORCAN MEATBALLS IN TOMATO AND PINE NUT SAUCE

ALBÓNDIGAS MENORQUINAS

SERVES 4

8 OUNCES/225 G GROUND BEEF

8 OUNCES/225 G GROUND PORK

¼ CUP/45 G SOBRASSADA, OR 1 TEASPOON PIMENTÓN DULCE (SWEET PAPRIKA) MIXED WITH 1 TABLESPOON EXTRA-VIRGIN OLIVE OIL

1 EGG

2 GARLIC CLOVES, MINCED

SALT AND FRESHLY GROUND BLACK PEPPER

⅓ CUP/50 G PLAIN DRY BREADCRUMBS

¼ CUP/60 ML DRY WHITE WINE, PLUS MORE FOR MOISTENING HANDS

¼ CUP/60 ML OLIVE OIL

1 POUND/455 G RIPE MEDIUM TOMATOES, HALVED CROSSWISE, SEEDED, AND GRATED (SEE PAGE 339)

1 MEDIUM-LARGE ONION, FINELY CHOPPED

2 TEASPOONS SUGAR

HEAPED 2 TABLESPOONS PINE NUTS

1 SPRIG FRESH THYME

1 BAY LEAF

1. In a bowl, blend the beef, pork, sobrassada, egg, and 1 of the garlic cloves. Season with salt and pepper. Add the breadcrumbs and work into a smooth paste. Moisten your hands with wine and roll the mixture into 1-inch-/2.5-cm-diameter meatballs with about 1-tablespoon portions. There should be 28 to 32 of them.

2. In a cazuela, heavy casserole, large sauté pan, or deep skillet, heat the olive oil over medium-high heat and cook the meatballs in single-layer batches, turning frequently, until browned on the outside, 5 to 7 minutes. Transfer to a platter and cover to keep warm.

3. In the cazuela over medium heat, prepare a sofrito with the tomatoes, onion, and remaining garlic clove, following the directions on page 39. Stir in the sugar and season with salt.

4. Return the meatballs to the pan. Add the wine, pine nuts, thyme, bay leaf, and 1 cup/240 ml water and bring to a boil. Reduce the heat to low and simmer uncovered for 20 to 30 minutes, turning the meatballs and swirling the pan from time to time to keep them from sticking. Add in a bit more water if needed to keep the tomato sauce loose. Serve from the cazuela.

STEWED MEATBALLS WITH CUTTLEFISH

ALBÓNDIGAS CON SEPIA

SERVES 6

Pork and cuttlefish or squid might seem like an unlikely couple in many kitchens, but they are a popular pair along much of the Mediterranean coast, and are found together in other recipes, such as traditional "mixed" paella and squid stuffed with fresh pork sausage.

8 OUNCES/225 G GROUND PORK

8 OUNCES/225 G GROUND BEEF

1 EGG

1 GARLIC CLOVE, MINCED

2 TABLESPOONS PACKED MINCED FRESH FLAT-LEAF PARSLEY

SALT

⅓ CUP/50 G PLAIN DRY BREADCRUMBS

1 CUP/240 ML DRY WHITE WINE, PLUS MORE FOR MOISTENING HANDS

¼ CUP/60 ML EXTRA-VIRGIN OLIVE OIL

1 MEDIUM ONION, FINELY CHOPPED

1 POUND/455 G CLEANED CUTTLEFISH OR SQUID (CALAMARI) STEAKS, CUT INTO 1-INCH-/2.5-CM-SQUARE PIECES, OR SQUID TUBES CUT INTO FAT RINGS

3 RIPE MEDIUM TOMATOES, HALVED CROSSWISE, SEEDED, AND GRATED (SEE PAGE 339)

1½ CUPS/360 ML FISH STOCK (PAGE 335), VEGETABLE STOCK (PAGE 335), OR WATER

10 UNSALTED TOASTED ALMONDS WITHOUT SKINS

10 TOASTED HAZELNUTS WITHOUT SKINS

1 THIN SLICE BAGUETTE, DAY OLD OR TOASTED

¾ CUP/110 G FRESHLY SHUCKED PEAS OR FROZEN PETIT POIS

FRESHLY GROUND BLACK PEPPER

1. In a bowl, blend the ground meats, egg, garlic, and 1 tablespoon of the parsley. Season with salt. Add the breadcrumbs and work into a smooth paste. Moisten your hands with wine and roll the mixture into 1-inch-/2.5-cm-diameter meatballs with about 1-tablespoon portions.

2. In a cazuela, heavy casserole, large sauté pan, or deep skillet, heat the olive oil over medium-high heat and brown the meatballs, turning frequently, about 5 minutes. Transfer to a platter and cover to keep warm.

3. Add the onion to the cazuela and cook over medium heat until it begins to soften and turn pale, about 5 minutes. Add the cuttlefish, increase the heat to medium-high, and cook until it has thrown its liquid, about 5 minutes. Add the tomatoes, reduce the heat to medium-low, and cook until pasty, about 20 minutes, dribbling in 2 or 3 tablespoons water once or twice during cooking to keep it from drying out.

4. Return the meatballs to the pan, cover with the wine and stock, and bring to a boil. Reduce the heat to low and simmer uncovered for 30 minutes.

5. Meanwhile, prepare a picada with the almonds, hazelnuts, bread, and the remaining 1 tablespoon parsley, following the directions on page 39.

6. Stir the picada into the meatballs and add the peas. Cook uncovered for 10 minutes, or until the cuttlefish is tender and the sauce has the consistency of thick gravy. Season with pepper. Serve from the cazuela.

GRILLED BEEF TENDERLOIN WITH BLUE CHEESE SAUCE

SOLOMILLO DE BUEY AL QUESO PICÓN

SERVES 4

Queso Picón Bejes-Tresviso from Cantabria is a compact, ivory-fleshed, blue-veined cheese. While its persistent and bold flavors are highly appreciated on their own, the cheese makes an excellent base for creamy sauces. Around northern Spain, you find different local blue cheeses used the same way to the same stunning effect—in Galicia along the central Río Miño with queixo do Cebreiro, for instance, or in Asturias with queso de Cabrales or queso de Valdeón in León. These same regions also produce excellent beef. An older animal, with a brilliant-to-slightly dark-red tone and deeper flavors, is perfect to use with this bold sauce.

4 OUNCES/115 G BLUE CHEESE, SUCH AS PICÓN, CABRALES, VALDEÓN, OR ROQUEFORT, CUT INTO PIECES

2 TABLESPOONS BRANDY OR COGNAC

⅔ CUP/165 ML HEAVY CREAM

FRESHLY GROUND BLACK PEPPER

EXTRA-VIRGIN OLIVE OIL FOR OILING PAN

FOUR 7- OR 8-OUNCE/200- OR 225-G BEEF TENDERLOIN STEAKS ABOUT 1½ INCHES/4 CM THICK, OR 2 BONELESS RIB-EYE STEAKS, ABOUT 1 POUND/455 G EACH

FLAKY SEA SALT

1. In a saucepan, warm the cheese and brandy together over low heat, stirring until melted and creamy, about 3 minutes. Add the cream and season with pepper. Stir for a few seconds over low heat until combined. Remove the pan from the heat. It will thicken as it begins to cool.

2. Preheat a grill pan, griddle pan, or large, heavy skillet over medium-high heat and lightly oil. Generously season the steaks with salt flakes and lay them in the pan, grilling as desired, turning only as needed with tongs.

3. Transfer the steaks to a platter. Rewhisk the sauce and spoon about half over the steaks. Serve them immediately with the remaining sauce in a bowl to add as desired.

"*Fricandó*, despite its clearly French origin, has acquired—like cannelloni, soundly Italian—a certificate of naturalization among us, and both have become, thanks to Catalan culinary genius and wit, dishes that are essentially ours." So gushed the great, late food historian Néstor Luján. Despite fricandó's foreign roots, he insisted, since the early nineteenth century, the Catalans have made it clearly Catalan.

This dish braises thin slices of veal with dried mushrooms and sweet wine. The most typical mushroom here is the small, aromatic, and flavorful *moixernon* (St. George's mushroom). Some larger dried mushrooms might need more soaking time.

BRAISED VEAL WITH DRIED MUSHROOMS

FRICANDÓ AMB MOIXERNONS

SERVES 4 TO 6

6 TABLESPOONS EXTRA-VIRGIN OLIVE OIL, PLUS MORE FOR OILING PAN

2 POUNDS/910 G BONELESS VEAL, THINLY SLICED ABOUT ¼ INCH/½ CM THICK

SALT AND FRESHLY GROUND BLACK PEPPER

ALL-PURPOSE FLOUR FOR DREDGING

1 MEDIUM ONION, FINELY CHOPPED

2 RIPE MEDIUM TOMATOES, HALVED CROSSWISE, SEEDED, AND GRATED (SEE PAGE 339)

1 GARLIC CLOVE, MINCED

SCANT 1 CUP/15 G DRIED MUSHROOMS, PREFERABLY MOIXERNONS (ST. GEORGE'S OR FAIRY RING MUSHROOMS)

¾ CUP/180 ML MUSCATEL, VINO RANCIO, SWEET SHERRY, OR ANOTHER SWEET WINE

1½ CUPS/360 ML LIGHT BEEF STOCK (PAGE 336) OR WATER

1. In a cazuela, heavy casserole, large sauté pan, or deep skillet, heat 4 tablespoons of the olive oil over medium-high heat. Season the veal with salt and pepper, lightly dredge in flour, and pat to shake off the excess. Quickly brown in single-layer batches that don't crowd the pan, about 30 seconds on each side. Transfer to a large platter. Add a bit more oil to the pan if needed between batches.

2. Add the remaining 2 tablespoons olive oil to the cazuela, reduce the heat to medium-low, and prepare a sofrito with the onion, tomatoes, and garlic, following the directions on page 39.

3. Place the dried mushrooms in a small bowl, cover with warm water, swish them around, and immediately pour off the water. Cover the damp mushrooms with 2 cups/480 ml warm water and let soak for 1 hour.

4. Return the veal to the pan and turn to coat. Pour in the Muscatel, turn over the pieces of veal, and let the alcohol burn off for 2 minutes before pouring in the stock. Bring to a simmer, reduce the heat to low, and partly cover the pan. Cook, just letting bubbles slowly break the surface for 45 minutes, turning over the meat from time to time to keep it from sticking.

5. Drain the mushrooms, reserving the liquid. Add the mushrooms and ½ cup/120 ml of the reserved liquid to the pan and cook uncovered for 30 minutes, or until the veal is very tender. Add more reserved liquid if needed. The sauce should be like gravy. Serve from the cazuela.

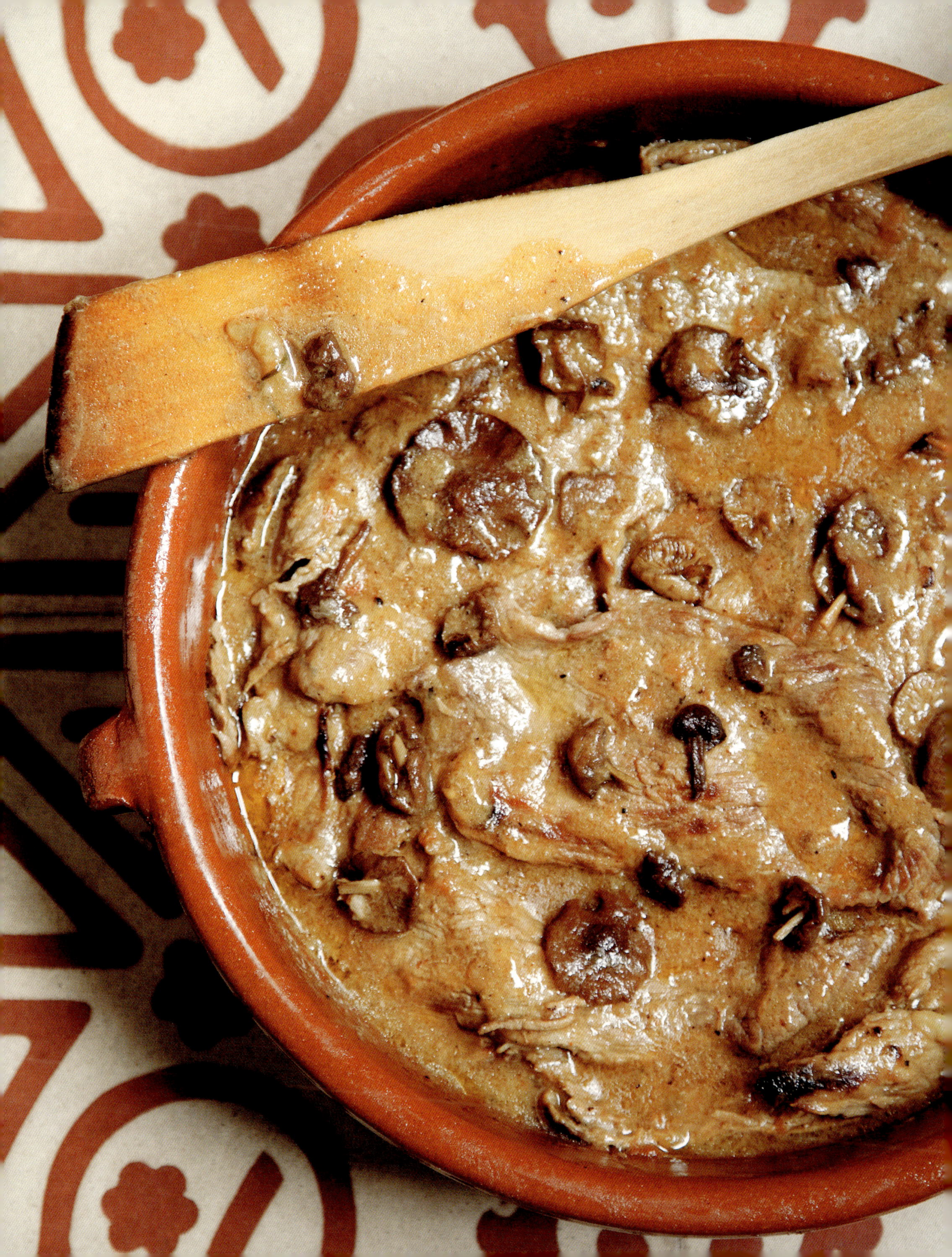

CHAPTER 12

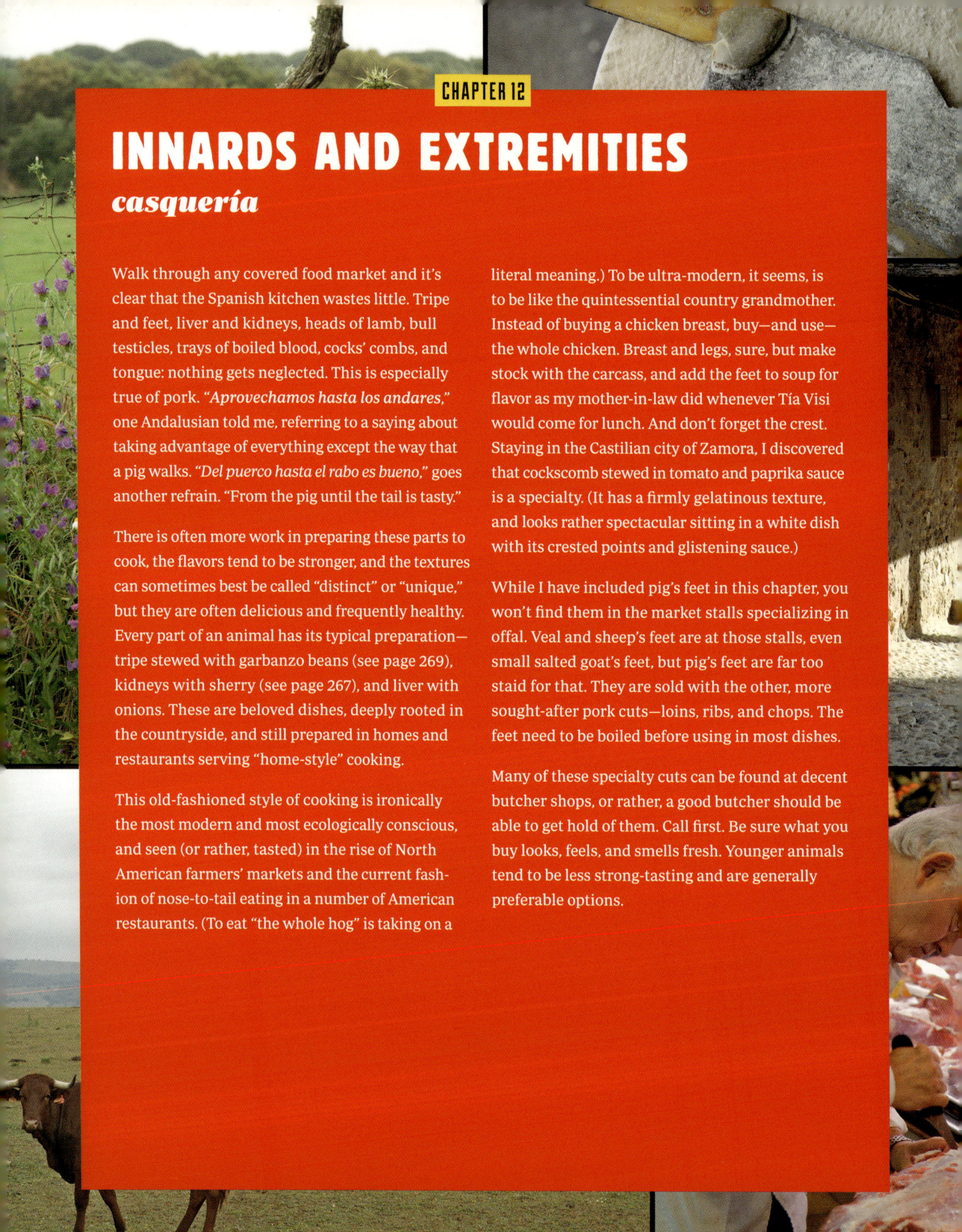

INNARDS AND EXTREMITIES
casquería

Walk through any covered food market and it's clear that the Spanish kitchen wastes little. Tripe and feet, liver and kidneys, heads of lamb, bull testicles, trays of boiled blood, cocks' combs, and tongue: nothing gets neglected. This is especially true of pork. *"Aprovechamos hasta los andares,"* one Andalusian told me, referring to a saying about taking advantage of everything except the way that a pig walks. *"Del puerco hasta el rabo es bueno,"* goes another refrain. "From the pig until the tail is tasty."

There is often more work in preparing these parts to cook, the flavors tend to be stronger, and the textures can sometimes best be called "distinct" or "unique," but they are often delicious and frequently healthy. Every part of an animal has its typical preparation—tripe stewed with garbanzo beans (see page 269), kidneys with sherry (see page 267), and liver with onions. These are beloved dishes, deeply rooted in the countryside, and still prepared in homes and restaurants serving "home-style" cooking.

This old-fashioned style of cooking is ironically the most modern and most ecologically conscious, and seen (or rather, tasted) in the rise of North American farmers' markets and the current fashion of nose-to-tail eating in a number of American restaurants. (To eat "the whole hog" is taking on a literal meaning.) To be ultra-modern, it seems, is to be like the quintessential country grandmother. Instead of buying a chicken breast, buy—and use—the whole chicken. Breast and legs, sure, but make stock with the carcass, and add the feet to soup for flavor as my mother-in-law did whenever Tía Visi would come for lunch. And don't forget the crest. Staying in the Castilian city of Zamora, I discovered that cockscomb stewed in tomato and paprika sauce is a specialty. (It has a firmly gelatinous texture, and looks rather spectacular sitting in a white dish with its crested points and glistening sauce.)

While I have included pig's feet in this chapter, you won't find them in the market stalls specializing in offal. Veal and sheep's feet are at those stalls, even small salted goat's feet, but pig's feet are far too staid for that. They are sold with the other, more sought-after pork cuts—loins, ribs, and chops. The feet need to be boiled before using in most dishes.

Many of these specialty cuts can be found at decent butcher shops, or rather, a good butcher should be able to get hold of them. Call first. Be sure what you buy looks, feels, and smells fresh. Younger animals tend to be less strong-tasting and are generally preferable options.

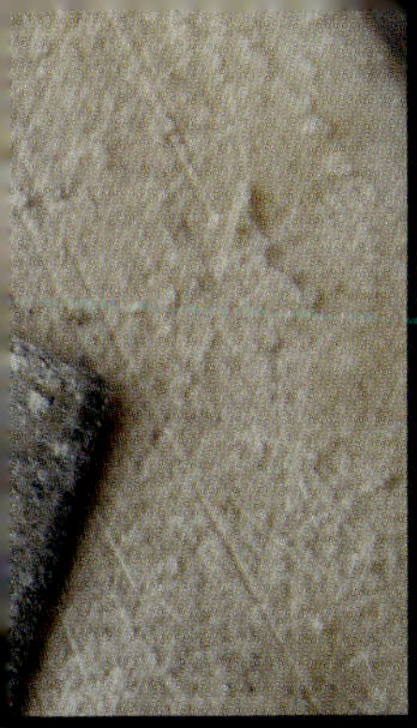

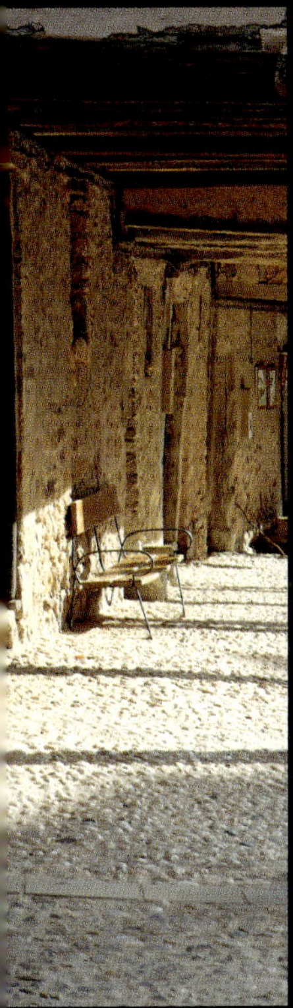

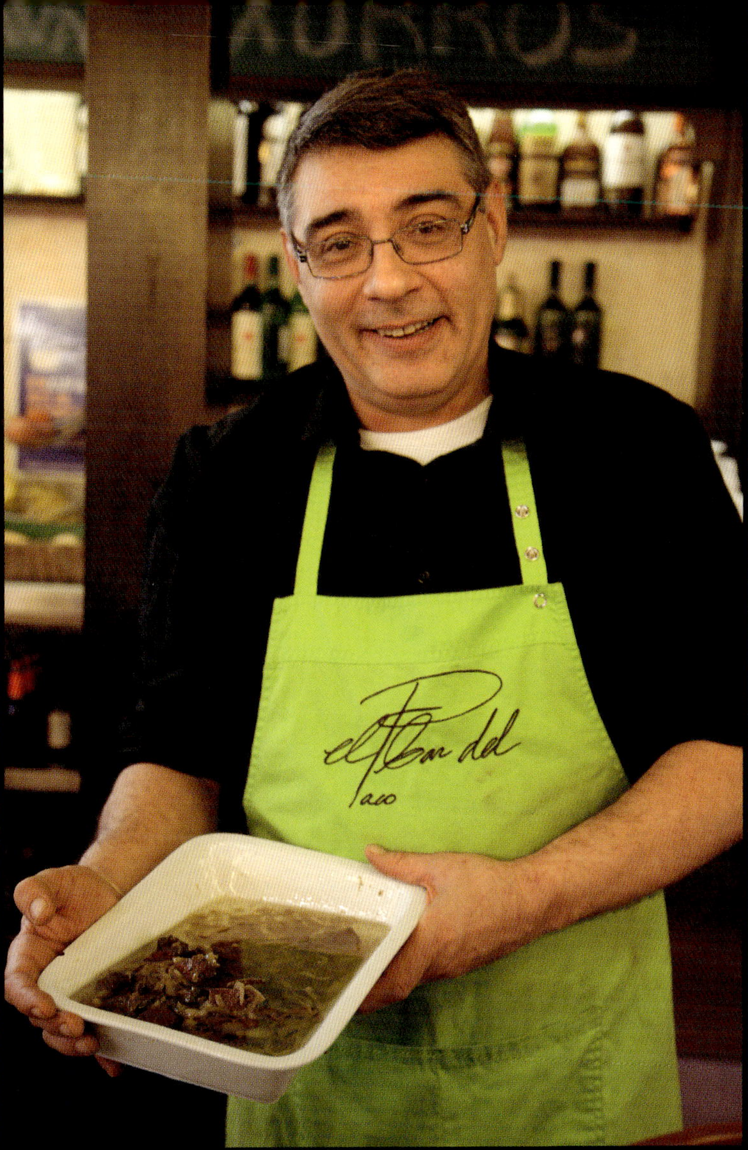

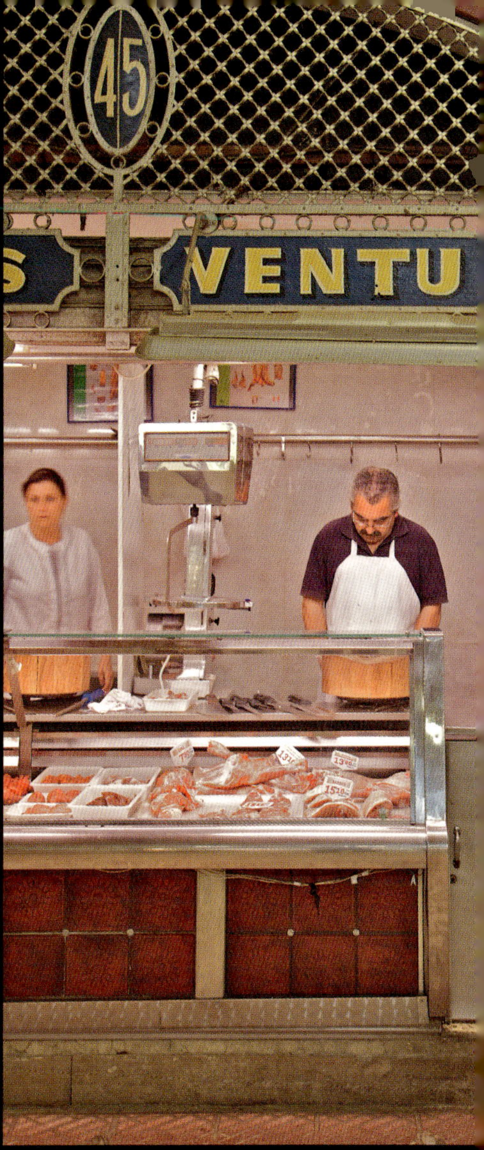
45
VENTU

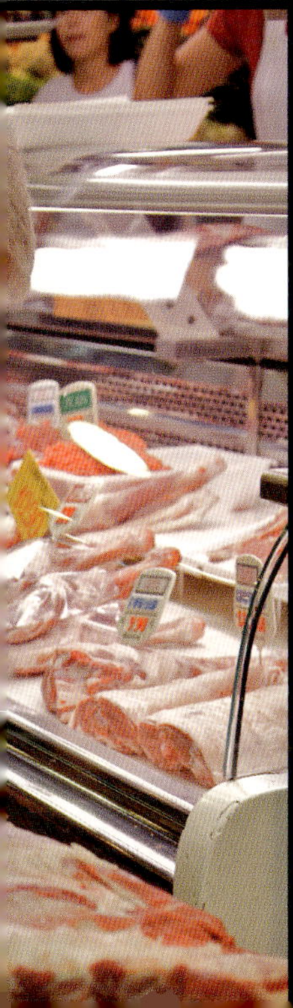

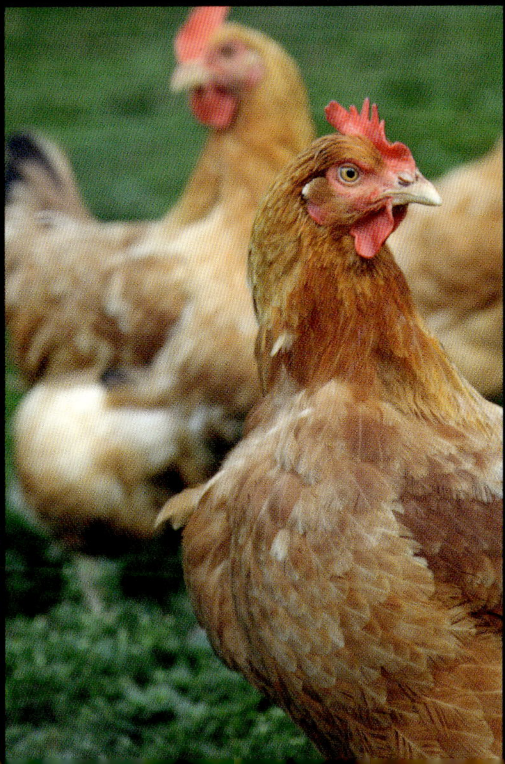

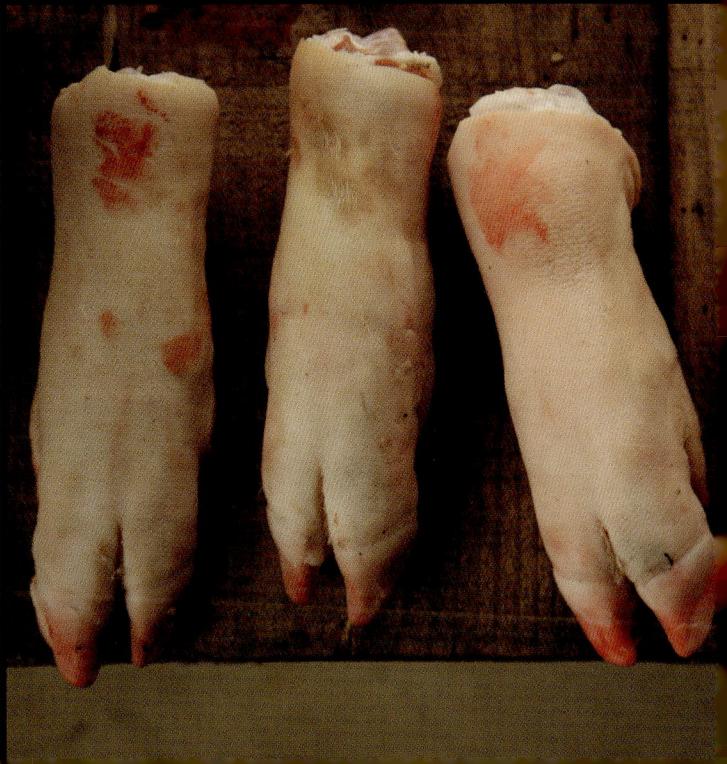

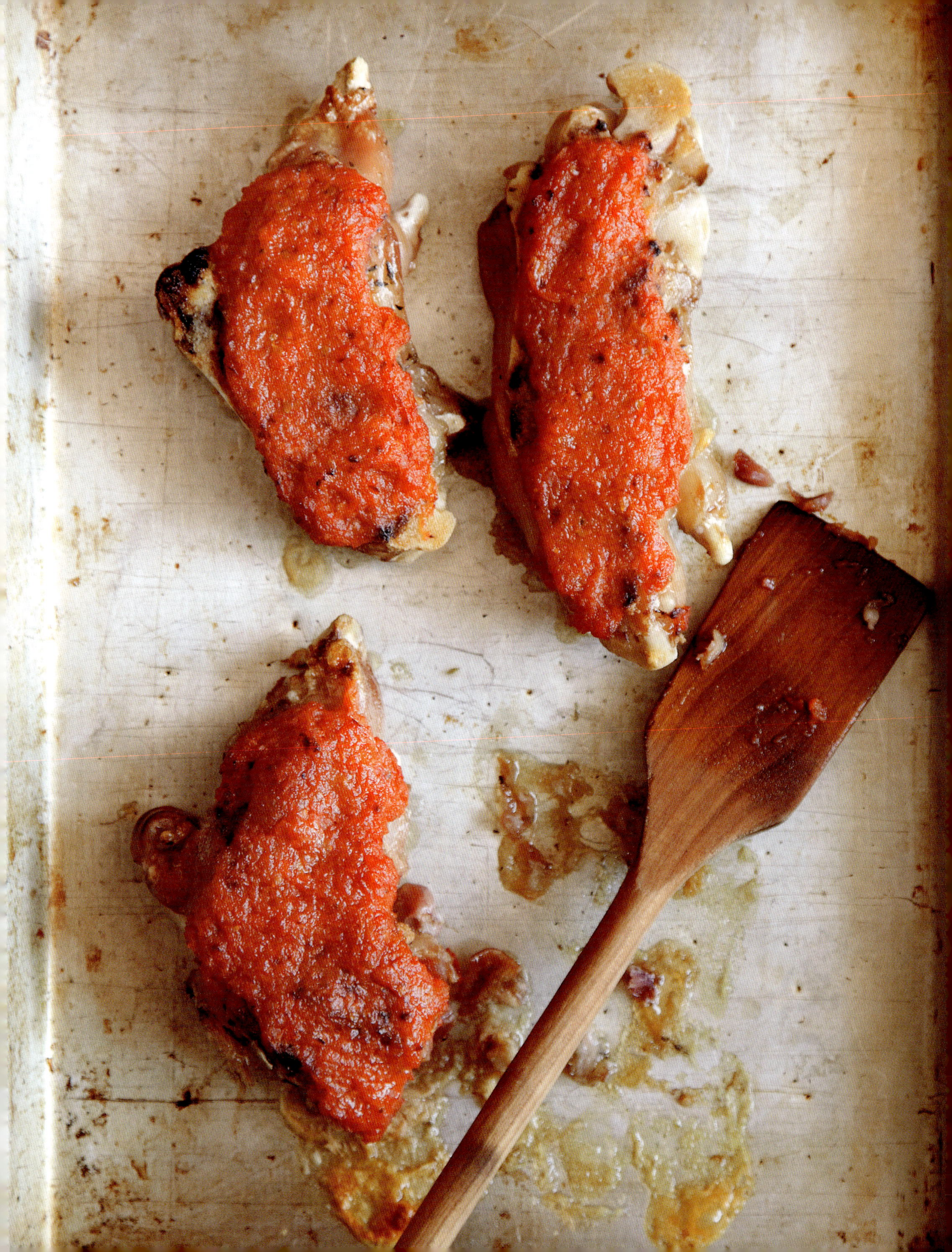

ROASTED PIG'S FEET

MANITAS DE CERDO AL HORNO

SERVES 4

In markets, pig's feet are not found at the stalls selling organ meats, tripe, and other extremities, but rather with loins, ribs, and other choice parts of the pig. They are beloved by many cooks. Case in point: Josep Lladonosa i Giró's comprehensive cookbook *El gran llibre de la cuina catalana* (The Big Book of Catalan Cooking) lists sixteen different main dishes with pig's feet (yet just ten for chicken).

I've adapted this favorite recipe from another grand book of Catalan cooking, Jaume Fàbrega's *El gran llibre de la cuina de les àvies* (The Big Book of Grandmothers' Cooking). Substitute pine nuts for the hazelnuts in the recipe, if desired, and add a pinch of ground cinnamon to the picada. The final texture of the dish should be a touch crunchy. It is a winter dish and I usually serve it with a green salad with fresh cheese and pomegranates (see page 49).

4 PIG'S FEET, SPLIT IN HALF LENGTHWISE BY YOUR BUTCHER
2 CARROTS, HALVED LENGTHWISE
2 MEDIUM ONIONS, QUARTERED
1 LEEK, ROUGHLY CHOPPED
2 GARLIC CLOVES, PEELED
12 BLACK PEPPERCORNS
1 BAY LEAF
10 SPRIGS FRESH FLAT-LEAF PARSLEY
SALT
½ CUP/60 ML DRY WHITE WINE
1 SLICE COUNTRY-STYLE BREAD
3 TABLESPOONS EXTRA-VIRGIN OLIVE OIL, PLUS MORE FOR DRIZZLING
4 RIPE MEDIUM TOMATOES, HALVED CROSSWISE, SEEDED, AND GRATED (SEE PAGE 339)
¼ CUP/30 G TOASTED HAZELNUTS WITHOUT SKINS
2 TABLESPOONS SWEET OR MEDIUM WHITE WINE
SALT AND FRESHLY GROUND BLACK PEPPER

1. If the feet have not been precooked, clean and boil them. Scorch any remaining hairs on the feet with a flame or shave off with a disposable razor. Wash well with plenty of water.

2. In a stockpot or another large pot, put the feet, carrots, onions, leek, garlic, peppercorns, bay leaf, 1 parsley sprig, and 1 teaspoon salt and cover with the wine and about 3 quarts/3 L water. Bring to a boil over high heat, reduce the heat to medium-low, cover the pot, and gently boil for 2 hours, or until very tender. Carefully remove the feet from the pot and drain. Discard the vegetables, herbs, and liquid. After boiling, handle carefully so that the feet keep their shape as much as possible.

continued

3. Trim the crusts and tear the bread into three or four pieces. In a small skillet, heat 1 tablespoon of the olive oil and fry the bread until golden, about 1 minute, turning as needed. Remove and reserve. Add the remaining 2 tablespoons olive oil and the tomatoes to the skillet and prepare a simple sofrito by cooking them over medium heat until dark and pasty, 10 to 15 minutes. Add a touch of water to loosen it. There should be at least ⅔ cup/165 ml of sofrito. Set aside.

4. Meanwhile, prepare a picada with the reserved bread, the hazelnuts, and 1 to 2 tablespoons water, following the directions on page 39. Stir in the wine to make the paste spreadable.

5. Preheat the oven to 350°F/180°C/gas mark 4.

6. Line a rimmed baking sheet or llauna (see page 187) with parchment paper and arrange the pig's feet facing cut-side up. Season with salt and pepper and spread with the picada. Bake for 30 minutes. Watch that the picada doesn't burn.

7. Remove the baking sheet from the oven and spoon the sofrito over the pig's feet. Lightly drizzle olive oil over the top.

8. Turn the oven to broil, and place the baking sheet on a higher rack. Broil until the edges of the feet are brown and slightly crunchy, about 5 minutes. Watch that the tomato sauce doesn't scorch. Transfer the feet to a serving dish and serve immediately.

VEAL KIDNEYS IN SHERRY

RIÑONES DE TERNERA AL JEREZ

SERVES 4

Veal kidneys are rich in protein, iron, and vitamins, with a smooth, firm texture and bold flavor. Cooked with sherry, they are a delicious southern classic. But they do take some work to first purge them of their strong, acrid odor before they are ready to be stewed in the sherry sauce. When buying, freshness is paramount. Look for whole, very fresh kidneys.

2 VEAL KIDNEYS, 1½ TO 1¾ POUNDS/680 TO 800 G TOTAL
SALT
3 TABLESPOONS WINE VINEGAR
5 TABLESPOONS EXTRA-VIRGIN OLIVE OIL
2 MEDIUM ONIONS, THINLY SLICED
2 GARLIC CLOVES, MINCED
1 TEASPOON ALL-PURPOSE FLOUR
1 PINCH SAFFRON THREADS, DRY-TOASTED AND GROUND (SEE PAGE 340)
FRESHLY GROUND BLACK PEPPER
1 CUP/240 ML DRY SHERRY
½ CUP/120 ML LIGHT BEEF STOCK (PAGE 336) OR WATER

1. Clean the kidneys. Slice them open in the middle and cut away the central white nucleus and any fat from the lobes. Sprinkle with salt, rub, and rinse well under running water. Cut into pieces slightly larger than bite-size.

2. In a bowl, soak the kidneys with 1 quart/1 L water and the vinegar for 15 or 20 minutes. Drain, rinse well under running water, and drain again. Pat dry with paper towels.

3. In a sauté pan or skillet, heat 3 tablespoons of the olive oil until smoking. Fry the kidneys over high heat in single-layer batches that don't crowd the pan, until they are cooked through and have expelled their liquid, 4 to 5 minutes per batch. (Add more oil to the pan if necessary between batches.) Transfer to a colander to drain of any impurities for 15 minutes. Rinse well under running water.

4. In a clean sauté pan or skillet, heat the remaining 2 tablespoons olive oil over medium heat. Add the onions and cook until very soft and translucent, about 15 minutes. Add the garlic and cook for 1 minute. Stir in the flour and saffron and season with pepper. Moisten with the sherry, add the stock, and bring to a simmer. The sauce should be very loose but not watery.

5. Let the sauce reduce for a few minutes if needed. Add the kidneys, reduce the heat to low, and gently cook, stirring from time to time, for 6 to 8 minutes without letting the kidneys boil in the sauce, until the flavors have blended. Taste for seasoning, adjust as needed, and serve.

VEAL TONGUE WITH CAPERS

LENGUA DE TERNERA CON ALCAPARRAS

SERVES 4

Veal tongue is a traditional part of the Spanish country kitchen, and prepared in a wide variety of regional ways. In the Basque country, for instance, you can find it with walnuts or in a sauce with a bit of apple. I learned this exquisite preparation in the Balearic Islands. The base of the sauce—stewed onions, carrots, and tomatoes—is almost sweet, and offers an ideal contrast to the pungency of capers. Capers grow abundantly in Menorca and Mallorca, often wild in the rockeries near the sea. Serve with potatoes—either fried (see page 132) or puréed (see page 117).

1 VEAL TONGUE, ABOUT 2¼ POUNDS/1 KG
2 BAY LEAVES
8 BLACK PEPPERCORNS
3 TABLESPOONS EXTRA-VIRGIN OLIVE OIL
1 MEDIUM ONION, FINELY CHOPPED
1 CARROT, FINELY CHOPPED
2 GARLIC CLOVES, MINCED
4 RIPE MEDIUM TOMATOES, PEELED, SEEDED, AND ROUGHLY CHOPPED
GENEROUS 1 PINCH SUGAR
½ CUP/120 ML DRY WHITE WINE
1 CUP/240 ML BEEF STOCK (PAGE 336), CHICKEN STOCK (PAGE 336), OR WATER
SALT AND FRESHLY GROUND BLACK PEPPER
1 TEASPOON ALL-PURPOSE FLOUR
¼ CUP/32 G DRAINED CAPERS

1. Bring a large pot of water to a boil. Rinse the tongue and add it to the water along with the bay leaves and peppercorns. Boil for 1½ to 2 hours, or until tender—the tines of a fork should pierce it easily. Transfer to a cutting board until cool enough to handle. Peel off the skin and discard. Trim away the fat, gristle, and any tough sections at the root end.

2. In a cazuela or heavy casserole, heat the olive oil over medium heat and prepare a sofrito: Add the onion and cook until soft and translucent, 8 to 10 minutes. Add the carrot and garlic and cook until they have softened and turned a yellowish orange color, about 8 minutes. Add the tomatoes and sugar and cook until pulpy, about 10 minutes, adding water from time to time to keep moist. Add the wine and cook for 2 minutes. Stir in the stock, lower the heat to medium-low, and simmer until the carrot is very tender and the sauce has concentrated, about 15 minutes.

3. Pass the sauce through a food mill and return it to the cazuela. The sauce should be very loose. Add water if needed. Season with salt and pepper, stir in the flour, and bring the sauce to a simmer over medium heat.

4. Cut the tongue crosswise into ¼-inch-/½-cm-thick slices. Cut the slices at the base in half again, so that the pieces are roughly the same size.

5. Lay the tongue in the sauce and turn over to coat. Add 2 tablespoons of the capers, cover the pan, and cook for 2 or 3 minutes, until the tongue pieces are hot. Scatter the remaining capers over the top. Serve immediately.

GALICIAN-STYLE TRIPE WITH GARBANZO BEANS

CALLOS A LA GALLEGA CON GARBANZOS

SERVES 6

Stewed tripe is one of the emblematic dishes of the central Spanish tablelands. *Callos a la madrileña*—eaten not just in Madrid, but similarly in Castilla, Extremadura, and elsewhere—usually include calf's feet, a dozen lamb's feet, and so on. This recipe, based on ones I have eaten along the northwest corner of Galicia, is simpler and includes garbanzo beans and chorizo.

Good butchers and Latino markets usually stock tripe, or they can get it with a day's notice.

- 3 CUPS/200 G DRIED OR 3 CUPS/500 G CANNED GARBANZO BEANS
- 1 POUND/455 G CLEANED AND PRE-BOILED TRIPE, PREFERABLY HONEYCOMB
- 2 MEDIUM ONIONS; 1 PEELED, 1 FINELY CHOPPED
- 5 CLOVES
- SALT
- 2 TABLESPOONS EXTRA-VIRGIN OLIVE OIL
- 4 GARLIC CLOVES, MINCED
- 3 RIPE MEDIUM TOMATOES, HALVED CROSSWISE, SEEDED, AND GRATED (SEE PAGE 339)
- 3 OUNCES/85 G SPANISH CHORIZO, CUT INTO ROUNDS
- 1 TABLESPOON MINCED FRESH FLAT-LEAF PARSLEY
- 1 TABLESPOON ALL-PURPOSE FLOUR
- ½ TEASPOON GROUND CUMIN
- ½ TEASPOON SPANISH PIMENTÓN DULCE (SWEET PAPRIKA)
- ½ TEASPOON SPANISH PIMENTÓN PICANTE (SPICY PAPRIKA)

1. If using dried garbanzo beans, soak them overnight and boil following the directions on page 343. If using canned garbanzos, drain, rinse, and place the garbanzo beans in a saucepan with 3 cups/720 ml water. Bring to a boil, remove from the heat, cover the pan, and leave them in the liquid until ready to use.

2. Rinse the tripe well under running water. Cut it into 1½-inch-/4-cm-square pieces. Stud the peeled onion with the cloves. In a large pot, add the tripe and studded onion, a pinch of salt, and cover with water. Bring to a boil over high heat and boil for 10 minutes. Drain and discard the water, onion, and cloves. Rinse and drain the tripe.

3. In a cazuela or heavy casserole, heat the olive oil over medium heat, and prepare a sofrito with the chopped onion, garlic, and tomatoes, following the directions on page 39. When the sofrito is ready, add the chorizo and cook for 5 minutes. Stir in the parsley, flour, cumin, and both types of pimentón.

4. Drain the beans, reserving about 3 cups/720 ml of the liquid.

5. Add the tripe, beans, and 2 cups/480 ml of the reserved liquid to the cazuela. Simmer over medium heat for 15 minutes, until the flavors are blended. The sauce should be very loose and require a spoon to eat. Stir in a bit more of the reserved liquid if necessary. Serve in bowls.

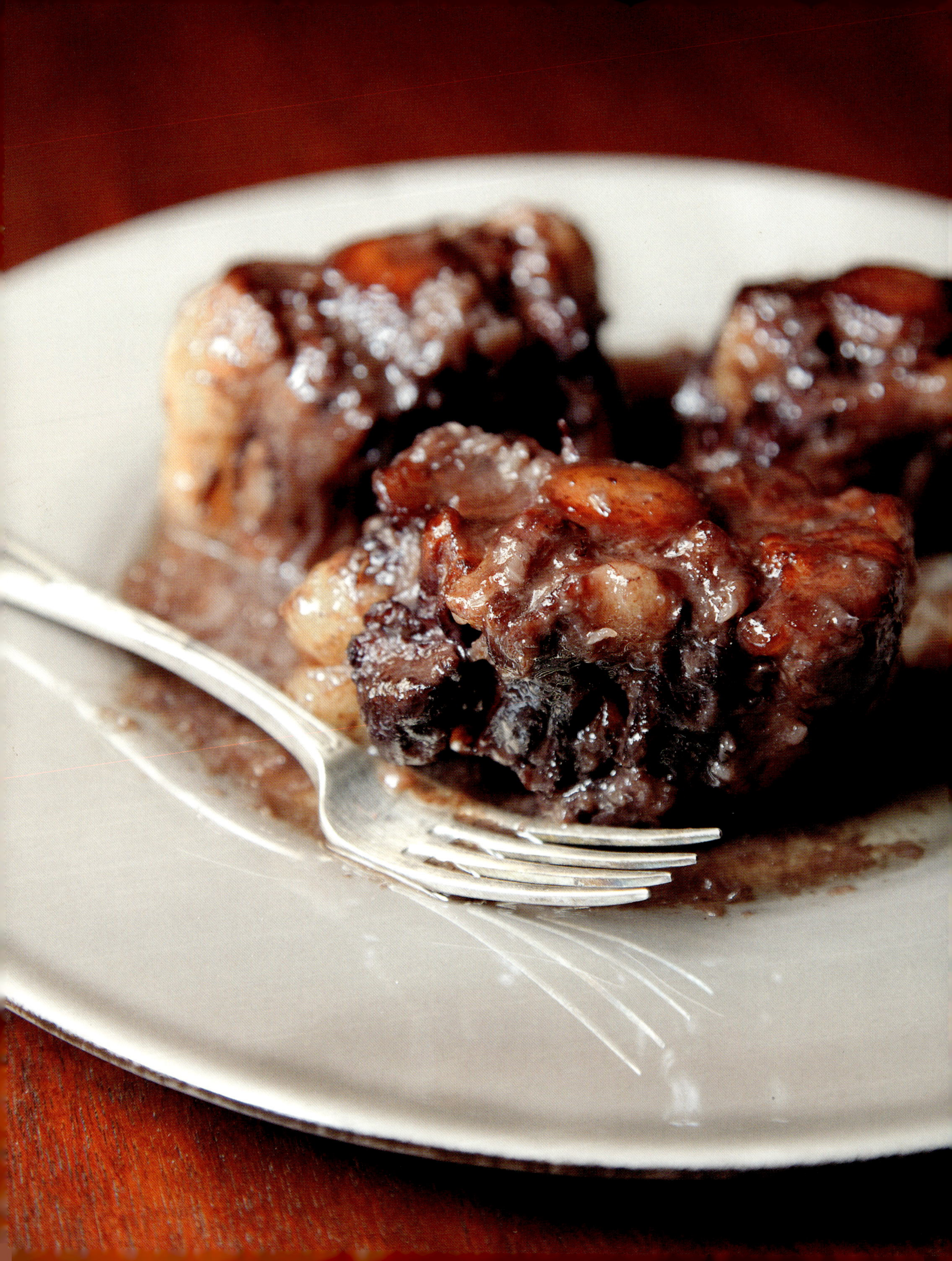

BRAISED OXTAIL STEW

GUISO DE RABO DE BUEY

SERVES 4

This rich, legendary Spanish dish hails from Extremadura and Andalucía (especially around Córdoba). It's bony and requires hours of braising, but the fatty meat becomes incredibly tender and the sauce velvety and almost decadently rich.

The sauce can be passed through a food mill before serving, but after so many hours of braising, it is not really mandatory. Serve the oxtails with Puréed Potatoes with Extra-Virgin Olive Oil (page 117).

4 POUNDS/1.8 KG OXTAILS

¼ CUP/60 ML OLIVE OIL

SALT AND FRESHLY GROUND BLACK PEPPER

ALL-PURPOSE FLOUR FOR DREDGING

2 LEEKS, WHITE AND TENDER GREEN PARTS ONLY, FINELY CHOPPED

1 ONION, FINELY CHOPPED

1 CARROT, CHOPPED

3 GARLIC CLOVES, CHOPPED

¼ CUP/60 ML BRANDY, COGNAC, OR OLOROSO SHERRY

2 CUPS/480 ML RED WINE

2 PINCHES FINELY CHOPPED FRESH THYME

1 BAY LEAF

PINCH FRESHLY GRATED NUTMEG

1. Ask your butcher to cut the oxtails into 1½- to 2-inch/4- or 5-cm sections, separated at the joints so that the bones don't splinter.

2. In a cazuela, large sauté pan, or deep skillet, heat the olive oil over medium-high heat. Season the oxtails with salt and pepper and lightly dredge in the flour, shaking off the excess. Working in single-layer batches that don't crowd the pan, brown the oxtails, turning as needed, 6 to 8 minutes per batch. Transfer to a platter.

3. Add the leeks, onion, carrot, and garlic to the cazuela and cook until the leeks and onion are tender, about 10 minutes. Pour in the brandy and, as the alcohol burns off, return the oxtails to the pan. Pour in the wine and 3 cups/720 ml water. Add the thyme, bay leaf, and nutmeg. Bring to a simmer, reduce the heat to low, and simmer uncovered until the meat is very tender and comes away from the bone in whole pieces without breaking, 3 to 4 hours. Add more water as needed to keep the sauce moist and loose.

4. Remove the pieces of oxtail and pass the sauce through a food mill, if desired. Return the sauce to the pan along with the oxtails, and loosen with a touch of water if necessary. Reheat the sauce and oxtails until very hot. Serve immediately.

CHAPTER 13

DESSERTS, SWEETS, AND FRUITS
postres, dulces y frutas

Peeled back, the archaeology of a cuisine reveals its sources and influences, its history and ancestors. In the Spanish kitchen, you can see it clearly in the sweets and *respostería* (baked goods). Every culture (or colony) has brought new influences, ingredients, and traditions to the peninsula, and added to the expanding *recetario* (recipe collection).

In classic antiquity, the ancient Greeks and Romans (I imagine; there are few records) utilized the ample honey, nuts, and flour at their disposal. The Moors brought true sweet splendor during their reign on the peninsula by introducing citrus fruits, sugarcane, and methods for processing sugar and showed what magic could be wrought from a base of almonds, lemons, and sugar. From abroad came the scent of cinnamon, nutmeg, and cloves, and, with the colonizing of the Americas, chocolate. Sweetened with sugar to rid its bitterness, and perfumed with vanilla and cinnamon, chocolate quickly found favor in Spain. Vanilla arrived in the peninsula in the fifteenth century from Mexico and Brazil. To these ingredients, add flour, eggs, milk, olive oil or butter, honey, dried fruits like raisins, and other nuts—hazelnuts, walnuts, pine nuts, and chestnuts—from the pantry, and you can create a whole wide world of *dulces* (sweets).

Many typical pastries are prepared for specific religious celebrations, such as buñuelos around Easter and round *panellets* with pine nuts (see page 291) and *huesos de santos* (filled marzipan "saints' bones") for All Saints' Day. At Christmas, shortbread *polvorones* are favorites, along with *turrón* (nougat) and various marzipans. In Valencia, the Balearic Islands, and Catalunya, delicate, tubular *neules* are one of the oldest Christmas sweets. First recorded in a celebration of Jaume I in 1267, according to Néstor Luján, their shape took on their more familiar cylindrical form in the fourteenth century. *"Cada cosa al seu temps i per Nadal, neules,"* goes an archaic refrain ("Everything has its time and for Christmas, neules").

Fresh fruit is an important part of the meal, and is usually served following the main course and before dessert (or strong coffee). Sometimes, it gets special treatment and *becomes* dessert. That might be as simple as tossing orange pieces with heady extra-virgin olive oil and a dollop of honey (see page 292). Usually, though, it means something more elaborate like figs baked in the oven with a splash of sweet dessert wine (see page 296), or pears poached in red wine (see page 295).

And in summer, there are sorbets. *Sorbete*, writes Inés Eléxpuru in *La cocina de al-Andalus* (The Cooking of al-Andalus), is derived from the Arabic word *sherbet*, from *sharbah* (to drink). Using ice stored in caves or natural wells—they could conserve the ice through the month of July—the Moors added "the essence of violets, bananas, roses, or melons, among many others." These proved, she continues rather effusively, "effective against summer thirst and the boredom of caliphs and high-society who spent the lethargic hours of the afternoon in the shade of a jasmine tree, leaning against the *azulejos* [glazed decorated tiles] of the patio and being soothed by the gentle bubbling of the fountain."

So many choices for a fruity finish—elegant, often light, always tasty options. From season to season, a perfect way to end a meal.

MEL FLAVIÀ
COLLITA PRÒPIA
ELABORACIÓ ARTESANA
MIL FLORS
(ROMANÍ, FARIGOLA)

TOASTED BREAD WITH CHOCOLATE, EXTRA-VIRGIN OLIVE OIL, AND SEA SALT FLAKES

PAN CON CHOCOLATE, ACEITE DE OLIVA VIRGEN EXTRA Y ESCAMAS DE SAL MARINA

SERVES 4

While a favorite these days of creative chefs, this is, at heart, an afternoon kids' snack—given at day care centers, schools, and kitchen tables. For my father-in-law, who grew up near the Arbequina olive region of Les Garrigues, it was this or a piece of bread sprinkled with sugar and moistened with red table wine. But as Gerard Veà—producer of Les Garrigues' most celebrated olive oil—once showed me, it isn't just for kids. He offered me this perfect version, using plenty of his family's own fruity, aromatic oil. Simple, sure, but a pure adult indulgence. Especially when using chocolate by Enric Rovira, Oriol Balaguer, or another of Spain's foremost chocolate makers.

12 SLICES BAGUETTE
12 THIN PIECES HIGH-QUALITY CHOCOLATE, ½ TO 1 INCH/1.25 TO 2.5 CM SQUARE
EXTRA-VIRGIN OLIVE OIL
FLAKY SEA SALT

1. Preheat the broiler.

2. Place the baguette slices on a baking sheet and slide them under the broiler. Toast slightly, turning as needed, until the edges are fringed golden. Remove from the oven. Turn off the broiler but close the door to keep the oven warm.

3. Lay a piece of chocolate atop each slice of bread and slide back into the warm oven. Leave in the heat only long enough to just soften the chocolate; do not let it completely melt. Once the edges begin to droop—but the chocolate still has a "bite" to it—remove from the oven.

4. Transfer the bread to a serving platter. Liberally drizzle each with olive oil and generously scatter salt flakes over the top. Serve immediately.

CREAMY VANILLA CUSTARD

NATILLAS

SERVES 4

Whereas Spanish egg flans (see page 278) should be firmish and jiggly, *natillas* are creamy. After all, the name is a diminutive of *nata* (cream). This velvety dessert has a lush texture and hints of vanilla. (Or cinnamon. Substitute a small cinnamon stick for the vanilla here if desired.) Often a Galleta María cookie—a thin, round, tea biscuit sold in most Latino grocery stores as "Marie Biscuits"—is set on top while the custard is still warm. This tends to make them soggy, so I prefer to place the biscuit on top just before serving. The classic serving dish to pour the custard into to set is a *cazuelita*, a small terra-cotta casserole.

½ VANILLA BEAN
4 CUPS/950 ML WHOLE MILK
8 EGG YOLKS
½ CUP/100 G SUGAR
1½ TABLESPOONS CORNSTARCH
4 THIN COOKIES, PREFERABLY GALLETA MARÍA OR ANOTHER ROUND, FLAT TEA BISCUIT FOR GARNISHING

1. Slice the vanilla bean open and scrape out the seeds with the tip of a knife into a heavy saucepan; drop in the pod. Add 3½ cups/830 ml of the milk to the pan and bring to a simmer over medium heat; do not let it reach a boil. Remove from the heat and let infuse for 10 minutes.

2. In a bowl, whisk the egg yolks and sugar until spongy. Dissolve the cornstarch in the remaining ½ cup/120 ml milk and stir into the eggs. Slowly pour into the saucepan of milk while whisking continually.

3. Over low heat, stirring continually and not letting it reach a boil, cook the custard until it thickens; stirs with a heavier, silken creaminess; and can coat the back of the spoon, about 8 minutes.

4. Pour the custard through a conical strainer or chinois into a clean pitcher and discard the solids. Divide the custard among cazuelitas or parfait or dessert glasses. Let cool to room temperature. Cover the surface with plastic wrap and refrigerate until chilled. Serve chilled with a biscuit on top of each custard.

CREAMY RICE PUDDING

ARROZ CON LECHE

SERVES 6

In many homes, the onset of colder weather can be detected in the soothing aromas of simmering *arroz con leche*. It is the homiest and most comforting of desserts, the kind of dish referred to as *de siempre* or *de todo la vida*, which both mean "from always" or "from forever." In the dairy-rich regions of Asturias and Cantabria, it is especially popular.

The history of this rice pudding is a long one, and many scholars argue that it traveled from India to Persia and on to Spain during the Moorish rule of the peninsula, adapting to the land and tastes. In Spain, it uses highly absorbent short-grain rice that becomes wonderfully plump and chewy, and is usually flavored by some citrus peels. The final texture should be creamy. Arroz con leche is frequently spooned into individual terra-cotta *cazuelitas* (casseroles) to cool and serve.

1 CUP/200 G SHORT-GRAIN RICE
7 CUPS/1.7 L WHOLE MILK
PEELS OF 1½ ORGANIC LEMONS, WHITE PITH SCRAPED AWAY
1 CINNAMON STICK
¾ CUP/150 G SUGAR
1 TABLESPOON BUTTER, CUT INTO PIECES
SALT
GROUND CINNAMON FOR DUSTING

1. In a large saucepan, bring 2 cups/480 ml water to a rolling boil. Add the rice and boil for 30 seconds. Dump into a strainer. Drain but do not rinse the rice (to avoid washing away more starches).

2. In the saucepan, add the milk, lemon peels, and cinnamon stick and bring to a boil over medium heat. Return the rice to the pan and stir to break up any clumps. Reduce the heat to low and gently boil for 30 minutes, stirring frequently to keep it from sticking or scorching, or a skin from forming on the surface (possibly causing it to boil over). Stir in the sugar, butter, and a pinch of salt and cook for 5 minutes more, or until the rice is plump and chewy. The consistency should be runny, as it will thicken further once it cools. (Stir in more milk toward the end if needed.)

3. Remove and discard the cinnamon stick and lemon peels. Divide the rice among small cazuelitas, ramekins, or dessert bowls and let cool to room temperature. Cover with plastic wrap and refrigerate until chilled.

4. Serve chilled, lightly dusted with ground cinnamon.

BASQUE WALNUT PUDDING

INTXAURSALSA

SERVES 4

A sibling of sorts to *arroz con leche* (Creamy Rice Pudding, facing page), this ancient, bucolic Basque dessert smacks of the region's many farms and verdant valleys so rich in dairy cows and walnut trees. But as rustic as it is, *intxaursalsa* finds a place on many Basque tables on Christmas Eve. It's simple, and requires only patience in letting it slowly reduce down to a creamy, soothing dessert. (The name literally means "walnut sauce" in the Basque language.) Traditionally, cooks crushed the walnuts to a paste in a large mortar and pestle, or used a rolling pin to mash them on a hard surface. It should go unsaid, but grinding them in a food processer is significantly easier.

The dessert will thicken up more once it cools, and the slight graininess of the ground walnuts will soften. This dessert is best served at room temperature.

2½ CUPS/285 G WALNUT PIECES
4 CUPS/1 L WHOLE MILK
1 CINNAMON STICK
½ CUP/100 G SUGAR

1. Coarsely grind the walnuts.

2. In a heavy saucepan, bring the milk and cinnamon stick to a boil over medium heat, stirring so that it does not scorch. Add the walnuts and sugar, reduce the heat to low, and gently simmer, stirring frequently to keep from scorching, until it has reduced by about one-fourth to a creamy, saucy consistency, about 45 minutes. (Add in a touch more milk if needed, or, conversely, let it reduce a bit longer.) Remove the pan from the heat and let cool.

3. Remove and discard the cinnamon stick. Ladle the sauce into bowls and serve at room temperature.

CITRUS-AND-CINNAMON-SCENTED FLAN

FLAN CON AROMAS CÍTRICOS Y CANELA

MAKES 8 FLANS

At home we like our flan less eggy and with a creamier, lush texture, flavored with an infusion of cinnamon and lemon and orange peels— a lovely nod to the profuse Moorish influences in the Spanish kitchen. Individual flan molds or ramekins that hold 5 to 6 ounces/150 to 175 ml are ideal. The final texture should be a bit jiggly, just as this Spanish expression indicates: *"Como un flan"* (like a flan) means to be shaking with nerves or fear.

3 CUPS/720 ML WHOLE MILK
PEEL OF 1 ORGANIC LEMON, WHITE PITH SCRAPED AWAY
PEEL OF 1 ORGANIC ORANGE, WHITE PITH SCRAPED AWAY
1 CINNAMON STICK
6 TABLESPOONS/300 G SUGAR, PLUS 1 CUP/220 G
6 EGGS
FRESH WHIPPED CREAM FOR GARNISHING (OPTIONAL)

1. In a saucepan, bring the milk, citrus peels, and cinnamon stick to a boil over medium heat, stirring to keep the bottom from scorching. Remove from the heat and let the flavors infuse for 20 minutes or so as it cools.

2. Meanwhile, preheat the oven to 300°F/150°C/gas mark 2. Arrange eight flan molds, fluted brioche molds, ramekins, or custard cups in a baking pan.

3. In a small saucepan, dissolve the 6 tablespoons/80 g sugar in 3 tablespoons water over medium heat. When it reaches a boil, reduce the heat to medium-low and simmer without stirring until caramelized into a rich amber color, 8 to 10 minutes. Immediately pour into the molds, tilting them as needed to cover the bottoms evenly before the caramel hardens.

4. In a large bowl, whisk the eggs with the remaining 1 cup/220 g sugar. Strain the milk, discarding the cinnamon stick and citrus peels. In a slow, steady stream, while whisking continually, pour the milk into the egg-sugar mixture. Divide the custard evenly among the molds.

5. Bring a saucepan of water to a boil. Pour the hot water into the baking pan until it reaches halfway up the outside of the molds. (Do not splash any water into the molds.) Gently slide the pan into the oven and bake until the flans are set, about 50 minutes. A knife tip should come out clean when inserted just off center.

6. Remove from the oven, take the molds from the water bath, and let cool to room temperature. Refrigerate until well chilled.

7. To serve, unmold the flans by running the tip of a thin knife around the top edge of a flan, covering the mold with a dessert plate, and inverting, jiggling the mold until the flan is released. Let the caramel run over the top and down the sides. If desired, garnish with fresh whipped cream, either encircling the flans or surrounding them with a series of swirled peaks.

SPONGY YOGURT CAKE

BIZCOCHO DE YOGUR

MAKES 1 ROUND 11-INCH/28-CM CAKE

This is *the* all-purpose Spanish cake. Moist with a slightly crumbling texture, it is prepared with olive oil instead of butter, and yogurt instead of milk. In fact, most popular written recipes give measurements based on a standard individual yogurt container, as in "1 container of yogurt, 1 yogurt container olive oil, 3 yogurt containers sugar . . . " Instead of dusting with powdered sugar, slather some creamy lemon spread (see page 325) or a favorite fruit preserve on top.

1½ CUPS/330 G SUGAR
½ CUP/120 ML PLAIN UNSWEETENED YOGURT
3 EGGS
2 CUPS/255 G ALL-PURPOSE FLOUR, PLUS MORE FOR PAN
2 TABLESPOONS BAKING POWDER
½ CUP/120 ML OLIVE OIL
FINE ZEST OF 1 ORGANIC LEMON
BUTTER FOR GREASING PAN
POWDERED SUGAR FOR DUSTING

1. Preheat the oven to 350°F/180°C/gas mark 4.

2. In a large bowl, vigorously beat the sugar, yogurt, and eggs with an electric mixer until well combined. Blend the flour and baking powder and gradually add them to the bowl along with the olive oil and lemon zest. Mix until combined but not overly beaten.

3. Grease an 11-inch/28-cm round or springform cake pan or an 8-inch/20-cm square cake pan with butter and dust with flour; shake the pan and discard the flour that does not stick. Pour the batter into the pan.

4. Bake until done but still spongy (a toothpick poked into the center will come out clean), 25 to 30 minutes. Do not open the oven during baking. Remove from the oven, let cool, and remove from the pan. Before serving, dust with powdered sugar.

When we go to Sinarcas, the rural village of my mother-in-law's family on the Valencian border with Castilla–La Mancha, we leave bearing a hefty country care package, from homemade blood sausages to bottles of wine from the village cooperative and, when the season is right, just-picked almonds in their shell.

One part of the package, though, never makes it home from Sinarcas—Tía Encarnita's spongy cake. Sometimes she makes a plain one (see page 279), but more often than not she adds pear or apple slices to the batter. If we are there in winter, she adds some walnuts from the village, too. She wraps up a big piece, but by the time we are back in Barcelona, there are never more than crumbs left.

SPONGY CAKE WITH PEARS AND WALNUTS, SINARCAS STYLE

BIZCOCHO CON PERAS Y NUECES AL ESTILO DE SINARCAS

MAKES ONE 11-INCH/28-CM CAKE

3 EGGS
1 CUP/200 G SUGAR, PLUS MORE FOR SPRINKLING
½ CUP/120 ML MILD OLIVE OIL OR SUNFLOWER OIL
1 CUP/240 ML MILK
1¾ CUPS/215 G ALL-PURPOSE FLOUR
2 TABLESPOONS BAKING POWDER
½ CUP/55 G ROUGHLY CHOPPED WALNUTS
1½ TO 2 RIPE BUT QUITE FIRM PEARS, SUCH AS ANJOU, BOSC, CONFERENCE, OR BARTLETT, PEELED, QUARTERED, AND THINLY SLICED LENGTHWISE

1. Preheat the oven to 350°F/180°C/gas mark 4.

2. In a large bowl, vigorously beat the eggs and sugar with an electric mixer until pale and frothy. Stir in the olive oil and milk. Blend the flour and baking powder and gradually add to the bowl so the eggs don't lose their volume. Fold in the walnuts.

3. Line an 11-inch/28-cm round or springform cake pan or an 8-inch/20-cm square cake pan with parchment paper.

4. Pour the batter into the pan. Layer the pear slices over the top. Lightly sprinkle with sugar.

5. Bake until done and golden on top but still spongy (a toothpick poked into the center will come out clean), about 30 minutes. Do not open the oven during baking. Remove from the oven and let cool before serving.

FIESTAS

THE THREE KINGS
Los Tres Reyes Magos

The winter holiday season does not climax in Spain with Christmas, but rather, a dozen days later on the Epiphany, January 6. The evening before, the Three Wise Men, or Magi, and their entourages arrive, parading through towns and throwing candy to those lining the streets to welcome them.

Just as the wise men traveled from the east to pay homage to the baby Jesus and bring gifts—gold, frankincense, and myrrh—today they also come bearing gifts. In Spain, each king represents a different continent: Melchior from Europe, Gaspar from Asia, and Balthasar from Africa. Children write a letter to their favorite king with a wish list of presents. At home, kids polish and set out their shoes and leave a snack for the kings and water for the camels. They awake to find presents stacked around their shoes.

Though little ones might beg to differ, that day is about more than gifts. January 6 is also celebrated with families gathering for a festive midday meal. Like many households, for us it is the third large family lunch in two weeks, and the food served does not adhere to an exact tradition—as the Christmas meals do—but changes from year to year.

There is one constant, though: a circular cake called *roscón de reyes* decorated with large crystals of sugar and colorful candied fruits that represent jewels—the diamonds, rubies, and emeralds on the robes of the kings. Inside there is a small figurine (or coin) and a fava bean. Whoever gets the figurine is king for the day; whoever gets the fava bean has to pay for the roscón.

Some food historians date the roscón tradition to the eighteenth century; others, centuries before that, and a few point to it being inherited from the Romans, who celebrated Saturn and the lengthening of days after the winter solstice. Whatever the origin, the tradition remains strong.

This poem is recited when the roscón is carried out to the table:

He aquí el roscón de reyes	Here is the Kings' [Day] roscón
tradición de un gran banquete,	tradition of a great feast,
en el cual hay dos sorpresas	in which there are two surprises
para los que tengan suerte.	for those who have luck.
En él hay, muy bien ocultas,	Inside, hidden very well,
una haba y una figura;	a fava bean and a figurine;
el que lo vaya a cortar	he who cuts the roscón
hágalo sin travesura.	should do no mischief.
Quien en la boca se encuentre	Whoever finds in their mouth
una cosa un tanto dura,	something a little hard,
a lo peor es el haba,	the worst case is the fava bean,
o a lo mejor la figura.	or better the figurine.
Si es el haba lo encontrado	If it's the fava bean that you find
este postre pagarás,	this dessert you will pay,
mas si ello es la figura	but if it is the figurine
coronado y rey serás.	you will be crowned king.

After all these years, I've yet to get the crown.

COUNTRY MUFFINS

MAGDALENAS

MAKES ABOUT 20 MUFFINS

These muffins made with olive oil (instead of butter) are a country staple in central Spain. My introduction to them came during the family paella of my mother-in-law. Until a couple of years ago, one of her elderly aunts, who grew up in the rural interior of the country, arrived each weekend for the paella carrying a bag of *magdalenas* to accompany the after-lunch coffee. An elderly widow who wore all black apart from a flowing, colorful scarf wound theatrically around her neck, Tía Visi always brought far too many muffins, and sent the excess home with my wife and me to have as a snack with a bowl of strawberries or to dip into our morning café con leche. For years, there always seemed to be at least a few magdalenas around our kitchen, and it wasn't until she had passed away that I ever bought them in the bakery or began to make them myself.

A generous pinch of sugar on top will caramelize into a round disc like a coin.

4 EGGS
1½ CUPS/330 G SUGAR, PLUS MORE FOR SPRINKLING
1 CUP/240 ML WHOLE MILK
½ CUP/120 ML MILD OLIVE OIL OR SUNFLOWER OIL
ZEST OF 1 ORGANIC LEMON
2½ CUPS/315 G ALL-PURPOSE FLOUR
2 TABLESPOONS BAKING POWDER

1. Preheat the oven to 350°F/180°C/gas mark 4.

2. In a large bowl, whisk the eggs and sugar with an electric mixer until pale and frothy. While continuing to beat, slowly add in the milk, olive oil, and then the lemon zest. Mix the flour and baking powder together and fold them into the batter with a spatula.

3. Line muffin tins with paper liners.

4. Spoon the batter into the paper liners, filling them about two-thirds to three-fourths full to allow room for the muffins to expand. Place a generous pinch of sugar (in a single pile) on the surface of each one, just slightly off center.

5. Place the muffin tin on the middle shelf of the oven and bake until golden, 15 to 20 minutes. Do not open the oven during baking.

6. Remove from the oven, sprinkle a pinch more sugar evenly over the muffin tops, and let cool on wire racks. Store in a sealed container lined with paper towels in a dry, cool place. These are best eaten within a few days.

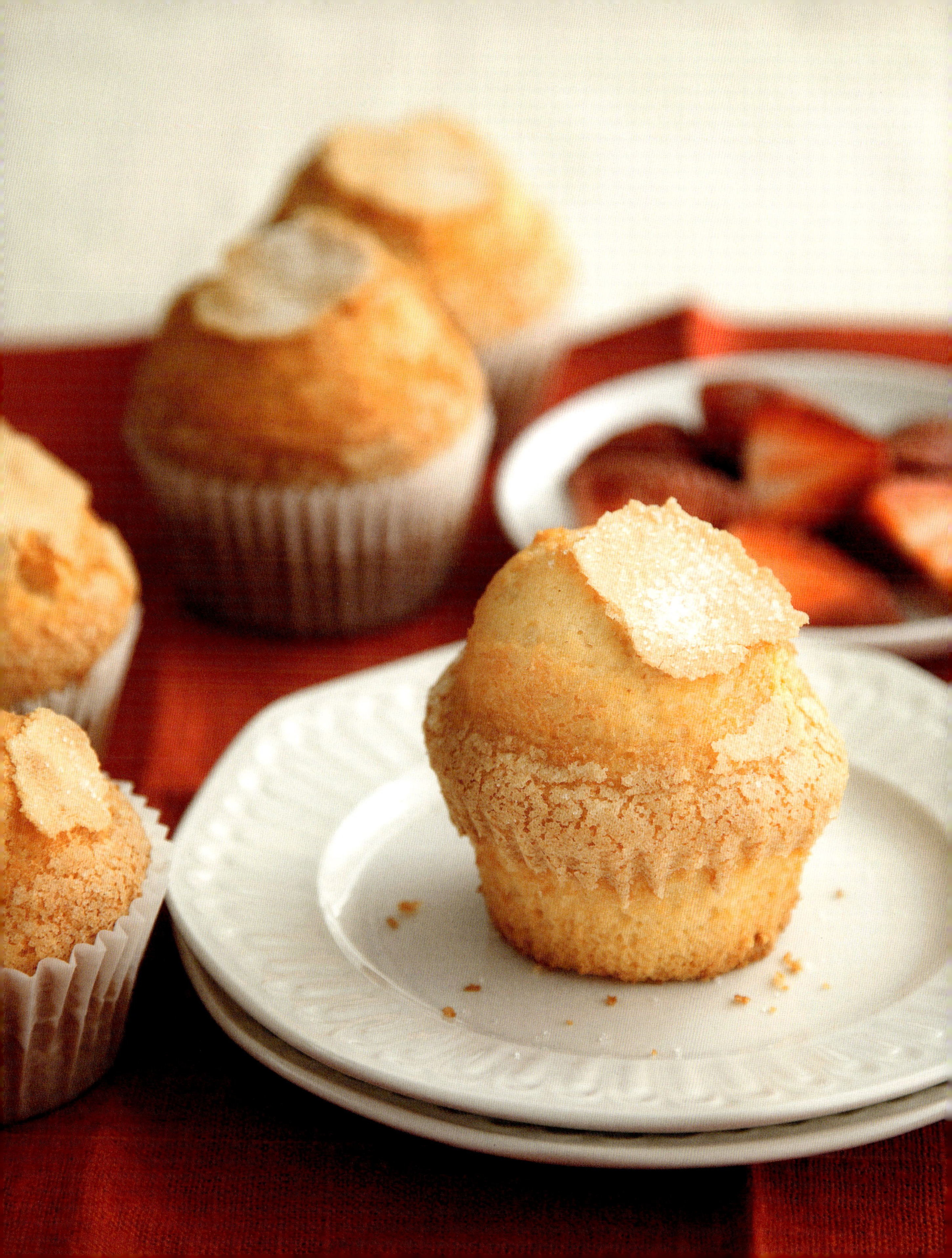

FIESTAS

ALL SAINTS' DAY
Día de Todos los Santos

The first of November is Día de Todos los Santos, or All Saints' Day, an ancient Catholic tradition to honor saints (both known and unknown). Today, Spaniards commemorate it by visiting cemeteries with chrysanthemums, scrubbing marble headstones, replanting flowers, and tidying up graves. But, like all traditions here, the day is also celebrated with specific foods.

Chestnuts are most associated with the occasion. In places like Jerte, Extremadura, and around Aracena in northern Andalucía, groups of friends go into the forest to pick and then roast chestnuts together. In towns and villages around Spain, chestnuts—the best come from Galicia—are sold from little wooden street-corner shacks, roasted over squat, charcoal-burning braziers. Scooped still warm into rolled paper cones (marked with charcoal-dusted fingerprints), they are sold by the half dozen. The blackened shells are peeled away to reveal the soft, nutty-tasting flesh.

The chestnut's consort is the sweet potato. A distant cousin of the potato and native of South America, where it has been cultivated for thousands of years, the sweet potato arrived in Europe sometime in the sixteenth century. *Boniatos*, as they are called in Spain, are elongated tubers, reddish brown, with sweet, deep-orange flesh. The same corner shacks that roast chestnuts roast these, too, and they are taken home for an indulgence.

There are special *dulces* (sweets), too. In Castilla, they eat the wonderfully named *hueso de santo* (bone of a saint)—cylindrical white marzipan filled with *dulce de yema* (candied egg yolk). In Catalunya, the main sweetmeats for this day are *panellets*, marzipan cookies typically rolled in toasted pine nuts (see page 291) and eaten with a glass of *moscatel* (Muscatel), a sweet, golden dessert wine made from muscat grapes. And, across the country, there are *buñuelos de viento* (literally "fritters of the wind"), fried, sweet fritters that are also prepared during Lent. During Lent, the "wind" refers to the fritter's airy texture, but for All Saints' Day, tradition says that by eating one you release a soul from purgatory.

This is also the time when the quince fruit begins to ripen. My wife's grandmother prepared quince paste (see page 323) with the season's first pieces of fruit from their tree for All Saints' Day, something of a tradition that we have taken over at home when local quince start arriving in our neighborhood markets.

With these treats, autumn has, at last, truly arrived.

There are three main versions of crêpe-like filloas in Galicia. Two are savory kinds from the interior, ancient dishes once cooked during the winter *matanza*, the important pork butchering season, and during the Carnival festivities in February. Of these, one is prepared with a simple stock made of pig's feet, the other with blood from the pig. This recipe is—regrettably for some, happily for most—a third version, *al natural*. More similar to French crêpes, this is by far the most popular of the trio.

But even if these crêpes are "sweet," it is typical to use a piece of *tocino* (fat back) to grease the pan between frying. That, surely, gives them a distinctive Spanish touch.

GALICIAN CRÊPES WITH FRESH WHIPPED CREAM AND HONEY

FILLOAS DE LECHE CON NATA MONTADA Y MIEL

MAKES ABOUT TWELVE 10-INCH/25-CM CRÊPES; SERVES 4

6 EGGS
2 CUPS/480 ML MILK
SALT
2 CUPS/255 G ALL-PURPOSE FLOUR
1 TABLESPOON BRANDY OR COGNAC
BUTTER FOR GREASING PAN, OR A PIECE OF TOCINO (FAT BACK)
POWDERED SUGAR FOR DUSTING
FRESH WHIPPED CREAM FOR GARNISHING
HONEY FOR DRIZZLING

1. In a large bowl, beat the eggs with the milk. Add a pinch of salt and begin adding the flour while continuing to beat, until it has the consistency of a smooth, loose, and thin batter. Let sit for 1 hour in a cool place. Add the brandy and whisk again.

2. Preheat a 10-inch/25-cm nonstick skillet or crêpe pan over medium heat. Grease the pan with butter using a piece of folded paper towel or pastry brush. Ladle in about ⅓ cup/75 ml batter and immediately swirl and slightly roll the pan to evenly coat the bottom in a thin layer of batter. Cook until bubbles appear in the surface and the edges begin to just curl away from the sides of the pan, about 1 minute or so. Loosen with the help of a thin spatula and then flip. Cook on the other side until golden, about 1 minute.

3. Transfer to a plate and repeat until all of the batter is used, greasing the pan between each crêpe. Place a sheet of parchment or wax paper between each. Reheat the first ones briefly in the pan before serving.

4. Dust with powdered sugar and serve with the whipped cream and honey to add as desired.

The Galician city of Santiago de Compostela lies at the end of the famous, thousand-year-old pilgrimage route that crosses northern Spain, called *El Camino de Santiago* (The Way of St. James). It is a spectacular city, with a marvelous cathedral dating to the early thirteenth century that holds the remains of the Apostle Saint James (Santiago in Spanish). For many gastronomes, though, the city is best known for giving its name to this ancient almond tart.

Tartas de Santiago are prepared all across Spain these days, but an authentic one does not have a crust and is made without flour. Officially—and it *is* a protected product with a seal of guarantee—ground almonds make up at least one-third of the weight of the total ingredients and sugar another one-third. Eggs, butter, lemon zest, and perhaps some liqueur make up the remaining. The top generally has the distinctive dusting of powdered sugar that's been done over a simple template, leaving the gothic-looking Cross of the Order of St. James visible. It is easy to do. Cut out a piece of butcher paper, lay it on top of the cooled cake, and sift the powdered sugar over top.

GALICIAN ALMOND TART

TARTA DE SANTIAGO

MAKES ONE 10-INCH/25-CM TART

¼ CUP/60 G UNSALTED BUTTER, PLUS MORE FOR GREASING PAN
1⅓ CUPS/275 G SUGAR
5 EGG YOLKS
2 CUPS/225 G GROUND ALMONDS
ZEST OF 1 ORGANIC LEMON
ALL-PURPOSE FLOUR FOR PAN
½ CUP/65 G CHOPPED ALMONDS
POWDERED SUGAR FOR DUSTING

1. Preheat the oven to 400°F/200°C/gas mark 6.

2. In a large bowl, cream the butter and sugar with a mixer. Add the egg yolks one by one, blending each into the batter before adding the next. Work in the ground almonds and the lemon zest.

3. Grease a 10-inch/25-cm springform pan with butter and dust with flour; shake the pan and discard the flour that does not stick. Pour in the batter. Once the batter has settled, generously sprinkle the chopped almonds over the top.

4. Bake for about 25 minutes, or until the top is golden and slightly chewy. Remove and let cool in the pan. Transfer to a serving plate.

5. Before serving, dust with sifted powdered sugar. If desired, place a cut-out of the cross of St. James (see illustration) on top before dusting.

TRADITIONS

CELESTIAL TEMPTATIONS
tentaciones celestes

Over the centuries, the historical repository for the rich tradition of sweets in Spain has been in convents and monasteries. To learn more about *dulces monacales* or *dulces de convento* (monastery or convent sweets), I spent some time in Arcos de la Frontera. An ancient city founded before the Roman era, perched on a massive cliff with sweeping views over rolling groves of olives trees, Arcos de la Frontera came to prominence as a Moorish town during the tenth- and eleventh-century reign of the Caliphate of Córdoba. The best sweets in this stunning Andalusian *pueblo blanco* (white town) are prepared by the nuns at the Convento del Corpus Christi of the Mercedarias Descalzas. These "Barefoot Mercedarians" specialize in pastries made with almonds—namely dense, round *alfajores* that have flour, nuts, honey, and a touch of aniseed and cinnamon—that they sell through a revolving window that keeps the cloistered nuns out of sight.

When I asked a baker in Arcos about this, he smiled. The valued ingredients for such traditional pastries always took money to procure or produce, and often substantial time to prepare. "Look who used to enter a convent," he said. "Cultured, noble people . . . people with money." Thus they could keep the wealthy traditions alive over time, even as the surrounding area had long periods of poverty, he explained. "The pastries haven't evolved for centuries."

He wasn't too far wrong. For instance, the first details for *tocino de cielo*, a flan-like egg dessert, date back to 1324 by the nuns of the Convento de Espíritu Santo in nearby Jerez de la Frontera. Of the versions I have eaten in Andalucía, the sweet seems about the same as it must have been back in the fourteenth century.

Another interesting tradition is the abundance of monastery sweets that call for many egg yolks. This comes in part from sherry and wine producers, who used egg whites for fining, or clarifying, wines. (Some still do. I have watched a man at a famous winery in La Rioja cracking eggs one by one into what looked like an old-fashioned set of scales, separating the yolks and whites in a series of plummeting levels.) The yolks were often given to a convent or monastery in town. The most famous of these sweets are candied egg yolks called, simply, *yemas* (egg yolks), or sometimes *yemas de Santa Teresa* after the sixteenth-century Carmelite nun St. Teresa de Ávila. (Yemas became popular during her lifetime in the Castilian town of Ávila.) Yolks are laboriously worked with sugar and a touch of lemon juice until they have a delicate, creamy consistency before being rolled in sugar and individually wrapped in waxed paper. These medieval candies dissolve in the mouth as you barely bite down.

While I enjoy buying such dulces monacales from certain monasteries on my travels around Spain, I get most at a wonderful shop in Barcelona's Gothic Quarter called Caelum. It sells only goods from monasteries and convents located around the country. It is one of my favorite spots in the city, and a place I always take visitors. It has a small café, and you can sit and have a cup of tea and individually sample the dozens of celestial temptations that they sell.

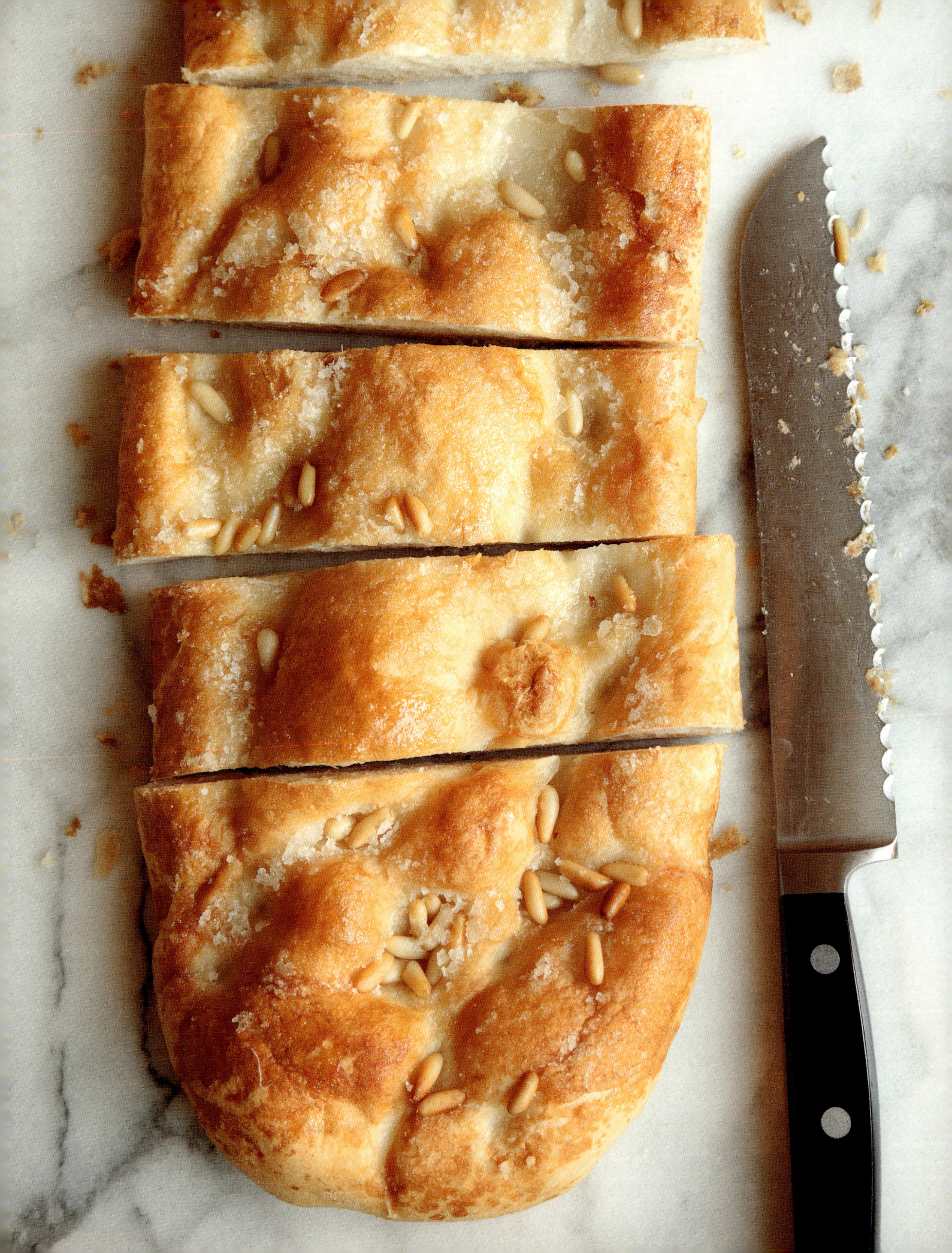

FLATBREAD WITH PINE NUTS, SUGAR, AND ANISE

COCA DE AZÚCAR CON PIÑONES Y ANÍS

MAKES 2 COCAS, ABOUT 14 BY 6 INCHES/ 36 BY 15 CM EACH

Cocas are flat, oval breads that can be savory, prepared either alone or as a base for topping like a rustic pizza (see page 70). But frequently they are sweet. In Mallorca, bakers prepare a version with candied dried fruit for San Juan on June 23 and 24, while on the mainland, you find *coca de llardons* (or *chicharrones*) topped with sugar, pine nuts, and fried pork rinds (with some fat), an interesting combination of flavors and textures.

This sugar-topped favorite version of the recipe also goes by the Catalan name *coca de forner*. (*Forner* means "baker," from *forn*, "oven.") The dough is savory—the sweetness comes from sprinkling the top with sugar before baking. Watch that the pine nuts don't blacken during baking.

4 CUPS/510 G ALL-PURPOSE FLOUR, PLUS MORE FOR WORK SURFACE

2 TEASPOONS SALT

1 TABLESPOON FIRMLY PACKED FRESH BAKER'S YEAST (SEE NOTE, PAGE 86) OR 2 TEASPOONS ACTIVE DRY YEAST

¼ CUP/60 ML EXTRA-VIRGIN OLIVE OIL, PLUS MORE FOR OILING BOWL AND BRUSHING DOUGH

⅓ CUP/50 G PINE NUTS

SUGAR FOR SPRINKLING

ANISETTE OR ANISE EXTRACT FOR DRIBBLING

1. In a large bowl, combine the flour and salt, crumble in the yeast, add the olive oil, and begin working in about 1½ cups/360 ml warm water until it forms a moist, sticky ball. Let sit for 5 minutes. Transfer to a lightly floured work surface and knead by hand for about 10 minutes, until the dough is supple and elastic and still slightly sticky. Or use a mechanical bread hook.

2. Place the dough in a large, lightly oiled bowl, cover with plastic wrap, and let rest at warm room temperature for 1½ hours, or until it has doubled in size.

3. Line two baking sheets with parchment paper or silicone baking mats.

4. Transfer the dough to a work space and divide in half. Form by hand into oblong rolls and transfer to the sheets.

5. Preheat the oven to 425°F/220°C/gas mark 7.

6. Gently stretch and press out the dough with your fingertips into ovals just over ½ inch/1.25 cm thick, about 14 inches/36 cm long, and 5 or 6 inches/ 13 or 15 cm wide. Generously brush with olive oil, cover with plastic wrap, and let sit for 15 minutes to rise again.

7. Sprinkle over the pine nuts and then very generously sprinkle the cocas with sugar. Shake some drops of anisette over the top. Bake until lightly golden and rich brown in places, 20 to 25 minutes, rotating the pans halfway through baking. Cool on wire racks before serving.

DESSERTS, SWEETS, AND FRUITS

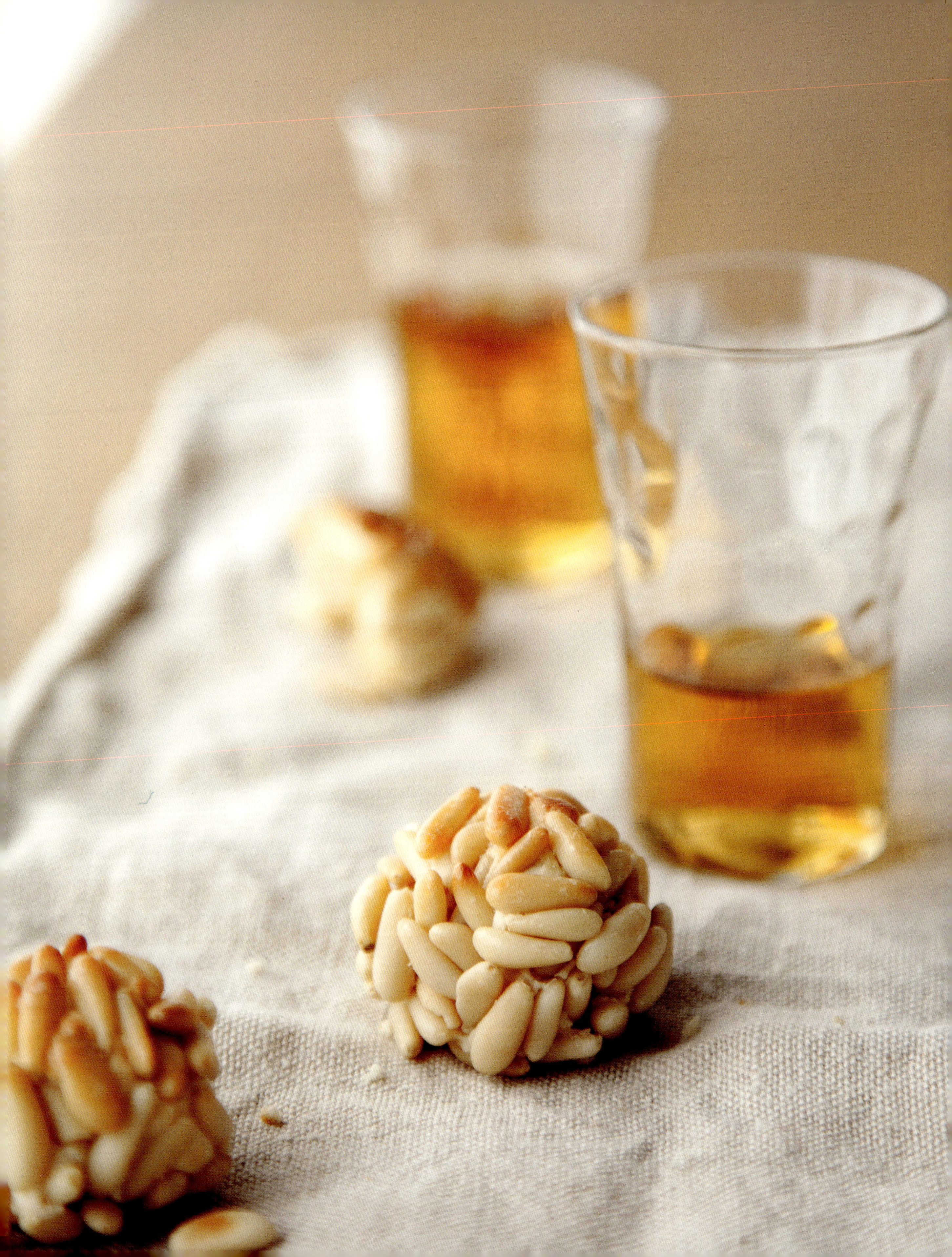

MARZIPAN COOKIES ROLLED IN PINE NUTS

PANELLETS DE PIÑONES

MAKES 24 TO 30 COOKIES

Like other traditional celebrations in Catalunya and Aragón, All Saints' Day is marked with specific foods, including roasted sweet potatoes and chestnuts. The biggest indulgence, though, is found in *pastelerías*: trays of *panellets*. Panellets are marzipan cookies made from a base of almonds, sugar, and sweet potato. The best known are these, perfectly round and rolled in pine nuts. Not all of the pine nuts will stick when rolled; they need to be pressed one by one into the gaps. Find help and be patient; it's worth it, for the cookies are sublime. They come out of the oven quite soft, but will firm up slightly as they cool. Serve with glasses of sweet white wine.

6 OUNCES/170 G SWEET POTATO, YAM, OR POTATO WITH PEEL, SCRUBBED
2 CUPS/225 G GROUND ALMONDS
1 CUP/200 G SUGAR
ZEST OF 1 ORGANIC LEMON
1 EGG
1½ CUPS/225 G PINE NUTS

1. Bring a saucepan of water to a boil, add the sweet potato, and gently boil until tender, about 30 minutes. (If using potato, reduce the cooking time by 5 or 10 minutes.) Remove with a slotted spoon and drain. When cool enough to handle, remove the peel and discard. Transfer the sweet potato to a large bowl, mash with the back of a fork, and let cool.

2. Add the ground almonds, sugar, and lemon zest to the bowl. Gently work the mixture by hand until it holds together. At first it will feel dry and crumbling, but it will gradually moisten as you work the dough. Cover and refrigerate for 30 minutes to chill the dough and make forming the cookies easier.

3. Preheat the oven to 425°F/220°C/gas mark 7.

4. Separate the egg, placing the white in one bowl and the yolk in another, and beat each with a fork. Place the pine nuts in a pie pan or wide bowl. Line one or two baking sheets with parchment paper or silicone baking mats.

5. Form the cookies by rolling about 1 tablespoon of dough into a ball. Roll it in egg white and then in the pine nuts. Patiently cover the cookies with pine nuts as needed. Place the cookies 1 inch/2.5 cm apart on a baking sheet. Brush lightly with the egg yolk.

6. Bake the cookies until the pine nuts are lightly browned, 12 to 14 minutes. Watch that the pine nuts don't burn. Transfer to a wire rack to cool. The cookies will keep in an airtight container for up to 5 days.

ORANGES WITH EXTRA-VIRGIN OLIVE OIL AND HONEY

NARANJAS CON ACEITE DE OLIVA VIRGEN EXTRA Y MIEL

SERVES 4

Combining these three iconic, bold ingredients makes a surprising, delicious dessert that is highly popular in Andalucía. Having eaten many variations of this in the south, I always prefer it with the orange pieces chopped up—thus juicier and eaten with a spoon—rather than prepared with the orange sliced into rounds and eaten with a small fork and knife. Both are typical, though.

This recipe needs at least a half hour to sit before eating. Prepare it before lunch or dinner, allow the flavors to meld during the meal, and it will be perfect for dessert. Choose a bold, even sharp extra-virgin olive oil and a highly aromatic honey to complement it. Serve with a couple of sweet biscuits or cookies.

4 RIPE VALENCIA ORANGES
2 TABLESPOONS EXTRA-VIRGIN OLIVE OIL
2 TABLESPOONS HONEY

1. Working over a large salad bowl to catch any juices that fall, peel the oranges and remove as much of the white pith as possible. Cut crosswise into ½- to ¾-inch-/1.25- to 2-cm-thick rounds and then roughly chop into pieces. Place in the bowl.

2. Drizzle over the olive oil and honey while turning the orange pieces with a spoon to blend.

3. Let sit at room temperature for at least 30 minutes. Before serving, stir and divide among dessert bowls.

EARLY SPRING STRAWBERRIES WITH RED WINE VINEGAR

FRESAS CON VINAGRE DE VINO TINTO

SERVES 4

Spain's main strawberry-growing area—some 90 percent of it—is around Huelva, in the southwestern part of Andalucía that abuts Portugal, with the remaining production found largely in Extremadura, Valencia, and the Maresma area of the Costa Brava north of Barcelona. (The industry is large: Spain is the world's second-largest exporter of strawberries, after the United States.) Their arrival in markets across the country in early spring—or even at the end of winter—is eagerly awaited. Perhaps sometimes a bit too eagerly. From my mother-in-law, I learned that a splash of red wine vinegar helps to pull out every bit of flavor from the fruit, especially those early ones that need a slight nudge toward sweet juiciness. The vinegar goes untasted; it simply draws the succulent juices from the strawberries. Choose plump, brilliantly colored strawberries. Don't clean or stem them until ready to prepare.

1 POUND/455 G FRESH STRAWBERRIES
1 TEASPOON RED WINE VINEGAR
2 TEASPOONS SUGAR

1. Rinse, stem, and quarter the strawberries. Place them in a bowl. Dribble with the vinegar and sprinkle with the sugar. Swirl the bowl and then carefully turn over the strawberries with a large spoon to mix. Cover and refrigerate for at least 1 hour, turning over with a spoon from time to time.

2. Spoon the strawberries and any juice into individual dessert bowls and served chilled.

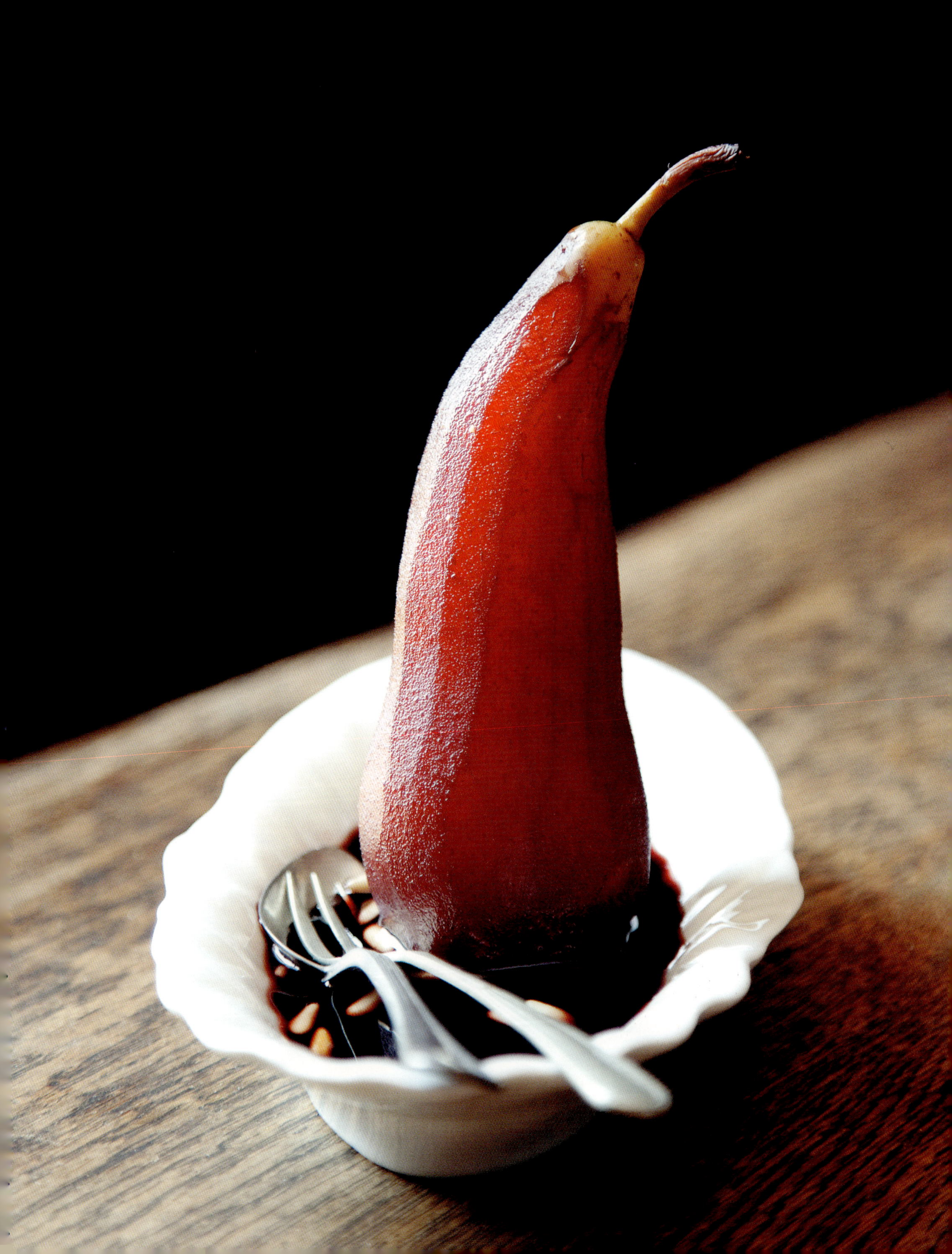

PEARS POACHED IN RED WINE

PERAS AL VINO TINTO

SERVES 6

Widely enjoyed from the central heartland of the country outward to the coasts, this is an elegant dessert—and also an excellent way to use a half bottle of leftover red wine. The pears, carefully stewed in wine aromatized with cinnamon and lemon peel, take on a bold ruby color. The final syrupy sauce should be a touch sweet, but not cloyingly so. This will allow the sweet freshness of the pears to surface and the warm tones of the wine to blossom.

6 RIPE BUT QUITE FIRM PEARS, SUCH AS ANJOU, BOSC, CONFERENCE, OR BARTLETT, ABOUT 3 POUNDS/1.4 KG TOTAL

HEAPING ¼ CUP SUGAR

2 CUPS/480 ML MEDIUM RED WINE

1 SMALL CINNAMON STICK

PEEL OF ½ ORGANIC LEMON, WHITE PITH SCRAPED AWAY

¼ CUP/35 G PINE NUTS, DRY-TOASTED (SEE PAGE 340)

1. Peel the pears without removing the stems, leaving them whole. Trim the bottoms so that the pears can stand upright.

2. In a large, deep sauté pan, dissolve the sugar in the wine over medium heat, add the cinnamon stick and lemon peel, and set the pears gently in the liquid, laying them down on their sides. Bring the liquid to a boil, reduce the heat to medium-low, and simmer uncovered for 40 minutes, or until the pears are tender but not mushy. As they cook, swirl the pan and baste the pears from time to time (to keep the coloring and flavoring even), as well as turning them occasionally, being careful as they scar easily. (To turn, grasp by the stem with your fingers and use a spoon to cup the bottom of the pear.)

3. Remove the pan from the heat and let cool, swirling it from time to time (to keep the coloring even). Transfer the pears and liquid to a large bowl, cover, and refrigerate until chilled.

4. Place a chilled pear upright on each dessert plate—preferably a white one, to show off the color of the syrupy sauce—by holding the stem and cupping the bottom with a spoon. Drizzle some of the liquid over the pears. Sprinkle some pine nuts around the pooled sauce before serving.

BAKED FIGS

HIGOS AL HORNO

SERVES 4

The farmhouse we've rented in Menorca for the summer has a row of fig trees planted above one of the long rockeries. There are a couple of different varieties, including the most appreciated local one called *figaflor*. In August, when the trees overlap in their ripening, and their flowing abundance offers more figs than we can eat fresh, I begin preserving them in marmalade to take back to Barcelona. But I also save plenty to prepare for dinner guests in a local way—baking the figs for a sweet, juicy dessert called, in the local dialects of the Balearic Islands, *figues al forn*. Serve with a small fork and knife but also a spoon in order to get all of their lovely juices. They are delicious with natural yogurt, fresh whipped cream, or even vanilla ice cream.

¼ CUP/50 G SUGAR
12 FRESH FIGS, ABOUT 1 POUND/455 G TOTAL
½ SMALL RIPE LEMON
1 TABLESPOON SWEET DESSERT WINE, SUCH AS MUSCATEL

1. Preheat the oven to 350°F/180°C/gas mark 4.

2. In a small saucepan, bring ½ cup/120 ml water and the sugar to a boil while stirring to dissolve the sugar. Remove the pan from the heat.

3. Gently rinse the figs and trim the stems flush to where the fruit begins to curve outward. In a baking dish, set the figs upright. Squeeze the lemon and dribble the sugar water over the top.

4. Bake for 15 minutes. Sprinkle the wine over top of the figs and bake for another 15 minutes, or until the figs are tender and succulent. Watch that the tops do not burn.

5. Remove from the oven and let cool. Divide the figs among dessert plates. Spoon the burgundy-hued syrup from the baking dish over the top. Serve at room temperature, or cover and refrigerate until slightly chilled.

The name of this rustic dessert, the eminent Catalan gastro-historian Néstor Luján argues, derives from what was given to itinerant musicians playing at village festivals during the autumn harvests. Curiously, *postres* is always plural here—"desserts" in Catalan—not singular, even when referring to a single dish. Perhaps the musicians had to make do with the nuts for more than one meal? While the classic combination includes almonds, hazelnuts, walnuts, raisins, and prunes, other dried fruits are added to the blend, often depending on what can be found in the pantry.

Today there is no Catalan dessert more emblematic of the countryside than a platter of nuts and dried fruits and some Muscatel or another sweet wine. The wine comes to the table in a *porró*, a thin-spouted glass beaker. (In Spanish, it's called a *porrón*.) Held at arm's length, the porró is tilted downward and a stream of wine is shot straight into the mouth. The wine surely aided digestion, but I can't help but see it as part of the musicians' pay, too. Apart from not needing to dirty glasses, the porró, Luján added, served another purpose. It limited the amount of wine that could be gulped to an "honest" amount, surely no small consideration with those wily minstrels.

MUSICIANS' DESSERT

POSTRES DE MÚSIC

SERVES 4 TO 6

¼ CUP/30 G TOASTED ALMONDS
¼ CUP/30 G TOASTED HAZELNUTS
¼ CUP/30 G WALNUT HALVES
2 TABLESPOONS PINE NUTS, DRY-TOASTED (SEE PAGE 340)
¼ CUP/35 G SEEDLESS RAISINS
4 TO 8 DRIED APRICOTS
4 TO 8 DRIED FIGS
4 TO 8 PRUNES
MUSCATEL OR ANOTHER SWEET DESSERT WINE

On a platter, arrange the almonds, hazelnuts, walnuts, pine nuts, raisins, apricots, figs, and prunes in an attractive manner by type. Serve with glasses of Muscatel.

MENORCAN GIN
gin de Menorca

The bean-shaped island of Menorca is small—just 27 miles/43 km long and between 6 and 12 miles/10 and 20 km wide—and strikingly rural. Mahón (called Maó in *Menorquí*, the distinct Catalan dialect spoken here), the island's largest city, has a population of just 30,000 (out of an island total of 90,000). It sits at the head of a lengthy, finger-thin inlet dotted with tiny islands and sheltered by hills. Some claim it is the finest port in the entire Mediterranean. The English surely thought so.

Britain gained control of Menorca in 1708 during the War of Spanish Succession, and then negotiated to keep it through the Treaty of Utrecht after the war ended. They moved the island's capital from ancient Ciutadella to Mahón, and used it as their main Mediterranean seaport for most of the eighteenth century. Their clearest fingerprints today are seen in the Georgian-style architecture, with its obvious references to the classicism of Palladio, and distinctive ruddy red walls that deepen in late summer afternoons to almost scarlet.

Their tastiest legacy, though, is *ginebra*, a locally made gin that is aromatic, woodsy, and distinctly herbal. Menorcans began distilling gin to supply the British flotilla, and kept on doing so after the flotilla pulled out two hundred years later. Made with wine alcohol (most gins are distilled from grain or malt) and flavored with juniper berries (from the Pyrenees mountains) and wild aromatic herbs local to the island, gin remains an important part of Menorca's gastronomic DNA.

The main manufacturer today is the Pons family, which has been bottling and selling gin under the Xoriguer label for the last century. The factory is located at the end of the city's magnificent port, just across from where ferries from Barcelona, Valencia, and Palma de Mallorca arrive. Still made in wood-fired stills and stored in vast oak barrels, the gin is bottled in distinctive green glass bottles. The label carries an image of the family's eighteenth-century windmill, which gives its name to the brand.

Locals drink *gin de Menorca* with a slice of lemon—then it's called a *pellofa*—or with lemon juice and lemon soda. This is the festive *pomada* (see page 315), a key ingredient to any Menorcan fiesta.

MENORCAN GIN SORBET

SORBETE DE GIN DE MENORCA

MAKES A SCANT 1 QUART/1 L

In summer, sorbets help mitigate the startling Spanish heat. Their roots, says esteemed Spanish food writer María Jesús Gil de Antuñano, date back to the ancient tradition of mixing the pulp of fruit with honey and snow. Introduced on Spanish soil during the Muslim rule, using snow gathered in the Sierra Nevada outside Granada and stored in caves, the techniques for making sorbets might have changed, but they have lost little of their original appeal. Today, there are various sorbets prepared across the country, with lemon being the most popular.

This interesting, elegant sorbet comes from Menorca and is prepared with lemon juice and the island's most famous and distinctive product, gin (see facing page). I have adapted a recipe from Josep Borràs and his son Damià's book *La cuina del menorquins* (The Cuisine of the Menorcans). It is, of course, easiest to prepare in a sorbet (or ice cream) maker, but it can be made with a bowl and fork by gradually adding the gin and breaking up the liquid as it freezes. That is the method that the Borràs pair uses, and the one I follow when I make it at home. For best results, use a rounded bowl as opposed to a container with straight sides.

1½ CUPS/300 G SUGAR
1 CUP/240 ML FRESHLY SQUEEZED LEMON JUICE
¼ CUP/60 ML FRESHLY SQUEEZED ORANGE JUICE
8 TABLESPOONS/120 ML MENORCAN XORIGUER GIN OR ANOTHER GIN, PREFERABLY WINE-BASED
1 EGG WHITE, AT ROOM TEMPERATURE

1. In a saucepan, bring 1½ cups/360 ml water to a boil with the sugar, stirring to dissolve. Reduce the heat to low and gently boil for 5 minutes. Remove from the heat. Strain the lemon and orange juices through a cheesecloth and into the syrup. Let cool completely. Pour into a bowl. Place in the freezer.

2. When the juice begins to freeze, scrape the edges of the bowl with a fork or spoon, and stir in 2 tablespoons of the gin. Return to the freezer. When the juice begins to freeze again, scrape the sides, add another 2 tablespoons gin, and freeze again. Repeat this two more times, until all of the gin has been added.

3. When the mixture has the consistency of slushy granita, prepare the egg white. In a clean bowl, beat the egg white with a mixer over medium speed to soft peaks that are opaque and still moist. Fold it into the gin mixture. Return the bowl to the freezer. When it is nearly frozen, whisk with a fork. Freeze a final time. (Keep in the freezer for up to 1 week.)

4. To serve, scoop into balls and place in chilled sorbet glasses or small bowls.

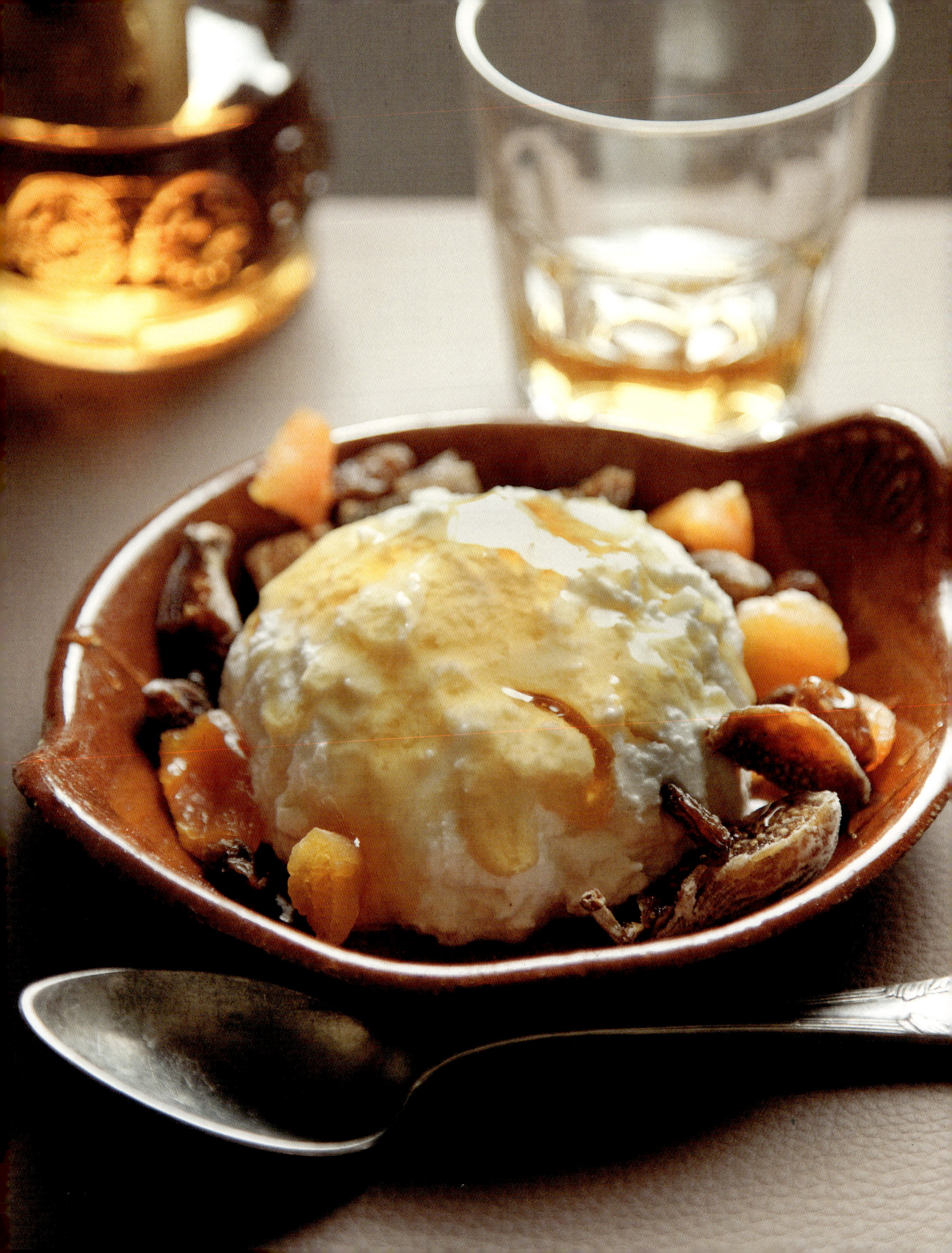

FRESH CHEESE WITH HONEY

MEL I MATÓ

SERVES 4

Fresh cheese drizzled with honey and garnished with nuts and dried fruit couldn't make for a simpler dessert. In Castilla (and indeed around Spain), the slightly firm *queso fresco* from Burgos is a favorite choice, while in Catalunya and along the Pyrenees mountain range, it's mató. Mató is a soft, textured cheese, a bit grainy, made with pasteurized milk from cows, sheep, or a mixture of the two. (Originally it was from goat's milk, though it is considered too heavy and greasy for many today.) Farmer cheese or ricotta is a good substitute. Traditionally *mel i mató* (literally "honey and mató") is served with one of the lovely, bright dessert wines from the Mediterranean—those from Valencia and Alicante are especially nice—such as Muscatel or *vino rancio*. The latter is a sweet, fortified, and aged wine whose name translates literally to "rancid wine." It is anything but. It is a bright, aged wine, oxidized by the sun in large glass jugs.

½ CUP/70 G ROUGHLY CHOPPED MIXED NUTS, SUCH AS WALNUTS, HAZELNUTS, ALMONDS, AND PINE NUTS

2 CUPS/400 G MATÓ, FRESH FARMER CHEESE (SEE NOTE), QUESO BLANCO, MEXICAN QUESO FRESCO, OR FRESH UNSALTED PART-SKIM RICOTTA

4 TABLESPOONS HONEY

½ CUP/70 G ROUGHLY CHOPPED MIXED DRIED FRUITS, SUCH AS FIGS, APRICOTS, AND RAISINS

MUSCATEL, VINO RANCIO, OR ANOTHER SWEET DESSERT WINE

1. In a small ungreased skillet, warm the nuts over medium-low heat, stirring constantly, until fragrant, 2 to 3 minutes.

2. Mound ½ cup/100 g of the cheese attractively on each dessert plate. Drizzle each with 1 tablespoon of the honey and sprinkle with the nuts and dried fruits. Serve with glasses of dessert wine.

NOTE: Farmer cheese is a type of cottage cheese. Most of the liquid is drained off, giving it a firm consistency and rich flavor. You can find it in the dairy case of most North American supermarkets.

INGREDIENTS

SPANISH CHEESES
quesos españoles

The vast and varied selection of cheeses in Spain bespeaks a lengthy history and distinct traditions. They began in different places: in monasteries; along the ancient pilgrim route to Santiago de Compostela; with shepherds in isolated hamlets and farmers in rural valleys. There are more than one hundred distinct cheeses across Spain—from the mountains along the French border to Galicia (where cheese—*queso*—is called *queixo* in Galician), from Andalucía to Catalunya (where it is called *formatge* in Catalan) and the Canary Islands. Cheese is made from the milk of cows, sheep, and goats, with some blending two or even three different types of milk. There are fresh cheeses, cured ones, blue-veined cheeses, ones with firm, toothy textures, others that are grainy or even crumbly. Nearly thirty Spanish cheeses have been awarded Denominación de Origen (D.O.) or Indicación Geográfica Protegida (I.G.P.) status.

Starting in the very northwest of the country and moving roughly clockwise, here are a dozen standouts.

Queixo Tetilla (Galicia): The word *tetilla* means "nipple" or "teat," which refers to the shape of this tender Galician cow's-milk cheese. Flavors are fresh, sometimes buttery; aromas pleasantly milky; and the texture creamy and a touch elastic. The rind is smooth and pale gold. Minimum aging is seven days.

Queixo do Cebreiro (eastern area of Lugo in Galicia): An unpressed cow's-milk cheese that has a mushroom-like shape from spilling out of the top of the mold. Sold both fresh and cured, it has yogurty aromas and a milky, slightly bitter flavor. Its origins are attributed to Benedictine monks who established a hospital for pilgrims in the mid-ninth century in the village of O Cebreiro. Back in the eighteenth century, it was the most expensive cheese in Spain.

Idiazábal (Gipuzkoa in the Basque Country and northwestern Navarra): Made from the milk of the Latxa and Carranzana breeds of sheep, this firm, smooth cheese is smoked over beech wood, alder, cherry wood, and green hawthorn to add a distinctive aroma and flavor. (In the lower valleys, you can also find it unsmoked.) That flavor, though, should be light rather than intense or overpowering, retain the classic tastes of sheep's-milk cheeses, and have a final sensation of delicateness lacking any bitterness. It is ideal with quince paste and some walnuts.

Queso de Cabrales (Asturias): An intense blue cheese aged for two to four months on wooden shelves inside the natural caves of the Picos de Europa mountains. Usually made with only cow's milk, it's sometimes blended with sheep's or goat's milk. The cheese has a soft, somewhat sticky rind and ivory-white interior riddled with a profusion of blue veins. The consistency is slightly granular, the aroma intense and penetrating, and the flavor milky and salty with slightly acidic notes and a spiciness that deepens with tasting—and persists. Wonderful.

Formatge l'Alt d'Urgell i la Cerdanya (Catalan Pyrenees): A cured cow's-milk cheese from the Pyrenees mountains in northwest Catalunya. This firm, ivory-toned cheese has an up-front, persistent flavor, milky, with notes of both a slight saltiness and vague sweetness.

Tupí (Catalan Pyrenees): Grainy, ivory colored, and spreadable, this fermented shepherd's cheese is made using hard, leftover goat's cheese. The cheese is grated, moistened with olive oil and *aguardiente de orujo* (like grappa, a distillation from pomace), and aged in small clay pots (called *tupí* in Catalan) where the cheese ripens into characteristic sharp, aggressive, and piquant flavors. Strong and greasy, and utterly delicious.

Mató (Catalan Pyrenees): Fresh mató has a soft, slightly granular texture, at times almost sandy, with a milky, salt-free freshness. It can be made from the milk of cows or goats or a blend of the two. It ideally partners with honey and some dried nuts for a dessert.

Queso Mahón (Menorca): In preparing this cow's-milk cheese, the curds are placed in a bag (as opposed to a hard mold) that is knotted and pressed. The final form is a flattened, boxy shape with soft corners. The rind has a golden-orange hue from being rubbed with olive oil, lard, and *pimentón* (paprika). There are four levels of curing—*tierno* (aged 21 to 60 days), *semicurado* (2 to 5 months), *curado* (5 months), and an even longer-aged one called *añejo*. Wedges of añejo are bold, salty, and even somewhat brittle.

Queso de Tronchón (Aragón): Found in the mountainous Maestrazgo range, and containing a mix of goat's and sheep's milk, it is molded into a roundish form with a crater in the top and bottom and aged from 3 to 8 months. It has a glossy butter-yellow rind, while the interior is ivory colored, springy, with a smooth texture, and pleasing dairy aromas. Cervantes twice mentions the cheese in the second part of *Don Quixote*, most memorably when a messenger tells Sancho Panza: "If your lordship wants a drink, although warm, pure, I have a gourd full of expensive wine, with I do not know how many slices of Tronchón cheese, which will serve as an attention-getter and wake-up to your thirst, in case it's sleeping."

Queso Manchego (La Mancha): Spain's most famous cheese is made exclusively from the Manchega breed of sheep that graze the herby, dry scrub of La Mancha in the center of the country. A bold, classic cheese, with older wheels becoming sharp and slightly grainy.

Torta del Casar (central plains of Extremadura): This unique and ancient sheep's cheese is aged for 60 to 90 days in humid conditions and turned over every day until ripe. To eat, you slice the top off like a lid and spoon out the pale-yellow cheese. It's soft and spreadable, greasy and stiffly creamy, with smooth but intense aromas and slightly bitter flavors. Best at room temperature spread over crackers or toasted bread. One of Spain's great delicacies.

Queso Zamorano (Zamora in Castilla y León): A pressed, compact sheep's-milk cheese from the Churra and Castellana breeds in the northwestern meseta. Cylinder-shaped with a yellowish rind, the compact, ivory-toned interior has a smooth texture and milky, buttery flavors. Tastes are intense, and lightly piquant in longer-aged cheeses. Minimum maturing is 100 days.

CHAPTER 14

DRINKS
bebidas

Of Europe's three and a half million hectares of vineyards—95 percent of those dedicated to wine production—28 percent are in Spain. That is more than in France (25 percent) or Italy (23 percent). A bottle of wine on the table is a fundamental part of a Spanish meal. While vintages and celebrated winemakers might be appreciated, many in the country buy their table wine from the local cooperative. Co-ops, of course, bottle their vino, but also usually sell it by the liter from huge casks. For this, you take your own container to fill under the tap.

Wines are usually enjoyed on their own, though sometimes they get a festive makeover in the form of sangria. I have a mixed relationship with this often sugary drink, but recently have begun preparing, and enjoying, naturally sweetened versions with both red wine (see page 311) and white wine (see page 313). It is possible to make sangria using Cava, local champagne-style bubbly, though I don't recommend it. A headache is almost guaranteed.

A simpler *tinto de verano* (summer red wine) is red wine cut with some *gaseosa*, a plain, sweet carbonated soda (usually La Casera brand) served over ice cubes with a slice of lemon. This is a favorite drink of summer café terraces, beachside *chiringuitos* (seasonal restaurants, commonly not much more than a shack), and backyards among friends. It is also an excellent way to use the tail end of a bottle that has been open for a couple of days. (Especially one of those rougher-edged bottles from the co-op.)

Homemade liqueurs and liquors remain popular. In Galicia, *licor de café* (see page 316), *licor de guinda* (a small, sour cherry-like fruit), and *licor de hierbas aromáticas* (aromatic herbs) are all popular. These are prepared using as a base *aguardiente*, a strong and clear spirit made from the residue of grape-pressings like Italian grappa or French marc. In Navarra and the Basque Country, the most famous home liqueur and fine digestive is called *pacharán*, made by infusing sloe berries in anisette.

Perhaps the most common *digestivo*, though, is a shot of brandy or rum added to coffee as an after-lunch tonic. Or a morning one. (I am still shocked at the popularity of this. Pull off at any rural roadside café in the morning to see just how common it is.)

While at times it may seem otherwise, not all Spanish drinks are alcoholic or spiked with alcohol. There are lush milky drinks like *leche merengada* (see page 308), or refreshing, slushy granitas made from lemon (see page 309) or coffee to quench a summer's thirst.

And, of course, the well-known and beloved hot drinking chocolate (see page 306). Is there a more soothing way to begin a cold day than with a cup of that? Or, like many, end it, in the wee hours of the morning after a late night out?

HORCHATA
de
Chufa
Natural
Qué Rica!
y LIMON
GRANIZADO
ELABORACION ARTESANA

SPANISH CINNAMON-SCENTED DRINKING CHOCOLATE IN THE CUP

CHOCOLATE A LA TAZA CON CANELA

SERVES 4

When sixteenth-century Spanish conquistadors arrived in modern-day Mexico, report Rosa Tovar and Monique Fuller in *3,000 años de cocina española* (3,000 Years of Spanish Cooking), they found Mayans drinking chocolate "with hot chile pepper, ground corn, or certain flowers." Sent back to Spain, sweetened with honey or sugar, chocolate swiftly became popular. According to Tovar and Fuller, "The Spanish immediately perfumed the already sweet chocolate with vanilla, also from the Americas, and spices imported to Europe, such as cinnamon, cloves, coriander, or black pepper." While Spain has become more conservative in its spicing over the centuries, drinking chocolate—generally now only lightly flavored with vanilla or cinnamon—remains roundly popular at festivals, in bars and cafés, and in homes.

I have adapted Tovar and Fuller's recipe, which I particularly like because it adheres to the more original sense of the drink—thick, dark, a touch bitter, with a lingering taste of cinnamon in the back of the throat. It is a bold drink for chocolate lovers. To smooth or soften the flavor, use milk, or at least some milk, instead of water.

While I call it "drinking" chocolate, "dipping" chocolate is probably more accurate for its consistency. As goes a typical saying that my wife likes to repeat, *"Las cosas claras y la chocolate espeso."* (That is, "Things [as in ideas] should be clear and chocolate thick.") Serve it with spoons and a piece of spongy cake like bizcocho (see page 279), a magdalena muffin (see page 282), or, even better, hot churros.

1 SMALL CINNAMON STICK
8 OUNCES/225 G CHOCOLATE THAT IS AT LEAST 50% COCOA, BROKEN INTO PIECES
1 TABLESPOON CORNSTARCH
3 OR 4 TABLESPOONS SUGAR OR MORE

1. In a saucepan, bring 1¾ cups/420 ml water to a boil with the cinnamon stick and boil for about 2 minutes to perfume the water. Remove the cinnamon stick. Add the chocolate and stir to dissolve.

2. In a small cup, dissolve the cornstarch in 3 tablespoons cold water and stir into the chocolate. Over medium heat, bring to a boil, stirring without stopping until it thickens and dribbles, more than runs, off the spoon, 5 to 8 minutes. Stir in the sugar. Taste for sweetness, and add more sugar if desired.

3. Serve immediately in low, wide tea or coffee cups (not mugs).

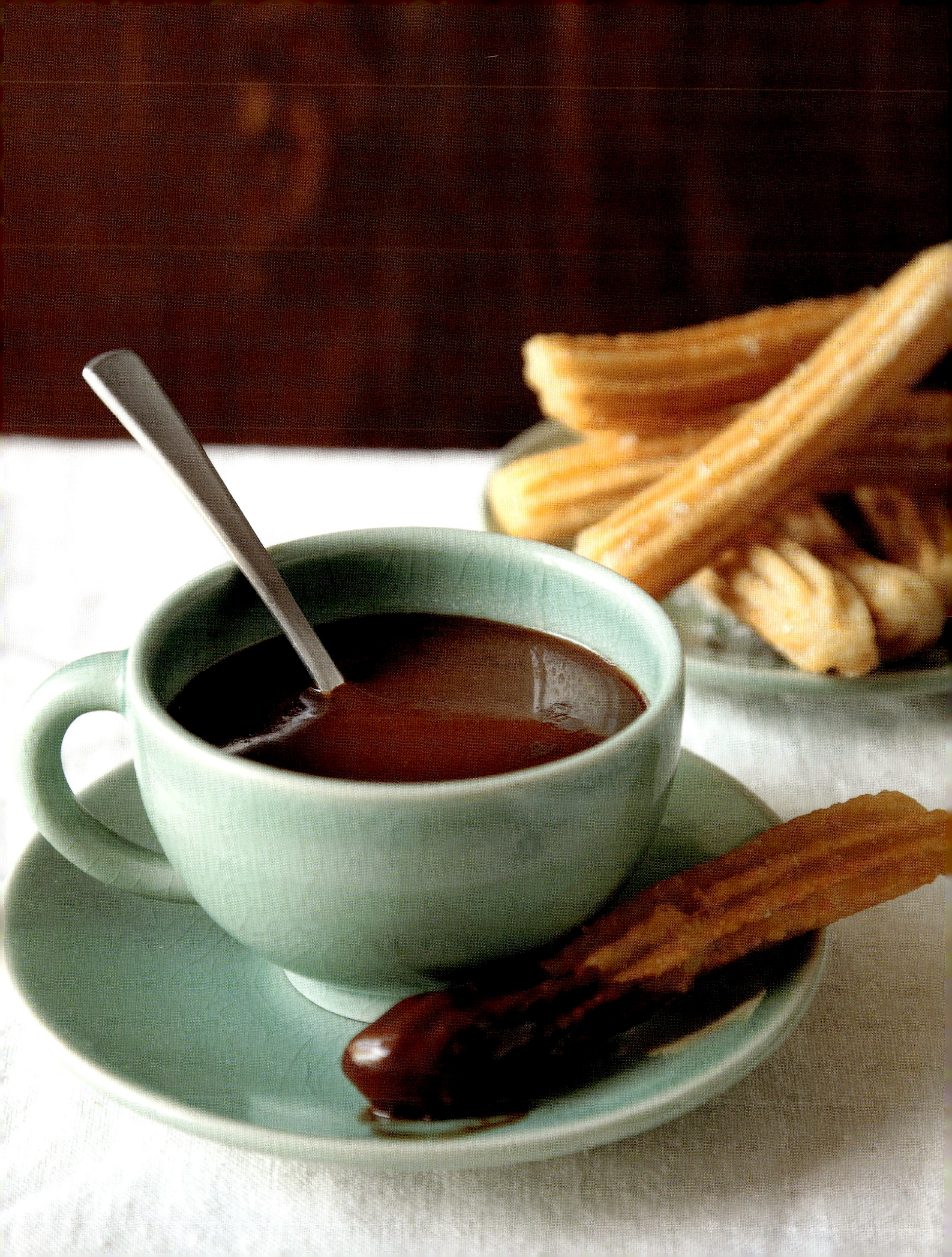

MERINGUED MILK

LECHE MERENGADA

SERVES 6

This is another sweet drink that shows its Moorish influences in the pronounced cinnamon and citrus flavors. Like *granizados* (slushy granitas) along the Levant, this is a drink once prepared for Sundays or festivals, or sipped around a village café table set out on the plaza in the late afternoon. The tradition of preparing leche merengada, though, has sadly begun to fade somewhat, and its popularity has been replaced by the broad assortment of ever-growing commercial drinks available. Serve very cold, almost slushy. It is filling and delicious.

1 QUART/1 L MILK
½ CUP/100 G SUGAR
1 SMALL CINNAMON STICK
PEEL OF 1 LEMON, WHITE PITH SCRAPED AWAY
2 EGG WHITES, AT ROOM TEMPERATURE
GROUND CINNAMON FOR DUSTING (OPTIONAL)

1. In a large saucepan, add the milk, sugar, cinnamon stick, and lemon peel and bring to a boil over medium heat, stirring to keep the milk from scorching. Remove the pan from the heat to let cool and the flavors infuse.

2. Pour into a wide stainless-steel or glass bowl and place in the freezer until nearly frozen but still slightly runny.

3. In a clean bowl, beat the egg whites with a mixer over medium speed to soft peaks that are opaque and still moist. Fold the egg whites into the milk.

4. Spoon into glasses and lightly dust with cinnamon, if desired. Serve very cold with tall spoons and straws.

The Spanish tradition of drinking ices dates back to the Moorish rule of the country, using snow collected in the Sierra Nevada, the stunning range of mountains southwest of Granada. Although you can find a (limited) array of granizado flavors today, the two classics—lemon and coffee—remain the most popular.

Generally, when prepared at home, the liquid is never quite allowed to freeze and is shaken or stirred from time to time until slushy. It can be done using either a bowl or plastic bottles. (I give directions for both.) Another method that also works is to freeze it completely, and then thaw in the refrigerator, shaking and breaking up with a spoon once it is nearly slush.

SLUSHY LEMON GRANITA

GRANIZADO DE LIMÓN

MAKES ABOUT 1¾ QUARTS/1.6 L

4 ORGANIC LEMONS, SUCH AS THIN-SKIN MEYERS
1 CUP/200 G SUGAR
FRESH MINT LEAVES FOR GARNISHING

1. Scrub the lemons. If waxed, dunk the lemons in boiling water and firmly wipe off the wax. Zest the lemons into a large bowl, grating only the yellow part. (The white pith is bitter.) Halve the lemons crosswise and juice them into the bowl. Drop in the lemon peels. Add 6 cups/1.4 L water. Let sit for 30 to 40 minutes.

2. Pour the liquid through a fine-mesh strainer into a large bowl. Press the lemons to get all of the liquid from them, straining that liquid, too. Stir in the sugar until completely dissolved.

3. *To freeze using a bowl:* Pour the liquid into a large glass or plastic bowl. Cover tightly. Place in the freezer. When it begins to freeze, stir with a fork or wire whisk. Repeat two or three times, never letting it completely freeze, until slushy, at least a couple of hours.

To freeze using plastic bottles: Place a funnel over a clean 2-quart/2-L plastic or glass bottle (or two smaller ones) and pour in the liquid. Close tightly. Place in the freezer. When it begins to freeze, shake. Repeat two or three times, never letting it completely freeze, until slushy, at least a couple of hours.

4. Ladle or pour into glasses. Garnish with mint leaves and serve with straws.

DRINKS

SANGRÍA

A big glass or terra-cotta *jarra* (pitcher or jug) of icy, fruit-filled, and spiked wine is perhaps Spain's most iconic beverage. Sangria!

Generally prepared with red wine, chopped fresh fruits, a shot or two of liqueur, sugar to sweeten it, and a carbonated beverage to fill it out, it's chilled and served over plenty of ice. Sangria jugs come with a pinched spout to keep the fruit and ice from sloshing out and a wooden spoon to give it a final, vigorous stir before pouring into glasses.

Spaniards particularly enjoy it during casual summer barbecues, on seaside terraces, and in *chiringuitos* (seasonal beach cafés) that dot the country's lengthy coastline. It's refreshing and fruity, sure, but above all, casual and often festive.

My introduction came more than fifteen years ago when I moved to Barcelona. That first summer, the woman I had followed to Spain and I spent many weekends swimming in the coves along the Costa Brava, or from the long, white beaches in Tarragona. For a late lunch, we'd find a shady terrace and order fried squid (see page 92), steamed octopus doused in olive oil and paprika (see page 91), and spicy potatoes, along with a jarra of sangria. Here we'd linger as the sun eventually softened and the pine trees turned deeper shades of green.

So I have good memories of drinking sangria, but less so of the drink itself. Too many bars and beachside cafés serve watered down, over-sweet, headache-inducing versions, and over the years my wife and I, like most of our friends, stopped drinking it.

But then not long ago, I sampled a version very different than I remembered. It was sophisticated and more complex in its flavors, and sweetened naturally with fresh fruits. That reawakened our interest, and—at least at home—we began to give the classic drink another chance, making versions with red wine as well as white wine for our (usually surprised) friends who came to dinner.

The key to good sangria, I learned, begins with the choice of wine, namely very young and fruity. For reds, that means plummy ones that carry touches of forest fruits, strawberries, and raspberries, even hints of vanilla. The second is the liqueur. A triple sec will add a touch of citrus, while the brilliant yellow Licor 43 some vanilla notes. But a tiny amount of Licor 43 is enough—any more and it becomes overpowering and cloying. And finally, ripe and sweet fresh fruit such as peaches, apricots, pears, certain (nonacidic) apples, and fresh berries. That's it.

Good—or at least different—sangria is mostly about what to omit, says Antoni Cot, the owner of my local wine shop: no orange juice (you don't want to find pulp), no sugar, no citrus or acidic fruits (that would need sugar), and no fizzy water. Ideally no ice, either, which will water the drink down as the cubes melt. And chilled, but not below 50°F/10°C, at which point the cold begins to stifle the wine's aromas and flavors. (Antoni was quite adamant about this last part.)

These new versions of red wine sangria (see facing page) have been especially successful with appetizers and tapas that are both salty and sweet. White wine sangria (see page 313), on the other hand, prepared with melon, fresh berries, and orange and lemon peels, is light and lovely, fruity, and perhaps more elegant than festive.

These are a long way from those sticky-sweet versions once so enjoyed along the coast. For me, it's the rekindling of an iconic drink by getting closer to its origins.

SUMMER RED WINE SANGRIA

SANGRÍA DE VINO TINTO

MAKES ABOUT 1 QUART/1 L; SERVES 2 TO 4

The classic Spanish sangría is bold with red wine, fruity, and a touch sweet with sugar. This recipe has two of those three attributes. The sweetness here is natural, coming from the fruits themselves. Cointreau, made from both sweet and bitter orange peels, gives the sangria lovely citrus flavors. Avoid adding fizzy water or wedges of citrus fruit (add anything more than peels and it will need sugar), or chilling too deeply. The flavors and aromas of the wine and fruit should come clearly through. While flavors will be diluted by adding ice, in summer—when the temperature soars—adding a couple of cubes to the glass is a temptation that, like most people, I find impossible to resist.

Serve the sangria among friends for an informal, festive drink. It goes well with most tapas. The best pairing? Perhaps dates wrapped in slices of bacon (see page 75), whose lovely salty sweetness is nicely complemented by sangria—as is strong chorizo from Navarra and some tinned *berberechos* (cockles) given a dash of sherry vinegar.

2 RIPE APRICOTS, PEELED, PITTED, AND THINLY SLICED
1 RIPE JUICY PEACH, PEELED, PITTED, AND CHOPPED
1 RIPE PEAR, PEELED, CORED, AND CHOPPED
PEEL OF 1 ORANGE, WHITE PITH SCRAPED AWAY
PEEL OF 1 LEMON, WHITE PITH SCRAPED AWAY
ONE 750-ML BOTTLE YOUNG, FRUITY RED WINE
¼ CUP/60 ML COINTREAU
1 SMALL CINNAMON STICK (OPTIONAL)
LARGE ICE CUBES (OPTIONAL)

1. In a large glass pitcher, jar, or punch bowl, combine the pieces of fruit and citrus peels, pour in the wine and Cointreau, and gently stir. Add the cinnamon stick (if using). Cover tightly with plastic wrap and refrigerate for at least 2 hours, or until chilled.

2. To serve, pour into wine glasses with a few pieces of fruit in each. Add 1 or 2 ice cubes if the weather is hot.

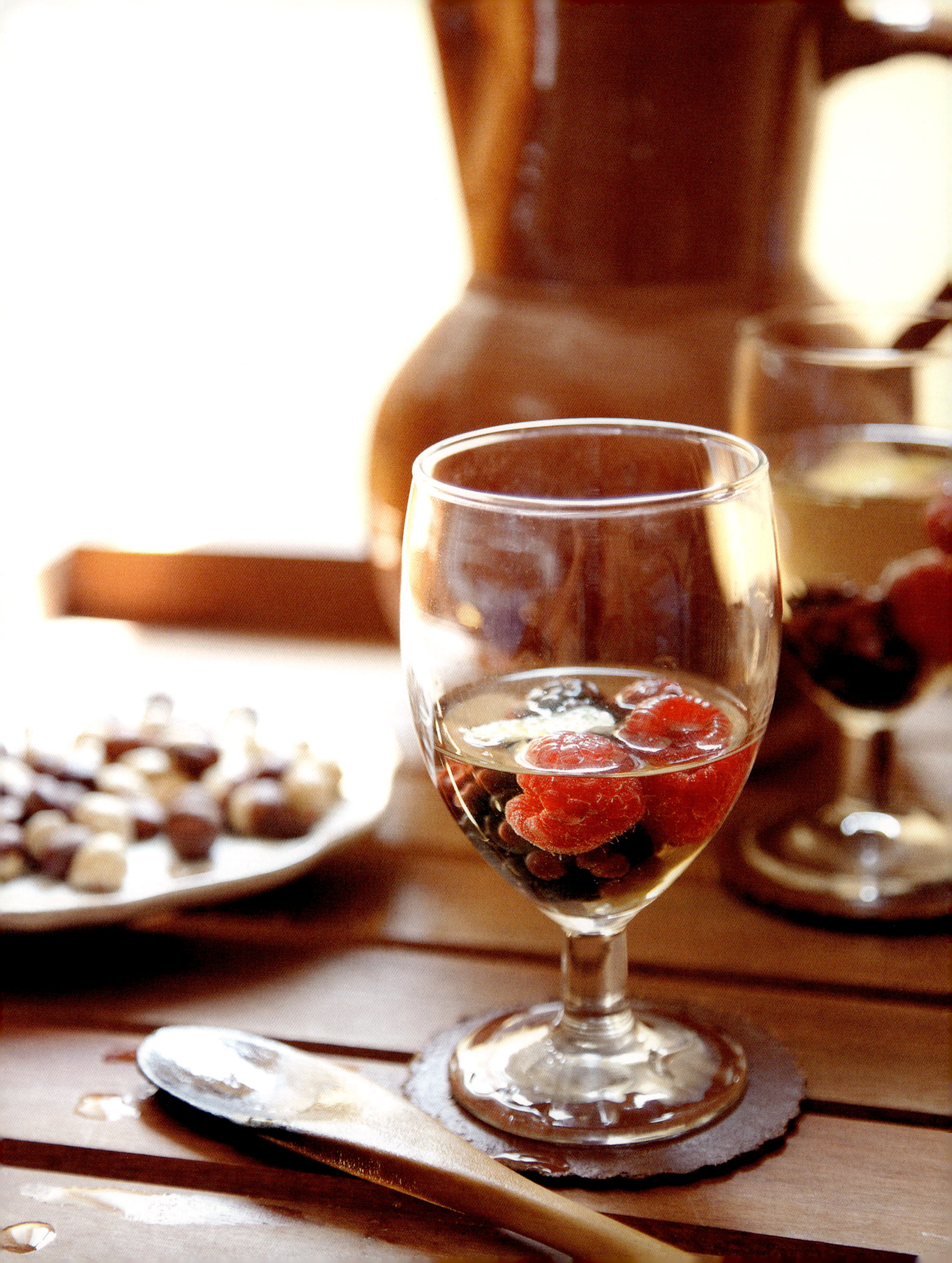

WHITE WINE SANGRIA WITH FRESH BERRIES

SANGRÍA DE VINO BLANCO CON FRUTOS DEL BOSQUE

MAKES ABOUT 1 QUART/1 L; SERVES 2 TO 4

This is a lighter, more sophisticated version of the classic red wine sangria. While best with fresh summer berries, it can be made out of season using frozen ones. Adding some small pieces of honeydew or another summer melon will add a mellow fruity touch.

2 CUPS/455 G MIXED FRESH BERRIES, SUCH AS BLACKBERRIES, RASPBERRIES, STRAWBERRIES, AND RED CURRANTS

PEEL OF 1 ORANGE, WHITE PITH SCRAPED AWAY

PEEL OF 1 LEMON, WHITE PITH SCRAPED AWAY

ONE 750-ML BOTTLE YOUNG, FRUITY WHITE WINE

¼ CUP/60 ML COINTREAU OR TRIPLE SEC

1. In a large glass pitcher, jar, or punch bowl, combine the berries and citrus peels, pour in the wine and Cointreau, and gently stir. Cover tightly with plastic wrap and refrigerate for at least 2 hours, or until chilled.

2. To serve, ladle some sangria with pieces of fruit into wine glasses.

DRINKS

SPANISH WINES
vinos de España

With food comes, of course, wine, so fundamental to the Spanish table—and, for many, part of the daily table. From unlabeled bottles of *vino de la mesa* (table wine) from the local cooperative to cellared vintages produced in the celebrated bodegas of La Rioja, Ribera del Duero, or Priorat; from the whites of Penedès, Rueda, and the Galician Rías Baixas to the *rosados* of Navarra and *Costers del Segre*, Spain has ancient viticulture traditions, world-class producers, and well over a million hectares of vines. There are around seventy wine regions with *Denominación de Origen* (D.O., Denomination of Origin) status. Three regions have a more esteemed, stricter status, *Denominación de Origen Calificada* (D.O.C. Qualified Denomination of Origin): La Rioja, Ribera del Duero, and Priorat.

Wine's importance in Spain cannot be understated. Take La Rioja, where it is king. The region in the northern part of the country is not much bigger than the American state of Delaware, contains only 1 percent of Spain's total area, and has a population of just 300,000 people (with half of those living in the capital, Logroño). Yet there are, by my count, well over 500 wineries on the registry, producing wine from grapes grown by tens of thousands of producers, including such well-known bodegas as R. López de Heredia, Marqués de Murrieta, Marqués de Legarda, Marqués de Riscal, La Rioja Alta, and Muga. Local legend says that Noah's grandson Tubal planted the first vines in La Rioja, though it was probably not until (!) the ancient Romans ruled the area. Traditions for making wines here date from the Middle Ages with monastic life.

The "modern" industry in Spain (and in La Rioja) was stimulated in the 1850s when the odium and then phylloxera outbreaks ravaged vines in France, sending producers south to Spain to buy and, in some cases, stay. Such French influences as long aging in oak barrels remain hallmarks and give the classic Rioja red its mellow, regal tones. As elsewhere in Spain, most wineries in La Rioja have adopted new technologies while remaining faithful to tradition.

A few, though, ardently adhere to the old ways. One of those is R. López de Heredia-Viña Tondonia in Haro. Mercedes López de Heredia, a fourth-generation winemaker passionate about the traditional craft, acknowledges that little has changed in the process since her great-grandfather founded the legendary bodega in 1877. There are no stainless-steel vats or computers controlling the fermentation process; every step is strictly manual. They use only grapes from their vineyards, eschew chemicals, and ferment with natural yeast. The winery has four full-time barrel-makers and their onsite cooperage uses only American oak from the Appalachian mountains. Before bottling, the wine isn't filtered, "just allowed to sit longer" as Mercedes put it, and naturally settle. Below the immaculately preserved original buildings (and a stunning, but jarringly modern tasting room and visitor's "pavilion" designed by Pritzker Prize–winning architect Zaha Hadid) are cellars with 13,000 oak barrels and 1.4 million bottles of wine aging under heavy coats of dust.

On a recent summer day, sipping a classic, full-bodied Viña Tondonia reserva—gentle, silky, aromatic—Mercedes noticed me struggling to identify the bouquet of flavors I was tasting. She said, "My grandfather used to say, 'The best wine is the one you can't describe. The balance is perfect.'" And wines like this are about as close to perfect as possible.

Two things are certain to be present at every village fiesta in Menorca: horses—magnificent stallions with braided manes and head finery parading among the crowds—and a lemony gin cocktail called *pomada*. One key ingredient is local, herbal-tasting gin (see page 298); another is lemons. Once made using only fresh lemon juice, it now generally includes a carbonated lemon beverage like Kas *limón*, too. (See Sources, page 345, for where to find Kas lemon soda.)

A friend named Cesc Segura introduced me to pomada in Menorca, and I still find his version of the drink to be the best. He combines the lemon juice, sugar, and gin in an empty water bottle, shakes to blend the ingredients, and then places it in the freezer. The Kas is added just before serving so that it retains its fizz. He uses equal proportions of gin, Kas, and fresh lemon juice, plus 1 tablespoon of sugar per lemon that he squeezed, but that depends on the tartness of the lemons. The drink should be sweetish, but still a touch tart, with the lovely aromas of juniper, pine, and the Mediterranean herbs of the gin coming through the lemon. Basically, you should be able to *taste* the gin, not just *feel* it.

MENORCAN GIN COCKTAIL WITH FRESH LEMON JUICE AND LEMON SODA

POMADA

SERVES 4

1 CUP/240 ML FRESH LEMON JUICE
SUGAR
1 CUP/240 ML MENORCA XORIGUER GIN OR ANOTHER GIN, PREFERABLY WINE-BASED
ICE CUBES
1 CUP/240 ML KAS OR FANTA LEMON SODA OR ANOTHER LEMON-FLAVORED CARBONATED DRINK

1. In a bowl, add the lemon juice and 1 tablespoon sugar per lemon used when juicing. Stir to dissolve. Taste and add more sugar if it is still extremely tart. (The lemon soda will sweeten the drink a touch more.) Pour into a glass jug or water bottle along with the gin. Place in the freezer until very cold.

2. Fill four tall glasses with ice, pour in the lemon and gin mixture, and add the lemon soda. Serve very cold.

In Galicia, *aguardiente*—a clear and potent spirit distilled from grape pressings like Italian grappa and French marc—is commonly used to make some wonderful home liqueurs. *Licor de hierbas*, infused with a dozen aromatic herbs, is a brilliant, emerald-yellowish drink. Around the area of Ourense, not far from the northern Portuguese border, the most famous and popular home licor is prepared with coffee. Sweetened with sugar and aromatized with cinnamon and orange peel, the taste of the coffee comes through, so choose the roast with care. Some people add in a piece of dark chocolate for its seductive cacao notes.

Aficionados recommend letting it *reposar* (rest) for *at least* one year before drinking, but a few weeks after filtering the mixture into a bottle is all it lasts in our home before I start sipping it. Normally it is drunk very cold, often in squat *chupito* (shot) glasses taken from the freezer. Nonconformists, though, have been known to add a shot of it to a *cortado*, an espresso cut with a bit of hot milk.

ORENSE-STYLE COFFEE LIQUEUR

LICOR DE CAFÉ AL ESTILO DE OURENSE

MAKES ABOUT 1 QUART/1 L

1 CUP/200 G SUGAR

3½ OUNCES/100 G GROUND COFFEE

PEEL OF 1 ORANGE, WHITE PITH SCRAPED AWAY

1 CINNAMON STICK

ONE 700-ML BOTTLE AGUARDIENTE DE ORUJO, GRAPPA, OR MARC, OR ANOTHER WINE SPIRIT

1. In a saucepan, bring ¾ cup/180 ml water to a boil. Add the sugar, stir until it dissolves, and then let boil for 2 minutes. Remove from the heat, and stir in the coffee until dissolved. Add the orange peel and cinnamon stick, and let cool for a few minutes before pouring in the aguardiente. Stir to blend, and let completely cool.

2. Cover and let sit for 7 to 10 days, stirring one or two times each day.

3. Filter the liqueur through a paper coffee filter, change the filter, and filter a second time. Pour into one or two sterilized glass bottles.

4. Store in a dry, cool, and dark place for 6 months, or until the liquid takes on a deep, rich coffee flavor.

5. Place in the freezer at least 2 to 3 hours before serving. Serve very cold, ideally between 46° and 50°F/8° and 10°C, in small glasses.

AGUARDIENTE DE ORUJO

The word *aguardiente* means "burning water," and sipping the potent spirit, it often feels just like that. (Or, more specifically, like "water that burns.") Aguardiente is a high-grade alcohol distilled from *orujos*, the pressing of grape skins, seeds, and stalks. In Italy, this pomace brandy is called grappa, and in France *eau-de-vie de marc* or just *marc*. In parts of Spain, it goes by the name *aguardiente de orujo*, or just aguardiente, or just orujo.

In Spain, such spirits have a lengthy tradition. It began after the Arabs in Spain taught the locals the principles of alcohol distillation sometime in the ninth century. Today, orujos are most typical in two regions. The first is the valley of Liébana, in the southwest of Cantabria, with production centered around the town of Potes. This is an area that produces little wine—and not such great wine, at that—but very good orujo. Distilled at low temperature, the orujos from Liébana are smooth and flavorful, even elegant.

The second region is Galicia. An *orujo gallego* is usually called aguardiente (or, in Galician, *aguardente*). Some are plain, others infused with herbs. There are aged aguardientes, too, called *envejecidos*, which have an amber color and smoother bite.

While some like a shot of it in the morning for strength more than flavor—they call it *matar el bicho*, literally "to kill the bug"—aguardiente is generally drunk as a *digestivo* after a meal. It should be at room temperature, or slightly warmed in the hands, to fully appreciate its flavors and aromas (often recalling grapes). The water-clear spirit can also be mixed with sorbets, especially lemon; added to pastry dough; or dashed into an espresso. Around Ourense, it is the base for making homemade licor de café, a popular regional coffee liqueur (see facing page).

Aguardiente is also an excellent and typical preserver for fruits. In Galicia, cherries (see page 320) and their more acidic counterpart, guindillas, are favorites to conserve this way with some cinnamon and coffee beans. Sometimes in the center of the country you find trout in aguardiente. In the Catalan Pyrenees, aguardiente is blended with grated aged cheese and fermented in earthenware pots into an emblematic mountain cheese called tupí. Soft and spreadable, a touch greasy, and highly aromatic, rustic tupí carries a heady mountain snap.

Clearly, many homemade preparations use the spirit—and sometimes even the aguardiente is homemade. Both Galicia and Potes have a tradition of home-distilled orujos. Some of them are even smooth. Most, though, are pure burning water.

CHAPTER 15

SWEET AND SAVORY HOMEMADE CONSERVES
conservas caseras

How to preserve the spoils of a season to enjoy all year long, or at least long enough to use before they can rot? How to store them in order to survive winter? Or a long voyage—the Phoenicians sailing across the Mediterranean, the Basques across the North Atlantic in search of whales and cod, the conquistadors heading to the New World in search of silver and gold. People have been struggling with these questions from the beginning.

Whether it is quince, tomatoes, or asparagus, pork or partridge, even anchovies, there is a traditional time to harvest, slaughter, or hunt, a time of abundance and even prime flavor. From the lengthy tradition of preserving, born out of practicality and perfected with centuries of trials and errors, we now have what can best be called delicacies. Using smoke, salt, alcohol, olive oil, and vinegar, even honey, and then technology brought about with Nicolas Appert's early nineteenth-century successes in canning, the lifespan of countless products was extended. And, in many cases, their flavors changed for the better. I would vigorously argue that desalted salt cod is superior in flavor and texture to fresh cod, that the flavors created in curing a leg of ham are far more complex than any other way it can be prepared, and that tinned cockles carry richer nuances of the sea than they do fresh.

Spain is unusual in its love for—and vast array of—conserves, and no country has guarded, or expanded, the tradition as strongly. Using the best products available, these *conservas* are some of the most sublime gourmet goods produced in Spain.

Times have changed. Seasons have gotten longer. (Or, as my wife's aunt says, "Seasons were shorter then, and we had to grab it when it was ripe.") We have freezers and markets that stock products that, though not in season locally, are somewhere else. (Or flown in from abroad.) Yet homemade conserves remain a key part of the country *despensa* (pantry). Marmalades, tomato sauces, quince paste (see page 323), stewed vegetables, dried herbs, cherries macerating in a clear spirit with a cinnamon stick and a couple of coffee beans (see page 320), or dried fruits in sweet wine (see page 326)—these are the flavors of a grandmother's pantry, flavors of the countryside well-organized along tall, narrow shelves.

Indeed, there remains an almost inexpressible pleasure in opening a jar of marmalade put up in late summer and spreading it on a slice of toast deep into the short days of winter. Spooning a couple of cherries (see page 320) that I began soaking in spring into a champagne glass for guests in January makes me giddy.

There is also an ample range of savory preserves. The finest for me are the broad range of escabeches, vinegar and olive oil marinades often flavored with onions, carrots, and herbs. Partridge or quail (see page 330), bonito tuna, sardines (see page 332), mussels—you name it. Even oysters.

With a handful of notable exceptions—jams and marmalades being the most obvious—most home conserves are prepared these days to be eaten sooner rather than later.

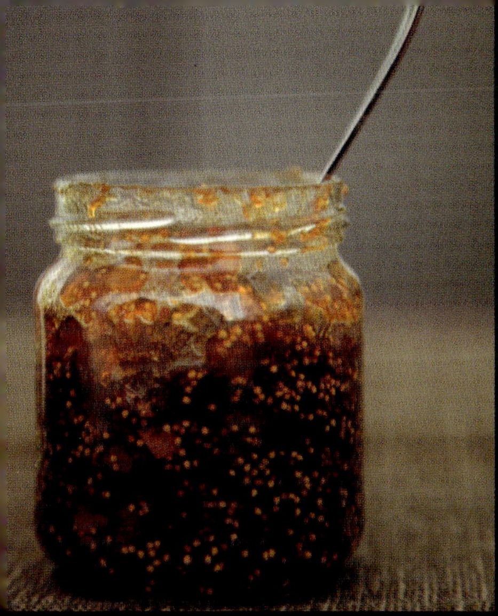
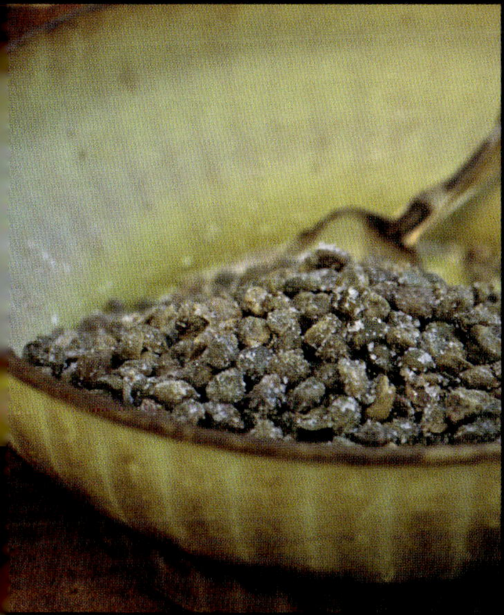
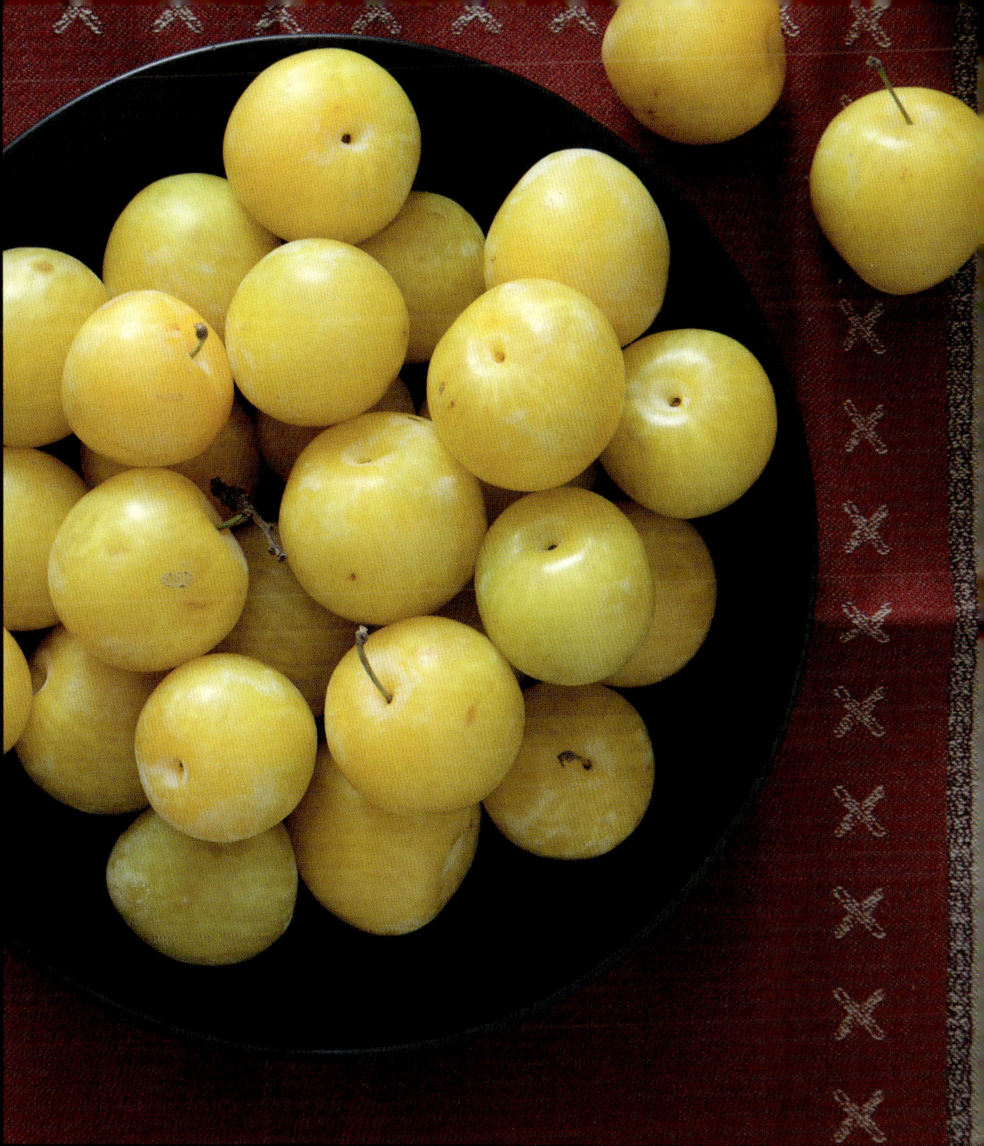
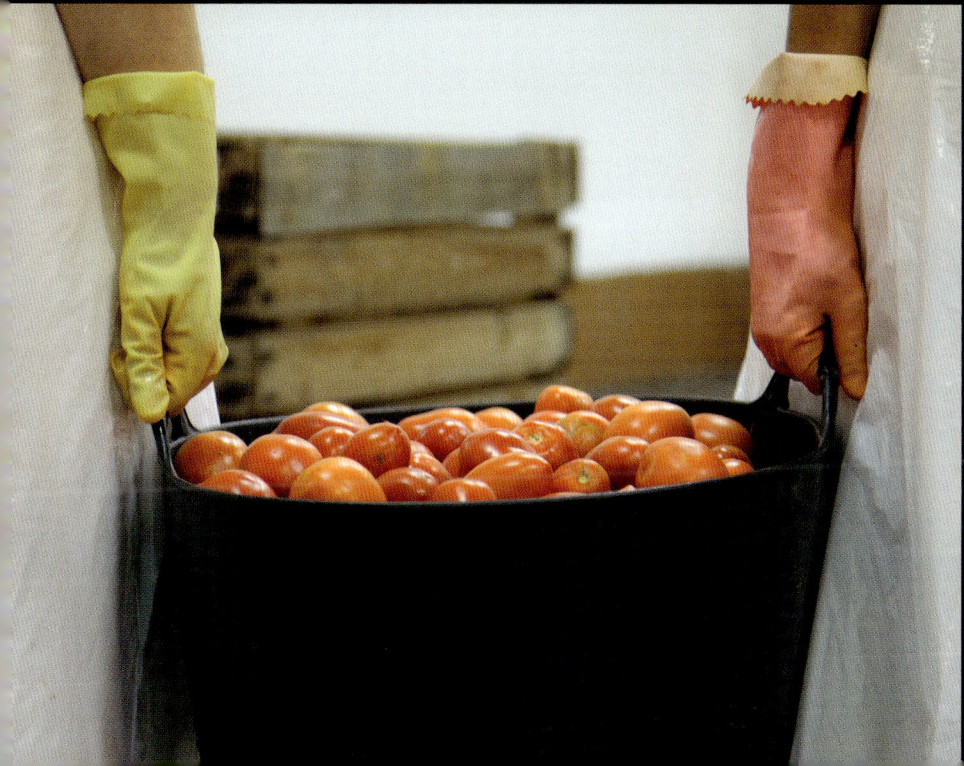
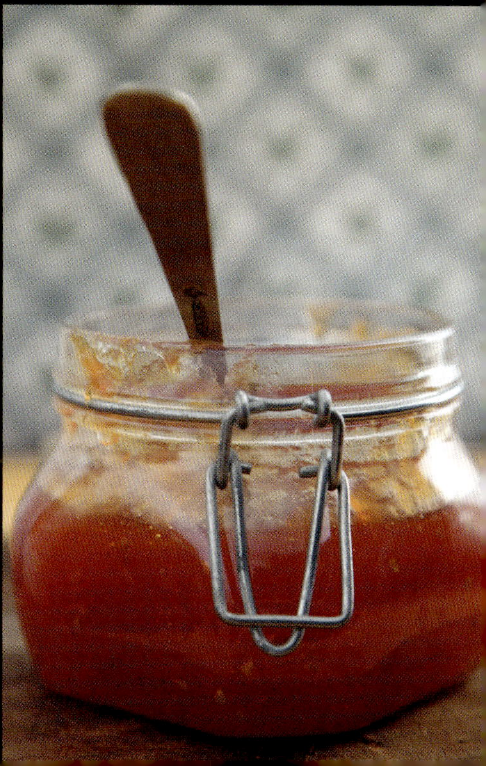

Lassoed just inside the Castilla y León border with Galicia, the area of Bierzo is particularly fertile. At the end of cherry season, *cerezas* and their smaller, more acidic counterparts called *guindas* are preserved in *aguardiente* (alcohol distilled from pressed grape skins, like Italian grappa; see page 317 for more on this spirit). The fruits' flavors deepen and soften over the summer and autumn months, and are ready to be enjoyed during the round of Christmas festivities and throughout Bierzo's rainy, foggy winter months. Sipped, the liquid is smooth, vaguely sweet, flavorful. But, be warned—bite into one of the cherries, where the alcohol has concentrated, and it feels like your mouth is on fire.

Sometimes these cherries are more than an adult aid to digestion following a heavy meal. I've met grandmothers in the region who give a cherry to their grandchildren when they have a stomachache. Does it work? I asked one. She replied, "Well, if it doesn't, at least they'll go to sleep."

CHRISTMAS CHERRIES IN AGUARDIENTE

CEREZAS EN AGUARDIENTE

MAKES TWO 1-PINT/500-ML JARS

1¼ POUNDS/570 G UNBLEMISHED FRESH CHERRIES WITH STEMS
6 COFFEE BEANS
2 CINNAMON STICKS, BROKEN IN HALF
½ CUP/100 G SUGAR
2½ CUPS/600 ML AGUARDIENTE DE ORUJO, GRAPPA, OR MARC

1. Rinse and then gently wipe the cherries with a clean kitchen cloth and let dry completely. Clip the stems ½ inch/1.25 cm above the fruit. (The stem will keep the inside of the cherry from turning mushy.)

2. Into each of two 1-pint/500-ml sterilized wide-mouthed glass canning jars, place 3 coffee beans and 1 cinnamon stick. (The broken halves should lay flat in the bottom of the jar.) Add the cherries one by one, jiggling the jar to settle them close together without mashing or damaging. (Leave enough space at the top to be able to cover with the aguardiente.) Into each jar, sprinkle ¼ cup/50 g of the sugar and then pour in about 1¼ cups/300 ml of the aguardiente or enough to completely cover the cherries.

3. Tightly screw the lids closed and invert the jars. Turn them gently back and forth until the sugar is largely dissolved.

4. Store in a dry, cool, and dark place for 6 months, or until the liquid takes on a characteristic brown color.

5. To serve, spoon out a couple of cherries into a glass dessert bowl or cocktail glass. Strain some liquid through a paper filter into each glass.

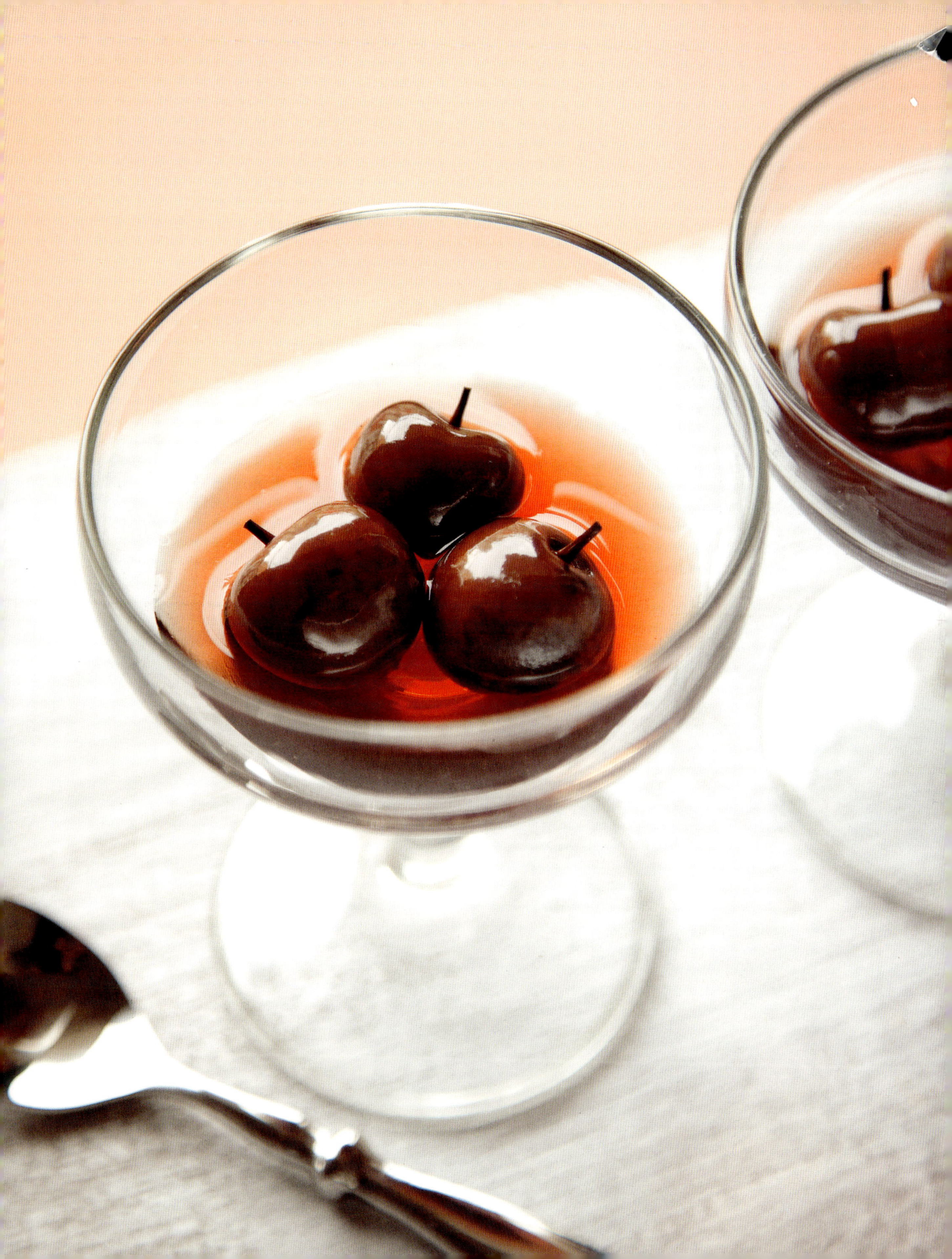

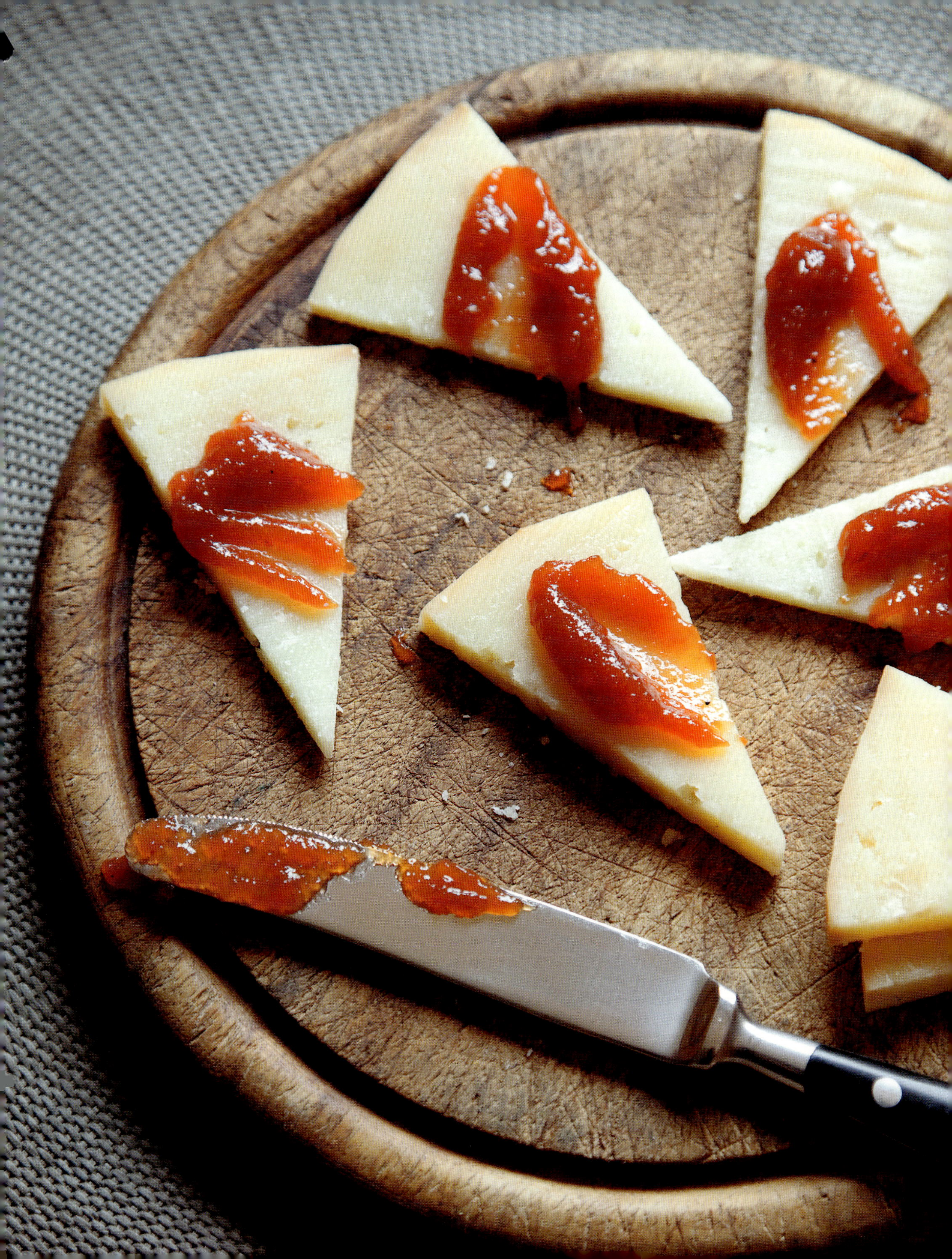

CREAMY QUINCE PASTE

CREMA DE MEMBRILLO

MAKES ABOUT 3 CUPS/720 ML

Membrillo is a dense, pressed quince paste found across Spain, but it is especially popular in the central heartland. It is a stunning combination paired with some wedges of aged Manchego cheese or smoky Basque Idiazábal cheese. This recipe is the softer, creamier version more common in many homes. It's spreadable and spoonable as opposed to sliceable, and particularly fruity rather than densely sweet. This recipe is similar to the one that my wife's grandmother prepared with the first quince from their tree each year for All Saints' Day on November 1.

Generally, recipes call for an equal weight of sugar to usable quince flesh—in this case about 3 cups/600 g sugar—but a slight tartness from the quince is lovely here and I tend to use less sugar.

½ LEMON
2 POUNDS/910 G RIPE MEDIUM QUINCES
2 CUPS/400 G SUGAR

1. Fill a large bowl with cool water. Squeeze the lemon into the bowl and then drop it into the water.

2. Quarter the quinces, removing and reserving the heart and seeds. Do not peel. Put the pieces of quince into the bowl of lemon water (to stop them from discoloring).

3. Put the cores and seeds in a heavy saucepan and cover with 1 quart/1 L water. Bring to a boil, cover the pan, and briskly boil for 45 minutes, or until the natural pectin has been released from the seeds. Strain and reserve the liquid (there should be 2 to 2½ cups/480 to 600 ml), discarding the cores and seeds.

4. Drain the quinces. Peel and cut them into small pieces, and add to the saucepan along with the sugar. Combine enough water with the reserved liquid to make 2½ cups/600 ml and add. Cover the pan and cook over low heat for 30 minutes, stirring occasionally with a wooden spoon. Remove the lid and cook, stirring from time to time, as it turns yellowish and then a scarlet color, the liquid mostly evaporates, and the quince is very tender, about 1 hour. Add in some water if necessary to keep it from scorching. Remove from the heat and let cool slightly.

5. Pass the quince and liquid through a food mill. Return to the pan and stir well while bringing it back to a simmer over medium-low heat. A wooden spoon dragged across the pan should leave a trail. Add in a touch more water to loosen if it feels too dense.

6. Remove the pan from the heat and cool slightly before spooning the paste into two small ceramic dishes, shallow bowls, or wide-mouthed glass canning jars to let set. Once cool, cover tightly. It will keep, covered, in the refrigerator, for 2 to 3 weeks.

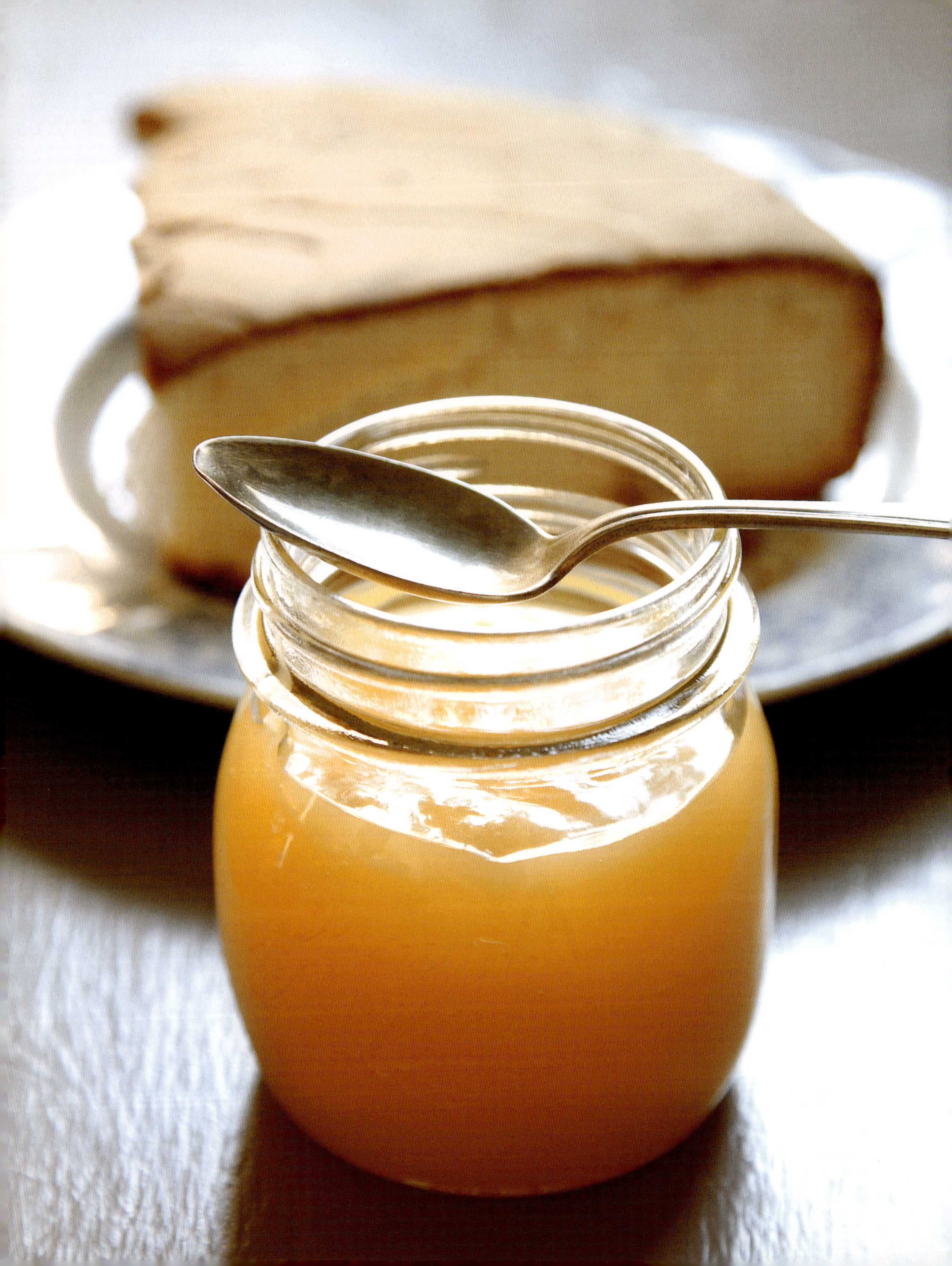

Lemons have been part of the Spanish landscape for many centuries and are an important ingredient in countless cakes, pastries, and desserts. In Galicia, cooks sometimes convert them into a creamy sweet spread with eggs, sugar, and butter. It's downright gorgeous in its luminous golden yellow color, and the generous hit of tart-sweetness is simply divine. Similar to English lemon curd, it perhaps shows some relatively modern influences from Great Britain. One of those surely came during the century that the British navy used the estuary of Arousa, on the western Galician coast, for fleet maneuvers. (That stopped with the outbreak of the Spanish Civil War in 1936.) Galicia is the part of Spain that lies closest to the British Isles, and links between the regions are deeply felt in Galicia's strong Celtic heritage. (Or at least heard. The traditional Galicia musical instrument is the *gaita*, similar in sound to the bagpipe.) This recipe is loosely adapted from one of Galicia's greatest literary chroniclers and food writers, Álvaro Cunqueiro. It is excellent spread over a piece of flaky bizcocho cake (see page 279) or slice of toast, or else dolloped on a bowl of natural yogurt.

CREAMY LEMON CURD

CREMA DE LIMÓN

MAKES ABOUT 3 CUPS/720 ML

3 RIPE MEDIUM ORGANIC LEMONS
4 EGGS
2½ CUPS/500 G SUGAR
¼ CUP/60 G BUTTER, CUT INTO PIECES

1. Scrub the lemons. If waxed, dunk the lemons in boiling water and firmly wipe off the wax. Zest the lemons into a bowl, grating only the yellow part. (The white pith is bitter.) Halve the lemons crosswise and juice them into the bowl. Whisk in the eggs and then the sugar. Spoon the mixture into a small saucepan or metal bowl along with the butter.

2. Heat a large pan of water on the stove, and place the saucepan inside in the manner of a water bath. Over low heat, heat the mixture, stirring continually with a wooden spoon to keep the eggs from curdling, until it turns a paler color and coats the back of a spoon, 8 to 12 minutes.

3. Pour through a conical strainer or chinois and into sterilized wide-mouthed glass canning jars. Let cool completely, tightly cover, and refrigerate. It will keep up to 2 weeks in the refrigerator.

DRIED APRICOTS MACERATED IN SWEET WINE

OREJONES MACERADOS EN VINO DULCE

MAKES ONE 1-PINT/500-ML JAR

In Barcelona, I buy most of my nuts at a small shop that has been roasting them in a metal tumbler by a wood fire since 1851. Casa Gispert has the best—and best selection of—nuts as well as dried fruits from around Spain: hazelnuts from Tarragona, marcona almonds, three kinds of prunes, three kinds of dried figs, dates from Alicante. I have taken inspiration from their shelves laden with marmalades, nuts, honey, and macerated fruits for my own preparations. Gispert macerates dried apricots in *mistela*, a fortified wine—made, nearly always, with *garnacha* (Grenache) grapes—whose fermentation has been stopped by adding alcohol to it. At home I like to use Muscatel for its honeyed, fruity aromas and bright clear-gold vibrancy. The apricots are excellent with yogurt, ice cream, or on their own, and even alongside a chicken roasting in the oven (see page 220).

8 OUNCES/225 G ORGANIC DRIED APRICOTS

1¼ CUP/320 ML MUSCATEL OR ANOTHER SWEET FORTIFIED WINE, PLUS MORE FOR TOPPING UP

1. Wipe the apricots with a clean, dry cloth if needed.

2. Into a 1-pint/500-ml sterilized wide-mouthed glass canning jar, place the apricots and jiggle to settle. They should fill about two-thirds of the jar. Pour in the wine. Close the jar tightly and label. Check the level of the wine during the first days to see how much the apricots have absorbed, topping up as needed to keep covered.

3. Store in a dark, cool place for at least 1 month and up to 6 months.

TOMATO MARMALADE

MERMELADA DE TOMATE

MAKES A GENEROUS 1 PINT/500 ML

This is an end-of-the-summer marmalade, when tomato vines are at their most generous, and you find, in the markets, great stacks of brilliant red *tomates* bursting with flavors. A dollop of this marmalade is perfect spooned onto a wedge of aged sheep's-milk cheese or with some fresh but strong-flavored goat cheese. At home, we also like it with grilled fresh pork sausages.

3 POUNDS/1.4 KG RIPE TOMATOES
2½ CUPS/500 G SUGAR
1 TABLESPOON FRESHLY SQUEEZED LEMON JUICE

1. Blanch and peel the tomatoes following the directions on page 339. Working over a bowl to catch all of the juices, seed and core the tomatoes. Cut them into chunky pieces. There should be at least 2 pounds/910 g of flesh.

2. In a large, heavy saucepan, add the tomatoes and their juices along with the sugar and lemon juice. Bring to a boil over high heat. Reduce the heat to medium-low and simmer, stirring from time to time, until thick and glazy, with the tomatoes somewhat dissolved and the liquid evaporated, about 1 hour. Remove the pan from the heat, and let cool for a few minutes.

3. Spoon the marmalade into sterilized glass canning jars, leaving one finger space at the top. Wipe the jars clean and seal. Store in the refrigerator and use within 1 month.

SWEET PRESERVED TOMATOES WITH THYME

TOMATES CONFITADOS CON TOMILLO

MAKES TWO 1-PINT/500-ML JARS

This recipe comes from Can Ravell, a superb delicatessen and restaurant in Barcelona beside Mercat de la Concepció. Opened in 1929 by the father of the current owner, Josep Ravell, it carries the finest preserves from Spain and beyond. (See page 237 for more about Can Ravell.) They also preserve some of their own—white asparagus from Navarra in spring, and, using a recipe from his grandmother, sweet tomatoes in summer. When Josep was a boy, his grandmother served these tomatoes with some anchovy fillets and a good dousing of extra-virgin olive oil for a salad, or else alongside white rice and a fried egg (and a glass of red wine) for a quick dinner. I learned this recipe from Josep, and in our house we more or less follow his grandmother's lead on how to eat them.

2 POUNDS/910 G RIPE MEDIUM TOMATOES
½ CUP/100 G SUGAR (SEE NOTE)
SALT AND FRESHLY GROUND BLACK PEPPER
2 TABLESPOONS EXTRA-VIRGIN OLIVE OIL, PLUS MORE FOR COVERING
FINELY CHOPPED FRESH THYME FOR SPRINKLING

1. Preheat the oven to 250°F/120°C/gas mark ½.

2. Blanch and peel the tomatoes following the directions on page 339. If the tomatoes are large, remove the seeds with a spoon. For small or medium tomatoes, trim just the top of the core and leave the seeds.

3. In a small saucepan, prepare a syrup by dissolving the sugar in 2 tablespoons water over medium heat. Remove from the heat.

4. In a baking dish, arrange the tomatoes. Season with salt and pepper. Spoon the syrup and the olive oil and generously crumble the thyme over the top. Bake for 1¼ hours, or until darker red and tender but not collapsing. Turn off the oven and let the tomatoes gradually cool in the oven.

5. Gently lift out the tomatoes and place them in sterilized glass canning jars, leaving one finger space at the top. Pour in the liquid from the pan. Top off with more oil until the tomatoes are covered. Seal and label. Store in the refrigerator and use within 2 weeks.

NOTE: If the tomatoes are particularly ripe and sweet, decrease the amount of sugar to ⅓ cup/75 g.

SWEET AND SOUR PRESERVED ONIONS

CEBOLLA AGRIDULCE

MAKES ABOUT 1½ CUPS/360 ML

The fertile northwest corner of Castilla y León, tucked into the region near Asturias and Galicia, is well known for its pantry preserves—chestnuts in syrup, cherries in aguardiente (see page 320), roasted peppers, and the like. These delightful preserves are adapted from Moncloa de San Lázaro, a small preserves company in the village of Cacabelos. The key, I learned from a group of women making preserves there one summer, is to patiently cook the onions until soft and translucent, without browning—what they called *pochar* (literally "to poach")—before adding the sugar and vinegar. Serve with cheeses (warmed goat cheese makes for a particularly pleasing combination), or on the side of a beefy grilled steak.

2½ POUNDS/1.2 KG RED ONIONS
3 TABLESPOONS EXTRA-VIRGIN OLIVE OIL
6 TABLESPOONS/80 G SUGAR
¾ CUP/180 ML RED WINE VINEGAR
1 TEASPOON AGED SHERRY VINEGAR OR BALSAMIC VINEGAR

1. Peel the onions. Chop into ½-inch/1.25-cm pieces, leaving some a bit longer and rectangular shaped.

2. In a large skillet or sauté pan, heat the olive oil over low heat. Add the onions and cook slowly, stirring frequently, until translucent, about 30 minutes. Sprinkle in the sugar and cook, continuing to stir frequently, until it begins to darken to a soft brown tone, about 20 minutes. Add the vinegars, and cook, stirring, until the vinegar evaporates, 5 to 10 minutes, and the onions are reddish brown. Remove from the heat and let cool.

3. Spoon the onions into sterilized glass canning jars, leaving one finger space at the top.

4. Store in the refrigerator and use within 2 weeks. Serve at room temperature or slightly chilled.

QUAIL IN ESCABECHE MARINADE

CODORNICES EN ESCABECHE

SERVES 2 TO 4

Castilla–La Mancha is the land of escabeche, the ancient olive oil and vinegar marinade, most famously used to prepare the red-legged partridge so abundant in autumn. Quail—smaller, with slightly more delicate meat, and found year-round in the markets—are an excellent alternative. They need to sit for at least a couple of days in the marinade to allow the flavors to blossom and penetrate. Eat with the fingers, getting every last shred of lush, tender meat from bones as delicate as toothpicks.

4 CLEANED WHOLE QUAIL OR SQUAB (NOT BONELESS), ABOUT 6 OR 7 OUNCES/ 170 OR 200 G EACH

2¼ CUPS/540 ML EXTRA-VIRGIN OLIVE OIL, PLUS MORE IF NEEDED

1 MEDIUM ONION, HALVED CROSSWISE AND THINLY SLICED

2 MEDIUM CARROTS, CUT CROSSWISE INTO ¼-INCH-/½-CM-THICK ROUNDS

1 GARLIC HEAD, UNPEELED, CLOVES LOOSENED SLIGHTLY

HEAPED 1 TEASPOON BLACK PEPPERCORNS

1 BAY LEAF, PREFERABLY FRESH

1 SPRIG FRESH THYME

1 SPRIG FRESH ROSEMARY

1 CUP/240 ML WHITE WINE VINEGAR

1. Wash and dry the birds. Singe off any remaining feathers over an open flame. Wipe clean with a damp cloth. Clean the cavities, while leaving the birds whole. Truss the legs with cotton kitchen string to help them keep their shape and cook evenly.

2. In a large sauté pan or deep skillet, heat ¼ cup/60 ml of the olive oil over medium heat. Add the quail and gently brown, turning as needed, about 6 minutes. Transfer to a platter.

3. Add the onion, carrots, and garlic to the pan and cook over medium heat until fragrant, about 2 minutes. Add the peppercorns, bay leaf, thyme, and rosemary and then pour in the remaining 2 cups/480 ml olive oil along with the vinegar. Once the liquid reaches a simmer, return the quail to the pan, cover, and simmer over low heat until very tender, about 1 hour. The quail are done when the meat begins to come away from the bone and a leg jiggles in the socket. Remove from the heat and let cool for about 30 minutes.

4. Gently transfer the quail to a clean wide-mouthed glass jar or deep bowl. Completely cover with the liquid from the pan. If the marinade does not cover them, top up with more olive oil. Once completely cool, cover and refrigerate for at least 1 day to allow the quail to take on the escabeche's characteristic flavors. Store in the refrigerator for up to 4 days.

5. Remove from the refrigerator 1 or 2 hours before serving. Strain the liquid, reserving the carrots. Spoon some of the liquid over the quail and serve at room temperature with a few carrot rounds on the side.

INGREDIENTS

ANCHOVIES
anchoas

Salting fish goes back millennia on the Iberian Peninsula, beginning with the Phoenicians who established salt pans on the southern coast and in Alicante. Using salt is a simple and natural way of conserving fish, and especially useful for anchovies, which spoil quickly. Anchovies are salted and packed into barrels to draw away their moisture and keep bacteria from forming, but also to ferment and take on their distinctive flavors. Since the nineteenth century, the finished fillets have been commercially packed in sealed jars or flat tins to keep even longer. The difference in flavor between fresh and cured anchovies is probably greater than with any other preserved seafood.

There are two main industries of anchovies in Spain. One is from l'Escala on the Catalan Costa Brava, using Mediterranean anchovies and packing them in salt that has some black pepper added. L'Escala sits beside the important Greek and Roman ruins of Empúries, which have vestiges of ancient salting workshops. The city was abandoned in the third century, but the methods were continued by local fishermen. In the sixteenth century, the first commercial anchovy factories were established in l'Escala. The industry grew, and there were once dozens of factories in l'Escala. Today there are just two, though both make sublime anchovies using methods that have, in many ways, changed little over the centuries.

The second, larger, and for many, superior, anchovy production comes from the Cantabrian Sea, along the southern end of the Bay of Biscay. The epicenter of the industry is in Santoña. The town dates its anchovy canning industry to the arrival in 1880 of an Italian named Giovanni Vella Scaliota. Drawn by the quality of the anchovies in the bay, he settled here and eventually perfected the techniques for canning them. Salting, filleting, and canning the anchovies remains as tedious and time-consuming as it was a century ago. But, happily, the flavors remain as well.

The standard method followed in Santoña begins with catching the small, silvery fish during their prime season, from March to June, when the young anchovies are rich in fats, oils, and flavors. The fish are handled with particular care on the boats and, once brought into shore, salted as soon as possible. Workers (nearly all women) gut the fish and remove the heads, and then place them in a fan pattern into barrels with salt between each layer. With a weight on top of the open barrel, they are gently pressed for a number of months. The pressing removes the fat so that the fish can begin maturing (fermenting) and take on their characteristic heady aromas, bold flavors, and supple texture. For high-quality brands, this step lasts a minimum of eight months. The fish are then removed from the barrels, cleaned, and filleted. Any remaining bones are plucked out with tweezers. Rolled into soft cloth, the fillets are gently squeezed to remove excess moisture before being gently laid one by one into flat tins and covered with oil. The top producers pack the fillets in extra-virgin olive oil.

To fully enjoy, carefully extract the fillets from the tin, rinse in water to remove the oil, and then gently pat dry with a paper towel. Place in a shallow dish, drizzle some fresh extra-virgin olive oil over the top, and give them a generous grating of black pepper. I recommend eating anchovies on a slice of toasted country bread. The fillets should be bold, and slightly salty, but not disagreeably so.

FRESH SARDINES IN ESCABECHE MARINADE

SARDINAS EN ESCABECHE

SERVES 4

Just as quail and partridge in escabeche preserve the flavors of the dry, herb-scented central *meseta* (tablelands), sardines in this oil-and-vinegar marinade retain those of the saline Mediterranean. The boldly flavored, silvery fish hold their own here. Aside from grilling over open embers on an Andalusian beach, for me this is the best way to prepare sardines. Period.

16 FRESH WHOLE MEDIUM SARDINES, ABOUT 1 POUND/455 G TOTAL
1½ CUPS/360 ML EXTRA-VIRGIN OLIVE OIL, PLUS MORE IF NEEDED
SALT
ALL-PURPOSE FLOUR FOR DREDGING
½ CUP/120 ML WHITE WINE VINEGAR
6 TO 8 GARLIC CLOVES, LIGHTLY CRUSHED IN THE PEEL
2 OR 3 BAY LEAVES
3 SPRIGS FRESH THYME
12 BLACK PEPPERCORNS
1 TEASPOON SPANISH PIMENTÓN DULCE (SWEET PAPRIKA)

1. Gently scale the sardines with a fish scaler or dull butter knife. Remove the innards by holding a sardine with one hand and with the other, rocking the head first upward breaking the neck, then downward, and finally firmly pulling it away to draw out the entrails. Run a finger through the cavity to make sure it's clean. Rinse and pat dry with paper towels.

2. In a large skillet, heat 3 tablespoons of the olive oil over medium heat. Season the sardines with salt, lightly dredge in flour, and cook until the skin is golden brown, 2 to 3 minutes. Turn gently to avoid breaking the skin, and cook on the other side until golden, about 2 minutes. Transfer to a rectangular earthenware, ceramic, or glass dish. Lay the sardines in side by side, alternating head-tail directions so that they fit snugly together.

3. In a saucepan, add the remaining 1⅓ cups/315 ml olive oil, the vinegar, garlic, bay leaves, thyme, and peppercorns and bring to a boil. Remove from the heat, let cool for a few minutes, and then stir in the pimentón.

4. Swirl the marinade in the pan to blend and then pour the oil and herbs over the fish to completely cover. If the marinade does not cover them, top up with more olive oil. Let cool to room temperature. Cover with plastic wrap and refrigerate for at least 1 day to allow the sardines to take on the escabeche's characteristic flavors. Store in the refrigerator for up to 4 days.

5. Remove from the refrigerator about 1 hour before serving and serve at room temperature with some of the marinade spooned over the top.

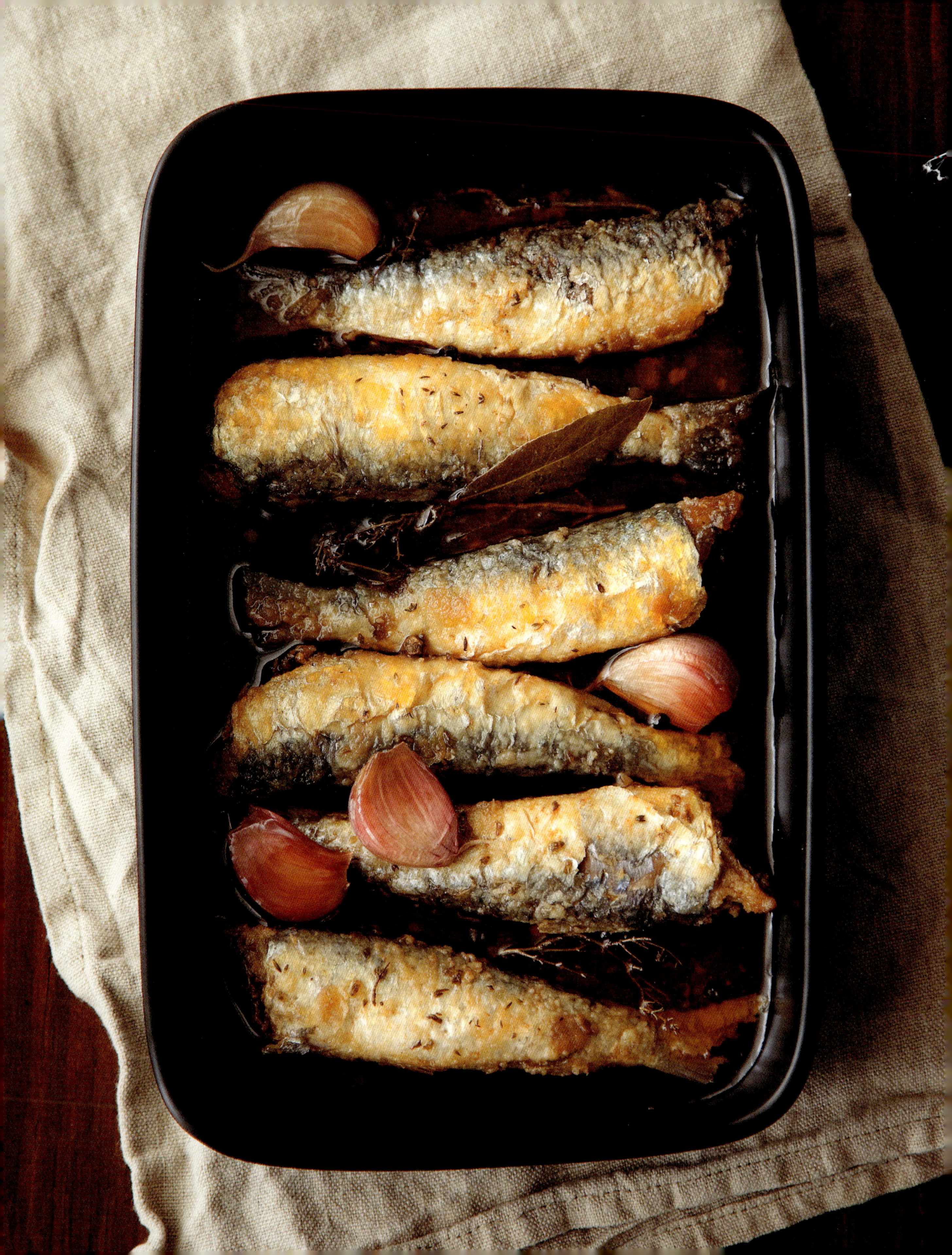

A GLOSSARY OF BASIC RECIPES AND TECHNIQUES

Vegetable Stock 335
Fish Stock 335
Chicken Stock 336
Beef Stock 336
Mayonnaise 337
Allioli 337
Béchamel Sauce 338
Blanching and Peeling Tomatoes 339
Grating Tomatoes 339
Cleaning Artichokes 339
Cleaning Wild Mushrooms 339
Dry-Toasting Pine Nuts 340

Using Saffron 340
Preparing Fresh Snails for Cooking 340
Preparing Preserved Snails for Cooking . 341
Desalting Salt Cod 341
Cleaning Mussels 341
Purging Clams of Sand 341
Cleaning Squid and Cuttlefish 342
Cutting a Chicken into 8 or 10 Pieces 342
Cutting a Rabbit into 8 or 9 Pieces 342
Perfect Hard-Boiled Eggs 342
Cooking Dried Garbanzo Beans 343
Cooking Dried White Beans 343

VEGETABLE STOCK

CALDO DE VERDURAS

Sautéing the vegetables in 1 or 2 tablespoons of olive oil until browned before adding the water will bring a more savory depth to the flavors of the stock.

MAKES 2 QUARTS/2 L

- SALT
- 4 CARROTS, HALVED LENGTHWISE AND QUARTERED CROSSWISE
- 2 CELERY STALKS, QUARTERED CROSSWISE
- 2 TURNIPS, HALVED LENGTHWISE AND HALVED CROSSWISE
- 1 PARSNIP, HALVED LENGTHWISE AND HALVED CROSSWISE
- 1 ONION, QUARTERED
- 1 LEEK, HALVED LENGTHWISE AND QUARTERED CROSSWISE
- 10 BLACK PEPPERCORNS
- 1 BAY LEAF
- 1 SPRIG FRESH THYME
- 10 SPRIGS FRESH FLAT-LEAF PARSLEY

In a stockpot or another large pot, bring 8½ cups/2.1 L water to a boil over high heat and season with salt. Add the carrots, celery, turnips, parsnip, onion, leek, and peppercorns; reduce the heat to medium-low; cover the pot; and simmer for 1 to 1½ hours.

Remove the pot from the heat; add the bay leaf, thyme, and parsley; and infuse for 20 minutes as the stock cools. Strain the broth through a conical strainer. Gently press out the remaining liquid from the vegetables. Discard the solids.

Store in the refrigerator for up to 3 days or freeze for up to 3 months.

FISH STOCK

CALDO DE PESCADO

If desired, sauté the onion, leek, and celery in 1 tablespoon of olive oil until soft and aromatic before adding the other ingredients. For a more concentrated caldo, gently simmer uncovered for 1½ hours.

MAKES 2 QUARTS/2 L

- 2 POUNDS/910 G SMALL SOUP FISH OR ASSORTED HEADS AND BONES OF FIRM, WHITE-FLESHED NON-OILY FISH
- 1 MEDIUM ONION, ROUGHLY CHOPPED
- 1 LEEK, ROUGHLY CHOPPED
- 2 CELERY STALKS, ROUGHLY CHOPPED
- 12 BLACK PEPPERCORNS
- ½ CUP/120 ML DRY WHITE WINE
- SALT
- 1 BAY LEAF
- 1 SPRIG FRESH THYME
- 10 SPRIGS FRESH FLAT-LEAF PARSLEY

In a stockpot or another large pot, begin heating 8½ cups/2.1 L water over high heat. As the water heats, add the fish, onion, leek, celery, and peppercorns; pour in the wine; and season with salt. Once it reaches a boil, reduce the heat to medium-low, partly cover the pot, and simmer for about 30 minutes, skimming any foam that floats to the surface.

Remove the pot from the heat; add the bay leaf, thyme, and parsley; and infuse for 20 minutes as the stock cools. Strain the broth through a conical strainer. Gently press out the remaining liquid from the fish and vegetables, and discard the solids.

Store in the refrigerator for up to 3 days or freeze for up to 3 months.

CHICKEN STOCK

CALDO DE POLLO

Absolutely fundamental to the Spanish kitchen, chicken stock gives a strong boost of flavor to countless dishes.

MAKES 2 QUARTS/2 L

2 POUNDS/910 G BONE-IN CHICKEN LEGS OR BACKS AND NECKS, SKIN PULLED OFF AND EXCESS FAT TRIMMED
SALT AND FRESHLY GROUND BLACK PEPPER
2 CARROTS, HALVED LENGTHWISE AND QUARTERED CROSSWISE
1 CELERY STALK, QUARTERED CROSSWISE
1 TURNIP, HALVED LENGTHWISE AND HALVED CROSSWISE
1 PARSNIP, HALVED LENGTHWISE AND HALVED CROSSWISE
1 MEDIUM ONION, QUARTERED
1 LEEK, HALVED LENGTHWISE AND QUARTERED CROSSWISE
10 BLACK PEPPERCORNS
1 BAY LEAF
1 SPRIG FRESH THYME
10 SPRIGS FRESH FLAT-LEAF PARSLEY

Using a cleaver or poultry shears, cut the chicken into large pieces. Rinse. Lightly season with salt and pepper.

In a stockpot or another large pot, add the chicken and cover with 8½ cups/2.1 L cold water. Over high heat, bring the water to a boil. Skim off any foam that floats to the surface. Add the carrots, celery, turnip, parsnip, onion, leek, and peppercorns; reduce the heat to medium-low; cover the pot; and simmer for 1 hour.

Remove the pot from the heat, add the bay leaf, thyme, and parsley, and infuse for 20 minutes as the stock cools. Strain the broth through a conical strainer. Gently press out the remaining liquid from the chicken and vegetables, and discard the solids.

Store in the refrigerator for up to 3 days or freeze for up to 3 months.

BEEF STOCK

CALDO DE CARNE

For a quicker, paler beef stock, skip the roasting and simply add the bones and vegetables to the pot, cover with cold water, bring to a boil, skim off the foam, and gently boil for 2 hours. (In Spain, they call this *fondo blanco*, literally "white background," but meaning a paler as opposed to a darker stock.) For a bolder, stand-alone stock that can be used as a soup broth, add ½ cup/60 ml red wine once the vegetables have browned, stirring for 2 minutes to let the alcohol burn off and scraping to get anything stuck from the bottom of the pan before continuing with the recipe.

MAKES 2 QUARTS/2 L

3 POUNDS/1.4 KG BEEF OR VEAL MARROWBONES, RINSED
SALT
1 TABLESPOON OLIVE OIL
2 LEEKS, WHITE AND TENDER GREEN PARTS ONLY, ROUGHLY CHOPPED
2 CARROTS, ROUGHLY CHOPPED
2 CELERY STALKS, ROUGHLY CHOPPED
1 GARLIC CLOVE, LIGHTLY CRUSHED IN THE PEEL
2 MEDIUM TURNIPS OR PARSNIPS, HALVED
10 PEPPERCORNS

Preheat the broiler. Lightly season the bones with salt. On a baking sheet or in a roasting pan, arrange the bones and slide into the oven. Broil until browned, turning as needed, 10 to 15 minutes.

Meanwhile, in a large stockpot, heat the olive oil over medium heat and add the leeks, carrots, celery, and garlic. Cook until browned, about 10 minutes. Add the turnips, peppercorns, and browned bones and their juices from the pan; season with salt; and cover with 3 quarts/3 L cold water. Bring to a boil, reduce the heat to medium-low, partly cover the pot, and gently boil for 2 hours, skimming off the fat that floats to the surface.

Remove the pot from the heat and let cool. Strain the broth through a conical strainer. Gently press out the remaining liquid from the vegetables, and discard the solids.

Store in the refrigerator for up to 3 days or freeze for up to 3 months.

MAYONNAISE

SALSA MAYONESA

To form a smooth emulsion, it is important that all of the ingredients are at the same temperature. Use a light or mild olive oil—not extra-virgin, which makes the mayonnaise quite heavy. Blending mild olive oil with sunflower oil will make an even lighter mayonnaise. The easiest way to prepare this recipe is with an immersion hand blender, though a food processor works, too. Instructions for both methods follow. It is frequently spelled *mahonesa*, which clearly reflects its origin in Mahón, Menorca.

MAKES ABOUT 1 CUP/240 ML

1 EGG, AT ROOM TEMPERATURE
SALT
WHITE WINE VINEGAR
¾ CUP/180 ML MILD OLIVE OIL, OR A BLEND OF MILD OLIVE OIL AND SUNFLOWER OR CANOLA OIL

Using an immersion hand blender: In a tall, narrow, and cylindrical container (ideally just wider than the shaft), add—in this order—the egg, a pinch of salt, some drops of vinegar, and the olive oil. While still turned off, place the blender shaft in the bottom of the container. Turn on the blender to three-fourths speed and begin blending. Once the emulsion begins to form, slowly bring the end of the shaft up through the oil and just out, and then slowly back down to the bottom. Bring it up once more and out. Total blending time is 30 seconds to 1 minute. The emulsion should be creamy, without any oil pooled on the surface. If needed, lower the shaft slowly back down to the bottom and out again.

Using a food processor: Add the egg, a pinch of salt, and some drops of vinegar. Begin whirring the food processor and add in the olive oil in a very slow but steady stream until all of the oil has been used and the emulsion has thickened to the consistency of creamy mayonnaise. It should not have any oil pooled on the surface. Total blending time is about 1 minute.

Transfer the mayonnaise to a bowl. Cover tightly with plastic wrap and refrigerate until ready to serve, for up to 2 days. Just before serving, rewhisk with a fork.

ALLIOLI

This classic garlicky mayonnaise-like emulsion sauce, so typical in Catalunya, Valencia, Murcia, and the Balearic Islands, is prepared with the ingredients that make up its composite name: garlic (*all*) and (*i*) olive oil (*oli*). It's served alongside grilled meats and sausages, many rice and fideo pasta dishes, and even with steamed vegetables. Note that the Spanish spelling has just a single "l"—*alioli*—and in Murcia and in some other places, some people combine the Spanish words for garlic (*ajo*) and oil (*aceite*) and call it *ajoaciete* instead. In Provence, there is a similar emulsion, *aïoli*.

Once, cooks prepared allioli in a mortar, mashing the garlic and then, almost drop by drop, incorporating the olive oil, moving the pestle in the same direction and in the same rhythm, until a pale, potent paste was produced. More common now, and much quicker, is using an egg (or egg yolk) to bind the emulsion that is whirred with an immersion hand blender (though a food processor works fine, too). Lighten the sauce by blending equal parts mild olive oil and sunflower oil.

MAKES ABOUT 1 CUP/240 ML

continued

1 GARLIC CLOVE, MASHED
1 EGG, AT ROOM TEMPERATURE
⅛ TEASPOON SALT
⅛ TEASPOON WHITE PEPPER
WHITE WINE VINEGAR
1 CUP/240 ML MILD OLIVE OIL, OR A BLEND OF MILD OLIVE OIL AND SUNFLOWER OR CANOLA OIL

Using an immersion hand blender: In a tall, narrow, and cylindrical container (ideally just wider than the shaft), add—in this order—the garlic, egg, salt, pepper, some drops of vinegar, and the olive oil. While still turned off, place the blender shaft in the bottom of the container. Turn on the blender to three-fourths speed and begin blending. Once the emulsion begins to form, slowly bring the end of the shaft up through the oil and just out, and then slowly back down to the bottom. Bring it up once more and out. Total blending time is 30 seconds to 1 minute. The allioli should have thickened to the consistency of a creamy mayonnaise without any oil pooled on the surface; if not, lower the shaft slowly back down to the bottom and out again.

Using a food processor: Add the garlic, egg, salt, pepper, and some drops of vinegar. Begin whirring the food processor and add in the olive oil in a very slow but steady stream until all of the oil has been used and the emulsion has thickened to the consistency of creamy mayonnaise. Total blending time is about 1 minute.

Transfer the allioli to a bowl. Cover tightly with plastic wrap and refrigerate until ready to serve, for up to 2 days. Just before serving, rewhisk with a fork.

BÉCHAMEL SAUCE

SALSA BECHAMEL

Numerous Spanish dishes use this creamy white sauce. There are different levels of consistency, from runny to thick, though the recipes in this book call for a medium sauce. When using béchamel in a dish from this book, follow the quantities and ingredients given in that recipe.

MAKES ABOUT 2 CUPS/480 ML

2 CUPS/480 ML MILK
2 TABLESPOONS BUTTER
2 TABLESPOONS FLOUR
PINCH SALT
PINCH FRESHLY GRATED NUTMEG

In a saucepan, heat the milk over medium heat nearly to a boil; do not let it boil. Remove from the heat, cover the pan, and keep hot.

In a large, heavy saucepan over low heat, melt the butter. Sift in the flour and cook, whisking, as it bubbles and the flour loses its raw taste and takes on a lightly toasted color, about 1½ minutes.

Over medium-low heat, gradually begin adding in the hot milk a ladleful at a time, incorporating each addition completely into the paste by whisking before adding more milk, 10 to 12 minutes total. It should be creamy and free of any lumps, and thickly coat the back of the spoon. Stir in the salt and nutmeg and remove from the heat.

Use immediately or store by letting it cool and refrigerate for 1 to 2 days with plastic wrap laid directly on the surface.

BLANCHING AND PEELING TOMATOES

An easy method for peeling tomatoes is to blanch them first.

Fill a large bowl with cold water. Remove the stem of each tomato and score an "X" in the bottom with the tip of a knife. In a large pot, bring about 2 quarts/2 L water to a rolling boil. Set the tomatoes in the water and boil until the skins begin to split, 15 seconds to 1 minute, depending on their ripeness. Immediately remove with a slotted spoon and plunge into the cold water to stop any further cooking. Once the tomatoes have cooled, drain and peel.

GRATING TOMATOES

Grating tomatoes is a recommended alternative to peeling and finely chopping, and a way to maximize the sweet flesh that lies close to the skin.

Cut the tomatoes in half crosswise. Gently squeeze the seeds into a bowl and then run a finger through the seed cavity to remove any remaining seeds. Cup a tomato half in one hand and slowly grate it on a box grater until the skin peels back and all the flesh has been grated away. Discard the flattened skin. Repeat with the remaining tomato halves. Strain the liquid from the seeds (press with the back of a spoon to get all of the juices) and add to the grated pulp.

CLEANING ARTICHOKES

Fill a large bowl with cool water. Cut a lemon into wedges, squeeze into the water, and then drop it into the bowl. The lemon will keep the trimmed pieces of artichokes from darkening too much.

Working with one artichoke at a time, rinse under cold running water. Cut or pull away the tough outer petals and trim away any fibrous parts. Cut the trimmed artichokes into eighths. Peel away the outside of the stem. Immediately drop the trimmed artichokes into the lemon water. Repeat with the remaining artichokes. Leave in the water until ready to use. Drain and pat dry with paper towels.

CLEANING WILD MUSHROOMS

As a general guide, mushrooms found in the wild should only be cleaned with a soft brush to remove any soil and then wiped with a damp cloth. Mushrooms purchased in markets or shops—grown in humus that may not be as natural as that in the woods—should be dunked and swished around quickly in a few changes of very cold water, drained well, and patted dry with paper towels. Wait to do this until just before cooking, and do it quickly to keep them from absorbing any liquid. Because of their irregular honeycombed surface, morels may need more attention with a brush and damp cloth to remove any grit.

DRY-TOASTING PINE NUTS

Heat a small ungreased skillet over medium-low heat, add the pine nuts, and toast, stirring frequently, until golden and aromatic, about 3 minutes. Immediately transfer to a plate to stop them from cooking further.

USING SAFFRON

Saffron's potent color and aroma mean that only a pinch (or, at most, two) of threads is required. The threads need to be either dry-toasted and crushed in order to fully maximize their flavor and color, or else steeped in warm liquid.

To dry-toast: Heat a small ungreased skillet over medium-low heat, add the saffron threads, and toast for 2 to 3 minutes, or until aromatic and the threads have turned a shade darker in color. Place the toasted threads in a small sheet of paper that has been folded in half, crumble with your fingers—be sure they are dry—from the outside, and then shake the saffron from the paper into the dish (this prevents any saffron from sticking to your fingers). Alternatively, transfer the toasted threads from the skillet to a mortar, pound into a powder, and add to the dish. Swirl 2 tablespoons water in the mortar to get all of the crushed saffron.

To steep: Place the threads in ½ cup/120 ml hot water and infuse for 20 to 30 minutes. Incorporate the brilliant golden and highly aromatic liquid into the dish. Discard the threads.

PREPARING FRESH SNAILS FOR COOKING

While fresh snails bought in markets no longer need to be purged before using, they *do* need to be cleaned and then boiled before being prepared in a sauce or added to a rice dish. It is important that the snails are brought slowly to a boil. The snail will emerge from the shell and then not quite be able to retract back inside, making the meat easier to extract and eat. A snail dropped into boiling water will quickly retract and be much harder work to eat.

2¼ POUNDS/1 KG FRESH, LIVE SNAILS
WINE VINEGAR
SALT
1 GARLIC CLOVE, UNPEELED
2 BAY LEAVES
1 SPRIG FRESH THYME

Scrub the snails clean of slime and grit using plenty of water, a bit of wine vinegar, and salt. Rinse very well with running water.

Put the snails in a large pot and cover with water. Over low heat, slowly bring the water to a boil, allowing at least 30 minutes. When the water breaks a boil, remove the pot from the heat, and dump the snails in a large colander to drain. Rinse the snails with running water and clean the pot. Return the snails to the pot, cover with fresh water, and bring to a boil over high heat. Add the garlic, bay leaves, and thyme; reduce the heat to medium-low; and gently boil uncovered for 30 to 60 minutes, depending on how the snails will be cooked. (If they will be stewed or braised, 30 minutes is enough; if they will be used in rice dishes, boil for 60 minutes.) They are now ready to use according to the recipe instructions.

PREPARING PRESERVED SNAILS FOR COOKING

Snails preserved in brine and sold in jars or vacuum packed should be given a quick boil before being incorporated into a dish. Add a sprig of thyme or a bay leaf to this quick boil if desired.

1 POUND/455 G PRESERVED SNAILS WITH SHELLS

Drain the brine and rinse the snails with plenty of running water.

In a large saucepan, put in the snails, cover with abundant fresh water, bring to a boil over medium heat, and gently boil for 3 or 4 minutes. Strain the snails in a large colander and rinse with running water. They are now ready to use according to the recipe instructions.

DESALTING SALT COD

Dry salt cod—bacalao—needs to be desalted before using. Soaking in water removes the salt, rehydrates the cod, and softens the flesh. The process takes at least 36 hours to 2 days, changing the water at least four to six times; fatter loin pieces can take as long as 4 days; the thickest loin pieces can take even longer.

Rinse the pieces under cool running water. Place skin-side up (to keep the salt from concentrating here) in a bowl and cover with fresh water. Change the water immediately, rinse out the bowl, and refill with cool water. Arrange the pieces in the bowl skin-side up. Place the bowl in the refrigerator and let the cod soak for 12 hours. Drain, rinse out the bowl, change the water, and soak for another 12 hours. Change the water every 6 to 8 hours or so for the next 24 hours. Place the pieces skin-side down during the final 12 hours. Drain the cod, rinse, and gently squeeze out some of the excess water. Place in a strainer—with the skin side up again—and let drain for at least 30 minutes. (For certain recipes where you don't want any salty moisture running into the sauce, I recommend draining for significantly longer.)

To check if it is ready, take a pinch of the fish and taste. It should be slightly salty but not disagreeably so. (If it is too salty, change the water and continue to soak.) Carefully debone. Use according to the recipe instructions.

CLEANING MUSSELS

Only clean mussels once you are ready to use them, as debearding can tear and kill a mussel. Discard any with cracked or broken shells. Trim, debeard, and scrape the outside of the shell clean with a paring knife. Gently rinse a few times until the water runs clear.

PURGING CLAMS OF SAND

Discard any clams with cracked or broken shells. Fill a large bowl with cool water. Add 1 teaspoon of salt for every 1 quart/1 L water and dissolve. Set the clams in the water and soak for 30 minutes. Dump out the water, rinse out the bowl, and soak for another 30 minutes in clean, unsalted water. Drain, set in a dry bowl, cover with a damp paper towel, and place in the refrigerator for 15 minutes or so before using.

CLEANING SQUID AND CUTTLEFISH

When buying whole squid or cuttlefish, make sure that the skin, head, and arms are intact and bright, and they have a pleasant sea smell.

Hold the squid or cuttlefish in one hand, grasp the tentacles with the other, and pull the body out from the tube. Trim the head below the "beak" and discard. Gently cut away and reserve the mercury-colored ink sac behind the eyes. Remove the transparent quill from the tube and discard. Run a finger through the tube and remove any gelatinous substance. Gently wash in a bowl of water. Rub away the light, purplish membrane on the outside of the tube with a kitchen cloth. Remove the "wings" on the head and reserve. Cut the tube and tentacles as desired.

CUTTING A CHICKEN INTO 8 OR 10 PIECES

Place the chicken breast-side up on a cutting board. Using poultry shears, cut the neck as close to the body as possible. Remove the wings. Cut away the legs by slicing through the skin, loosening, and then bending at the joint; cut through the joint at the ball and socket, and then cut away the leg, keeping the blade against the backbone. Separate the legs into drumsticks and thighs by cutting through the joint between them. Cut the ribs from the backbone. Separate the breastbone lengthwise into two parts. There should be eight serving pieces (plus the backbone). To get ten serving pieces, halve each of the breasts crosswise at an angle so that they are about even-sized pieces.

CUTTING A RABBIT INTO 8 OR 9 PIECES

Open the cavity and pull out the organs, reserving the liver if desired. Cut away the hind legs and separate them from the loin, and then do the same with the forelegs. Cut the loin crosswise into two or three pieces. Working between rib bones, cut the ribcage crosswise into two pieces. There should be eight or nine serving pieces. Rinse under running water and pat dry with paper towels. Trim any excess fat, as it won't melt away when cooked. Carefully pick out any shards of bone.

PERFECT HARD-BOILED EGGS

A perfect hard-boiled egg has a creamy, brilliant golden yolk (that is not ringed with greenish gray), and whites that are supple (not rubbery) in texture.

MAKES 6 HARD-BOILED EGGS

6 EGGS, AT ROOM TEMPERATURE

Place the eggs in a medium saucepan and cover with at least 1 inch/2.5 cm water. Bring to a boil, reduce the heat to medium-low, and gently boil for 9 to 10 minutes.

Meanwhile, fill a large bowl with ice water.

Transfer the eggs with a slotted spoon to the ice water to cool.

To peel, gently roll one under your palm to crack, and then peel away the shell.

COOKING DRIED GARBANZO BEANS

Garbanzo beans need to be soaked overnight before cooking. In "hard" or chlorinated city water, soaking them with some baking soda will help soften. If soaking time much exceeds 16 hours, change the water. Never presoak for more than 24 hours. To help soften them during cooking, garbanzo beans are added to boiling water (unlike other pulses). For the same reason, add salt only at the end. Gently shake the pot—don't stir with a spoon—to keep them in perfect shape.

MAKES ABOUT 6 CUPS/1 KG COOKED GARBANZO BEANS

1 POUND/455 G DRIED GARBANZO BEANS
1½ TEASPOONS BAKING SODA (OPTIONAL)
1 SMALL ONION, PEELED
1 GARLIC CLOVE, UNPEELED
1 BAY LEAF
1 SPRIG FRESH OR DRIED THYME
1½ TEASPOONS SALT

Rinse the beans with cold water. In a large bowl, dissolve the baking soda (if using) in plenty of cold water. Add the beans, place the bowl in a cool spot, and soak for 12 hours. Drain, rinse away any yeasty or fermenting odors, and drain again.

In a large, heavy pot, bring 10 cups/2.4 L water to a boil over high heat. Add the beans, onion, garlic, bay leaf, and thyme. Return to a boil, reduce the heat, cover the pot, and gently boil until tender, between 1½ and 2 hours, gently shaking (not stirring) from time to time. Add the salt once the beans begin to soften. If the pot needs more water during cooking, add boiling water.

Remove the pot from the heat and leave the beans in the water until ready to use. Drain and discard the onion, garlic, and herbs.

COOKING DRIED WHITE BEANS

White beans need to boil gently so that they don't break. "Use little water so they don't dance and fly though the water," advises the woman in my neighborhood market, from whom I buy most of my dried and cooked beans. "Keep the heat very low. And season with salt only at the end."

MAKES ABOUT 6 CUPS/1.2 KG COOKED BEANS

1 POUND/455 G DRIED WHITE BEANS
1 SMALL ONION, PEELED
1 GARLIC CLOVE, UNPEELED
1 BAY LEAF
1 TEASPOON EXTRA-VIRGIN OLIVE OIL
SALT

Rinse the beans with cold water. Place them in a large bowl, cover with plenty of cold water, place in a cool spot, and soak for 8 hours. Drain, rinse away any yeasty or fermenting odors, and drain again.

In a large, heavy pot, add the beans, onion, garlic, and bay leaf; cover with no more than 1½ inches/4 cm cold water (about two finger spaces); and put over high heat. Just as it begins to show signs of boiling, skim off the foam, reduce the heat to low, and add the olive oil. Cover the pot and very gently boil until tender, about 2 hours, though it depends on the type, size, and age of the beans. Gently shake (don't stir) the pot from time to time. If the pot needs more water during cooking, add cold water. Season with salt at the end of cooking.

Remove the pot from the heat and leave the beans in the water until ready to use. Drain and discard the onion, garlic, and bay leaf.

SELECTED BIBLIOGRAPHY

Andrews, Colman. *Catalan Cuisine*. Boston: Harvard Common Press, 1988.

Arazo, María Ángeles. *Recetas de cocina del Mercado Central de Valencia*. Valencia: Asociación de Vendedores del Mercado Central de Valencia, 2002.

Bajraj, Graciela. *La cocina tradicional de nuestras fiestas*. Barcelona: Alba, 2009.

Bar Pinotxo. *Pinotxo*. Barcelona: Viena, 2004.

Barrenechea, Teresa. *The Cuisines of Spain*. Berkeley (CA): Ten Speed Press, 2005.

Batista, Josep M. *Ravell*. Barcelona: Viena, 2005.

Berasategui, Martín. *La joven cocina vasca*. Alegia (Gipuzkoa, Spain): Hiria Liburuak, 1996.

Borràs, Josep, and Damià Borràs. *La cuina del menorquins*. Barcelona: Columna, 1998.

Carmona, Julio. *Mermeladas y conservas del convento: Recetas del Monasterio de Santa Paula de Sevilla*. Barcelona: Scyla, 2005.

Cunqueiro, Álvaro, and Araceli Filgueira Iglesias. *Galicia: Cocina tradicional*. León (Spain): Everest, 2009.

Davidson, Alan. *North Atlantic Seafood*. Berkeley (CA): Ten Speed Press, 2003.

———. *The Tio Pepe Guide to the Seafood of Spain and Portugal*. Málaga: Santana, 2002.

De Castro, Mercedes, ed. *Guía del turismo gastronómica en España*. Madrid: Anaya Touring Club, 2008.

Díaz Lafuente, Antonio. *Fogones granadinos*. Granada: Ediciones Miguel Sánchez, 2000.

Díaz Yubero, Ismael. *Las estrellas de la gastronomía española*. Madrid: Alianza, 2008.

Eléxpuru, Inés. *La cocina de al-Andalus*. Madrid: Alianza, 1994.

Fàbrega, Jaume. *El gran llibre de la cuina de les àvies*. Barcelona: Magrana, 2005.

Felpeto Lagoa, Matilde. *Recetas de la cocina familiar gallega*. 2nd ed. Vigo (Spain): NigraTrea, 2006.

Fernández, Sofía, and Víctor Alperi. *Cocina y gastronomía de Cantabria*. Madrid: Pirámide, 1998.

Font, Marga. *Mallorca: Gastronomia i cuina*. Menorca: Triangle Postals, 2007.

Fundació Institut Català de la Cuina. *Corpus del patrimoni culinari català*. Barcelona: La Magrana, 2011.

Fuster, Xim, and Manel Gómez. *Menorca: Gastronomia i cuina*. Menorca: Triangle Postals, 2005.

Gil, Francisco J. *La cocina del mar en Galicia*. Vigo (Spain): NigraTrea, 2005.

Gil de Antuñano, María Jesús. *El libro de cocina*. 4th ed. Madrid: El País Aguilar, 2007.

Hermanas, Clarisas. *Cocina monacal*. Barcelona: Planeta, 1997.

Koehler, Jeff. *La Paella: Deliciously Authentic Rice Dishes from Spain's Mediterranean Coast*. San Francisco: Chronicle Books, 2006.

———. *Rice, Pasta, Couscous: The Heart of the Mediterranean Kitchen*. San Francisco: Chronicle Books, 2009.

Lladonosa i Giró, Josep. *El gran llibre de la caça*: Barcelona: Empúries, 2005.

———. *El gran llibre de la cuina catalana*: Barcelona: Empúries, 1991.

Llona Larrauri, Jesús, and Garbiñe Badiola. *País Vasco: Cocina tradicional*. León (Spain): Everest: 2009.

Luján, Néstor. *Como piñones mondados*. Barcelona: Círculo de Lectores, 1996.

———. *Diccionari Luján de gastronomía catalana*. Barcelona: La Campana, 1990.

Luján, Néstor, and Juan Perucho. *El libro de la cocina española*. Barcelona: Tusquets, 2003.

March, Lourdes. *El libro de las conservas, las hierbas aromáticas y los frutos silvestres*. Madrid: Alianza, 1999.

———. *El libro de la paella y de los arroces*. Madrid: Alianza, 1985.

Martín, José Luis. *Gourmetquesos*. Madrid: Grupo Gourmets, 2003.

Millo, Lorenzo. *La gastronomía de la Comunidad Valenciana*. Valencia: Prensa Valenciana, 1992.

Molina González, Manuel. *Cocina tradicional de Priego de Córdoba*. Priego de Córdoba (Spain): Ayuntamiento de Priego de Córdoba, 2005.

Norman, Jill. *Herbs & Spices: The Cook's Reference*. New York: DK, 2002.

Ortega, Simone. *1080 recetas de cocina*. Madrid: Alianza, 1996.

Ortega, Simone, and Inés Ortega. *El libro de los platos de cuchara*. Madrid: Alianza, 2004.

Petràs, Llorenç. *La millor cuina dels bolets*. Barcelona: Empúries, 2000.

Prádanos, Jorge, and Pedro Gómez Carrizo. *El gran diccionario de cocina*. Barcelona: RBA Libros, 2003.

Real Academia Española. *Diccionario de la lengua española*. 22nd ed. Madrid: Espasa-Calpe, 2003.

Riera, Ignasi. *Diccionari de la cuina catalana*. Barcelona: Edicions 62, 2002.

Santonja, Elena. *Diccionario de cocina*. Madrid: Alderabán, 1997.

Seguí, Montserrat. *Cocinar es facil*. 2nd ed. Barcelona: Queralt Seguí, 2000.

Seijo Alonso, Francisco G. *La cocina alicantina*. Alicante (Spain): Instituto de Estudios Alicantinos, 1973.

Solé i Torné, David. *El romesco: Història, tècniques i receptes*. Valls (Spain): Cossetània, 2003.

Solsten, Eric, and Sandra W. Meditz, ed. *Spain: A Country Study*. Washington (DC): GPO for the Library of Congress, 1988.

Spínola, Carlos. *Gastronomía y cocina gaditana*. 11th ed. Cádiz: Ediciones Gastronómicas del Sur, 2005.

Tovar, Rosa. *Arroces*. Madrid: El País Aguilar, 2003.

Tovar, Rosa, and Monique Fuller. *3,000 años de cocina española*. Pozuelo de Alarcón (Madrid): Espasa, 2006.

Vázquez Montabán, Manuel. *La cocina de los finisterres*. Barcelona: Zeta, 2008.

———. *La cocina del mestizaje*. Barcelona: Zeta, 2008.

Wright, Clifford A. *A Mediterranean Feast*. New York: William Morrow, 1999.

SOURCES

There are now a number of specialty Spanish shops and cookware retailers with (in most cases) storefront locations as well as online and phone ordering. As well, many Spanish products can be found at better supermarkets like Whole Foods or Trader Joe's; purveyors of fine foods such as Dean & DeLuca; and at specialty international import shops. Italian or Portuguese grocery shops often have similar ingredients (like salt cod and squid ink), Latino markets also have some overlap, and Asian markets are often a good source for squid ink and seafood. A good butcher should have, or be able to order, tripe, kidneys, pig's feet, rabbit, and the like, and a good fishmonger will be able to get hold of monkfish, sardines, bones for stock, cuttlefish, and so on. For cookware, Sur la Table and Williams-Sonoma often carry paella pans and other specialty pieces. Amazon.com offers a wide variety of options and suppliers.

SPECIALIST SPANISH SOURCES

Delicias de España DELICIASDEESPANA.COM
From this Miami-based company with three shops, you can find most of what you need, including top-level Iberian jamón, various chorizos, salted pork bones (from the jamónes that they cut), fideo pasta and cannelloni sheets, and a wide selection of dried Spanish pulses. They also carry excellent preserved, ready-to-eat snails in the jar from the Navarra company Rosara.

Despaña DESPANABRANDFOODS.COM
Begun as a chorizo factory in 1971, the New York City–based Despaña has grown into a comprehensive retailer of Spanish products with a shop in Jackson Heights and a SoHo food boutique. They take orders by phone (718-779-4971) and ship. They carry the most obvious Spanish products: Spanish rices and fideo pasta, morcilla with onions, chorizo, top-quality jamón ibérico, dried choricero peppers and choricero paste, dried ñora peppers, packets of squid ink, and salt cod. Next door to their SoHo space is a shop dedicated to Spanish wines and spirits, including Galician aguardiente, Navarran pacharán (sloe berry–infused anisette), and Spanish vermouth, and you should be able to get Menorca Xoriguer gin. They also stock Kas lemon soda.

La Tienda TIENDA.COM
This online store carries an enormous range of Spanish products, plus many harder-to-find items, including dried ñora peppers, fideos, morcilla with rice and also with onions, Mallorcan sobrassada, a wide selection of Spanish cheeses, jamón ibérico de bellota, Spanish pulses, salt cod, packets of squid ink, and plenty of tinned delicacies.

The Spanish Table SPANISHTABLE.COM
Their four stores (Seattle, Berkeley, Mill Valley, and Santa Fe) and online ordering offer most Spanish products and cookware, along with three types of morcilla (plain, with onions, and with rice), Catalan blood sausage (botifarra negre), Mallorcan sobrassada, fuet and other cured sausages, jamón ibérico, salted pork (jamón serrano) bones, packets of squid ink, salt cod, Spanish lentils, and Kas lemon soda.

SPECIALIST MEAT, GAME, AND SEAFOOD

D'Artagnan DARTAGNAN.COM
An excellent source to order rabbit, venison, wild boar, and wild red-legged partridge and wood pigeon.

DeBragga DEBRAGGA.COM
Look here for marrowbones and New Zealand–raised venison.

Nicky USA NICKYUSA.COM
This Portland, Oregon, company offers a wide selection of top-quality wild boar, venison, rabbit, lamb, goat, quail and quail eggs, partridge, and dried wild mushrooms.

Octopus Garden 718-946-9221
This Brooklyn store carries all manner of fresh cephalopods, including squid, octopus, and cuttlefish.

Wild Edibles WILDEDIBLES.COM
An excellent New York seafood market that sells and ships whole turbot and gilt-head bream (they call them by their French name, *dorade royale*), and fresh cockles. They can sometimes get frozen land snails.

FOR THE PANTRY

Kalustyan's KALUSTYANS.COM
This New York City emporium of imported foodstuffs and spices opened in 1944 and stocks a number of Spanish products, including sherry vinegars, olive oils, rices, brown Pardina lentils, many types of whole dried chiles, and so on.

Spice House THESPICEHOUSE.COM
Look here for a vast array of spices, including Spanish smoked sweet paprika from La Vera and saffron from La Mancha.

Wagshal's WAGSHALS.COM
Based in Washington, D.C., Wagshal's well-stocked delicatessen and gourmet market carries cured jamón ibérico delicacies and can get partridge, quail, boar, and so on. They also ship fresh cuts of Iberian pork.

Zingerman's ZINGERMANS.COM
This Ann Arbor, Michigan, delicatessen and mail-order emporium stocks Bomba rice, various sherry vinegars, excellent olive oils, Spanish chorizo, cured pork loin and jamón, smoked Idiazábal cheese, and marcona almonds.

COOKWARE

Bram Cookware BRAMCOOKWARE.COM
This Sonoma, California shop dedicated to clay cookware sells a wide range of terra-cotta cazuelas, from small sizes perfect for tapas to larger ones for braising and stewing.

Fante's Kitchen Wares Shop FANTES.COM
This longtime specialist cookware shop stocks a massive array of pots, pans, and tools, including paellas, Spanish ceramic mortars, and assorted sizes of terra-cotta cazuelas.

La Paella PAELLAPANS.COM
An online store that specializes in paella pans made from a range of materials (carbon steel, enameled steel, stainless steel). They also carry tripods for preparing paella outdoors, as well as gas burners and leg supports for the large pans. The store also sells terra-cotta cazuelas and ceramic mortars.

INDEX

A

Aguardiente, 317
    Christmas Cherries in Aguardiente, 320
    Orense-Style Coffee Liqueur, 316
Ajada Sauce, Galician, 169
Ajo blanco con uvas, 59
Albariño, 204
Albóndigas con sepia, 258
Albóndigas menorquinas, 257
Alcachofas al horno, 113
Allioli, 337–38
    Quince Allioli, 240
All Saints' Day, 284, 291
Almejas al oloroso de jerez, 197
Almejas con gambas, 94
Almejas en salsa verde, 196
Almonds
    Chicken Braised in Saffron, Almond, and Egg Yolk Sauce, 212
    Curly Endive with Xató Sauce, 47
    Fresh Cheese with Honey, 301
    Galician Almond Tart, 286
    Lobster in a Nutty Chocolate Sauce, Costa Brava Style, 205
    Marzipan Cookies Rolled in Pine Nuts, 291
    Musicians' Dessert, 297
    picada, 39
    Romesco Sauce, 170–71
    Stewed Lentils with a Nutty Chocolate Picada, 43
    White Gazpacho with Grapes, 59
Alubias blancas con almejas, 41
Anchovies, 331
    Andalucía-Style Deep-Fried Fish, 164
    Belgian Endive with Cabrales Blue Cheese Sauce and Anchovy Fillets, 48
    Catalan Flatbread with Roasted Red Peppers, 70–71
    Curly Endive with Xató Sauce, 47
    Fresh Anchovies in Vinegar, 88
    Spanish Potato Salad, 56
    Winter Green Salad with Fresh Cheese and Pomegranate Seeds, 49
Andalucía-Style Deep-Fried Fish, 164
Apricots
    Dried Apricots Macerated in Sweet Wine, 326
    Fresh Cheese with Honey, 301
    Musicians' Dessert, 297
    Summer Red Wine Sangria, 311
Arcos de la Frontera, 287
Arroz caldoso de bogavante, 148–49
Arroz caldoso de pollo de corral, 150
Arroz con leche, 276
Arroz de montaña, 151
Arroz negro con allioli, 144–46

Artichokes
    Artichoke Egg Tortilla, 126
    cleaning, 339
    Creamy Artichoke and Leek Soup, 27
    Rabbit Paella with Artichokes and Red Bell Peppers, 138–39
    Roasted Artichokes, 113
Asparagus
    Eggs Scrambled with Tender Green Garlic Shoots, Asparagus, and Shrimp, 128
    Fresh White Asparagus with Crispy Shards of Dry-Cured Jamón, 109
    Green Asparagus in Vinegar Marinade, 107
Atún encebollado al estilo de Barbate, 175

B

Bacalao. *See* Salt cod
Bacalao a la vizcaína, 183
Bacalao con pasas de avia Lola, 185
Bacallà a la llauna, 187
Bacon
    Dates Wrapped in Bacon, 75
    The Ritz's Madrid-Style Cocido, 20–21
    Shepherd's Migas with Grapes, 161
    Smashed Potatoes and Cabbage Topped with Streaky Salt Pork, 119
Baker's Oven-Roasted Potatoes, 116
Balearic-Style Baked Stuffed Eggplant, 104
Barbate-Style Tuna in Caramelized Onions, 175
Basque Fresh Tuna and Potato Stew, 31
Basque Leek Soup, 26
Basque Walnut Pudding, 277
Beans. *See* Garbanzo beans; Green beans; White beans
Béchamel Sauce, 338
Beef, 234
    Beef Stew, 32
    Beef Stock, 336–37
    Braised Oxtail Stew, 271
    Catalan Two-Course Soup, 22–23
    cecina, 256
    Grilled Beef Tenderloin with Blue Cheese Sauce, 259
    Menorcan Meatballs in Tomato and Pine Nut Sauce, 257
    Pyrenees Mountain–Style Penne Pasta with Ground Meat and Pâté, 155
    The Ritz's Madrid-Style Cocido, 20–21
    Stewed Meatballs with Cuttlefish, 258
    Stuffed Tomatoes, 103
Beets, Roasted, in Vinegar, 114
Belgian Endive with Cabrales Blue Cheese Sauce and Anchovy Fillets, 48
Berberechos al vapor, 198
Berenjena frita con salmorejo, 106

Berenjenas rellenas al horno, 104
Berries
    Early Spring Strawberries with Red Wine Vinegar, 293
    White Wine Sangria with Fresh Berries, 313
Biscay-Style Salt Cod with Choricero Pepper Sauce, 183
Bizcocho con peras y nueces al estilo de Sinarcas, 280
Bizcocho de yogur, 279
Blood sausage, 256
    Pinotxo's Garbanzo Beans with Blood Sausage, Raisins, and Pine Nuts, 42
    The Ritz's Madrid-Style Cocido, 20–21
    Seared Morcilla de Burgos with Roasted Green Peppers and Fried Eggs, 252
Boar, wild, 224
Bogavante con chocolate, 205
Boquerones en vinagre, 88
Botifarra amb mongetes i allioli, 251
Brandada de bacallà, 87
Brandade
    Piquillo Peppers Stuffed with Salt Cod Brandade, 188
    Salt Cod Brandade on Toast, 87
Bread, 67
    Catalan Flatbread with Roasted Red Peppers, 70–71
    Country Bread Rubbed with Tomato and Olive Oil, 68
    Flatbread with Pine Nuts, Sugar, and Anise, 289
    Salt Cod Brandade on Toast, 87
    Shepherd's Migas with Grapes, 161
    Toasted Bread with Chocolate, Extra-Virgin Olive Oil, and Sea Salt Flakes, 274
Bream
    Marinated Seafood Salad, 50
    Salt-Baked Gilt-Head Bream, 174
    Seafood Fideuà with Allioli, 153
    Velvety Menorcan Fish Soup, 28–30
Buñuelos de Cuaresma, 184
Buñuelos de viento, 184, 284
Butifarra blanca, 256
Butifarra cocida, 256
Butifarra negra, 256

C

Cabbage
    Catalan Two-Course Soup, 22–23
    The Ritz's Madrid-Style Cocido, 20–21
    Smashed Potatoes and Cabbage Topped with Streaky Salt Pork, 119
Cachelos, 116
Cádiz-Style Potatoes in Vinaigrette, 74

Cakes
- Spongy Cake with Pears and Walnuts, Sinarcas Style, 280
- Spongy Yogurt Cake, 279

Calamares fritos, 92
Calçots, 120–21
Caldereta de langosta, 28
Caldereta de pescado, 28–30
Caldo de carne, 336–37
Caldo de pescado, 335
Caldo de pollo, 336
Caldo de verduras, 335
Callos a la gallega con garbanzos, 269
Caña de lomo, 254
Canelones de carne, 157–59
Canelones rellenos de setas, 160

Cannelloni
- Cannelloni Stuffed with Meat, 157–59
- Cannelloni Stuffed with Mushrooms and Pine Nuts, 160

Can Ravell, 237, 328
Caracoles de año nuevo, 232
Carne mechada, 243
Carrots, Torre del Bosc Braised Rabbit with, 222
Castilian Garlic Soup, 25
Catalan Flatbread with Roasted Red Peppers, 70–71
Catalan Shredded Salt Cod, Tomato, and Olive Salad, 54
Catalan Two-Course Soup, 22–23
Cazuela de Pilar, 228
Cazuelas, 213
Cebolla agridulce, 329
Cecina, 256
Celery and Lemon Granita, Slushy, 177
Cerezas en aguardiente, 320

Cheese, 302–3
- Belgian Endive with Cabrales Blue Cheese Sauce and Anchovy Fillets, 48
- Cannelloni Stuffed with Meat, 157–59
- Cannelloni Stuffed with Mushrooms and Pine Nuts, 160
- Fresh Cheese with Honey, 301
- Grilled Beef Tenderloin with Blue Cheese Sauce, 259
- Penne Pasta with Tomatoes and Fresh Sausage au Gratin, 156
- Pyrenees Mountain–Style Penne Pasta with Ground Meat and Pâté, 155
- Winter Green Salad with Fresh Cheese and Pomegranate Seeds, 49

Cherries, Christmas, in Aguardiente, 320
Chestnuts, 284
- Pork Tenderloin with Purée of Chestnuts, 246–47

Chicken, 208
- Cannelloni Stuffed with Meat, 157–59
- Catalan Two-Course Soup, 22–23
- Chicken Braised in Saffron, Almond, and Egg Yolk Sauce, 212
- Chicken Croquettes, 79–80
- Chicken Stock, 336
- Chicken with Samfaina, 216
- Chicken with Shallots and Orange and Cinnamon Sauce, 214
- cutting into pieces, 342
- The Mayoress's Stewed Christmas Chicken, 217
- Mountain-Style Rice with Chicken and Fresh Sausage, 151
- The Ritz's Madrid-Style Cocido, 20–21
- Roast Chicken with Prunes, 220
- Soupy Rice with Free-Range Chicken, 150

Chipirones en su tinta, 206–7
Chistorra, 254

Chocolate
- Lobster in a Nutty Chocolate Sauce, Costa Brava Style, 205
- Spanish Cinnamon-Scented Drinking Chocolate in the Cup, 306
- Stewed Lentils with a Nutty Chocolate Picada, 43
- Toasted Bread with Chocolate, Extra-Virgin Olive Oil, and Sea Salt Flakes, 274

Chocolate a la taza con canela, 306
Chorizo, 254
- Castilian Garlic Soup, 25
- Galician-Style Tripe with Garbanzo Beans, 269
- La Rioja–Style Stewed Potatoes with Chorizo, 118
- The Ritz's Madrid-Style Cocido, 20–21
- Shepherd's Migas with Grapes, 161

Christmas Cherries in Aguardiente, 320
Chuletas de cordero al ajo cabañil, 239
Chuletas de cordero con miel, 242
Ciervo adobado a la plancha, 226
Citrus-and-Cinnamon-Scented Flan, 278

Clams, 192
- Clams in Green Sauce, 196
- Clams with Oloroso Sherry, 197
- Clams with Shrimp, 94
- Grilled Razor Clams, 195
- purging of sand, 341
- Shellfish Paella, 141–42
- Steamed Cockles, 198
- White Beans with Clams, 41

Coca de azúcar con piñones y anís, 289
Coca de forner, 289
Coca de llardons, 289
Coca de recapte, 70–71
Cochinillo asado, 249
Cocido madrileño de Ritz, 20–21

Cocidos, 24
- Catalan Two-Course Soup, 22–23
- The Ritz's Madrid-Style Cocido, 20–21

Cockles, Steamed, 198
Codornices a la plancha con ajo y vino blanco, 229
Codornices en escabeche, 330
Coffee Liqueur, Orense-Style, 316
Conejo a la brasa con berenjenas, calabacines y allioli, 221
Conejo de torre del bosc, 222

Conserves, 190–91, 318
- Christmas Cherries in Aguardiente, 320
- Creamy Lemon Curd, 325
- Creamy Quince Paste, 323
- Dried Apricots Macerated in Sweet Wine, 326
- Fresh Sardines in Escabeche Marinade, 332
- Quail in Escabeche Marinade, 330
- Sweet and Sour Preserved Onions, 329
- Sweet Preserved Tomatoes with Thyme, 328
- Tomato Marmalade, 327

Cookies, Marzipan, Rolled in Pine Nuts, 291
Córdoba-Style Salmorejo, 62
Costillas de cerdo en adobo, 81
Costillas de cordero con allioli de membrillo, 240
Country Bread Rubbed with Tomato and Olive Oil, 68
Country Muffins, 282
Crema de alcachofas y puerros, 27
Crema de limón, 325
Crema de membrillo, 323
Crema de setas de temporada, 35
Crêpes, Galician, with Fresh Whipped Cream and Honey, 285
Croquetas de pollo, 79–80
Croquetas de trucha y jamón ibérico, 76–77

Croquettes
- Chicken Croquettes, 79–80
- Trout and Dry-Cured Iberian Jamón Croquettes, 76–77

Cuaresma, 184

Cucumbers
- Classic Andalusian Gazpacho, 60
- Córdoba-Style Salmorejo, 62
- Piriñaca, 178
- White Gazpacho with Grapes, 59

Curly Endive with Xató Sauce, 47
Custard, Creamy Vanilla, 275
Cuttlefish. *See* Squid or cuttlefish

D

Dates Wrapped in Bacon, 75
Dátiles con bacón, 75

Desserts, 272, 287
- Baked Figs, 296
- Basque Walnut Pudding, 277
- Citrus-and-Cinnamon-Scented Flan, 278
- Creamy Rice Pudding, 276
- Creamy Vanilla Custard, 275
- Early Spring Strawberries with Red Wine Vinegar, 293
- Flatbread with Pine Nuts, Sugar, and Anise, 289
- Fresh Cheese with Honey, 301
- Galician Almond Tart, 286
- Galician Crêpes with Fresh Whipped Cream and Honey, 285
- Marzipan Cookies Rolled in Pine Nuts, 291
- Menorcan Gin Sorbet, 299
- Musicians' Dessert, 297
- Oranges with Extra-Virgin Olive Oil and Honey, 292
- Pears Poached in Red Wine, 295
- Spongy Cake with Pears and Walnuts, Sinarcas Style, 280
- Spongy Yogurt Cake, 279
- Toasted Bread with Chocolate, Extra-Virgin Olive Oil, and Sea Salt Flakes, 274

Día de Todos los Santos, 284
Dorada a la sal, 174

INDEX / **347**

Drinks, 304. *See also* Wine
    Menorcan Gin Cocktail with Fresh Lemon Juice and Lemon Soda, 315
    Meringued Milk, 308
    Orense-Style Coffee Liqueur, 316
    sangria, 310
    Slushy Celery and Lemon Granita, 177
    Slushy Lemon Granita, 309
    Spanish Cinnamon-Scented Drinking Chocolate in the Cup, 306
Duck with Pears, 210–11
Dulces de convento, 287
Dulces monacales, 287

E

Eggplant
    Balearic-Style Baked Stuffed Eggplant, 104
    Chicken with Samfaina, 216
    Fried Eggplant Strips with Salmorejo, 106
    Grilled Rabbit with Eggplant, Zucchini, and Allioli, 221
    Roasted Red Peppers, Eggplant, and Onions, 72
Eggs, 122
    Artichoke Egg Tortilla, 126
    Chicken Braised in Saffron, Almond, and Egg Yolk Sauce, 212
    Citrus-and-Cinnamon-Scented Flan, 278
    Creamy Vanilla Custard, 275
    Eggs Scrambled with Mushrooms and Dry-Cured Jamón, 130
    Eggs Scrambled with Tender Green Garlic Shoots, Asparagus, and Shrimp, 128
    Fried Eggs with Fried Potatoes and Slices of Dry-Cured Iberian Jamón, 132
    Perfect Hard-Boiled Eggs, 342
    Potato and Onion Egg Tortilla, 124
    Salt Cod Egg Tortilla, 127
    Seared Morcilla de Burgos with Roasted Green Peppers and Fried Eggs, 252
    Tender Spinach Leaves with Spanish-Style Poached Eggs, 112
Embutidos, 254
Empanada de lomo, 85–86
Empanada with Marinated Pork and Roasted Red Peppers, 85–86
Empedrat de bonito del norte, 55
Endivias con queso de cabrales y anchoas, 48
Ensalada de invierno con queso fresco y granada, 49
Ensaladilla rusa, 56
Epiphany, 281
Escalivada, 72
Escudella i carn d'olla, 22–23
Espaldita de cabrito al horno con patatas y cebollitas confitadas, 236–37
Espárragos blancos frescos con virutas de jamón, 109
Espárragos verdes en vinagreta, 107
Espinacas con garbanzos, 36
Espinacas con piñones y pasas, 110
Esqueixada de bacallà, 54
Estofado de buey, 32

F

Fideos, 134
    Fideos in the Cazuela with Pork Ribs, 152
    The Ritz's Madrid-Style Cocido, 20–21
    Seafood Fideuà with Allioli, 153
Fideos a la cazuela, 152
Fideuà amb allioli, 153
Figs
    Baked Figs, 296
    Fresh Cheese with Honey, 301
    Melon or Fresh Figs with Slices of Dry-Cured Jamón, 57
    Musicians' Dessert, 297
Filloas de leche con nata montada y miel, 285
Fino, 51
Fish, 162. *See also* Anchovies; Salt cod; Sardines; Trout; Tuna
    Andalucía-Style Deep-Fried Fish, 164
    Baked Turbot with Basque White Wine, 173
    Fish Braised in Romesco Sauce, 170–71
    Fisherman's Suquet, 165
    Fish Stock, 335
    Galician-Style Hake with Garlic Ajada Sauce, 169
    Grilled Swordfish Steaks with Piriñaca, 178
    Marinated Salmon on the Grill with Galician Potatoes, 182
    Marinated Seafood Salad, 50
    Monkfish Steaks with Saffron, 166
    Salt-Baked Gilt-Head Bream, 174
    Seafood Fideuà with Allioli, 153
    Velvety Menorcan Fish Soup, 28–30
Fisherman's Suquet, 165
Flan, Citrus-and-Cinnamon-Scented, 278
Flan con aromas cítricos y canela, 278
Flatbread
    Catalan Flatbread with Roasted Red Peppers, 70–71
    Flatbread with Pine Nuts, Sugar, and Anise, 289
Fresas con vinagre de vino tinto, 293
Fricandó amb moixernons, 260
Fritura de pescado, 164
Fruits, 272. *See also* Sangria; *individual fruits*
Fuet, 254

G

Galician Ajada Sauce, 169
Galician Almond Tart, 286
Galician Boiled Potatoes with Paprika, 116
Galician Crêpes with Fresh Whipped Cream and Honey, 285
Galician Fair-Style Octopus with Paprika on Potatoes, 91
Galician-Style Hake with Garlic Ajada Sauce, 169
Galician-Style Tripe with Garbanzo Beans, 269
Gambas al ajillo, 93
Gambas a la plancha, 202

Garbanzo beans
    Catalan Two-Course Soup, 22–23
    cooking dried, 343
    Galician-Style Tripe with Garbanzo Beans, 269
    Pinotxo's Garbanzo Beans with Blood Sausage, Raisins, and Pine Nuts, 42
    The Ritz's Madrid-Style Cocido, 20–21
    Spinach with Garbanzo Beans, 36
Garbanzos de Pinotxo, 42
Garlic
    Allioli, 337–38
    Castilian Garlic Soup, 25
    Eggs Scrambled with Tender Green Garlic Shoots, Asparagus, and Shrimp, 128
    Garlicky Shrimp in Olive Oil, 93
Gazpacho
    Classic Andalusian Gazpacho, 60
    White Gazpacho with Grapes, 59
Gazpacho andaluz, 60
Gin, 298
    Menorcan Gin Cocktail with Fresh Lemon Juice and Lemon Soda, 315
    Menorcan Gin Sorbet, 299
Goat, 234
    Roast Shoulder of Kid Goat with Potato and Shallot Confit, 236–37
Grandma Lola's Lenten Salt Cod with Raisins, 185
Granitas
    Slushy Celery and Lemon Granita, 177
    Slushy Lemon Granita, 309
Granizado de apio y limón, 177
Granizado de limón, 309
Grapes
    Shepherd's Migas with Grapes, 161
    White Gazpacho with Grapes, 59
Green beans
    Spanish Potato Salad, 56
Guiso de rabo de buey, 271

H

Hake
    Andalucía-Style Deep-Fried Fish, 164
    Fish Braised in Romesco Sauce, 170–71
    Galician-Style Hake with Garlic Ajada Sauce, 169
    Monkfish Steaks with Saffron, 166
Ham. *See* Jamón
Hazelnuts
    Curly Endive with Xató Sauce, 47
    Fresh Cheese with Honey, 301
    Musicians' Dessert, 297
    picada, 39
    Roasted Pig's Feet, 265–66
    Romesco Sauce, 170–71
    Stewed Lentils with a Nutty Chocolate Picada, 43
Higos al horno, 296
Hueso de santo, 284
Huevos fritos con patatas fritas y lonchas de jamón ibérico, 132

I

Intxaursalsa, 277

J

Jamón, 16, 133, 254
    Castilian Garlic Soup, 25
    Chilled Melon Soup with Crispy Jamón, 58
    cocido, 256
    Eggs Scrambled with Mushrooms and Dry-Cured Jamón, 130
    Fresh White Asparagus with Crispy Shards of Dry-Cured Jamón, 109
    Fried Eggs with Fried Potatoes and Slices of Dry-Cured Iberian Jamón, 132
    Melon or Fresh Figs with Slices of Dry-Cured Jamón, 57
    Navarra-Style Trout with Dry-Cured Jamón, 181
    New Year's Day Snails in Spicy Tomato Sauce, 232
    Roasted Artichokes, 113
    Trout and Dry-Cured Iberian Jamón Croquettes, 76–77

L

La Mancha–Style Sautéed Onions, Zucchini, Tomatoes, and Peppers, 102
Lamb, 234, 238, 241
    Grilled Lamb Chops with Honey, 242
    Grilled Lamb Rib Chops with Quince Allioli, 240
    Shepherd's-Style Lamb Chops with Potatoes and Zesty Vinegar-Garlic Sauce, 239
Langoustines
    Shellfish Paella, 141–42
La Rioja–Style Stewed Potatoes with Chorizo, 118
Latas, 190–91
Leche merengada, 308
Leeks
    Basque Leek Soup, 26
    Creamy Artichoke and Leek Soup, 27
Lemons, 276
    Citrus-and-Cinnamon-Scented Flan, 278
    Creamy Lemon Curd, 325
    Menorcan Gin Cocktail with Fresh Lemon Juice and Lemon Soda, 315
    Menorcan Gin Sorbet, 299
    Slushy Celery and Lemon Granita, 177
    Slushy Lemon Granita, 309
Lengua de ternera con alcaparras, 268
Lent, 184
Lentejas estofadas, 43
Lentils, Stewed, with a Nutty Chocolate Picada, 43
Licor de café al estilo de Ourense, 316

Lobster
    Lobster in a Nutty Chocolate Sauce, Costa Brava Style, 205
    Soupy Rice with Lobster, 148–49
Lomo de cerdo a la sal con dos salsas, 245
Lomo embuchado, 254

M

Macarrones de los Pirineos, 155
Macarrones gratinados, 156
Magdalenas, 282
Manitas de cerdo al horno, 265–66
Manzanilla, 51
Markets, covered food, 131
Marmitako, 31
Marzipan Cookies Rolled in Pine Nuts, 291
Mayonnaise, 337
The Mayoress's Stewed Christmas Chicken, 217
Meatballs
    Menorcan Meatballs in Tomato and Pine Nut Sauce, 257
    Stewed Meatballs with Cuttlefish, 258
Mejillones a la vinagreta, 95
Mejillones con sofrito, 199
Mel i mató, 201
Melon
    Chilled Melon Soup with Crispy Jamón, 58
    Melon or Fresh Figs with Slices of Dry-Cured Jamón, 57
Melón e higos frescos con lonchas de jamón, 57
Menorcan gin, 298
    Menorcan Gin Cocktail with Fresh Lemon Juice and Lemon Soda, 315
    Menorcan Gin Sorbet, 299
Menorcan Meatballs in Tomato and Pine Nut Sauce, 257
Mercados, 131
Merluza a la gallega con ajada, 169
Mermelada de tomate, 327
Migas, Shepherd's, with Grapes, 161
Migas de pastor con uvas, 161
Milk, Meringued, 308
Monkfish
    Fish Braised in Romesco Sauce, 170–71
    Fisherman's Suquet, 165
    Marinated Seafood Salad, 50
    Monkfish Steaks with Saffron, 166
    Seafood Fideuà with Allioli, 153
Morcilla. *See* Blood sausage
Morcilla de Burgos con pimientos asados y huevos fritos, 252
Mountain-Style Rice with Chicken and Fresh Sausage, 151
Muffins, Country, 282
Mushrooms
    Braised Veal with Dried Mushrooms, 260
    Cannelloni Stuffed with Mushrooms and Pine Nuts, 160
    cleaning, 339
    Cream of Seasonal Mushrooms, 35
    Eggs Scrambled with Mushrooms and Dry-Cured Jamón, 130

    Sautéed Wild Mushrooms, 100
    wild, 33
Musicians' Dessert, 297
Mussels
    cleaning, 341
    Mussels in Sweet Sofrito Tomato Sauce, 199
    Mussels in Vinaigrette, 95
    Shellfish Paella, 141–42

N

Naranjas con aceite de oliva virgen extra y miel, 292
Natillas, 275
Navajas a la plancha, 195
Navarra-Style Trout with Dry-Cured Jamón, 181
New Year's Day Snails in Spicy Tomato Sauce, 232

O

Octopus, Galician Fair-Style, with Paprika on Potatoes, 91
Olive oil, 16, 63
Olives, 66
    Catalan Flatbread with Roasted Red Peppers, 70–71
    Catalan Shredded Salt Cod, Tomato, and Olive Salad, 54
    Curly Endive with Xató Sauce, 47
    Salt Cod, Orange, and Olive Salad, 53
    Spanish Potato Salad, 56
    Winter Green Salad with Fresh Cheese and Pomegranate Seeds, 49
Onions, 16
    Barbate-Style Tuna in Caramelized Onions, 175
    calçots, 120–21
    La Mancha–Style Sautéed Onions, Zucchini, Tomatoes, and Peppers, 102
    Potato and Onion Egg Tortilla, 124
    Roasted Red Peppers, Eggplant, and Onions, 72
    Sweet and Sour Preserved Onions, 329
Oranges
    Chicken with Shallots and Orange and Cinnamon Sauce, 214
    Citrus-and-Cinnamon-Scented Flan, 278
    Menorcan Gin Sorbet, 299
    Oranges with Extra-Virgin Olive Oil and Honey, 292
    Pork Tenderloin in Orange Sauce, 248
    Salt Cod, Orange, and Olive Salad, 53
Orejones macerados en vino dulce, 326
Orense-Style Coffee Liqueur, 316
Oxtail
    Braised Oxtail Stew, 271
    The Ritz's Madrid-Style Cocido, 20–21

P

Pa amb tomàquet, 68
Padrón Green Peppers, 73
Paella de conejo con alcachofas y pimientos rojos, 138–39
Paella de marisco, 141–42
Paellas, 134
    pan for, 143
    Rabbit Paella with Artichokes and Red Bell Peppers, 138–39
    Shellfish Paella, 141–42
    tips for, 136–37
Pan con chocolate, aceite de oliva virgen extra y escamas de sal marina, 274
Pan con tomate, 68
Panellets de piñones, 291
Papas aliñás, 74
Paprika, 101
Partridge, 224, 230
    Toledo-Style Partridge, 231
Pasta, 134
    Cannelloni Stuffed with Meat, 157–59
    Cannelloni Stuffed with Mushrooms and Pine Nuts, 160
    Catalan Two-Course Soup, 22–23
    Fideos in the Cazuela with Pork Ribs, 152
    Penne Pasta with Tomatoes and Fresh Sausage au Gratin, 156
    Pyrenees Mountain–Style Penne Pasta with Ground Meat and Pâté, 155
    The Ritz's Madrid-Style Cocido, 20–21
    Seafood Fideuà with Allioli, 153
Patatas a la riojana, 118
Patatas panaderas al horno, 116
Pâté, Pyrenees Mountain–Style Penne Pasta with Ground Meat and, 155
Pato con peras, 210–11
Pears
    Duck with Pears, 210–11
    Pear Compote, 245
    Pears Poached in Red Wine, 295
    Quince Allioli, 240
    Spongy Cake with Pears and Walnuts, Sinarcas Style, 280
    Summer Red Wine Sangria, 311
Peas
    Spanish Potato Salad, 56
    Stewed Meatballs with Cuttlefish, 258
Peppers
    Biscay-Style Salt Cod with Choricero Pepper Sauce, 183
    Catalan Flatbread with Roasted Red Peppers, 70–71
    Chicken with Samfaina, 216
    Classic Andalusian Gazpacho, 60
    Córdoba-Style Salmorejo, 62
    dried red, 16
    Empanada with Marinated Pork and Roasted Red Peppers, 85–86
    green, 16–17
    La Mancha–Style Sautéed Onions, Zucchini, Tomatoes, and Peppers, 102
    La Rioja–Style Stewed Potatoes with Chorizo, 118
    Marinated Seafood Salad, 50
    The Mayoress's Stewed Christmas Chicken, 217
    Mussels in Vinaigrette, 94
    Padrón Green Peppers, 73
    pimentón, 101
    Piquillo Peppers Stuffed with Salt Cod Brandade, 188
    Piriñaca, 178
    Rabbit Paella with Artichokes and Red Bell Peppers, 138–39
    Roasted Red Peppers, Eggplant, and Onions, 72
    Romesco Sauce, 170–71
    Seared Morcilla de Burgos with Roasted Green Peppers and Fried Eggs, 252
    Shellfish Paella, 141–42
    Shepherd's Migas with Grapes, 161
    Soupy Rice with Free-Range Chicken, 150
Peras al vino tinto, 295
Perdices a la toledana, 231
Pescadito frito, 164
Pez espada a la plancha con piriñaca, 178
Pheasant, 224
Picada, 38–39
Pilar's Cazuela with Snails and Rabbit, 231
Pimentón, 101
Pimientos del Padrón, 73
Pimientos del piquillo relleno de brandada de bacalao, 188
Pinchos morunos, 83
Pine nuts, 111
    Cannelloni Stuffed with Mushrooms and Pine Nuts, 160
    dry-toasting, 340
    Flatbread with Pine Nuts, Sugar, and Anise, 289
    Fresh Cheese with Honey, 301
    Grandma Lola's Lenten Salt Cod with Raisins, 185
    Marzipan Cookies Rolled in Pine Nuts, 291
    Menorcan Meatballs in Tomato and Pine Nut Sauce, 257
    Pinotxo's Garbanzo Beans with Blood Sausage, Raisins, and Pine Nuts, 42
    Pork Tenderloin in Orange Sauce, 248
    Spinach with Pine Nuts and Raisins, 110
Piñones. *See* Pine nuts
Pinotxo's Garbanzo Beans with Blood Sausage, Raisins, and Pine Nuts, 42
Piquillo Peppers Stuffed with Salt Cod Brandade, 188
Piriñaca, 178
Pisto manchego, 102
Polbo á feira con patatas, 91
Pollo asado al horno con ciruelas pasas, 220
Pollo con chalotes y salsa de naranja y canela, 214
Pollo con samfaina, 216
Pollo en pepitoria, 212
Pollo navideño de la alcaldesa, 217
Pomada, 315
Pomegranates
    removing seeds from, 49
    Winter Green Salad with Fresh Cheese and Pomegranate Seeds, 49
Pork, 234. *See also* Bacon; Jamón; Salt pork; Sausage
    Cannelloni Stuffed with Meat, 157–59
    Catalan Two-Course Soup, 22–23
    Chilled Pork Loin, 243
    Empanada with Marinated Pork and Roasted Red Peppers, 85–86
    Fideos in the Cazuela with Pork Ribs, 152
    Menorcan Meatballs in Tomato and Pine Nut Sauce, 257
    Pork Ribs in Adobo Sauce, 81
    Pork Tenderloin in Orange Sauce, 248
    Pork Tenderloin with Purée of Chestnuts, 246–47
    Pyrenees Mountain–Style Penne Pasta with Ground Meat and Pâté, 155
    The Ritz's Madrid-Style Cocido, 20–21
    Roasted Pig's Feet, 265–66
    Salt-Baked Pork Loin with Two Sauces, 245
    Spicy Marinated Pork Skewers, 83
    Stewed Meatballs with Cuttlefish, 258
    Stuffed Tomatoes, 103
    suckling pig, 249
    wild boar, 224
Porrusalda, 26
Postres de músic, 297
Potatoes, 98
    Baked Turbot with Basque White Wine, 173
    Baker's Oven-Roasted Potatoes, 116
    Basque Fresh Tuna and Potato Stew, 31
    Basque Leek Soup, 26
    Beef Stew, 32
    Cádiz-Style Potatoes in Vinaigrette, 74
    Fisherman's Suquet, 165
    Fried Eggs with Fried Potatoes and Slices of Dry-Cured Iberian Jamón, 132
    Galician Boiled Potatoes with Paprika, 116
    Galician Fair-Style Octopus with Paprika on Potatoes, 91
    Galician-Style Hake with Garlic Ajada Sauce, 169
    La Rioja–Style Stewed Potatoes with Chorizo, 118
    Marinated Salmon on the Grill with Galician Potatoes, 182
    Potato and Onion Egg Tortilla, 124
    Puréed Potatoes with Extra-Virgin Olive Oil, 117
    The Ritz's Madrid-Style Cocido, 20–21
    Roast Shoulder of Kid Goat with Potato and Shallot Confit, 236–37
    Salt Cod Brandade on Toast, 87
    Shepherd's-Style Lamb Chops with Potatoes and Zesty Vinegar-Garlic Sauce, 239
    Smashed Potatoes and Cabbage Topped with Streaky Salt Pork, 119
    Spanish Potato Salad, 56
Prawns. *See* Shrimp or prawns
Prunes
    Musicians' Dessert, 297
    Roast Chicken with Prunes, 220
Puddings
    Basque Walnut Pudding, 277
    Creamy Rice Pudding, 276
Puré de patatas, 117
Pyrenees Mountain–Style Penne Pasta with Ground Meat and Pâté, 155

Q

Quail, 224
    Grilled Quail with Garlic and White Wine, 230
    Quail in Escabeche Marinade, 330
Quince
    Creamy Quince Paste, 323
    Quince Allioli, 240

R

Rabbit, 208
    cutting into pieces, 342
    Grilled Rabbit with Eggplant, Zucchini, and Allioli, 221
    Pilar's Cazuela with Snails and Rabbit, 228
    Rabbit Paella with Artichokes and Red Bell Peppers, 138–39
    Torre del Bosc Braised Rabbit with Carrots, 222
Raisins
    Fresh Cheese with Honey, 301
    Grandma Lola's Lenten Salt Cod with Raisins, 185
    Musicians' Dessert, 297
    Pinotxo's Garbanzo Beans with Blood Sausage, Raisins, and Pine Nuts, 42
    Spinach with Pine Nuts and Raisins, 110
Rape con azafrán, 166
Remojón de naranja, 53
Remolachas asadas en vinagre, 114
Revuelto de ajetes con espárragos y gambas, 128
Revuelto de setas y jamón, 130
Ribera del Duero, 218–19
Rice, 134, 147
    Black Rice with Allioli, 144–46
    Creamy Rice Pudding, 276
    Mountain-Style Rice with Chicken and Fresh Sausage, 151
    Rabbit Paella with Artichokes and Red Bell Peppers, 138–39
    Shellfish Paella, 141–42
    Soupy Rice with Free-Range Chicken, 150
    Soupy Rice with Lobster, 148–49
Riñones de ternera al jerez, 267
The Ritz's Madrid-Style Cocido, 20–21
Rodaballo al horno con txakoli, 173
Romesco de pescado, 170–71
Romesco Sauce, 170–71
Roscón de reyes, 281

S

Saffron, 168, 340
Salads, 44
    Belgian Endive with Cabrales Blue Cheese Sauce and Anchovy Fillets, 48
    Catalan Shredded Salt Cod, Tomato, and Olive Salad, 54
    Curly Endive with Xató Sauce, 47
    Marinated Seafood Salad, 50
    Piriñaca, 178
    Salt Cod, Orange, and Olive Salad, 53
    Spanish Potato Salad, 56
    White Bean Salad with Bonito del Norte Tuna, 55
    Winter Green Salad with Fresh Cheese and Pomegranate Seeds, 49
Salchichón, 254
Salmon, Marinated, on the Grill with Galician Potatoes, 182
Salmón marinado a la parrilla con cachelos, 182
Salmorejo
    Córdoba-Style Salmorejo, 62
    Fried Eggplant Strips with Salmorejo, 106
Salmorejo cordobés, 62
Salpicón, 50
Salsa bechamel, 338
Salsa mayonesa, 337
Salt, 16
    Salt-Baked Gilt-Head Bream, 174
    Salt-Baked Pork Loin with Two Sauces, 245
Salt cod, 162, 184
    Biscay-Style Salt Cod with Choricero Pepper Sauce, 183
    Catalan Shredded Salt Cod, Tomato, and Olive Salad, 54
    Curly Endive with Xató Sauce, 47
    desalting, 341
    Grandma Lola's Lenten Salt Cod with Raisins, 185
    Piquillo Peppers Stuffed with Salt Cod Brandade, 188
    Salt Cod Baked in the Tin, 187
    Salt Cod Brandade on Toast, 87
    Salt Cod Egg Tortilla, 127
    Salt Cod, Orange, and Olive Salad, 53
Salteado de espinacas tiernas con huevos escalfados, 112
Salt pork
    The Ritz's Madrid-Style Cocido, 20–21
    Shepherd's Migas with Grapes, 161
    Smashed Potatoes and Cabbage Topped with Streaky Salt Pork, 119
Samfaina, Chicken with, 216
Sangria, 310
    Summer Red Wine Sangria, 311
    White Wine Sangria with Fresh Berries, 313
Sangría de vino blanco con frutos del bosque, 313
Sangría de vino tinto, 311
Sardinas a la brasa con granizado de apio yl limón, 176
Sardinas en escabeche, 332
Sardines
    Fresh Sardines in Escabeche Marinade, 332
    Grilled Sardines with Slushy Celery and Lemon Granita, 176
Sauces
    Allioli, 337–38
    Béchamel Sauce, 338
    Blue Cheese Sauce, 259
    Galician Ajada Sauce, 169
    Pear Compote, 245
    Quince Allioli, 240
    Romesco Sauce, 170–71
Sausage, 254, 256
    Castilian Garlic Soup, 25
    Fresh Pork Sausages with White Beans and Allioli, 251
    Galician-Style Tripe with Garbanzo Beans, 269
    La Rioja-Style Stewed Potatoes with Chorizo, 118
    Menorcan Meatballs in Tomato and Pine Nut Sauce, 257
    Mountain-Style Rice with Chicken and Fresh Sausage, 151
    Penne Pasta with Tomatoes and Fresh Sausage au Gratin, 156
    Pinotxo's Garbanzo Beans with Blood Sausage, Raisins, and Pine Nuts, 42
    The Ritz's Madrid-Style Cocido, 20–21
    Seared Morcilla de Burgos with Roasted Green Peppers and Fried Eggs, 252
    Shepherd's Migas with Grapes, 161
Scallops, Baked, in the Shell, 201
Seafood, 162, 192. *See also individual seafood*
    Marinated Seafood Salad, 50
    Seafood Fideuà with Allioli, 153
    Shellfish Paella, 141–42
    tinned, 190–91
Setas salteadas, 100
Sheep, 234, 238. *See also Lamb*
Shepherd's Migas with Grapes, 161
Shepherd's-Style Lamb Chops with Potatoes and Zesty Vinegar-Garlic Sauce, 239
Sherry, 51
    Clams with Oloroso Sherry, 197
    Veal Kidneys in Sherry, 267
Shrimp or prawns, 192
    Andalucía-Style Deep-Fried Fish, 164
    Black Rice with Allioli, 144–46
    Clams with Shrimp, 95
    Eggs Scrambled with Tender Green Garlic Shoots, Asparagus, and Shrimp, 128
    Garlicky Shrimp in Olive Oil, 93
    Grilled Shrimp, 202
    Marinated Seafood Salad, 50
    Seafood Fideuà with Allioli, 153
    Shellfish Paella, 141–42
Snails, 224
    New Year's Day Snails in Spicy Tomato Sauce, 232
    Pilar's Cazuela with Snails and Rabbit, 228
    preparing, 340–41
Sobrassada, 254
    Menorcan Meatballs in Tomato and Pine Nut Sauce, 257
Sofrito, 38–39
Solomillo de buey al queso picón, 259
Solomillo de cerdo a la naranja, 248
Solomillo de cerdo con puré de castañas, 246–47
Sopa de ajo castellana, 25
Sopa fría de melón con crujiente de jamón, 58
Sorbete de gin de Menorca, 299
Sorbets, 272
    Menorcan Gin Sorbet, 299

Soups, 18
- Basque Leek Soup, 26
- Castilian Garlic Soup, 25
- Catalan Two-Course Soup, 22–23
- Chilled Melon Soup with Crispy Jamón, 58
- Classic Andalusian Gazpacho, 60
- Córdoba-Style Salmorejo, 62
- Cream of Seasonal Mushrooms, 35
- Creamy Artichoke and Leek Soup, 27
- The Ritz's Madrid-Style Cocido, 20–21
- Velvety Menorcan Fish Soup, 28–30
- White Gazpacho with Grapes, 59

Spanish Cinnamon-Scented Drinking Chocolate in the Cup, 306
Spanish Potato Salad, 56
Spinach
- Spinach with Garbanzo Beans, 36
- Spinach with Pine Nuts and Raisins, 110
- Tender Spinach Leaves with Spanish-Style Poached Eggs, 112

Squid or cuttlefish
- Black Rice with Allioli, 144–46
- cleaning, 342
- Deep-Fried Squid, 92
- Seafood Fideuà with Allioli, 153
- Shellfish Paella, 141–42
- Small Squid in Their Own Ink, 206–7
- Soupy Rice with Lobster, 148–49
- Stewed Meatballs with Cuttlefish, 258

Stocks, 17
- Beef Stock, 336–37
- Chicken Stock, 336
- Fish Stock, 335
- Vegetable Stock, 335

Strawberries, Early Spring, with Red Wine Vinegar, 293
Suquet de pescadors, 165
Sweet potatoes, 284
- Marzipan Cookies Rolled in Pine Nuts, 291

Swordfish Steaks, Grilled, with Piriñaca, 178

T

Tapas, 64
Tart, Galician Almond, 286
Tarta de Santiago, 286
The Three Kings, 281
Tinned delicacies, 190–91
Tió de Nadal, 96–97
Tocino de cielo, 287
Toledo-Style Partridge, 229
Tomates confitados con tomillo, 328
Tomates rellenos, 103
Tomatoes
- Beef Stew, 32
- Black Rice with Allioli, 144–46
- blanching and peeling, 339
- Catalan Shredded Salt Cod, Tomato, and Olive Salad, 54
- Chicken with Samfaina, 216
- Classic Andalusian Gazpacho, 60
- Córdoba-Style Salmorejo, 62
- Country Bread Rubbed with Tomato and Olive Oil, 68
- Fideos in the Cazuela with Pork Ribs, 152
- Grandma Lola's Lenten Salt Cod with Raisins, 185
- grating, 339
- La Mancha–Style Sautéed Onions, Zucchini, Tomatoes, and Peppers, 102
- Menorcan Meatballs in Tomato and Pine Nut Sauce, 257
- Mussels in Sweet Sofrito Tomato Sauce, 199
- New Year's Day Snails in Spicy Tomato Sauce, 232
- Penne Pasta with Tomatoes and Fresh Sausage au Gratin, 156
- Piriñaca, 178
- Pyrenees Mountain–Style Penne Pasta with Ground Meat and Pâté, 155
- Rabbit Paella with Artichokes and Red Bell Peppers, 138–39
- The Ritz's Madrid-Style Cocido, 20–21
- Roasted Pig's Feet, 265–66
- Romesco Sauce, 170–71
- Seafood Fideuà with Allioli, 153
- Shellfish Paella, 141–42
- sofrito, 39
- Stuffed Tomatoes, 103
- Sweet Preserved Tomatoes with Thyme, 328
- Tomato Marmalade, 327
- Veal Tongue with Capers, 268

Torre del Bosc Braised Rabbit with Carrots, 222
Tortilla de alcachofas, 126
Tortilla de bacalao, 127
Tortilla de patatas y cebolla, 124
Tortillas, 122
- Artichoke Egg Tortilla, 126
- Potato and Onion Egg Tortilla, 124
- Salt Cod Egg Tortilla, 127

Trinxat de la cerdanya amb rosta, 119
Tripe, Galician-Style, with Garbanzo Beans, 269
Trout, 179
- Navarra-Style Trout with Dry-Cured Jamón, 181
- Pan-Fried Trout with Thyme and Walnuts, 179
- Trout and Dry-Cured Iberian Jamón Croquettes, 76–77

Truchas a la navarra, 181
Truchas con tomillo y nueces, 179
Tuna
- Barbate-Style Tuna in Caramelized Onions, 175
- Basque Fresh Tuna and Potato Stew, 31
- Curly Endive with Xató Sauce, 47
- Spanish Potato Salad, 56
- White Bean Salad with Bonito del Norte Tuna, 55

Turbot, Baked, with Basque White Wine, 173
Turkey, 213

V

Vanilla Custard, Creamy, 275
Veal, 234
- Beef Stew, 32
- Braised Veal with Dried Mushrooms, 260
- Cannelloni Stuffed with Meat, 157–59
- Veal Kidneys in Sherry, 267
- Veal Tongue with Capers, 268

Vegetables, 98. *See also individual vegetables*
- tinned, 190–91
- Vegetable Stock, 335

Venison, 224
- Grilled Marinated Venison Steaks, 226

Vieiras al horno, 201
Vinegar, 17

W

Walnuts
- Basque Walnut Pudding, 277
- Fresh Cheese with Honey, 301
- Musicians' Dessert, 297
- Pan-Fried Trout with Thyme and Walnuts, 179
- Spongy Cake with Pears and Walnuts, Sinarcas Style, 280

White beans
- cooking dried, 343
- Fresh Pork Sausages with White Beans and Allioli, 251
- White Bean Salad with Bonito del Norte Tuna, 55
- White Beans with Clams, 41

Wine, 304, 314
- Albariño, 204
- Baked Turbot with Basque White Wine, 173
- Dried Apricots Macerated in Sweet Wine, 326
- Grilled Quail with Garlic and White Wine, 229
- Pears Poached in Red Wine, 295
- Ribera del Duero, 218–19
- sangria, 310
- Summer Red Wine Sangria, 311
- White Wine Sangria with Fresh Berries, 313

Winter Green Salad with Fresh Cheese and Pomegranate Seeds, 49

X

Xató, 47

Y

Yogurt Cake, Spongy, 279

Z

Zucchini
- Grilled Rabbit with Eggplant, Zucchini, and Allioli, 221
- La Mancha–Style Sautéed Onions, Zucchini, Tomatoes, and Peppers, 102